Creative Drama in the Classroom

Nellie McCaslin

Fifth Edition

Creative Drama in the Classroom

PLAYERS PRESS, Inc.
Studio City, California

Creative Drama in the Classroom

Copyright 1990 by Longman

All rights rescrved. No part of this publication may be reproduced, stored in a retrieval system, or transmitted in any form or by any means, electronic, mechanical, photocopying, recording, or otherwise, without the prior permission of the publisher.

Reprinted under special agreement with the Publisher.

Players Press, Inc.
P. O. Box 1132
Studio City, CA 91614

Library of Congress Cataloging-in-Publication Data

McCaslin, Nellie
    Creative drama in the classroom / Nellie McCaslin. -- 5th ed.
        p.   cm.
    Includes bibliographical references.
    ISBN 0-88734-604-9
    1. Drama in education.   I. Title.
  PN3171.M25   1990b   89-63227
  371.3'32--dc20   CIP

Acknowledgments

"The Paddygog" by Charles Van Riper reprinted with permission from Avery Color Studios and Cully Gage from *The Northwoods Reader* (1977).

"The Story of Noah's Ark" by Penny Jones. Reprinted by permission of the author.

"Jack and the King's Daughter" by Rex Stephenson. Reprinted by permission of the author.

"Threads" by Ann Klotz. Reprinted by permission of the author.

"Little Burnt Face" from *Red Indian Fairy Book* by Frances J. Olcott. Copyright 1917 and © renewed 1945 by Frances Jenkins Olcott and Houghton Mifflin Company. This version of "Little Burnt Face" was adapted from *Legends of the Algonquin Indians* by C. G. Leland, 1894, Houghton Mifflin Company. Reprinted by permission of Houghton Mifflin Company.

This version of "Jack and His Animals" by Sinead de Valera in *Irish Fairy Tales*. Published by C.J. Fallon Educational Publishers, Dublin, Ireland, 1973.

"The Doughnuts" from *Homer Price* by Robert McClosky. Copyright 1943, renewed © 1971 by Robert McCloskey. All rights reserved. Reprinted by permission of Viking Penguin, a division of Penguin Books USA, Inc.

"The Old Man and the Goombay Cat" by Kitty Kirby. Copyright ©by Kitty Kirby. By permission of the author.

"The Wise Old Woman" from *The Sea of Gold and Other Tales* by Yoshiki Uchida. Copyright © 1965 by Yoshiki Uchida. Reprinted by permission of Charles Scribner's Sons.

"The Night the Elephants Marched on New York" from *Seven Sound and Motion Pictures* by Joanna H. Kraus. Reprinted by permission of New Plays, Inc., Bethel, Conn.

"Rimouski" from *In One Basket* by Shirley Pugh. Copyright © 1972 by Shirley Pugh. Reprinted by permission of Anchorage Press of New Orleans.

"Jump and Jiggle" from *Another Here and Now Storybook* by Lucy Sprague Mitchell. Copyright © 1937 by E. P. Dutton & Co., Inc. Renewed 1965 by

To Nadine Miles, Professor Emeritus, whose classes at Case Western Reserve University stimulated my intellectual curiosity, awakened my social consciousness, and turned a love of theatre into a lifelong commitment.

The arts improve human life: the quality of our thoughts, acts, choices—the cultural events that make us who we are.

They help all learning by educating feeling: the beliefs, emotions, insight and intuition to deal with information.

They are basic to "the basics": drama and story-telling ground speaking/reading; visual arts ground verbal learning; and "trying out" grounds common sense, estimation (math) and hypothesis.

Creative Arts improve confidence, awareness, expression, self-concept, concentration, problem solving, motivation and the use of unique thought styles.

They teach the generic skills needed in work/leisure: inter-acting with and "reading" others; being creative, spontaneous, flexible, adaptable, persistent with good judgment.

Creative Arts promote social bonding: cooperation is essential to many activities in music/dance/drama/ art.

Teaching the arts is a highly complex and difficult task requiring the skills of artist and teacher.[1]

---

1. The Forum for Arts and Media Education (Ontario Institute for Studies in Education; *and* Faculty of Education, University of Toronto).

Contents

Foreword

For the past twenty years or more, Nellie McCaslin's *Creative Drama in the Classroom* has been one of the best sellers in educational drama. And no wonder: it was a clear, precise, and valued handbook for beginning teachers; and it was a book they could grow with. Everywhere in the world where drama teachers gathered, you could see a copy of it under someone's arm. Now she has revised it thoroughly, cut away a little dead wood, and added significant new material to suit the changing times.

This new book is truly for the 1990s, and it will be the standard reference for the twenty-first century. Although this is its fifth edition, it contains so much that is new that it will gain a further generation of enthusiastic readers. It is so packed with rich information, so full of valuable materials to use, and so infused with wisdom, that it is an essential tool for beginning teachers and leaders in creative drama who can go on to expand its ideas as they enrich their experience.

I wonder if its readers realize how fortunate they are? When I began teaching creative drama in 1948, there was virtually nothing to help me. Caldwell Cook's *The Play Way* (1917) was long out of print, as was the work of Winifred Ward, and it was the rare library that had a copy of either. There were no other drama teachers whom I could ask for help. Most principals and administrators had never heard of "creative drama." Parents thought it was acting for the theatre. When I went to my first job, I faced classes of 40 or 50 inner city secondary students—rough, tough, and street-wise—entirely on my own. I was thrown on my personal resources and my struggles in the classroom were both exciting and painful.

"You're the drama man, I hear," said the principal, looking at me severely over his glasses. "Well, we don't do any drama *here!*"

"But—"

"No, no drama *here!*" he exclaimed with the finality of thunder. So I had to slip creative drama into my teaching whenever I thought no one was looking. But one day, when my 14-year-old slow learners were acting what happened on Columbus' journey (and Harry was the fish swimming under Columbus' ship), the principal came into the back of the classroom. He beckoned me over.

"I thought I told you that we don't do any drama here?" he said in a loud stage whisper.

"But," I explained, "we're doing social studies. You see—"

"Look!" he said angrily, pointing at Harry. "I know drama when I see it! And *that's* drama!"

I managed to get him to talk to the students, to question them about what they knew of the voyages of discovery. They were so full of information and excitement (after all, they'd *been there!*) that he was quite overwhelmed. By the end of the year in the same school I was teaching nothing but drama. This real story says little about me except that I am persistent. But it says a lot about drama as a learning medium.

Over forty years later, the world has changed. Teachers can now be trained in drama from beginning to doctoral level. There are plenty of good books and journals available. There are master-teachers helping others—either in person, or on tape and film. Increasingly schools employ drama teachers. Virtually anyone who wishes to teach drama, and who has the necessary ability, can do so.

Creative drama has *grown up*. And one of the reasons it has come of age is that *Creative Drama in the Classroom* has been available for over twenty years. For example, some years ago it was common to hear that *this* method of teaching drama was better than *that,* or that X should not be used in the drama classroom while Y should be. One of the main things we learn from Nellie McCaslin's book is that these issues are quite insignificant. She says that "there are many ways of approaching the study of drama; become familiar with different approaches, then follow the method that is right for you and the students you teach." That is very wise.

What is most important is that students are practically engaged in *creating drama*. That sounds simple but it is more complex than it appears. For example, there are many different kinds of dramatic acts. Drama is acting "as if" which we can identify when:

1. A student acts the role of another character and also transforms the environment into something different—"I am a spaceman in a space-ship."
2. A student keeps the same self but transforms the environment—"I, myself, am in a space-ship."
3. A student acts the role of another character in the actual environment— "As I eat my breakfast in real life, I am a spaceman."

If any of these events are taking place, the students are creating drama. The key in each case is the intention, aim, or purpose of the student. Clearly not merely action is involved but also mental activity. The creative imagination is *the thinking function* of action which also has *a doing function.* These two functions are the joint focus of creative drama. If the student is engaged in both of them, then creative drama is taking place. (We should note that this is a direct analogy with how we all operate in life—through thinking and acting.)

Which method the teacher uses is not as important as whether the students are *really* dramatizing or whether they are not. If they are, the method the teacher is using is probably the right one. This accounts for the enormous range of activities in this book: from spontaneous improvisation and playmaking in the classroom to puppetry and poetry, from mime to speech, from therapy to participation, and from play to appreciation. There are also whole new chapters on circus arts and Theatre-in-Education, or T.I.E. Creative drama is *a way of working* and Dr. McCaslin shows that it can be used not only in schools but in recreation and libraries, church and community groups, recreation and leisure, and all kinds of other activities.

When players, children or adults, are engaged in creative drama they create a microcosm of life. We can say the same about plays performed on a stage in a playhouse, but there is a difference. In the theatre, the work has been cut and added to, polished and honed, because its *necessary* purpose is that *the audience* must feel it to be such a microcosm. But with creative drama an audience is not *necessary.* It may possibly be present but it is unlikely. In creative drama the purpose of the playing is *for the players.* They draw on real life for their materials, just as they model themselves on real life in their actions, to create drama spontaneously and, thus, satisfy their needs as human beings. This may be for learning—in which case creative drama is part of education. Or it may be for therapy, or for recreation, or for a plethora of other purposes.

What is most interesting is that, in the drama field, *distinctions between activities are NOT clear and precise oppositions.* That is to say, although there is a difference between the extremes of creative drama and theatre, there is "a grey area" between them. For example, in 1966 some fifty teenagers and I, on a ten day residential course, used creative drama to explore a whole series of subjects from the Old and New Testament; on the eleventh day we staged them in a school hall in front of their parents like a medieval Mystery Cycle—around the sides of the hall with the audience sitting in the middle on swivel chairs and, thereby, participating in the action. Was this creative drama? Was it theatre? It was both, of course—and other things, too. During the ten days, the students also used creative puppetry, made their own costumes, used playmaking to form their creative drama into scenes, and made specific decisions (like the use of swivel chairs). The key question the reader will ask is: how did I, as the teacher, know *when* to initiate such an activity?

If a beginning teacher asks such a question, or asks "What do I do on a wet Friday afternoon?" or if a recreation leader asks, "What do I do now?" there is no one answer. Everything depends on *the teacher's or leader's judgment of the students' needs at a specific moment.* What this book provides is a rich resource upon which the teacher or leader can draw in order to make effective decisions. The prime *AIMS* of the creative drama teacher or leader are to ensure that:

1. the players create drama in its thinking and acting functions;
2. the activity satisfies their own personal and social needs; they may not be conscious of these needs which can be tacit, or implicit in what they do, so the teacher must infer them; and
3. the activity meets the end-in-view; i.e., education, recreation, therapy, etc.

People interpret these aims differently. While this is true between countries where different societies make particular demands upon teachers, it is also the case from one teacher to another in the same community. That is why Nellie McCaslin asks all teachers to identify the approach which is best for them. Thus the teacher's main *TASKS* are threefold:

1. to *diagnose* the students' needs through the inter-active skill of "negotiation"—"seeing things from their viewpoint" (which is also a criterion for dramatic thinking);
2. to *design* activities which will likely satisfy them; and
3. to *assess* whether this happened effectively.

Beginning teachers will find that the author provides a splendid guide to fulfilling these aims and undertaking these tasks.

Nellie McCaslin has been an integral part of many changes in creative drama, both past and present, and she appropriately devotes her last chapter to New Directions. Creative drama is always on the knife-edge of the future and change is its constant companion. This is what makes it a challenge for the good teacher. Like our experience in everyday life, teaching creative drama resembles "a high-wire act": we are all proceeding onwards in the "here and now," one step at a time, as we face "what happens next." But then, no one said it was going to be easy. . . .

Richard Courtney
Ontario Institute
for Studies in Education

Preface

Preparing the fifth edition of a book is an intimidating, albeit exciting, prospect, challenging the author to question what can be added that has not been said in previous editions or in other texts in the field. In the case of *Creative Drama in the Classroom,* a number of new texts have been published since the fourth edition, five of which were addressed to the specific needs of the elementary school teacher and several to specialists in related disciplines. These books, in addition to others already on the market, made me wonder whether there is need for yet another. In spite of this burgeoning literature, however, so much has been developing in and expanding the field that I was compelled to conclude that yes, there is a need, and yes, I am eager to begin work on a new edition.

As I started planning the content, I was aware of the changing profile of students enrolled in my classes. Whereas when I first began to teach I could anticipate young theatre and education majors, today they are outnumbered by students interested in drama therapy, social work, recreation and leisure-time activities, religion, deafness education, and even business, with many more foreign students at the graduate level. This new population is a challenge to the instructor, who must rethink the objectives and adjust the content to meet these varied interests and needs. Far from being a disadvantage, however, the variety of backgrounds and experiences these students bring with them enriches a group immeasurably, and I feel fortunate to have the stimulation and pleasure of teaching so many of these interesting and interested men and women.

I am also aware of the changing titles of university departments, which range from being called theatre, drama, theatre arts, performing arts, fine arts, or simply arts, film and theatre, music and dance, dance and drama, and communication arts and sciences. This variety indicates an expanding content and a closer relationship among all arts forms than previously existed. Some departments take a conservatory approach, whereas others are an integral part of a college of liberal arts or a school of education. Today's graduates have more career choices open to them, including teaching, community service, drama as therapy, and acting and the technical areas of the professional and nonprofessional stage.

As I surveyed the field, I was tempted to change the title of the book, but I refrained, concluding that it was not necessary since I was starting from the same base as in all former editions. The rationale for a fifth edition lies in the new directions, directions that admittedly are perceived from my own experience and reported with my own emphases. The emphases have not changed; indeed, they have, if anything, become stronger. Chief among them is the value of creative expression for children, drama that is guided but not directed and is nonjudgmental. This is not to suggest that "anything goes" but rather that honest efforts must be respected and students encouraged to take risks and learn to work cooperatively with others. Second is performance. In the fourth edition I cited performance as being a natural development of creative drama and often a desirable end, when culminating a successful unit of work. Now I am prepared to go a step further and argue with those who regard all performing by children as undesirable. The reasons behind their point of view, which I shared for many years, was based on a response to the wooden acting and boredom of children, who were forced to endure long periods of rehearsal in an effort to attain a level of perfection that could not and should not have been expected. This aim, unfortunately, too often led to a second undesirable practice: that of putting the so-called talented children on stage at the expense of their classmates, who may have needed the experience far more than they did. Furthermore, such productions were often in the hands of teachers who had no background in the theatre arts, yet were required to put on a play or present some kind of public performance. This practice resulted in a painful experience for both players and audience, rather than the pleasure that playmaking should be. Therefore, to do away with performance was a necessary step in the shifting of priorities from product to process. Even so, and I must be cautious in my advocacy of performing by children, the audience and the playing space should be selected with care, for strange spectators and large auditoriums can destroy all of the benefits that can be derived from sharing work with others in a familiar and intimate setting. I should still, however, not endorse putting very young children on a stage.

Among the other changes in my perception of creative drama as it is taught today are the values of the new uses that have been discovered. There is, for instance, drama as a tool for the teaching of writing; drama as therapy, a rapidly developing field; clowning and circus arts, an exciting experiment; puppets and human players performing together, rather than separately; participatory drama, in which creative drama and formal theatre merge; and Theatre-in-Education, or T.I.E. These new uses must be introduced and handled with care, or they risk going down with other good ideas that failed because too little preparation preceded practice. The growing interest in T.I.E. and the circus arts has suggested entire chapters on these subjects.

Attending plays has also taken on new dimensions, as television has become the primary source of popular entertainment in America. Sponsors and producers of children's plays, concerned that live theatre was being replaced by television, recognized their responsibility to provide more than an hour of entertainment if they hoped to compete with such formidable competition. This meant that children's theatre faced new restraints: It must guard against fare so weighted in favor of education that it loses the excitement and aesthetic appeal of the living theatre at its best; yet it should not, in an effort to amuse, be lacking in substance. When content and entertainment are held in balance and well performed, the result is a rich experience, which children in an affluent society should not be denied. To this end, fundamental changes are taking place.

The art of storytelling, which lost favor with the advent of television, has undergone a renaissance in the past twenty years. Professional storytellers now abound, and conferences in which storytelling techniques are the focus draw large numbers of students, teachers, and librarians. Amazing to me is the ease with which practitioners and public alike are accepting these changes, which I hope are not fads, "in" one year and "out" in five. Fortunately, research is being carried on in many quarters, testing the results of pilot projects and experiments that seem to be successful. My question at this juncture is not what is new but rather where lines should be drawn, for an author's temptation is to include material that may not be germane to the stated subject of a book, in this case creative drama.

Few teachers and students have had sufficient experience in the performing arts to feel secure. On the other hand, many who have studied formal theatre techniques have had no experience with children. There is little doubt that the creative leader eventually will find his or her own way, but if the following chapters hasten the process by offering a point of view and ways of working, they will have served their purpose.

It is not my intention to provide either a recipe book or a collection of exercises that go no further. Exercises are valuable in drama as they are in the other arts, but they are rarely ends in themselves and should not be used as such. Rather, they should be regarded as preparation for work in greater depth or as warm-ups. Many activities are fun; all of them strengthen players in different ways. Included as an important component of teaching drama, they help to develop concentration, imagination, and the use of body, voice, and speech. By merely repeating them endlessly, however, they are little more than charades, leading administrators to question their validity in the curriculum. Although I tend to work through the progression I have outlined in this book, it may not be the best for every teacher. There are many ways of approaching the study of drama: become familiar with different approaches and then follow the method that is right for you and the students you teach.

Particularly important is avoiding getting caught up in theory, for this can confuse as well as explain.

This book is intended as a college text for students who are preparing for both classroom teaching and/or specializing in drama education. It has been conceived, as have all of the earlier editions, from a point of view rather than organized along specific age levels, for I believe the philosophy to be the same for all, regardless of the age or grade level. Indeed, recent workshops for senior adults have shown that many creative drama techniques designed for children are equally effective in working with this older population.

I have added numerous new activities, stories, and poems in an effort to enrich the content. A conscious decision was made to emphasize practicality rather than theory; any theory that is included is, in general, implicit, serving as a guideline for activities I have found to be successful. I believe that a good experience in drama and theatre, regardless of the reason for providing them, enhances the quality of life, and it is to this end that I am most deeply committed. To bring satisfaction and joy into the lives of *all* children and to awaken a respect and caring concern for all living creatures are the ultimate goals of an enlightened society.

The bibliography has been revised and updated. Familiarity with the literature in the field not only helps to build a better background for teachers but should strengthen their awareness of the values of drama. It also helps to discourage a tendency to espouse a single method or point of view. My hope is that students will begin to devise some original techniques geared not to an arbitrary age level or method but to their individual circumstances.

A problem that plagues most teachers of the arts is evaluation of student work. Although many of us would prefer not to give grades at all, we can and should assess both individual and group progress. One way that I have found helpful is the use of a chart in which criteria for growth and development are listed. It has been suggested that I include a checklist in this edition similar to the one I designed for my teacher resource books, *Creative Drama in the Primary Grades* and *Creative Drama in the Intermediate Grades.* Although those books were written specifically for the classroom teacher, the principle is the same: to measure the growth of the student rather than to assign a grade for a product. It is hoped that the inclusion of guidance in pupil evaluation in the appendix will prepare college students for the evaluative process that inevitably lies ahead of them.

I want to acknowledge the inspiration that has come from my many friends and colleagues in this country and abroad. In the earlier editions I listed the names of persons to whom I felt particularly indebted. That list has expanded to the point that it would be impossible to name them all. But their thinking and work have continued to shape my views, just as their writing has contributed so richly to our field. I also want to acknowledge my appreciation of the pioneering work being done in the areas of drama therapy and special education. Although teachers of the arts have long recognized the value of drama for the handicapped, little had been done to provide opportunities for hands-on participation. The federal legislation in the midseventies forced us to take a closer look at our offerings in the arts and their availability to the handicapped. The lacks that were revealed resulted in a number of new programs and improved facilities; most important, however, was a heightened awareness of the needs of *all* handicapped persons.

I want to express my gratitude to practitioners and producers across the land, who responded to my call for photographs. I cannot thank them enough for their generosity. The pictures they sent not only enhance the book but add a dimension by showing readers some of the approaches and kinds of work being done in the different regions of the country. My thanks also go to my students who continue to raise questions that I must answer. Their desire to learn stimulates my own thinking, and their observations cause me to reconsider and often modify some of my views.

In addition to the above, I owe special thanks to the following friends and colleagues, who have read the manuscript and made helpful suggestions in areas of their expertise. Deepest gratitude goes to John Hodgson for the chapter on T.I.E.; to Andrew Burnstine and Jean Paul Jenack for the chapter on clowning and circus skills; to Robert Landy for checking the information on drama therapy; to Daty Healy for her careful proofreading of the entire manuscript; and finally to my editor, Gordon T. R. Anderson, for his continuing guidance, as I traveled this road once again.

Nellie McCaslin
New York City

1 Creative Drama: An Art, a Socializing Activity, and a Way of Learning

A socializing activity. (*Courtesy of Jamaica Arts Center, Arts Partners, New York City.*)

*Creative drama in its truest and deepest sense cannot
be stereotyped. It's like a river—always on the move—
making connections:*
connecting river banks
connecting starting points and destinations;
connecting through improvisation
action and reaction
initiative and response
thinking and feeling;
relations between
people
ideas
even centuries!

—JULIE THOMPSON, **Former director, Children's Centre
for the Creative Arts, Adelphi University**

*F*ew adults would deny the importance of the arts
in the education of their children. To enjoy the arts and appreciate the richness
they can add to human life, however, some preparation is needed. For most
children, that preparation is, or should be, given in school. The questions,
therefore, concern not so much an educational philosophy as practical matters of
budget, time, and place in the curriculum; grade-level allocation; and local
priorities. Although music and the visual arts have long held tenure in the
curriculum of many schools, the theatre arts have not. Now, however, despite
budget cuts, drama is being mandated in a number of states. The most valid
argument offered in support of this action is the most obvious. Of all of the arts,
drama involves the participant the most fully: intellectually, emotionally, physically, verbally, and socially. As players, children assume the roles of others, where
they learn and become sensitive to the problems and values of persons different
from themselves. At the same time, they are learning to work cooperatively in
groups, for drama is a communal art, each person necessary to the whole.

As spectators, children become involved vicariously in the adventures of
characters on the stage. It is also an opportunity to become acquainted with
literature and to enjoy the visual arts through scenery and costumes. Discipline is
an important element of the theatre, both on and off stage, but it is a discipline
readily accepted in much the same way that an athletic team is willing to suspend
personal wishes and interests for the sake of group goals and interests. Drama is
the first art we discover as toddlers and the last we relinquish in old age. Since
the advent of television, drama has come into our living rooms, into hospitals,
and into nursing homes, making the performing arts available as long as we live.
Although we may deplore the number of hours that *children* spend in front of the
screen, for the housebound and the patient, television provides theatre, music,

dance, news, and sports, enabling the viewers to escape the physical and geographic boundaries of their beds and chairs.

The child who is given an opportunity to participate in creative drama in a comfortable and nonpressured classroom and to see plays of high quality has advantages that extend into all areas of life. With such an abundance of riches, it is easy to understand the widespread belief that drama and theatre constitute an elaborate art form, difficult to implement and expensive to maintain. Actually, nothing is further from the truth. Creative drama needs no special equipment, no studio, and no stage; time, space, and an enthusiastic, well-prepared leader are the only requirements. As for theatre, most actors can perform anywhere, provided the play does not depend on special effects or sophisticated staging. Professional touring companies are prepared to perform in all-purpose rooms and cafeterias. A stage may enhance the production, to be sure, but it is seldom a necessity. There are aesthetic values to be found in beautiful visual effects, but they are not necessary to the majority of plays designed for young audiences. Sincerity, sensitivity, and intelligent planning are the most important components of an effective performance. In many communities, the local university or civic theatre offers plays to which classes are bused during school hours at little or no cost to the children. Many of these productions are excellent, sensitively played, and tastefully staged. In recent years, an educational component has become an important service offered by producers. Workshops for children following a performance, special workshops for teachers, and an effort to relate plays to the curriculum enrich the experience.

In summary, the theatre arts are the least difficult of the arts to implement, with the greatest potential for learning. They have a place in our schools on all levels because they constitute a subject in its own right, to be treated seriously, not added as a frill or an enhancement if the budget permits. Moreover, in the best arts programs, students learn the basic skills through the process of creative drama, for the commonly held objectives of education are remarkably similar to the objectives of creative drama. Let us compare them.

Educational Objectives

One of the most frequently stated aims of education is the maximal growth of the child both as an individual and as a member of society. To achieve this aim, certain educational objectives have been set up. Although these objectives vary somewhat, there is general agreement that knowledge and appreciation of and skills in the arts are essential. The modern curriculum tries to ensure that each child will:

1. *Develop basic skills in which reading, writing, arithmetic, science, social studies, and the arts are stressed*
2. *Develop and maintain good physical and mental health*

3. *Grow in ability to think*
4. *Clarify values and verbalize beliefs and hopes*
5. *Develop an understanding of beauty, using many media, including words, color, sound, and movement*
6. *Grow creatively and thus experience one's own creative powers*[1]

Although other objectives are mentioned, these six are most frequently listed in the development of educational programs designed for today's world and the complex problems that life offers.

The most enthusiastic proponent of creative drama would not go so far as to claim that its inclusion in the curriculum will ensure the meeting of these objectives. But many objectives of modern education and creative drama are unquestionably shared. Among them are:

1. Creativity and aesthetic development
2. The ability to think critically
3. Social growth and the ability to work cooperatively with others
4. Improved communication skills
5. The development of moral and spiritual values
6. Knowledge of self

Before we discuss creative drama in greater detail, some definitions are in order. The terms *dramatic play, creative drama, playmaking, role playing, children's theatre,* and *participation theatre* often are used interchangeably, although they have different meanings. The following definition will clarify the meanings as they are used in this text.

Definitions

Dramatic Play

Dramatic play is the free play of very young children, in which they explore their universe, imitating the actions and character traits of those around them. It is their earliest expression in dramatic form, but must not be confused with drama or interpreted as performance. Dramatic play is fragmentary, existing only for the moment. It may last for a few minutes or go on for some time. It even may be played repeatedly, if the child's interest is sufficiently strong; but when this occurs, the repetition is in no sense a rehearsal. It is, rather, the repetition of a

---

1. Robert S. Fleming, *Curriculum for Today's Boys and Girls* (Columbus: Charles E. Merrill, 1963), p. 10.

creative experience for the pure joy of doing it. It has no beginning and no end and no development in the dramatic sense.

It has been stated that "dramatic play helps the child develop from a purely egocentric being into a person capable of sharing and of give and take."[2] In dramatic play children create a world of their own in which to master reality. They try in this imaginative world to solve real-life problems that they have, until now, been unable to solve. They repeat, reenact, and relive these experiences. In the book *Understanding Children's Play,* the authors observed that through this activity children are given an opportunity to imitate adults, encouraged to play out real-life roles with intensity, to dramatize relationships and experiences, to express their own most pressing needs, to release unacceptable impulses, to reverse the roles usually taken to try to solve problems, and to experiment with solutions. If encouraged, by providing the place, the equipment, and an atmosphere in which a child feels free, dramatic play is a natural and healthy manifestation of human growth.

Creative Drama and Playmaking The terms *creative drama* and *playmaking* may be used interchangeably since they refer to informal drama that is created by the participants.[3] As the name *playmaking* implies, this activity goes beyond dramatic play in scope and intent. It may make use of a story with a beginning, a middle, and an end. It may, on the other hand, explore, develop, and express ideas and feelings through dramatic enactment. It is, however, always improvised drama. Dialogue is created by the players, whether the content is taken from a well-known story or is an original plot. Lines are not written down or memorized. With each playing, the story becomes more detailed and better organized, but it remains extemporaneous and is at no time designed for an audience. Participants are guided by a leader rather than a director; the leader's goal is the optimal growth and development of the players.

The replaying of scenes is therefore different from the rehearsal of a formal play in that each member of the group is given an opportunity to play various parts. No matter how many times the story is played, it is done for the purpose of deepening understanding and strengthening the performers rather than perfecting a product. Scenery and costumes have no place in creative drama, although an occasional property or piece of a costume may be permitted to stimulate the

---

2. Ruth Hartley, Lawrence K. Frank, and Robert M. Goldenson, *Understanding Children's Play* (New York: Columbia University Press, 1964), p. 19.

3. Definition of *creative drama* accepted by the Children's Theatre Association of America in 1977: "Creative drama is an improvisational, nonexhibitional, process-centered form of drama in which participants are guided by a leader to imagine, enact, and reflect upon human experiences. Although creative drama traditionally has been thought of in relation to children and young people, the process is appropriate to all ages."

imagination. When these things are used, they should not be considered mounting or production. Most groups do not feel the need of properties of any kind and are generally freer without them.

The term *creative drama* is used to describe the improvised drama of children from age five or six and older, but it belongs to no particular age level and may be used just as appropriately to describe the improvisation of high school students. The young adult is more likely to label it *improvisation,* which indeed it is, but the important distinction is that it has form and is, therefore, more structured than dramatic play. At the same time, it is participant centered and not intended for sharing, except with the members of the group who are not playing and are, therefore, observers rather than audience.

The word *drama* is also used to mean literature. In the present context, however, it is used to mean a play that is developed creatively by a group, as opposed to one that abides by a written script. When dialogue is written by either teacher or children, it automatically ceases to be spontaneous drama, although it may, indeed, be a fine example of creative writing. This occasionally happens, and when it does, the results may be doubly rewarding. Nevertheless, whether it is simple or elaborate, if the play is to be properly described as creative drama, it must be improvised rather than written.

Children's Theatre   The term *children's theatre* refers to formal productions for children's audiences, whether acted by amateurs or professionals, children or adults, or a combination of both. It is directed rather than guided; dialogue is memorized, and scenery and costumes usually play an important part. Since it is audience centered, it is essentially different from creative drama and dramatic play. The child in the audience is the spectator, and the benefits derived are aesthetic.

What do children gain from attending good children's theatre? They gain much. First, there is the thrill of watching a well-loved story come alive on a stage. There is the opportunity for a strong, vicarious experience as they identify with characters who are brave, steadfast, noble, loyal, beautiful. Emotions are released as they share the adventure and excitement of the plot. Finally, they learn to appreciate the art of the theatre if the production is tasteful and well done.

We are speaking now of children in the audience, not in the play. Although there is much that is creative and of value for the performer, it is generally agreed that participation in creative drama is far more beneficial than public performances for all children up to the age of ten or eleven. Occasionally, there is an expressed desire to put on a play, and when this comes from the children themselves, it is probably wise to grant the request. There are times when sharing is a joy and a positive experience, but it is to be hoped that formal play production would be infrequent. Certainly, if it is done, the production should be simple and all precautions taken to guard against the competition and tension that so often characterize the formal presentation of a play. For junior and senior high school students, however, a play is often the desired culmination of a semester's work. To deprive students of the experience would be to withhold the ultimate satisfaction of communicating an art.

Some leaders in the field believe that any performance in front of an audience is harmful because it automatically interferes with the child's own free expression. I agree up to a point, but the theatre is, after all, a performing art, and when the audience is composed of understanding and sympathetic persons, such as parents or members of another class, performance may be the first step toward communicating a joyful experience. Without question, however, very young children should not perform publicly. Those in the middle and upper grades may not be harmed if their desire and the right occasion indicate that the benefits outweigh the disadvantages. A performance is a disciplined and carefully organized endeavor, involving a variety of skills that children of elementary school age do not and should not be expected to possess.

I am not speaking here of the professional child actor, who, most educators agree, is in grave danger of being damaged by exploitation and the pressures of performance. The same dangers, however, are present whenever children are used for ends other than their own growth and development. When children are trained rather than guided, praised extravagantly instead of encouraged, or featured as individuals rather than helped to work cooperatively with others, they risk losing all positive aspects of the experience. Ironically, this leads to poor theatre as well, for ensemble, that most desirable quality of good theatre, is achieved through the process of working together, not by featuring individual players.

Role Playing The term *role playing* is used most often in connection with therapy or education. It refers to the assuming of a role for the particular value it may have to the participant, rather than for the development of an art. Although all art may be considered to have certain curative powers, it is not the primary purpose of either creative drama or theatre to provide therapy or make use of drama to solve social and emotional problems. Role playing is what the young child does in a dramatic play, but it is also a tool used by psychologists and play therapists.

Acting is, in a way, an extension of dramatic play. According to Richard Courtney, "Play, acting and thought are interrelated. They are mechanisms by which the individual tests reality, gets rid of his anxieties, and masters his environment."[4]

Drama Therapy Drama therapy is similar to role playing in its stated purpose. Its use assumes a problem, for which this type of treatment is indicated.

---

4. Richard Courtney, *Play, Drama, and Thought* (New York: Drama Book Specialists), p. 177.

An art form. (*Courtesy of Arts Partners; photograph by Frank Stewart.*)

Physically handicapped, mentally retarded, emotionally disturbed, and culturally disadvantaged children may derive great benefit from its use, provided the therapy is in the hands of a competent and sensitive therapist. The distinction between role playing and therapy, therefore, consists more of degree than of kind. *Role playing* may be considered preventive, in that it provides an opportunity for all children in a group to develop sensitivity toward the feelings of others and encourages changes of attitude through understanding. *Therapy* is the dramatic technique used for its curative power in helping a patient to solve problems that frighten, confuse, or puzzle her. "It is in itself both a form of comfort and reassurance, and a way of moving on toward new attitudes about these things."[5]

New Techniques in Drama and Theatre Education

Although the following techniques have been in use in England since the midsixties, they are only now becoming generally known and accepted in this country. The terminology, however, is not always clearly understood here nor, indeed, is it always used to mean the same thing; therefore I am defining the more common terms in order that references in later chapters will be understood.

5. Peter Slade, *Child Drama* (London: University of London Press, 1954), p. 119.

Participation Theatre

This is a technique, originated by Brian Way in England, which permits the audience to become vocally, verbally, and physically involved in the production.[6] Children are invited to suggest ideas to the actors from time to time during the enactment of a play. Frequently, the audience, if not too large, is invited to come into the playing area to assist the cast in working out these ideas. Skillfully handled, this can be an exciting technique.

All theatre involves participation the moment the attention is captured. An audience feels, thinks, laughs, applauds, and occasionally speaks out; in our time, unlike earlier periods, adult audiences are expected to sit quietly whether or not the performances please them. The child audience, however, less inhibited and unschooled in these conventions, wants to do more, to become actively engaged as it suspends all disbelief. It identifies with the protagonist and participates in the action to the extent that conditions and authority permit. The younger the audience, the more natural the involvement. The point to be made here is that the Brian Way Method offers a new approach to children's theatre by combining the formal with the informal in its attempt to establish a closer relationship between actor and audience. The line commonly drawn between creative drama and children's theatre disappears as the spectator becomes participant.

Developmental Drama

The term *developmental drama* has been used primarily by Richard Courtney in Canada. Although one occasionally finds it in the literature here, Courtney's definition is the best and clearest we have.

> Developmental drama is the study of developmental patterns in human enactment. Drama is an active bridge between our inner world and the environment.

---

6. Brian Way, *Audience Participation* (Boston: Baker's Plays, 1981). In this book Way begins with a description of his study of the child audience. Based upon his observations, he tells how he developed a play structure in which spaces were left open for audience input and actual physical participation. This meant, first, reducing the size of the audience to a managable group of no more than two hundred and fifty persons, preferably seated in the round. Next was the training of his actors to handle the technique: how to invite children's responses, how to involve them in the action, and how to get them back into their seats when their part in the play was finished.

Lifting the barrier between actors and audience removed the controls that exist in the theatre, however, and it had to be replaced by a sense of security on the part of the actors and an involvement in the *play*, not in the *release* from restrictions on the part of the audience. Although the Way method might be summed up in the single word *trust*, its success depends on experience in a theatre where, periodically, actors and audience merge. Participatory theatre has been most successful with younger children, although a skilled, experienced company can provide a rich and meaningful experience for any age level.

Thus the developments studied are both personal and cultural, and each is in interaction with the other. These studies overlap with other fields: with psychology and philosophy on a personal level, and with sociology and anthropology on a cultural level. Despite the use of these allied fields, however, the focus of study within developmental drama is always the *dramatic act*. From these theoretical considerations, implications can be drawn for specific practical fields.[7]

Drama-in-Education

D.I.E. (Drama-in-Education) is the use of drama as a means of teaching other subject areas. It is used to expand children's awareness, to enable them to look at reality through fantasy, to see below the surface of actions to their meanings. The objective is understanding rather than playmaking, although a play may be made in the process. Attitudes rather than characters are the chief concern. Exponents of DIE say that this technique can be used to teach any subject.

Classroom teachers find it a valuable tool for involving children in the study of a topic. Rather than dramatizing a story or developing a play, children project themselves into a dramatic moment of the topic at hand (i.e., a mine disaster, a strike, a gold rush, an election, etc.); from there they go on to examine and learn more about the topic. They *become* the persons in the situation as they study it. The teacher brings in source materials and guides the study. A play may result but it is not the purpose of this use of drama.

Theatre-in-Education

T.I.E. (Theatre-in-Education) is a British concept that differs from traditional children's theatre in its use of curricular material or social problems as themes. Performed by professional companies of actor–teachers, it presents thought-provoking content to young audiences for educational purposes rather than for entertainment. It must entertain to hold their attention, but that is not the primary purpose. The intent is to challenge the spectator and push him or her to further thinking and feeling about the issue. John O'Toole described it as follows:

> T.I.E. (Theatre-in-Education) was conceived as an attempt to bring the techniques of the theatre into the classroom, in the service of specific education-al objectives. . . . its aim was more than to be entertaining and thought-provoking, or to encourage the habit of theatre-going. . . . First, the material is usually specially devised, tailor-made to the needs of the children and the strength of the team. Second, the children are asked to participate; endowed with roles, they learn skills, make decisions, and solve problems, so the programs' structures have to be flexible . . . to respond to the children's contributions within the context of the drama and still to uphold the roles. . . .

7. Richard Courtney, *Re-Play* (Toronto: Ontario Institute for Studies in Education, 1982), p. 5.

Third, teams are usually aware of the importance of the teaching context, and try to prepare suggestions for follow-up work, or to hold preliminary workshops for classroom teachers.[8]

Special Techniques

The following terms are used in referring to special techniques used by some teachers of creative drama.

Side Coaching. This is a technique practiced by some teachers as a way of encouraging and strengthening players. The teacher offers suggestions from the sidelines to keep the improvisation going.

Teaching in-Role. The teacher takes an active part in the drama to deepen and extend the belief in established circumstances. This technique breaks the division between leader and group but is not necessarily continued after the group is going well.

Parallel Work. All students work at the same time, doing the same thing in different groupings (i.e., individual, pairs, two or more groups) to give everyone an equal opportunity for active simultaneous involvement. With all students participating there are no spectators.

Values in Creative Playing

Television has made us a nation of spectators. Children view it from infancy, and surveys reveal that they spend more hours in front of the screen each week than they spend in school. The current craze for video games has intensified this situation; therefore, it is more important than ever that we make opportunities available for children to experience participation in the arts. Creative drama is an ideal form for this participation, with its inclusion of the physical, mental, emotional, and social abilities of the participant.

There is general agreement among teachers of creative drama that important values can be gained from creative playing. Depending on the age of the children, the particular situation, and the orientation of the leader, these values may be listed in varying order. It is the contention of this book, however, that in spite of these differences, certain values exist in some measure for all, regardless of age, circumstances, or previous experience. To be sure, the activities must be planned with the group in mind and the emphasis placed upon the needs and interests of those involved. The five- or six-year-old needs and enjoys the freedom of large movement and much physical activity, but this should not deny a similar opportunity to older boys and girls. Adult students in early sessions also gain freedom and pleasure when given an opportunity to move freely in space.

---

8. John O'Toole, *Theatre-in-Education* (London: Hodder and Stoughton, 1976), p. vii.

The ten- or eleven-year-old enjoys the challenge of characterization and often creates with remarkable insight and understanding. Young children, however, can also create on their level, although they cannot be expected to compete with children who are older. In other words, it is not a question of assigning different values to various age levels; it is a matter of accepting basic values that exist on all levels, varying more in degree than in kind. Specifically, these values may be listed as follows:

An Opportunity to Develop the Imagination

Imagination is the beginning. To work creatively, it is necessary, first, to push beyond the boundaries of the here and now, to project oneself into another situation or into the life of another person. Few activities have greater potential for developing the imagination than playmaking. Little children move easily into a world of make-believe, but as we grow older, this amazing human capacity is often ignored or even discouraged. The development of the imagination to the point where the student responds spontaneously may take time in some cases, but it is the first step toward satisfying participation.

The sensitive teacher will not demand too much in the beginning but will accept with enthusiasm the first attempts of a beginner to use imagination to solve a problem. Once the players have had the fun of seeing, hearing, feeling, touching, tasting, or smelling something that is not there, they will find that their capacity grows quickly. Holding the image until they can do something about it is the next step, but the image must come first. Through drama, the imagination can be stimulated and strengthened to the student's everlasting pleasure and profit. We learn through experience. Unless we want a child to experience everything—which is impossible—we are obliged to give up the idea except by way of theatre. Through participation in drama and vicariously through attendance at plays, we can provide realistic experiences in acceptable and exciting ways.

An Opportunity for Independent Thinking

A particular value of creative playing is the opportunity it offers for independent thinking and planning. Although the drama, both informal and formal, is a group art, it is composed of the contributions of each individual, and every contribution is important. As the group plans together, each member is encouraged to express his or her own ideas and thereby contribute to the whole. The leader recognizes the part each child plays and the value that planning has for the child. If the group is not too large, there will be many opportunities before the activity is exhausted. Thinking is involved in questions such as: Who are the characters? What are they like? What part do they play? Why do they behave as they do? What scenes are important? Why? How can we suggest this action or that place?

The evaluation that follows is as important as the planning: indeed, it is preparation for a replaying. Children of all ages are remarkably perceptive, and their critical comments indicate the extent of their involvement. A well-planned session in creative drama provides exercises in critical thinking as well as an opportunity for creativity.

Freedom for the Group to Develop Its Own Ideas

Through creative drama an individual has a chance to develop and grow. This is also true of the group, in which ideas are explored, evaluated, changed, and used. As a group of any age works together under sensitive and skilled leadership, the members learn to accept, appreciate, and stimulate each other. Every teacher has experienced a group in which the dynamics were such that all seemed to produce more because of their association. This is not to suggest that creative drama is a magic formula for successful teamwork, but it unquestionably offers a rare opportunity for sharing ideas and solving problems together. The formal play, whatever problems it may pose, cannot offer a group this same challenge. The written script imposes a structure in which free improvisation has no place. There are values in formal production, to be sure, but the major emphasis is on the product, rather than on the participants.

The strength, incidentally, that is acquired through this kind of planning and playing together is a valuable asset when, at some later date, the group decides to give a formal play. Far from limiting the players, improvisation strengthens techniques and builds individual and group rapport.

An Opportunity for Cooperation

When a group builds something together, it is learning a valuable lesson in cooperation. Social differences may be forgotten in the business of sharing ideas and improvising scenes. Teachers who guide children in creative drama cite numerous examples of social acceptance based on respect for a job well done and the bond that develops from the fun of playing together. As an illustration, Jack entered a neighborhood class in drama that several of his third-grade schoolmates attended. It was obvious that he was an outsider, and the leader despaired of his ever becoming a part of the group. For the first three or four sessions, he contributed nothing and was chosen by no one, regardless of activity.

Then one day the children were dramatizing the story of *The Stone in the Road*. They wanted a farmer character to drive along the road with a donkey cart. Several attempted to pantomime the action, but each time the children insisted that "he didn't look like he was really driving." Suddenly Jack, who had been sitting on the sidelines, put up his hand and volunteered to try it. The vigorous and convincing pantomime he created as he guided his cart around the stone astonished the class. His position in the group changed at that moment, and although he never became one of the leaders, he was accepted and often sought out. Working together in an atmosphere of give-and-take is an experience in democratic partnership; it provides an opportunity for the Jacks in a group to contribute their skills and have them accepted. Or, as a college student once put it after her first experience of being in a play: "Now I know what John Glenn meant by 'we.' It was all of us working together who did it!"

An Opportunity to Build Social Awareness

Putting oneself in the shoes of another is a way of developing awareness and human understanding. By the time a player has decided who a character is, why she behaves as she does, how she relates to others, and the way in which she handles her problems, the player has come to know a great deal about her. Even the very young or inexperienced player may glimpse insights that help in understanding people and, therefore, in living. Both literature and original stories provide the player with this opportunity to study human nature.

In one class of ten-year-olds, the teacher began the morning by asking the children to think of someone they had seen on their way to school who had attracted their attention. It was suggested that the person should have interested them enough to become a character in a play. Immediately, every hand went up, and a variety of people were described. After a period of telling what they looked like, where they were, who they might have been, and what they were doing, the teacher asked the class to select three who would be good subjects for original stories. The class was then divided into three groups, six or seven in a group, and given an opportunity to make up a story about the person of their choice.

The first group decided upon the character Peter suggested—an old man whom Peter described sitting on the steps of his apartment building. The children decided that the old man might have been a school janitor who, in his retirement, spent the morning watching the children go to school. Having reached this decision, it was no time at all until they had developed a plot in which the old man's memory of having once saved a child's life became a sudden reality: A boy had run across the street after his ball, and the old man, in an automatic reaction, had rescued him from being hit by a car. The story, with its throwback scene imposed on the present, was dramatic and exciting both to the players and to the rest of the class; more than that, however, was the warm and sympathetic portrayal of the old man. Two adults who were in the room that day have spoken many times of the scene. If the memory remained with the observers, is it not likely that the children, who created the play, must have grown in the process?

A Healthy Release of Emotion

Much has been said about the thinking, both creative and critical, that characterizes creative drama. Another value is of equal importance: the opportunity to feel and release emotion. As children grow up, the opportunity for

A way of learning. (*Courtesy of Arts Partners; photograph by Frank Stewart.*)

emotional response is too often restricted to television and movies. Although there is value in being a spectator, the deep involvement of active participation is lacking.

Control of emotion does not mean suppression of emotion. It means the healthy release of strong feelings through appropriate and acceptable channels. At some time, all people feel anger, fear, anxiety, jealousy, resentment, or negativism. Through the playing of a part in which these emotions are expressed, the player may release them and thus relieve tension. "By permitting the child to play freely in a setting of security and acceptance, we enable him to deal satisfactorily and healthfully with his most urgent problems."[9]

Better Habits of Speech

To many teachers, a primary value of creative drama is the opportunity it offers for training in speech. There is a built-in motivation for the player who wishes to be heard and clearly understood. Volume, tempo, and pitch, as well as diction, are involved in a natural way; no other form of speech exercise captures the player to the same degree or offers so good a reason for working on speech. The little girl who can barely be heard in a classroom recitation will be reminded by her fellow players to speak up or the lines will be lost. The boy with the strident tone will also be told when his voice is too loud or inappropriate for the character he is portraying. Being, in turn, a giant, a prince, a king, an old man, or an animal offers further opportunity for developing variation of tone and expression. In creative drama, the concern is less for a standard of speech than it

9. Hartley, Frank, and Goldenson, *Understanding Children's Play,* p. 16.

is for audibility, clarity, and expression. Although the teacher does not dwell on speech as the major objective, she can point out its importance, and the children will accept the validity of her suggestion.

Not only articulation but also vocabulary is served through this form of oral expression. Conceptual thinking and the cognitive aspect of language are encouraged when words are put into practical use. For the young child, the culturally disadvantaged child, or the student with a foreign language background, vocabulary can be built and distinctions in word meanings made clear through participation in creative drama. Even abstract learnings may come more readily when words are acted or shown.

An Experience with Good Literature

The story one plays makes a lasting impression. Therefore, the opportunity to become well acquainted with good literature, through dramatizing it, is a major value—not that every story chosen will be of high literary quality. But many will be, and the leader usually discovers that these are the stories that hold interest longest. Both folk tales and modern tales provide fine opportunities for acting. Bruno Bettelheim has advanced powerful arguments for the folk and fairy tale, a genre that has in recent years been questioned as to its relevance for the modern child. In addition to the narrative interest of these tales, there are important psychological reasons why they continue to have value and why they should be used, though not to the exclusion of contemporary literature. A program that includes a variety of material helps to build appreciation and set a standard for original writing. Television shows and comic books attract temporary interest, but put beside a story that has stood the test of time, they rarely sustain attention. Believable characters, a well-constructed plot, and a worthwhile theme make for engrossing drama. What better way of discovering and learning to appreciate literature?

An Introduction to the Theatre Arts

Art is said to represent the human being's interpretation of life, expressed in a way that can be universally recognized and understood. The theatre offers many examples. Although creative drama is primarily participant centered, like theatre, it deals with the basic conflicts in life and thus offers young players their first taste of the magic and make-believe of the theatre. In their imagination, a chair becomes a throne; a stick, a wand; a change in lighting, a difference in time; and a character, a human being in whom they believe and with whom they can identify. Listening, watching, and becoming involved are required of the theatre audience. Children who are introduced to the theatre first through playing are going to look for more than superficial entertainment when they attend a performance. If we can visualize drama/theatre as a continuum, with dramatic play at one end and formal theatre at the other, we can follow a logical sequence leading from a child's earliest attempts at make-believe to creative drama to the finished product, in which there must also be belief.

Recreation

Implicit in everything that has been said so far, yet different and of value in itself, is the opportunity for recreation, or "re-creation," that drama/theatre affords. Under certain types of circumstances such as camp, community centers, after-school activity programs, and neighborhood clubs, the highest priority of drama may indeed be recreation. Drama is fun. It exists for the pleasure of the players, and it expresses free choice. It may also, in time, lead to serious work or even a lifelong avocation. Many universities today have programs in leisure studies, in which the constructive use of our increased free time is the focus. The human impulse to play makes drama one of the most popular activities in a recreation program.

Creative Drama for the Special Child

Creative drama offers an opportunity for children with handicapping conditions to participate in a performing art. Because of its flexibility, drama can be a joyful and freeing adventure for groups of all ages. Special needs can be served by adjusting emphases and activities. Often the experience of participation in drama for these children serves to stimulate interest in other subjects and, in so doing, strengthens skills and awakens latent abilities.

Values for the Teacher

What do teachers get from creative drama? Probably the most important thing is a perspective on every child in the class. A child's participating in drama reveals his or her imagination, skill in problem solving, and ability to work with others.

What if an exercise fails? The teacher should not be discouraged. No activity is foolproof, and no idea stimulates every class equally well. But we learn as the children do, by doing. Be prepared; then take the risk. The worst thing that can happen is that *one* lesson will not go as you had hoped it would. You will discover more from your flops than from your successes.

Although I do not suggest that special study of creative drama is unnecessary to its practice, I believe that the average classroom teacher, because of preparation and experience, is better equipped to teach it than he or she may realize. The reason? Drama does not require mastery of the kinds of technical skills that are required for the teaching of music, dance, or the visual arts. Drama does, however, demand sensitivity to and a knowledge of children; the goals and principles of education and some knowledge of child psychology—these things the classroom teacher already possesses. If we enjoy the theatre, and most of us do, sharing this interest with children should be a pleasure. Skill comes with experience. Experience, combined with study under well-prepared leaders, leads to an ease and ability that marks the professional.

Summary

Creative drama, whether in the classroom or in the camp or community program, may be regarded as a way of learning, a means of self-expression, a therapeutic technique, a social activity, or an art form. Children are helped to assume responsibility, accept group decisions, work together cooperatively, develop new interests, and—particularly in a classroom situation—seek new information. Drama is the most completely personal, as well as the most highly socialized, art form we have.

The values of informal play are many, and the leader will discover these and others as the group moves and grows. Not all values listed will be manifested at once, or perhaps ever, for the creative process is slow and takes time to develop. Also, leaders do not all hold the same priorities. They arrange them according to their situations and interests. More will be said on this point later.

The arts help us to develop a humane and enlightened society, for they point out our objectives:

They reflect our values, leading us to question them in time.
They express our feelings and sensitize us to the feelings of others.
They help us to grow.
They give us lifelong pleasure.

In these ways the arts are both means and ends, neither exclusively one nor the other.

It is often observed that few persons perform on their highest level. This is true of the beginning player, child or adult, who, through shyness or actual fear, needs encouragement and acceptance. The sensitive leader recognizes this and tries to create an atmosphere of mutual trust. In his or her acceptance of every child and what the child has to offer, the leader has taken the first big step toward building self-confidence. Freedom will follow, learning will occur, and an ordinary room will become a place in which exciting things can happen.

2 Imagination Is the Beginning

Encouraging dialogue through the puppet. *(Courtesy of Tamara Hunt, University of Hawaii at Manoa.)*

*Imagination is but another name for absolute power
and clearest insight, amplitude of mind, and reason in
her most exalted mood.*

—WORDSWORTH, The Prelude

*I*magination and creativity are two words we hear a great deal these days. Whether we are able to define them precisely or whether we merely have a sense of their meanings, we use them freely and in regard to a variety of people and a multitude of activities. Although it is not the purpose of this book to go into the subject in either length or depth, the terms *imagination* and *creativity* have been used in describing the art of creative drama. Therefore, some definition is required.

Imagination

The *fact* of imagination has long been recognized, but it is only recently that the *value* of imagination has been hailed. Shakespeare described imagination as the spark that makes humans the "paragon of animals." Today, not only the artist but also business people, scientists, military leaders, and educators describe imagination as the magic force that goes beyond the mastery of facts and techniques in the search for new ideas.

Suzanne Langer called imagination . . . "probably the oldest mental trait that is typically human—older than discursive reason; it is probably the common source of dream, reason, religion, and all true general observation."[1]

John Allen, in *Drama in Schools,* described imagination as free flowing, open-ended, transformational. "Artistic discipline is a constraint—but here lies the paradox—only until the discipline has forced the material into its appropriate pattern; then there follows a sense of freedom and exaltation that is the ultimate reward of all artistic creation."[2] Thus can the trivial be transformed into the significant through a creative act, and the ordinary into something unique.

Creativity

Creativity may be defined in a number of ways. It may be thought of in terms of product or process, depending on whether we are concerned with the solution to a problem or the way in which the problem is solved. If creativity is

1. Susanne K. Langer, "The Cultural Importance of the Arts," in *Aesthetic Form and Education,* ed. Michael F. Andrews (Syracuse, N.Y.: Syracuse University Press, 1958), p. 6.
2. John Allen, *Drama in Schools* (London: Heinemann Educational Books, 1979), p. 70.

interpreted as process, it is considered as a new way of seeing, a different point of view, an original idea, or a new relationship between ideas. Inventiveness and adaptation are often included in the thinking of those who believe creativity to be a way of working.

If, on the other hand, creativity is defined in terms of product, it is best illustrated by works of art (poems, stories, paintings, music, dance), scientific inventions, and new arrangements or designs. There has been great interest in the study and measurement of creativity in recent years, and a considerable body of data has appeared. One assumption accepted by psychologists doing research is that creativity is not a special gift possessed by a fortunate few but, rather, a human capacity possessed to some degree by everyone. It has been found, incidentally, that many individuals learn more if permitted to approach their studies creatively.

According to some authorities, the beginning of creative thinking may be found early in the life of the infant, in "manipulative and exploratory activities."[3] In his or her awareness of human expression, gestures, and sound, the baby is first observer and then investigator. It is but a short step from here to the baby's own experimentation, at which point the infant becomes creator. Drama, both informal and formal, is the artistic creation of human beings, based on their observation of human life—selected, arranged, and heightened.

The words *observer, investigator,* and *creator* are of particular interest to the teacher of creative drama. One leader held a discussion on the subject of creativity and imagination with a group of eight-year-olds in a creative drama class. Their dialogue ran something like this:

TEACHER: What does creativity mean to you?
PATRICIA: I think it means to make.
DENISE: No, not to make. To make up.
TEACHER: Can you explain the difference?
KENNY: Well, if a man made a pair of shoes, he'd be creating.
TEACHER: Do you all agree with Kenny?
DENISE: No, I think only the first pair of shoes would be created. If the man made a lot of others like them, they'd just be made—not made up.
TEACHER: Then everything that's made is not created?
DENISE: *(sticking to her original point)* Only the things that aren't copied.
TEACHER: How do you feel about copying?
PATRICIA: You don't get any fun out of copying.
CATHY: I think it's all right to copy some things.
TEACHER: What kind of things, Cathy?
CATHY: Well, like good manners. And words. You wouldn't know what to do lots of times if you didn't have something to copy.

---

3. E. Paul Torrance, *Creativity,* What Research Says Series (Washington, D.C.: National Education Association of the United States, 1963), p. 5.

TEACHER: Then you don't think copying is always a bad thing to do? *(General agreement that it is not.)*

DENISE: Just the same, you shouldn't use somebody else's mind. You want a thing to be just yours.

ALAN: You have to know what to copy and what not to. Sometimes it's hard to know which is which.

TEACHER: How would you explain imagination? Dean?

DEAN: You think of something that isn't there.

TEACHER: Would anyone like to add to that?

BILLY: Yes, it isn't that it isn't there. It's more like you make yourself believe.

PATRICIA: You see, outside of you it isn't real. Inside your head, it's there.

TEACHER: Do you enjoy using your imagination?

JOHN: Oh, yes. Because you can make anything happen.

PATRICIA: Sometimes they're silly things. What we do isn't always good.

TEACHER: What do you mean, "not good"?

PATRICIA: I mean, some children have better ideas than others.

TEACHER: But you still want a chance to try them all out?

DENISE: Oh, yes. It's better for an idea to be yours than good.

BILLY: I think using your imagination means being creative. It means making up something that wasn't ever there before.

The discussion went on like this for some time, but it was obvious that the terms *creativity* and *imagination* held real meaning for the children. Their observations—that it is important to have ideas and the freedom to try them out—are basic to good work in creative drama.

One of the most delightful views toward creativity was expressed by Professor Franz Cizek of the Vienna School of Arts and Crafts in 1921. Although he was not referring to drama, his attitude is that of many successful teachers in any of the arts. The following "Conversation with Cizek" is included verbatim for its insight and relevance to this chapter.

"How do you do it?" we asked at last, when we had looked at some hundreds of the productions of Professor Cizek's pupils, each more delightful and original than the last.

"But I don't do," he protested with a kind of weary pity for our lack of understanding. "I take off the lid, and other masters clap the lid on—that is the only difference."

"Children have their own laws which they must needs obey. What right have grown-ups to interfere?"

"And do many of your children go in for art afterward?" we queried.

"Not as a rule. They go into all sorts of professions and trades. That's quite right. That's what I like. I like to think of art coloring all departments of life rather than being a separate profession."

". . . What a pity all children don't come to you."

"Yes, it is a pity," he assented, shaking his head rather mournfully. "There is so much of the summer and the autumn but the spring never comes again."[4]

Creativity refers both to the cognitive and the affective life and is the result of conscious and unconscious effort. In the anthology *Essays on Creativity,* the point is made repeatedly that "ideas are born from stimulation from within and without, but such stimulation must be grasped, filtered and used."[5] Working together, students and teacher can accomplish this to the satisfaction of all. A creative act does not happen once; it is an ongoing process, which with encouragement and guidance becomes a way of life. Rollo May put the whole thing very simply when he said that creativity is the act of repatterning the known world into meaningful new configurations.

Beginning Exercises for Imagination

The first day the class meets, the leader will do well to begin with the simplest exercises in which imagination is involved. Regardless of age level, there must be an opportunity for the participants to go beyond the here and now, but they cannot, and should not, be expected to handle a story or create an improvisation. It is also wise to begin with the entire group, if space permits. This removes all thought of audience, thereby diminishing fear and self-consciousness.

How the leader begins will be determined by the age, experience, and number in the group, as well as the size of the playing space. If the group is fortunate in having a very large room, physical movement is an excellent opening exercise. Music or even a drumbeat will enhance the mood and help to focus the attention. One simple and very effective way of beginning is to have the group walk to the beat of the drum. As the group becomes more comfortable and relaxed, the beat can be changed: rapid, double time, slow, and so on. The participants, in listening for the change in beat, forget themselves and are usually able to use their entire bodies. Galloping, skipping, and hopping are fun for younger children and good exercise for those much older. Adults find freedom and pleasure in physical movement and when it is over sit down relaxed and better able to go on to the next assignment.

From the purely physical body movement, the teacher may move on to mood. For example, if the group has been walking to a beat, he may suggest that there is green grass underfoot. "How does it feel to you? Your feet are tired. Think what it is like to put them down on soft, cool grass. Take off your shoes. (Some will do so at this suggestion.) Walk on it. Feel it."

4. Franz Cizek, in "Some Conversations with Cizek," in *The Child as Artist,* booklet issued by the Children's Art Exhibition Fund, 1921.

5. Stanley Rosner and Lawrence Abt, *Essays on Creativity* (Croton-on-Hudson, N.Y.: North River Press, 1974), p. 192.

Soon the steps will become more flexible as the image of grass grows stronger. The teacher might suggest, next, that there is ice underfoot. "It is hard, slippery, difficult to walk on, dangerous." The movement usually changes perceptibly now as the participants imagine the difficulties of crossing an icy pavement. Muscles are tensed and bodies stiffen. It is here that one or two may lose their balance or even slip and fall down as they get into the spirit of the situation. The teacher's acknowledgment of their efforts offers encouragement and usually stimulates further invention. As participants imagine that they are running across hot sand, stepping over puddles, crossing a creek, wading through snow, each suggestion stretches the imagination a little more. When the exercise is over, most groups will have moved far from the first stiff, self-conscious steps without realizing when, or how, or even that they have done it.

Inside a bubble bigger than they are, children can pretend they are touching the sky, riding in a space ship, or looking around the inside of a whale. This huge plastic bubble was made by Indiana University's Children's Theatre director, Professor Dorothy Webb, who uses it to teach creative drama to graduate education students. Once inside the bubble, the imagination is not subjected to the confines of familiar boundaries and thus we have an environment for creativity, she explains.

Games known to all the participants might come next. Tossing a ball is a familiar activity, and the players by this time usually respond eagerly. The teacher may suggest that they are using a tennis ball, then a basketball, and next a beach ball or a ping-pong ball. The players experience little difficulty shifting from one

*I*nside the plastic bubble—what do they see? *(Courtesy of Dorothy Webb, Indiana University.)*

ball to another and have fun showing its size and weight as they throw and catch it. Lively groups sometimes drop the ball, run for it, lose it, or carry the assignment much farther than the leader suggested. Favorite activities such as flying kites, jumping rope, playing hopscotch, and playing with jacks provide other opportunities for using the imagination. How long this goes on is best left to the discretion of the teacher, who can tell when the interest begins to wane.

A pantomime of seasonal sports might be the culmination of the various exercises and a means of tying them together. If the class is large, this may be the time to subdivide into smaller groups, with each taking a particular game or sport. However the teacher proceeds from here, he or she will find that imagination has been sparked and the next step will be easier. The chapter on movement includes a more detailed discussion of ways in which movement, dance, and mime can be used as both means and ends.

With the first meeting of any group the leader's goal is to create an atmosphere in which the players feel comfortable; the next step is to stimulate their imagination. There are various ways of doing this, and each of us has his or her own favorite methods, but a good teacher is always looking for fresh ideas. Sometimes a nondramatic, quiet approach is preferable to physical activity. The following game was introduced by a drama teacher from Israel, and I have used it successfully on several occasions with different age levels.

The class is seated in a circle on the floor. After introducing themselves, the students are asked to put some personal object in the center of the circle. (The more unusual the object, the better.) The teacher then goes around the circle, asking the players to try to remember to whom each object belongs and to return it to its owner. This is followed by each person's selecting another player's object and making up a story about it. Improvisations using the objects or stories told about them may follow, depending on time and interest. If the exercise simply stops with the stories, it will have given the class a chance to get acquainted before moving into active group work.

Another quiet exercise that captures the attention of most groups requires a blackboard and colored chalks. One student after another goes up to the board and puts a mark or drawing on it. When everyone has had a turn, second turns are taken. The size of the class determines whether or not there may be third and fourth turns. The mural created by the class is then described and interpreted. The more abstract it is, the more imaginative the interpretations will probably be. This activity may be a springboard to improvisation or may simply remain a means of drawing a group together. In either case, it is effective with both children and adults in engaging and holding the attention.

Sometimes an idea or activity that stimulates one group won't work with another. Do not be discouraged; try something else. Remember, this is the first time the class has met as a group, and it takes some groups longer than others to become cohesive. Children's games can be used with most groups. Ones that any number can play and that are not too complicated, with the players entering at different times, are usually the best.

*Tw*o chairs become a racing car. *(Photograph by Amy Kargman.)*

Fruit Bowl

This is a familiar game, which is adaptable to groups of all ages and abilities. It may be used as a warm-up or an activity while waiting for everyone to assemble. As the players enter the room, they are given names of a fruit to remember—such as "apple" or "banana." Players sit in a circle with the leader standing in the center. When the leader calls out "apple," all who are named apple change places; when she calls out "banana," those players change places. When she calls out "fruit bowl," everyone in the circle must get up and exchange places with someone else. The values are obvious: all players must move; there is no winning or losing; concentration is necessary; and the leader can expect total participation. Variations in the game can be made, but however it is played, the leader should always stop and turn to another activity or to the problem of the day before the players become bored.

Games are generally thought of as warm-ups or enjoyable activities. They are both of these and more, for they have other values. One is the framework for communication they provide a group. Another is the imposition of rules that develop discipline and self-control in the players. A third is the social nature of the game, especially important in drama, where interpersonal relationships are an integral element.

Deliberate brainstorming for ideas is often a successful way of starting a first session with older or more experienced players. Find out:

What interests them
What their concerns are
Whether there is a controversial subject they would like to explore

With young adults this may lead into explosive confrontation, but after working together on a topic for a while, they are usually receptive to suggestions and different ways of dramatizing it. It may even become the focus of an original play, continuing on for a number of class meetings.

Concentration

If imagination is the beginning, concentration—the capacity to hold an idea long enough to do something about it—must come next. It is not enough to glimpse an idea; the image must be held long enough for action to follow. Inexperienced players of any age may have difficulty here, for self-consciousness and fear of failure are paralyzing and distracting agents. It is now that the teacher needs to encourage every effort, however small, to free the player of self-doubt. This is difficult in some cases: the player may never have excelled at anything and so does not believe that he or she has anything worthwhile to offer. Many children, on the other hand, become involved easily. Concentration poses no problems for them because of their freedom from fear and their willingness to experiment.

Organization

Concentration and organization go hand in hand. Once the players are able to focus their attention on their material, they can get down to the business of organizing it. They have ceased to think about themselves and are ready to decide things such as who their characters are, what they are doing, and the overall form the improvision will take. If the group is working on a story, the organization will more or less follow the plot. The characters are related to a logical sequence of events, and it is up to the players to decide how they will handle them.

If, on the other hand, the group is creating an original situation—pantomime or improvisation—a different kind of planning is involved. More guidance is required, since there is no structure to follow, but if children feel free to experiment, they come up with surprising and often delightful results. "Organization" does not mean the imposing of a conventional form but rather means an arrangement of parts or material to achieve order. Older groups, or groups that have had more exposure to television, movies, and theatre, are less inclined to experiment with organization although, with encouragement, they can be helped to find the challenge in "trying it another way." Organization is order, and until it exists in some form, the participants rarely find satisfaction in creative playing.

Self-Expression

So far we have been talking about exercises that may or may not be expressive. Creative drama implies self-expression, hence the necessity of the participants' involvement beyond merely imitating an action. How do they feel when the kite soars high in the air? Who is winning the ball game? How do we know? How many jacks have they won? Do they enjoy picking flowers in the woods? What are their feelings as they fish or row their boat against a strong current? These are the kinds of questions we may ask as the players grow more confident.

We are not concerned with the quality of the children's performance yet; rather, we are concerned with their developing freedom and the ability to express themselves. Each child has something to say, something that he or she alone can offer, provided the opportunity and the encouragement are given. No one has put this any better than Hughes Mearns:

> You have something to say. Something of your very own. Try to say it. Don't be ashamed of any real thought or feeling you may have. Don't undervalue it. Don't let the fear of what others may think of it prevent you from saying it. Perhaps not aloud but to yourself. You have something to say, something no one in the world has ever said in just your way of saying it—but the thing itself is not half so important to you as what the saying will be to you.[6]

Communication

Although communication is the responsibility of the formal theatre, and therefore not our primary concern, there comes a time when the participants want to share their work in creative drama, and this sharing involves communication skills. It has been stated that, for the younger child, public performance is undesirable; for the older child, under the right conditions, it may do no harm. But unless the class is exceptionally small, there will be periods when some are observers an some are participants. It is to these periods that communication pertains. This is the audience that is not an audience in the usual sense. On the other hand, the observers want to see and hear, and they become deeply involved in the situation. Participants soon learn that they must move on to the next stage of development: that of making themselves clear, of being heard and understood, and of being interesting—in short, of communicating.

Communication comes about naturally in the discussion periods that follow each playing. One procedure, used successfully by many teachers, is the playing, discussing, replaying method. To describe it more fully, the teacher begins with the story or situation, which she either reads or tells to the group. This is

6. Hughes Mearns, *Creative Power* (New York: Dover Publications, 1958), p. 259.

followed by class discussion, in which the characters are enumerated and described, the plot is reviewed, and the scenes are planned. No matter how simple the situation, it is important that it be thoroughly understood before the first playing. The group will decide which characters are necessary to the plot, which ones may be eliminated, or whether others should be added. Often a story that is excellent to read takes considerable adapting to make it good drama.

When the teacher is sure that the group has all details well in mind, he or she is ready to suggest playing it. Asking for volunteers usually brings a show of hands from which the teacher will choose the first cast. The players come forward, while the rest of the class remain in their seats. After they have finished the scene, the teacher leads a general discussion. This evaluation period covers the plot and the way the children have handled it. The players themselves always have criticisms to offer, but the observers also have reactions to share. Children's criticism is honest and their observations are keen. Because the observers anticipate playing the story themselves, they are as deeply involved as the players. Questions such as these help to guide the discussion:

1. Did they tell the story?
2. Was anything important left out?
3. What did you like about the way they began it?
4. Did we understand the ending?
5. When we play it the next time, what might we add or leave out?

The questions are naturally more specific when we have a particular story in mind. There will be further discussion of characters, their relationships, and their motives, but these things usually come after a second or third playing. Finally, when the teacher feels that a number of important points have been made and the class is growing eager to resume playing, a second group is given a chance to play the same scene. This group, having the benefit of observation and discussion, will probably succeed in developing more detail and clearer characterizations. This does not necessarily happen, for the first group to volunteer may have been the stronger.

At any rate, when the second cast has finished, a new evaluation period is in order. It is always interesting to hear the different kinds of comments that this second discussion evokes. A third playing, a fourth, even a fifth, may follow, depending on the interest of the children and the length of the period. It is a good idea to take the cue from them as to when to move on to the next scene. As long as the scene holds their interest, they will continue to grow in their understanding of it. The teacher will become increasingly sensitive to their involvement as they work together.

When the group works from another source, the questions will be different. The following are general but may be helpful in suggesting how to begin a discussion.

1. Who were the people in the drama?
2. How did their home (or occupation, school, way of life, values, etc.) differ from ours?
3. How did they communicate with each other without (a telephone, common language, automobile, etc.)?
4. What was the problem they faced?
5. Were there other ways of solving it? Shall we try one of them?

If the class has made a study of a particular society, an earlier period in history, or an institution, the questions will be more specific. Often a discussion will take off in another direction; as long as it does not continue at too great a length, it is interesting to see where it leads and what the concerns of the class are. If it appears to be tangential and unrelated to the topic, it is time to guide it back into more productive channels.

As the group gains experience, its ability to communicate increases. Younger children, because of their more limited vocabulary, communicate more easily through body movement and facial expression. Older children are not only better able to express themselves verbally but also enjoy improvising dialogue. The adult student, depending on background and previous experience, will feel more comfortable in one medium or the other, but most comfortable with oral discussion.

Discipline

As young teachers will tell you, discipline is one of the most difficult problems they face. It scarcely seems necessary to ask why this is so, let alone ask the more basic question of why discipline is necessary. But once it has been established, both teaching and learning become a far more pleasant and satisfying experience. Part of the problem is misunderstanding of John Dewey's philosophy, believing that freedom consists of allowing students to do as they please. Contrasting with this is the traditional approach, again misinterpreted to mean arbitrary authoritarian rule. The dream of most teachers today is a classroom in which freedom reigns within a structure that supports, encourages, and protects the rights of each individual. This means *order*, or the insistence of ground rules to which all adhere. Ideally, self-discipline can be achieved, permitting each member of the group to pursue his or her own interests and goals, while respecting the rights of others.

According to C. M. Charles, order in the classroom:

1. Facilitates learning
2. Fosters socialization
3. Permits democracy

4. Fills a psychological need
5. Promotes a sense of joy[7]

After all, teachers and students are working toward the same end: the best learning, under the most favorable conditions, in the best possible learning environment.

Problems in Creative Playing

Sooner or later, the teacher of creative drama, or the classroom teacher who uses creative drama, is bound to encounter problems. They may be simple problems of time and space: periods that are too short; space that is inadequate; classes that are too large. These problems can be solved, though the solutions are not always easy. They call for adaptability and ingenuity on the part of the leader and present difficulties that are discouraging and sometimes defeating. Other problems confronting the leader even under ideal circumstances are the individual problems he or she finds in the group. Discipline has come to mean punishment in our society. This is not the original meaning of the word, nor is it the sense in which it is used here. Rather, it signifies order or control, a control preferably of oneself.

It has been stated many times that self-consciousness is the greatest obstacle to creative playing. Self-consciousness, or fear, takes many forms. The shy child and the show-off are examples of the two forms in which self-consciousness is most frequently encountered in children. The insensitive child is also a problem, for he or she usually lacks friends and so finds it difficult to work cooperatively in a group. Finally, there is the handicapped child, whose physical, mental, or emotional problems pose special difficulties for the leader.

We must keep in mind that in drama players are exposing themselves more than in any other art form or activity. Therefore, our handling of behavior problems implies awareness of their causes. Insensitivity on the leader's part can damage a player whose vulnerability is evidenced by a conspicuous form of behavior. There is great interest in drama as therapy at present, but this is a special field for which the average teacher—even the specialist in creative drama techniques—is not trained. Every teacher is aware of the therapeutic value of the arts, even though the primary purposes are educational, social, and aesthetic. But because there are, in every group, those children (or adults) who experience real difficulty in expressing themselves, consideration must be given to their problems. If the problem is severe, it should be handled by a therapist and not the classroom teacher; in many cases, an intelligent, sympathetic effort to build

---

7. C. M. Charles, *Building Classroom Discipline* (White Plains, N.Y.: Longman, 1985), pp. 7–15.

self-respect and bring fun into the lives of the players can go a long way toward solving problems.

Timidity

Timid children are the most common problem the teacher encounters but one that creative drama can help. Such children are usually quiet in a class, preferring to sit in the back of the room and let others do the talking. Their fear of making a mistake, or even of being noticed, causes them to withdraw, even though underneath they are eager to express their ideas and take part. They are usually not happy children, for their feeling of inadequacy inhibits both expression and communication.

The little girl who never volunteers will need special encouragement to try doing a part, no matter how simple. The teacher who gives her this opportunity to show her peers what she can do may be taking the first step in helping her build a better self-image. If the child is successful, it will be less difficult for her a second time. The teacher will be wise to praise her warmly for whatever contribution she makes. Remember that, for the little girl, the very fact of getting up in front of the class is a big achievement.

There was eight-year-old Patty, who was referred to a Saturday-morning play group because of her excessive shyness. At first she took part only when the whole group was moving and then because it would have been more conspicuous to remain seated than to get up with the others. After several weeks (probably five or six sessions), she did a pantomime of a child finding a kitten. Her honest joy and tenderness as she fondled its soft body drew spontaneous admiration from the other boys and girls in the class. This was the breakthrough. From that day Patty's eagerness to play was apparent. Her voice was small—inaudible at first—but grew stronger in proportion to her growing self-confidence. This was no sudden miracle; in fact, it took three years for the transformation to take place. Patty's feelings of inadequacy had been so deep seated that many successes were necessary to convince her that she had something to offer that her peers would accept. She became not only one of the most vocal children in the group but also an unquestioned leader. Whether she would have found her way anyhow, no one can say. Creative drama as a technique was deliberately used, and the change during her three years in the class was striking.

Exhibitionism

The show-offs are just as much in need of help as shy children, but they rarely elicit the same kind of sympathetic attention. Their problem is also one of uneasiness, and in trying to prove their importance, they do all of the wrong things. Their behavior will range from monopolizing the class discussion to interfering with the work of the other children (pinching, pushing, interrupting). They may deliberately use a wrong word for the sake of a laugh. They are conscious of the effect they are having and so have difficulty concentrating on what they are doing.

An example is John, a nervous little fellow of nine, with facial mannerisms and a habit of interrupting. John was accepted by the others: he amused them. For more than a semester John's work was erratic. He seemed unable to get involved in a part for more than a minute or two, and then he would look around the room to see what effect he was having on the rest of the class. There was no sudden or dramatic incident that effected a change; rather, it was a long period of working under the patient guidance of a teacher who took every opportunity to praise his honest expression and help him to find satisfaction in getting attention legitimately. By the end of a year, John was able to work cooperatively with the group much of the time and forego showing off. His problem was still not entirely solved, but he had learned something of the give-and-take of working together and the pleasure of recognition that comes from work that is honest.

Arline was a high school student whose weight problem caused her great embarrassment. She expressed this by comic behavior and exhibitionistic antics. For years Arline had been the class clown, deliberately tripping, using a wrong word, or misunderstanding a simple question. In this way she made people laugh at what she did before they had a chance to laugh at the way she looked. Successful coping with her problem in this manner had created a behavior pattern that was hard to break. Through improvised drama, where there was no audience to impress, Arline gradually came to understand something of motivation and, finally, to trust and accept herself. True, the slapstick occasionally took place but less and less often as the years passed, and she was able to get the laughs for the right reasons. Beneath the clowning there was an intelligent, sensitive adolescent, who today is a successful educator. Undoubtedly, there were other methods that could have been used effectively, but Arline liked theatre and elected to participate. It was obvious that through the use of creative drama she learned how to believe in herself and perhaps to lay the foundation for her future work in special education.

Sometimes the teacher may be forced to ask the disruptive child to go back to her seat. Not punishment but the consequences of unacceptable behavior will teach the child that creative dramatics demands consideration and teamwork.

Isolation

The isolate or loner is often a child who cannot relate to the group. He or she may work hard and have good ideas and the ability to present them effectively but is always in isolation. It must be said that this is not necessarily a problem. Indeed, it may be indicative of superior talent and high motivation. Independence is a desired goal, whereas isolation, which is the result of an inability to relate to others, is a problem. Through movement and dance all members of a group are drawn together naturally; they discover the meaning of interdependence as well as individual effort. For the person who has real difficulty in relating to his or her peers, this is a natural way of becoming a part of the group.

Insensitivity

Insensitive players are similar to, but different from, the show-offs in that they are usually rejected by the others and do not understand why. Their clowning brings no laughter, and they have great difficulty in making friends. They tend to reject the ideas of others and criticize their efforts, often harshly. Playing a variety of roles may cause them to gain insights and develop an awareness of the feelings of others. Patient attention to their problem in human relations may, in time, help them to listen and learn to accept suggestions from their peers. Theirs is a difficult problem, but once they have begun to feel some small acceptance, they will prefer belonging to going it alone. Again, we are not talking about the extreme personality disorder but about the human being who is experiencing difficulty in working cooperatively with others.

Distraction

Every teacher has experienced the easily distracted player—the one with imagination, interest, and enthusiasm, whose concentration is broken at any unexpected sight or sound. Often this is a hyperactive child but not always. I have had college students whose ability to remain involved in an exercise was so fragile that the slightest noise in the corridor or the appearance of someone at the door would destroy it. Unfortunately, this stops the other players, making it necessary to build back the situation, but rarely is the same degree or depth of involvement achieved that was present before the interruption.

Physical Handicaps

Children with handicaps need special attention. Moreover, their teachers need orientation to their special needs. Although the classroom teacher may have a child who is disabled or who has a speech defect, he or she is not going to be equipped to practice therapy or to give time for all of the help these special children merit. If the teacher has one or two children in a group who are handicapped, he or she will treat them essentially the same as the others. These children need sympathy, understanding, and encouragement. The teacher must know what can be expected of them and then try to adapt the activities to their capabilities. Often such a child will be in therapy, and if the teacher can work with the therapist, he or she will be able to receive helpful suggestions about the therapist's approach.

For example, Marcia, who has a cleft lip and is seeing the speech therapist regularly, will benefit from an opportunity to use speech in a legitimate and pleasurable way. The teacher will not have the time to give her all of the attention she needs, but in treating her like the others and encouraging her in her efforts, the teacher will be contributing to her social growth and, in some measure, to her treatment.

It is a common phenomenon that the stutterer often speaks fluently when cast in a play. Although there is no proof that acting ever cured a stutter, children who tend to repeat or whose anxiety causes them to stutter often find relief in speaking as someone else. Regular participation in either informal or formal dramatics may have a therapeutic effect in encouraging successful oral expression.

All people gain in self-respect when their ideas are accepted and put into effect. The child with a problem has a special need for acceptance, and the teacher tries to find the best way in which to meet it. Creative drama provides an ideal opportunity to help timid children overcome their inhibitions; provides show-offs with a better way of getting attention; guides insensitive children to some awareness of the feelings of others; works with the handicapped to find their avenue of self-expression; and broadens the horizons of the disadvantaged. "How drama can be used today, how the play-acting impulse can be harnessed to help people grow, to develop greater sensitivity to themselves and to their fellow human beings, to become more spontaneous and outgoing, to discard old fears and insecurities, has attracted the interest of many who are working in the various fields of human relations."[8]

Today's children are subjected to pressures and demands, which, if not greater than in the past, are certainly new and different. Not only inner-city children but the children of affluent and suburban communities reflect the changes in values and mores. The pressures they feel often result in bizarre and unpredictable behavior, causing problems for teachers and creating difficulties when freedom is encouraged. The creative drama instructor is particularly vulnerable to these problems, for he or she is dealing with the emotional and social, as well as the intellectual, aspects of child development.

Although freedom is essential to creativity, it is often necessary to impose restraints in the beginning or until children become more comfortable with the group and the leader. Social mobility, broken homes, television programs, the violence in our society, and economic problems are among the causes given for discipline problems. It is not the purpose of this text to explore the causes, but it is important for us to be sensitive to unusual behavior and to try to deal with it with understanding, compassion, and firmness. Although we cannot accept certain antisocial behavior in a child, it is important for him or her to know and understand what is being rejected. In other words, we do not reject the *player*, but we do reject behavior that interferes with the freedom of others to express their ideas and feelings. One person cannot be permitted to dominate the group, regardless of his or her needs.

8. Jack Simos, *Social Growth through Play Production* (New York: Association Press, 1957), p. 16.

Evaluating Children's Responses

A question that always comes up is how to evaluate children's responses. This is difficult to answer, for progress varies from one child to the next. The teacher has different expectations for each child and what may be extraordinary growth for one is scarcely an adequate performance for another. (The word *performance* as used here means work, not theatre performance.) Let me explain. The shy child, described earlier, may take a long time to come out of his or her shell; therefore the slightest offering the child makes to the group—idea, vocal or physical expression, ease in working with peers—indicates growth. The overly aggressive child, who learns to harness his or her energy in deference to others, has also made progress. With the overcoming of individual problems, and every child has them, albeit less severe than the ones cited earlier, there has been progress. Beyond that, each teacher has social, intellectual, and aesthetic goals he or she hopes will be met.

Have the individuals in the class become a group, willing and able to work together? Is there easy give-and-take?

Is each child an integral part of the group, sharing without fear or need to impress?

Is there sincerity in the work?

Is physical movement becoming freer, more expressive?

Have verbal skills improved—speech, voice and diction, vocabulary, and the ability to express ideas orally?

Depending on the focus, have other goals been met? Use of resource materials, integration of learnings, involvement in subject?

Is there vitality in the group? Eagerness to begin; reluctance to stop at the end of the period?

Does the noise level reflect activity, industry, enthusiasm?

The teacher may want to make "before and after" tapes of the class. These are often more revealing than the teacher's recollections, written notes, or check sheets in showing the progress made from the beginning to the end of the year. My own concern, however, is that no matter how valuable such records are—and there is value—there is also a danger of losing the spirit of creative drama in the quest for proof of its effectiveness. If evaluation can be done quietly, perhaps by student teachers or aides, it is a valuable record for the teacher, to be shared judiciously with staff and administration. The purpose of the class, however, determines the type and use of tests and measurements.

For teachers who may need further help in evaluating growth, a chart is included in the appendix. Although some sort of evaluation is usually required, and actually not regarded as unreasonable by most teachers, it remains a difficult task. We do not want to inhibit freedom nor do we suggest a right or wrong way to perform. As teachers, we see how the arts stretch children. They engage them wholly by challenging their imagination, which calls all of the thought processes in operation. By exercising a variety of abilities, the arts draw on human resources and potentials that might otherwise lie idle and perhaps even atrophy. In that process, the arts create bridges between children and other aspects of their lives, including other subjects in the curriculum. Instead of a curriculum of isolated learnings, students begin to make connections that are vital to understanding the relations and interrelations between different areas of the world around them. More important, it teaches students to expect such connections and to seek them out.

Summary

Imagination is the spark that sets off the creative impulse. Concentration (the capacity to hold an idea long enough to do something about it) and organization (the design or arrangement of the parts) are necessary to satisfying self-expression. Communication—the bridge to others—comes last and is less the concern of creative drama than of the formal play.

In all creative work there are obstacles. They must be recognized and overcome. They may be problems of time and space or the more difficult ones of human relations. Wise leaders learn first to identify the problems and then to look for solutions. They will remember that they are neither therapists nor theatre directors but teachers, guiding players, whatever their age, in the medium of informal drama. Brian Way has suggested the role of the teacher in these words:

> Schools do not exist to develop actors but to develop people, and one of the major factors in developing people is that of preserving and enriching to its fullest the human capacity to give full and undivided attention to any matter in hand at any given moment.[9]

Activities and exercises are suggested not as ends in themselves but as means to self-expression and a springboard to other more extensive projects. Some prose and poetry are also included as illustrations of what can be used and how; with a point of view and a creative approach, it is hoped that the leader will be able to find additional materials relevant to his or her own and the group's interests and needs.

---

9. Brian Way, *Development through Drama* (New York: Humanities Press, 1967), p. 15.

3

Play

Robert (age one) imitating his dog retrieving a stick. *(Courtesy of Alexandra Plotkin.)*

Man only plays when he is in the fullest sense of the word a human being; and he is only fully a human being when he plays.

— FRIEDRICH SCHILLER

*T*o ask the question "What is play?" is to prompt a score of answers. All of us recognize play in the young, but a precise definition of it eludes us, perhaps because play takes many forms and can move in opposing directions. The one, toward games, sports, and ritual; the other, toward drama, in which the players assume the roles of others. The first is structured, whereas the second is free and fluid. Even so, with this distinction in mind, there is no neat separation between them, for the players can shift suddenly from a game with rules to a world of fantasy, in which anything and everything is possible. Moreover, participants in dramatic play will often stop midway to give directions, explain an action, or answer a question.

Although play begins in infancy with a parent, caretaker, or sibling, it is between the ages of two and four that it includes more than one other player at a time. It is at this point that play enters a highly social phase. British educator Donald Baker, in the article "Defining Drama: From Child's Play to Production," maintained that play is a form of exploration of self and one's environment.[1] It also, he said, enables the child to create order and give meaning to the chaotic mass of random sense impressions with which he or she is bombarded daily. A third function can be seen in the way that play meets the child's need for security. In the rhythmic stamping or beating of a spoon on a surface, the young child is able to make a predictable noise at predictable intervals; through this pattern of sound and movement, the child's need for security is answered. It is further reinforced by repeating in play events the child has witnessed or experienced in life. In replaying trips to the doctor's office or other disturbing encounters, the child is coming to terms with life; this, according to Baker, is as fundamental a function of play as it is of drama.

Dressing up is often an element of play, though it is not always included and is not necessary. Children love to dress up but do not need a complete costume; often a hat, shawl, or apron will suggest a wealth of characters. Cheerleaders' uniforms are an example of dressing for a ritual in which the participants have an opportunity to create appropriate actions of their own. Examples of play may be found in all countries of the world, at different periods in history, and on every

1. Donald Baker, "Defining Drama: From Child's Play to Production," *The Journal of Curriculum Studies* (London: Collins and Sons, Ltd.) 15, no. 1 (May 1973).

age level. Play is inherent in human beings, and the child early manifests an impulse to engage in it.

One of the best examples of play in its earliest stage is to be seen in the rough and tumble of kittens and puppies as they explore the use of their bodies. Clumsy at first, they chase, leap, attack each other, fall down, and scramble up again, learning the skills and controls that will be needed later on. Their need for security is also evident, however, for if the game becomes too rough or the unexpected occurs, they will immediately withdraw to the safety of a familiar corner—even a cage. Every movement they make is preparation for adult life, though at the moment it is a release of energy in play, joyous and free.

A Historical Overview of Play

Primitive societies released the impulse to play through tribal expressions of hope, joy, fear, desire, sorrow, hatred, and worship. What primitive people felt strongly, they danced or mimed. From their sacred play came ritual; poetry, music, and dance were a part of their play. Philosophy and wisdom found expression in words.

In ancient Greece religious celebration resulted in contests, and these contests gave birth to dramatic forms or plays. As highly organized as they were later to become, these contests could be considered the creative expression of the people from whose ranks individual playwrights emerged. During the Middle Ages, drama had its rebirth in the church. Authorship of the scripts is unknown, but there is proof that the performers were amateurs, whose participation was voluntary. Professionalism had no part in these plays, which served a religious and educational purpose. The involvement of the audiences was probably great as they responded to the dramatization of the Bible stories and moral tales as enacted by their neighbors.

In more recent periods in the Western world play became ritualized, as process culminated in product with a conventional form, structure, and rules. Theatre is a typical example of the institutionalization of an art form with a playhouse; regular times, hours, and lengths of performance; and established rules for the writing and production of plays. This does not preclude creativity and brilliance of product, but it does impose order and form; process, on the other hand, by its own definition, is fluid and free.

Our modern preoccupation with making big business of play has resulted in its decline, and this decline is our loss. True play does not know professionalism, for it is a voluntary activity, based on, but different from, the business of everyday life. Joy and freedom are the hallmarks of play, with the rules and limits established by the players. True play, though free, creates order—indeed, *is* order. Whereas people may play alone, one of the basic characteristics of play is the teamwork involved; through play, the participants are drawn closely together.

Some Theories of Play

The phenomenon of play has fascinated philosophers, educators, psychologists, and anthropologists through the ages. Studies reveal a persistent search for the meaning of play and its role in life, civilization, and culture. Theories range from its being an expression of surplus energy, a means of relaxation, and an escape from reality to a concern with its importance in the development of higher intelligence and the learning process. Some psychologists have viewed play as a way of working through unconscious pressures; some have discerned a close relationship between play and the creative process, signifying that art is actually one aspect of play. Regardless of theory, however, there is consensus on play as being a profoundly important activity in the process of human development. According to Richard Courtney, whose scholarly work on the subject encompasses all areas, "Play, initially, and the arts subsequently, develop imaginative constructions whereby people function in the world. The arts are expressions of imagination through which the personality develops, and upon which cognitive and abstract ways of working with the environment are built."[2]

To Adam Blatner, American psychiatrist and author of *The Art of Play,* the pivotal concept in relation to play is spontaneity or the opposite of habit.[3] Blatner pointed out the importance of "if" in the study of play, a word often used by actors in discussing a method of acting. This temporary suspension of reality by the actor is necessary if he or she is to become someone else in a situation created by a playwright. Play does not belong to the young, as we are prone to think, but is, or should be, a part of our life for as long as we live. Unfortunately, in our modern society it is often discouraged or at least overpowered by structured games and the compulsion to win.

One of the most popular theories of play was advanced by Herbert Spencer, who expressed the idea that play in both animal and human behavior is the result of surplus energy.[4] This theory is illustrated in the physical activities of the young of all species, who are yet to feel the burden of responsibility and whose bodies are young and resilient. Other psychologists explain play as a way of achieving relaxation and rest, not a refutation of the surplus energy theory but a further observation.

Aristotle's theory of catharsis has been seen by some philosophers as a safety valve for pent-up emotions. This is expressed by acts of aggression and play fighting, as well as in laughter. Karl Groos, writing at the end of the nineteenth century, believed play to be a necessary factor in the development of intelligence and preparation of the young for adult life. It is make-believe, through which

---

2. Richard Courtney, *Re-Play* (Toronto: Ontario Institute for Studies in Education, 1982), p. 157.

3. Adam Blatner and Allee Blatner, *The Art of Play* (New York: Human Sciences Press, 1988).

4. Herbert Spencer, *The Principles of Psychology* (New York: D. Appleton and Co., 1914).

youth gains mastery over its world. Play, in his view, is at a lower stage of development than art, but it is nevertheless a means toward that end, though not an end in itself.[5]

Johan Huizinga, whose work is widely read and admired in America, regards play as a cultural phenomenon. Huizinga is in agreement that it is a form of relaxation and fun, but he also sees in it a serious side, through which art forms are created. Music, poetry, and dance have an affinity with play. "In the turning of a poetic phrase, the development of a motif, the expression of a mood, there is always a play element at work."[6] This theory of play as fundamental to art has been repeated by other philosophers, educators, and psychologists, including Rudolph Laban, and Ruth Hartley and Robert Goldenson, coauthors of *The Complete Book of Children's Play.* Hartley and Goldenson said that through play a child is able to discipline the imagination and thus enter into the adult world of the arts and sciences.[7]

Freud's explanation of play as the projection of wishes and the reenactment of conflicts in order to master them is a theory held by many drama therapists. He believed that art, like play, offered an escape from the familiar world of reality. Both Erik Erikson and Bruno Bettelheim concurred with this theory, arguing that in externalizing problems and pressures, the player is able to control them. In play an unpleasant experience can be resolved, an enemy beaten, or a problem satisfactorily solved and put to rest. Witness children "playing school" and exorcising a bad experience through repetition of it in play, or a reversal of roles, sometimes collapsing in laughter at the outcome. The situation is weakened by playing it. For example, if the teacher is perceived as a villain in the drama and is made into the victim, the comedic value of the reversal is therapeutic; moreover, the conflict makes for good drama, over which the players have complete control.

Piaget did not oppose the theories cited, but as an educator, he viewed play primarily as an important aspect of the learning process. A child enjoys play and takes it seriously, a process through which learning takes place. Perhaps it is the word *serious* that gives us trouble. Although play *is* serious to children, they know they are playing and enjoy it; therein lies their freedom.

Similar to the above is the view of Everett Ostrovsky, who believes that what a child hopes for, fears, or wishes is buried in play. The player learns his or her limits and those of the surrounding world through exploration and experimentation, both of which are ingredients of play. Although there is a wide range of

5. Karl Groos, *The Play of Animals,* trans. Elizabeth Baldwin (New York: D. Appleton and Co., 1898).

6. Johan Huizinga, *Homo Ludens: A Study of the Play Element in Culture* (Boston: Beacon Press, 1955), p. 132.

7. Ruth E. Hartley and Robert M. Goldenson, *The Complete Book of Children's Play* (New York: Cromwell, 1975).

speculation as to the meaning of play, the theories cited are among the most commonly known and accepted. One finds more agreement than argument among the proponents. The fact that today we recognize the value of play is reflected in such events as the conference "The Power of Laughter and Play," held in Toronto in 1988 at the Institute for the Advancement of Human Behavior. The two-day conference included lectures and workshops on humor as a healing tool, play as a way to alleviate stress, expressive movement, and designing playful experiences; all were conducted by well-known physicians, educators, and psychologists. This is only one of many similar conferences on play as a way to better physical and mental health.

One has only to watch a group of children playing in an empty lot or a playground to accept the truth of these observations. Children play almost as soon as they move, and through their playing, they learn. In their own dramatic play, the three- or four-year-olds try on the roles of those about them; they observe their activities and learn by pretending to be and do. They enter the various worlds of their family and neighbors, interpreting and reenacting. First they observe; then they respond, repeating in play what has made a strong impression on them in life. Not unlike primitive people, young children express their feelings through movement and words, creating more complex situations as they grow older, with the boundaries stretched but the rules still clearly established. By the time they are ready for school they have learned much about the world they live in, and a large part of their learning has come about through their play.

The impulse to play, if encouraged, can become a continuing way of learning, a medium of expression, and eventually an art form. Many teachers have realized the potential of play and have made drama an integral part of their programs. Others have rejected it on the grounds that it is frivolous and therefore unrelated to serious learning. The fact that children give it their most serious attention escapes the teachers' notice; the children are made to feel that play is unworthy and therefore something to be left outside the schoolroom door. When this happens, the joyful and creative element of their free play is extinguished, perhaps never to be rekindled. Other teachers, and it is to them that this book is addressed, ask how they can keep the play impulse alive, that it may enhance learning and thus enrich the lives of their pupils.

Jon and Rumer Godden, in their recollections of a childhood spent in India, wrote with feeling about play, its magic, and its privacy. When asked, as they often were by their parents, what they were playing, the reply was generally "nothing."

> Or if that were too palpable a lie, we would give a camouflage answer like "Mothers and Fathers," which we never played or, with us, another improbable play, "Shops." . . . Yet if we had told what we were playing no one would have been much the wiser, because our plays were like icebergs, only three-tenths

seen, the rest hidden, inside ourselves. It was what we thought into our play that made its spell.[8]

According to Richard Courtney, "Play is the principal instrument of growth. Without play there can be no normal adult cognitive life; without play, no healthful development of affective life; without play, no full development of the power of will."[9]

Marie Winn wrote in her book *The Plug-in-Drug* that the child can work out difficulties through play, assuming the roles of adults in his or her life, redressing grievances and reenacting scenes that have caused distress. "In play he can expose, and perhaps, exorcise, fears that he cannot articulate in any other way; more important, perhaps, is the opportunity imaginative play affords the child to become an active user rather than a passive recipient of experience."[10] In our television world, this is an important contribution.

One of the most delightful and understanding treatments of the subject is to be found in Virginia Glasgow Koste's *Dramatic Play in Childhood: Rehearsal for Life*. In this book she offered three main reasons for valuing play:

> That is the time when most people are most expert and constant in playing; that is the time when they most freely externalize their playing so that it is possible to see and hear it; and that is the time when the power of play as a means of growth and accomplishment can most effectively be nurtured for a stronger rising generation of adults.[11]

The text is rich with examples of children at play. Although she purposely eschewed the scholarly approach, Koste presented effective evidence of learning, imagination, and social growth. Valuable insights are to be found in this early stage of human development, which is preparation for the next—creative drama. That it is also the root of drama and theatre is an obvious conclusion to Peter Slade, whose theory of child drama is based on this premise.

Ritual

Games, sports, and ritual are closely related to play. Whereas sports are like theatre and are designed for an audience, games and drama exist for the participants. A sport is held in a particular place; a game, wherever players may assemble. Ritual may be defined as the observance of a set form or series of rites.

---

8. Jon Godden and Rumer Godden, *Two under the Indian Sun* (New York: Knopf, 1966), p. 55.
9. Richard Courtney, *Play, Drama, and Thought* (New York: Drama Book Specialists, 1974), p. 204.
10. Marie Winn, *The Plug-in Drug* (New York: Viking, 1977), p. 95.
11. Virginia Glasgow Koste, *Dramatic Play in Childhood* (New Orleans: Anchorage Press, 1978), p. 6.

*P*lay soon leads to drama. *(Courtesy of Tom Behm, University of North Carolina, Greensboro.)*

We think of the ritual as having religious significance, but it is more inclusive than that. The repetition of an act or set of acts is also ritual. This is important to remember when working with children, for their games often assume a ritualistic form. Movement and chants play an important part in them. By beginning a creative drama session with the familiar—movement, rhythms, songs, or group games that all know—the leader is using ritual to draw class members together and make them comfortable. Like play, ritual has been defined in different ways. They range from some psychologists' use of the term to describe certain types of compulsive behavior to the most general terms, that is, pronouncing any formal behavior or repetition of a word, phrase, or sign as ritual. A handshake, a salutation or greeting, applause at the end of a play, or familiar repeated action of any kind thus qualifies as ritual. This interpretation is so inclusive that it becomes almost meaningless.

In an article in *The Children's Theatre Review,* Lawrence O'Farrell made a case for ritual as a creative resource for drama. His article clears up some of the confusion that has surrounded it by listing the components that distinguish ritual as a special event, different from everyday life. These components are easily recognized by the following characteristics:

1. Tradition.
2. Presentational acting, by which is meant that the players are conscious of the effects they are creating within their symbolic roles.
3. Stylization of both verbal and nonverbal communication.

4. Order: any spontaneous actions are framed within a prescribed structure.
5. The use of symbols and sensory stimuli to evoke concentration.
6. The collective identification of the participants.[12]

It is common belief that with so many prescribed elements, ritual is automatically disqualified as a creative activity. This is not the case, however, as O'Farrell points out, for by providing a supportive setting, participants in a ritual are enabled to express themselves freely and to indulge in divergent thinking, if given the opportunity. When a ritual is extended, it falls into three distinct stages. The first stage detaches the subject from the traditional form; the second offers the opportunity for creative expression; and the third returns the subject to the original structure. In the process, however, a change has taken place. A familiar example is the improvised portion of a hymn; the soloist, secure in the knowledge of the music, and inspired by it, improvises a section of his or her own, then returns to the music as written. So it is in the study of a culture. The teacher brings materials to the class to stimulate interest in the life and customs of a particular people. At some point, if encouraged, the class moves on to another stage in which creative drama, based on some aspect of the subject, takes place. Moving back again, the activity is seen in the context of the study, but change has taken place, for the study has been enriched in the process.

Tradition, presentational acting, stylization, order, appropriate symbols, and unity or collective identification with the subject characterize it as ritual drama. Far from discouraging creativity, the structure focuses it and strengthens the players. In concluding his article, O'Farrell said, "Not only can ritual embrace any subject, it can also include any dramatic method. Participants can speak, move, freeze, dance, sing, play, and perform feats of skill. Importantly, they do all of these varied activities in a special way."[13]

The Benefits of Play

It has been implied, if not stated, throughout the preceding pages that the benefits of play are enormous, ranging from temporal pleasure to lifelong satisfaction. On a practical level, dramatic play in childhood is what Virginia Koste called "a rehearsal for life."[14] And, indeed, we can see in the free play of children their perception of adult roles and adult relationships. In her text she cites case after case to illustrate the point. Hughes Mearns, in describing his experience as a young teacher in the thirties, wrote that the creative spirit and

---

12. Lawrence O'Farrell, "Making It Special: Ritual as a Creative Resource for Drama," *Children's Theatre Review* 33, no. 1 (1984): pp. 3–6.

13. Ibid., p. 6.

14. Virginia Glasgow Koste, *Dramatic Play in Childhood* (Lanham, Md.: University Press of America, 1988).

*P*laying witch. *(Courtesy of Synthia Rogers, Dallas Theatre Center; photography by Cindy Harlow.)*

creative impulse are found and flourish in children's play.[15] Although Mearns was writing about education, he was committed to the philosophy that only through the spirit of play could creative power be released. A teacher, respecting this power, is able to draw the best from each student, whether it be poetry, exposition, art, dance, or drama.

Blatner listed the benefits as applicable to four important areas of life: the personal–emotional, the social, the educational, and the cultural. These areas are improved, he said, when augmented with the following skills, learned in childhood in play:[16]

Flexibility of mind
Initiative and improvisation
Humility and a sense of humor
Effective communication
Inclusiveness, or the ability to interact and be at ease with others
Questioning, or looking for alternative solutions
Problem solving, or the learning of new techniques and strategies

Many educators regard creativity as the most valuable benefit of play. Whether the teacher approaches play from an art or academic background, the

15. Hughes Mearns, *Creative Power* (New York: Dover Publications, 1958).
16. Blatner and Blatner, *The Art of Play*, p. 37.

freedom inherent in play is perceived as fertile ground from which the imagination can soar.

Role play is seen as therapeutic as well as aesthetic. Its cultivation is particularly important when our lives are controlled by the suppression of emotion, often resulting in psychic fatigue. Children can express their feelings in play. The adults in today's highly competitive and structured world, however, find themselves detached from play and even alienated as a result. When preserved, the ability to play or be playful helps to recreate the spirit and refresh the body. It is a common experience to be tired at the end of a working day and then take part in a favorite activity or play a game with friends and afterward "feel like a new person."

Ashley Montagu discussed the benefits of play at length in his recent book *Growing Young.*[17] By keeping spontaneity alive, he contended, adults will find their later years rich and rewarding rather than barren of interest. His thesis was forcefully stated when he wrote, "In the child's imagination lies the power to know, and to create an environment, his own reality, and so it is with adults—those of us who continue to use our imaginations, for if you will keep your dreams and dream new ones, you will never grow old."[18]

Summary

Play may be the language of the young, but it is not their exclusive property. Play changes as we grow older. It acquires more structure, and it loses some of its freedom and spontaneity, as we assume serious responsibilities, but the spirit of play is within us, ready to be called. Play is also a way of reliving experiences and working out conflicts; it is an important technique of the drama therapist. Therapists, working with older groups, find that by recalling early happy experiences, creative drama is often stimulated.

Play has a recognized relationship with the arts, particularly theatre and dance. Socially, it brings us together, for it has a bonding power that contributes to our mental health and satisfaction.

Finally, play refreshes and rejuvenates through activities in which the players find satisfaction. To quote Huizinga, "As a regularly recurring relaxation, it becomes the accompaniment, the complement, in fact, an integral part of life in general. It adorns life, amplifies it and is to that extent a necessity both for the individual—as a life function—and for society by reason of the meaning it contains, its significance, its expressive value, its spiritual and social associations, in short, as a cultural function."[19] In every period of history, play has served a significant purpose, interpreting and affecting the lives of the people.

17. Ashley Montagu, *Growing Young* (New York: McGraw-Hill, 1981), p. 159.
18. Ibid.
19. Huizinga, *Homo Ludens,* p. 9.

4 Movement and Rhythms

A dance class sponsored by Arts Partners, an Inter-Agency collaboration. *(Courtesy of Carol Sterling, director, New York City Board of Education.)*

*M*ovement is a natural response to a stimulus and therefore an important element of drama. Indeed, movement, dance, mime, and drama merge in the expression of feelings and ideas. Theatre began with movement; its origins were closely linked with religious and magical rites. Gradually, the elements of conflict, character, plot, and dialogue were added. When this happened, the theatre as an art form was born.

Early human beings, in attempting to order their universe, explain natural phenomena, and pray to their gods, used rhythmic movement to express themselves; this, in time, became dance. An entire tribe might take part or perhaps only the young men or the most skilled of the dancers. As the movements were repeated, they became set and took on special meanings. These meanings were understood by both performers and spectators and were taught to the young, thus serving an educative as well as a religious purpose.

Every society has its rituals, and ritual and theatre are never far apart. Traditional garments, body paint, and masks are worn to enhance the performance. Although not theatre in the modern sense, these tribal dances are nevertheless closely akin to it in the use of body, voice, rhythm, and costume to help express strong feelings and ideas in a form the community understands. As danced movement, therefore, drama is the oldest of the arts. Out of the rites and rituals of dance came myth; and out of myth, story or plot. It was but a short step from plot to play.

Children and Movement

Creative movement deals with the elements of dance but is more spontaneous. Children move naturally; by encouraging such movement, the teacher can help children to express themselves through physical activity, thereby creating their own styles of movement, gaining confidence in their bodies, and developing spatial awareness. It is easy to move from here to either dance or drama. Drama differs from dance because it involves a linguistic element; the older the players, the greater the dependence on words to communicate meaning. The teacher of creative drama hopes to develop ability and ease in the use of both verbal and nonverbal expression; starting early is an important factor in achieving these goals.

Like primitive people, the preschool children use their bodies to express their strongest emotions and communicate their needs and desires. Children's posture, for instance, shows us how they feel, regardless of what they may say. We read much about body language these days. This form of nonverbal communication includes any posture as well as reflexive or nonreflexive movement of the body that conveys emotion to the observer. Although most of this popular writing concerns the adult, the attitudes and feelings of children and animals are just as clearly revealed by their movements and expressions. A leader can learn much about the members of a group of any age from the postures they assume, their ability to relax, and the use they make of the various parts of their bodies.

A young child tends to express physically what an adult states in words. For example, when asked how a horse moves, a small child is more apt to gallop than to describe the gait. Asked the height of a very tall person, the child will stand on tiptoe to reach as high as possible. Although the majority of children walk before they can talk, this early use of the body to express emotions and describe or give information is a phenomenon common to most boys and girls, regardless of their linguistic development.

Rhythms classes for young children build on this natural impulse. What happens in the class is well described by an experienced teacher of rhythms and dramatic play. The children remove their shoes and stockings as they enter a gym or large, free, unencumbered space. Music is provided by a pianist or a recording, or "if we are lucky, it is music created by the children themselves." Then, as if by signal, the children respond to changing rhythms. If the music is fast, wild, free, so are their movements. If it becomes slower, quieter, softer, so will be their movements. The idea is for the children to listen to what the music says and then to transfer it into bodily activity. "To one child the rhythm may suggest the rhythm of a galloping pony; to another it may mean the branches of a tree buffeted in a wind storm; a third may think of the whirling arms of a threshing machine." The teacher does not suggest what the children should do or ask them questions but, by watching, is usually able to tell what is in the mind of each child. In the middle grades rhythms may be based on units of study: Indians, Greek mythology, the great West, the jungle. "These are samples of the big rhythmic activities that appeal so strongly to growing, energetic youngsters."[1]

Children with language problems tend to find great satisfaction in movement. The physicality of dance/movement circumvents their disadvantages in verbal skills, thus providing another reason for its inclusion, particularly in the beginning. In addition to these conscious and unconscious expressions, however, there is the physical pleasure a child derives from moving, a pleasure that leads into play, dance, sports, and exercise for its own sake. Today, unfortunately, television constantly bombards the eyes and ears of children, giving information of all kinds but at the expense of their movement experience and natural creative response. In bringing children indoors, they are made passive spectators rather than active participants in games and sports in open areas. Most children enjoy moving their bodies and discovering different ways of exploring a space. As they gain physical control, they prefer running to walking, and they enjoy finding new methods of locomotion that are energetic and fast. Running, skipping, galloping, hopping, jumping, leaping and rolling stretch the muscles and help children to gain a mastery of their bodies as they try out different things they can do. Because

---

1. All quotations in this paragraph are from *Rhythms by Mary Perrine,* as told to Henrietta O. Rogers (New Canaan, Conn.: The New Canaan Country School Monograph, Spring 1951).

movement is so natural an expression, it is the ideal way of beginning work in creative drama.

Peter Slade used the term *natural dance* to describe dance that is not tied to a set of rules or complicated techniques but rather is improvised and personal in style. He further identified it as the bridge between the primitive and the sophisticated or between natural inclination and a disciplined art form.[2]

Elizabeth Polk, movement therapist and for many years professor of dance at Adelphi University, placed a special emphasis on skipping for young patients. She saw the skip as much more than alternating right and left hops; she described it as "an upward movement, a joyous way of going places."[3] It begins with the jump; next is the one-legged jump, which is a hop. If the child has a rhythmic sense, the hop easily turns into a skip. As to the value of the skip, she viewed it as twofold: coordination of movement and pride in achievement, which strengthens self-esteem. This achievement helps to develop the self-control and discipline that are needed in the classroom and in life.

Teachers and leaders of older groups find that their goals may be reached more easily and quickly if, instead of a verbal approach, they begin with physical activity. Actors call these activities warm-ups and declare them an effective way to relax and tone the muscles of their backs, legs, arms, and necks in preparation for a performance. Through rhythmic exercise a group can be drawn together and released in an objective and pleasurable way.

Rhythm, an element of movement, supplies structure and enjoyment. Rhythm is apparent in many of the games and chants of children and is the basis of music and dance. In fact, music and dance are frequently taught together through the medium of song, rhythm, and the employment of toy or rhythm instruments. This is called music-movement and is advocated by many educators. Émile Jacques Dalcroze thought of using the body as a musical instrument by treating rhythm, with its roots in physical movement, as the organizer of musical elements.

Classes in movement are most successful when taught in a large room, where students have plenty of space in which to move freely. Too large an area, such as a gymnasium or a playground, on the other hand, presents problems; for large, unconfined space can lead to chaos, not freedom, dispersing the group rather than bringing it together. Therefore boundaries should be established and maintained.

Leotards, pants, jump suits, or comfortable old clothing of some kind should always be worn; rhythm sandals or bare feet prevent slipping on a hardwood floor. Piano accompaniment is an asset, if the leader can play or has an accompanist; if not, a drum is perfectly satisfactory. Later on, recorded music will help suggest mood and possible characterization. In the beginning, however,

2. Peter Slade, *Natural Dance* (London: Hodder and Stoughton, 1977).

3. Elizabeth Polk, "Teaching Children to Skip," *New York State Journal of Health, Physical Education and Recreation* 29, no. 2 (June 1976): 2.

and for most purposes, percussion instruments are all the leader needs to give the beat and suggest or change rhythms. One advantage of the drum, incidentally, is that it permits the leader to move about freely and watch the group. This freedom of movement is not possible while playing a piano or changing tapes and records.

In a movement class it is usually a good idea to begin work with the entire group, unless the class is so large or the room so small that the participants bump into each other. In that case, the leader should divide the class into two parts, working first with one and then with the other and alternating every few minutes to hold the interest of all. Beginning with a large circle, the leader should beat a good rhythm for walking. When all are moving easily and without self-consciousness, the beat can be changed to something faster, such as a trot or a run. Shifting the rhythm to a gallop, a skip, a hop, a jump, and then back to a slow-motion walk not only is good exercise, but it holds the participants' attention as they listen for the changes. Depending on the pupils' ages, more complicated rhythms can be added. The participants themselves can take turns beating the drum or clapping new combinations. Why rhythmic movement first? According to Marjorie Dorian, teacher of dance and author of books on the subject, it encourages spontaneous movement within a disciplined framework. This is the goal of the teacher of creative drama as well as the teacher of dance.

> The arts, through the common denominator of rhythm, can best be served by an introduction to rhythmic movement, both disciplined and expressive. Through rhythm the child experiences the dynamic changes of opposites: soft and loud, fast and slow, much and little: qualities that make us sensitive to everything around us. Through the measurement of time and space he becomes aware of the limitations that eventually give him strength to pursue other disciplines.[4]

As teachers, we have tended to think of creative drama as concerned primarily with developing intellectual and linguistic abilities, whereas we have thought of movement as concerned only with the control and use of the body. Actually, movement and body language are part of creative drama. It is the combined mental, physical, vocal, and emotional involvement that distinguishes creative drama from all other art forms and gives its special value.

Instruments

Although the drum is the most commonly used instrument when working on rhythms, there are other instruments that add variety and are not difficult to obtain. Some of these are triangles, bells, and gongs for metal sounds; sticks and castinets for wood sounds; and shaking instruments like maracas or gourds with pebbles inside. Imaginative leaders and groups will find or invent other

---

4. This is a summary of the philosophy presented by Marjorie Dorian in *Ethnic Stories for Children to Dance* (San Francisco: BBB Associates, 1978).

instruments of their own. Trying out different objects to discover what sounds they make is an exercise in itself and one most children enjoy.

One of the values of using different instruments is the discovery of the qualities of sound they produce. This in turn helps the student to feel the rhythm in a special way. For example, slow drumbeats might suggest waves washing up on the shore of a lake, whereas the sound of castinets might bring hailstones or raindrops to mind. In telling a story in movement, the use of several percussion instruments will stimulate the imagination, often giving different results from those obtained with the use of a single drum.

Records and tapes are excellent, but percussion instruments are recommended primarily because the teacher has complete control over them—stopping, starting, changing the rhythm, and so on according to the immediate need. The terms *largo, allegro, legato,* and *staccato* can be introduced at this time; they have special meanings that describe rhythms clearly and, incidentally, add to a growing vocabulary.

Remember that you do not have to have real instruments to suggest rhythms or sounds. The following things work very well and encourage use of the imagination.

> For *drumming* try objects found in every school room or home: wastepaper baskets turned upside down, pans, table or desk tops, boxes, coffee cans with plastic covers, wash tubs.
> For *sharp noises* use sticks, pencils, rulers, stones, spoons.
> For *shaking* noises try cans with pebbles, rice, or beans inside; gourds; anything that can be rattled.
> For *thunder* use a sheet of aluminum (shake it).
> For *ringing* sounds use bells, water glasses and jars filled with different amounts of water, metal against metal.

For many kinds of sounds the human voice can supply the quality of sound desired. Try having the class hum together, shout, blow, and sing.

Rhythmic Activities

The following activities are designed to help the student discover the drama in movement. In the early stages the leader works within the group, moving out when the participants are secure and able to move without support. The teacher does not *show* the groups what to do but supports, in every way possible, honest effort, involvement, and the development of individual ideas.

> 1. Take the group on a journey over a desert, across a river, up a hill, over both smooth and rough ground, over slippery rocks, through tall grass, and into an open field. Vivid imaging stimulated by rhythmic accompaniment makes this a favorite game of young children and a challenge to older ones.
> 2. Have the group listen to different beats and then imagine what gaits or

A workshop in movement. *(Courtesy of Creative Arts Team.)*

characters they suggest, such as an Indian chief striding, an old man shuffling, a toddler, a young woman running for a train, a delivery boy with a heavy load, or a night watchman on his rounds. Try moving like these characters.

3. Do the same things with moods. Have the group first listen and then tell whether the beats sound happy, sad, proud, excited, sneaky, angry, or shy. Have the group move together to the same beats, expressing these moods.

4. "Snail" is a good beginning game for establishing a common rhythm. Have the group form a single file, each putting his or her hands on the shoulders of the person in front. The leader moves to the center of the room with the line following. Chanting "snail, snail, snail, snail," the group moves into a shell-like formation. When the players can move in no further, they reverse and move back into their original circle.

5. Rhythms can suggest people working or moving in unison. Try beats that describe the following: an assembly line, a marching band, robots, motorcycles, athletes warming up, workmen using picks, joggers, and so on.

6. Not only young children but adult actors enjoy suggesting different animals through rhythmic movement. Try to find rhythms for the following:

Horses	Chickens	Mice
Cats	Cranes	Frogs
Rabbits	Kangaroos	Sea gulls
Snakes	Monkeys	Pigeons

7. Carrying this activity a step further, have children suggest the movements of a puppy, who at first is wobbly on his feet and then, in time, becomes more sure of himself. Finally, he carries himself proudly, runs, leaps, and even learns to stand up on two legs and beg for food.

8. City children will enjoy the "trash can." A group of ten to twelve children are huddled together as if in a trash can. Suddenly a gust of wind comes along and topples the can, letting all of the trash fall on the pavement. When the wind blows, the papers fly in all directions. Suggest that they decide what they are: cardboard cartons, paper napkins, crusts of pizza, newspapers, and so on. Children who are not in this one can be the wind, shifting, changing, becoming stronger and then weaker.

9. An imaginative exercise that requires a little more experience is the creation of fantastic creatures. Ask the class to imagine strange or fanciful animals and then to show with their bodies what the animals are like. How do they look? What are they made of? What do they eat? How do they move? Breathe? Sleep? This exercise can be a source of fun and relaxation as well as a challenge.

10. The following is a quieting exercise to be used after vigorous movement. Sitting in a circle on the floor, the group creates different rhythms and sounds. Clapping hands, snapping fingers, tapping knees, and brushing the floor softly with the hands are among the sounds that can be made in this position. Have each child put two and then three of these sounds together in a rhythmic sequence. The group listens carefully and tries to repeat the sequence.

From Rhythms to Dramatic Play

Dramatic play, the child's earliest effort to reproduce life situations and to try out the roles of others, is based on imitation. Through imitating the actions and behavior of others, the young child masters reality and gains self-confidence. Movement thus merges with improvisation, as the drama takes shape. Words, the last element to be added, will be scanty at first, for the vocabulary of the preschool child is limited. In fact, much older players in creative drama classes tend to say less than they have planned and feel. In time, however, the need for words is felt: when that moment comes, natural dialogue is born. This is why movement is preferred to a verbal beginning for every age level.

Virginia Koste, in her book *Dramatic Play in Childhood: Rehearsal for Life*, observed that "Ironically one backlash of the creativity craze has been the neglect, the ignoring of imitation with all of its implications in human learning and art."[5] She urged us to restore imitation to its rightful place, for it is through observation and imitation that children learn. Knowledge of others and their

5. Virginia Koste, *Dramatic Play in Childhood* (New Orleans: Anchorage Press, 1978), p. 19.

ways of doing things enables children to invent new forms and create dramas and characters of their own. "Holding the mirror up to nature" is a necessary function; imitation is a fault only when it discourages inventiveness and encourages dependency and copying.

Observation and Imitation

Here is an exercise for observation and imitation that younger children enjoy. It is suggesting movement through the "—ly" game. The entire class can play it together, or one person can begin and the others follow his or her interpretation. In this way every child is assured of the opportunity to create a movement. Words used might be *lazily, quickly, slowly, curiously, wearily, sleepily, noiselessly, loudly, angrily, happily, joyfully, thankfully*, and *sheepishly*. Incidentally, playing this game is also a way of learning new words.

Similar to this exercise is the beating out of rhythms. Each child beats a rhythm for the others to follow. After each has had several turns, variations of the game can be played. One child can go into the center and begin a rhythm, change it suddenly, and tap the one who will begin the next. This has endless possibilities and is an excellent exercise for encouraging close observation and imitation.

Movement Activities

In the preceding activities we were especially concerned with rhythms and the use of the body. All movement is concerned, however, with *where* and *how* the body is used:

*A*rhythmetics. *(Courtesy of the Kaleidoscope Dance Company and Mary Sichel; photograph by Teri Bloom.)*

A. *Where* the body moves refers to:
   1. Level (high, low, medium)
   2. Direction (forward, backward, left, right, in diagonals)
   3. Shape of the movement
B. *How* the body moves refers to:
   1. Energy (much or little)
   2. Time (sudden or sustained)
   3. Flow (free or tight)

The next group of exercises may be used to work on the *where* or the *how* of moving. Try the following to show *where* movement takes place.

Low movement: caterpillar, duck, seal, shallow pool of water, young plant emerging from the earth
High movement: airplane, high cloud, person on stilts, wire walker, kite
Horizontal movement: swinging bell, elephant's trunk, lion pacing in a cage, someone paddling a canoe, someone on a swing
Up-and-down movement: seesaw, plane, bird, bat, ball bouncing, elevator, falling star, Jack-in-the-box, rocket, piece of machinery

Try the following to show *how* movement takes place.

Fast movement: arrow, fire engine, express train, leaf in a storm, jet plane, speedboat, racehorse, top, skateboard
Slow movement: clock, farm horse, melting ice, tugboat, turtle, freight train pulling out of the station, movie in slow motion
Turning movement: curling smoke, merry-go-round, revolving door, spool of thread, figure skating, top
Strong, heavy movement: chopping wood, bulldozer, tank, stormy waves, digging in concrete
Soft, light movement: balloon, butterfly, flickering candle, soap bubble, kitten, kite, elf, leaf
Sharp movement: bucking bronco, cuckoo clock, cricket, grasshopper, juggler, woodpecker
Floppy, loose movement: clothes on a line, rag doll, mop, loose sail, straw hat blowing down the street, long hair blowing, flag in the breeze
Smooth movement: airplane, cat, fish swimming, syrup pouring, skating, rainbow forming, automobile on a throughway
Twisted movement: octopus, pretzel, knot, piece of driftwood, crumpled paper, tangled chain

Change in movement:
   1. A candle standing tall and straight burns down to a pool of wax
   2. A piece of elastic, stretched and then released

3. A paper drifting to the sidewalk and then picked up by a sudden gust of wind
4. A board slowly breaking away from the side of an old building and then falling off
5. A toy train moving rapidly, running down and stopping, and then being rewound, repeating the sequence

The following images suggest being, using or doing, and feeling through movement.

Water
Being: bubbles, rushing water, rain, whirlpool, quiet pool, surf
Using: blowing bubbles, carrying water, hosing the lawn, water skiing, wading in shallow water
Feeling: weightlessness of floating, walking in water, walking against the tide
Fire
Being: bonfire blazing, forest fire raging, smoke puffing, match being lighted
Using: building a fire, putting out a fire, being warmed by a fire
Feeling: hot, warm, sleepy from a fire, choking from the smoke of a fire
Air
Being: soft summer air with only a slight breeze blowing
Using: pumping air into a tire, blowing up a balloon, breathing good, clean air
Feeling: warm air, cold air, polluted air, pleasant cool air

Try to suggest the following ideas in dance and then in pantomime. They may be expressed differently or they may be much the same, depending on the one moving. Each student must move as he or she feels, for there is no right or wrong way. At this stage sincere involvement is the major goal.

1. Offering a prayer
   Giving thanks
   Asking for rain in a time of drought
2. Casting a magic spell on someone
   Being under a magic spell
   Trying to throw off a spell
3. Feeling frightened
   Investigating the cause of your fear
   Feeling relief at discovering that your fear was groundless
4. Feeling joyful
   Showing what has made you so happy
   Sharing your joy with others
5. Feeling very angry
   Showing what has made you so angry
   Resolving your anger by doing something about it

Now take one of the above ideas and combine the three parts of it so as to create a simple story.

Partner Activities

The activities so far have been planned for the whole class. Working in pairs or with partners is more difficult, because the movements must be synchronized. Try the following simple exercises as a starter.

1. Have each member of the group take a partner. Have them put their hands on each other's shoulders and then push to see who is the stronger. Working with a partner in this way helps the individual move from group work to individual work without feeling self-conscious.
2. Next try the theatre game of having one person lead another whose eyes are closed. Have the class walk around the room in pairs until all are moving easily together. Reverse roles and try it again.
3. Divide the group into pairs, with one person standing at each end of the room. To the beat of the drum, they:
   a. Walk toward each other, meet, and part
   b. Walk toward each other, meet, and clash
   c. Walk toward each other, meet, and go off together
4. Have one person begin a movement and the partner pick it up and continue it.
5. Have one person begin to make or do something and the partner complete it.

Activities on a Theme

The activities that follow are different from the preceding in that they involve group cooperation. Although simple in themselves, they become more complex in their dependency on interaction. Three themes are suggested, but the children as well as the leader will think of others in which the entire class is asked to contribute to a single theme.

1. *The Old Men's Dance.* This is an actors' exercise that most children enjoy. The class is divided in half and placed in two lines facing each other. There may be music with a strong rhythm or a drumbeat as accompaniment. The child at the head of one line invents a step or movement of some part of the body. The child across from him or her repeats the step and adds another one. The second person in the first line repeats both movements and adds another. This continues until everyone in the class has contributed a step or movement to the dance. The larger the class, the more difficult it becomes to remember all the steps, but the exercise is a good warm-up for a group, as well as a good activity at the end of class, particularly when too little time is left to begin on new material.

2. *Building a Zoo.* This is fun for younger players. Each child creates a different animal in movement, eventually having them all move into imagined cages around the room. The teacher can be the zoo keeper, working "in-role" with the class.

3. *Making a Train, Being Ants, Being Boats.* Younger players enjoy this exercise. The problem here is one of precision. The players follow each other in a line, maintaining equal distances between themselves and the children preceding them. The leader (first car, ant, boat, etc.) determines the speed, direction, and rhythm.

Telling Stories in Movement

Pure dance has no describable story. Mime, on the other hand, uses movement to narrate or describe. Mime can range from the classic form that captures the essence of a person or action to the imitative form that reproduces an action realistically and in detail. There is a trend at present to add sound to enhance the situation or help tell the story. This is a new direction in the art of mime, which requires as much skill as silent theatre. Indeed, all forms of movement and mime demand concentration, practice, and precision. In time, a personal style can be developed that characterizes the work.

Myths and legends lend themselves to mime and mimetic movement. They are generally simple in plot and deal with universal themes and feelings.

Action–reaction. (*Photograph by Anne Jackson.*)

THE BAT'S CHOICE
A Tale from India

This legend comes from India and offers various possibilities for creative movement.

In India they tell why the bat hides by day and comes out only at night. Many, many years ago there was a war between the birds and the animals. The bat, who had wings like a bird but a body like an animal, watched them fight but could not make up his mind which side to join. Finally, he decided he would go to the winning side. That appeared to be the animals, so he went over to them, declaring his everlasting loyalty.

Then suddenly things changed. With the help of the eagle, the birds began to overcome the animals. Now the bat wondered whether he had made a mistake; perhaps he would be better off with the birds. Until he could be sure, however, he hid in a tree and watched. When peace was finally reached, the bat found himself unpopular with both sides. And so it is to this day that he hides in a tree by day and comes out at night, when the birds and most of the animals are asleep.

This simple legend lends itself equally well to dance and mime. The birds and animals suggest movement, whereas the plot is so simple that it can be told easily without words. There is plenty of action to make it interesting. If the group prefers to use dialogue, however, the story can be improvised. Another way would be to have a narrator tell it while the group pantomimes the action. In a story of this kind, any number can play. It is included to show the possibilities in a simple tale with a strong conflict and minimal characterization. More specifically, the tale can be told first in movement and then retold with the addition of animal noises. Little children love to tell it in this way, and older students discover they lose all inhibitions when there is no demand for words.

Although many stories that can be expressed in dance can also be dramatized as plays, The Bat's Choice *is particularly good example. Indeed, it can be extended into another dimension by comparing the Bat's behavior to the behavior of human beings, who shift their positions from one side to another. I have tried this story with all age levels, after first working in movement and then combining movement with animal sounds. Young children usually apply the theme to a playground or school situation, whereas older children see a more and deeper implications, from the conflict of loyalties in a broken home to peer pressure and power plays. College students carry the theme much further into areas of personal commitment and political and social issues. Not every story can be extended to this degree but folk tales often can because they have been preserved for this quality of wisdom and morality.*

THE TURNIP

The old Russian folktale of pulling up the turnip can be told completely in movement. Although the tale is about individuals rather than groups, there are so many characters and the tale is so short that everyone in the class can have a turn. It is a very amusing situation but also one that requires skill and control to prevent its becoming a series of pratfalls. Although the story is a simple comedy, there is the basic truth that by pulling together, a difficult task can be accomplished.

It was autumn and time for the turnips to be harvested. Grandfather went out to the garden and bent down to pull the first one. But this turnip was different from any turnips he had ever planted. It refused to come up! So, after trying unsuccessfully with all his might, he called his wife to help him.

When grandmother came out and saw what he wanted, she put her arms around his waist, and together they pulled and pulled. Still the turnip would not budge. Then granddaughter came out to the garden to see what was happening. Putting her arm around grandmother's waist, she pulled grandmother, who pulled grandfather, who pulled the turnip. But the turnip refused to come up.

(The story continues in this way with any number of characters included, each one pulling the one before him. Sometimes it is told with the granddaughter's dog pulling her and a beetle pulling the dog, followed by a second, third, and fourth beetle all pulling at the end of the line.)

Finally, when all pull together, the turnip comes up!

THE PASTA POT

The old Italian tale of the witch and her pasta pot can be told in dance just as easily as with improvised dialogue. It is a simple story line.

The witch, Nona, had a magic pasta pot. One day, as she put the pot on the stove, her servant Anthony heard her chanting the words, "Boil and bubble, pasta pot. Make me some pasta, nice and hot." What Anthony did not see were the three magic kisses that Nona threw at the pot when she had eaten her fill.

Then, telling him to stay and guard the cottage, but not to touch the pot, Nona left. She had no more than gone out the door, however, when Anthony, eager to see if the magic worked for him, looked at the pot and chanted the words he had heard her say. No sooner were the words out of his mouth than the water began to boil and the pot to fill up with pasta. Anthony was greatly pleased with himself and ate heartily, but to his dismay the pasta continued to roll out of the pot. He couldn't stop it!

The neighbors, seeing the pasta rolling out the door of the cottage, rushed in to find out what was happening. They all tried to stop it but it only kept on coming. At this moment Nona returned. She threw three magic kisses in the direction of the pot and at once the pasta stopped. She gave Anthony a beating for disobeying her; then, seeing how frightened he had been, she forgave him. They and their neighbors joined together in a dance.

Players of any age will find this a humorous tale that can be handled in a variety of ways, depending on the interpretation. With the help of a drum and other instruments, children will find appropriate rhythms and movements by which to tell the story. Try out some movements. Decide what best expresses the old witch, Nona. How would Anthony move and show his feelings: curiosity, delight, dismay, helplessness, relief, enjoyment of the dance at the end? How would you suggest pasta boiling in a pot? Running over? Rolling out the door? What are the neighbors like? What are their feelings? Can you make up a group dance at the end? The players may want to use a folk dance here instead of creating one. There are many ways in which the story can be told and every group will find a way of its own.

Little children enjoy making up stories involving a variety of rhythms. For example, a story might go something like this: "I went for a *walk* in the park. It was a lovely morning and I *skipped* happily down a path. Soon I met an old man, *shuffling* along with a pack on his back. Next I met some pigeons *strutting* across the path in search of food." This can go on as long as you want, adding persons and animals with clearly observable gaits. The teacher, working with the children, suggests the rhythms with drumbeats. A little practice and the story will take on embellishments, providing a rich opportunity for imaginative ideas and ways of showing them.

THE STORY OF MA-UI

The Hawaiian Islands are rich in myths and legends, some of which offer excellent material for movement and creative dance. "The Story of Ma-ui" is one of them. Players of all ages will find ideas that can be expressed physically, perhaps even better than vocally—certainly, just as well. The story is simple and direct, with a theme reminiscent of folk tales around the world.

There was a time, long ago, when the sun raced across the skies of Hawaii so rapidly that the fruit had no time to ripen on the vines and the fishermen could not catch any fish. The days were short and the nights were long. The earth was so cold and dark that plants froze on their stems. These beautiful islands, as we know them today, were inhospitable to life, and the people wondered how much longer they would exist or where they could go if they left. One day a small boy named Ma-ui decided that he would catch the sun and make it slow down. Then perhaps the plants and trees would have time to grow and mature, and the fishermen could wait for a catch before it was night again. He told his grandmother of his plan. At first she feared for his life and tried to dissuade him; but when he begged her not to stop him, she gave him a magic stick and a piece of rope and fearfully bade him goodbye.

The next day Ma-ui climbed to the top of Mt. Haleakala to wait for the sun to rise. The trip was long and hard, but at last Ma-ui stood where he could see the day break. When the first ray of the sun appeared on the mountaintop, Ma-ui jumped high in the air. Quickly he threw his rope around the ray and wrestled with it. Finally, with the help of his magic stick, he mastered it and tied it to the twisted trunk of a tree. Then he made it promise to slow down or he would not let it escape. The sun saw the magic stick in the small boy's hand and promised never to race across the skies over Hawaii again. From that day forth the flowers blossomed and the trees grew straight and tall. The fruit ripened on the vines and the fishermen had time to catch the fish so that the people had plenty to eat again.

Many different movements and rhythms can be found in this story. One way to begin is with a discussion of all the movements that are mentioned. Then the entire group can work on them together, using a drumbeat to set the rhythms. A warm-up composed of walking, running, jumping, stretching, curling up, falling, and rising might precede work on the story. Some of the rhythmic patterns that the group might try next are:

The sun, racing across the sky
The flowers, stretching and trying to grow and then wilting and withering
The fishermen, casting their lines and pulling them in as the sun goes down
The people, trudging back to their homes, exhausted and cold
Ma-ui, climbing the mountain and jumping to catch the sun's ray
The sun, slowing down in its course across the sky
The slower rhythms found at the end of the story

After the class has worked on the movements long enough to become free and thoroughly acquainted with the story, they will be ready to try playing it in its entirety. Although the tale can be told in pantomime or improvised with spontaneous dialogue, The Story of Ma-ui *can be beautifully conveyed through dance or simple creative movement. Older groups may want to add a Hawaiian dance at the end or to combine speech and movement. There is no best way of handling it; it was included in this chapter because it offers unusual opportunities for creative movement.*

THE LITTLE SNOW GIRL

The Russian folk tale of "The Little Snow Girl," or "Snow Maiden," has often been dramatized and makes a charming play with dialogue, dance, and music. It is equally effective, however, when performed entirely in dance. Even young children, knowing the story, can create movement appropriate to the characters. Whereas it can be done in a longer version, including a scene in the woods, it can be done by quite young children if that portion is eliminated and the story limited to the old people, the snow girl, and the village children.

There once lived in a small Russian village an old couple named Maria and Ivan. They had always wanted children of their own but, having none, used to watch the children of the village at play. One winter day they were at the window of their cottage as usual, watching the children playing games in the snow. When the children tired of their games and ran off, Ivan and Maria went outdoors and decided to make a snow maiden just like the little girl they had always wished they had. When it was finished, it was so beautiful that the two old people stood back and looked at it in silence. Imagine their astonishment to have it slowly come alive and dance about the yard. "It is our own little girl," they said. "Please stay here and live with us."

The Snow Girl agreed to stay but said she would melt in the house and would have to live outside until spring came, when she would have to go away, but she promised to return when the snow fell again.

(If a longer version of the story is desired for an older group, there is one that includes the Snow Girl's trip up the mountain with some of the village children.)

The children climbed, occasionally stopping for breath, as the path grew steeper. Finally, it began to grow dark and the children knew it was time to turn back so as to get home before nightfall. But the little Snow Girl wanted to go further, so they left without her. For a while all was well, then suddenly it grew quite dark and she realized that she could no longer see the path. The cold did not bother her but she knew that the old couple would worry about her if she didn't return. She sat down on a rock when along came a grey Wolf, who offered to take her home on his back. She was afraid of the Wolf, however, so she thanked him and said she would wait until morning when she could find her way home.

"Very well," said the Wolf, and he went on his way.

Next came a Brown Bear. Once again, the Snow Girl declined the offer of help, so he shuffled off, leaving her alone. Last came a Red Fox, leaping over the snow drifts. When he saw the Little Snow Girl, he stopped and offered to take her down the mountain side on his back. Now she was not afraid of the Red Fox, so she thanked him and said she would like to ride down to the village on his back. When they reached the cottage, it was dark and the old people were overjoyed to see her. "What can we give you in return for bringing our little girl home?" they asked.

"A fine fat hen," the Fox replied. "Very well," they said but when they reached the corner of the house, they stopped and looked back. "After all," the old woman argued, we have our little girl back. We are poor, and we have so few hens, why not put some stones in the sack, then send the dog after the Fox to chase him away?" The old man did not want to do it but she insisted, so he finally filled the sack with stones and sent the dog after him.

But when they turned back, they were stricken to see the Little Snow Girl moving away. "You do not love me as much as a hen," she said. "I can stay no longer." And then she was gone.

The old people were very sad. All that spring and summer they grieved. When the first snowflakes fell the following winter, they stood at the door of their cottage as they had so many times before, realizing they had lost what was dearest to their hearts through their own deception and greed. Suddenly, out of the swirling snowflakes, a small figure emerged. It couldn't be—but it was—their Little Snow Girl. "You have suffered enough," she said. "I have come back because I believe you are truly sorry. I will stay with you every winter as your own child for as long as you live."

Appropriate music will help the children create movement to tell the story and suggest the dialogue without speaking. Piano music or taped music, including some Russian folk tunes, can set the mood for children playing in the snow, the snow flakes swirling, the old people, and the animals. Telling the entire story in movement is an ambitious undertaking, but a group that really likes it will find The Little Snow Girl *not only enjoyable but work that they will want to show others.*

THE FULL MOON FESTIVAL

Moon cakes are sold in Chinese communities throughout America in the fall of the year. These hard dry cakes can be found, beautifully packaged, four to a box, in Chinese stores. The legend that is told about them is suggested here as one that can be told in movement as well as in words. Like all folk tales and legends, this one also requires that the class be thoroughly familiar with the details before trying to express it in dance.

Once upon a time, there were ten suns in China. The suns were big and bright and they burned houses, so that the people were frightened by them. There were also at that time outlaws who stole from people and sometimes even killed them. The people were terrified but could not stop them any more than they could stop the sun's rays. All they could do was to hide in their homes and hope that neither the suns nor the outlaws harmed them.

One day a man, who knew how to use a sword skillfully, came to the village and killed the outlaws and nine of the suns. The villagers were so grateful that they decided to make the hero their ruler. For years he ruled wisely and well. Then, after a time, he became greedy and foolish. He wanted to live forever and never lose his power. He had heard of a drug that gave the one who took it eternal life, so he sent one of his servants to find it.

His wife, who was kind and generous, realized what would happen if he should live forever; it would be the same as it was before he came and saved the people. So, when the servant returned with the drug, she decided the only way to keep her husband from taking it, was to take it herself. Suddenly, she noticed tiny clouds forming at her feet. Then she felt herself becoming very light. Gently, the clouds lifted her to the sky, where she lived all of her life and never grew old.

The day that she went to the moon was September 18th, and that is why the people celebrated the Full Moon Festival at that time of the year, for saving them from the evil ruler.

Percussion accompaniment is all that is needed, although Chinese music helps to establish the mood and stimulate the imagination of the children. The legend can be told and then danced, or it can be told in movement and mime as the teacher tells it. The mixture of delicacy and violence is typical of many of the Chinese folk tales, and American children usually like performing them.

FROM TYL EULENSPIEGEL'S MERRY PRANKS

This is a made-to-order tale for dancing. Moreover, children love the little rascal who can outwit the staid and unimaginative townsfolk. The story can be told easily in movement with music and the beat of a drum. There are many tales of Tyl, and this one may stimulate a class to want to dance or dramatize some of the others.

The adventures of Tyl Eulenspiegel are known throughout the world. This lovable little rascal was always up to some mischief but he was never found out until after he had gone away. On this particular occasion, Tyl was dancing along the bank of a river. The people so enjoyed his performance that they tossed coins generously in his cap and soon he had quite a collection. In response to their applause, he promised them another performance the following day. Then he hopped on a rope tied to trees on each bank of the river. He did not know, however, that someone had cut the rope on the other side and when he was halfway across, the rope broke, causing him to fall into the water!

Tyl, not one to be daunted, climbed out, his coins safely packed away in his sack. Suddenly he had an idea. He boasted that he could dance on the rope in anyone's shoes, no matter how small or large, if only they would tie up the rope again. Collecting another sack full of shoes, he danced his way across the river, then tossed the bag of shoes back to the villagers, saying that he had never said he would put on the shoes! Before the people could find their own shoes, Tyl had disappeared off into the woods.

A list of music to evoke mood and stimulate movement is included at the back of the book. Most of the titles are readily available. I have found these selections extremely helpful, particularly if the teacher does not play an instrument or needs to give all of his or her attention to the class. There are other occasions when simple percussion is a preferred method; it is an advantage when the leader wants to shift rapidly from one rhythm to another or to talk and beat the drum simultaneously.

Summary

Movement—the basis of play, ritual, games, dance, and theatre—is a natural beginning for work in creative drama. Physically, the whole body is involved: torso, arms, legs, head, and neck. Through the use of the body, muscles are stretched and relaxed. Posture and coordination improve with regular exercise. Because the entire group can take part at one time, the possibility of self-consciousness is lessened. Persons of all ages and backgrounds usually find it easier at first to become involved through movement rather than through verbalization. This is particularly true of younger children, those for whom English is a second language, and persons with special problems and needs. Often in the rhythms and patterns of a child's movement the problems in the child's inner life are revealed. This is why movement and dance are recommended as treatment, serving both diagnostic and therapeutic purposes.

Imitation and observation are as much a part of movement as creativity. The leader encourages imagination but discourages the cliché. Through movement, therefore, children experience both discipline and freedom. By moving into the rituals of the group (and here the word *rituals* is used in its broadest sense), a feeling of belonging is engendered. Rhythm, that underlying flow and beat, captures the mover in what was described earlier as an experience both objective and pleasurable. Taught together, rhythms and dramatic play provide a sound foundation for acting. "Dance–drama" encompasses the disciplines of both arts and is, therefore, a powerful tool for creative expression.

5

Pantomime:
The Next Step

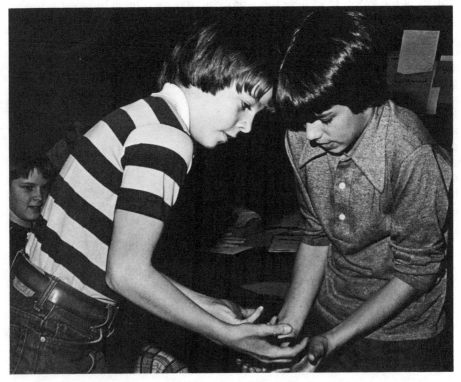

Absorption during "Pass the Ball." *(Courtesy of Lou Furman, Washington State University.)*

*P*antomime is the art of conveying ideas without words. Children enjoy pantomime, and for the young child this is an excellent way to begin creative drama. Since many of a child's thoughts are spoken entirely through the body, the five- or six-year-old finds pantomime a natural means of expression. Group pantomimes of the simplest sort challenge the imagination and sharpen awareness. In kindergarten, basic movements such as walking, running, skipping, and galloping prepare for the creative use of rhythms. Music can set the mood for people marching in a parade, horses galloping on the plains, toads hopping in a field, racing cars on a track, or children skipping on a fine autumn day. In other words, rhythmic movement becomes dramatic when the participants make use of it to become someone or something other than themselves.

For older children and adults, pantomime is advocated because it encourages the use of the entire body and relieves the players of having to think of dialogue. Here, also, group pantomime should precede individual work. Familiar activities such as playing ball, flying kites, running for a bus, or hunting for a lost object get the group on its feet and moving freely. If the entire class works at one time, self-consciousness disappears and involvement is hastened. Fifteen or twenty minutes of this sort of activity, changed frequently enough to hold the group's interest, makes for relaxation and readiness to move on to a more challenging assignment.

Others for whom pantomime is especially satisfying are children who do not speak English and those with speech and hearing problems. The child who has an idea but not the words to express it can convey meaning, often very successfully, through body language. I have had speech-handicapped students of all ages present characters, stories, and ideas in pantomime with clarity and artistry. Another benefit, in addition to the obvious one of building self-confidence, is motivation for developing skill in the language arts. Having succeeded in sign language, children are encouraged to express themselves in words and writing as well. Pantomime, incidentally, has become a familiar art form in the past ten to fifteen years. One of the benefits of television is the opportunity it affords all persons to enjoy the performing arts, including skilled professional mime.

Class Size

Although creative rhythms can be carried on successfully with any number, pantomime requires a group of no more than fifteen to twenty. If a class is very large, the teacher should make every effort to divide it so that half the group is involved with some other activity at that hour. Pantomime demands individual attention, and every child should be assured the opportunity of participation each time the class meets. This is true whatever the age level, for growth depends upon repeated experiences in exercises that increase in difficulty.

Length of Class Period

The length and frequency of class meetings depend upon the situation (school, club, or camp) and the age of the players. With very young children, daily experiences for ten to fifteen minutes are ideal, whereas for older children, two or three meetings a week for forty-five minutes or an hour work out well. With club groups, the meeting may be only once a week; this is less desirable but may be the only possible arrangement. High school students and young adults can be absorbed for as long as two hours, but in general, more frequent meetings of shorter length are preferable.

In schools in which creative drama is a definite part of the curriculum, the teacher can look forward to regular meetings throughout the year. Where it is not, it will be up to the classroom teacher to introduce it whenever and however he can. He will probably use pantomime in connection with other subjects that, if imaginatively done, can be of value as a tool for teaching and a creative experience for the class.

Playing Space

A stage is generally used for formal rehearsals, whereas a large room is more desirable for creative drama. Little children enjoy moving all over the room and should be encouraged to do so. The younger the group, therefore, the larger the space required. If a large room is not available, a classroom in which all chairs have been pushed aside will do. Space makes for freedom; a small or cramped area inhibits it. As was said in the preceding chapter, however, too large an area can present other problems, particularly for a beginning or uncontrolled group. Boundaries are needed, as the leader soon discovers; there is greater freedom when there are clear boundaries of both time and space than when neither exists. An auditorium with a stage and chairs is least desirable as a playing space for a beginning group of any age, since it inevitably leads to a concept of performance with stage techniques before the players are ready for it. Under any circumstances, seating children on the floor in a semicircle where all can see, hear, and be heard is the most satisfactory arrangement.

Imagination

Whatever the space, the teacher will try to see that it is kept uncluttered and that the players are seated in a circle or semicircle around it. Having engaged in rhythms and group activities, the players are now ready for pantomime. There are many ways of proceeding, but one that has proved effective is having the class handle a small, nondescript object (such as a small box or blackboard eraser) as if it were several different items. For example, the teacher calls six or seven players to the center, hands one the object and tells the child that it is a diamond bracelet, the most beautiful piece of jewelry the teacher has ever seen.

I have found this activity an ideal way of beginning with a new group. It involves several players yet offers each one an opportunity to interpret an action in his or her own way. It is uncomplicated: only one thing is required at a time. Finally, because it is so simple, it does not tempt players to imitate each other; on the contrary, they soon begin to enjoy the different ways they can think of to do it. The teacher will then ask the players to:

1. Handle the object.
2. Look at it.
3. React to it.
4. Pass it along to the next person.

When each has had a chance to handle and react to the object, the teacher may say that it is now a kitten with very soft fur. The same group again takes it and reacts to it. The next time it may be a wallet—dirty and torn—with nothing in it. The fourth time it is passed, it becomes a knife or a glass of water filled to the brim or perhaps an old, valuable manuscript. Each time it is handed around, the group invests it with more of the qualities of the suggested object. The idea is to stimulate the imagination and help the players realize that it is not the property used but their own imaginations that turn an eraser first into a bracelet, then a kitten, then a wallet, and finally a knife or a glass of water.

The observers are as interested as the players in the growing reality that develops. Depending on the time at their disposal, the teacher may repeat the exercise with another group or move on to a new exercise. Some of the questions that might be asked of the observers are:

1. How did we know it was a bracelet?
    "One player held it so that the diamonds sparkled in the light." "John held it as if it were very expensive." "Linda tried it on." "Charles looked for the price tag."
2. Why did we know it was a kitten the second time the eraser was passed?
    "One stroked its head." "Another girl put it close to her cheek as if it were alive." "Barbara held its legs carefully when she gave it to Lois." "They all held it as if it were soft and round."

Questions put to the players might be:

1. What did the wallet look like to you?
    "It was dark green leather." "It was old and torn." "There was a faded snapshot in the front." "It had a hole in the bottom." "It was muddy because it had been lost in the yard."
2. You were careful not to let any of the objects drop, but you handled them differently. Why?

"The bracelet was valuable." "I didn't want it to get broken." "The kitten was alive, and that made it different from all the others." "When I jiggled the glass, the water almost spilled."

Questions like these push the players to stronger visual images and greater power of observation.

Another exercise that serves to excite the imagination is the suggestion that a table in the middle of the room is covered with a variety of small objects. Each participant must go up and pick out one thing, showing, by the way he or she handles it, what it is. Although this is an individual exercise, it can be done with several persons at once so that the attention is not focused on a single player. By having the rest of the class seated in a semicircle, some observers will see one player and some another. This is fun for all, and what self-consciousness may have existed in the beginning will soon be gone.

Concentration

Many children will be able to concentrate on the activities; but some, for whom this is the first experience of this sort, will not, so the next step is to work on "holding the image." One good exercise is to have the class hunt for a ring that has been lost. A few minutes of searching usually involves them in the assignment. If it does not, the teacher might actually hide a ring and ask them to find it. The reality that comes with the second playing demonstrates clearly the difference between pretending to hunt and really looking. Other good group exercises for developing concentration are:

1. Watching a plane come in
2. Looking at a funny movie
3. Smelling smoke in the woods
4. Listening for the lunch bell to ring

Sense Images

The class is now ready for some specific exercises involving the five senses. This might be introduced by a discussion of the ways in which we find out what is going on around us. We see; we hear; we touch; we smell; we taste. Individuals may do the following, using no props, but trying to "see" what is suggested.

1. Enter a very large room in which you have left your sweater.
2. Go into the dark closet to look for your sweater.
3. Go into your own room to get your sweater.
4. Try to find your sweater among a dozen in the locker room.

Exercises for the sense of hearing might include:

1. Hearing an explosion
2. Listening to a small sound and trying to decide what it is
3. Listening to a military band coming down the street
4. Hearing a dance orchestra playing a popular tune on the radio

Exercises for the sense of smell might include:

1. Coming home from school and smelling cookies baking in the kitchen
2. Walking in the woods and smelling a campfire
3. Smelling different perfumes on a counter
4. Smelling something very unpleasant and trying to decide what it is

Exercises for the sense of taste might include:

1. Eating a piece of delicious chocolate candy
2. Trying a foreign food that you have never tasted before and deciding you like it
3. Biting into a sour apple

Exercises for the sense of touch might include:

1. Touching a piece of velvet
2. Touching a hot stove
3. Touching or holding an ice cube
4. Touching or holding some sharp nails

These are only a few suggestions, and the leader will think of many more. Whatever is suggested, however, should always be within the experience of the players. Practice in actual hearing and observation is good exercise and may be introduced either beforehand or at any point that the teacher thinks it of value. For instance, the teacher might ask the players to:

1. Close your eyes for one minute and listen to all the sounds you can hear.
2. Go to one corner of the room and describe all of the things that you see.
3. Touch one object and describe it as completely as possible.

What we are trying to do is to "lead children into experiences that will involve them in touching, seeing, tasting, hearing, and smelling the things in their world. We also want them to become involved in experiences that will lead to imagining, exploring, reasoning, inventing, experimenting, investigating, and selecting, so that these experiences will not only be rich in themselves but lead to personal creative growth."[1]

Performing an Action

There is no right or wrong order and no prescribed length of time the group should spend on one kind of exercise. Generally, the older the players, the longer the attention will be sustained, but this does not always hold true. At any rate, a pantomime guaranteed to capture the interest of every player, regardless of age, is "making or doing something." In the beginning the teacher will offer suggestions, but later the players will have ideas of their own. Some good suggestions might be:

1. Playing video games
2. Taking clothes to the laundromat
3. Feeding your dog
4. Getting dressed
5. Selecting books in the library
6. Turning on a favorite television program
7. Buying a pizza and taking it home
8. Riding on a crowded bus and going past your stop
9. Packing your backpack
10. Choosing food in a cafeteria

Again, let it be stressed that particularly in working with disadvantaged children, or with children in urban areas, the activities suggested should be those in their environments. "Washing clothes" rather than "fishing in a brook" is familiar to these children and can, therefore, be easily imagined and acted. This, incidentally, also helps children to respect their own ideas and regard their own experiences more positively.

Pantomimes of actions will grow more complicated as the players put them into situations. The above might be inherent in such scenes as the following:

1. You are getting ready for a birthday party for your sister and must set the table. What are you going to put on it? Are there decorations? A cake? Favors? Presents? What dishes and silver will you use? Is it a surprise? Are you alone?
2. You are baking your first cake. No one is home, so you must read and follow the recipe yourself. What will you put in it? What utensils do you need? Is it a success?

1. Earl Linderman and Donald W. Herberholz, *Developing Artistic and Perceptual Awareness* (Dubuque, Iowa: William C. Brown, 1964), p. x.

*M*akeup and mime workshops for young people. *(Courtesy of Honolulu Theatre for Youth; photograph by Jody Perry Belknap.)*

3. You have a new puppy and have come home from school to take care of it. What do you feed it? How much? How big is he? What kind of dog?
4. You are getting up on a Saturday morning. Today it has begun snowing so you must dress to go out and play. What do you wear? Is it cold? Are you excited about it? Do you take time to comb your hair? Eat your breakfast?
5. It is after dinner and you have been told to do your homework. There is a television show you would like to see, but you know you should study. What is the assignment? Do you like the subject? Is it hard? Easy? Boring? What is the show you want to see? Is anyone else in the room? What do you finally do about it?

Mood and Feelings

Somewhere along the way, feelings have crept into the pantomimes so that a specific assignment on mood will now be appropiate. The teacher may want the group to talk about feelings first, or perhaps this will come about as a result of a particularly good job one of the players has done. The teacher might even ask the class what kinds of feelings they have experienced, and their reponses will often include many more than she has anticipated. Anger, fear, happiness, excitement, pride, curiosity, vanity, anticipation, sorrow, and hatred are some feelings that seven- and eight-year-olds have enumerated.

This might be a time to break the class into groups of four or five, with each group taking one feeling to pantomime. Delightful results are always forthcoming when working on mood. One group showed excitement through a scene on Christmas Eve, when they crept downstairs to look at the tree and presents. Another asked if they could act out the story of *Pandora's Box* because it was such a good example of curiosity. Another group chose fear and set their scene in a tent at a summer camp. They were campers who heard a strange noise at night and imagined it to be a bear, but it was only their counselor coming back.

It soon becomes obvious that more than one emotion is usually involved in a situation of any length. Therefore, the next step will be to show change of mood. Situations like the following help the players to move from one mood to another.

1. You are a group of friends taking a hike in the woods. It is a beautiful day and you find strawberries and wildflowers. You stop to have your lunch, but when you are ready to move on, you discover that you have wandered from the path and are lost. Your happy mood changes to panic. Where are you? Should you go on or turn back? Is there any familiar landmark to guide you? Suddenly one of the girls finds a broken flower lying on the ground. As she picks it up, she realizes that it is on the path, and she must have dropped it when she looked for a picnic spot. Panic turns to relief as the group starts for home.

2. A group of boys discover a cave (or it could be the basement of an empty building). They go in, curious as to what they may find. One of them stumbles over a box. The boys open it and find money and jewels. Excitement grows as they realize they have found hidden treasure. Then they hear voices; men are approaching. Terrified, the boys hide. The men go past, not seeing them. The boys stuff a few coins in their pockets and run, escaping from danger.

3. A group of people get into an elevator in a big downtown building. Suddenly, it stops between floors. Their poise turns to fear as the operator pushes one button and then another, and nothing happens. Suddenly, she gets it started and the elevator moves, taking the passengers down to the ground level.

4. You are a group of children who come into your schoolroom one morning and find a monkey scampering about. First you are startled and then amused by his antics. Finally, the man who has lost him comes in and catches him, taking him away. You are sorry to see him go as he waves good-bye to you from his owner's shoulder.

5. You are going on a field trip to which you have looked forward for a long time. You get in the bus, but the bus will not start. After a few minutes, the driver lets you know that he cannot make it go, and so your trip must be postponed. Disappointed, you get out. Suddenly, the engine starts. You turn around and see the driver motioning for you to get back in. Your happiness is great because you can now go after all.

6. You are sitting in a movie. First you are watching a very dull short subject. How do you feel when it seems to be going on forever? Then it changes

to a hilariously funny cartoon. How do you react? At last, the feature begins and you are absorbed.

7. It is a very hot summer afternoon and you are on your way to the dentist. As you approach the building where his office is located, the traffic lights go out. Cars slow down, and lights in store windows go out. Everything comes to a stop, and you begin to realize that there is a massive power failure. How do you react? Do you try to go on, or do you decide to go home? Show what happens as you visualize the event. No two persons in the class will see it the same way because you will react according to where you live in relationship to the dentist's office and your past experience with blackouts.

8. It is early in the morning and you have an appointment for a job interview in an hour and a half. You have had your breakfast and are going out to empty the garbage when a gust of wind suddenly blows the door shut. Unfortunately, no one else is home, and you cannot get back into the house. How do you solve your problem?

9. Another garbage situation: You are dressed and ready for your job interview. You are taking the garbage out to empty it in the can on the curb, but your mind is on the interview and you forget to do it. You take the bus the short distance to the employment office, go in, and as you are beginning the interview, you are aware of a very bad odor. Suddenly, you realize that you are still carrying your garbage! What do you do with it? How do you manage such an embarrassing situation?

10. You are invited to dinner at the home of your club advisor. You help yourself liberally to the potato salad, which you like very much but when you take your first bite, you think something is wrong with it. Should you go on eating it or leave a large serving on your plate? Say something to your hostess? You look around the table; what are the others doing?

11. You are on a plane and the stewardess brings in the meals. You enjoy yours and eat heartily, finally scooping up the last spoonful of pudding with chocolate sauce. Suddenly, the plane gives a lurch, and the sauce is spilled on your lap. What can you do? There is a passenger in the aisle seat, and the sauce is rapidly spreading over your skirt or pants.

Mood can be created in countless ways, among them through the use of pictures, colors, light, music, and rhythms. The following ideas have been put into practice successfully with widely varying results.

1. The leader selects a picture or photograph that will evoke a strong emotional response. If the picture is realistic, the leader might, after all in the group have had a chance to look at it closely, ask questions such as: who is in the picture? Why do you think she is there? What is she doing? What does she seem to be feeling? Why do you think she feels that way?

The discussion that results will lead into possibilities for pantomime or even improvisation, if the group is ready for it. A story can be built from the meanings and mood the children find in the picture. Instead of a composition in which persons are represented, however, a picture of a place may be shown. Country roads, city streets, the platform of a railroad station, a deserted house, a stretch of empty beach, woodlands—all are springboards if the mood evoked is one that kindles the emotions and arouses our curiosity. Where do you think this is? Why is no one around? What feelings do you have when you look at it? What is there about it that makes you feel this way?

After some discussion the leader will be ready to continue with questions leading to a scene laid in the place portrayed. Who might come along? Where is he or she going? Does he meet anyone? Anyone else? What do they talk about? Do? Feel? In very little time most groups will fill the canvas with characters, often involving them in an imaginative situation laid in the scene depicted. For example, a deserted house could take the group in several directions. It might be the site of buried treasure (still a favorite theme of eight- to ten-year-old boys), important documents, or a fascinating archaeological discovery. It might, on the other hand, be the home a family has had to leave sorrowfully. Why? What has happened? Perhaps a son or daughter returns to say a last good-bye. Perhaps he or she meets a friend and finds something left behind, something meaningful. Or perhaps it is the home of a famous person who has come back after an absence of many years to see his old neighborhood once more. Does anyone see him? Does anyone recognize him? What happens if they do? How does he feel about his home? What kind of reception is he given? How do his old neighbors react?

2. Instead of a realistic painting, an abstract composition might be shown. Color, dark and light contrasts, design, the brush strokes—all will stimulate imaginative response. Not what the picture may *mean* but what it means to the viewer is the object of this exercise. Younger children tend to respond to the abstract composition more quickly than older players, perhaps because they do not feel the need for realistic detail and appreciate the fact that the artist's expression is direct and free like their own. Movement, rather than story, will usually be the response to this experience, although some children move naturally from physical movement into character.

3. As stated elsewhere, music is a powerful stimulus to creativity. Use of rhythms to suggest kinds of movement, characters, or animals is a popular and highly successful way of working. From this to the heightening of characterization is a natural next step. Actually, only the beat of a drum is necessary, although music, particularly if the leader is able to play the piano, can enrich the activity. Recordings of orchestral music are an extremely effective means of establishing mood and may be used as we used pictures to stimulate the imagination, in a pattern of listening and responding. A leader with no formal background in music can guide the

group not in the sense of a lesson in music appreciation but in the sense of encouraging listening and imaginative response. Again, young children seem to respond more spontaneously to music than older children, who have learned to be concerned with structure, theme, and melody. Careful selection of the music to be used is necessary. Thereafter, the procedure is much the same as that followed with the pictures. How does it make you feel? Show us. Where are you? Who are you? Are there others with you? What might be happening?

To create a story from music takes time, but after several experiences in listening and responding the group will be ready to proceed with the creation of characters, an original situation suggested by the music and perhaps some dialogue. Again, music is a way of inducing the flow of creative energy and, because of its abstract quality, may produce a mood more readily than other stimuli.

Characterization

Until now, we have been pantomiming activities and working to induce mood or feeling. The next step is characterization. Some participants will already have suggested characters different from themselves, but the teacher can use either the same exercises or new ones to start the group thinking in terms of characterization.

Again, situations involving groups are a good way to begin.

1. You are a group of people waiting for a bus on a city street. Each one of you will think of someone special to be: an elderly woman going to see her grandchildren, a businessman late for work, a girl on her way to high school, a blind man who needs help getting on the right bus, a young man beginning a new job, and so on.
2. You are pilgrims who have gone to a shrine where, once a year, one wish is said to be granted. Decide who you are and what it is you want. You might be a crippled man who wants to walk again, a poet who wants very much to have her work published, a young mother who wants her sick baby to be cured. The teacher may wish to play with the group and be the statue at the shrine who indicates which wish is to be granted. This is a good situation to pantomime because it offers an opportunity to work on both characterization and strong motivation.
3. You are people in a bus terminal. Some of you are going on trips, others returning; still others are meeting friends or relatives. There may be a porter, a woman selling tickets, a man selling newspapers and magazines, and so on. By your behavior, let us know who you are and how you feel as you wait for the buses to arrive and depart.

Some individual pantomimes stressing character are suggested:

1. You are a robber who is entering a house at night. While you are there, the people return unexpectedly. You listen and finally make your escape, having stolen nothing.
2. You are a neighborhood gossip. You have a party line, and one of your favorite pastimes is listening in on other people's conversations. This afternoon you hear some very good news, some bad news, and then some remarks about yourself and your habit of listening in on your neighbors. How do you react? What do you do?
3. You are a child who has wanted a dog for a long time. One day you overhear your parents talking about it in the next room. Your mother does not want a dog, but your father thinks it is time you had one. They discuss reasons for and against it. How do you react to their arguments and what is the final decision?
4. Two of you will be a customer and a storekeeper in a shop in a foreign country. You do not know each other's languages. The customer decides, in advance, on three things he needs to buy and tries to convey what they are to the clerk through pantomime. Who are you? What are the three things? How does it turn out? (This is an exercise that the entire class can do in pairs.)

Another exercise is to take one action and do it as three people. For example:

1. You go into a restaurant to order a meal. Do it as:
    a. A teen-aged boy who is very hungry
    b. A middle-aged woman who has very little appetite and sees nothing on the menu that she wants
    c. A very poor man who is hungry but must limit his choice to what he can afford
2. You are trying on dresses in a shop. Do it as:
    a. A very fat woman who has trouble being fitted
    b. A young girl, looking for a pretty dress to wear to a dance
    c. A secretary who is trying to find the most appropriate dress to wear on her first day at work in a new job
3. You are visiting an art museum. First you look at the exhibition as:
    a. An artist who knows the painter whose work is on display
    b. A woman who thinks she should go to museums but does not appreciate the pictures
    c. An elderly man who has been ill and is enjoying visiting his favorite museum for the first time in many months
4. You are exercising in a gymnasium. Do the exercises first as:
    a. A young woman who loves all athletics
    b. A fat man whose doctor has advised him to exercise to lose weight
    c. A child who has never seen gymnasium equipment before

For each of these exercises, consider what each participant does and how he or she feels about it.

Pantomime Suggested by Other Means

Some exercises are fun to do and stimulate inventiveness, but they have nothing to do with familiar actions, mood, or characters. These exercises are good as a change and may be introduced any time the leader feels the group needs a new type of stimulation. Some ideas are:

1. Beat a drum and ask the group to move in any way the drumbeat suggests.
2. Ask each person in the class to represent a mechanical appliance. He does not operate it, he *becomes* it. Some very imaginative representations may be expected, such as a pencil sharpener, an egg beater, a lawnmower, a hair drier, or a record player. This is a challenging exercise, guaranteed to break down all inhibitions.
3. Give each person a color and ask that he or she suggest it by means of movement, attitude, or characterization. This, incidentally, may be followed up with an improvisation in which the color becomes a person. For example: Mr. White, Mrs. Black, Mrs. Blue, Mr. Green, Mr. Red, and Mrs. Yellow might be people at a tea. What are they like? How do they talk? How can we distinguish one from another?
4. Each person selects a property and acts according to what it suggests to him or her. The following are usually good for stimulating imaginative reactions: a gnarled stick, a ruler, a gold bracelet, a broken dish, a sponge. Again the players do not use the properties; they become characters suggested by their qualities.
5. Be puppets. Try to imagine what it feels like to be controlled by strings. Imagine that you are being controlled and then dropped by the puppeteer. Although there is an element of characterization involved, it is the feeling of the inanimate object being manipulated that interests us.
6. Have the group listen to orchestral music. Suggest that they try to identify the various instruments. Then have the children *be* the instruments—not the musicians playing them but the instruments themselves. If they are enjoying the exercise, suggest that each child select a different instrument to be until a whole orchestra has been assembled. This particular activity will probably not last longer than one session, but it is fun and a means of stretching the imagination.
7. Put up a sheet at one end of the room with a light behind it. Have the children pantomime something behind it. See what happens. The magic quality of a silhouette never fails to stimulate an immediate desire to try out ideas. This particular activity, incidentally, is an excellent one for the

timid child who feels less exposed behind a sheet than out in the open. Practice in acting behind the sheet leads to inventiveness: What happens when the actor is close to the sheet? Far from it? Approaches or leaves it? How can a figure be exaggerated? Enlarged? How is humor obtained? Then try acting out nursery rhymes and stories in shadow.

8. The leader discusses growth and growing. It is suggested that the group conceive of themselves as seeds, buried deep in the earth. It is dark and they are quiet. Then spring arrives with rain, sun, and wind. What happens to the seeds? Do they break through the earth? Can we feel them push and grow? As summer comes, the plants grow taller. What are they going to be—flowers or trees? Tall, short, bushy, weak, or strong? Feel the warm rain, the hot sun, the breeze blowing, the final push to maturity. Poetry written about the springtime ties in well with this exercise.

9. Either the teacher or the class composes a story in which a variety of sounds are listed and described. It is great fun to act out the sounds and/or what is making them. For example, one child wrote the following narration for the others to act.

> I woke up in the morning to the sound of my ALARM CLOCK going off. I opened my CLOSET DOOR, which squeaked. Then I turned on the FAUCET and the water made a rushing sound in the sink. After that I ran downstairs to breakfast. The coffee was PERKING in the pot. The BACON was frying in a pan. The TOAST popped up in the toaster. The RADIO was playing but the MUSIC was drowned out by the STATIC.
>
> Outside I heard my father MOWING the lawn and an AIRPLANE was flying low overhead. It was going to be hot and my mother turned on the FAN. Suddenly down the street I heard the noise of the SCHOOLBUS, its engine chugging. I ran out the front DOOR, which slammed and I ran down the walk, my SHOES clattering. My DOG barked as I climbed aboard a very noisy BUS.

An exercise like this stimulates awareness as well as imagination in the attempt to suggest or reproduce sounds and the objects making them.

10. Mirror images are popular and great fun for actors of all ages. Two players face each other, one being herself and the other her mirror image. Whatever the person does, her image must reproduce precisely. With practice this can become a skilled performance, challenging to the players and fascinating to those watching. Greater awareness as well as the ability to work together are developed in the process. Older groups may ask to repeat this exercise from time to time, realizing the possibilities for technical improvement.

11. Older players often find the following exercise rewarding. Imagine yourself shut up in a box. How large is it? Can you stand up? Move around? Get out? Let us see the box—its sides, floor, top. Suppose the box becomes larger. What do you do? It grows smaller. What happens to you then?

This is an exercise that may be repeated many times with the players improving their technique as they try to imagine and suggest in every way possible the experience of being encased in a box.

12. The following exercise is for older children or adults. Each member of the group writes a letter of apology for something he or she has done or might have done. Then the leader asks two players to go to the telephone. One gives the apology and the other whatever response he feels is appropriate. Next, the first player faces the other person and makes his apology in person. Finally, he reads the original letter aloud, and the group comments on which apology has the greater reality, how the two improvisations have gone, and why. This is an interesting exercise, which may be carried out with each member of the group, time and interest permitting.

As the group progresses, organization improves, and situations often develop into simple plots. The players are learning to use their entire bodies to express ideas and are ready to add dialogue. Although improvisation, or informal dialogue, is the subject of the next chapter, the teacher will want to alternate exercises in pantomime and improvisation. No matter how advanced the group, pantomime is always good to work on from time to time because of the type of practice it offers.

Starting Places

The following *situations* are suggested as starting places to set children thinking. The younger or less experienced the group, the more preliminary work

What do they see? (*Courtesy of Tom Behm, University of North Carolina, Greensboro.*)

in the form of pantomime and discussion is needed. Group pantomimes related to the situation will stimulate movement, whereas discussing the topic and asking questions about it helps to stir the imagination. When all seem to be ready, divide the class into several small groups to develop simple narratives. Each group will come up with its own ideas as to plot and characters. This can be a one-time activity or the beginning of a creative play done entirely in pantomime.

A beggar comes to the door	"April Fool!"
A house is for sale	A wrong number on the telephone
The tallest sunflower in town	Delivery of a package you didn't order
A magic sandal	A substitute teacher appears in your room one morning
A bracelet found in an alley	Your bus "pass" is missing
A puppy in a box left in a doorway	A new uncle from abroad

Starting places may also be *locations.* See what the class can do with some of them, again beginning with pantomimes as warm-ups and discussion questions to start the flow of ideas. When everyone is ready to begin work, divide the class into groups to develop narratives to be told through mime.

Making a Machine

There are many variations on this exercise, which has great appeal for older students. One way of beginning is for the leader to start a regular beat and ask one person to come into the center of the room and begin a movement. When the movement has been stabilized, a second person comes forward with another movement that relates to the first. This continues until as many as a dozen players become parts of a machine, each one contributing a movement that is coordinated with the rest. The effect can be interesting and dynamic when all players are working together.

This exercise may be made more interesting by adding sounds. Each player makes a noise appropriate to her movement. When all parts of the machine are moving rhythmically together, the sounds enhance the effect. This exercise requires imagination, inventiveness, concentration, cooperation, and the ability to sustain both sound and movement until the mechanical quality is established. The machine can run indefinitely, or it can break down, either stopping or falling apart.

The group may also start with a particular machine in mind (threshing machine, wrecking equipment, ice cream machine, sewing machine, etc.); or a machine may develop from the activity of the players. As a group gains experience, the results will become more precise and sophisticated. Incidentally, this is a technique that can be incorporated effectively into an improvisation, and it is often far more interesting than the use of conventional props.

Some teachers find that acting a story while it is read aloud is a good transition from pantomime to dramatization. Many stories can be done in this way, though some lend themselves to it better than others.

The Paddygog is a good example. It is filled with opportunities for all kinds of pantomime, much of it unusual and therefore interesting to children. It also offers an opportunity for learning about another time and region of our country. The more action, obviously, the better for miming a narrative. Each time it is played, the teacher can expect it to be richer in detail. Stories acted while read help the more timid or inexperienced children to follow the plot and feel the sense of accomplishment that comes from successful dramatization.

THE PADDYGOG
CULLY GAGE

"The Paddygog" comes from the Northwoods of Michigan's upper peninsula. According to the author, it is still a strange and isolated area, bounded on the north by Lake Superior and on the south by Lake Michigan. It was once inhabited by French Canadians, Finns, Indians, Cornish miners, and other immigrants, who lived a rough life in a harsh environment. Through sharing their ethnic tales and local yarns, community ties were strengthened and the most colorful of the stories preserved.

Several summers after my father's death, my daughter and her family were vacationing with me at his old house in the village where I spent my youth. One morning, Jennifer, then eight, found me on the porch when she returned from playing with the village's current crop of youngsters.

"Grampa," she said. "We kids found a great big paddygog up there by the grove. What's a paddygog, Grampa?"

I had to confess that I didn't know, but that I would sure like to see one if she could lead me to it.

Up the old familiar street we went, hand in hand, Jennifer chattering all the way.

"It's awful heavy, Gramp, and big like this." She held her hands together in an arc above her head.

"And there's a big long chain on it and it's in the leaves by a big tree and it's kinda dirty, and that's what the other kids called it. A paddygog, Grampa."

She led me to the vacant space where our Town Hall stood before it burned down and then to a big maple tree.

"See! See! There it is, Grampa."

Jennifer pointed to a huge rusty iron triangle that lay half-hidden in the leaves and grass.

I recognized it immediately. It was Paddy's gong, the one he beat with a crowbar to celebrate the top o' the mornin' on St. Patrick's Day. It brought back a host of memories.

Patrick Feeny, Paddy as he was called by all the kids who adored him, was our village blacksmith.

My dad always claimed there were only two indispensible men in town: him, the town doctor, and Paddy, the blacksmith. The preacher and others were way down the list.

Dad fixed up the bodies.

Paddy repaired the things. He was not only a blacksmith, but a gunsmith and mechanic of great competence. He could fix anything from a watch to a broken logging derrick 30 feet tall. Moreover, his services were cheap. Paddy never set a price.

"Sure, and you can pay me what you think it's worth," he'd say. "Pay Paddy when you can."

That's how he operated and it was a shame how many people cheated him or didn't pay at all.

M. C. Flinn, the stingy old proprietor of our general store, probably took advantage of Paddy more than anyone else. Flinn used to say disapprovingly whenever his name was mentioned in connection with Paddy, "No way to run a business. No way to run a business." But Paddy never seemed to mind even when some of his customers complained about his being too slow.

He certainly worked terribly hard, not only in the smithy, but late at night in his home. Any evening a passerby could see him at the workbench by the front window, taking a gun or clock apart and putting it back together again. He especially liked clocks. His house was full of them. Said they kept him company. No one else did. People only came to see Paddy when they needed him.

But the smithy was his first love. I can see him yet, a huge man, built square to the floor from the shoulders down, in a sooty leather apron and ragged under shirt, his heavy hammer clanging a piece of white hot iron, fresh from the forge, until it turned cherry red. Then Paddy would plunge it hissing and smoking into the water barrel. It was almost as good as the Fourth of July to visit the blacksmith shop.

A single man, Paddy dearly loved children and always made us welcome though he'd built a bench back by the stanchions to keep us out of the way of sparks and bits of hot metal that sometimes shot from his anvil. Once in a while he'd even let us help pump the huge bellows on the forge until the fire roared, but we had to keep out of his way when he was shoeing one of the great draft horses the loggers and farmers brought in.

Paddy had a way with those horses. He'd lead them in, half crooning to them all the way till they were in place. Then he'd shove up his stool, take a monstrous hoof in his lap and start paring it with a knife as our eyes bugged out. The horses never seemed to mind a bit.

First he'd measure the hoof with big calipers, then sort through a barrel for a new shoe, heating it red, bending it over the anvil. Then he'd cool it and nail it home with mighty blows, rarely more than two whops to a nail.

After the horse had been led away, Paddy would give us the hoof parings for our dogs or he'd save them for the trappers. They claimed you couldn't find better bait for wolves or coyotes than those parings.

Then Paddy would come over to our bench to give us a ginger snap from the big tin on the shelf. He'd pour himself a cup of tea and tell us wonderful tales of the wee people, the leprechauns of the ould sod of the Ireland he had loved, but left as a boy.

Like many powerful men, Paddy had a soft voice. His had a special "lilt to it" though, like he was talking music. This, along with his brogue, made us hang on every word lest we miss something.

He'd tell us gory tales of the wars between the old kings of Ireland from whom he claimed to be descended.

"Sure it is, me bhoys, that ivery Irishmon has a wee bit iv king's blood in him, that he has."

It was a little hard to imagine Paddy wearing a crown. His face was always so covered with soot that his eye holes gleamed white, but you could sure feel some hint of strange royalty just the same, especially when he told his tales about the slaughter of Shannon's Ford and stories of castles and dungeons. Paddy loved the land he'd left and he opened the windows of our isolated little world when he told of tinkers with high wheeled covered carts, long stone walls that curved across soft green hills and the smell of "taters" baking in the ashes of a peat fire hearth.

Perhaps it was because several generations had sat on that bench that no one protested when Paddy went on his week long St. Patrick's Day spree.

At daylight he'd crank the chain that held the huge steel triangle that we called Paddy's gong down from the rooftree of the smithy. Then he'd take a sledge or crowbar to it till the reverberations woke half the town. I can hear the sound of it still, half boom and half clang, echoing from the hills that nestled our valley.

St. Patrick's Day!

Paddy Feeny was making sure that no one forgot the Irish.

But just the gong's great clanging flood through town wasn't enough.

Paddy always got out his big goose gun, at least an eight gauge with a barrel so big it was terrifying, and he'd shoot that off: first downtown, then in front of the post office and finally at the uptown post office. It sounded like someone had touched off a cannon! Everyone in the village knew then that it was St. Patrick's Day!

After he'd fired the goose gun, Paddy would visit old Mrs. Murphy. They'd have a cup of tea and talk about old times and maybe they'd sing a few Irish songs together. Then Paddy went to Higley's saloon, bought 10 bottles of rye whiskey and proceeded to get "polluted to the gills" for a whole week. Paddy never drank at any other time, but he sure laid a real drunk on then. He didn't do a lick of work either, just sang Irish songs or keened between bottles. Anyone who needed some iron work or horse-shoeing done made sure it was finished before St. Patrick's Day or they put it off till the week after. Year after year, Paddy "cilibrated" in the same way.

It was early February when people of the village suddenly realized just how important Paddy was to them and stopped taking him for granted.

He was doing something he'd done hundreds of times—fitting a huge steel rim on a heavy wheel from a logging wagon—and his knees just sagged and he fell on his face there on the brick floor of the smithy. Some men slid him onto a couple of boards and carried him over to his house while others ran for my father. The news spread swiftly through the village and dad had to shoo people out of the house before he could get to feel Paddy's pulse and put on the stethoscope.

"A massive heart attack," he concluded. "Go get the priest."

Unfortunately, Father Hassel had gone to Marquette that morning to see his bishop, but when he returned that evening, Paddy had rallied considerably. He still got the last rites and the lights of the Catholic Church burned all night as Masses were said for a soul that had seldom seen the inside of the confessional.

For three weeks Paddy lay abed. He received more attention then than he had in thirty years. He was never left alone for a minute. One or another of the neighbor women took turns hovering over him day and night. Dad said it wasn't so much their nursing as his digitalis and nitroglycerin that pulled Paddy through, but he was finally able to totter over to the smithy to offer advice to a strapping young lad who was clumsily trying to fill in.

"Now don't you let Paddy do a damn thing," my father warned. "He isn't even to lift a hammer. If he wants to sit on the bench with the kids for half an hour or so at a time, that's all right, but he's got to take it real easy for a long time or he's a dead man.''

We made sure there was always one of us to sit on the bench with Paddy, but he didn't tell us any stories. He would run out of breath if he tried to talk very much.

Even after Paddy could get around, the townspeople made sure he was cared for. They cooked his meals, cleaned his house and watched over him constantly, showing in a thousand little ways how much they really cared. He couldn't even go to the outhouse without someone watching to make sure he came out again after a reasonable time. Paddy gradually improved enough to joke with the women about nagging him back to health.

According to dad, however, who examined Paddy almost every day, his apparent recovery was not a true reflection of Paddy's condition.

"Paddy's in bad shape," he told my mother. "I don't like what I hear in my stethoscope and his pulse is still none too regular. He could go anytime."

I sure felt bad when I heard him telling her that.

When the middle of March approached, the whole village began to worry again, especially after they heard that Paddy had sent Jim Pillion to bring his usual 10 bottles of rye from the saloon.

Dad blew his top, went over to Higley and read him the riot act for sending the whiskey and he tried to find it in Paddy's house.

"You drink half a bottle of that rotgut, Paddy, and you're dead. I tell you, you can't touch a drop of it. Now where did you hide it?"

But Paddy wouldn't tell.

"Now, Doctor," he said with that wide old grin of his, "a wee bit from the bottle nivver killed an Irishmon yet. An Irishmon will cilibrate the day, that he will, so long as he has a heart in him, will he not?"

Dad managed only to take away the goose gun.

"If Paddy tries to climb that hill, he'll be gone before he gets a quarter of the way up it," he told the neighbors. "And if he tries to take a sledge to that triangle gong of his, that'll do him in too. You watch him now. Paddy just can't do that kind of thing in his condition. I tell you he's got to take it easy for a long, long time."

But dad knew the nature of the Irish and he worried. So did the rest of the village.

I don't know who first got the idea, but I think it started in school. Some kid, probably a regular on Paddy's bench, thought that if we could hold a real slam bang St. Patrick's Day celebration in Paddy's honor the night before the day came, then he wouldn't feel he had to go through his old routine and kill himself.

"We'd cilibrate' for him."

The idea caught hold and grew so fast and spread so far that no one could stop it. My dad felt all the excitement might be more than Paddy could stand and he still worried.

"Well, I don't know," he told us at the dinner table. "It might just keep him from banging that gong and drinking that booze if he sees all of us sharing his Irish insanity. At least he'll find out that the whole town likes and respects him after all these years of neglect and Paddy's sure got that much coming. I just hope it won't hurt him."

Well, we really celebrated that St. Patrick's Day Eve and Paddy didn't even know that the whole doings were in his honor until he got out of Old Man Marchand's rig and entered the Town Hall.

It was full of people cheering him. It was full of green streamers and paper shamrocks three feet high. And it was full of Finns and French-Canadians, Indians, Swedes and "mixed stuffs," each with a bit of green on him to show he was Irish too. School kids were parading across the stage singing, "Where the River Shannon Flows" and other Irish songs.

And the speeches, too many of them, all telling Paddy how much he'd meant to the whole town. Old Mrs. Murphy was even trying to teach a bunch of little school kids how to do an Irish jig for him.

At the end of it all, Paddy was presented with a huge grandfather clock, a token of our esteem.

Paddy Feeny weathered it all and enjoyed every minute of it. After the clock presentation, he stood up, held out his arms to all of us and shouted, "Erin Go Bragh," and was driven home.

He went to bed and died in his sleep.

Everyone felt terrible, but the next day, St. Patrick's Day, the men hauled Paddy's big triangle up to the Town Hall, hung it by a chain to the roof piece and rang it till sundown. They rang it again the next year and on St. Patrick's Day every year after until the Town Hall burned down.

After my grand-daughter showed me her paddygog, I got a crew together and we hung the huge triangle from a big limb of the maple tree. Since Jennifer is half Irish, I lifted her up so she could be the first to bang it with a hammer and I gave each of the other kids a dollar so they would remember to ring it next St. Patrick's Day.

Many regions of the country have published material on local history, including local anecdotes and yarns. They are well worth exploring as material little known outside the region, yet giving colorful pictures of life lived in the United States at an earlier time. Often they can be tied in with social studies units and so serve a double purpose, to the enrichment of both. Pictures, artifacts, other stories also help the time and place to come alive.

THE DOUGHNUTS
ROBERT McCLOSKEY

"Homer Price" is one of the most amusing boy stories of recent years, and the doughnut episode is the favorite. Robert McCloskey won the Caldecott Award in 1942 for "Make Way for Ducklings," but any one of his other stories might well have won it.

One Friday night in November Homer overheard his mother talking on the telephone to Aunt Agnes over in Centerburg. "I'll stop by with the car in about half an hour and we can go to the meeting together," she said, because tonight was the night the Ladies' Club was meeting to discuss plans for a box social and to knit and sew for the Red Cross.

"I think I'll come along and keep Uncle Ulysses company while you and Aunt Agnes are at the meeting," said Homer.

So after Homer had combed his hair and his mother had looked to see if she had her knitting instructions and the right size needles, they started for town.

Homer's Uncle Ulysses and Aunt Agnes have a very up and coming lunch room over in Centerburg, just across from the court house on the town square. Uncle Ulysses is a man with advanced ideas and a weakness for labor saving devices. He equipped the lunch room with automatic toasters, automatic coffee maker, automatic dish washer, and an automatic doughnut maker. All just the latest thing in labor saving devices. Aunt Agnes would throw up her hands and sigh every time Uncle Ulysses bought a new labor saving device. Sometimes she became unkindly disposed toward him for days and days. She was of the opinion that Uncle Ulysses just frittered away his spare time over at the barber shop with the sheriff and the boys, so, what was the good of a labor saving device that gave you more time to fritter?

When Homer and his mother got to Centerburg they stopped at the lunch room, and after Aunt Agnes had come out and said, "My, how that boy does grow!" which was what she always said, she went off with Homer's mother in the car. Homer went into the lunch room and said, "Howdy, Uncle Ulysses!"

"Oh, hello, Homer. You're just in time," said Uncle Ulysses. "I've been going over this automatic doughnut machine, oiling the machinery and cleaning the works . . . wonderful things, these labor saving devices."

"Yep," agreed Homer, and he picked up a cloth and started polishing the metal trimmings while Uncle Ulysses tinkered with the inside workings.

"Opfwo-oof!!" sighed Uncle Ulysses and, "Look here, Homer, you've got a mechanical mind. See if you can find where these two pieces fit in. I'm going across to the barber shop for a spell, 'cause there's somethin' I've got to talk to the sheriff about. There won't be much business here until the double feature is over and I'll be back before then."

Then as Uncle Ulysses went out the door he said, "Uh, Homer, after you get the pieces in place, would you mind mixing up a batch of doughnut batter and put it in the machine? You could turn the switch and make a few doughnuts to have on hand for the crowd after the movie . . . if you don't mind."

"O.K." said Homer, "I'll take care of everything."

A few minutes later a customer came in and said, "Good evening, Bud."

Homer looked up from putting the last piece in the doughnut machine and said, "Good evening, Sir, what can I do for you?"

"Well, young feller, I'd like a cup o'coffee and some doughnuts," said the customer.

"I'm sorry, Mister, but we won't have any doughnuts for about half an hour, until I can mix some dough and start this machine. I could give you some very fine sugar rolls instead."

"Well, Bud, I'm in no real hurry so I'll just have a cup o' coffee and wait around a bit for the doughnuts. Fresh doughnuts are always worth waiting for is what I always say."

"O.K.," said Homer, and he drew a cup of coffee from Uncle Ulysses' super automatic coffee maker.

"Nice place you've got here," said the customer.

"Oh, yes," replied Homer, "this is a very up and coming lunch room with all the latest improvements."

"Yes," said the stranger, "must be a good business. I'm in business too. A traveling man in outdoor advertising. I'm a sandwich man, Mr. Gabby's my name."

"My name is Homer. I'm glad to meet you, Mr. Gabby. It must be a fine profession, traveling and advertising sandwiches."

"Oh no," said Mr. Gabby, "I don't advertise sandwiches, I just wear any kind of an ad, one sign on front and one sign on behind, this way. . . . Like a sandwich. Ya know what I mean?"

"Oh, I see. That must be fun, and you travel too?" asked Homer as he got out the flour and the baking powder.

"Yeah, I ride the rods between jobs, on freight trains, ya know what I mean?"

"Yes, but isn't that dangerous?" asked Homer.

"Of course there's a certain amount a risk, but you take any method a travel these days, it's all dangerous. Ya know what I mean? Now take airplanes for instance . . ."

Just then a large shiny black car stopped in front of the lunch room and a chauffeur helped a lady out of the rear door. They both came inside and the lady smiled at Homer and said, "We've stopped for a light snack. Some doughnuts and coffee would be simply marvelous."

Then Homer said, "I'm sorry, Ma'm, but the doughnuts won't be ready until I make this batter and start Uncle Ulysses' doughnut machine."

"Well now aren't you a clever young man to know how to make *doughnuts!*"

"Well," blushed Homer, "I've really never done it before but I've got a receipt to follow."

"Now, young man, you simply must allow me to help. You know, I haven't made doughnuts for years, but I know the best receipt for doughnuts. It's marvelous, and we really must use it."

"But, Ma'm . . ." said Homer.

"Now just *wait* till you taste these doughnuts," said the lady. "Do you have an apron?" she asked, as she took off her fur coat and her rings and her jewelry and rolled up her sleeves. "Charles," she said to the chauffeur, "hand me that baking powder, that's right, and, young man, we'll need some nutmeg."

So Homer and the chauffeur stood by and handed things and cracked the eggs while the lady mixed and stirred. Mr. Gabby sat on his stool, sipped his coffee, and looked on with great interest.

"There!" said the lady when all of the ingredients were mixed. "Just *wait* till you taste these doughnuts!"

"It looks like an awful lot of batter," said Homer as he stood on a chair and poured it into the doughnut machine with the help of the chauffeur. "It's about *ten* times as much as Uncle Ulysses ever makes."

"But wait till you taste them!" said the lady with an eager look and a smile.

Homer got down from the chair and pushed a button on the machine marked, "Start." Rings of batter started dropping into the hot fat. After a ring of batter was cooked on one side an automatic gadget turned it over and the other side would cook. Then another automatic gadget gave the doughnut a little push and it rolled neatly down a little chute, all ready to eat.

"That's a simply *fascinating* machine," said the lady as she waited for the first doughnut to roll out.

"Here, young man, *you* must have the first one. Now isn't that just *too* delicious!? Isn't it simply marvelous?"

"Yes, Ma'm, it's very good," replied Homer as the lady handed doughnuts to Charles and to Mr. Gabby and asked if they didn't think they were simply divine doughnuts.

"It's an old family receipt!" said the lady with pride.

Homer poured some coffee for the lady and her chauffeur and for Mr. Gabby, and a glass of milk for himself. Then they all sat down at the lunch counter to enjoy another few doughnuts apiece.

"I'm so glad you enjoy my doughnuts," said the lady. "But now, Charles, we really must be going. If you will just take this apron, Homer, and put two dozen doughnuts in a bag to take along, we'll be on our way. And, Charles, don't forget to pay the young man." She rolled down her sleeves and put on her jewelry, then Charles managed to get her into her big fur coat.

"Good night, young man, I haven't had so much fun in years. I *really* haven't!" said the lady, as she went out the door and into the big shiny car.

"Those are sure good doughnuts," said Mr. Gabby as the car moved off.

"You bet!" said Homer. Then he and Mr. Gabby stood and watched the automatic doughnut machine make doughnuts.

After a few dozen more doughnuts had rolled down the little chute, Homer said, "I guess that's about enough doughnuts to sell to the after theater customers. I'd better turn the machine off for a while."

Homer pushed the button marked *"Stop"* and there was a little click, but nothing happened. The rings of batter kept right on dropping into the hot fat, and an automatic gadget kept right on turning them over, and another automatic gadget kept right on giving them a little push and the doughnuts kept right on rolling down the little chute, all ready to eat.

"That's funny," said Homer, "I'm sure that's the right button!" He pushed it again but the automatic doughnut maker kept right on making doughnuts.

"Well I guess I must have put one of those pieces in backwards," said Homer.

"Then it might stop if you pushed the button marked *"Start,"* said Mr. Gabby.

Homer did, and the doughnuts still kept rolling down the little chute, just as regular as a clock can tick.

"I guess we could sell a few more doughnuts," said Homer, "but I'd better telephone Uncle Ulysses over at the barber shop." Homer gave the number and while he waited for someone to answer he counted thirty-seven doughnuts roll down the little chute.

Finally someone answered, "Hello! This is the sarber bhop, I mean the barber shop."

"Oh, hello, sheriff. This is Homer. Could I speak to Uncle Ulysses?"

"Well, he's playing pinochle right now," said the sheriff. "Anythin' I can tell 'im?"

"Yes," said Homer. "I pushed the button marked *Stop* on the doughnut machine but the rings of batter keep right on dropping into the hot fat, and an automatic gadget keeps right on turning them over, and another automatic gadget keeps giving them a little push, and the doughnuts keep right on rolling down the little chute! It won't stop!"

"O.K. Wold the hire, I mean, hold the wire and I'll tell 'im." Then Homer looked over his shoulder and counted another twenty-one doughnuts roll down the little chute, all ready to eat. Then the sheriff said, "He'll be right over. . . . Just gotta finish this hand."

"That's good," said Homer. "G'by, sheriff."

The window was full of doughnuts by now so Homer and Mr. Gabby had to hustle around and start stacking them on plates and trays and lining them up on the counter.

"Sure are a lot of doughnuts!" said Homer.

"You bet!" said Mr. Gabby. "I lost count at twelve hundred and two and that was quite a while back."

People had begun to gather outside the lunch room window, and someone was saying, "There are almost as many doughnuts as there are people in Centerburg, and I wonder how in tarnation Ulysses thinks he can sell all of 'em!"

Every once in a while somebody would come inside and buy some, but while somebody bought two to eat and a dozen to take home, the machine made three dozen more.

By the time Uncle Ulysses and the sheriff arrived and pushed through the crowd, the lunch room was a calamity of doughnuts! Doughnuts in the window, doughnuts piled high on the shelves, doughnuts stacked on plates, doughnuts lined up twelve deep all along the counter, and doughnuts still rolling down the little chute, just as regular as a clock can tick.

"Hello, sheriff, hello, Uncle Ulysses, we're having a little trouble here," said Homer.

"Well, I'll be dunked!!" said Uncle Ulysses.

"Dernd ef you won't be when Aggy gits home," said the sheriff.

"Mighty fine doughnuts though. What'll you do with 'em all, Ulysses?"

Uncle Ulysses groaned and said, "What will Aggy say? We'll never sell 'em all."

Then Mr. Gabby, who hadn't said anything for a long time, stopped piling doughnuts and said, "What you need is an advertising man. Ya know what I mean? You got the doughnuts, ya gotta create a market . . . Understand? . . . It's balancing the demand with the supply . . . That sort of thing."

"Yep!" said Homer. "Mr. Gabby's right. We have to enlarge our market. He's an advertising sandwich man, so if we hire him, he can walk up and down in front of the theater and get the customers."

"You're hired, Mr. Gabby!" said Uncle Ulysses.

Then everybody pitched in to paint the signs and to get Mr. Gabby sandwiched between. They painted "SALE ON DOUGHNUTS" in big letters on the window too.

Meanwhile the rings of batter kept right on dropping into the hot fat, and an automatic gadget kept right on turning them over, and another automatic gadget kept right on giving them a little push, and the doughnuts kept right on rolling down the little chute, just as regular as a clock can tick.

"I certainly hope this advertising works," said Uncle Ulysses, wagging his head. "Aggy'll certainly throw a fit if it don't."

The sheriff went outside to keep order, because there was quite a crowd by now—all looking at the doughnuts and guessing how many thousand there were, and watching new ones roll down the little chute, just as regular as a clock can tick. Homer and Uncle Ulysses kept stacking doughnuts. Once in a while somebody bought a few, but not very often.

Then Mr. Gabby came back and said, "Say, you know there's not much use o' me advertisin' at the theater. The show's all over, and besides almost everybody in town is out front watching that machine make doughnuts!"

"Zeus!" said Uncle Ulysses. "We must get rid of these doughnuts before Aggy gets here!"

"Looks like you will have ta hire a truck ta waul 'em ahay, I mean haul 'em away!!" said the sheriff who had just come in. Just then there was a noise and a shoving out front and the lady from the shiny black car and her chauffeur came pushing through the crowd and into the lunch room.

"Oh, gracious!" she gasped, ignoring the doughnuts, "I've lost my diamond bracelet, and I know I left it here on the counter," she said, pointing to a place where the doughnuts were piled in stacks of two dozen.

"Yes, Ma'm, I guess you forgot it when you helped make the batter," said Homer.

Then they moved all the doughnuts around and looked for the diamond bracelet, but they couldn't find it anywhere. Meanwhile the doughnuts kept rolling down the little chute, just as regular as a clock can tick.

After they had looked all around the sheriff cast a suspicious eye on Mr. Gabby, but Homer said, "He's all right, sheriff, he didn't take it. He's a friend of mine."

Then the lady said, "I'll offer a reward of one hundred dollars for that bracelet! It really *must* be found . . . it *really* must!"

"Now don't you worry, lady," said the sheriff. "I'll get your bracelet back!"

"Zeus! This is terrible!" said Uncle Ulysses. "First all of these doughnuts and then on top of all that, a lost diamond bracelet . . ."

Mr. Gabby tried to comfort him, and he said, "There's always a bright side. That machine'll probably run outta batter in an hour or two."

If Mr. Gabby hadn't been quick on his feet Uncle Ulysses would have knocked him down, sure as fate.

Then while the lady wrung her hands and said, "We must find it, we *must!*" and Uncle Ulysses was moaning about what Aunt Agnes would say, and the sheriff was eyeing Mr. Gabby, Homer sat down and thought hard.

Before twenty more doughnuts could roll down the little chute he shouted, "SAY! I know where the bracelet is! It was lying here on the counter and got mixed up in the batter by mistake! The bracelet is cooked inside one of these doughnuts!"

"Why . . . I really believe you're right," said the lady through her tears. "Isn't that *amazing?* Simply *amazing!*"

"I'll be durn'd!" said the sheriff.

"OhH-h!" moaned Uncle Ulysses. "Now we have to break up all of these doughnuts to find it. Think of the *pieces!* Think of the *crumbs!* Think of what *Aggy* will say!"

"Nope," said Homer. "We won't have to break them up. I've got a plan."

So Homer and the advertising man took some cardboard and some paint and printed another sign. They put this sign

FRESH DOUGHNUTS
2 for 5¢
WHILE THEY LAST
$100.00 PRIZE
FOR FINDING
A BRACELET
INSIDE A DOUGHNUT
P.S. You have to give the
bracelet back

in the window, and the sandwich man wore two more signs that said the same thing and walked around in the crowd out front.

Then . . . The doughnuts began to sell! *Everybody* wanted to buy doughnuts, *dozens* of doughnuts!

And that's not all. Everybody bought coffee to dunk the doughnuts in too. Those that didn't buy coffee bought milk or soda. It kept Homer and the lady and the chauffeur and Uncle Ulysses and the sheriff busy waiting on the people who wanted to buy doughnuts.

When all but the last couple of hundred doughnuts had been sold, Rupert Black shouted, "I GAWT IT!!" and sure enough . . . there was the diamond bracelet inside of his doughnut!

Then Rupert went home with a hundred dollars, the citizens of Centerburg went home full of doughnuts, the lady and her chauffeur drove off with the diamond bracelet, and Homer went home with his mother when she stopped by with Aunt Aggy.

As Homer went out of the door he heard Mr. Gabby say, "Neatest trick of merchandising I ever seen," and Aunt Aggy was looking sceptical while Uncle Ulysses was saying, "The rings of batter kept right on dropping into the hot fat, and the automatic gadget kept right on turning them over, and the other automatic gadget kept right on giving them a little push, and the doughnuts kept right on rolling down the little chute just as regular as a clock can tick—they just kept right on a comin', an' a comin', an' a comin', an' a comin'."

I have seen some superb work done in pantomime by high school students, who loved the medium as an art form and whose disciplined study of it made good theatre. Few groups can or will carry it that far, but working in mime with good literature as a base benefits players and spectators alike.

Although The Doughnuts *is suggested here as rich material for pantomime, there is no reason why it cannot also be used for improvisation. The scene at the end in the doughnut shop offers an opportunity for a large group of children to create characters. The period and small-town life call for some background study, and most children today respond readily to the situation and humor. However, we do not want to lose the flavor of the writing, which was one of the reasons for including it.*

Summary

Pantomime, while good practice at any time, is usually the most satisfactory way of beginning work in creative drama. Although it is not necessary to follow a prescribed program of exercises, it is easier for many groups to begin with familiar activities and then move on to mood or feeling, and finally characterization. By starting with movement and then pantomime, the players learn to express themselves through bodily action, without the additional problem of dialogue. Younger children accept this as a natural means of expression, and older children and adults find it easier to begin with pantomime than with improvisation or formal acting. Pantomime sharpens perception and stimulates the imagination as the players try to remember how actions are done and what objects are really like, as to size, weight, and shape. Recalling emotion demands concentration and involvement: How do you feel when you are happy, tired, angry, excited, anxious, etc.? Close observation of people is a means of developing believable characters whose bearing, movement, and gestures belong to them and whose behavior seems appropriate. Although pantomime is considered here as a medium of expression, it may become an art form in itself. Mimes like Marcel Marceau have demonstrated its power to communicate with people of all ages and backgrounds, when a high level of artistry is achieved. The past fifteen to twenty years have witnessed a heightened interest in mime, in part stimulated by artists such as Marceau and other skilled performers who have studied with him, and the recent popularity of clowning and circus arts. Television, as a visual medium, is also responsible for our orientation to "things seen" and our close observation of visual techniques. Whereas radio captured the listening public of fifty years ago, it is television that has created today's audience for the performing arts on all levels.

6

Improvisation: Characters Move and Speak

*H*igh school drama students perform in a play written by a local high school student playwright. (*Courtesy of Honolulu Theatre for Youth; photograph by Ross Gaspar.*)

*I*mprovisation is difficult at first. Dialogue does not flow easily, even when it has been preceded by much work in pantomime and a thorough understanding of the situation or story. With practice, however, words do begin to come, and the players discover the possibilities of character development when oral language is added. Dialogue is apt to be brief and scanty at first, but usually begins to flow rapidly once the children become accustomed to it. Players aged seven and older enjoy the opportunity of using words to further a story and more fully describe the characters they are portraying. It is a good idea to begin with simple situations so as to get accustomed to using dialogue before attempting more ambitious material.

Many of the situations suggested in the previous chapter on pantomime can be used, although they were designed with movement in mind. Frequently, children will begin to add dialogue of their own free will, as they feel the need of expressing ideas in words. When this happens, the leader accepts it as a natural progression from one step to the next. Younger children, players for whom English is a second language, or older students who lack self-confidence, will usually wait until they are urged to try adding dialogue. The teacher will not expect too much and will accept whatever is offered, knowing that more will be forthcoming the next time. The author recalls a sixth-grade class that was acting *The Story of Roland.* Although fond of the story and well oriented to the background, the first time it was played, one scene went like this: "Hello, Roland."—"Will you marry me?"—"Why, Roland, I'd love to." The final playing, after several had tried and discussed it, was a charming scene with all the necessary exposition and appropriate vocabulary.

Since even the simplest stories present complications for the beginner, some preliminary exercises are suggested. The purpose here is to give emphasis to dialogue rather than to the memorization or plot. Sometimes just one scene of a story can be improvised to advantage. The teacher will feel his way, and if interest is sustained better with excerpts from favorite stories, he may prefer them to exercises.

Sounds, incidentally, can stimulate imagination and lead the listener to the creation of an improvisation. For example, the teacher can beat a drum or tambourine, knock, ring bells, or make any other kind of sound. This works particularly well with younger children but is also a good exercise to use from time to time with those who are older.

Simple Improvisations Based on Situations

The following improvisations may be done with various age levels, although the backgrounds of the players will determine the appropriateness. In some cases, the situations are better for older players.

1. You are a group of people in a subway station. It is six o'clock in the evening. In the center is a newsstand, at which newspapers, magazines, and candy are sold. It is run by a woman who has been there for many years. She knows the passengers who ride regularly and is interested in them and all the details of their daily lives. Decide on who you are going to be—a secretary, an actress, a businessman, a cleaning woman, a shopper, a policeman, a teenager, a stranger in town, and so on. Then let us know all about you through your conversation with the proprietor of the newsstand while you are waiting for your train.

2. The scene is a toyshop on Christmas Eve. It is midnight, and the owner has just closed the door and gone home. At the stroke of twelve the toys come alive and talk together. They may consist of a toy soldier, a rag doll, a beautiful doll, a clown, a teddy bear, a jack-in-the-box, and so forth. Let us know by your conversation and movements who you are and why you were not sold.

3. You are a committee from your school, assigned the job of selecting a gift for your teacher, who is retiring. Each of you has an idea of what you think is appropriate, and you have only a certain amount of money to spend. The scene takes place in a large gift shop. Let us know who you are and what you want to buy. What is the decision you finally make?

4. This improvisation is good on a high school or college level. The scene is a meeting of the student council. You have the job of questioning a student who is reported to have stolen the examination questions for a history class. He is brought before you, and you ask him questions. What is each one of you like? How do you handle the situation? Is he guilty or not? What is your final decision and what do you do about it?

5. This improvisation is also probably better for older students, although it has been done by ten- and eleven-year-olds. You are a group of people returning for your thirty-fifth reunion from high school or college. Who are you? What has happened to you since you last saw each other? Have you been happy, successful, or unsuccessful? Let us know all about you through your conversation.

6. You are a group of young women in a suburban community. One of you has invited the new neighbor in to meet the rest of the group. Coffee is served and you talk together. All seems to be going well when the hostess notices that an expensive silver tray is missing from her coffee table. One by one, you begin to suspect the newcomer. Why do you suspect her? Did she take it? Is it found? Where? If she took it, why did she? Let us know what each one of you is like by your reaction to this situation. How does it turn out?

7. This improvisation is good with children. You are a group of children in an apartment house. It is Valentine's Day, and you are gathered in the front hall to look at and count your valentines. You see one child in the

building going to her mailbox, and you notice that she did not receive any. How do you feel about this? What is each one of you like? Do you decide to do anything about it? If so, what do you do?

8. You are a group of children who live near a very cross, elderly woman. She chases you away from her property whenever you come near it. This particular morning, you see that someone has broken her fence and ruined many of her flowers. For the first time you feel sorry for her. What do you do? How does she react to you? Do you all agree as to whether you should help her? Do your actions change her attitude toward children?

9. A new child has entered your class at school. He does not speak English, and some of the children laugh at him. When recess comes, you all go out to the playground. How does each of you treat him? How does he react to you? You are all different so you will each feel differently toward him. Do you finally take him in, or do you exclude him? Try changing roles so that different players have the experience of trying the part of the new child. Does the improvisation change as you all think more about the situation?

10. The scene is a small bakery. One of you is the owner, one of you a child who helps him on Saturdays, and another is a beggar. It is not busy this particular morning so the owner goes out for coffee. While he is gone, a beggar comes into the shop and asks for some bread. The girl (or boy) knows that she should not give away the bread but she feels sorry for the old man. What do they say to each other? What does the owner say when he comes back? Try changing parts in this improvisation to see if it will turn out differently.

Improvisations Suggested by Objects

Not only situations and stories motivate improvisation; some very imaginative results can be obtained by the use of objects or properties. Try some of the following suggestions as springboards.

1. An object (any object) is put in the center of the circle where all the players can see it. Look at it, without speaking, for three or four minutes. Try to think of a story about it. Where might it have come from? How did it get here? What does it make *you* think of? Each of you will have an original story to tell; tell it.

2. This time, divide the class into groups of three or four. An object is presented, and each group is asked to make up an improvisation about it. Perhaps the property is a wooden spoon. When used with one class, the following ideas were suggested and these situations improvised.

a. The scene was a settler's cabin over one hundred years ago. The family had very few household items and so they prized each one. Among them was a wooden spoon. In this scene it was used to stir batter for cornbread and then was washed and put carefully away.

b. The scene was a museum and the spoon, a relic from the Indians who once inhabited the region. The characters were the curator of the museum and two children who were visiting it. The curator answered their questions by telling the history of the spoon.

c. The scene was a cave. Three boys were hiking and found the spoon. They used it to dig and discovered an old box of coins that had been buried there. They took the old spoon home with them for good luck.

d. The scene was an industrial arts class. The boys were making things of wood, and a blind boy carved the spoon. It was so well done that the teacher said she would display it as one of the best things made in her class that year.

e. The scene was a dump. The old wooden spoon was the speaker as he told the other pieces of trash how he had been used and handed down from one generation to the next. Finally, his family became rich and threw him away because they considered him too old and ugly to be of further use to them.

Any object can function as a springboard, and no two groups will see it in exactly the same way. Among the kinds of properties that suggest ideas are:

A velvet jewelry box	An old hat
An artificial rose	A cane
A foreign coin	A quill pen
A feather duster	An old dog leash
A bell	

An improvisation with unusual interest was developed from a whistle by a very imaginative group of ten-year-olds. They decided that it was a policeman's whistle, made of silver and bearing an inscription. They laid the scene in his home on the day of his retirement from the force; the characters were the policeman, his wife, and his grandson. The policeman came in that evening, took off his whistle, looked at it nostalgically a long time, and then laid it on the supper table. His grandson, coming into the room at that point, begged him to tell the story again of how he had received it. As the story began, there was a throwback scene in which the policeman was rescuing a child from burning in a bonfire many years before. He was honored for his bravery and given an inscribed silver whistle, which he treasured for the rest of his life. At the finish of the story, the throwback scene faded, and some neighbors came in with a cake and presents for him. The improvisation was effective both in its good dramatic structure and the reality of the characterizations.

Not every group is able to develop an improvisation to this degree, but occasionally one will, and when it happens, it is an inspiration to the rest of the class. Incidentally, it is nearly always the result of the play's having been based on familiar material so that the players are sure of the dialogue and can identify easily with the characters. Again, respect for their background and acceptance of the ideas that come out of it not only make for comfort but also bring forth ideas that the teacher probably would not have thought of. Children of foreign background have a wealth of material on which to draw, but too often it remains an untapped source because they have been made to feel that it is unworthy of consideration. Both the stories they have been told and the details of their everyday life contain the basic ingredients of drama. For example, one group of boys, who lived in a housing project, played a scene in an elevator. The situation was simple but had reality. Two boys, having nothing to do, decided to ride up and down in the elevator, angering the tenants and almost causing a tragedy because one man on a high floor was ill and waiting for the doctor. Whether or not this had been an actual experience the teacher did not know, but the situation contained reality, humor, and drama, with characters who were believable.

One final example of the use of properties was an improvisation done by a group of high school girls. They had been asked by the teacher to empty their purses and select the six most unusual or interesting objects. The objects they finally chose were a newspaper clipping, a snapshot, a lipstick in a Japanese case, a key ring with a red charm, a pocket knife, and a purse flashlight. Within minutes they had created a mystery, prompted by and making use of every one of the properties they selected. There were six players, and their preparation time was approximately ten minutes.

Improvisations from Costumes

Similar to the use of objects or props, and equally effective in stimulating ideas, are pieces of costume. Garments such as hats, capes, aprons, shawls, tailcoats, and jewelry will suggest different kinds of characters. Innumerable examples could be given of situations that grew from characters developed this way. For example, to one boy, a tailcoat suggested a musician, down on his luck and playing his violin on a street corner for pennies. A feathered hat helped a little girl create a lady of fashionable pretensions and become a comic character in her extravagant dress and poor taste. A shawl suggested witches, grandmothers, people in disguise, or a scene laid in very cold weather.

It is wise for the teacher on any level, working anywhere, to keep a supply of simple and sturdy costumes available for this kind of use. If children experience difficulty in getting into character, a piece of a costume may sometimes be all that is needed to provide the necessary incentive. Costume used in this way is not dressing the part but is an aid to more imaginative thinking.

Improvisations from Characters

In Chapter 5, an illustration was given of an improvisation created from a character. This is a successful method of starting, as well as a way of encouraging, observation. If the group is small and has had some experience, original monologues are good practice and fun for the players. If the class is large, however, this is probably not a wise assignment, unless the monologues are kept short.

To create from a character, the teacher can ask each member of the class to think of a particularly interesting person she has noticed that day, or sometime during the week. This is followed by questions such as:

Who was he?
What was he doing?
Did he have anything to say?
How did he dress?
How old was he?
What special thing about him attracted your attention?

One girl offered as a character a woman who served the hot vegetables in her school cafeteria. Although the woman was bad tempered, the girl had observed that she was always extremely generous in her servings and did her job more efficiently than anyone else. The group, which chose her as a heroine for their story, decided that she might have been a refugee. Because she had experienced hunger during that period in her life, she was determined that all plates would be generously filled, now that food was available. Her irritability they attributed to her own unhappy experiences and her separation from her family. The scene that the children improvised, using this particular character as an inspiration, was thoughtful, sympathetic, and interesting to the class.

Another improvisation based on an actual person was the story of an elderly woman whom one child noticed every day, sitting on the front porch of her house. The group, which chose her for a heroine, decided that she was really very rich but miserly and was saving her money for the day when her son would come home. They agreed that he had gone into the army several years before and had not returned. Although he had been reported missing, his mother clung to the hope that he would come back some day, and so she sat on the porch— waiting by day and counting her money by night. The group decided to have him return, so the story had a happy ending.

A fantasy was the result of another character study. Two of the children described a well-dressed old man whom they saw coming home every morning around eight o'clock. They decided that he must have an interesting occupation and so made him a wizard, who helped the good people and punished the evil through the power of his magic cane. This became a modern fairy tale filled with highly imaginative incidents.

Improvising "The
Tortoise and the Hare."
(*Courtesy of the New
Canaan Country
School.*)

Improvisations from Clues

Older players enjoy creating improvisations from clues. The following
exercises can be done to build characters. With these clues, what kinds of
persons do you imagine? In an improvisation, create a character who is suggested
by:

Raw vegetables	Hair dryer	Checkbook
Cane	Television	Belt
Book	Hat	Stick
Coca-Cola	Fur piece	Bag

The following exercise is good for experienced players. Select a place where
a number of strangers might gather. This could be an air terminal, a bus stop, a
grocery store in the morning before it opens, a parking lot, a picket line. One
person enters and is soon joined by another. They get into a conversation.
Another comes in and then another, until a large group has assembled. The class
can decide in advance whom each will be or, what is harder, will come into the
group as the character, making those already there decide whom he is. This has
wonderful possibilities for character study and simple plot development.

Biography

This exercise is suggested for older players. The leader chooses a character (real or fictional) and describes her briefly. After some general discussion, the class is divided into five or six small groups, each representing a period in the character's life. Each group then plans its interpretation of the character at a given time. The periods could be:

Birth to age six
Six to twelve years
The teens
The twenties
The thirties or forties
Later life
Old age

The persons in the first scene would have to be members of the family, neighbors, or others. The character about whom the scenes are built need not actually appear in each one, but the scenes must be related in some way to his or her life. This is an excellent way to study a character; if a historical person is used, it will lead to research. If it is not a real person, it is a challenge to the imagination. "Biography" implies not only representing the character but other significant persons in the character's life.

Improvisations for Two

Try to imagine yourself in the following situations:

1. You receive a letter in the mail telling you that you have won first prize in a poster contest. Tell your mother the good news.
2. Your dog has been hit by a car. When you come home from school, your mother meets you and tells you what has happened.
3. You have been warned not to go down a dark street by yourself at night. This evening, however, you are in a hurry and decide to go anyway because it is a shortcut. About halfway down the block you hear footsteps behind you. You look over your shoulder and see someone hurrying toward you. You hurry also; so does the other person. You decide to slow up; so does the person who is following you. By this time you are frightened, but it is too late to turn back. You start to run and so does he. You run faster; so does he. Finally, you reach the corner, but the light has turned red. As you stand there alone waiting for it to change, a friend comes up. It was the friend who was following you, but neither of

you recognized the other, and both of you had been running to get to the brightly lit corner. You have a good laugh when you discover each other.

4. You are trying on shoes to take to camp. The clerk does not have what you want and tries to sell you something else. Should you take her suggestion?

5. You are moving to a new neighborhood today. Your best friend comes around to say good-bye to you. Although you are looking forward to your new home, you are sad to leave the old neighborhood. What do you say?

6. Your aunt, whom you have never met, has come for a visit. You answer the door. What is she like? What do you say to each other?

7. You have found a kitten that you want very much to keep, but your mother has said you cannot have a pet. Try to persuade her that the kitten needs a home.

8. A salesman comes to the door. He insists on demonstrating a vacuum cleaner, although you tell him you have one. How do you handle the situation?

9. You have been wanting ice skates for your birthday. Your grandmother, who always selects the right presents, comes to the door with a box in her hands. When you open it, you find it contains stationery. What do you say to each other?

10. You wore your sister's bracelet on a picnic and, when you get home, discover you have lost it. Now you must tell her what happened.

Improvisations for Three

1. You and your friend are going to the playground. Your little sister wants to go with you, but if she does, you cannot go into the area reserved for older children. What do you do?

2. You are delivering papers. You throw one toward a house, but instead of landing on the porch, it breaks a window. Both the man and his wife come to see what has happened.

3. You and your friend find a five dollar bill on the sidewalk. You want to keep it, but at this moment a woman comes down the street looking for something. You are certain she has lost it. What do you do?

4. You tried out for a leading part in a play but were put in the chorus. You try to be a good sport when you talk to the teacher and to the girl who was cast in the part you wanted.

5. Your mother has just given your old rag doll to your younger cousin, who is visiting you. Neither of them knows how much the doll means to you. You try to pretend it is all right.

6. You see the girl across the aisle cheat on a test when the teacher steps out of the room. He suspects that there has been cheating and asks you

and the girl to stay after class so he can find out about it. What does each one of you say and do?

7. You are delivering flowers for a neighborhood florist. On this particular day you are carrying a very large plant, and you lose the address. You think you remember it, however, so you go to what you hope is the right door. It is the wrong address, but the person who answers the door accepts the plant, then discovers the mistake. You have left by that time. How do all three of you work things out?

8. Three of you are getting refreshments ready for a party. It is said that "too many cooks spoil the broth." This happens when all of you put salt in the chocolate pudding, thinking that it is sugar and needs sweetening. This can be a very funny situation. How do you handle it?

9. You are falsely accused of cheating on an examination. You are angry and upset. The three persons involved are your teacher, the principal of the school, and you.

10. Your two best friends are running for president of your class. You meet on the playground. What do you say? How do you handle the situation?

11. You are in a laundromat, waiting for a washing machine. One is ready, except that the person who put the clothes in it has not returned for them. One woman tells you that you have a right to remove the clothes and use the machine. Another says that you should wait, because the owner is coming back in a few minutes. Meanwhile, you are in a hurry. What do you decide to do? Does the person who left the clothes return soon? How does the situation turn out? (This has several possible endings.)

12. You are at the checkout counter of a supermarket. The cashier is checking off your items when you realize that you forgot to get the milk. You run back for it. This annoys the person behind you. Then you discover that you don't have enough money to pay the bill so you have to return some items. By this time the cashier and two people behind you are annoyed. You put the things back on the shelves and return, but when you pick up your shopping bag, which the cashier has packed for you, it splits open. Now you are angry too. This makes everyone laugh, including you; suddenly the annoying situation becomes funny.

Other Suggestions

Unfinished stories can also be used to stimulate thinking. If the teacher introduces a character and sets the scene, the group is given the problem of completing the story. Although this is more an exercise in plotting than in character, the action is motivated by the character: an interesting character makes for an interesting plot.

One club group showed an unusual interest in holidays, so the teacher used this as a springboard for the entire year. She brought in stories about Halloween, Thanksgiving, Christmas, New Year's Day, Valentine's Day, St. Patrick's Day, April Fool's Day, Memorial Day, and the Fourth of July. Sometimes the group acted out the stories she read to them; sometimes they made up stories of their own, suggested by the occasion. One day they observed that there was no holiday in August. The result was an original play, which they called *A Holiday for August.* It was to be a festival of children's games, which developed into a particularly attractive summer pageant. August was the narrator, who began by telling of his disappointment that no one had ever thought to put a holiday in his month. At the conclusion, he expressed his joy that the children had made him special with a festival of games played in his honor.

Television, films, and open discussion of heretofore taboo topics have affected the subject matter that has come into creative drama sessions in recent years. While most children still enjoy working on the material the teacher brings in, their own experiences and problems often surface when they are given a chance to express their own ideas. Broken homes, divorce, racial discrimination, illness and death, values, and social issues of all kinds can be disturbing problems to children, problems the leader must be prepared to deal with if or when they come up. The following improvisations are purposely open-ended to allow for the players' interpretations.

"You End It!" Improvisations

1. The personnel officer in a store is faced with a difficult decision. Business has been poor lately and the president of the company has said that two employees must be let go. The personnel officer calls in the last three people he hired and discusses the problem with them. After they leave, he must decide which two will go and which one to keep. The three are then called back into the office and told. The decision has been made on the basis of what has been said, the quality of the work, and what was expected of them.

2. The scene is a courtroom. A woman has been apprehended for selling on a street corner what is suspected of being stolen jewelry. Two or three witnesses are called up front to tell what they have seen or know. Then the woman is called up to give her explanation of how she came by the articles she was offering for sale. The judge decides whether or not she is guilty of having stolen property.

3. Take a well-known story and instead of ending it as written, stop before the final action and end it differently. For example, take *Rumplestiltskin.* Imagine that the miller's daughter does not spin straw into gold. How would you end the story?

4. A small group of people are hiking in a national park. It is a beautiful day and they go farther into the forest than they had intended. Suddenly, they

realize that it is growing dark. They turn to go back, but discover there are two paths and they cannot remember which one they had been following to arrive at their present location. A decision must be made quickly: one path will lead them back to their campsite; the other may be fraught with danger and they will be hopelessly lost. What will they decide to do? Why do they make this decision?

5. The scene is a country fair. A raffle is being held and the person calling the winning numbers announces the number for the grand prize. Two people rush forward and claim to be the winners. When they show their tickets, however, the two tickets are identical. The person in charge calls a stranger from the crowd (in this case, from the class) and asks him or her to make the decision. This is to be done by pulling one of the tickets from a hat.

All of the above situations are open-ended. They are to be played as regular improvisations until the end, when someone or the group itself must make an important decision. Players may use details they observe, information they gather, or intuition in arriving at the decision; there is no right answer because each time the situation is improvised, it will be done differently and the variations will affect the decision.

The leader can make up other situations if the group enjoys the open-ended format. If the group is composed of very young children, simpler situations can be created for them, including nursery rhymes. For example, suppose you stopped "Humpty Dumpty" before the last line:

> Humpty Dumpty sat on a wall,
> Humpty Dumpty had a great fall;
> All the king's horses and all the king's men . . .

Can they put him together again or not? If so, how do they do it? The players make the decision.

Here are some other ideas:

1. Arrange furniture and props so as to create an environment or setting. What does it suggest to the players? Create an improvisation that might take place in this setting.
2. Divide the group into two subgroups, representing opposite sides of an idea or issue. Improvise in individual groups first; then bring the two groups together with the aim of reaching a solution.
3. Create a plot from one of the following phrases:
   a. "Can you spare a dime?"
   b. "Got a cigarette?"
   c. "May I have a cup of coffee?"
   d. "Do you have the time?"
   e. "Which way to Main Street?" (or any familiar street)

4. Tell or read the group a short story. Then have them improvise it. Next, create a scene that might take place *after* the ending of the original story.

5. Two friends meet after many years. One, who was once very attractive, is now greatly changed; she is obviously down on her luck. The other, who had been plain, has been successful.

Improvisations with Problems for Discussion

The following situations involve problems. Older players may enjoy first improvising them and then discussing the options with the rest of the class.

1. You are in a gift shop in a terminal. Over the glass and china counter there is a sign that says if you break anything, you will have to pay for it. Your sweater sleeve accidentally catches a glass dish, and it falls to the floor and breaks. It is so noisy in the terminal that no one sees or hears it. What are you going to do?
   a. Go to the clerk with the broken pieces and explain what happened.
   b. Decide to do nothing, hoping you can get away with it.

2. Your class is competing in a play festival. The group about to go on is very good. Suddenly, you see their most important prop lying on the floor outside the stage door. You realize that if they lose it they won't be able to replace it, and any substitute prop will probably upset the actors. What are you going to do?
   a. Pick up the prop and give it to the stage manager.
   b. Hide the prop in a trash basket, in an effort to make them do less than their best.

3. You are invited to a party in a very beautiful home. Your mother says you should dress up, but your friends say they are going to wear blue jeans. One of them says she has no dress clothes. What will you do?
   a. Try to persuade your friends to dress up.
   b. Dress up; then change into blue jeans at the last minute.
   c. Wear your best clothes and find that everyone else is dressed casually.
   d. Try to help the one who has nothing dressy to wear.

4. You are buying a birthday present for your sister or brother. You know exactly what she or he wants. You find two different gifts, one cheap and the other expensive. You also see something you want for yourself. If you buy the expensive item, it will take all your money. If you buy the cheap item, there will be enough money left for you to get what you want too.
   a. You decide on the expensive gift.
   b. You decide on the cheap gift and get yourself what you want as well.

5. Just before a game you fall and hurt your knee. You don't know whether it is going to ruin your playing or not. What do you do?
   a. Say nothing about it and play. The knee lets you down.
   b. Explain and stay out of the game. The team is angry and upset.

6. There has been a bad flood in your neighborhood, and many families have had to leave their homes quickly. Your mother invites some people to stay in your house till the crisis is over.
   a. One of them is a boy or girl you dislike.
   b. You have to give up your room to a family.
   c. You decide to help in any way you can.

The following situations are suggested for older students, who are faced with similar problems. Having several groups work on them at the same time and then enact them for the entire class gives an opportunity for good discussion. Two groups rarely come up with identical reactions and solutions. The problems make for good drama, perhaps because they have reality for the players, and they combine imagination, and emotional and intellectual involvement in the situations.

THE TELEPHONE

A young girl answers the telephone. The caller is a boy in her class who asks her to go to the movies with him on Saturday night. Although she does not like him particularly, she has nothing else planned, and she does want to see that film. So she agrees to go and hangs up. A few minutes later the telephone rings again; this time it is one of her girl friends, who is going to have a party, to which she really wants to go. She accepts but, after she hangs up the phone, realizes that she will have to get out of the first invitation or call her girl friend back and explain why she must decline after all.

(Stop for discussion.) What should she do? Discuss all solutions suggested. Then try them all out. What was the best decision and why?

THE RECORD

Two or three young people are playing records in a record shop. One of them accidentally scratches a record badly. It is destroyed as far as sales are concerned and should be reported at once. However, there is a discussion about it because if it is slipped back into the album, no one will know who did it and the girls will be gone before it is discovered. One urges this solution; the one who scratched it is uncomfortable with that but realizes that if she pays for the record, she will be unable to buy anything else. The third has yet a different idea as to what to do about it.

(Stop for discussion.) What can they do? What should they do? Try out all the ideas. What was the best solution and why?

THE KENNEL

A young person has a part-time volunteer job in an animal shelter. Not only does he or she love working with the animals but it gives school credit for learning outside the classroom. The student has been doing very well and on occasion is left alone to fill water bowls, clean cages, etc. One day he/she opens a cage door too far and a cat leaps out and is suddenly gone. He/she knows it is in the kennel but finding a grey cat among all the cages and supplies seems impossible. Should he/she call a staff member and explain what happened? If so, will he/she not be allowed to return? Or is it better to say nothing, hoping that it won't be noticed right away? Hunt for the cat?

(Stop for discussion.) What does he or she do? What was the best solution?

THE PARTY

A girl is home alone. Her parents are out for the evening and have told her not to let anyone in and to call them if a problem arises. She is watching television when the doorbell rings. She hears voices and knows they are those of her friends. She goes to the door and they burst into the room. She tries to explain that her parents are out but they take it as an invitation to stay. They order from the deli, play records, and have a party. As time goes on the party gets out of hand and a valuable piece of pottery is accidentally broken. There is silence as they realize that it has all gone too far.

(Stop for discussion.) What should be done? What can be done? What will happen when the adults find out about the party and the broken pottery? Try out the various solutions. What was the right thing to do?

THE DOOR-TO-DOOR SALESMAN

A child is at home alone when a salesperson comes to the door. She explains that her mother is not there but the salesperson goes on to show products and leave the brochure. For some reason the child is fascinated with the product but knows she has no right to order it. She also has great difficulty saying "no." So she orders it. The salesperson goes away but the consequences of the action lie ahead. Should she confess? Tell her mother that the salesperson insisted? Say nothing?

(Stop for discussion.) Try out all of the ideas.

In each situation adults and peers are involved. Their reactions differ. An interesting thing to do with these problems is to have the students shift from child to adult roles to get a better understanding. If they respond very positively to the activities, perhaps they would like to suggest some of their own, either problems they have had to face or some they can imagine. This is an exceptionally effective activity for high school students.

Improvisations for Older Players

The following improvisations are suggested for older players. In working on them, ask the following questions: Who am I? Where does the scene take place? What has preceded it both recently and earlier in the life of the character? Where does the action take place? You won't have all the answers, so to start you will have to think the situation through carefully. Next come these questions: What is the action? What is the problem? What is the conflict that follows? How is the conflict resolved?

Staying Out too Late

CHARACTERS:
MOTHER
FATHER
DAUGHTER
GRANDMOTHER

Time: midnight on a school night

Place: the family's living room

The daughter, who is in high school, has repeatedly stayed out too late at night. This particular evening she agreed to be home by eleven o'clock and it is now approaching midnight. The family is waiting for her, each reacting to the situation in his or her own way. Think through each character, deciding on the motivation for attitude and action.

The Shopping Center

CHARACTERS:
SEVERAL RESIDENTS OF THE TOWN OPPOSED TO A SHOPPING CENTER
SEVERAL RESIDENTS IN FAVOR OF IT
DEVELOPER, WHO IS EAGER TO START THE PROJECT
OWNER OF THE MEADOW, WHO SEES TWO SIDES OF THE SITUATION

Time: 8:00 P.M.

Place: Town hall of a very small town

A developer wants to buy a beautiful meadow on the edge of a small town and put up a shopping center and parking lot. Some of the residents think it a good idea but others are violently opposed. For one thing, it will mean destroying a lovely meadow and razing three nineteenth-century farmhouses that are the pride of the town. The owner of the land is not sure which way to go. Decide who you are and how you feel. Then, according to the questions asked above and the information you have about the situation, you will find your motivation and will act on the proposal.

THE PLAYGROUND OR A GYM?

CHARACTERS:
GROUP OF NEIGHBORHOOD CHILDREN
PLAYGROUND DIRECTOR
COMMUNITY LEADER

Time: a summer morning

Place: the playground

A new gymnasium is being proposed for the site of a children's playground. The children have just heard about it and most of them are upset. The playground director is not sure where he or she stands but tries to comfort them by talking about it. The community leader comes along and is very enthusiastic about the idea. He offers strong arguments in favor of it. Decide who you are, how you feel about the proposal, and why you feel as you do. The more you know about yourself, your past use of the playground, and your fear or interest in the new gym will help you discuss the proposal.

Make up other situations in which there are conflicts and characters caught up in them. A strong situation could become the plot for a play. Situations such as these offer excellent opportunities for developing dialogue. Arguments must be clear, well presented, and motivated by the interests, needs, and values of the characters stating them. Most players like the challenge of controversial real-life situations.

One particularly effective exercise for older players makes use of suspense stories as a springboard. After the class has heard or read the story, there is a discussion of plot, characters, motivation. Some of the more suspenseful phrases are written on the board. They might be:

The howling wind
Creaking stairs

Screeching owl
Rapid footsteps
Dark, lonely street
Squeaking hinges

Then the class puts the phrases into sentences. (For example: "The frightened boy walked down the dark, lonely street." "He heard squeaking hinges.") Next, extend the sentences into stories. Finally the class selects one story to enact.

This exercise can be further extended by discussing the improvisation and offering suggestions as to how it might be done differently or even changed. One way to change an improvisation would be to tell the story from the viewpoint of another character (e.g., to tell the story of *Hansel and Gretel* from the witch's point of view or "Humpty Dumpty" from the standpoint of the king's men). This is a challenging assignment, which can be used in the teaching of the language arts as well as serving as an exercise in creative drama.

Improvisations Based on Stories

The most popular and, in many ways, most satisfactory form of improvisation for children is based on good stories. Although making up original stories is a creative exercise, a group endeavor rarely achieves the excellence of a story that

Group improvisation. (*Courtesy of Synthia Rogers, Dallas Theatre Center; photograph by Cindy Harlow.*)

has stood the test of time or has been written by a fine author. Improvising from a story is a way of introducing literature, and when a story is well chosen it offers good opportunities for acting. Chapters 8 and 9 illustrate the ways in which both simple and more complicated stories have been approached.

Good stories on any level should have literary quality, worthwhile ideas, correct information, and dramatic values. Children up to the age of ten and eleven like fairy tales and legends. Older children may still enjoy them but tend to prefer adventure, biography, and stories of real life. Frequently, the real-life stories, because of their length, will have to be cut or the incidents rearranged. This is a learning experience that, if the group has had some experience, should not be too difficult.

Sometimes groups will want to act plays they have seen. This can be a worthwhile activity, although the tendency is to try to do it exactly as it was presented on the stage. Nevertheless, working on reenactment of a play can be a valuable period of time spent with a good piece of literature and is to be preferred to the reproduction of television shows or enactment of stories from comic books.

To present the right story, the leader must, first, know the group well. One leader, who was later to achieve remarkable success, told of her first experience as a young teacher at a settlement house in a disadvantaged urban area. Nothing she brought to the children in her drama group captured their interest. Improvisation seemed an impossible goal, though the group was alert and lively when she saw them on the street. Finally, she hit upon the idea of asking them to tell her stories they knew. Hesitantly at first, then willingly, legends and family anecdotes came. She tried them. Not only was the material a success—the group doubled in size. Parents began to look in. Before the end of the year, an activity that had seemed doomed to failure became the most popular in the settlement. Some years later, the drama department was to achieve nationwide recognition as an arts center. The search for material had led to the children themselves. Their cultural heritage, and their creative use of it under intelligent and sensitive guidance, was the first step.

The leader should prepare in advance for improvisation of the story, but avoid any preconceived ideas as to how it should be done. Improvisation is a group project with ideas contributed by both children and leader. The teacher is ready to offer suggestions but must be equally receptive to those of the players.

He should not expect the product to be perfect. Improvisation is never twice the same, and although repetition usually leads to greater fluency and richness of detail, each performance does not necessarily "top" the preceding one.

Role Playing

Although it was stated in the first chapter that role playing as therapy is not the job of the creative drama teacher or the classroom teacher using creative drama techniques, some teachers have tried it with reported success. The purpose is educative rather than therapeutic, and the situations examined are common to all. Human conflicts and the ways in which problems are solved can promote social growth. Family scenes, school situations, and playground incidents give opportunity for interaction and group discussion. Discussion is the most important aspect of role playing, according to some teachers, for it is during these periods that various points of view are presented and attitudes clarified. The teacher must accept all ideas, giving the boys and girls a chance to express themselves without fear of disapproval. He or she will pose questions such as: how do you think the father felt? The brother? The mother? What did the man next door think when you broke his window? How do you think he felt the third time it happened? If you were he, how would you feel?

Exchanging roles is a good way to put oneself in the shoes of another, in order to understand that person. One teacher gave a demonstration of role playing done with her group of junior high school girls, who lived in a neighborhood with a growing Puerto Rican population. The girls had had difficulty in accepting the newcomers, and the teacher's introduction of role playing, as a way of helping them understand the problem, led to the following improvisation. The scene was the planning of a school dance by a small clique. The committee wished to exclude the newcomers but could accomplish the exclusion only by making them feel unwelcome. This led to a serious breakdown in group relations. The period spent in playing the situation reportedly did much to restore peace and communication. The problem was faced squarely, and the girls were able to discuss their own attitudes and feelings. Later, when the improvisation was done as a demonstration for a university class, it made a tremendous impression. The insights expressed through the honesty of the players proved the value of the experiment. The teacher did not claim to be a therapist but was an intelligent and experienced classroom teacher who was deeply troubled about a condition that was interfering with the work of the class.

Peter Slade, in *Child Drama,* summarized the use of role playing in this way: "I would go so far as to say that one of the most important reasons for developing child drama in schools generally is not actually a therapeutic one but the even more constructive one of prevention."[1]

It must be pointed out that playing the part of a fictional character also demands identification with the character and his or her problems. Exchange of parts gives all of the players a chance to experience both sides of a conflict. The real-life conflict that the group itself experiences is stronger than the fictional one, and the solution, if found, is of practical benefit.

Summary

Improvisation is the creation of a situation in which characters speak spontaneously. There are many ways of introducing improvisation, but some

---

1. Peter Slade, *Child Drama* (London: University of London Press, 1954), p. 119.

groundwork in pantomime is the best preparation. Once the players have achieved a sense of security in movement, they are ready to add dialogue. Dialogue does not come easily at first, but continued practice on familiar material usually induces the flow. There are many points of departure and some of the most successful are those described in this chapter: improvisation from situations, objects or properties, sounds, characters, ideas and stories. A good program is one that makes use of all, though the teacher will be flexible in his or her approach, using those methods that lead to the greatest success for the group. Stories should be chosen with care and include both familiar and new material. Although the leader will probably want to start with the known, he or she will find this an excellent opportunity to widen horizons by bringing in good literature with dramatic content.

Role playing is a kind of improvisation that has as its specific objective the social growth of the individuals involved. There may well be a place for it in the school or club program, but it must not be confused with creative dramatics as art. Both, however, are participant centered and in that respect differ from theatre. When observed by others, improvised drama of any kind should be considered as demonstration and not as performance.

There is a great interest in improvisation today, and several professional theatre groups specialize in it. This, like the commedia dell'arte of the sixteenth century, is the development of improvisational theatre by adult actors to a high level of artistry. Although older boys and girls are able to become skilled improvisational actors, the purpose of improvisation with children is not to entertain others but rather to provide the children with a medium of self-expression. The leader or teacher, whether working in school, camp, or club program, tries to stimulate the imagination, free the individual to create, guide the group, and build confidence. Evaluating the results with the group ultimately leads to richer performance and personal growth.

Improvisation, as the student progresses, generally moves in the direction of product or theatre art. The beginning level is creative drama, with an emphasis on personal and group development. The second level, as described by Margaret Faulkes-Jendyk, is an awareness of the dramatic art form. It is still process and "personal development continues with special emphasis on expansion of experiences."[2] The final level is improvisational theatre art and is achieved by only the few. There is a natural progression from one level to the next, though not all students are equally interested in going on to develop the skills demanded of the serious theatre artist.

A final word of warning: theatre games and warm-ups are fine, but they can be carried to extremes. A group needs to advance and will become bored when there is a continued absence of substance with no obvious long-range goals. A

---

2. Margaret Faulkes-Jendyk, "Creative Drama—Improvisation—Theatre," in *Children and Drama,* 2d ed., ed. Nellie McCaslin (New York: Longman, 1981), p. 19.

perceptive graduate student, after observing four different groups of children for several months, recently remarked: "on a physical level the work was good but the mental content was lacking. They did nothing for the entire semester but movement and games."

Although most children enjoy impromptu activities, they tire of repeating them indefinitely and want to get on to something more demanding and ambitious. Whether this be story dramatization, original plays, or integrated projects, there comes a time when the group must progress or lose interest. It cannot remain on one level. Ideally, the move will be gradual as the participants grow in confidence, self-control, the ability to work together, appreciation, and the development of their skills. By making use of theatre games and exercises, which become increasingly difficult (always planned carefully in advance), they are able to handle longer assignments and a culminating project of which they can be proud.

One good way of proceeding is to begin a session with a group game while the children assemble—almost in the nature of a ritual involving everyone. When all have arrived, have them do some physical activity as a warm-up and then a game or two. By this time they will be ready to start or resume work on a major project. Any falling off in attendance is always a warning: pay attention to it. A group must respect its work, and to accomplish this, the work cannot be too easy or too repetitious.

7 Puppetry and Mask Making

Shadow puppet. (*Courtesy of Milton Polsky.*)

*P*uppets and masks are an important part of theatre history, predating the play as we know it by centuries. In many countries of the world puppetry enjoys the status of a fine art, designed and performed for adults, whereas in our country it is generally regarded as children's entertainment. In recent years, however, there has been an awakened interest in puppetry as an art form, resulting in a new popularity, and its value as a teaching tool has been recognized. Besides providing an alternative or an adjunct activity, to creative drama, puppetry and mask making each offer wonderful incentives for improvisation.

One could say that puppetry starts with dramatic play, when dolls and toys are manipulated to perform various roles and actions. The young child's game of "Peek-a-Boo," with the hands hiding the face, illustrates an early concept of the mask. As children grow older, they assign both mask and puppet more specific functions and handle them with greater dexterity. A child's first awareness of the mask as a mask, however, probably occurs about the age of four or five, when he or she wears it as part of a Halloween costume. Children of that age put on masks, confident that they are hidden from view and disguised as ghosts, witches, or monsters. Puppets and masks have much in common; in fact, at times they are indistinguishable from each other. In this chapter some of the ways in which both can be made and combined with creative drama are discussed. Although each form merits a book in itself, the limitations of space and content preclude more than the most elementary discussion. There are, however, a number of excellent texts concerning both forms on the market, and it is hoped that the teacher interested in incorporating puppets and masks into the curriculum will investigate those texts listed in the bibliography.

Puppets

In the minds of many persons puppetry is associated with the field of entertainment for very young children, although it is equally at home in the classroom. Today, with the popularity of the Muppets and other puppet characters on television, children learn about puppets at an early age and become acquainted with some of the techniques of handling them. This familiarity suggests to teachers ways in which they can include puppets either as special craft projects or as tools for teaching other subjects. A further, and particularly valuable, use is a social or therapeutic one: through the puppet shy or troubled children are often able to express what they cannot state as themselves. Best of all, perhaps, because these engaging little creatures are such fun to make and manipulate, puppets capture the child's attention and hold it in a variety of situations.

What is a puppet? Contrary to what many think, puppets are not dolls, although they often resemble them. Puppets are "actors" who come to life with the help of a puppeteer. Almost any object can be a puppet: a toy, a tool, a hairbrush, a lollipop, a spoon, a broom. Even the hand can be a puppet, if you move it and speak so that the hand appears to be doing the walking and talking. Just to prove it, try out a few things. Kneel behind a table and move an object along the edge of it. Keep moving. Here are a few things that can be used.

A wooden spoon. Make it walk, run, jump, disappear.

A toy. A teddy bear or a rag doll will do. They are soft and move in different ways from the spoon. Sometimes toys make fine puppets but it is not a good idea to depend on them. The puppets you make yourself will almost always be better.

A pencil. A ruler. A lollipop. An artificial flower. They will all become different characters when you start moving them. Now try holding one in each hand. What happens when a pencil and a ruler meet?

Your own hands. What can they do that the other things couldn't do? Hands make wonderful movements. Let them walk, dance, jump, fight, bow, march off.

Look around for some other objects that have not been mentioned. Invent actions for them and decide what kinds of characters they seem to be. Remember that *you* make the puppet. It is not alive until you move it.

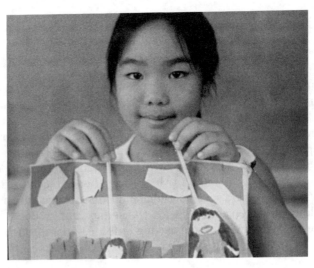

Puppets, operated from above. (*Courtesy of Tamara Hunt, University of Hawaii at Manoa.*)

Making Puppets

There are many different kinds of puppets. Some hang from strings; some are fastened to sticks called rods. Others slip over the hand like gloves. Some puppets are as tall as a person and must be pushed or moved from inside. Because the string puppet is the most complicated to make and manipulate, it is not recommended for the beginner or for the elementary school classroom. The hand puppet with its many variations is the most satisfactory for any age level, and the classroom teacher will find it within his or her capabilities, regardless of previous experience. The hand puppet includes the bandana puppet, the finger puppet, the paper bag puppet, the flat puppet, the shadow puppet, the sock puppet, and the glove puppet.

Bandana Puppets

The easiest one to begin with is the bandana puppet. Put a bandana or cloth over the hand. Let the first and middle fingers be the head of the puppet and put a rubber band around them for the neck. The thumb and little finger are the arms. Put rubber bands around them in order to hold the cloth in place. Imagine that the hand is the actor. Have the puppet you have made clap its hands, shake its head, and fall down.

There are many more things you can do in making a bandana puppet. For instance, try cutting a hole in the middle of the bandana and poking the first finger through it. Next, take a styrofoam ball with a hole scooped out for your finger and use it for a head. Heads can be made out of many different things: a small paper cup, an apple (after cutting out the core), or a ball. The bandana puppet can be quickly made by the teacher, but making one is also within the capability of young children.

Finger Puppets

Finger puppets are the smallest of all puppets. They slip on the fingers and can be played with as they are or used with larger hand puppets to show different-sized characters. For instance, a finger puppet might be an elf, with a hand puppet as a human being. One way to make a finger puppet is to sew it using felt. First, make a pattern. Put the hand down flat on a piece of paper and draw around the fingers with a pencil. Be sure to add a little extra material all around to allow for the sewing. Next, cut out the paper patterns and pin them on a piece of felt. You will have to cut two shapes for each puppet. Put the two shapes together and sew around the edges. Leave the bottom open for your finger.

Another way to make finger puppets is to cut the fingers off an old glove. White gloves are the best because you can put faces on them. Slip the glove fingers over your own and you will have five little puppets! You can cut circles and paint faces on them; when the paint is dry, they can be pasted on the puppets.

Paper Bag Puppets

The paper bag puppet is one of the best puppets with which to begin because bags come in all sizes and are easily obtained. Also, if you happen to tear the bag, there are many more around. Adults, children, giants, and elves can all be suggested with different sizes of paper bag. Small bags fit on the hands, whereas big bags will go over the head. If a bag is worn on the head, holes will have to be cut out for the eyes and mouth. Next, paint or draw a face on the bag. You can use your hands, your head, or even your feet for puppets. Hands work best, however, because you can do so many more things with them. You can paint and paste on paper bags and, if the paper is strong enough, you can sew through them. A bag can be just a head or a whole puppet.

Flat Puppets

Flat puppets are also often called rod puppets and are included here because they are easy to handle and can be used with other kinds of puppets. Flat puppets are a little like paper dolls. They can be cut out of lightweight cardboard, colored, and pasted-on tongue depressors or sticks. When the puppet is firmly attached to the stick, hold it in your hand just below the edge of the stage or table top. As it is moved, it will seem to be walking by itself. Animals make good flat puppets because you have to draw only the side view. Incidentally, if you would like to show your puppet moving in both directions, cut out two shapes and paste them together with the stick in between. Color both sides and your animal can be moved from either left or right. One more advantage to flat puppets: they are easy to keep in good condition as they don't take up much space when put away in neat piles.

Shadow Puppets

Flat puppets can be used for shadow shows also. To give a shadow show, all you need are some flat puppets, a sheet, and a lamp placed behind the sheet. When you move the puppets behind the sheet, they cast shadows on it. The closer they are to the sheet, the stronger the shadow, or silhouette, will be. Shadow puppets may be made more exciting if parts of them within the outside boundaries are cut out and backed by colored gelatins. Stores that handle stage lighting equipment carry relatively inexpensive gelatins in a variety of colors. Older children love the challenge of making these puppets, which in some ways resemble stained-glass windows. The strong light shining through the gelatin brings out the richness of the color and creates a magical effect. In the Oriental theatre, where shadow plays originated, one can still see performances using puppets made of wood or hide decorated with elaborate openwork patterns. Older students enjoy making puppets of this kind with colored gelatin pasted over the open areas. The stylized result can be beautiful and effective.

*H*and-held puppets. (*Courtesy of Tova Ackerman, Brooklyn College.*)

Sock Puppets

A sock makes a very good puppet because it stretches, yet won't slip off the hand. You can do many things with a sock puppet, such as making it into a mouth. Take one of your own old socks and put your hand inside it. Put your fingers into the toe and your thumb into the heel. You now have the upper and lower jaws of a mouth. Bring them together in a big bite. By adding eyes and other markings, you can create a bird, a wolf, a crocodile, or a dragon. You can make a puppet mouth more exciting by sewing a piece of red felt inside it and adding another piece for a tongue. So many children's stories have animal characters that the "mouth" is a useful puppet to have on hand.

Glove Puppets

The glove puppet needs more sewing than the other types. It has to be cut out of two pieces of cloth sewn together. It may also have a separate head. First, take a piece of strong cotton cloth and double it. Felt is good, if you have it, because it won't ravel. Other fabrics will do, however, so use what you have on hand, provided they are sturdy.

Cut a pattern of newspaper for your puppet. There should be a head and two arms, and the pattern must be large enough to fit the hand. Pin the pattern to the material and trace around it. Then remove the pattern and cut out the puppet. Keep the two pieces of cloth together and sew around the edges, remembering to leave the bottom open for your hand to go through. A felt puppet is ready to use as it is. A puppet made of softer material should be turned inside out to keep it from unraveling.

Children will want to put a face on the puppet. Eyes, nose, and mouth can be drawn or embroidered on it. Buttons make excellent eyes and yarn makes good hair. A little stuffing makes the head rounder. If you want to make a separate head, a lightweight material such as styrofoam or papier-mâché, for instance, works well. It is a good idea to decorate the head first and then slip it over your first and second fingers or just your first. Although it is harder to handle a puppet with a separate head than a puppet that is all in one piece, most children learn how to manage it with practice.

Giant Puppets

Some puppeteers use puppets as tall as they are or even taller. These giant puppets must be made of lightweight material so they can be pushed from behind or inside or carried. Unless you have a large area in which to perform, you probably will not be making life-sized puppets; for those who want to try, however, here are some suggestions. An easy way is to put a paper bag or papier-mâché head on a broomstick or pole. Then hang a blanket or cape on the broomstick and have the manipulator hide inside the covering. He can then carry the stick as he, in fact, "merges" with the puppet.

Another way to make a giant puppet is to use a tall, narrow cardboard box. A face and clothes can be painted on the box, which the puppeteer pushes from behind. A variation of this, and one which can be very effective, is to take a piece of cardboard decorated on one side and manipulate it from behind.

The inspiration for giant puppets has probably come from two main sources: the Japanese puppet theatre, with life-size puppets requiring two or three persons to manipulate them, and the Bread and Puppet Theatre of Glover, Vermont. This company tours part of the year, always before holiday seasons and often in between. Some of the puppets are eighteen to twenty feet tall, although in a production they are combined with smaller puppets, thus adding to the effectiveness of each one. For one thing, the variation in size aids in suggesting not only difference in character but also in importance (i.e., supernatural or powerful). Giant puppets can perform only in areas like a church or loft that offer sufficient height and space for them to be handled with ease. Should this unusual company be performing in your community, I urge you to see them, and, if possible, arrange for children to attend a performance, for the experience stimulates originality and inspires experimentation. The Bread and Puppet Theatre also combines puppets and masks, thus breaking down all preconceived ideas about what a puppet is or should be.

Materials

Just as a costume closet or box is handy to have for creative drama, so is a supply of scrap materials necessary for making puppets. You probably will not have to purchase anything because most of what you need will be in your own or the children's homes or in the school. Scraps of paper and fabrics, boxes of all sizes, sticks, styrofoam, lollipops, apples, balls, and paper bags are all useable. Ribbons, yarns, sewing materials, paper cups, paper napkins, discarded decorations, old socks, and gloves will all find a use as somebody's puppet.

Holding the Puppet

There are different ways of holding puppets, so it is suggested that you use the one that works best for you. Because younger children have short fingers they will have to experiment to find a comfortable way to hold the puppet. Some puppeteers put their first and second fingers in the neck, their fourth and fifth fingers in one arm, and their thumb in the other. Puppets can be held either in front of you or over your head. Again, use whichever way is easier for you. If you are playing for a long time, it is usually more comfortable to work the puppet in front of your face.

If you decide to hold your puppet that way, you will be seen by the audience. This doesn't matter. The audience, if you have one, will soon forget you are there. If you want to hang a curtain between you and your puppets, you will need a stage. A dark, lightweight piece of cloth at the back of the stage will hide you and make your puppets stand out. If the cloth is semitransparent, you can see through it without being seen by the audience.

Some Basic Actions

Moving the puppet's head up and down means "yes." Shaking it from side to side means "no." When the puppet's hands point to itself, it means "me" or

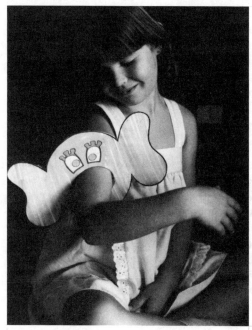

An arm becomes an elephant's trunk. (*Courtesy of Tamara Hunt, University of Hawaii at Manoa.*)

"mine." Moving one of its hands toward its body means "come here." Waving its hand may mean either "hello" or "goodbye."

Walking, running, and jumping can be suggested by the way you move the puppet across the stage. Try not to lift it up in the air. You will soon get the knack of holding it down, so that it seems to be doing all the moving.

When two persons are puppeteering together, the chances are they will each be holding a puppet. This is more difficult than playing alone, but it is also more fun. Each has to watch out that the puppets don't bump into each other. Also, when one puppet is speaking, the other one should remember to listen. Occasionally, there will be a scene for three puppets. This takes some doing, for three people will have to work together backstage, or one person will have to handle two puppets. It is a good idea at first to use stories that have no more than two characters on the stage at one time.

The Puppet Stage

It is not necessary to have a stage, for puppets can act anywhere. All you need is a smooth surface about three feet long. A table, a coffee table, a bench, or a box will do. In a setting with windows opening on a porch, one group of children used the windowsill for the stage. Another idea for a stage is a cardboard box with the front and back cut off. Making such a stage takes some work, as well as requiring a place to store it when not in use. But a stage with a lamp placed in front of the box to light it adds a professional touch.

Scenery

You do not need scenery any more than you need a stage, but sometimes you may want it. If you do, make it of cardboard or stiff paper and be sure to fasten it securely so that it won't fall down. Doll furniture can be used if it is the right size, but a simple background is usually all you will want. You don't even need that if the puppets tell the audience where the story takes place.

Stories for Puppet Plays

It is a good idea to work without scripts because you have your hands full just moving the puppets. If you know the story you are presenting very well, you can make up the dialogue as you go along, just as you do in creative drama. Besides, it will sound more natural if you do. Although many stories that are good for creative playing are also good with puppets, not all work well. One thing must be kept in mind: there is very little room backstage. Therefore, stick to stories in which no more than two or three characters are on stage at the same time. Often you can arrange the scenes so as to have no more than two, but some stories will lend themselves to the puppet theatre better than others. Here are three examples.

LITTLE INDIAN TWO FEET'S HORSE

This story can be played just as it is, or it can be made longer by adding adventures. Since Indian Two Feet is a little boy who talks to himself, we know what is happening. You can make the horse move by bending your hand so that the arm of the puppet becomes its front legs. Try out some movements until you find the ones that are right. The horse may be a flat puppet instead of a glove puppet, if you wish.

CHARACTERS:
LITTLE INDIAN TWO FEET
HIS HORSE

Little Indian Two Feet wants a horse more than anything else in the world. He often walks on the prairie, dreaming of the horse he will someday own. His father has told him that he can have a horse when he is older. That seems far away to a boy of ten! So one morning Little Indian Two Feet decides to go out to see if he can find a horse. Perhaps if he hunts long enough he'll see one on the prairie, a horse that no one owns. He walks and he walks. He calls and calls, but no horse answers. He climbs a hill, he looks over it, and he calls again. Still no horse comes to him.

He manages to cross a wide stream by a meadow. Two Feet walks in the tall grass until he is tired, but there are no horses grazing anywhere. Finally he decides to lie down and rest before starting home. In no time at all Two Feet falls fast asleep. While he is sleeping, a pony appears. It is a colt, one of the wild ponies that run loose on the prairie. In fact, it is so young that it knows no fear. Since it has never seen a boy before, it steps up to look at him. The pony puts his soft nose against Two Feet's cheek and rubs against it. Two Feet awakens with a start! He can hardly believe his eyes. He sits up and touches the pony's shoulder. "Did you come to me?" he asks. "Do you want to go home with me?"

The pony nods his head as if to say "yes." Little Two Feet puts his arm on the pony's neck and the two of them go off together. Little Indian Two Feet has found his horse at last.

THE TALKING CAT
(A French Canadian Folk Tale)

This French Canadian folk tale works better for puppets than for human actors. One of the characters is a ventriloquist, which makes it ideal for the puppet stage.

CHARACTERS

TANTE ODETTE, AN OLD WOMAN
CHOUCHOU, HER CAT
PIERRE, A WORKMAN
GEORGES, HIS FRIEND

There is an old woman, who is fooled into believing that her cat can speak. Tante Odette lives alone on her farm, deep in the Canadian woods. She is careful and thrifty, always keeping a pot of soup on the stove for herself and her old gray cat, Chouchou. She takes good care of her small farm. But as the years go by, she sometimes complains that the work is becoming too much for her. She talks to Chouchou about the chores that have to be done and how she must save her money for later. Often she says to him, "How I wish you could talk, Chouchou. Then I should not be so lonely."

One evening as Tante Odette is sitting by the fire there is a knock at the door. When she opens it, she sees a man in workman's clothes with a red sash tied around his waist.

"I am looking for work," he says politely, "If you can give me some chores, all I ask is a bowl of soup and a night's sleep in your barn."

"Go away," says Tante Odette. "I do not need anyone to help me. Besides, I have only enough soup for myself."

Just as she is about to close the door in his face, an amazing thing happens. Chouchou speaks! "Wait a minute," he says. "You are getting older, and it would be a good idea to have a strong young man on the place."

Tante Odette can't believe her ears. She looks at the man; then she looks at the cat. "Well, if you think so, Chouchou."

"I certainly do," says the cat. "Ask him to come in and join us in a bowl of soup."

The old woman invites the man in and asks him to supper. "It's only cabbage soup and bread, but we like it."

The man thanks her. When he has finished his supper, he tells her tales of his travels and the different places he has worked. But he says that now he would rather stay in one place, even though he wouldn't make any money. He tells her his name is Pierre. As time goes on both the old woman and Chouchou become very fond of him.

One day Chouchou says to Tante Odette, "Why don't you give Pierre meat and cakes? He works hard. I'm sure he gets very hungry."

"But we have no meat," she replies.

"Then let him go to the store in the town and buy some meat. He will not waste your money."

Pierre appears in the doorway. "I heard what your cat said just now. He's very wise. Let me strike a good bargain."

The old woman goes to a chest of drawers and takes out some money. "Mind you don't waste it," she tells Pierre.

When Pierre has gone, she turns to Chouchou. "How is it that you never spoke in all the years that I've had you and now you are giving me advice?"

But as always, when they are alone, Chouchou says nothing.

The next day when they finish their dinner of meat and cakes, Pierre is in a very good mood and Tante Odette says that she has never enjoyed a meal so much! "Why don't you let Pierre move into the house?" asks the cat.

"What?" says the old woman.

"Winter is coming and it will soon be cold in the barn. We have plenty of room inside."

Pierre says that he would like this very much. And so he moves in.

A few weeks later when the old woman is alone in the house, there is a knock at the door. She opens it and to her surprise, she sees a working man standing there. He is wearing a red sash just like Pierre's.

"Have you seen a workman who calls himself Pierre?" the newcomer asks.

"A man by that name works for me," the old woman says.

"Is he a good worker?"

"A very good worker," she says; and she tells of all the things Pierre can do.

"It certainly sounds like the same man. One more thing, can he throw his voice? Is he a ventriloquist?"

"Throw his voice? Oh, no! I could not stand having anyone around who did that."

"Then it can't be the same person," says the man, as he turns to go.

At this moment Pierre comes to the door. "Georges!" he shouts, "My old friend!"

"Pierre! I've been searching for you everywhere. I want you to go with me to get furs. You know they pay good money for furs in the city. How about it?"

Pierre thinks for a moment. "If I go with you, I'll make money, but it will be cold. If I stay here, I have a good job, food, and a warm place to sleep. What shall I do, Chouchou? You're a wise cat."

"Stay here," the cat answers. Then the cat turns to the old woman. "Why don't we pay him some wages? You have money in the chest. Surely he's worth a few pieces of gold."

The old woman doesn't know what to do. Finally she says, "Very well. I can give you a small wage, if you'll stay."

"Good!" says Pierre. "Then I'll stay." He says goodbye to his friend and walks with him down the road.

The old woman looks at Chouchou. "I don't believe he throws his voice, do you?"

There was no answer. She stares at Chouchou, who says nothing as usual.

Just then Pierre returns. "It will be a much better winter for me here than in the north woods. And I can earn money at the same time, thanks to your cat."

The cat bows and speaks.

"That's all right, Pierre. Fair is fair." Then Chouchou looks at the old woman. "Well, we may as well sit down at the table and celebrate the way it has all worked out."

THE FISHERMAN AND HIS WIFE

This is another good story for puppets to play. You don't need any scenery. If you want to show the different houses, you can draw pictures of them and put them up behind the puppets.

CHARACTERS:

THE FISHERMAN

HIS WIFE

THE FLOUNDER

A poor Fisherman lives with his wife in a cottage by the sea. Every day he goes down to the shore to catch a fish for their supper. When his luck is good, he has enough fish to sell to their neighbors. One morning the Fisherman goes out as usual and sits down in his favorite fishing spot. Suddenly there is a tug on his line. He pulls and he pulls.

"What have I caught?" asks the Fisherman. He gives another tug on his line and up comes the biggest flounder he has ever seen.

Then, to his amazement, the fish speaks. "Please let me go. I have done you no harm."

The Fisherman can't believe his ears. "You can talk? I have never heard of a fish that could talk."

"I was once a prince," says the Flounder sadly. "An evil spell was put on me, and I am doomed to spend the rest of my life as a fish."

"I am sorry if I've hurt you," says the Fisherman, taking the hook from the fish. "Go back to your home in the sea."

"Oh, thank you," the Flounder says. "You have saved my life. If I can ever do anything for you, call on me. I'm never far away."

The Fisherman promises the Flounder that he will do so. Then, eager to tell his wife about his strange adventure, he packs up and goes home. When he has finished his tale, his wife scolds him for his stupidity. "That's just like you! Why didn't you ask him for a nice house and some food for our dinner? He was a magic fish, and you let him go."

"I'm sorry, wife," says the Fisherman. "I didn't think of it."

"Well, go back down to the sea and ask for a house like our neighbor's, with enough food to last us a year."

"Very well," replies the Fisherman. So he goes down to the place where he had caught the Flounder and calls out:

> "Oh, fish of the sea,
> come listen to me.
> For my wife, my wife, the plague of my life,
> Has sent me to ask a boon of thee."

Scarcely does he finish when the Flounder appears.

"What can I do for you?" the fish asks politely.

The Fisherman tells him.

"No sooner asked than granted," says the fish. "Go home and you will find a house like your neighbor's."

The Fisherman hurries home, and there is a beautiful stone house where his little cottage had been. His wife appears at the door, delighted with their good fortune.

For a time the Fisherman and his wife live happily. Then one morning his wife, who is always discontented, says, "I don't know why you asked for this house. I should like a castle with servants to wait on me."

"This house is plenty good enough," says her husband.

"No," she replies. "Go back and tell the fish I must have a castle."

The Fisherman doesn't want to do her bidding, but at last he agrees. He goes down to the sea and again calls out:

> "Oh, fish of the sea,
> come listen to me.

For my wife, my wife, the plague of my life,
Has sent me to ask a boon of thee."

In a flash the Flounder appears. "Nothing easier," he says, after the Fisherman explains the matter to him. "Go home to your castle."

Then the Flounder disappears and the Fisherman returns home. Instead of the stone house, there is a great castle with towers and walls surrounding it. His wife is overjoyed. But after a time, she again becomes discontented.

She sends her husband back to the Flounder many times. She wants to be the richest woman in the world. Then a Queen. Next, an Empress. And finally, Goddess of the Universe. Each time her husband begs her to be content with what they have, but she will not listen. And each time the fish grants her wish—until the last one.

"What is it now?" the Flounder asks the Fisherman.

"Oh, gracious Flounder," replies the Fisherman, "my wife wants to be Goddess of the Universe."

"Never!" declares the Flounder angrily. "I will grant no more wishes. Your wife can return to her cottage."

There is a loud noise like a clap of thunder and the fish disappears. Then the Fisherman goes home, where he finds his wife in the doorway of their humble cottage.

Puppets as Teaching Aids

Puppets also make excellent teaching aids because of their power to hold and sustain the attention of a class; and, in doing so, they facilitate learning. Unlike some curricular materials, puppets are not limited to any one area of

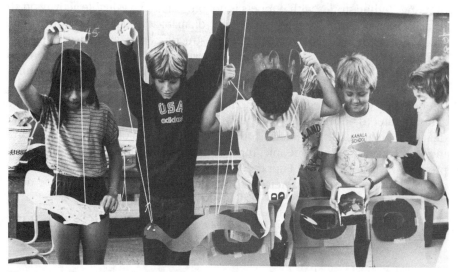

The complete experience: Making and manipulating the puppets. (*Courtesy of Tamara Hunt, University of Hawaii at Manoa.*)

study. They can be used to teach any subject, ranging from the language arts to science and math. They can be combined with other teaching materials and they can be used alone. Moreover, puppets cost little or nothing to make. As has already been stated, their value lies in their mobility, not in their beauty or complicated construction. Those made by teachers and children are usually more satisfactory than commercial puppets. If puppets are purchased, however —and there are many on the market—they should be selected for their durability, avoiding the nonwashable and perishable.

The degree of sophistication of puppets that students create depends on the age and previous experience of the students. Although the simple puppets of young children can be wonderfully effective, experienced older groups find a challenge in making more elaborate ones. It cannot be repeated often enough, however, that a good puppet is one that can be manipulated easily; the most beautiful puppet in the world is a failure if it does not move easily and well. Another consideration, and an important one, is the child's perception of his or her work. In other words, "it is not what the puppet looks like that counts but rather how the child feels about the puppet . . . a rabbit puppet made by a child does not have to look like a real rabbit—the child needs only to believe in it.[1]

Probably the most extensive use made of puppets as a teaching tool is in the area of the language arts. According to John Warren Stewig, "Children generate more verbal language during dramatic play than in any other situation."[2] In both creative drama and puppetry, extemporaneous speaking is involved; use of the puppet has the added advantage, however, of shielding the speaker who may be shy or weak in verbal skills, thus enabling him to communicate through his puppet. A skillful teacher makes use of the opportunity afforded by this communication to open up new areas of learning and tune into a student's thinking. Telling stories with puppets is not only fun but a valuable activity on all levels. The move from storytelling to story dramatization is a natural next step, involving dialogue, character study, play structure, and growth in language competency. The use of puppets in the teaching of poetry has also proved successful in promoting the appreciation and writing of this form of literature.

Some teachers have found puppets invaluable aids in the study of elementary science and environmental education; the writing of original skits on these subjects, later to be enacted by puppets, is strong motivation in two areas that are difficult for many children. Social studies provide a wealth of puppetry opportunities for the study of other people, other countries, historical events, and current problems. "Famous People Puppets" is suggested as an activity for intermediate grades.[3] Puppets provide exercise in bilingual education also: this can be done

---

1. Tamara Hunt and Nancy Renfro, *Puppetry in Early Childhood* (Austin, Tex.: Nancy Renfro Studios, 1982), p. 24.

2. John Warren Stewig, *Teaching Language Arts in Early Childhood* (New York: Holt Rinehart and Winston, 1980), p. 123.

3. Bojabi Treehouse, *Puppetry—A Tool for Teaching* Brochure (New Haven Public Schools, 1973).

by way of dramatic sketches or taught directly by a familiar mascot puppet. The mascot, incidentally, is often able to hold the attention of the most restless group, a phenomenon observed by anyone who has ever used puppetry with children. In short, there is no area of the curriculum that cannot be enhanced by these appealing little creatures who come alive in the most inexperienced hands, teaching and entertaining simultaneously. Their popularity with all kinds and ages of groups practically insures success.

THE STORY OF NOAH'S ARK

A puppeteer who works with the New York City Board of Education has a number of scripts that can be adapted for a hands-on experience in the primary grades.[4] One delightful script, which works very effectively, is "The Story of Noah's Ark." I have included it here because it can be expanded to include as many animals as needed and is simple enough for even the youngest children to perform.

"The Story of Noah's Ark" is a puppet pageant with parts for up to three classes. The roles of Noah and his family and the technical stage business (the flood and sound effects, etc.) should be handled by an older class (third or fourth grade), while the younger children "march on" the animals and "dance" the fish. One advantage of having three classes share responsibilities is the presence of three teachers to help organize the children during the performance. The younger classes can sit out front and watch the show until it is time for them to come on stage.

Teacher A concentrates on helping his or her class make the fish and rehearse dancelike movements for them when it is time for them to appear on stage. Teacher B has his or her class study animals, collects pictures, perhaps takes the class to the zoo, and helps them make stick puppet animals. Once the puppets are made, all that the class has to do is march its animals on and off the stage in the performance. Teacher C's class makes people puppets, the ark, the two doves, the rain, and so on. He or she assigns parts and rehearses the children in their parts.

Teacher A remains backstage to help throughout, while Teacher B sends the children up from the auditorium when it is time for them to perform. Teacher C narrates the story and cues in the children. He or she may insert dialogue, should the children miss their cues.

It is desirable for the children to perform at least twice, with discussion between performances about how the show might be improved. It is also a good idea to have two casts as insurance against absence and also because children learn from watching each other. Four performances in two days will service most schools, at the same time enabling both casts to perform twice. In general, the fewer combined rehearsals and the more performances, the better for all.

---

4. Penny Jones' Early Childhood Puppet Theatre, Ltd.

How to Stage "The Story of Noah's Ark": Noah and his family stand behind a low screen, holding their puppets above their heads or hold them above the top of the table or desk, while kneeling behind it. All of the other children sit in the audience until they are called on stage or to the playing space. To avoid congestion the children cross from one side of the stage to the other and then go back to their seats in a continuous clocklike circle of movement. The animals march on and off to marching music. Slow waltz time music is good for the movement of the fish.

Space is left in the script for dancing and music, if desired. The ark entertainment is optional but it is an excellent opportunity to include songs the children know and want to sing. Animals songs are particularly appropriate, as are water and rain songs.

If the pageant is given in a classroom, a table or desk is satisfactory for the puppet stage. If it is given on a platform or stage in an auditorium, then a screen, which is two dimensional, is better.

Properties and Scenery: Scenery is unnecessary but props are essential to this play. All props, however, can and should be made by the children as part of the experience.

The Ark—A flat cut-out of cardboard, shaped like an ark and attached to a long stick. It is large enough for several puppets to appear behind it at one time and it should be moved by a child with a steady hand so that it can rise and fall with the flood waters

Rainbow—A cardboard cut-out painted in bright colors

Mountain—A cardboard cut-out

Fish and animals—Cardboard cut-outs taped to sticks and decorated in the colors of the animals they represent. The fish should be made of flexible paper and painted on both sides so that they can turn while swimming.

Doves—Two identical paper birds, one with a leaf in its beak, on long wires

Noah's family—Cardboard cut-out puppets taped to sticks

Sound effects:

    Rain—Plastic bags that make a noise when rustled

    Thunder—A sheet of thin metal or aluminum pan that rumbles when shaken

Apples, corn, and honey—Cardboard cut-outs of bags taped to sticks

Flood—A long piece of light blue fabric raised and lowered by two children, one at each side of stage

The script of "Noah's Ark": The cast of Noah's family sit backstage waiting for their turns, while the rest of the children sit out front, watching and waiting to be sent backstage. The Narrator sits at one side of the stage so as to be able to monitor both backstage and audience area.

Five children each holding a sign reading "The Story of Noah's Ark" walk across the stage, stopping center long enough for the audience to read the words.

NARRATOR: This is *The Story of Noah's Ark*. Once there lived a good man named Noah. (Noah pops up, looks around, and leaves. As each member of his family is introduced, that puppet pops up, then leaves.) He had a wife named Esther. They had three sons, Ham, Shem, and Japheth. But the rest of the world was very bad, so God decided to have a flood to wash it clean and start all over again. He wanted to save the animals, and he liked Noah. So he told Noah to build an ark—a boat big enough to hold his family and two of every animal in the world. Then, when the flood came, they could all just float away in the ark. Noah called his sons.

NOAH: (Appears, looks around, and calls loudly.) Shem, Ham, Japheth, come here! We have to build a boat. I'll make the design and you get the wood. (The sons appear.)

SHEM: What, father?

NOAH: There's no time to talk now. I'll tell you later. Just get the wood.

HAM: All right. (They leave.)

NARRATOR: And so they began to build. They hammered and they sawed. (Sounds of hammering.)

SHEM: I'm tired. It's hard working day and night like this.

HAM: (Off stage) Ow! Watch out for my fingers!

JAPHETH: (Off stage) I'm sorry, the hammer slipped. I'm very tired. I need sleep.

NARRATOR: Finally the ark was finished. (The ark slowly rises to the stage on the right side but remains partially hidden. Rachael, Sarah, and Ruth appear and admire it. Shem, Ham, and Japheth are at the other side of the stage.)

RACHAEL: That's a fine looking boat you made.

SHEM: Thank you.

SARAH: It looks strong, too.

HAM: It is.

RUTH: It better be. I can't swim! (They leave.)

NARRATOR: Then the women filled the ark with food—bags and bags of it. (Rachael enters carrying a bag of apples.)

RACHAEL: Here's another bag of apples. (Disappears behind the ark.)

SARAH: Here's the last of the grain. (Disappears behind the ark.)

RUTH: Someone help me with the honey. It's heavy. (Disappears.)

MRS. NOAH: Don't drop it! (Disappears behind the ark.)

NARRATOR: Finally the storerooms were filled with food. Suddenly Japheth saw something on the other side of the hill.

JAPHETH: Look, look what's coming!

(The whole family crowds center stage.)

RACHAEL: Animals!

SARAH: They're coming here!

RUTH: You mean they're going to be on the boat, too? Oh, no!

MRS. NOAH: Now, Ruth, there's plenty of room for *all* the animals, for the universe includes the beasts and birds as well as human beings. Get on the boat, everyone, so we can show the animals where to go. Come on!

(The following lines should be divided among the family members and spoken rapidly so as to suggest the general hubbub.)

ALL: I want to be upstairs! I want to be downstairs! I want to be in front. I like the back. Don't push. Who's going to show the animals where to go? Me! Me! I'll help. We'll all help.

NARRATOR: (By this time the family have all gone behind the ark.)

And so the animals came.

In a long, long line, two by two,

The elephant and the kangaroo.
Cows and baboons, camels and raccoons;
Cats, bats and rats; dogs, frogs and hedgehogs.
All these and many more came to the door.
Even the aardvarks came to the ark.
(While the Narrator speaks, the children in the audience are lining up their animals, ready to go back stage and march them on the ark. Marching music accompanies the procession, which can be of any length, depending on the number of animals crossing, two by two. One cat turns around when it reaches the ark and scampers off stage left.)
NARRATOR: Finally, they were ready for the flood. But before he closed the door, Noah told his family to check one more time to see if all the animals were safely inside.
RACHAEL: We have only one cat!
SARAH: Where's the other one?
RUTH: There he goes—running away!
MRS. NOAH: Go, catch him. We need two cats. Hurry!
(The entire family disappears behind the ark; the cat runs out, then turns around and runs the other way. They all chase it except Japheth, who waits and catches him.)
JAPHETH: Got him!
NOAH: (As Japheth goes behind the ark) All right, everybody inside. I feel the first drop of rain. The rain began to fall. It rained and it rained. (Sound effects of rain.) Thunder cracked! (Sound effects.) Lightning flashed. (Lights are clicked on and off.) It was a terrible storm. (Repeat sound effects.) Pretty soon there was a lake. (Floor cloth is lifted up by the two children.) The lake got deeper. The water rose higher and higher until it reached the ark. (The cloth is lifted up to the ark.) The ark began to rock and then to float. It rained for forty days and forty nights. And the wind blew. (Children in the audience blow.) And the lightning flashed. The thunder cracked. And the waves rose and fell. (Sound effects are louder and cloth lashes the ark.) At last it stopped. (Sound effects gradually stop.) The fish came out to play. (Slow music as children glide their fish back and forth. They glide in a pattern, perhaps one at first, then two, and finally all together.)
For a time Noah and his family looked at the fish. Then they grew tired of watching, and wanted to do something themselves.
RACHAEL: I'm tired.
SARAH: Me, too.
RUTH: I'm tired of just sailing around with nothing to see but water. Why don't we make our own entertainment?
MRS. NOAH: Good idea. Let's sing?
NARRATOR: (This is an open place in the script where the children may sing songs if they want to.) Well, they sang until they were tired of singing.
RACHAEL: I'm tired of singing.
SARAH: Me, too.
RUTH: I'm sick of this ark and the animals and the same old faces. Won't we *ever* get somewhere?
MRS. NOAH: I have a dove. Maybe he can find some dry land now that the rain has stopped. Come, little dove. Spread your wings. Fly over the water to see what you can see. Bring us something from land.
NARRATOR: (The dove comes up and flies off stage right.)
The dove flew East but he came back with nothing.

MRS. NOAH: Oh, dear. Try again, little dove. This time go West.
(The dove flies off stage left.)
NARRATOR: This time he came back with an olive leaf. (This is the second dove, who has the leaf in his mouth.)
NOAH: Look, everybody, the dove has found land! The water must be going down.
ALL: Hooray! (All appear, then go back down again.)
NARRATOR: They drifted for a few more days. Then suddenly the ark bumped into the side of a mountain.
ALL: (Ad lib. lines like:) What was that? It must be a rock. It's land!
NARRATOR: The water kept going down. (Flood cloth begins to go down.) And down. And down. At last they were able to leave the ark, but they were not sure they wanted to. After all, what if there was another flood?
RACHAEL: I'm scared of leaving the ark.
SARAH: Me, too.
SHEM: I don't think we should take a chance.
HAM: I don't either.
RUTH: I can't swim.
NARRATOR: Just then there was a clap of thunder. (Sound effect.) But it wasn't a storm this time. It was a rainbow. (The rainbow is held up.)
JAPHETH: Look! Isn't it beautiful!
NOAH: I think this is a sign that everything is going to be all right now. We can leave the ark and start the world all over again. And they did.
ALL: (Divide up the lines) I'll go North. I'll go South. I'll see you in the spring. I'll take the cows and start a herd. I'll take the sheep. Goodbye, goodbye!

The children march off the animals, two by two. If desired, they can go around the audience. Next go the family, the fish, and the sound effects

The circus. (*Courtesy of George Latshaw, puppeteer.*)

children behind them. The parade circles the audience, returns, and takes a
bow on the stage; then they march out, with monitors collecting the puppets
at the door.

Puppets as Therapeutic Tools

Puppets have been used effectively as both diagnostic and therapeutic instruments. It is understood that neither the classroom teacher nor the creative drama specialist is a therapist; nevertheless, the puppet offers insights often undiscernible in other situations, and the sensitive teacher will take note of them. For the puppet becomes a nonthreatening little friend in whom a child can confide, entrusting his or her most private thoughts and feelings without fear of censure. This friend has access to the child's inner world and is also able to speak to the outer world as an intermediary.

Puppetry provides socially accepted avenues for the discovery, expression, and release of emotions and attitudes. Therapists do not aim at well-rehearsed, finished performances; rather, they use puppets to encourage and help motivate patients and students in clinical and educational settings. Some professional puppeteers have engaged in special ongoing programs. George Latshaw, a well-known puppeteer, worked with a group sponsored by the National Committee, Arts for the Handicapped, using puppets with severely handicapped children. Latshaw's puppets played and interacted with children in classrooms, often eliciting response from those who had until then been detached from others or lacked verbal skills.[5] In their use of puppetry the classroom teacher and the therapist share a similar goal. Thus the teacher will find puppetry an exceptionally effective way of drawing out children who are reluctant to participate in creative drama. Here are a few exercises to stimulate expression of strong feelings.

1. Try to find ways of showing that the puppet feels:
   Angry
   Excited
   Shy
   Tired
   Happy
   Curious
   Scared
   Hungry
2. Next, see if you can put actions with a feeling:
   Curious—and looks into a box
   Angry—and hits someone

5. *Puppets—Art and Entertainment* (Washington, D.C.: Puppeteers of America, 1980), p. 9.

Happy—and claps its hands for joy

Thoughtful—and comes up with an idea

3. Most of us get into trouble at one time or another. Do you remember a particular time when you got into trouble? Was it your fault? Did you think you were punished unfairly? How did you feel about it? Let your glove puppet be the other person in this story and you be the finger puppet. Act it out.

4. Talking with your puppet is fun. Like a conversation with a person, it builds as it goes along.

   a. Imagine that your puppet is mischievous. You ask it to do something and it refuses. It thinks of reasons why it won't do what you ask. How do you handle the puppet? Who wins in the end?

   b. Imagine that your puppet is angry, and try to find out what is wrong.

   c. Imagine that your puppet can't speak English. Try to make it understand you.

   d. Imagine that your puppet's feelings are hurt. Can you say or do anything to make it feel better?

5. The puppet is *you*. Talk to it, imagining that you are one of the following: your mother, your best friend, the owner of a candy store in your neighborhood, your teacher, a new child on the block.

6. Try out the following verse as you look into your own inner world. Some children are amazingly perceptive in comparing their inner and outer selves.

> I have two Selves or so I'm told.
>> My Outside and my In.
> And if I take a thoughtful look
>> I'll see myself within.
> Although I know my Outside Self,
>> I see it every day,
> My Inside Self seems hidden,
>> So neatly tucked away.
> It seems so strange I cannot touch
>> Or taste or hear or see. . . .
> I only *feel* all those things
>> That are inside of me.
> Both my Selves are special
>> That's what I'm about.
> Feeling on the *Inside,*
>> Showing on the *Out.*
> —Tamara Hunt

7. Did you ever get a present that you didn't want? Or *not* get one that you wanted more than anything else in the world? Make up a story about what happened and how you felt about it.

8. It is fun to make up stories. Here are a few ideas for starters, but soon all members of in the class will be coming up with ideas of their own.

A MISTAKE

CHARACTERS:
YOU
YOUR FAMILY (they talk offstage)

You come to breakfast early one morning and no one is up yet. You call your mother, but she tells you to be quiet; she is trying to sleep. You find some food to eat; then you get your books and pack a lunch. You call to your family and tell them they are all going to be late. You run out of the house but a minute later you come back in. Your father calls to ask who it is. You tell him that the school bus isn't there. He laughs and says, "Of course, not. Did you forget? Daylight Saving Time is over!"

SPACE TRAVELER

CHARACTERS:
YOU
A PERSON FROM ANOTHER PLANET

Imagine you are walking in the country, when you meet a person from another planet. The spaceship has landed in a field nearby. He (she) wants to know who you are, where you live, what you do, and what you eat. Then he (she) tells you all about him (her) self. Can you understand each other's language? How do you communicate?

GEORGE, THE TIMID GHOST

CHARACTERS:
FATHER GHOST
GEORGE

There was once a timid ghost named George. He lived with his parents at the edge of a cemetery not far from town. He wanted very much to be able to scare people like a proper ghost but every time someone approached him, he ran away. "Someday," he often said to himself, "I'll be as spooky as the rest of my family. Someday, but not today."

One night George's father decided that it was time to teach his son a lesson. When it was quite dark, George's father showed him how to sneak up behind someone without being heard, and to say "Boo." "Never hurt anyone," his father warned him. "Just give them a little scare."

George was eager to learn all of his father's tricks, so he practiced saying "Boo" in different tones of voice. He jumped out from behind trees and he ran back and forth, waving his arms in the air.

"Good," said his father approvingly. "You're going to be the scariest ghost in town."

George strutted back and forth after his father went into the house. "I'm going to be the scariest ghost in town."

Suddenly he heard the sound of somebody running behind him. He froze in his tracks, determined this time not to run away. This is an unfinished story. What happened next? You make up the ending.

Masks

Closely related to the art of puppetry is the art of mask making. A brief section on masks is included in this chapter because mask can be either part of a puppet project or an extension of creative drama. Interesting experimental work with mixed media is being done these days in which the human actor, often masked, and the puppet are used in the same production. In the case of life-sized puppets, the human body actually merges with that of the puppet in order to move it. When this happens, it is difficult to say which one is the performer: the

Paper-plate masks. (*Courtesy of Tamara Hunt, University of Hawaii at Manoa.*)

human being or the puppet. Young children have no problem with this, for in their own play they assume both animate and inanimate roles simultaneously. Older children and adults, however, faced with an inanimate or grotesque character to act, often find that the wearing of a mask helps to stimulate the imagination and free them of their inhibitions. Not that a mask is necessary to performance but the teacher who enjoys arts and crafts may find mask making a relevant activity.

In one imaginative production given by a small professional group, human actors, puppets, actors wearing masks, and a larger-than-life cardboard figure were used together. In this way the group were able to suggest more characters than they had actors to play and to suggest size differences involving adults, children, a giant, and other fantastic characters. The effect was both childlike and smart, suggesting ways in which a teacher might solve problems otherwise insoluble.

Many persons link the mask with theatre, even though its functions go far beyond costume and performance. The mask is used in a variety of ways, but its four major functions are:

To act as a protective covering for the head or face (ski and fencing masks)
To function as a disguise or concealment
To describe or identify a character (in a play)
To serve as a symbol (religious and ritualistic rites)

In children's theatre the mask is commonly used in costuming an animal or a fantastic creature, though stage makeup is preferred by many directors and costumers.

Background

Historically, masks and makeup have enjoyed wide popularity throughout the world. Tribal societies have worn them in performing religious rites and rituals. The primitive human being thought that by putting on the face of another he gained power over him. For example, if the hunter wore the skin and mask of an animal, he believed it would bring him a good day of hunting. In time the mask or facial paint became stylized and more elaborate, as it was embellished by generations of wearers. The masks of primitive tribes were thought to be potent in other ways as well. They could release the wearer's personality by concealing it, and they became symbols of a universal awareness of gods or a creative force in the universe.

In the ancient Greek theatre the mask served the practical purpose of projecting the actor's features and amplifying his voice. The mask was larger than the human face and was made with protruding lips that created resonance. Thus the masks of comedy and tragedy gave the actor in the huge amphitheatres, where the performance took place, an objective reality larger than life.

In the Oriental theatre, on the other hand, the mask was part of an elaborate costume, designed primarily for its aesthetic appeal rather than its practical use. Japanese masks, familiar to audiences today, are colorful, decorative, and smaller than the human face. Although they suggest the characters in a play, they make no attempt at realistic representation. The audience, knowing the story, recognizes the symbolism in the mask and the actor's movements and is appreciative of the skill of the highly trained performers.

In the commedia dell'arte, the Italian traveling theatre of the sixteenth and seventeenth centuries, the mask was an essential part of the actor's costume. Special masks represented stock characters and were always associated with them. A character's actions and appearance were thus closely connected; in fact, the covering of the face seemed to have an effect on the actor's body, making it freer and more expressive. An example of this connection may be found in Punch, a descendent of the commedia character, whose flesh-colored face with its great red nose and bulging eyes are as familiar to us as his outrageous behavior. His face and his actions go together in more ways than one.

Clowns, who prefer greasepaint to the mask, observe a unique tradition relating to mask. Each clown creates his own face and is careful never to copy that of another. A clown's face is, therefore, an individual creation to be respected as long as he or she lives.

Most children are fascinated with these various uses of masks and attitudes toward them and enjoy inventing masks of their own. One of the most creative projects I have ever seen involved puppets and children wearing paper-bag masks, both made by a class studying a unit on North American Indians. Because the mask has been used by so many people at so many different periods in history, it is a valuable resource for the teacher and a magic prop for the child who makes and wears it.

Types of Masks

The mask may cover the entire head, the face, or the upper part of the face only, leaving the lower part exposed. The simple half-mask, worn on Halloween or at masked balls, is a well-known example. The obvious advantage of the half-mask is its comfort. It is cooler than the mask that covers the entire face and it makes speaking easier. Speaking through the mouth of a mask is difficult and distracting for the inexperienced performer.

Masks may be simple, elaborate, beautiful, and grotesque, but except for the representation of animals, they are rarely realistic. The values of mask making are many and are implicit in this brief discussion. They provide an extension of the drama lesson; they reveal aspects of a culture in which the mask is an important artifact, and they release the wearer from his or her inhibitions. Many children feel freer when they are shielded from view by even a partial face covering. Children project their feelings and ideas through a mask, while they, themselves, remain hidden. The mask serves the same purpose as the puppet in this respect.

In fact, some interesting research has been done on the use of masks and makeup in therapy.

The teacher will be wise to avoid using the commercial masks sold in stores around Halloween, just as he or she should avoid commercial puppets. One of the values of including the mask in a classroom is the opportunity it offers for imaginative construction and design. This is particularly valuable for a child who is shy about acting but who has interest and ability in arts and crafts. In using a commercial mask or puppet, the teacher misses a rich opportunity for teaching.

Makeup is another form of mask. It is not the purpose of this text to go into its application for the stage: however, the makeup that persons create themselves provides valuable insights for the leader and drama therapist. Nancy Breitenbach, a therapist working in Paris, described her innovative work with makeup as "a form of free association," helping children through its use to discover who they are, what they want others to believe they are, and whom they would like to be. In an article published in England, she listed the response of children of different ages to makeup and described how it released them into drama.[6] In her opinion, the eventual removal of makeup, resulting in the reappearance of the child's familiar face, brings an affirmation of personal strength; strong feelings can be expressed and yet the individual will return to his or her normal state with a greater degree of confidence in his or her social well being.

Greasepaint applied to a child's face by an adult, on the contrary, tends to place the emphasis on the outer rather than the inner aspects of character. This is not to say that the formal, scripted play produced with costume and makeup is without value. It is simply not germane to a text on creative drama, and the art of makeup is therefore left until later, when the student is ready for formal play production.

Materials

Like puppets, masks can be made of a variety of materials. The older the student, the more complicated the techniques one can introduce, and the more experimentation one can anticipate. Students who are particularly interested in the craft of mask making will bring in many materials, often combining them in interesting and original ways. Myths and animals are always good sources of inspiration, for they remove the possibility of using the human face as a model, thus releasing the imagination to create new and wonderful designs.

For very young children the paper bag mask is by far the easiest and cheapest to make. It is also the most satisfying because it can be completed in a single class period. The brown paper bag from the grocery store slips comfortably over the head, and holes can be cut in it for the eyes and mouth. Younger children need help in locating the right places; once the holes are cut out, however, the

---

6. Nancy Breitenbach, "Secret Faces." *British Journal of Dramatherapy* 3, no. 2 (Autumn 1979): 18–23.

mask is ready for decoration. Strips of colored paper can be pasted on the bags for hair, moustaches, and even eyelashes. Paint, chalk, and crayons can be used to color them. Older children, studying a particular culture or tribal society, may paste or sew on feathers, cloth, jewelry, buttons, and so on.

Cardboard boxes can be used effectively to suggest robots and stylized characters. These are more difficult to work on than bags, and it is often hard to find boxes of the right size and shape. Because both bags and boxes cover the entire head, they muffle speech and limit freedom of movement. As a follow-up activity, however, after a class has worked on material dramatically, masks have value in extending the learnings. When they are incorporated in a project that is further developed for an audience, they offer an added dimension for the observers.

Paper Plate Masks

Masks made of plain white paper plates are recommended for the middle grades because of their shape, toughness, and availability. To make the mask appear three dimensional, cut two slits about two inches deep and about two inches apart on the edge of the plate. By overlapping the sides adjacent to each slit and stapling them back together again, a chin is formed, making the mask fit on the child's face. As with the paper bag mask, holes for eyes, mouth, and nose must be cut in the appropriate places. A nose that protrudes from the face can be made of construction paper and pasted on the plate, further adding to the three-dimensional quality. From here on experimentation with other materials is fun and will make each mask unique.

The Bread and Puppet Theatre. (*Photograph by Antony Bacewicz.*)

Papier-Mâché Masks

Papier-mâché is a substance made of pulped paper or paper strips moistened with thin wheat paste (wallpaper paste). The paper used may be newspaper, tissues, napkins, or toweling. Wheat paste may be secured from any hardware store (follow directions on the package).

You will need a form or mold to work on. This may be made of modeling clay, or you may use a wig form or a large round balloon as a foundation. Be sure the mold is lightly greased with oil or cold cream. It may then be covered with strips of *torn* paper (approximately one by ten inches) dipped in paste. Apply strips diagonally, bandage fashion, wherever possible and overlap them. Two layers of paper are usually enough. Paper pulp (soft paper torn into small pieces and soaked in paste and then squeezed out) may be added to build a nose, eyebrows, lips, and so on. Allow this to dry for two to three days before removing from form.

When dry, it will be firm and brittle. Holes for the eyes, nose, and mouth may be cut with a razor blade, X-acto, or mat knife. If you use a balloon blown to larger than head size, you can make a whole head mask (e.g., animal). Leave open at the base and trim so that the form will slip over the head and rest on the shoulders.

Basic forms for whole head coverings may be made of chicken wire, covered with cheesecloth, and then layers of papier-mâché added. This will require tin snips to cut the wire; be careful that all wire ends are bent under and covered with papier-mâché. The dry head or face mask may then be painted or decorated with cut paper. Feathers, yarn, or paper strips may be added for whatever effect you want. If you spray the mask with a lacquer or plastic finish (Krylon), it will add to its durability.

Unless you want to cover the entire head, which is uncomfortable for the wearer, let it be a face mask and fasten it with elastic across the back of the head. A scarf, hat, or wig will complete the disguise.

Activities for Masks

Although masks are fun to make just in themselves, they are even more fun and more satisfying when they serve a purpose: for instance, when they are worn in a play or creative drama class or when they carry out a theme. Sometimes, on the other hand, the mask will suggest an idea to the wearer.

1. *Pandora's Box* Pandora's Box contains a variety of evil spirits. Try making masks to represent them. Players who have created movements for the spirits will love adding masks; this is a perfect example of the relationship that exists between mask and movement.
2. *A Circus* A circus calls for clowns, animals, a ringmaster, and any number

of sideshow characters. Every person in the class can invent a different mask for a circus parade.

3. *Holidays* Although Halloween comes to mind first as an occasion for mask making, every holiday contains possibilities. Take Valentine's Day, Fourth of July, or St. Patrick's Day. What about your birthday? Every child in the class might try making a mask of himself or herself. It may look like you, or it may be simply your own invention.

Summary

Puppetry and mask making provide an added dimension to creative drama as well as being arts in their own rights. Although it has been stated repeatedly throughout the chapter that the types of puppets and masks described are simple, requiring no previous experience or special course work, it is always wise to try out an assignment before giving it to a class. In this way you can foresee any problems that might arise and solve them yourself in advance. Gathering materials and providing enough space for construction is important. As in creative drama, the encouragement of original ideas will help to prevent imitation of familiar television characters.

The teacher who includes puppets and masks in the curriculum will find them a rich resource. Regardless of the reasons for including them, the possibilities they offer are limitless. The major values may be summarized as follows.

1. Puppets and masks provide opportunities for developing motor skills. Tools and materials must be handled with care in order to construct puppets and masks that are sturdy and functional.
2. Dressing and decorating puppets require imagination. Each puppet must become a character, first through its costume and then in the way in which it is decorated and painted.
3. Puppets require control. It takes controlled fingers to manipulate a puppet so that it can perform as the operator wishes.
4. Puppets and masks offer an avenue of expression. Through them the operator expresses the thoughts and feelings of characters.
5. Both puppets and masks have therapeutic power. Through them, timid or withdrawn children can find release, whereas aggressive children learn to subordinate themselves to the personality of the characters they are presenting.
6. Puppetry demands cooperation. Children learn to take turns and work together for a successful performance.
7. Puppetry and mask making are inexpensive arts. Delightful results may be

obtained within the most limited budget. If there is no stage, a box will do until the teacher is able to construct something more permanent.

8. Puppets and masks may be ends in themselves or the means by which other ends are reached.

Given half a chance, the puppet engages the child as performer, playmate, teacher, and alter ego. The mask, though less versatile, is closely related, serving many of the same purposes.

8 Dramatic Structure: The Play Takes Shape

*T*he Wind in the Willows, adapted by Moses Goldberg. *(Courtesy of Tom Behm, University of North Carolina, Greensboro; photograph by W. C. Burton.)*

*I*f creative drama teachers are going to help children create a play, they must know something of the structure and fundamental dramatic elements that distinguish the play from other forms of literature. They will not be expected to become expert at playwriting or dramatic criticism, but their enjoyment will be greater and their guidance more helpful, if they have a basic understanding of the art form with which they are working. Although there is no rigid formula for writing a play, particularly in this period of experimentation, there are certain elements that are necessary to its existence.

First, a play is to be played. Until it finds life on a stage, it is not a play. Through the process of interpretation by actors and the mounting by costume and scenic designers, it is born, and it will live or die according to the communication it has for an audience. It is true that some plays have been popular in their own times but have failed to speak to subsequent generations of playgoers. Occasionally, a play that is badly received when it opens finds an audience later. All too often, however, the play that fails to please in its first production is discarded before there is another opportunity to tell whether or not it communicates with even a limited audience.

There are plays that are universal and timeless in their appeal; what they have to say is as true today as when they were written, and this truth is understood by persons of all races and national backgrounds. There are other plays, however, whose messages are more temporal. Couched in the language of the day, they speak to the men and women of their own times, presenting problems both serious and comic, to which contemporary audiences respond but to which those of another time or place are indifferent. This is not to discredit such plays but simply to observe that although they have found success as theatre pieces, they lack the universality and timelessness of the classics. What classics will come out of our own time must be left to future generations of playgoers to decide. The works of George Bernard Shaw, Eugene O'Neill, and Tennessee Williams are among those that have been translated into many languages and produced widely both at home and abroad. It is too soon to tell, however, to whom they will speak in the future.

As to plays for child audiences, there are not many that meet the criteria of good dramatic literature. This is true because the field is new and few professional playwrights have been attracted to it. Charlotte Chorpenning, Aurand Harris, Joanna Kraus, Flora Atkin, and Susan Zeder are among our best-known and most-produced American children's playwrights. We are not concerned with formal production or the printed script in this text; we are, however, concerned with the knowledge of drama that older children sometimes want to carry beyond the classroom. It is here where process and product merge and where knowledge of play structure and elementary theatre techniques are necessary. For this reason some attention is given to terminology and definition in this chapter.

Children are rarely concerned with linear structure. Their dramas may move backward or forward in time, absent characters may appear without explanation, and action in different times and places may take place simultaneously. This occurs not because children lack a sense of order but because they do not know the conventions of playwriting until they experience them in the theatre or until they are pointed out. Children have a logic of their own but need some help in communicating. Indeed, some of our modern playwrights, in creating new forms, are doing what children do naturally: letting form follow function instead of traditional rules.

The teacher, therefore, should not change children's work; in giving them a concept of structure, he or she will be helping them to express, improvise, and eventually, perhaps, write plays of their own. When they do this, they will want to communicate with an audience. Far from stifling their creativity, this knowledge will help to stimulate and focus it. Given boundaries, children are freer to express themselves than they are with no boundaries or form to follow.

Aristotle said that there were six elements in every tragedy. Although styles of playwriting have changed radically throughout the ages, we can still find these six elements in all plays, comedy and tragedy: fable (or plot), characters, thought (or underlying theme), language (dialogue), melody (mood, including cadence and sound of words), and, finally, spectacle (in our terminology, mounting). Although teachers will not burden children with the list or its origin, they will find these elements useful to keep in mind when questioning and guiding children in need of structure.

1. Plot

The plot is the story. It may be simple or complex, internal or external, but what happens between the opening scene and the final curtain is the action we call story or plot. Although tastes differ and styles change, a good plot holds the interest of the audience and is consistent. The most bizarre events must belong to it, and the outcome, whatever it may be, must seem logical. It involves exposition, complication, climax, and dénouement.

2. Characters

A play involves characters. It is their conflict that holds our attention, and it is through them that the playwright delivers the message. Whether tragic or comic, lovable or despised, a character must be believable and belong to the play. Even in fantasy, a character must have reality; a witch or a ghost, for example, though unrealistic in itself, must compel our belief through the consistency of its behavior.

The hero or heroine should be someone with whom the audience can identify. Whatever his or her faults or human weaknesses, our sympathy must be aroused, making us care what happens. Whether this person should be more good than bad is debatable, but we must accept the hero or heroine as real and his or her actions as true.

Characters respond to each other in a natural way. Although it is clearly established to whom the story belongs, there are other characters in the play who help to advance the plot through their involvement with it and their relationship to the hero, or protagonist. A skillful playwright develops character and situation through this interaction. Sometimes many characters are needed to tell a story; sometimes it is done better with one or two. The fewer there are, the greater the responsibility they have for telling the story, and the more the audience learns about them. The actor, however, must find in the most minor characters the answers or clues to questions such as:

1. Age of the character
2. Education and cultural background
3. Interests
4. Occupation or profession
5. Religion
6. Members of the family and the character's relationship to them
7. Social relationships
8. Physical appearance and health
9. Dominant mood
10. Qualities of personality

Good characters are at all times consistent. If they are not, either through the writing or the actor's interpretation, we cannot believe in them. A believable character, on the other hand, has a reality that exists for the audience long after the final curtain has been drawn. Even when a character is fantastic, he or she must be credible.

3. Theme or Thought

The theme is the underlying thought or basic idea upon which the play rests. Not every play has a well-defined theme; it may, however, be the most important element. If there is a theme, the story both springs from and expresses it.

4. Dialogue

Dialogue is the term given to the lines of the play. Good dialogue should belong to the characters, both in content and manner of speech. A noblewoman will not talk like a peasant, nor will a country boy talk like a prince. Although dialogue must be understood, the speech patterns of the characters must not be sacrificed. For example, a character of little education who comes from a particular region will use colloquial speech or appropriate dialect. Poetic dialogue has been employed in the drama during certain periods of history, but even this convention does not obscure the speech patterns and individuality of the characters. Unlike the novelist, who can explain actions and motives, the playwright must incorporate explanations into the speech of the characters. Although it appears easy, it can be much more difficult, and this is why improvising dialogue before attempting to write it is extremely helpful to the fledgling playwright, child or adult.

Dialogue also advances the plot. The playwright's job is to tell the story as economically as possible through the words of the characters. A soliloquy, in which only one person speaks, is a device used occasionally, but in general it is through conversation between two or more persons that characters are revealed and the plot is unfolded.

5. Melody (or Mood Created by Sound Effects, Music, and Vocal Sounds)

During the time Aristotle was writing, musical instruments were used as accompaniment to dialogue. Music enhanced the mood of the drama, and as we know, it is a very effective means of evoking emotion in the audience. The American musical is the most obvious example, although musical backgrounds in certain scenes of plays perform the same function. Sound effects, both on and off stage, are used in many plays to add credibility as well as mood, a device we take for granted.

The human voice is also a musical instrument, however, that, when trained, is capable of lifting the dialogue from a practical to a poetic level. Pitch, rhythm, tempo, emphasis, and tone are all qualities of voice that a good actor acquires to move the audience and express the feelings of the character. Although we do not list melody separately, preferring terms like *music* and *sound effects,* we are well aware of it as a necessary dramatic element of a play.

6. Spectacle

We use the word *mounting* to embrace all of the visual aspects of a production: direction, scenery, costumes, lighting, makeup, and properties. In the contemporary theatre, these things vary enormously in importance; some plays are given elaborate production whereas others are produced with minimal scenic effects. Modern costumes and little or no scenery are familiar to audiences, although the less scenery, the more lighting that is usually required to highlight a scene or change it. Color, line, and design also enter into the picture, particularly in producing plays for child audiences. The trend now is toward simplicity, even to the point of uniform costumes in some types of plays. The Paper Bag Players of New York, in their "revue" type of structure, use the uniform very effectively. It enables the players to move quickly from skit to skit and to use props rather than take the time to change costumes between scenes. Children do, however, enjoy a full-scale production despite their ability to imagine colorful scenery and costumes, and most producers are sensitive to which plays are best served by spectacle.

In addition to Aristotle's six elements, there are other terms used in discussing the theatre that children in the intermediate and upper grades should know. In fact, older children like knowing and using them; some of the following are the most common.

Conflict

Conflict is the basis of drama, whether comic or tragic. Without conflict, there is no resolution; with conflict, the interest is sustained to the end. The successful playwright resolves the conflict in a way that is satisfying and acceptable.

Climax

The *climax* is the high point of the play. A three- or five-act play will have more than one climax, but there will always be a point at which the interest is highest. This scene usually comes somewhere near the end, after which there is an untangling, or resolution.

Acts

Acts are the major divisions in a play. Short plays are generally written in one act. Longer plays may be divided into two, three, or even five acts, depending on the plot and the need to break it into parts. Although three acts are most often used, there is no right or wrong number. Many playwrights today use the two-act form with one intermission between them.

Scenes

Scenes are divisions within acts and are most often used to indicate a different time or place. A play does not have to have any particular number of scenes; the time covered and the locations in which the action takes place determine them. Many one-act plays are written in a single scene because they are concerned with a single action or plot.

Subplots

Sometimes longer plays tell two stories: the story of the major characters and another story of the minor characters *(subplot).* One-act plays rarely have subplots. Full-length plays frequently do.

Flashback Scenes

Flashback scenes are sometimes used to show an important event that happened at an earlier time, before the play began. The flashback is a device that helps to explain the behavior or attitudes of characters more dramatically than merely telling about them.

Dénouement

Denouement is the portion of the play that follows the climax. It may be long or short, depending upon the number of situations that need straightening out. In a children's play, the denouement and climax are often one, since children are satisfied once the conflict is settled, and long explanations at this point do not interest them.

Unity

Unity is the overall term applied to the integration of the various parts of the drama, making a smooth and consistent whole. Unity may be achieved in a number of ways, such as the creation of a single hero, a single action, a single idea, a single mood. On the other hand, a good play, no matter how many characters or episodes, can also be unified through the sensitive arrangement and organization of the various parts.

Dramatic Irony

Dramatic irony is the term used for letting the audience in on a secret. Suspense is usually greater when it is employed, and many comedy scenes are funnier because of it.

Structure

Plays are described as long or short, depending on whether they are a full evening's entertainment or consist of merely one act. The number of acts in a long play varies. Although many playwrights have used the three-act form, some prefer four or five or a series of episodes rather than the conventional division between acts. Scenes are the divisions within acts and usually occur when the time or place changes.

Comedy

Comedy is defined as a play that ends satisfactorily for the hero or heroine. Comedy may be funny, but this is not essential according to this definition. Many comedies are serious or satiric.

Tragedy

Tragedy is defined as a play that ends with the death or defeat of the leading character. Although fashions in playwriting change according to the times and public taste, the downfall of the protagonist places a play in the category of tragedy.

Prologue and Epilogue

Prologue and *epilogue* are the portions of the play sometimes placed at the beginning and end, to introduce the play or to establish atmosphere. Such scenes are not an integral part of the play, although a narrator may appear in the prologue and also be involved in the play. Many children's plays employ narrators or are written with prologues as a means of imparting necessary information to an audience composed of different age levels and theatre experience.

Narrator

The *narrator* is a person who tells or reads an exposition that ties the incidents together. It is a useful device when an extended period or a variety of scenes are included and is also a way of bridging the distance between actors and audience.

Theatre for Children

Children's theatre is above all good theatre. In this respect, it does not differ from theatre for adults. There are, however, special requirements that must be met if the children's play is to hold their interest as well as be worthy of their time and attention. The script contains the same basic elements—characters, dialogue, plot—but not all material appropriate to the adult audience is suitable for children. Action, for example, is particularly important: the playwright writing for children must remember that it is more important to "show" than to "tell." Speeches should be short; long, talky dialogue is lost on the audience. Although vocabulary is necessarily adapted to the age level of the audience, it should not be oversimplified but should rather add enrichment and an opportunity for learning new words.

In writing an adaptation of a classic or well-known story, the playwright must make every effort to retain the essential elements of the source material so as not to disappoint or offend the audience. Characters must be believable. Fantasy and fairy stories comprise a large segment of plays written for children; nevertheless, the characters in such plays must be endowed with credibility, exhibiting a pattern of behavior that is consistent.

Children on the Salt River Indian Reservation enjoy a performance. *(Courtesy of Lin Wright, Arizona State University, photograph by John Barnard.)*

If the playwright has suggested difficult technical problems, he or she must decide whether they can be carried out successfully or whether any modification of the effect will damage the play. By "technical problems" are meant things such as blackouts; characters who fly, disappear, or change into birds or animals; or unusual lighting and sound effects. What might be easily solved in the professional theatre can often pose an insoluble problem on the school stage, where equipment, budget, and technical assistance are limited.

Children's theatre, like adult theatre, should not depend on extravagant effects or gimmicks to stimulate interest; if such scenes are essential to the plot, however, and can be executed artistically, they will certainly add to the effectiveness of the play. Children do not demand theatricality, but there is no question that their enjoyment is enhanced by scenes that offer excitement and color. Many children's plays call for music and dance. Therefore, the actor in children's theatre should study both so as to be able to sing, dance, fence, and master any other performance skills demanded by the play. More will be said of this, however, in Chapter 16 on playgoing.

The following script is included as an illustration of a story that contains the basic elements of a play:

A worthwhile theme
A plot that holds interest
Characters who motivate the action
Believable dialogue
Melody
Spectacle or appropriate scenery and costumes

Like most folk material, *Apples in the Wilderness* may be enjoyed by a wide age range, although it is most popular with children under twelve. It can be produced simply in classroom, club room, or camp or on a stage. This is not to advocate formal productions by children of that age (the memorization of a script, long rehearsals, and performances for outside audiences), but an older group interested in giving plays for younger children would find this and other folklore worthwhile and fun to do. Should a younger group want to perform for other classes or friends, it is more desirable for them to create a play themselves than to use a printed script. It takes longer but is well worth the time and effort. Through the process of developing a play, they will have an experience in creative writing and working with others in a variety of ways. The actual performance should be low key, regarded more as a sharing than a showing.

On the other hand, the theatre is a performing art, and children today see so many shows on television that they accept performance as a usual, rather than an unusual, occurrence. The teacher or leader should emphasize process and discourage production; nevertheless, a sincere desire to perform on the part of the children should be respected. "To withhold the experience," as one young teacher observed, "is like refusing them the game after they have practiced for it." According to another teacher, the most serious drawback to performance by children is the adult. Whether it is the teacher who works for a perfect product, featuring some children at the expense of others, or the adult in the audience who gives excessive praise, laughs in the wrong places, or is insensitive to the children's efforts, it adds up to exploitation. Exploitation, pressure, and boredom are destructive both to children and theatre. An occasional show need be none of these things if the adults involved handle the situation judiciously. As John Allen said of drama in schools, "a school does not exist to create beautiful works of child art: what matters is the growth of the child and his ability to express himself in a variety of media."[1]

APPLES IN THE WILDERNESS
NELLIE MCCASLIN

One of the most delightful figures in American legendary history is Johnny Appleseed. A small man with a mission, he traveled the length and breadth of the Middle West, planting apple seeds and tending his orchards. Some thought he was crazy and some thought he was a saint, but he continued his work, asking nothing in return but the satisfaction of seeing his seedlings bear fruit. He was said to have given up the comforts of home and wealth for a life in the wilderness, where he made friends with the Indians and lived on intimate terms with animals, wild and tame. Several monuments have been erected in his honor, but the one that bears the inscription "Johnny Appleseed, Soldier of Peace. He went about doing good" probably sums up his contribution to his country better than anything else. His courage and his dream in the face of ridicule and danger make him indeed one of our giants.

CHARACTERS

STORYTELLER	FIRST MAN	
JOHNNY APPLESEED	SECOND MAN	
ANDREW HOLBROOK, *a settler*	THIRD MAN	
BETSY HOLBROOK, *his wife*	FOURTH MAN	*neighbors*
ANDY, *his older son*	FIRST WOMAN	
MARY, *his daughter*	SECOND WOMAN	
PETER, *his younger son*	THIRD WOMAN	
AL, *an old man with a fiddle*	OTHER NEIGHBORS	
JOE, *a young settler*		

TIME

About 1835 to 1865.

---

1. John Allen, *Drama in Schools* (London: Heinemann Educational Books, 1979), p. 23.

SCENE ONE

SETTING: *A settler's cabin in the Ohio wilderness. An evening in spring.*

STORYTELLER: America has had many giants but not all of them were big. Some of them, like Paul Bunyan and Pecos Bill, towered over their countrymen. Others were ordinary men with big ideas. And one of them was small. "Little Johnny Appleseed," they called him. For sixty years he trudged across the wilderness that is now the Middle West, sowing apple seeds and tending orchards.

Johnny Appleseed wasn't his real name, of course. He was christened Jonathan Chapman when he was born in Massachusetts. Some say he got interested in apples when he was just a baby in his nurse's arms. The end of a rainbow came right down in their apple orchard, turning the blossoms silver and gold. He reached out his hands to touch a branch and from that moment on loved apple trees better than anything else.

Others say it wasn't till he was a young man in Pennsylvania that he thought of planting the seeds that were left in the cider press. Whichever way it was, he turned his back on the life of ease he might have led and started west. Crazy? Maybe. Kindly? Certainly. Courageous? Yes!

He had many adventures in his life but most of them were something like this.

(The STORYTELLER *leaves as the curtains open. The scene is in the main room of a settler's cabin in the Ohio wilderness. The family has apparently just moved in, for the room is barely furnished with only a table, three or four chairs and a cupboard.* BETSY, *the settler's wife, a tired-looking young woman, is sitting on a chair near the fire and her two older children,* ANDY *and* MARY, *are tidying up the room. The youngest,* PETER, *is playing on the hearth.)*

BETSY: Here, Andy, sweep it into the hearth. *(The older boy sweeps into the hearth as his mother tells him.)* Mary, you can set the bowls on the table for supper.

MARY: All right, Mother. *(She does so.)* I can't reach the pitcher. *(She tries again.)*

BETSY: Wait. Let Andy get it for you.

ANDY: *(Going over.)* Here. I can do it. *(He takes the pitcher down.)* I can reach the top shelf this year without even standing on my toes. See?

BETSY: You've grown a lot since we came out to Ohio.

ANDY: I'm practically as tall as Father—

BETSY: It won't be long. And you're a big help, Andy. It's like having another man around the house.

MARY: *(Stretching to her tallest.)* I've grown, too.

BETSY: I should say you have. And so has little Peter. It's a good thing, too, with me laid up the way I've been and your father so busy.

MARY: It's almost time for him to come home, isn't it, Mother? Should I put the corn meal on to cook?

BETSY: Yes, you'd better. The days are getting so long, I almost forget it's supper time.

ANDY: I don't. I'm hungry.

BETSY: Of course, you are. Put the mush on to heat and cut some bread, Mary. Andy, you better bring in some more wood for the fire. You go along with him, Peter, and pick up some kindling. The box is almost empty.

PETER: All right, Mother. Come on, Andy. *(The two boys run out the door and* MARY *busies herself in setting the table.)*

BETSY: I'll make the tea for Father's supper. *(She starts to get up but sinks back, exhausted, in her chair.)*

MARY: I'll do it, Mother. You tell me how.

BETSY: Well, you boil some water first. We'll brew just enough for him, there's so little left. (MARY *puts the water on the fire.*) Now you might as well set the table for four. I don't feel like eating tonight.

MARY: *(Anxiously.)* Not anything, Mother?

BETSY: Maybe a little milk later. But your father'll be hungry, so get supper for the rest of you first.

ANDY: *(Running back in with* PETER *at his heels.)* Mother, Mother, there's a man coming out of the woods!

BETSY: *(Alarmed.)* What kind of a man, Andy? Are you sure it's not one of our neighbors?

ANDY: Oh, no. He was queer. Little and dressed in funny clothes, all ragged. With bare feet and—

PETER: And a big pan over his head!

ANDY: And a couple of dogs following him.

BETSY: *(Relieved.)* Then I'm sure there's nothing to be afraid of. A man with dogs—

ANDY: But he was so different, Mother.

(*At this moment a strange figure appears in the doorway. The man is as the boys described him: small, middle-aged, dressed in ragged clothes with a saucepan on his head and his feet bare. It is, of course,* JOHNNY APPLESEED.)

JOHNNY: Excuse me, ma'am. I was passing by and saw a clearing where it used to be a wilderness.

BETSY: We've just been here since March. I'm afraid we're not very well settled.

JOHNNY: It's good land along the Ohio River. You'll be glad you came.

BETSY: You know this country?

JOHNNY: For miles around. I've been tramping this territory since I was a young man. There's not much of it I haven't covered.

BETSY: For mercy's sake! Here we are, asking you questions and you tired from your journey. Come on in and rest.

JOHNNY: Gladly, ma'am. I am tired and your fire looks mighty good. *(He comes in, puts his knapsack on the floor and sits in the chair opposite her.)* So you've just been here since March?

BETSY: Yes. We came out from Pennsylvania. My husband heard the land was good. He'll be home for supper soon.

JOHNNY: *(Sympathetically.)* It's not easy, settling in the wilderness with three little ones.

ANDY: I'm twelve. I helped build this house—*(Looks at his mother.)*—along with the other men.

BETSY: I should say he did. I don't know what we'd have done without him these last three months.

JOHNNY: You're not well, ma'am?

BETSY: I had pneumonia when we first came here. And I don't seem to be getting my strength back very fast. In a little while, though—

JOHNNY: You'll be all right, if you'll just take it easy and rest.

BETSY: I try. But there's so much to do in a new place like this. *(To MARY.) Mary, put another place on the table. The stranger'll stay to supper.*

JOHNNY: I'm much obliged, ma'am. But I don't want to put you out.

BETSY: It's no trouble, if you want what we're having—corn meal and milk and bread.

JOHNNY: That suits me fine. I don't eat meat. And I've some molasses here to put on the mush. *(He reaches in his knapsack and pulls out a small jug.)*

ANDY: Molasses!

BETSY: *(Gratefully.)* We haven't tasted molasses for a long time.

PETER: *(Approaching the stranger cautiously, his curiosity now gets the better of him.)* What else do you have in your bag?

BETSY: Peter! That isn't polite.

JOHNNY: That's all right, ma'am. *(To the child.)* I've got quite a lot of things in here but there might be one would interest you especially. Let's see, now. *(The three children gather around him as he pulls out various bundles and boxes. Finally he draws out a ball.)* How's that, Peter? You like a ball?

PETER: *(Delighted)*. Oh, yes! *(He grabs it and begins to toss it.)*

BETSY: Thank the stranger, Peter.

PETER: Thank you, sir. *(He runs off with the ball.)*

JOHNNY: Now I think there might be something in here for a grown-up boy. *(He searches and then finally pulls out a tool.)* Here, we are! Some pliers for your own tool box.

ANDY: Oh, thank you, sir! This is the first tool I ever had of my own.

JOHNNY: And now, let me see. *(He pulls out a corncob doll, not quite finished.)* Yes—here's a doll. Not quite finished yet but after supper I'll carve her a head and—

MARY: *(Delighted with it.)* And I'll make her a dress from the quilt scraps we had left. Oh, thank you, sir.

BETSY: You're very kind to them. When you move around the way we have, you don't have room for toys. These will be all they've got.

JOHNNY: Wait, I've got something else. *(He pulls out a small leather bag.)* For you. Herbs. It's an Indian tonic and never fails to help a body gain strength. If I could have a cup of hot water, I'd brew some into tea.

BETSY: Mary, you put the pot on to boil. Look and see if it's ready.

MARY: It is, sir. *(She gets the pot and she and JOHNNY go over to the table, stage left.)*

JOHNNY: Now we put this in—let it steep—and you give your mother a cup every night. Make it strong. *(At this moment a tall, strong young man comes in the door. It is the settler, ANDREW HOLBROOK.)*

ANDREW: Well, I'm hungry tonight, all right. We cleared that big patch of woods behind the barn. Matthew and Al helped till the last brush was cut. *(He sees the stranger suddenly and stops.)*

BETSY: Father, here's a stranger who's staying to supper.

JOHNNY: If I'm not in the way, sir.

ANDREW: Of course not. You live hereabouts?

JOHNNY: No. Can't hardly say where I live. You see, I've got apple seeds in my sack and I'm planting 'em all through this river valley.

ANDREW: Apple seeds? You're not—? You must be Johnny Appleseed!

JOHNNY: *(Bowing.)* That's what they call me.

ANDREW: *(Shaking his hand warmly.)* Why, I've heard of you. Matthew Barnes, down yonder, has settled places all across this stretch of land and he told me how you've been planting orchards since—

JOHNNY: Since I was twenty-one. And that's a good while now.

ANDREW: Well, I'm Andrew Holbrook. And this here's my wife, Betsy. And Mary and Andy and Pete.

BETSY: We've had quite a visit already.

MARY: Is the tea ready yet, Mr. Appleseed?

JOHNNY: *(Hurrying back to the table)*. Well, I should say it is. Good and strong. *(To* ANDREW.*)* Herb tea, sir, for your wife. I know a lot about medicines and tonics. Almost as much as I do about apples.

(MARY *hands her mother the cup. She drinks it and looks up in astonishment.)*

BETSY: Why, it's good. Strong and hot—

JOHNNY: You take a cup every day and in no time your strength'll come back till you're strong as a Shawnee brave.

ANDY: How do you know, Mr. Appleseed?

JOHNNY: Well, you see I know because they made me a member of the tribe.

PETER: They did? Tell us about it.

JOHNNY: After supper. It's a long, long story.

MARY: Supper's ready!

BETSY: You all sit up to the table. I'll just drink my tea here by the fire. Maybe later, I'll feel like a bite.

(The others go to the table.)

ANDREW: *(To* JOHNNY.*)* You sit down there. You boys in your regular places.

MARY: *(Bustling around as she puts the food on the table.)* Here's the corn meal. And the bread. And the milk.

ANDREW: *(Joining hands about the table.)* Let us thank God for our food and the good land that provides it.

(They bow their heads and repeat the blessing.)

ALL: "Oh, Father in Heaven, we thank thee for this food. Bless it to our use and us to thy service. For Christ's sake. Amen."

JOHNNY: This is right good, Mary. I haven't tasted any corn meal since last fall. It was in Kentucky, where I went to look over the orchards I planted on my first trip west.

ANDY: How many apple orchards have you planted, Mr. Appleseed?

JOHNNY: Land sakes, boy, I lost count twenty-five years ago. I've planted as many as I could find the place for and now they're bearing fruit the whole length and breadth of the land.

ANDREW: It's a great thing you've done for us, Johnny. There isn't a settler in the West won't thank you for the orchards you provided.

JOHNNY: I've my bag of apple seeds yonder. It was my intention to set some out for you in the morning.

BETSY: It would be good of you, Johnny. Andy, here, will help.

ANDY: We can plant them in the field behind the barn, where you said there'd be an orchard some day.

ANDREW: I never thought it would be so soon. We'll be grateful to you, Johnny.

JOHNNY: Pshaw, we'll get out there the first thing in the morning and in no time we'll have those seeds in the ground.

BETSY: I declare, Johnny Appleseed, your being here has done us all good. I feel better already, just listening to you.

JOHNNY: *(Going over to her.)* It's the tea, ma'am. A cup of that a day and you'll be up and around in no time.

BETSY: I think I'd like some milk and bread.

MARY: I'll get it for you, Mother. Here, you sit in my chair while I pour your milk.

JOHNNY: *(Standing by the fireplace as* BETSY *goes to the table.)* You've a nice family, Andrew Holbrook. And it's a nice place you've started. Now, if you wouldn't consider it rude, I think I'd just like to sit here by the fire and rest myself.

ANDREW: You make yourself at home.

JOHNNY: That's the best part of traveling. I have so many homes.

(He nods and the curtains close.)

SCENE TWO

SETTING: *The same as Scene One, thirty years later. An evening in autumn.*

STORYTELLER: Most of Johnny's adventures were like the scene we have just shown you. Of course, sometimes he did meet up with Indians in the forest and he was always running across rattlesnakes and bears. But Johnny—well, he was a peaceful man and he always seemed to settle his differences without a fight.

The next scene is thirty years later in the same place. Johnny is an old man now. The Holbrooks are middle-aged and their children are all grown up. It's harvest time and all the neighbors are gathering for a party.

(The STORYTELLER *leaves as the curtains open on the second scene. The cabin is now well furnished and comfortable.* BETSY HOLBROOK *is putting the finishing touches on the table which has been pushed back against the right wall.* ANDREW *is building a fire.)*

ANDREW: Well, Mother, it's thirty years now we've lived in this place.

BETSY: They've been good years, too, Andrew. Once we got the land cleared and the first crops in, we've had good luck.

ANDREW: It's the Lord's blessing, Mother, not luck.

BETSY: You know, I always feel it started with little Johnny Appleseed. His coming by when we needed help most seemed like the turning point. From then on, things seemed to get better.

ANDREW: That orchard he planted is the best for miles around. It's too bad he never got back this way to see how it turned out.

BETSY: Nobody's heard of him for a long time, either. I wonder if he's still alive?

ANDREW: We'd have heard about it if he wasn't. Johnny Appleseed may have been a little man but he was a strong one all the same. It would be hard to find a man that had done more for others—and expected less in return.

BETSY: There's someone at the door, Andrew. Let them in.

(ANDREW goes to the door. Several neighbors are standing there.)

ANDREW: Good evening, neighbors. Welcome!

FIRST MAN: It's a cold night out. Might be the first frost.

FIRST WOMAN: Your fire feels good!

JOE: I hope you've got a lot of corn to husk! I feel just like husking.

SECOND MAN: Hoping you'll get a red ear, Joe?

THIRD MAN: *(As they all laugh at* JOE.*)* I remember how you helped us, Andrew Holbrook, when we moved out here five years ago. Not much of a harvest that winter.

(There is another knock on the door and ANDREW *goes to open it.)*

ANDREW: Welcome, neighbors. Did you see Andy on the way?

FOURTH MAN: He's down the road a piece. He'll be along.

THIRD WOMAN: How does it seem, Betsy, to have your last young one married and gone?

BETSY: Kind of quiet. It wasn't so bad when Mary and Andy left because they settled so close to home. But Peter's had Oregon on his mind for a long time. There was no talking him out of it.

FIRST MAN: I guess your folks couldn't talk you out of Ohio thirty years ago.

BETSY: Oregon seems so far away—

FIRST MAN: No farther'n this did from Philadelphia. When you got pioneering in your blood, distance don't make much difference.

(The door opens and in come ANDY *and* MARY *with their families.)*

ANDY: Hello, Mother. Hello, Father. Think we were never coming? *(As he takes off his coat.)* It wouldn't seem right not to have a harvest party—but it's sure funny without Peter!

SECOND WOMAN: You just keep still about your brother, Andy. You're only making your mother feel bad. Peter's a smart lad and this country's developing faster'n you and I can count to ten. He'll be back here with a fortune in his pocket before you know it.

THIRD MAN: What about the husking, Andy? The sooner we get to that, the sooner we dance!

ANDREW: There won't be much tonight. This is just the excuse for a party. *(He indicates the baskets of corn on the hearth.)* Here it is. And here's the baskets to put it in.

FIRST MAN: Well, I've started. *(He begins to husk furiously and the others soon join in.)* What about a song while we work?

SECOND WOMAN: That's a good idea. You start, Joe.

JOE: Well—*(He thinks a moment, then begins "Down in the Valley." The others join in.)*

THIRD MAN: *(As they finish it.)* Well, we're getting along fine, Joe. Let's keep it up. Start us another.

(JOE begins "The Little Mohee" or another American folk song. All join in, working rapidly as they sing.)

ANDREW: What do you say we let the corn husking go a spell and stretch our legs in a dance? You got your fiddle with you, haven't you, Al?

(AL, an old man, steps up with his fiddle. If no one on stage can play a fiddle, a record or piano music off stage can easily be substituted. The folk dance begins and soon all are dancing briskly to the music. There is general clapping when it is over. At that moment the door opens and a very small, very old man peers in. It is JOHNNY APPLESEED.)

JOHNNY: Sounds like a celebration—*(They all stop talking as they stare at him.)* I hope I'm not intruding—

AL: Well, I'll be switched! If it isn't Johnny Appleseed!

JOHNNY: *(Grinning and bowing.)* At your service.

ANDREW: We were talking about you only tonight. Wondering where you were and wishing you'd come this way again.

(All the people gather around him now, asking him questions and greeting him warmly.)

ANDREW: Before we wear poor Johnny out with answering questions, suppose we give him a chair and something to eat?

BETSY: We've more to offer you tonight than bread and milk. There's a whole supper on the table and pies made from the apples in our orchard.

JOHNNY: Apple pies? I'd like a piece.

BETSY: I'll cut you one. Everybody else, come up and help yourselves.

(Some stay with JOHNNY while others swarm about the table, filling their plates.)

JOHNNY: *(Tasting the pie.)* It's good, all right. So those orchards grew? I never got back this way to see 'em.

ANDREW: I should say they have. That last row you put in, though, was the best. Those apples were too good to make into pies. I've got a basket of 'em here. Nothing like 'em anywhere around. Taste one—

(JOHNNY takes one and so do several of the others.)

ALL: *(Ad lib their delight in the apples.)* What kind are they? Best I've ever eaten! Etc.

JOHNNY: Say, that's a jim-dandy!

ANDREW: What kind is it, Johnny? It's different from all the rest.

JOHNNY: I don't know. I thought I knew all the apples that grow but this one is different.

FIRST MAN: It ought to have a name —

SECOND MAN: What about calling it the "Appleseed Apple"?

THIRD MAN: That don't sound right.

(All think hard. Suddenly ANDREW *has an idea.)*

ANDREW: I have it! Jonathan Chapman. The perfect name. We'll call it the "Jonathan Apple."

ALL: *(Slowly at first.)* The "Jonathan Apple." *(More sure of it.)* The "Jonathan Apple." *(And then with a shout.)* The "Jonathan Apple"!

JOHNNY: I'm much obliged for the honor. I've called myself after the apples all these years but I never thought one would be called after me.

(The curtains close and the STORYTELLER *steps forward.)*

STORYTELLER: And that's how the Jonathan Apple got its name. That wasn't Johnny's last trip across the country but it was one of the last. He'd been working sixty years to bring apples to Americans and they say that when he finally died, it was in an apple orchard. Lots of places from New York State to Indiana have claimed to be his final resting place. But the most important thing is not where he died but what they put on his tombstone down in Ohio: "Johnny Appleseed, Soldier of Peace. He went about doing good." Sometimes that takes more courage than fighting. If that's so, then Johnny was a hero and a giant.

PRODUCTION NOTES

CHARACTERS

Eleven boys; five girls; extras.

COSTUMES

The men and boys wear simple settler's garments consisting of denim pants and plain or plaid shirts. The women and girls wear bodice dresses with full skirts. They may add aprons and shawls for variation. Johnny Appleseed wears eccentric clothing, which must be ragged. A pan on his head and bare feet distinguish him as a character from everyone else.

PROPERTIES

Broom; dishes; pitcher; kindling box; kettle; knapsack; corncob doll; ball; pliers; small bag of herbs; bag of seeds; knife; pots and pans; bread, corn meal, and milk; bushel baskets of corn; food for the party; basket of red apples; pie; fiddle.

SETTING

Fireplace; table; five or six chairs or a bench; cupboard; chest (not essential to action); details to furnish room more completely in Scene Two.

MUSIC

Record or piano for dance in Scene Two if there is no one who can play the fiddle.

Summary

Although the study of dramatic structure belongs to the upper rather than the lower grades, it is a part of playmaking on any level. The advancement of plot and the development of character depend on a structure of some sort. Younger players, unfamiliar with theatre conventions, often invent highly imaginative forms and this is not to be discouraged. The main thing to keep in mind is that structure is necessary to create order out of the profusion of ideas that a lively group offers. Breaking a story into scenes, finding the climax, listing the necessary characters, seeing where additional characters can be added or where extraneous material can be cut, all develop critical judgment and a sense of organization in young players.

Whether performing or writing, the student needs boundaries within which to work. Too rigid a boundary stifles creativity whereas its lack often causes good ideas to become dissipated. Form and content are of equal importance; creative drama offers a superb opportunity to shape material into a form that communicates with the spectator as well as expresses the thoughts and feelings of the player.

The dramatization of a favorite story, on the other hand, makes different demands on the group and is, in many respects, much easier to write than an original play. First, there is a plot that supplies the basic structure. Characters are clearly defined but must be given appropriate dialogue. In a play, dialogue serves three major functions: to describe the characters, to further the action, and to help show the time, place, and circumstances in which the story takes place. Because the players do not have to create an original narrative, they can focus their attention on characterization and believable dialogue. Time spent on improvisation before the actual writing is time well spent; then, when the group is ready to write the play, it will have a much clearer idea of what to include in each scene and how the characters would respond in the light of their circumstances, interpersonal relationships, and the period in which they lived.

Often new characters have to be added to flesh out parts of the story that the author has told through simple exposition. Sometimes characters and scenes need to be cut, if the plot is too long or too complicated for dramatic presentation. When such additions or deletions have to be made, young players need our help. Children are usually quick to find solutions, however, when a discussion is held as to how best to solve the problems. Questions such as "how do we know that . . ." or "what can we do to show . . ." or "can we think of a way to explain . . ." will elicit suggestions.

Whereas there are many values in the writing of an original script, most teachers find it more satisfactory to start with an adaptation of a well-known story. The players have the experience of working with a good piece of literature and from it will be better able to handle the additional problems that a totally original project presents, if or when they want to try one. Again, it must be emphasized that creative drama is participant centered. Product can never be totally separated from process, however; therefore, when a class is ready for the next step—the writing of a play or dramatization of a story for an audience—some knowledge of dramatic structure is necessary. This knowledge can be learned through improvisation or through the development of a script or, ideally, through a combination of both.

9

Building Plays from Stories

"The Little Match Girl," written and directed by Xan S. Johnson, University of Utah

*W*hen the group has had some experience with pantomime and improvisation, it will be ready to attempt to act a story. Groups of all ages welcome this next step and often have suggestions of their own to offer regarding favorite stories or material from other classes that they want to dramatize. Regardless of how well they may know the story, there is still some preliminary work to be done before improvisation begins. The teacher, well acquainted with the group by this time, knows the kind of material that will have an appeal and present the fewest difficulties. Success is important to future work, and the leader will want to select a story that he or she is relatively sure the group can handle.

There is a wealth of good literature readily available that both group and leader can enjoy and find worthy of their efforts. The stories and poems included in this and following chapters are illustrative of the kinds of material groups of all ages have used successfully. Suggestions are offered as to ways in which material may be presented and handled. It should not be inferred that these are the only or even the best ways of using the material; they are merely illustrations of the thinking done by some groups.

Folktales, legends, and fables are recommended material for use on all levels, though different age groups will view them according to their own maturity and experience. For younger children, stories should be simplified in the telling, whereas in working with older children, greater emphasis can be given to characterization. Meanings and insights come with experience as well as age; hence a really good story spans many age levels.

When the teacher has decided upon an appropriate story, she must decide whether it is better told or read. In general, telling the story is preferable because it establishes a closer rapport with the audience and gives the leader a chance to observe the listeners' responses and to clarify, as he or she goes along, any points that appear to puzzle them. This means that the teacher must be thoroughly familiar with the material; in fact, the beginning teacher will do well to practice telling the story aloud before presenting it to the group. This will add to the teacher's own self-confidence and help him or her develop greater variety and color in the presentation. A good voice and clear diction are certainly assets, but even more important is the teacher's ability to become involved in the material so that the story comes alive to the listeners. The teacher will probably find it easier to establish contact if he or she sits down, with the audience gathered closely around.

Experience in telling stories helps the teacher to avoid pitfalls such as forgetting parts and having to return to them out of sequence. The teacher will soon learn to proceed in order, holding the climax until the end, including as many details as the listeners are able to handle and as are necessary to the story. The teacher will avoid condescension and will adapt his or her vocabulary to the age and background of the group, taking advantage, at the same time, of opportunities to introduce new words and explain ideas that are strange or foreign. With a little practice, most leaders can develop an effective storytelling technique that stimulates enthusiasm for dramatization.

After the story has been told, and all questions answered, the children are ready to begin planning how they will handle it. A discussion should include a review of the plot and descriptions of the characters. When the leader feels that the group has the details well in mind, he or she will suggest that they try playing it. Asking for volunteers is a good way of starting: this gives the stronger ones a chance to try it first and the more timid ones an opportunity to become better acquainted with it before taking their turns. Casting is done on a voluntary basis the first two or three times. Later, the leader may suggest that other children try various parts. For instance, he or she might say, "Lynne hasn't had a chance yet. How would you like to try the princess this time, Lynne?" Or, "John has been the cobbler. Let's give Alan a chance to play it. And you, John, be one of the townsfolk." Or, "I know David has a strong voice. How about letting him be the giant?"

In other words, it is the development of each participant that concerns us. Later, when the group is ready to play the story for the last time, the leader might suggest those children who have brought the greatest reality to each part, but this is as close as we come to type casting.

The situation may be played any number of times, but the replaying should not be interpreted as rehearsal. It is hoped that with each playing the story will gain in substance and depth, that there will be deeper insights, and that the participants will develop greater freedom and self-confidence. The discussions preceding and following each playing are important aspects of creative dramatics, for it is during these periods that some of the most creative thinking takes place. Some questions that might precede the first playing are:

1. What do we want to tell?
2. Who are the people?
3. What are these people really like?
4. What are they doing when we first meet them?
5. Where does the first scene take place?
6. What kind of a house do they live in?

After the scene has been played once, more specific questions can guide the discussion. They might be:

1. Did they tell the story?
2. What did you like about the opening scene?
3. Did the people show that they were excited? (Angry, unhappy, etc.)
4. When we play it again, can you think of anything that would improve it?
5. Was anything important left out?

Throughout a year, there are often delightful results, and both the leader and group may honestly wish to share them with others. There is no reason why this should not be done, provided public performance was not the original intention. More often, however, the initial results will be crude and superficial. Dialogue will be scanty, despite the most careful planning. To the experienced leader, this does not represent failure. It is an early stage in the development of the group and may, at that point, indicate real progress. Acceptance of the effort, therefore, does not mean that the leader is satisfied to remain at this level but, rather, that he or she recognizes the efforts that have been made and is aware of the values to those who have taken part. As the leader works with the group, he or she will become more selective but in the beginning will accept all ideas simply because they have been offered. It is important for every member to feel that his or her ideas are worthy of consideration. In time, even eight- and nine-year-olds will learn to distinguish between contributions that advance the play and those that distract or have little to do with it.

The following group of stories have been chosen for inclusion here because of their simplicity. Most children are familiar with them and like them and need only to be refreshed as to the details. The first, *Caps for Sale,* is popular with younger children but equally interesting to older children, and even adults, because of the underlying theme. Very young children enjoy being monkeys and like to take turns acting the Peddler. Older children, however, quickly see a parallel between human behavior and the behavior of monkeys, hence find in this simple tale a meaning worthy of their thought and effort. Although *Caps for Sale,* or *The Peddler and His Caps,* is very well known, a brief synopsis of the story is included.

Caps For Sale

There was once a little old man who made caps. All year long he worked at them: red caps, pink caps, yellow caps, blue, green, and purple caps, caps with feathers and caps without. Every so often, when he had made a large enough number of caps to sell, he would put them in his pack and take them around to the villages. This particular morning he decided that he had plenty of caps to peddle, and since it was a very fine summer day, he took himself off. His cries of "Caps for sale" roused the townsfolk, and soon many of them were trying on caps and selecting the ones they wanted to buy. Butchers, bakers, shoemakers, mothers, children, and even the mayor himself, gathered around the little Peddler, trying on caps and admiring their appearances. Finally, the mayor, who had found nothing to his liking, took off his cap and tossed it back to the Peddler, suggesting that he come again some other day. "Not today, Peddler. Come back another time."

Reluctantly, all of the townsfolk followed his example, echoing the mayor's words that he return another day. Realizing that he could sell no caps in this village, the little Peddler departed. Before long, he passed by the edge of a woods and, feeling very sleepy, decided to lie down and rest. Soon, however, he fell fast asleep, his hats lying on the grass beside him. Now it happened that this part of the woods was inhabited by a band of monkeys. Monkeys are curious little fellows, and finding the Peddler asleep

Children in Hokulani School playing the story of "Caps for Sale." *(Courtesy of Tamara Hunt, University of Hawaii at Manoa.)*

under a tree, they decided to investigate the contents of his pack. First one, then another, cautiously approached. When they saw that the Peddler was wearing a cap on his head, the monkeys tried the caps on their own little heads. Then they scampered a distance away, chattering excitedly, for they were very much pleased with themselves. The sound of the chattering soon awakened the Peddler. He reached for his pack and was astonished to find it empty. Greatly puzzled, he looked about him to see where the caps might have gone. Suddenly he saw the monkeys. He called to them, pleasantly at first, and asked them to give back his caps. They only chattered, "Chee, chee, chee," pleasantly, in reply.

Then he shook his fist at them and demanded his caps, but they just shook their fists back. Angrily he stamped his foot at them but they only stamped their little monkey feet at him in return. He begged, and they begged; he moved a few steps away, and they moved a few steps away. Suddenly it occurred to him that the monkeys were doing everything he did. With a sweeping gesture, he removed his own cap and tossed it to the ground at his feet. Immediately all of the monkeys removed their caps and threw them down to the Peddler. He gathered his caps up as quickly as possible, then made a low bow and thanked the monkeys for returning them. Chattering happily, the monkeys also bowed; each was pleased with the trick he thought he had played on the other.

After telling the story, the leader will be wise to review the plot to make certain that it is clearly understood. From here on, there are many ways of proceeding. The leader may ask where the story begins and how many scenes the group sees in it. They may suggest two, three, four, or even five, although they usually come to the conclusion that three main scenes are necessary. They are:

1. The Peddler starts out on his travels.
2. He arrives in the village.
3. He stops to rest in the forest.

Some groups imagine a road running all around the room, with the three scenes laid in different areas. This enables the Peddler to move from one place to another and gives him an opportunity to talk to himself as he walks along. Since no scenery is used in creative dramatics, such an arrangement is perfectly feasible. Incidentally, one advantage of a large room in dramatizing this story is the amount of freedom it provides the players: they are not limited by the rows of seats or traditional stage area. When playing in an auditorium, however, the succession of scenes will follow a more conventional pattern, unless there is an apron (area in front of the curtain) to accommodate some of the action.

In discussing how the Peddler's occupation might be introduced, one group may suggest that he have a wife with whom he can talk over his plans for the day at breakfast. Another group may give him a helper; another, a son; and still another may insist that he lives alone and thus have him talk to himself.

Whether or not his trip down the road is considered a separate scene depends on the importance the group attaches to it, but the next major scene is certainly the village in which the Peddler attempts to sell his caps. One of the advantages of a story of this sort is the opportunity for characterization afforded by the villagers. As any number of villagers may be included, there is an opportunity for many children to take part. The mayor is always a favorite, though other delightful characters may be created; a shoemaker, a mother, a small boy, a farmer, a young girl, and a milliner are examples. The playing of this scene will be long or short, depending upon the characterizations and the fun the children have with it. Again, if a road is used to suggest the Peddler's travels, he will move along to a place designated as a part of the forest. If the group is small, the same children who were villagers can be monkeys. If the group is large, however, there is ample opportunity for others to play the monkeys. One of the best features of this particular story is the flexibility of the cast: whatever its size, the entire group can take part in it.

Regardless of age, children always respond to the monkeys, and the activity demanded by their antics is conducive to bodily freedom. There is such great opportunity for pantomime in the final scene that the leader might do well to begin with it, as a means of relaxing the group. By the time all have been monkeys, they are better prepared to begin on the story.

In this, and, indeed, in any story selected for dramatization, it is a good idea to work on small portions first rather than to attempt the entire story at once. No matter how well the children may know the material, it is another thing to improvise the scenes. Therefore, working on short bits, not necessarily in sequence, makes for more successful playing. In this respect, it is similar to rehearsing a play: the director does not attempt to run through the complete script until he or she has rehearsed each individual scene.

A word is in order here regarding the use of folk and fairy tales in creative drama. At one time they were the exclusive fare for dramatization and children's theatre. The reaction against them was based in part on a need for more diversified material and contemporary themes and in part on a question of whether modern children were interested in fantasy. Bruno Bettelheim's book *The Uses of Enchantment* has caused us to take a second look at traditional material. Yes, we do want to introduce new stories, but in seeking them we must take care not to discard the rich resources of the past. The psychological values of the fairy tale and the cultural insights offered by folk tales are important aspects of a child's experience. For this reason, as well as for the imaginative possibilities they offer, a number of folk and fairy tales are included in this and the next chapter. It is further hoped that the leader, in planning a unit or season, will offer material from both the old and the new, the fantastic and the real, the amusing and the serious. Variety and quality capture and hold the interest. Fantasy is not necessarily escape from reality; it can also be an instrument for the analysis of reality.

The Fir Tree Who Wanted Leaves

The German tale of the little fir tree who wanted leaves is a good choice for young children. Although it concerns an individual, it can be played by the group. No dialogue is necessary, but it may be added if and when the children want to use words. Music to create mood and suggest the changes will help the children play the story.

There was once a little fir tree who grew tired of his needles and wanted leaves like the other trees in the forest. One day, while he was complaining, a voice answered him, asking what kind of leaves he would like. "Oh, green leaves like the other trees," said the little fir. "I want leaves that are green in summer and change to red in the fall."

No sooner had he asked for them, than his needles changed into smooth, bright green leaves. The little fir tree thought he looked very fine indeed. All that morning he moved his branches and admired his appearance. Then, about noon, along came some goats. Seeing the fresh green leaves, they lifted their heads and greedily began to eat them. The poor little tree could do nothing to stop them, and soon all his leaves were gone.

He felt very sad. Finally he said, "I wish I had glass leaves. They would be pretty and no one would want to eat them."

Again, no sooner had he said the words than he found himself covered with sparkling glass. He was greatly pleased. "These leaves are much better than the others."

He moved his branches and watched them sparkle in the sunshine. About noon, however, a storm came up. The wind blew and the leaves hit against each other. They were so brittle that as the storm grew worse, all the glass was broken and fell to the ground.

The little fir was discouraged but not for long. "I know," he said, "I'd like gold leaves. They will sparkle, but the goats will not eat them and they cannot break."

Suddenly he was covered with yellow gold that gleamed in the sunlight. Surely he was the most beautiful tree in the forest! All day long he admired his leaves. Then, as night fell, he saw some robbers approaching. When they saw the little fir tree, they could hardly believe their eyes. "A gold tree," they said, "there's enough gold here to last us the rest of our lives!"

They began picking off the leaves and putting them in sacks on their backs. In no time at all, every leaf was gone. The little tree stood cold and miserable in the forest.

"I wish," he began, "I wish I had my needles back again. They were the best of all."

Quick as a flash his branches were covered with long, dark green needles. And he never wished for leaves again.

> *The theme of dissatisfaction with one's lot runs through folklore, and it is understood by young children. There are many ways in which this particular story can be handled. If the group is small, it can be played by individuals. Better, however, is group playing with some children being the leaves and others the goats, the wind, and the robbers. In this way the imagination is stretched as the players experiment with different ways to show how leaves, glass, and gold might look and move.*
>
> *The story lends itself to movement as well as to improvisation and offers rich possibilities for discussion and expressive playing.*

Fables are popular with some groups, though the obvious moral does not appeal to others. One advantage of a fable is its brevity. There is action as well as a quick and satisfying ending. There is little opportunity for character development, however, though some groups will fill in the plot with delightful and imaginative dialogue.

THE TORTOISE AND THE HARE

There was once a Hare who was forever boasting of his great speed. In fact, whenever more than two animals gathered together in the forest, he would appear and then take the opportunity of telling them that he could outstrip the best of them. Stretching his long legs proudly, he would declare, "No one has ever beaten me. When I race at full speed, there is no one who can pass me."

The other animals said nothing, for there was no one who wished to dispute him. One day, the Tortoise, who had been listening quietly, replied, "I accept your challenge. I will race you."

"That is a good joke," laughed the Hare. "I could go to the goalpost and back before you had passed the first marker."

"Save your breath until you've won," said the Tortoise. "I'm willing to race you."

The other animals, who were mighty tired of listening to the Hare's boasts, were only too glad to hear someone speak up, though they secretly wished it had been an animal with a greater chance of winning. Nevertheless, they cheered the little Tortoise on and helped draw up a course. Then they lined up on each side and the Cock called the start of the race: 1 — 2 — 3 — GO!

The Hare was gone and out of sight in a flash as his white cottontail disappeared through the bushes. The Tortoise kept his eyes straight ahead and never varied his pace. Presently, the Hare returned and danced around him, laughing at his slow progress. The Tortoise didn't say a word. Then, to show his scorn for the Tortoise he lay down under a tree. He yawned, shut his eyes, and finally curled up and took his afternoon nap. The Tortoise only smiled and plodded on. After a while, the Hare awoke from his sleep. He opened his eyes just in time to see the Tortoise crawl past the winning post. As fast as he could make his legs go, he could not get there in time to save the race. The Tortoise, slow as he was, had crawled steadily forward while the Hare had spent his time running in circles and taking a nap. "I've learned a lesson today," said the Hare, ashamed of himself for having made so much fun of his opponent. "It's hard work, and not speed, that wins the race."

> *After the leader has told the fable, there is a good opportunity for total group participation: all can be hares and then tortoises. Younger children particularly enjoy the physical movement of this story. After some preliminary pantomime, it can be played in its entirety, since it is so short. A large room lends itself to the race, which may be run in a wide circle or in repeated circling of the space. Unless the group is very large, all may take turns playing the two parts, with the rest participating as the other animals watching the contest. This is a highly satisfying story for use in a single period or as a change from a more ambitious undertaking. Discussion brings out the moral, which children of ages eight to ten comprehend easily.*

The Sun and the Wind and *The Country Mouse and the City Mouse* are favorite fables with many children. They also provide excellent opportunities for pantomime, as well as ideas for discussion. A group of fables, incidentally, makes a good program without taxing either teacher or players.

The stories that follow are longer than the Aesop fables, but they have the same advantages of a simple story line based on an amusing or intriguing idea. When a group has mastered the fable, it is ready to take on a longer and more detailed story. The following were selected for characterization, theme, ethnic background, and opportunities offered for group discussion.

THE TWO FOOLISH CATS

> *The following fable comes from Japan. It can be enjoyed by all ages, although I have found it to have particular appeal for younger children. The idea of fair play is well understood by even the youngest, and the trickster is*

always a popular character. The simplicity of the story precludes depth so far as character study is concerned, but there is a lesson in it if the leader wants to pursue it. "The Two Foolish Cats" *is fun and, for that reason alone, worth doing.*

There were once two cats who lived together in peace and harmony. They were good friends, sharing food and shelter. One day, however, each of them came upon a fresh, sweet rice cake on a path leading into a woods. Delighted with their discoveries, they showed their cakes to each other, comparing them for size and freshness. Now it happened that the larger of the two cats had picked up the smaller rice cake. "This is not fair," he said, "I am larger than you and therefore I should have the larger cake. Come, let us trade."

But the smaller cat refused. "No, I am smaller than you and I need more food so I can grow to your size. I wouldn't think of trading."

Well, this led to an argument, each cat insisting that he should have the larger of the two cakes. They accused each other of greediness and as they grew angrier they began to growl and spit. The argument went on for some time, neither one willing to give in to the other. Finally the bigger cat said, "Let us stop. We will get nowhere fighting like this. Let us go find the wise monkey who lives in the forest. If we ask him to divide our cakes equally, we shall each have our fair share and our argument will be over."

The smaller cat agreed, for he was hungry and wanted to eat his cake. So the two took themselves off to the forest to find the wise monkey. They looked in the bushes and tree tops, around rocks and behind the trunks of the trees, until at last they found him. They explained what they wanted but the old monkey replied that he must hear each side of the argument. The bigger cat began. Then the wise monkey said, "Stop. Let me hear the other."

The smaller cat spoke up. When he had finished, the old monkey nodded his head gravely. "I think I can solve your problem. Give me the rice cakes."

The cats handed them over eagerly. The monkey took one in each hand and weighed them with care. "Yes," he said, "this one is heavier. Let me take a bite out of it. Then they will be the same size."

But he took a very big bite and what had been the larger cake now became the smaller. "Dear, dear," said the monkey, "I shall have to take a bite out of *this* cake to even things up."

As you can imagine, he again took a large bite and the first cake became the larger. Paying no attention to the cats, who were anxiously watching their cakes disappear, the old monkey went from one to the other until both cakes were gone.

"Well," he said, "You asked me to solve your problem and I have done it. Without the cakes you have nothing to quarrel about." Whereupon he went off, leaving the two cats hungry and feeling very foolish indeed. But never did they quarrel again!

A discussion of greed and fair play is bound to follow. A small group will be able to play all three parts because of the brevity of the story. After playing and replaying the monkey, most children are ready to talk about his way of handling the problem. The humor must not be sacrificed for the moral, however; the value of the fable is its ability to convey a lesson in a humorous anecdote, usually told through animals.

DARBY AND JOAN

This story appeals to both boys and girls and is easy to play in a small area. There are only three characters, but the story is so short that, unless a group is large, every boy and girl may have a chance to try one of the parts.

Have you ever seen a little house about the size of a birdhouse, with two doors in front marked "Fair" and "Rain"? And have you ever noticed that a little woman stands in the doorway marked "Fair," and a little man in the doorway marked "Rain"? And, depending on the weather, that one is always out while the other is in? Well, this little man and woman are known as Darby and Joan, and the following story is told of how they came to be there.

Many years ago Darby and Joan lived happily in a little cottage together. As time went on, however, they began to quarrel. Regardless of how peaceably the day had begun, before long they were disagreeing and finding fault with one another. And so a spell was put on them: from that day forth, one must be out while the other was in, depending on the weather. Our story begins many years later. The day has been fair but the weather is beginning to change, and Darby is about to come out, allowing Joan to go inside and finish her housework. As they talk together, not seeing each other, they regret the quarreling that led to their punishment.

"How I wish I could see you, Joan. Do you realize it has been ten years since we sat down at the table together?"

"I know, Darby. I'm sure if we could be released from this spell, we should never quarrel again."

"Imagine not seeing one's own wife for ten years. It was too cruel a punishment."

As they are talking together, Darby notices someone approaching the cottage. He calls out, "It's beginning to rain. Won't you stop and rest here for a bit?"

The stranger, who is a Fairy in disguise, comes to the doorway and asks Darby why it is he is standing out in the rain while his wife stays in the house. He explains and sighs over their misfortune. The Fairy then tells him who she is and offers to release them from their spell, but only on one condition: that they never quarrel again. They agree joyfully and the Fairy goes off; but not without warning them that if they do quarrel, they will be put under the spell again, and this time it will be forever.

The old couple can scarcely believe their good fortune as they move their arms and legs stiffly and venture outside together. The rain is clearing, and they decide to have supper in front of the cottage. Darby brings out the table and chairs while Joan gets the food. Scarcely have they sat down to eat, however, when Darby criticizes the way Joan slices the bread. Joan replies with annoyance that if he objects, he can cut it himself. Furthermore, she notices that he is wearing his hat at the table. Before they know it, they are quarreling furiously.

Suddenly, the Fairy appears. The old people are stricken. They beg the Fairy for one more chance to try getting along, but she replies, "It is too late. You knew the condition and should have thought of the consequences."

Darby and Joan feel the spell coming on, and slowly move back into their old positions. The Fairy disappears with the old couple once more back in their doorways marked "Fair" and "Rain."

Children of all ages enjoy this story and have a grand time with the quarrel. First, playing the puppetlike figures while under a spell is a good pantomime for the entire group. Release from the spell gives practice in making the transition from a stiff, controlled stance to free movement. After all have tried it in pantomime, they will be ready to add dialogue. Darby and Joan *is a delightful little story that calls for strong feeling and changes of mood.*

The Peasant Who Dined with a Lord
A Ukrainian Folk Tale

Once in a small Ukrainian village there was a rich lord who would have nothing to do with the common folk. As a matter of fact, he was so proud and so greedy that he had little to do with anyone, save his servants. He had no family, and this gave rise to curiosity on the part of the villagers. Whenever a group of them gathered, their conversation was apt to be about the great lord: who had seen him pass by in his carriage, what he looked like, what clothing he wore. Some, who had never seen him, wondered what his servants had bought in the market that day.

One afternoon a poor peasant, overhearing one of these conversations, said laughingly, "Why spend time asking questions? You can find out by simply climbing over the wall and looking into the kitchen."

"When have you done that?" demanded one of the old men, who had dwelt in the village longer than any of the rest of them.

"Yes," said the others, "have you been inside those gates? Has the master asked you to dinner?"

The group laughed uproariously at the young peasant in his ragged clothes, but he answered impudently, "I could dine with him before the week is out, if I wished."

"Dine with a lord? You?" said one of them; then they all laughed again. "Why, if you so much as put one foot inside the courtyard in those clothes, he would have you thrown off the place!"

"Will you make a bargain with me?" asked the young peasant.

All nodded vigorously in agreement.

"Very well. If I dine with him, then will you each give me a sack of your best wheat and a bullock? If I do not dine with him, I will be your servant and do everything that you ask for one month."

All agreed to the bargain, certain that they would get the better of it. Whereupon the young man walked boldly into the courtyard of the great lord. As had been predicted, he was met at the gate by two servants, who started to chase him out. "Wait a minute," said the peasant. "I have good news for your master, but I can tell it only to him."

The lord, being told of the promised message, was curious about it, and asked that the bearer of good news be shown into the house. The peasant said that what he had to say must be said in private, so the lord ordered his servants to leave. "Now, what is it that is meant for my ears alone?"

"What," whispered the young man, looking cautiously about, "is the cost of a piece of gold the size of a horse's head?"

The lord could not believe his ears and asked that the question be repeated. He was sure that the peasant must have found a great treasure. He tried to discover why such a poor man would want to know the value of so much gold. But the peasant, who was far more clever than he appeared, simply said that if the lord did not wish to tell him, he would be on his way and find someone else who would. The lord, afraid that a great treasure was about to slip out of reach, said, "Why not stay and have dinner with me? We can talk while we eat."

He called his servants and ordered them to bring bread, fruit, meat, and cheese as quickly as possible. Then the two sat down at the table together. When they had eaten their fill, the lord said, "And now, tell me where is your gold the size of a horse's head?"

"I have no gold," replied the young man.

"You have no gold?" the lord repeated after him. "Then why did you ask what it was worth?"

"I just wanted to know, my lord. And it was a kind of bet."

The lord was very angry when he heard this, and he ordered the peasant out of the house.

"Peter Pan"—The Lost Children shoot down Wendy with bows and arrows. *(Empire State Institute for the Performing Arts. Courtesy of Patricia Snyder. Photograph by Tim Raab, Northern Photo.)*

"I am not as stupid as you think me," said the young man, courteously. "I have had a very good dinner and I have won a bet besides. Now I must go and claim my sacks of wheat and my bullocks."

And bowing low, the clever peasant left, chuckling all the while at the way he had outwitted both the villagers and the lord.

Folk tales telling of cleverness, especially on the part of ones who are young and poor, are popular with most people. Children love the double trick played in this story and are always eager to take turns being the peasant. Although there are only two major roles as the story is told, there is no reason why the villagers cannot be fleshed out, giving each of them his own motives and personal qualities.

The story can be played just as it is, or additional scenes can be added. It can lead to deeper character analysis or a study of the kind of society that is represented by the master and the peasants. Children are quick to detect greed, vanity, arrogance, and scorn, and they like to participate in a discussion of what they are and how they are found in our lives today. The humor amuses them because it functions on two levels.

LITTLE BURNT-FACE
(Native American—Micmac)
RETOLD BY FRANCES J. OLCOTT

This folk tale is an Indian version of Cinderella, but it is also a fascinating study of masks, or appearances. The Great Chief, who is a god, wears the mask of invisibility to everyone but Little Burnt-Face, who is pure of heart. Scarred and beaten by her envious sisters, she wears the mask of ugliness. When the god becomes visible to her, she is restored to her original beauty. In one version of this story the girl is called Little Scar-Face. Through the healing power of love, she is so transformed that she becomes known as Little Star-Face.

Once upon a time, in a large Indian village on the border of a lake, there lived an old man who was a widower. He had three daughters. The eldest was jealous, cruel, and ugly; the second was vain; but the youngest of all was very gentle and lovely.

Now, when the father was out hunting in the forest, the eldest daughter used to beat the youngest girl, and burn her face with hot coals; yes, and even scar her pretty body. So the people called her "Little Burnt-Face."

When the father came home from hunting he would ask why she was so scarred, and the eldest would answer quickly: "She is a good-for-nothing! She was forbidden to go near the fire, and she disobeyed and fell in." Then the father would scold Little Burnt-Face and she would creep away crying to bed.

By the lake, at the end of the village, there was a beautiful wigwam. And in that wigwam lived a Great Chief and his sister. The Great Chief was invisible; no one had ever seen him but his sister. He brought her many deer and supplied her with good things to eat from the forest and lake, and with the finest blankets and garments. And when visitors came all they ever saw of the Chief were his moccasins; for when he took them off they became visible, and his sister hung them up.

Now, one Spring, his sister made known that her brother, the Great Chief, would marry any girl who could see him.

Then all the girls from the village—except Little Burnt-Face and her sisters—and all the girls for miles around hastened to the wigwam, and walked along the shore of the lake with his sister.

And his sister asked the girls, "Do you see my brother?"

And some of them said, "No"; but most of them answered, "Yes."

Then his sister asked, "Of what is his shoulder-strap made?"

And the girls said, "Of a strip of rawhide."

"And with what does he draw his sled?" asked his sister.

And they replied, "With a green withe."

Then she knew that they had not seen him at all, and said quietly, "Let us go to the wigwam."

So to the wigwam they went, and when they entered, his sister told them not to take the seat next to the door, for that was where her brother sat.

Then they helped his sister to cook the supper, for they were very curious to see the Great Chief eat. When all was ready, the food disappeared, and the brother took off his moccasins, and his sister hung them up. But they never saw the Chief, though many of them stayed all night.

One day Little Burnt-Face's two sisters put on their finest blankets and brightest strings of beads, and plaited their hair beautifully, and slipped embroidered moccasins on their feet. Then they started out to see the Great Chief.

As soon as they were gone, Little Burnt-Face made herself a dress of white birch-bark, and a cap and leggings of the same. She threw off her ragged garments, and dressed herself in her birch-bark clothes. She put her father's moccasins on her bare feet; and the moccasins were so big that they came up to her knees. Then she, too, started out to visit the beautiful wigwam at the end of the village.

Poor Little Burnt-Face! She was a sorry sight! For her hair was singed off, and her little face was as full of burns and scars as a sieve is full of holes; and she shuffled along in her birch-bark clothes and big moccasins. And as she passed through the village the boys and girls hissed, yelled, and hooted.

And when she reached the lake, her sisters saw her coming, and they tried to shame her, and told her to go home. But the Great Chief's sister received her kindly, and bade her stay, for she saw how sweet and gentle Little Burnt-Face really was.

Then as evening was coming on, the Great Chief's sister took all three girls walking beside the lake, and the sky grew dark, and they knew the Great Chief had come.

And his sister asked the two elder girls, "Do you see my brother?"

And they said, "Yes."

"Of what is his shoulder-strap made?" asked his sister.

"Of a strip of rawhide," they replied.

"And with what does he draw his sled?" asked she.

And they said, "With a green withe."

Then his sister turned to Little Burnt-Face and asked, "Do you see him?"

"I do! I do!" said Little Burnt-Face with awe. "And he is wonderful!"

"And of what is his sled-string made?" asked his sister gently.

"It is a beautiful Rainbow!" cried Little Burnt-Face.

"But, my sister," said the other, "of what is his bow-string made?"

"His bow-string," replied Little Burnt-Face, "is the Milky Way!"

Then the Great Chief's sister smiled with delight, and taking Little Burnt-Face by the hand, she said, "You have surely seen him."

She led the little girl to the wigwam, and bathed her with dew until the burns and scars all disappeared from her body and face. Her skin became soft and lovely again. Her hair grew long and dark like the Blackbird's wing. Her eyes were like stars. Then his sister brought from her treasures a wedding-garment, and she dressed Little Burnt-Face in it. And she was most beautiful to behold.

After all this was done, his sister led the little girl to the seat next the door, saying, "This is the Bride's seat," and made her sit down.

And then the Great Chief, no longer invisible, entered, terrible and beautiful. And when he saw Little Burnt-Face, he smiled and said gently, "So we have found each other!"

And she answered, "Yes."

Then Little Burnt-Face was married to the Great Chief, and the wedding-feast lasted for days, and to it came all the people of the village. As for the two bad sisters, they went back to their wigwam in disgrace, weeping with shame.

Although this tale has been compared to Cinderella, *there is an element that the European story lacks. Although both have as heroine an uncomplaining household drudge, Cinderella's presence at the ball is made possible through the intervention of a fairy godmother; in the Indian story, however, Little Burnt-Face goes to the Chief's wigwam on her own, and there, because of her sheer goodness, she can see him. Thus it is not her outer beauty that attracts him but rather the beauty that lies inside. The thesis makes for discussion and even young children see the reason for the transformation from the ugly younger sister to the beautiful maiden, which she is.*

JACK AND HIS ANIMALS

"Jack and His Animals" is another tale of poetic justice but it is told with humor that children love. It is less familiar than "The Musicians of Bremen," but there is a similarity, and children respond to both of them. Playing the parts of animals appeals, but the underlying motive is one of compassion and a sense of responsibility giving the tale two levels rather than one.

Years and years ago there lived in that part of Ireland which is now County Tyrone a man named Lorcan with Brid his wife and Jack their only child, a boy in his teens.

They had been happy and fairly comfortable till the father lost his health. He had worked very hard to provide a good home for his wife and child but his health broke down under the strain of the hard labour.

Jack was a kind, loving boy. As he grew older he felt he should find some means of helping to make life easier and happier for his parents.

He was very fond of animals and had wonderful power in training them and winning their affection.

"Mother," he said one day, "I have thought of a plan to make life easier and more comfortable for you and my father. We have four animals here, the ass, the dog, the cat and the goat."

"Well, Jack Alanna, what do you mean to do?"

"You know, Mother, I have trained the animals to play tricks and I have thought that perhaps I could earn money by amusing the people who would see them performing."

"Certainly, Jack, you have done extraordinary work in teaching the beasts. Not only do they perform wonderfully but they also enjoy the play."

"Well, Mother, I will start on my travels at once and I promise you I will return home as soon as possible."

Jack made all things ready and set off. He took his fife with him.

The parents stood side by side at the window of the room where the poor invalid passed his days. They waved a loving farewell to their good son.

He, with the four animals, travelled on till they reached a field near a small town.

Jack placed the animals in a row, took out his fife and began to play. Immediately the four responded to the music. The ass began to bray, the dog to bark, the cat to mew and the goat to bleat.

In a little while most of the people in the neighbourhood assembled in the field to listen to the "band."

After a short time Jack stopped playing. Immediately the animals followed his example.

One old lady, a lover of animals who had been brought out to witness the performance, gave orders to have a good meal prepared at her house for Jack and his animals. Both man and beasts thoroughly enjoyed the food. She also gave Jack a good sum of money.

Jack wished to derive as much profit as possible from the long day.

He gathered his band together and started off to go to another town. When they reached it he arranged the animals in order on a patch of waste ground.

The music started. In a short time it seemed as if all the people of the town were gathered together to hear and see the strange band. The animals themselves seemed to enjoy the game.

Among the crowd was a rich man named Feilim, with Finola his wife and Maeve their seven-year-old daughter.

"Father, where are the man and the animals going now?" Maeve asked.

Jack himself answered the question. "We will travel a bit farther and reach a wood. We can sleep under the trees."

"Oh!" said Feilim, "rain might come on and you would have no shelter."

"There is a big empty shed near the back of our house," said Finola. "The animals could sleep there. You yourself can find a bed in the house."

Both Jack and his animals slept comfortably that night. They started off early next morning after having a good breakfast.

Feilim with his wife and daughter stood at the gate of the house to say goodbye. Maeve had been given a purse of money to put into Jack's hand. He was delighted to think of the joy the money would bring to his parents.

He travelled on till he came to a splendid mansion surrounded by trees. It was the home of a wealthy chieftain named Angus, Anna his wife, and their daughter, Eva.

They had been for years a very happy family but were now a sad one.

Eva was a beautiful girl and was as good as she was beautiful.

A marriage had been arranged between her and a fine young chieftain named Oscar.

All preparations had been made when a sad occurrence put an end to the joyful anticipation.

One lovely spring day Eva and two of her companions, Brid and Siobhan, went for a walk along a winding road known as The Witch's Lane.

It was so called because a wicked witch had her home there among the bushes and brambles.

The witch was feared by the people of the neighbourhood.

It was said she put cruel spells on anyone who dared to go near her dwelling place.

When the three girls came towards it Siobhan and Brid turned back but Eva went on.

"I am not afraid of the ugly old creature," she said.

She had gone only a very short distance when the hideous old hag rushed out from among the bushes.

She had a crooked stick in her hand.

With it she struck Eva on the mouth as she said:

> "Power of speech you'll ne'er regain
> All help and cures will be in vain
> Till strange, quaint music greets your ear
> And drives away all doubt and fear."

Laughing and cackling the witch rushed back towards her den.

In her savage delight she forgot the deep lake near her home. She stumbled over a large stone. In vain she tried to reach the brambles. The water seemed to drag her down, down. She was never heard of more.

Her wicked power had put poor Eva under a cruel spell. She was deprived of the power of speech.

Oscar wished the marriage to take place as arranged but Eva herself would not consent to such an arrangement.

Jack happened to select for his next performance a field near Eva's house.

The day was bright and sunny. The birds were singing and the blossoms were sprouting on the trees. Scenes of beauty and renewed life appeared on all sides.

Angus, his wife, daughter and Oscar were seated at the mid-day meal when they heard the sound of extraordinary music.

Eva loved music. She rushed without ceremony from the table and hurried to the place from whence the sound had come.

The parents and Oscar followed her. All four were amazed to see Jack and his band. The sight was a fantastic and funny one.

The poor donkey was getting tired but he kept on bravely with his part so as to hold his place in the orchestra.

The dog kept on changing the key from threatening growls to barks of joy and welcome.

The cat mewed loudly but now and again softened the tone to a gentle purr.

The meg geg geg of the goat was somewhat nasal but was constant and well sustained.

The parents and Oscar listened for a moment to the "choir" but what was their joy when they turned towards Eva and saw that she was laughing heartily.

"Oh! Father, Mother, Oscar," she cried, "the cruel spell is broken. The witch's prophecy has come true. Strange, quaint music has been my cure."

All the listeners came forward with generous money gifts.

Angus asked Jack what were his plans for the future.

"I will go home now to my parents," was his reply.

"Is your home far from here?"

"Well, it is a good distance."

"Oh! then we must find some means of sending you back."

"Do you remember, Father," said Eva, "there are wagons in the stables that would take more than twice the number of animals? And Jack himself could be sent home on one of the side-cars."

The triumphant march home began. Jack received a tumultuous welcome from all his neighbours and friends.

With great care and good food the father regained his health and both people and animals lived happily ever after.

An aspect of this tale that sets it apart is that Jack and Eva do not marry and live happily ever afterward but, rather, go their separate ways, having achieved the goals sought.

JACK AND THE HAINTED HOUSE
R. REX STEPHENSON

Most children love ghost stories. The following tale from the Blue Ridge Mountains is simple in structure; yet it has all the elements of a good ghost story for creative playing: a hero with whom children can identify, a scary situation that is resolved in the end, and strong dramatic action.[1] It is told here in the dialect of the region.

This is a story about a boy named Jack. Now Jack is a boy who lives way up in the Blue Ridge Mountains of Virginia. Old Jack, why, he is always getting himself into a fix. This tale is called *Jack and the Hainted House.* "Hainted" is what mountain folks say when they mean haunted. So this tale is gonna find Jack meetin' some ghosts and the like.

Well, one day Jack was walkin' in the woods and it commenced to get dark. Jack was lookin' for a good place to spend the night. Finally he came upon this house with a light in the window and he went up and knocked on the door.

When the door opened, an old man stepped out carryin' a candle. He had about the wildest bunch of hair that Jack had ever seen on anybody's head.

1. Published for the first time in this book.

"What can I do for ya, boy?" the old man asked.

"I'm lookin' for a place to spend the night and maybe get something to eat," answered Jack.

"Afraid I have no room here. Too crowded," the old man said, all the time studyin' Jack real careful with his candle.

"I'm awful hungry, too," Jack said.

"Well, I have a goose that I'll give ya. But you'll have to cook hit. Now then, a place to sleep. I got a little house over there you can stay in . . . if'n you want to." With that the old man handed Jack the goose and slammed the door in his face.

Jack took that goose and moved purty slow to the house. When he got there, Jack opened the door and went inside. But before he knew what was happenin' that door shut fast and he was trapped. Try as he would, Jack couldn't get that door open.

Well, all that work tryin' to get that door opened left Jack plumb tuckered out, so he looked around for a place to sleep. He spied a bed over in the corner, picked up a quilt, spread it over himself, and before a cat could of blinked twice, he was fast asleep.

Jack was just beginnin' to dream about bein' home and eatin' ash cakes and sorghum, when he felt this tuggin'-pull on that quilt. Well, the harder Jack pulled, the harder that tuggin'-pull was from the other end. Finally old Jack gave up and tore that quilt half-in-two and said, "I don't know who you are or what you are, but I guess I'll have to give ye half of this quilt if'n I'm gonna get any sleep tonight."

After Jack tore that quilt half-in-two, he went right back to sleep, but it wasn't long before he felt that tuggin'-pull on the quilt again. Jack pulled, but the other thing pulled harder and finally Jack fell on the floor. So Jack just gave that quilt to whatever it was and went someplace else to sleep.

Well, it wasn't long before Jack was fast asleep again, dreamin' of his maw's ash cakes and sorghum, when he heard these strange sounds. When Jack looked up, he saw these seven witches comin' in the room! Well, they surrounded Jack, but when they went to grab him, Jack jumped out of the way and all them witches bumped into one another. Well, old Jack, he jumped up and started yellin', "Get out of here, 'fore I beat the Devil out of ye!"

Well, to old Jack's surprise, those witches left. Jack went over to another corner of the room and decided he'd stay awake, to see if there was any other strange critters in that hainted house.

Hit wasn't long till these seven witches returned, not only makin' those scary sounds but carryin' a dead body. The witches left the body and disappeared again.

Well, Jack remembered something his grandpaw had told him. If you speak to a haint using the Lord's name, hit will talk back to you.

So Jack walked over to that haint and said, "What in the Lord's name are you doin' here?" That haint told Jack that he had been killed in this house many years ago by a robber, who was after his gold. The haint told Jack to go find the gold, which was hid in the fireplace, and to give one-third each to the haint's two sons, and, for doin' that, Jack could keep one-third for himself.

Well, Jack did just what that haint said, and you know Jack took the money and bought him a little piece of ground up on the mountain, and today he's got seven sons, jist as ornery as he was. And that's the story of Jack and the Hainted House.

The leader might begin by having all the children be witches. How do witches move, speak, carry the body, disappear? What makes them scary? Many children will want to try the parts of Jack, the old man, and the haint.

When all have had a chance to try their favorite parts, the group will be thoroughly familiar with the story. The mountain dialect provides a special quality of authenticity and distinguishes it from other ghost stories that may be more familiar. Older children will appreciate the humor.

JACK AND THE KING'S GIRL
R. REX STEPHENSON

The next tale comes from the same source. Whereas younger children enjoy the direct simplicity of the story line, older children find humor in the naive explanation of how Virginia became a state. If a program is planned for parents or another class, presenting two Jack Tales can be fun. Preceded by an explanation of their origin and background, the spectators as well as the performers learn about a different culture, where even today the stories from the Blue Ridge are told and enjoyed. In this tale music and dance are integral and offer an ideal opportunity for research into the dances and songs of the area. Ferrum College students, when presenting the tales, precede the performance with instrumental music using homemade instruments like the ones used by the mountain people in the old days. Except for a "store-bought" fiddle and perhaps a banjo, instruments were constructed by the musicians and consisted of a washtub drum, bottles filled with varying amounts of water and blown, spoons rattled like castinets, jugs, and so on. Making the instruments adds another dimension to the experience, costs nothing, and enhances the performance.

This is the story of Jack and the King's girl. Now, in this story, Jack is a grown-up boy. No longer is he that little fella that was always in trouble. His "bojangle" days are over.

His eighteenth birthday was the day Jack "set off" to seek his fortune. He was a might sad to leave home and say goodbye to his Maw and his two brothers, Bill and Tom. But, he was purty sure that there was lots to see in the world, and, this was the perfect day to start seeing it!

So, Jack walked and walked. He went up hills, round mountains, waded creeks, and finally crossed through Adney's Gap. This was all might hard goin', too, cause you see, the part of Virginia that Jack was raised in was made up mostly of hills and mountains, and, this was long ago, way before there were any roads—let alone bridges—in the Blue Ridge Mountains.

It started to get pretty dark after Jack crossed Adney's Gap, so, he cut some pine branches and made himself a bed under the stars. Then, while he was laying there thinking what a lucky fella he was—he fell asleep. Jack didn't hear the foxes that howled or the owl that "whood" all night long, he just slept soundly.

The next morning, Jack made some "ashcakes" and drank some buttermilk that his Maw had sent with him, and he found some blackberries that he ate for dessert. Then, on Jack went. It wasn't long till he reached Bear Mountain. He had to climb over Bear

Mountain "iffin" he was going to see the world. Up Jack went, climbing over rocks, goin' round trees, even grippin' hold of bushes in a couple of places cause it was so steep!

Jack finally got to the top, and then he started down the other side. This was a might easier than going up. When he got to the other side of Bear Mountain, Jack heard this music, and, he being a curious fella, went to see just what was going on.

Well! What was going on, was a party! And, right there, in that valley, the King of Virginia, and all the Dukes and Duchessess of the Blue Ridge, were having a party to celebrate the birthday of the King's daughter. They were all dancing, eating, and talking to one another, and having the best time.

So, Jack walks up to the King and says, "Hello, King, may I come to your party?" Jack asked nicely cause his Maw had raised him to be polite.

"I'd be proud to have you join us," the King said.

"Mighty nice party, King," Jack replied, then asked, "but, who is that pretty girl over there?"

"That's my daughter," the King answered, "and, this party is to celebrate her eighteenth birthday."

"Well, King, she is mighty pretty—mighty pretty," Jack said.

At that moment, the King's daughter looked at Jack and smiled. Jack smiled back, and then he declared, "You know, King, I think I'd like to marry your daughter."

"I don't want to hear any kind of talk like that," the King warned, "I won't let my daughter marry an ol' mountain boy like you!"

"King, I'm bound and determined to marry your daughter!" Jack avowed.

"Listen, Jack, if I hear any more talk like this from you—you and I will fight!" the King responded with a touch of finality in his voice.

Jack was still polite when he said, "Now, King, that'd be a might unneighborly of you, cause I think the little girl likes me."

Just then, the King noticed his daughter, again, smiling at Jack, and he raised up and exclaimed, "Jack, I'm mighty powerful, I'm the King, and I have an army!" The King snapped his fingers and in marched forty soldiers. They stopped directly in front of Jack, showed him their muskets and skinn'n knives, then marched around him three times till the King said, "Ya'll are dismessed. Now, Jack, you are welcome to stay at my party, but, keep away from my daughter!"

Jack didn't answer the King, but went over and got himself something to eat. There was lots of apple cider and ham biscuits and even some turnip greens. However, while Jack was eating, the King's daughter came over and asked him to dance the Virginia Reel with her.

They were going through the arch the other dancers made for them when the King's daughter said, "I'm might fond of you, Jack."

Jack quickly responded by asking, "How would you like to become my wife?"

"That would be fine," she answered, "but, my Paw would never allow me to marry a mountain boy like you."

"Well, why don't we just run away?" Jack asked.

"Let's go!" the King's daughter quickly replied, and off they ran headed in the direction of Jack's Maw's house.

When the king discovered they had run away, he ended that party pretty quick, and he got his army out searching for Jack and his daughter. They looked in every holler and on top of every mountain, but, they never even got close to them.

Well, Jack and the King's girl got married, but after about three months, they both felt they should go back and try to make friends with the King. So, back they went—up hills, round mountains, wadin' creeks, and crossing Adney's Gap until they came to the site of the party.

But, when they got there, there was nothing there except an old wooden sign. Beside the sign, an old man was smoking a corn cob pipe. Jack and the King's daughter walked up to the sign and read it: GONE WEST OF THE MISSISSIPPI, signed, the KING. Jack thought this sign curious, so, he said to the old man, "You know anything about the King leavin?"

"Yep, I do," the old man replied, "he left here so you and his daughter could have his Kingdom of Virginia."

So Jack and the King's daughter lived on that land where they had first met, and Jack was the King for a short piece, but later he "give it up" so we could have a democratic government and be part of the United States, and that's the true story of how Jack got married, and, how Virginia became one of the original thirteen states.

> *The above story is in the best tradition of oral history and folklore, according to Rex Stephenson, who said he first heard the tale when the troupe was on tour in a veterans' hospital in Kentucky. After the performance a patient came up to him and said he knew a "Jack tale" he was sure they had never heard. It was "Jack and the King's Daughter," and it ended with the departure of the king. Some time later in a creative drama workshop in a local school, Stephenson asked the children to imagine what might have happened after the king departed. The children discussed various endings and finally came up with the idea that Jack abdicated so that Virginia could become part of the United States.*

The preceding stories were selected for inclusion because of their simplicity and successful use with beginning groups of all ages. Although children's stories, each one has been used with both children and adults, and each age brings its own insights, meanings, and humor to the playing of the stories. There are many excellent stories just as suitable for beginning creative playing, and the interested leader will have no difficulty finding them. Tastes and interests of the group will guide the selection, though one of the values in creative drama is the opportunity it offers for introducing new material and good literature. One thing the leader will discover is that no two groups ever handle a story in the same way; if he or she is able to present it without a preconceived plan as to how it should be done, the leader will find that every group brings original ideas to its playing.

The procedures suggested are essentially the same, regardless of age level:

1. Presentation of the story
2. Organization of the material
3. Improvisation
4. Evaluation
5. Replaying

Evaluation is an important aspect of creative drama and leads into the replaying, which should acquire new depth and richer detail. Changing parts with each playing may not always make for a better performance, but it does give each participant a chance to play the part of his or her choice at least once. When the leader feels that the group has gone as far as it can with the story, he or she may suggest that the group cast it for final playing. This usually makes for a successful conclusion: the group has created something of its own and has found the last playing to be the most rewarding.

The older the participants, the more preliminary planning the leader can expect. Children, on the other hand, tend to move quickly into improvisation. Their dialogue will be brief, and the scenes shorter than planned, but their attack is direct. Children, less conditioned to the conventions of the proscenium stage, are likewise freer in their use of space, planning scenes in various parts of the room simultaneously. When the class is held in a room with a stage at one end, they are likely to use it as a particular place—perhaps a mountaintop or a distant land—rather than considering it as the central playing area. For every age group there are fewer inhibitions if a large room, instead of a stage, is used. Playing in the round reduces self-consciousness and is conducive to freer movement, since the scattered observers do not seem so like an audience.

When the group has shown that it can handle the problems of simple fables and stories, it is ready to move on to more demanding material. The following stories illustrate the possibilities offered for characterization and multiple-scene planning.

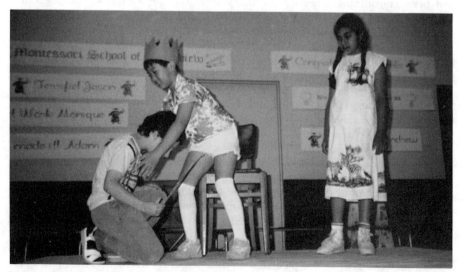

Third graders perform the Greek myth "Theseus and the Minotaur." *(Courtesy of Julie Thompson, Plainview, New York, Montessori School.)*

PROMETHEUS

Greek mythology is a rich and generally untapped source of material that can be successfully dramatized. One myth, which has been used many times with success, is the story of Prometheus, who stole fire from the gods. Basic human emotions and a dramatic story make it particularly appealing to children from seven to twelve. The idea of a formless earth stirs their imagination and provides an unusual opportunity for creativity. The story must be told carefully and in considerable detail, since not all children will be familiar with it. Although Greek myths are readily available, a brief synopsis of Prometheus is given here, with suggestions as to ways in which the leader may handle it.

The Greek gods and goddesses were believed to have dwelt on Mount Olympus, high above the earth. Ruling over them was the mighty Zeus. Among the young gods, most in favor with Zeus for his bravery in helping defeat the Titans, was Prometheus. One day Zeus and Athena, Goddess of Wisdom, were walking in the garden. They caught sight of Prometheus in the distance, looking down toward the earth. Zeus called to him and asked him what interested him, for he had often seen the young god staring down at the forests and mountains below.

Prometheus replied that he was troubled because the earth was so empty and silent, with no one moving about its surface. Zeus smiled, and said that for some time he had been considering a reward for the young god. "Prometheus," he suggested, "perhaps you would like to descend to the earth and fashion human beings out of soil." Prometheus was overjoyed.

"You are wise and kind," added Athena. "When you create them remember to give them strong bodies, keen minds, and tender hearts. Let them also see that there is a need for beauty as well as for the necessities of life."

"You may give them any gifts you wish except the gift of fire," continued Zeus. "That alone belongs to the gods and must remain on Olympus. When you have fashioned and are satisfied with your work, I will come down to earth and blow the breath of life into their bodies."

Prometheus was eager to begin and went off swiftly. Working with power and skill, he modeled his first human being upright and powerful, and called him "the Builder." Then he took more soil and made a second person, who was likewise tall and strong. Putting a few grains of corn in his hand, he named him "the Sower and Reaper." The third he pronounced "the Hunter," and to that one he gave a stone. The fourth he called "the Musician." Finally, he finished his fifth whom he proclaimed "the Thinker."

Scarcely had he stepped back to admire his efforts when the deep voice of Zeus was heard from Olympus. "We are pleased with your people, Prometheus. I shall now come down to blow life into them."

Miraculously, each statue came to life and breathed, and moved, and walked. As the days passed, Prometheus cared for his people and worked with them, teaching them to do the special jobs for which they had been created. They learned quickly and worked happily. One day, however, the seasons changed. The warm air was replaced by cold winds and snowy weather. The people were cold, and Prometheus was deeply disturbed as he watched them huddling together, trying to keep warm. Finally, he could bear it no longer. He knew he must give them fire.

When he called to Athena for help, she asked, "Do you care so much about your people, Prometheus?"

Prometheus declared that he did.

"Enough to risk the wrath of Zeus!" continued Athena. "He will surely punish you. The one thing he has forbidden them is fire."

"I have made my people, and I must help them, even though I suffer for it," replied Prometheus.

"Very well, then," said Athena. "I will help you find the fire to give them."

As swiftly as he had gone down to earth, Prometheus returned to Olympus to get the fire that he was determined his men and women should have. Then he called the five together and told them not to be frightened, but to learn to use their new gift. Just as he had taught them other things, he taught them how to use a fire for warmth and for the cooking of food. He warned them never to let the fire go out. The people were fascinated with the many possibilities of fire, and were soon warm and comfortable again.

It was not long, however, before Zeus learned what had happened. Angrily he told Prometheus that he had disobeyed, and must be punished for his act.

"I am ready to accept my punishment, great Zeus," Prometheus replied, "for I cannot let my people suffer from the wind and cold."

"A gift that has been given cannot be recalled," continued the god. "Human beings now possess fire, but you must pay the price. I shall have you bound by chains to yonder mountain. There you must remain forever and serve as an example to those who dare to disobey my laws."

So saying, Zeus sent his messenger, Hephaestus, down to seize Prometheus and put him in chains. The people were grieved when they saw the dreadful thing that happened to their creator and teacher, but their hearts were filled with gratitude for his great gift to human kind.

The discussion preceding the story can take many directions. It may begin with a consideration of human qualities and feelings. It may, on the other hand, begin with occupations and some pantomime suggesting them. It may begin with an analysis of the characters in the story and their conflicts. Eventually, in whatever way the story is introduced, there must be a focus on the characters, their behavior, and the consequences of Prometheus' act.

As in the other stories, the myth should be broken down into scenes before it is acted. Work in pantomime can easily be done with the whole group, for there is rich opportunity here. Together, the children can do the following actions: build a hut, hunt for food, plant a field, make a musical instrument (drum or pipe) and discover how to play it, suggest the beginning of human thought processes. Each activity gives scope for imaginative pantomime. Music may be helpful in stimulating movement, though it is not necessary. Children love playing the statues who come to life and learn to do the things for which they were intended. One whole period may easily be given over to these pantomime activities.

When the players are ready to begin the story, they may wish to take turns playing gods and people. If playing in a large room, the children may conceive of one end of it as Olympus and the other end as earth. Or, if there is a platform, they may decide to locate Olympus on a higher level. The plot calls for at least three scenes, though some groups may see it in five or six. More than one group has played it with use of a simultaneous setting, with Zeus and Athena observing and commenting, while Prometheus works. When this approach is used, the scenes may move back and forth without a break or scene division.

Prometheus is a story strong enough to hold the children's interest for three or four class sessions, with constructive discussion preceding and following each playing. If the group enjoys the story, other myths may be introduced, for there are many with fine dramatic action and values that children comprehend. Like the other stories in this chapter, Prometheus *gains depth and detail with each new playing. The young god's sense of responsibility and compassion for his people begins to emerge, adding another dimension to the character. The conflict between the law of Zeus and Prometheus' moral courage as he begins to feel for his men and women makes for powerful drama. The final playing can be most rewarding, as theme, story, character, and action are unified. The group that has become really involved in Prometheus' dilemma will have had a rich experience. This is a story better suited to an older group although even seven- and eight-year-olds can understand and play a simplified version.*

BLUE BONNETS

This Indian legend, telling how the first blue bonnet flowers appeared on the earth, is a story that appeals to children of middle and upper grades. Many Indian legends are excellent for improvisation, but this one has a special appeal since it is the story of a child and her sacrifice.

Yellow Star is a little Indian girl who lives with her father and mother in a village belonging to the Comanche tribe. As the story begins, the Chief calls his people together. He describes the trouble that has come to their village after many weeks without rain. The long drought has caused the brooks to dry up, vegetation is dying, and animals have left the parched plains in search of food. The people sit quietly in a circle around the campfire as they listen to their leader. Then they beat the drums and dance, praying to the Great Spirit for rain. At first, nothing happens. Then, suddenly, they hear the voice of the Great Spirit far in the distance. They stop, put down the drums, and listen: "You are being punished for your selfishness and greed. You have lived in a land of plenty for many years, but your people have not shared with their brothers."

The Chief begs for mercy, but the Great Spirit replies, "I will forgive your tribe and send you the water you need only when one among you sacrifices on the campfire that which is dearest to his heart."

Excitedly, the braves talk together. They suggest that one give his horse, another his jewelry, and still another offer his beautiful young squaw to the Great Spirit. No one, however, is willing to make a sacrifice for the sake of his brothers, and so they move from the campfire and start slowly off toward their homes. The Chief calls them. "Come to this place again in the morning. By that time one among you may have found the gift that will bring us all forgiveness."

The people slowly disappear, each hoping that someone will think of a way to save them. Only little Yellow Star remains. In her arms she carries her fawn-skin doll with its bonnet of blue jay feathers. The doll is her dearest possession. She realizes that she must throw it into the fire to please the Great Spirit, but it is not easy to part with her only toy. Finally, she reaches her decision, as night falls on the village, and she tells the Great Spirit that she is ready to give that which is dearest to her heart. She watches the doll burn slowly; then, seeing the blue feather bonnet lying in the ashes, she picks it up and throws it into the flames. To her amazement, the feathers do not burn but become small blue flowers. Yellow Star knows, then, that the Great Spirit has accepted her gift, and with a light heart she runs home.

The next morning, all of the Indians gather together as their Chief has commanded, but where only last night there was a campfire, there is now a huge bed of blue flowers. The people are mystified, for they cannot understand how flowers could have sprung up in the hard, dry earth.

Yellow Star's mother tells the Chief about the doll. "Surely," she says, "it must be a sign. Hundreds of flowers now grow on ground that was trampled and dry."

The people, however, are unwilling to believe her story, for why should the Great Spirit be satisfied with so small a gift as a child's fawn-skin doll? At that moment, there is a roll of thunder in the distance. The Chief knows now that the Great Spirit has accepted Yellow Star's offering. Again, he asks his people to beat their drums and give thanks that they have at last been forgiven. The first raindrops fall.

This charming legend gives an opportunity for total group participation. Since movement is an important element, a good beginning can be made with a dance around the campfire. The use of a drum aids enormously in building rhythms, as the Indians move and dance and pray. The leader can begin with the story, but before dialogue is attempted, practice in rhythmic movement helps the players to become involved.

Discussion of the story and its theme should precede the playing, inasmuch as this will deepen the understanding of a people different in custom, yet like us in their human strengths and weaknesses. When the group is ready to begin, it is again suggested that short scenes, rather than the whole story, be played first. For example, the opening scene, in which the Chief calls his people together and explains the seriousness of their situation, is enough for one sequence. Yellow Star's sacrifice is another. The players conceive of the story as taking place in one act, with a break to indicate passage of time, or they may see it as a play in two or three scenes. Because it is a story in which any number may participate, playing it in the round is desirable, if possible. Players and observers are one and are, therefore, involved to an unusual degree.

The part of Yellow Star is a favorite, but the Chief, the mother, and the selfish braves and squaws can all be built into characters who are believable and interesting. If this story finds favor, the leader may wish to bring other Indian legends to class. Most of them require little more than space for playing, since they are concerned with human beings in conflict with nature and with human weaknesses familiar to all.

THE OLD MAN AND THE GOOMBAY CAT
KITTY KIRBY

Stories and legends of the Bahamas are almost unknown in this country. Yet, like all places where people have lived, worked, played, and worshipped, it has a rich store of folklore. It waits only to be discovered. The following tale from the Bahamas makes wonderful material for creative playing.[2]

Cat Island was home to William T. His father and grandfather were born there. William's father had sold fish by day and had given organ lessons to the island children by night. He had been a "church-going" man. And, like his father, William T. was also a fisherman and gave organ lessons; but now he was getting old and could no longer see the notes.

His wife was dead, and his two sons and daughter had left the island. His only companion was a parrot named Penny. Penny had flown into the old wooden house one day after a tropical storm had swept over the island. She had just flown through the window and adopted old William T. Many afternoons the children would stop by the old man's house to say hello to Penny. The children called William T. Cousin Will-Yum, and loved to listen to stories of his boyhood. They would sit on the old wooden porch and listen attentively as William T. swung in his wornout hammock and drew in long breaths of smoke from his pipe. Then he would begin:

"When I was about sixteen, I was one of the best sea divers on the island. My father used to take me out in his small boat to the coral reefs. There we would dive down into the clear, blue-green water into a sea-garden. It was still—so still—we would swim through coral caves with plants all around us. There were hornlike plants and sea fans that looked like feathers. Pink plumeworms with spindly flower petals danced like angels. And bright, jewel-like fish were swimming all around us: red parrot fish, blue parrot fish, and silvery grunts."

As he spoke little girls' eyes would shine brightly as they listened, but the boys would be fidgety and impatient.

"Tell us about the sea monsters and how you set yourself loose from the water octopus," the little boys would beg.

---

2. Published for the first time in this book.

Penny knew these stories well, and would interrupt William T. each time he spoke of the sea fans, the grunts, and the parrot fish. Still, the children would never leave until the old man had finished his stories. Then, after picking some tamarinds from the century-old tamarind tree which shaded the old man's hut, the children would say good-bye to Cousin Will-Yum and Penny and leave.

William T. never needed a clock to wake him up in the mornings because every morning when the rooster crowed he knew it was time to get up and go fishing.

"Breakfast, Will-Yum Tee. Breakfast!" Penny squawked.

"Come, come, Penny. Give me some time to get hold of myself," answered the old man.

William T. fed Penny and fixed himself a bowl of hominy grits. Penny not only ate her own food, but she helped William T. with his, too.

"Such a glutton," said William T.

"Glutton, glutton!" repeated the parrot. "Yes, you are, but I don't know what I would do without you," said the old man as he put Penny back into her cage.

"Fish biting good today, Will-Yum Tee? Fish biting good today?" chattered Penny.

"Hope so, Penny. You know tomorrow is Goombay Day!" said the old man as he gathered up his fishing pots and said good-bye to the bird.

William T. started down the hilly steps and narrow lanes toward the fishing cove. He hoped that today would bring a good catch. He hadn't had much luck lately. Walking along, he passed barefoot boys and girls on their way to school. They reminded him of when he was a boy. Their faces broke into a smile when they saw him.

"Good morning, Cousin Will-Yum," said the children.

"Morn-in', children. Have a good lesson today and mind the teacher!" answered the old man.

The children giggled. William T. waved good-bye and continued on his way. He walked along the busy waterfront until he came to the edge of Rock Cove. Then he sat down on the warm, pink sand and took his shoes off because he had to wade a little before reaching his rock in the deep water.

"Fish biting good today, mon?" asked William T. as he climbed onto the rock.

"Hope so," answered the other old fishermen.

William T. sat down and began to bait his fishing-pot with pieces of conch.

"Mon, you still using that old fish-pot trap?" teased one of the fishermen.

"Never mind. 'Tis good enough," answered William T.

William T.'s father was known to have made the best triangle fishing-pot traps on the island. The method had been handed down to him from *his* father and he, in time, had taught it to William T. The old man was very proud of the fishing-pot trap and felt it was still good enough to use today. He was just about to lower his pot into the water when the cry of an animal brought him to his feet. The tormented cry grew louder. Leaving his pot behind, William T. went to see what was wrong. He walked to a nearby rock that jutted out into the water. Not too far from there he saw newcomers. They were teenage boys and they were having lots of fun throwing rocks and pebbles at a scrawny, old, black cat.

"Stop it! Can't you see you are hurting a poor, helpless animal?" shouted William T.

"Go 'way, you silly old man!" said the boys as they continued to torment the cat. "This is a fisherman's rock. You can't even bait a catch. You are too old!"

Shoving one of the boys aside with his elbow, William T. butted the other two with his head. The youths were so amazed at the strength of the old man they quickly ran to the other side of the rock. William T. looked down at the cat as it let out a mournful "meo-o-ow."

"They won't hurt you anymore," said the old man as he picked up the cat, and together they went back to his fishing spot.

The old man sat down and dropped his pot into the water. Then he and his newly found friend waited. The fish were not biting, and the old man had grown tired, so he pulled in his pot. The cat jumped into the wet pot and rolled over and over in it.

"Mon, you look like one big cat-ball!" said William T. laughingly. He laughed so loudly that all the other fishermen stopped to see what had happened.

"You catching cat instead of fish?" they teased jovially.

"Haven't seen a cat in a long time on the island," said another fisherman. "How did he get on the rock?"

"Don't know," answered William T. Then, looking at the cat, he kept on laughing as he watched it roll out of the pot.

With his head turning and his tail swishing, the cat pranced lightly over to one of the fisherman's baskets and with one swipe of his paw hooked a small porgy and ran back to William T.

"Tut, tut. That was not nice," said the old man, watching the cat devour its delicious dish. After finishing his meal the cat licked his whiskers and strolled over to William T. Settling himself on the old man's lap, the cat purred and purred and soon fell asleep.

Once more the old man lowered his pot into the water and hooked the ends to the edge of a rock alongside him. He sat there gazing out at the ocean at the hundreds of fishing boats looming over the waters. William T. thought to himself:

"Mon, what big boats! And listen to the sound of those engines and young fishermen singing. Not like the little boats that me and my father used. They even got machines to help catch fish. Look at the haul of Nassau groupers, jack-runners, margaret-fish, and the largest fresh conch that I've ever seen! You've got to be young and strong to carry all that load on your back. Big Goombay Day for them . . . and all that is left for us old fishermen are little fish that got away from the big nets."

He looked further up the rock and saw more newcomers.

"I wonder how long it will be before they take over this rock?" he thought. "My father and grandfather fished here, so in a way I inherited this rock." Then he thought of the young boys telling him he was too old for fishing.

At that moment the cat stirred on the old man's lap. William T. stroked the furry body. Somehow he felt calmer, and as he gazed out into the ocean the ripples of the water made him feel drowsy, and he drifted off to sleep.

Many hours passed. The old man was awakened by the tapping of the cat's paw on his arm. He looked around and saw that everyone had gone.

"I'm glad you woke me," said William T.

The cat pushed the fishing-pot with his two large paws and swung the handle from side to side.

"All right, all right! I'll hurry!" said the old man as he pulled in his meager catch. Showing them to the cat, he said, "I did not catch much fish, but you were good company." The cat blinked his eyes and purred.

With the catch over his shoulder and the cat under his arm, William T. climbed off the rock and waded in the water until he reached the pink, sandy shore. The cat jumped from the old man's arms.

"Don't get lost again," said William T. as he waved good-bye to the cat.

After walking for some time, William T. felt he was being followed.

"Meo-ow, meo-ow."

William T. turned around, and there, nosing into some seashells and fishbone along the road, was the cat!

"You are following me. I'd like to take you home, but I'm a poor fisherman and already have a bird that I can barely feed."

"Meo-o-ow," replied the cat mournfully.

As William T. started to leave, he thought he saw teardrops falling from the cat's eyes, but then he thought of Penny. He was late with her supper. So he hurried on his way.

The sun, shining like a large copper ball, was dropping lower and lower behind the fertile green hills. Tourists riding in bright blue surreys, pulled by horses wearing straw hats, nodded their heads in greeting to the old man as he hurried along. The soft night winds rustled the palm leaves of the coconut trees that stood tall and majestic all over the island. The air was also warm and fragrant with the smell of thousands of hibiscus plants. And lamplighters, flickering in and out of trees, lit up the night with their twinkling lights.

The old man trudged up the rocky steps until he reached his house on the top of the hill. From the porch came the sound of Penny.

"Will-Yum Tee, Penny wants supper! You're late! You're late!" squawked the parrot.

"Just now, Penny. I'm coming," said William T. But the parrot just kept on talking.

"Will-Yum Tee! Will-Yum Tee . . .!"

William T. opened the door, found his oil lamp, and lit it. He then washed his hands and mixed some dilly seeds and pumpkin seeds together. Then he went outside to feed Penny, who was still being talkative. While the old man was feeding Penny, the cat was making his way soft-footed around the side of the house. The cat leaped through an open window and landed silently on the cracked, wooden floor. William T. said good-night to Penny and went inside to prepare his supper.

"MEO-O-OW!"

"My goodness, you followed me. And how did you get in here?" asked the old man.

The cat nodded his head up and down, swished his tail, and turned around. Then before William T. knew what was happening, the cat tore across the kitchen of the two-room house and stopped suddenly in front of the table. Looking up at the bowl of coconut milk, he meowed and meowed.

"So you are still hungry? I will share some of my supper with you," said the old man. He gave the cat some coconut milk, mixed some okra and rice with his meager catch of fish, and went outside to cook it in his coal stove. Finally, William T. and the cat sat down to eat their supper.

After the old man and his little friend had finished eating, the cat stretched his two front paws, brushed his whiskers, blinked a cat blink, and yawned. Then he strolled across the room and curled up in an old, wornout chair. Staring straight at the old man, the pupils of his eyes grew large and bright. His mouth widened into a large grin. The fisherman noticed a strange look on the cat's face. Suddenly the wooden walls began to creak and the sound of bells and drums echoed throughout the room.

"Who's there? Who's there, mon?" he gasped.

William T. tried to get up, but he could not move. There rising up in front of him was an enormous cat of black, shimmering fur. His brilliant eyes, almost blinding the old man, were as green as the ocean. Around his neck he wore a necklace of coral seashells. His silvery whiskers sparkled as he smiled and swayed from side to side to the rhythm of the Goombay. The old man was dumbfounded and his mouth dropped open when the magnificent cat began to sing:

> Goombay fish is very nice.
> Eat it once, you eat it twice.
> Mix it with some okra and rice.
> Goombay fish is very nice.

Finally the fisherman found his voice. "A Goombay Cat!" he cried. "A Goombay Cat! Gracious! Heavens, am I dreaming?"

The singing and music stopped as suddenly as it had begun. William T. rubbed his eyes and looked again at the worn-out chair. There, staring, and smiling, was the scrawny cat. Shaking nervously, William T. got up and went outside to see if Penny had heard the singing and music too, but the parrot was sleeping soundly.

"My mind must be playing tricks," said William T. to himself as he went back into the house. Gazing curiously at the cat, he patted the animal several times and found him a place to sleep. Then he went off to bed muttering to himself.

"I, I, I, must be get-ting old . . . very old."

The next morning William T. was awakened by a light weight on his chest and a tickling on his cheeks. It was the cat sitting there and blinking at him.

"Morn-in'," chuckled the old man as he rubbed his rugged cheeks. "Your whiskers tickled me."

The cat leaped forward, leaped up in the air, turned three somersaults, and landed with a bounce on the old wooden floor.

"Mon, what a cat! You're sure feeling good this morning."

Looking at the cat and studying him for a moment, he remembered last night. Should he tell his friends about what happened? Would they believe him if he told them about the cat? Or might they say: Cousin Will-Yum is getting old . . . very old. Then he thought to himself—how did the cat get on the rock? And why was this island named Cat Island? Did some strange cats live here long ago? He decided to keep all this to himself, but someday he would tell the story to the children.

Bracing his back, he sat up on the edge of the bed. As he went to put on his shoes the cat pounced at them, pulling at the shoestrings.

"Don't tan-ta-lize me, mon. Let me put my shoes on in peace. I gotta hurry 'cause today is Goombay Day!"

But the cat would not let go.

"Don't vex me," said the old man impatiently. Just then a squawk came from the porch.

"Will-Yum Tee! Will-Yum Tee! Don't forget my breakfast! You're late! You're late!" screeched Penny.

The cat let go of the shoestrings and perked his ears toward the sound. Before William T. could stop him, the cat ran to a hole in the screen door and eased himself through the opening onto the porch. Suddenly the cat caught sight of the beautiful red bird with her flowing tail of brilliant green and yellow feathers. His eyes grew wide and bright as he meo-o-owed loudly. Seeing the cat, Penny flapped her wings furiously as she scuttled wildly around in her cage. Her ruby-red eyes glared in panic.

"Will-Yum Tee! Will-Yum Tee! Hurry! Hurry!"

Thinking something horrible had happened to Penny, William T. rushed outside; by now he was out of breath. He calmed down when he saw the cat just sitting there watching the wild performance of the bird.

"Come, come, Penny. He won't hurt you. He wants to be your friend."

Penny looked at William T. and then at the cat. With her beak held high, she moved to the corner of the cage.

"Come, Penny," he pleaded as he opened the cage door. Penny hesitated, then flew onto William T.'s shoulder, keeping an eye on the cat.

William T. was very happy and chuckled to himself as he went inside to prepare breakfast for his two friends. After breakfast was over, Penny quickly flew into her cage. She was very quiet. The cat followed William T. and watched him as he locked the cage door.

"Good-bye Penny. I'll bring you some sweet benny-cake for Goombay."

The cat looked up at Penny and winked his eye, but Penny only flapped her wings. The old man gathered his fishing-pot trap and threw it over his shoulder. He put his last piece of conch, which he had to use as bait, into his pocket; then he and the cat started on their way to Rock Cove.

William T. had seen many a Goombay morning, but somehow there was a strange and happy feeling about this one. The sky was so blue and wide it seemed to run right into the blue-green water. You could not tell where the sky began and the ocean ended. He was so happy that he began to whistle an old familiar tune. Looking down at his little friend, who was strutting gracefully to the rhythm of the tune, he began to sing:

> Got-ta catch fish, before big boats come.
> Got-ta get it done, before the mid-day sun.
> Got-ta catch fish to sell to ev-ry one.
> Got-ta catch fish, before the big boats come.

As he was singing he looked up at the sky. Not a cloud was in sight, and the sky was bluer than he had ever seen it. He could feel the heat from the blazing sun burning through the soles of his shoes. The sweat was running down his face. The old man and his friend stopped to rest a while under a shady silk-cotton tree.

"Good morn-in', Cous-in Will-Yum," said a group of women with shiny faces. They were carrying baskets on their heads filled to the brim with fruits: soursops, saperdilles, Spanish limes, casavas, tamarinds, and sea grapes.

"You are early, Cous-in Hilda, Rebecca, and Cous-in Eunice," said the old man.

"Yes, 'cause it's Goombay Day!" answered the women, swinging their brightly colored, well-starched dresses. Everyone was moving so fast no one noticed Cousin Will-Yum's new friend.

"Come, come let us hurry," said the old man to the cat as they moved along with the crowd. Nearing the waterfront, he and the cat stopped at the Open-Straw Market.

"Big boat in today for Goombay, Cous-in Will-Yum," hollered Auntie Hattie B. from her booth in the Open-Straw Market.

"Yes, child. I seen them big tourist ocean liners down by the Prince Charles stop. Lots of money mak-in' to you."

"We'll set up a table for you right by Cous-in Eunice on the waterfront," she said.

"Where did you get the cat?" asked Cous-in Hilda, noticing the cat for the first time. "Found him yesterday on top of the rock," answered William T.

Leaving the Open-Straw Market, William T. passed brightly decorated straw booths running along the waterfront. The sun illuminated the blue-green water till it sparkled a jade green. Multicolored seashell beads, big straw pocketbooks, gaily colored straw dolls, and straw hats bedecked with seashells lined the booths.

Suddenly the smell of smothered conch and pigeon peas and rice filled the air. William T. knew he was near the market range with its many booths full of steaming vegetables, sweet fruits, and dazzling pink and white conch shells. Cousin Charlie had his booth here.

Cousin Charlie was busy cooking conch smothered in tomato sauce, and pigeon peas, and rice for the festival. The succulent dish bubbled in a big, cast-iron skillet on an open fire.

The cat ran up to Cousin Charlie's stand, looked up, and meowed and meowed. He licked his tongue and kept his eyes on the smothered conch.

"Mon, where did you find this cat?" asked Cousin Charlie. "Why, I haven't seen one for a long time on this island."

"He found *me!*" laughed William T.

Cousin Charlie fixed a plate of smothered conch and rice and gave it to the old man and the cat.

"Thank you. We will have a good lunch today," said William T. as he and his little friend pushed their way through the Market Range and headed for the waterfront. When William T. and the cat arrived at the fishing rock, he noticed that the cat's back was arched high, his ears were turned up, and he was switching his tail vigorously in signs of anger. It was then that he looked around only to see the young boys who had taunted the cat yesterday. They were fishing not too far from the old man's spot.

"Come, come. They won't bother you," said William T. as he sat down to bait his fishing trap.

The cat flexed his muscles, his tail stood straight up, and his eyes grew large and bright as he watched the fishing trap being lowered into the blue-green waters. William looked at the cat. He gasped when he saw that once more the cat was changing in size. He began to tremble and broke out in a cold sweat as harmonious sounds of bells and drums swelled across the ocean. At that moment a gigantic wave rose up and the great cat leaped into the oncoming billowing waves.

"Help! Help!" cried William T. "My cat is in the water!"

But the other fishermen were so frightened by the crashing of the water against the rocks that they did not hear his cry.

Suddenly the music stopped and the waters were calm again. William T. noticed the fishing-trap was still in place, but there was a heavy tugging on it. He tried to pull the trap up, but it would not give. Again he cried for help. Hearing his call, his fishing companions came to his rescue. Together they grabbed hold of the fishing-trap and began to pull and pull. All at once out of the water came the trap-pot filled with hundreds of beautiful fish shimmering in the sunlight. And there amidst the miraculous catch nestled the cat.

"My *cat!* My *cat!*" cried William T. But the fishermen were so amazed by the miraculous catch they paid no attention to the cat.

"Mon, look at that catch! Biggest I've ever seen!" shouted one of the fishermen.

"Never seen so many fish in one haul," said another.

Tears of joy ran down William T.'s cheeks as he lifted the wet, shivering body out of the trap and cradled it under his tattered old coat.

"Are you all right, mon?" he whispered. The cat looked up at William T. and purred contentedly.

"Old man, how did you catch all those fish?" asked the teenage boys.

It was then that William T. looked at his fishing trap piled high with goggle-eyed fish: margaret fish, jack-runners, grunts, and Nassau groupers. He was so happy that he could not speak for a moment. He just stood there staring at his catch. Then, remembering the boys' question, he looked down at the cat and said:

"Just luck, mon. Just luck."

"Will you sell us some of your catch?" asked one of the boys.

"*No!* I will not sell you any of my catch . . . but I will give you some of them." He then shared many of his fish with his companions and the boys. The boys felt ashamed and sorry for the way they had treated the cat and the old man.

"May we help you carry your load off the rock?" asked the boys.

The cat purred; the old man smiled, and said he would like that very much.

News of Cousin William's catch spread all along the waterfront. Auntie Hattie B., Cousins Eunice, Hilda, and Rebecca, and all the women left the Goombay tables to see the great haul of fish. Even Cousin Charlie left the Market Range to see Cousin William's big catch. Children came from all over the island when they heard the news of the old man's catch. Now they danced around him, playing big bass drums and singing a song of the Goombay catch:

> Cous-in Will-Yum caught big catch!
> From the blue-green waters.
> He caught them in his fish-pot trap,
> From the blue-green waters.

While the children sang, the cat swished his tail to the rhythm of the song. William T. was so happy he began to sing too:

> Goombay Cat caught big fish,
> From the island wat-ters
> He caught them with a great big smile,
> From the island wat-ters.

The teenage boys walked tall, their heads held high, as they carried William T.'s catch to his table. William T. strutted proudly before them with the cat riding on his arm. It was a grand sight to see the joyous procession marching to their tables to begin the Goombay festival. Tables were quickly filled with fried chicken, sous, coconut cakes, and other delectable dishes.

"Well, mon," said William T., setting the cat by his table. "It's time for us to fix our table."

The old man was about to pick up his fish-pot when he heard the sound of the Goombay song! It lasted for a brief second, and when William T. looked down again the cat was gone! Where his little friend had stood was a shiny, coral, seashell necklace. He picked it up slowly and he knew that his little friend was now gone forever.

However, William T. was not sad. The beautiful necklace was left by the Goombay Cat to remind him that miracles still happen and that he wasn't so very old after all.

This tale gives information about the Bahamas in its description of the country, the plants, the foods, and the customs, including the legends told by the people. It could, therefore, be used in connection with a social studies unit on the islands. It could also be played purely for the narrative. William T. is an appealing character, but the others can be more fully developed than they are in this account of his strange experience.

After the children have decided which characters are necessary to the telling and which others may be added, they are ready to decide on the scenes. If they are playing in a large room, one end can be William T.'s cabin; the other, the fishing area. The middle of the room might be the village square. If the space is small, the scenes can follow in sequence. The procession at the end can be handled in a variety of ways. One group had it move around the playing space in a large circle; another had it weave in and out, suggesting that it was going into different parts of the village. Carefully selected music will suggest movement and a mood.

All can try playing William T.—showing how he moves, walks, sits, runs, handles his fishing pots, and rescues the cat. When the class is thoroughly familiar with the story, it will want to go on to the enactment of scenes. Again, by allowing small groups to play bits of the story, each will have an opportunity to contribute dialogue, characterization, and movement. Some groups can be villagers, creating individual characters and showing their love for William T. An experienced group might want to create earlier scenes in William T.'s life, showing what he was like when he was a

Elementary School students visit actors backstage after seeing a performance of "Cinderella." *(Courtesy of Honolulu Theatre for Youth; photograph by Norman Montigal.)*

boy. Groups handle the cat differently. One class wanted to have a child play the part when it became large. Another group used a "prop" cat in the scenes where it was small but had a large boy play the cat when it grew to enormous proportions. Still another imagined it throughout, using offstage sounds when the cat and the parrot spoke. This last was probably the most satisfactory solution, but it is good to let the class wrestle with the problem and come up with its own solution.

Some children chant the songs, but one group composed its own music to "Goombay fish is very nice." Superstition and the supernatural intrigue most children, so this aspect of the story usually has particular appeal. There is a rich opportunity here for learning and creative playing. The results will be as simple or as detailed as the children are able to make them.

THE WISE OLD WOMAN
YOSHIKO UCHIDA

This version of the Japanese folk tale "The Wise Old Woman" is included for several reasons.[3] First, it is a good story. The narrative holds the interest of the players and provides complications that make demands on them. Also, the characters may be interpreted in considerable depth. The situation, though extreme, can be discussed in relation to our attitude toward older people. How do we feel about them? How do we treat them? What value do older people have in our society? What have we to learn from them? Why do you think we react to them as we do? What has caused our attitude? What are the implications in this story for our own old age? These are some of the questions that might be asked.

Many long years ago, there lived an arrogant and cruel young lord who ruled over a small village in the western hills of Japan.

"I have no use for old people in my village," he said haughtily. "They are neither useful nor able to work for a living. I therefore decree that anyone over seventy-one must be banished from the village and left in the mountains to die."

"What a dreadful decree! What a cruel and unreasonable lord we have," the people of the village murmured. But the lord punished anyone who disobeyed him, and so villagers who turned seventy-one were tearfully carried into the mountains, never to return.

Gradually there were fewer and fewer old people in the village and soon they disappeared altogether. Then the young lord was pleased.

"What a fine village of young, healthy and hardworking people I have," he bragged. "Soon it will be the finest village in all of Japan."

Now there lived in this village a kind young farmer and his aged mother. They were poor, but the farmer was good to his mother, and the two of them lived happily

---

3. From *The Sea of Gold and Other Tales* (New York: Scribner's, 1965), pp. 61–71.

together. However, as the years went by, the mother grew older, and before long she reached the terrible age of seventy-one.

"If only I could somehow deceive the cruel lord," the farmer thought. But there were records in the village books and every one knew that his mother had turned seventy-one.

Each day the son put off telling his mother that he must take her into the mountains to die, but the people of the village began to talk. The farmer knew that if he did not take his mother away soon, the lord would send his soldiers and throw them both into a dark dungeon to die a terrible death.

"Mother—" he would begin, as he tried to tell her what he must do, but he could not go on.

Then one day the mother herself spoke of the lord's dread decree. "Well, my son," she said, "the time has come for you to take me to the mountains. We must hurry before the lord sends his soldiers for you." And she did not seem worried at all that she must go to the mountains to die.

"Forgive me, dear mother, for what I must do," the farmer said sadly, and the next morning he lifted his mother to his shoulders and set off on the steep path toward the mountains. Up and up he climbed, until the trees clustered close and the path was gone. There was no longer even the sound of birds, and they heard only the soft wail of the wind in the trees. The son walked slowly, for he could not bear to think of leaving his old mother in the mountains. On and on he climbed, not wanting to stop and leave her behind. Soon, he heard his mother breaking off small twigs from the trees that they passed.

"Mother, what are you doing?" he asked.

"Do not worry, my son," she answered gently. "I am just marking the way so you will not get lost returning to the village."

The son stopped. "Even now you are thinking of me?" he asked, wonderingly.

The mother nodded. "Of course, my son," she replied. "You will always be in my thoughts. How could it be otherwise?"

At that, the young farmer could bear it no longer. "Mother, I cannot leave you in the mountains to die all alone," he said. "We are going home and no matter what the lord does to punish me, I will never desert you again."

So they waited until the sun had set and a lone star crept into the silent sky. Then in the dark shadows of night, the farmer carried his mother down the hill and they returned quietly to their little house. The farmer dug a deep hole in the floor of his kitchen and made a small room where he could hide his mother. From that day, she spent all her time in the secret room and the farmer carried meals to her there. The rest of the time, he was careful to work in the fields and act as though he lived alone. In this way, for almost two years, he kept his mother safely hidden and no one in the village knew that she was there.

Then one day there was a terrible commotion among the villagers for Lord Higa of the town beyond the hills threatened to conquer their village and make it his own.

"Only one thing can spare you," Lord Higa announced. "Bring me a box containing one thousand ropes of ash and I will spare your village."

The cruel young lord quickly gathered together all the wise men of his village. "You are men of wisdom," he said. "Surely you can tell me how to meet Lord Higa's demands so our village can be spared."

But the wise men shook their heads. "It is impossible to make even one rope of ash, sire," they answered. "How can we ever make one thousand?"

"Fools!" the lord cried angrily. "What good is your wisdom if you cannot help me now?"

And he posted a notice in the village square offering a great reward of gold to any villager who could help him save their village.

But all the people in the village whispered, "Surely, it is an impossible thing, for ash crumbles at the touch of the finger. How could anyone ever make a rope of ash?" They shook their heads and sighed, "Alas, alas, we must be conquered by yet another cruel lord."

The young farmer, too, supposed that this must be, and he wondered what would happen to his mother if a new lord even more terrible than their own came to rule over them.

When his mother saw the troubled look on his face, she asked, "Why are you so worried, my son?"

So the farmer told her of the impossible demand made by Lord Higa if the village was to be spared, but his mother did not seem troubled at all. Instead she laughed softly and said, "Why, that is not such an impossible task. All one has to do is soak ordinary rope in salt water and dry it well. When it is burned, it will hold its shape and there is your rope of ash! Tell the villagers to hurry and find one thousand pieces of rope."

The farmer shook his head in amazement. "Mother, you are wonderfully wise," he said, and he rushed to tell the young lord what he must do.

"You are wiser than all the wise men of the village," the lord said when he heard the farmer's solution, and he rewarded him with many pieces of gold. The thousand ropes of ash were quickly made and the village was spared.

In a few days, however, there was another great commotion in the village as Lord Higa sent another threat. This time he sent a log with a small hole that curved and bent seven times through its length, and he demanded that a single piece of silk thread be threaded through the hole. "If you cannot perform this task," the lord threatened, "I shall come to conquer your village." The young lord hurried once more to his wise men, but they all shook their heads in bewilderment. "A needle cannot bend its way through such curves," they moaned. "Again we are faced with an impossible demand."

"And again you are stupid fools!" the lord said, stamping his foot impatiently. He then posted a second notice in the village square asking the villagers for their help.

Once more the young farmer hurried with the problem to his mother in her secret room.

"Why, that is not so difficult," his mother said with a quick smile. "Put some sugar at one end of the hole. Then tie an ant to a piece of silk thread and put it in at the other end. He will weave his way in and out of the curves to get to the sugar and he will take the silk thread with him."

"Mother, you are remarkable!" the son cried, and he hurried off to the lord with the solution to the second problem.

Once more the lord commended the young farmer and rewarded him with many pieces of gold. "You are a brilliant man and you have saved our village again," he said gratefully.

But the lord's troubles were not over even then, for a few days later Lord Higa sent still another demand. "This time you will undoubtedly fail and then I shall conquer your village," he threatened. "Bring me a drum that sounds without being beaten."

"But that is not possible," sighed the people of the village. "How can anyone make a drum sound without beating it?"

This time the wise men held their heads in their hands and moaned, "It is hopeless. It is hopeless. This time Lord Higa will conquer us all."

The young farmer hurried home breathlessly. "Mother, Mother, we must solve another terrible problem or Lord Higa will conquer our village!" And he quickly told his mother about the impossible drum.

His mother, however, smiled and answered, "Why, this is the easiest of them all. Make a drum with sides of paper and put a bumblebee inside. As it tries to escape, it will buzz and beat itself against the paper and you will have a drum that sounds without being beaten."

The young farmer was amazed at his mother's wisdom. "You are far wiser than any of the wise men of the village," he said, and he hurried to tell the young lord how to meet Lord Higa's third demand.

When the lord heard the answer, he was greatly impressed. "Surely a young man like you cannot be wiser than all my wise men," he said. "Tell me honestly, who has helped you solve all these difficult problems?"

The young farmer could not lie. "My lord," he began slowly, "for the past two years I have broken the law of the land. I have kept my aged mother hidden beneath the floor of my house, and it is she who solved each of your problems and saved the village from Lord Higa."

He trembled as he spoke, for he feared the lord's displeasure and rage. Surely now the soldiers would be summoned to throw him into the dark dungeon. But when he glanced fearfully at the lord, he saw that the young ruler was not angry at all. Instead, he was silent and thoughtful, for at last he realized how much wisdom and knowledge old people possess.

"I have been very wrong," he said finally. "And I must ask the forgiveness of your mother and of all my people. Never again will I demand that the old people of our village be sent to the mountains to die. Rather, they will be treated with the respect and honor they deserve and share with us the wisdom of their years."

And so it was. From that day, the villagers were no longer forced to abandon their parents in the mountains, and the village became once more a happy, cheerful place in which to live. The terrible Lord Higa stopped sending his impossible demands and no longer threatened to conquer them, for he too was impressed. "Even in such a small village there is much wisdom," he declared, "and its people should be allowed to live in peace."

And that is exactly what the farmer and his mother and all the people of the village did for all the years thereafter.

It is suggested that the major discussion of The Wise Old Woman *be held after several playings. By that time the story will have had an impact on the group, and the players will be ready to discuss the theme and its modern implications. This can lead into a discussion of stereotyping of age, the meaning of wisdom, and the social values in our society. The depth of perception will affect the playing of the story for as the children discover its meaning, they will find their playing enriched, more serious.*

JACQUES THE WOODCUTTER

*The final story, "Jacques the Woodcutter," is more sophisticated than
any of the preceding, but it appeals to older groups and even adult players.
The deception and its discovery lead to excellent discussions of parallel
situations in real life. The humor and boisterous behavior of the Prince and
the Peddler, on the other hand, are good fun as they build toward the climax.
The fact that these tales have persisted through many retellings is proof of
more than surface narrative; in enacting them, therefore, the teacher has an
opportunity to push beyond the story line into thoughtful questions of moral
and ethical behavior, action, and consequences.*

Jacques Cornaud lived at the edge of a forest with his pretty wife Finette.

Jacques was a woodcutter by trade. Each morning he went off into the forest to cut
down trees and chop them into firewood. As soon as he left the house, his wife Finette
would have a visitor—for she was not only pretty and charming, but a fine cook
besides. Not far away lived a good-for-nothing prince named Bellay, who was extremely
fond of eating.

Every day while Jacques was away working in the forest, the Prince would come to
the house and sit down to an enormous meal. Finette didn't mind cooking for him. She
had no other company during the daytime, and besides, when the Prince had finished
his meal he always left a gold piece under the plate.

But Jacques the woodcutter was not so well satisfied. At last he decided to speak to
his wife about it.

"Finette," he said, "I have nothing against the Prince, and I don't mind his little
visits to our table. But does he have to come so often?"

Finette promised she would speak to the Prince. Next morning Jacques went off to
the forest, and soon afterward Prince Bellay turned up as usual, with a smile on his lips
and a flower in his buttonhole.

"And what's on the menu today?" he asked, patting his stomach.

"Savory dumplings," said Finette. "But I have a message for you. My husband
thinks you come to the house too often."

Prince Bellay frowned (thinking was such hard work that it always made him
frown). "Too often?" he repeated. "Well, you know, he's right. I'm here every day. No
wonder he's annoyed! This will have to stop."

No more gold pieces, thought Finette. What a pity, just when she was beginning to
gather together quite a tidy sum! She decided she would try to change Prince Bellay's
mind.

"No more onion soup," she said.

The Prince stared at her. "No more onion soup?" he gasped. "Oh, I couldn't bear
that. Life without onion soup wouldn't be worth living."

"And for next week," said Finette, "I had planned a meal of roast pigeon. But now
we'll have to give up that idea."

"Roast pigeon!" exclaimed the Prince, licking his lips. "But couldn't I sneak in while he's away in the forest without his knowing?"

"He might come back during the day," said Finette. "Imagine how annoyed he would be then."

"You're right," groaned the Prince. "We must think of a plan to keep him away from the house."

When his food was at stake the Prince could think quite fast. After a moment he stopped frowning and smiled.

"I have it!" he said. "This will keep him away for at least two weeks, and by that time I can think of something else. Now listen carefully."

And he told Finette his plan. Thinking of the gold pieces, she listened carefully and promised to do as he told her.

That evening, when she saw Jacques coming home from the forest with his axe on his shoulder, she stuffed a handkerchief into her cheek so that it would look swollen. Then she lay down on her bed and began to moan.

"Oh Jacques, Jacques, I feel so awful!"

The woodcutter put down his axe and hurried to her bedside. "What is it? What's the matter?"

"Toothache," moaned Finette. "The worst I've ever had. Ohhh—I've been in agony ever since you left this morning!"

Jacques reached for his coat. "I'll go and fetch the doctor at once."

Finette moaned harder than ever. "No, the doctor can't help me. There is only one thing that will cure this toothache, and that is water from the Fountain of Paris."

"But dear wife," said Jacques, "by the time I go to Paris and back you could be seven times dead with the pain."

"No, no," said Finette, "I'll wait for you. But you must hurry if you are to be back soon. I've made you a sandwich for the road. It's on the kitchen table."

Jacques was tired after a hard day in the woods, but he was so kindhearted that he left at once and took the high road to Paris. No sooner had he gone than Finette got to work at the stove, and soon afterward Prince Bellay was sitting down to a delicious supper of roast pigeon and artichokes with pepper sauce.

Meanwhile Jacques had gone only a little way when he met an old man with a big wicker basket on his back. It was the peddler who often called at his home.

"Good evening, old friend," said the peddler. "And pray, where are you going with such a sad face?"

"To Paris," said Jacques. "My wife Finette is dying of toothache, and I must bring her some water from the fountain there."

The peddler shut one eye and chuckled. "Tut, tut," he said. "Your wife no more has the toothache than I have."

"You don't know Finette," said Jacques indignantly. "If she says she has toothache, then she has. She isn't like other women."

The peddler shut his other eye. "And she wants you to go all the way to Paris? Tell me, isn't there some reason why she'd like to have you out of the house?"

The woodcutter thought for a moment. "Well, there's that good-for-nothing Prince with the big appetite. But I can't believe she would send me all the way to Paris just for that."

"Well, old friend," said the peddler, opening both his eyes, "never mind about the

Fountain of Paris. It just so happens that I have some of its water with me now, so I can save you the trip. Here, you're too tired to stand. Jump into my basket and I'll give you a ride back home."

So Jacques climbed into the peddler's basket and rode back home. When they reached the cottage there was a fine smell of cooking in the air. The peddler chuckled and knocked on the door.

"Who's there?" cried Finette.

"Only the peddler and his basket, good lady. Will you open your door to a tired and hungry man?"

"The peddler, at this time of night!" said Finette. "Is a woman never to have any peace?"

Then they heard Prince Bellay's voice from the dining table.

"Let him come in, good Finette. He's an old man, and tired. If you put him in the kitchen with his basket, he won't disturb us."

"All right," said Finette. She let in the peddler and told him to sit down in the kitchen. The peddler thanked her and put his basket next to the stove.

At the dining table the Prince was finishing his roast pigeon. Having eaten so well himself, he felt kindly toward the rest of the world.

"Poor old fellow," he said. "He's probably come a long way with nothing to eat. Why don't we ask him in here to sup with us? These traveling men are always good company."

Finette was in good humor again. She invited the peddler to come in and share their meal.

"Bless you, good lady," said the peddler. "Never turn down an invitation, I always say. But you won't mind if I bring my basket along? It's my living, and I don't like to leave it behind."

"That great big basket in my dining room?" said Finette. "What an idea!"

"Oh, let him bring it if he must," said the Prince kindly. "He can put it in the corner where it won't trouble anybody."

Finette thought of the gold piece under the plate and decided not to object. So the peddler brought in his basket from the kitchen and put it in the corner behind his chair. He sat down to the table, smacking his lips, and soon made short work of the roast pigeon.

"Ah," he said when he had finished. "A fine meal, Hostess! With food like that, I'll wager you keep in good health."

"Indeed I do," said Finette. "I haven't had a day's illness in years."

At this there was a strange grumbling noise from the wicker basket in the corner. Finette turned pale, but the peddler chuckled in his beard and told her not to be alarmed.

"It's the heat in here," he explained. "Bring an old wicker basket in out of the cold, and you'll hear it grunt and creak like a live thing."

Prince Bellay was feeling cheerful after his meal. "No speeches after dinner here, Master Peddler," he said. "Instead, let's have a jolly song or two."

"A fine plan!" said the peddler. "Nothing would suit me better. But everyone in his place. You're a prince, and the chief guest here. It's proper that you should sing first."

The Prince was pleased, for he liked to think of himself as a gay fellow with a fine voice. He called for wine and sang a little verse that he had just made up:

> There is a good woman lives in a wood
> (Savory dumplings and pigeon pie)
> Who bakes and fries as a good wife should:
> Savory dumplings and pigeon pie —
> If Jacques won't eat them, why can't I?

"Bless me, that was well sung," cried the peddler, laughing and clapping his hands. "Why shouldn't you, indeed?"

The Prince beamed and called for more wine. "Now it's your turn," he said to Finette.

"No, no," said Finette. "Ask the peddler. He's a traveling man, and he must know all kinds of songs."

The peddler shook his head. "Everyone in his place," he said. "First the hostess and afterward the peddler."

Finette gave in. And here is the song she sang:

> My husband has gone to Paris town
> (Savory dumplings and pigeon pie)
> So eat and drink till the moon goes down
> (Savory dumplings and pigeon pie);
> He won't be back till the snowflakes fly.

"Excellent, excellent!" laughed the peddler. "Oh, my basket and I haven't had such a good time in a month of Sundays!"

"More wine," said the Prince. "And now, Master Peddler, will you warble us a tune in your turn?"

"Sir," said the peddler, "since there is nobody left but myself and my basket, I am at your service."

And here is the song he sang:

> I met a man on the broad highway.
> (We travel far, my basket and I.)
> The man would go, but I made him stay
> (We're full of surprises, my basket and I):
> And where he is now, who can say?

Finette didn't like the sound of this song, especially when she heard another grunt from the corner where the basket stood. But Prince Bellay was too full of wine and good food to take any notice. He clapped the peddler on the back and shouted with laughter.

"I declare," said the Prince, "you talk about that old basket of yours as if it were alive! If it's as good as you say, why don't you tell it to sing the next song?"

The peddler shut one eye and chuckled. "Bless me, why not?" he said. "It doesn't do much singing in the ordinary way — just creaks and groans — but I have a notion it will sing for you."

"We'll make sure of it," laughed the Prince. "Here, basket, have some wine."

And he poured a cup of wine over the basket.

"Enough!" said the peddler. "Now, basket of mine, let's hear what kind of voice you have."

The basket creaked, and then in a muffled voice it began to sing. And this was its song:

> Good wife, your toothache's cured, I see.
> (What was your medicine—pigeon pie?)
> The Prince has dined; he'll pay the fee:
> For savory dumplings and pigeon pie
> The price is a beating. Fly, Prince, fly!

And out of the basket sprang Jacques the woodcutter, shaking his fist. Never in your life did you see a prince leave a house so fast. He didn't stop running till he was safe in his castle, with the door locked and barred. And he never went near Finette's table again.

As for Finette, she gave up her ideas of becoming rich. Nowadays Jacques Cornaud the woodcutter has onion soup whenever he wants it, and roast pigeon with artichokes on special days. Sometimes the peddler calls on them, and he can be sure of a welcome and a fine dinner. While he is at the table his old wicker basket sits quietly in the corner. It creaks a little, but it doesn't say a word.

Summary

Because of the greater plot complications and length, all of these stories will demand more time in planning than the selections for younger players. There is sufficient content to absorb the interest of the average class for several sessions, depending on the length of the periods and the age of the participants. Characters are presented in greater depth; hence much more time must be spent on their development. Most groups like to consider such questions as:

1. What is the character really like?
2. Why does the character behave as he or she does?
3. What do others think of him or her? Why?
4. If the character is not like that, why do others think so?
5. How is the character changed, or what has he or she learned as a result of his or her actions?

As the participants grow in experience, they will find new ways of telling the story. Some will want to use narrators; others, many scenes; and some may rearrange the sequence of events altogether. As was said earlier, every group is unique, and the leader learns to expect an endless variety of ways in which the same material can be handled and interpreted. The growing self-confidence of the players releases ideas that lead to further thinking and experimentation. Each group, regardless of age, becomes more critical of its efforts as, with the help of the leader, it strives for a higher level of accomplishment.

10

Creating Plays
from Other Sources

Making a Menorah. (*Courtesy of Milton E. Polsky; photograph by Robert Iulo.*)

Where does one go to find good material for creative playing? There are many sources other than stories, and the longer one teaches creative drama, the more one finds. The children's room of the public library is the best source for literature: stories, biography, science, history, and other areas of interest. The creative drama teacher as well as the classroom teacher will be wise to investigate its shelves. What are the children's interests? Have any of them special interests they would like to share and pursue? There are also family anecdotes, family recollections with ethnic backgrounds, stories no one else knows. Consider them. They might make very good plays.

For example, a creative writing contest held every two or three years in New York City entitled "Stories My Grandparents Told Me" is a rich resource for dramatization. Lively characters, amusing and touching anecdotes, customs of other lands, and experiences of immigrants in America are all fodder for the adult playwright and actor, but they are equally good for the classroom, and children love sharing them. In addition, family tales help to build respect for the cultural backgrounds of both self and others. I have been one of the judges of this contest for several years, and I am always amazed at the variety of stories that are submitted. Children from eight to eighteen write their stories, which are first read by the classroom teacher. He or she then selects the six or eight best ones from each class and sends them to the sponsoring agency of the city, which in this case is the Police Athletic League (PAL). PAL next distributes the manuscripts among the judges, who read and place them in three categories: first, second, and third. More than one judge reads each story, so that they are assured of careful, professional evaluation. Finally, decisions are made and the ten winners in the three categories on the several grade levels are announced at a simple but effective ceremony and reception. Because the contest is open to both private and public schools in all five boroughs, many manuscripts are submitted and the interest runs high. I have often suggested at the ceremony that many of these stories would make wonderful plays and that I hoped they might be used in this way.[1]

Dramatizing Legendary Material

Myths, legends, and folk tales are particularly good for creative playing. First, these stories have been told and retold over the years so that the story line is clear and easily followed. Characters are generally well defined; have complete relevance to the plot; and, even in the case of the supernatural, have credibility. The theme is usually strong, for one generation has passed the tale along to the

---

1. Conducted by the Police Athletic League of New York; Kitty Kirby, director of Performing Arts.

next, carefully, if unconsciously, preserving the values of the culture. Primitive creation myths, explaining natural phenomena, are particularly good today in the face of our expanding body of information about the universe and the new kinds of questions we are asking.

A group might dramatize a well-known myth or legend, or, through the study of legendary material, develop a play of its own. A holiday, for instance, often has an interesting origin that would make good material with which to construct a play. Halloween is a good example.

Halloween

Of all of the holidays, Halloween must certainly be one of the top favorites of children. Their fascination with the supernatural, the dressing up in fanciful and grotesque costumes, the parties, the games, the tricks and treats (all to be forgiven in the spirit of the occasion), make for a holiday with appeal for every age. Even the commercialization of Halloween in the form of ready-made costumes, masks, crêpe-paper decorations, and packages of candy corn in the supermarket have not spoiled its appeal, though it has perhaps shifted the emphasis. At any rate, Halloween as a suggestion for dramatizing is guaranteed to elicit an enthusiastic response from the most resistant group. Let's take a look at Halloween to see what some of the possibilities are.

Its roots date from antiquity, thus providing a rich source of information for playmaking as well as the fun and the social activities associated with its celebration. As a holiday, therefore, Halloween enjoys great popularity because it offers interesting content, action, and an opportunity for dressing up. Fifth and sixth graders, with the help of the teacher, can learn about play structure through the process of building a creative drama from source material concerning this holiday.

The customs associated with Halloween spring mostly from three distinct sources: pagan, Roman, and Christian. The strongest influence was probably the pagan. Each year the Druids of Northern and Western Europe celebrated two feasts—Beltane, on the first of May, and Samhain, on the thirty-first of October. The latter was a fall festival, held after the harvest had been gathered, thus marking the end of summer and the beginning of winter. Their new year began on November first, so Halloween was actually New Year's Eve. Fortune telling was a popular custom on this holiday, as people were eager to learn what the new year held.

The Druids believed that the spirits of persons who had died the previous year walked the earth on this night. They lighted bonfires to frighten away the evil spirits. It is thought that the candle in a pumpkin is a descendent of this custom. One legend has it that a rogue named Jack was caught playing tricks on the devil. As punishment, Jack was doomed to walk the earth forever, carrying a pumpkin lantern to light his way.

To ward off evil spirits and also to imitate them and so frighten others, many persons took to the wearing of costumes and masks. This led to playing tricks, mixing fun with fear and superstition.

In Rome the festivities were mainly in the form of feasts honoring the goddess of fruits, Pomona. When the Romans invaded Britain, they took their customs with them. The traditional use of fruits and vegetables (apples, corn, nuts) may be derived from this intermingling of celebrations.

During the Middle Ages the Christians observed All Saints' Day, which fell on November first. The eve of that day was October thirty-first, which became known as Halloween, or hallowed evening. There is little, if any, Christian significance left; for most people it is a secular celebration, retaining only the outward trappings of ancient customs and rituals. Witches, ghosts, goblins, cats, bats, and pumpkins come to mind when we hear the word *Halloween.* (Recently, collecting money for UNICEF has replaced the traditional "treats" in many communities.) Because so much information is available and much of it not generally known, Halloween is a good choice for a program that can be researched, improvised, written, and, if desired, performed for the enjoyment of others. The tasks involved would be:

1. Looking up information about Halloween (the amount dependent on the age of the group and the time that can be devoted to it)
2. Improvising legendary material with the greatest appeal for the children
3. Developing a program or play by the group based on the information found
4. (Optional) Writing a script that has come out of the research and improvisation

Should this prove to be something the children want to perform for others, it will lead naturally into the next stage: a play for an audience. What we are concerned with here, however, is an understanding of dramatic structure, obtained through the process of creating an original play or group project. Later, if the group so desires, it might try creating a myth of its own. Children enjoy thinking of ways to explain phenomena, sayings, or characters for which they have no ready answers. Because an activity of this sort involves creative writing as well as creative playing, it is a way in which drama can be integrated naturally into the curriculum. Younger children might want to find their own explanations for things such as the Man in the Moon, Groundhog Day, Jack Frost, candles on a birthday cake, or perhaps local jokes and customs. Older children find intellectual stimulation in the study and dramatization of myths and legends. They may also want to try their hands at the writing of original science fiction. Our space age, far more familiar and acceptable to young people than we often realize, can be a powerful force for imaginative writing. The study of dramatic structure, through the creation of an original plot, is a sound and rewarding experience.

Class Projects

Sometimes a class interest will evolve into a project that can be dramatized. This can happen on any level, from preschool through high school. A fascination with butterflies in a preschool classroom is an example of the direction one such interest took. It was told to me by one of the teachers, who described the process in the following words.

BUTTERFLIES

During the Spring, the children (3–5 years) spent a lot of time studying the life cycle of the butterfly. We patiently watched eggs (in a butterfly "house") hatch into caterpillars, then form cocoons, and finally emerge as butterflies! Interest was high during the whole process, especially as the children waited the few days it took for the butterfly wings to dry. The day arrived when it was time to let them fly outside. With great ceremony the children lined up as one of them led the way, carrying the butterfly house outside into the sunshine. As the lovely creatures flew up in the air, the excitement the children had been feeling was hushed in the wonder of the moment. But that was not the end of the experience. The Kindergarteners wanted to know more. They found new information, such as the fact that Monarch butterflies migrate from Mexico to the north to lay their eggs. There were questions such as what would happen to them in a storm? The children were encouraged to explore, through movement, the stillness of a hanging cocoon, the developing action inside the cocoon, and finally flying as butterflies. Music from the "Grand Canyon Suite" by Aaron Copeland added new drama to their experience as they listened, moved, described their feelings and imagined what the Grand Canyon must look like to a butterfly. They reveled in the storm sequence, making the most of all the elements. A story line evolved through their improvisations, and they finally felt satisfied with the whole butterfly experience. Then, of course, they wanted to share it with their parents on the last day of school. Since only family members were there, the "work-in-progress" was an informal "family" sharing.

The numbers on the back of the pictures correspond to the following story: There were two butterflies, a Momma and a Poppa at their winter home in Mexico. As the sun grew stronger and stronger, Mom and Dad felt it was time to head North to lay their eggs. As they soared North their first stop was just over the border at the Grand Canyon. After flying for a bit they decided to land and take in the view. While doing so a terrific thunderstorm came up. The children represented different elements of the storm: clouds, rain, thunder, and lightning. With that, Mom and Dad Butterfly decided the Grand Canyon was a great place to visit but not a nice place to lay eggs and raise a family. So they flew and flew and flew, and finally came to a lovely island with a big city at one end and farms and fishing villages at the other, and a Montessori school right in the middle. This was it—what more could one ask for? With that Mom and Dad laid their eggs and went off to butterfly heaven (or in the kids' literalism of today, "you mean they died").

Kindergarteners form a cocoon—after patiently waiting, the butterflies begin to come out. (*Courtesy of Julie Thompson, Plainview, New York, Montessori School.*)

The children began by being eggs. Then they became hungry caterpillars and formed cocoons. After much patient waiting, they gradually began to come out. As their wings dried, they fluttered just a little, then soared about the room before flying back to Mexico for the Winter, to start the cycle all over again.[2]

An older group would do something different with the same topic. For children in the intermediate grades, it might go in the direction of science, creative writing, poetry, or dance, depending on the age and interest of the students and the teacher's background and guidance.

THREADS

An entirely different theme was developed by older girls through an interest in women living in America a hundred years ago. Although the following account describes the work of a high school class, the subject could easily be pursued in the upper grades or on the junior high school level. I learned of the

2. Julie Thompson at the Plainview Montessori School, Plainview, New York. The children were aged three to five.

project from the drama teacher, who helped her students develop the project. They went through the following steps: a study of the role of American women in the nineteenth century, including their occupations, arts and crafts, family life, and community service. Next they did improvisations based on the study. This was followed by playwriting, using the dramatic elements of the material, and, finally, a performance of the play for the rest of the school and their families. The project was an entire semester's work, which was made possible by the enthusiasm of the students and the skilled leadership of the teacher.

The making of "Threads," a full and detailed report of the project, is too long to include, but excerpts from it give a picture of the steps taken in creating and producing a play from a theme that captured the imagination of the students and teacher. What follows is taken directly from the writer's own words.

In the fall of 1986, a colleague lent me a lovely book entitled *Anonymous Was a Woman,* a collection of words and photographs about women and the works of art they regularly and anonymously created as part of their daily lives. The book was filled with journal entries and diaries of extraordinary women, and as I sat reading parts of it to my American literature class, I was struck by how dramatic this material was. Several months later, I approached the members of the Drama Club with the suggestion that we create a script of our own. The idea was not greeted with enthusiasm. Some complained that they wanted to do a *real* play, that they could *not* write their own script and that they didn't want to, anyhow. I had envisioned enthusiasm and inspiration, yet, against my better judgment, I set about trying to convince them that they *could* write a play, that other students had done it, that it would be a great experience. . . . They were unconvinced, but a few, probably to humor me, agreed to meet several times to brainstorm with me about subject possibilities . . .

In our first session, I suggested they list all the topics about women that they could think of, no matter how bizarre. They listed topics which included everything from the lives of Greek goddesses to a show about women in different professions. Ironically, they also mentioned wanting to explore several generations in a family and/or looking at a day in the life of a village—topics which we ended up including in *Threads.* Throughout these early conversations (and indeed, throughout the entire process) I had to fight my own instinct to impose my ideas upon them or to force them into directions I wished to them to take; yet, at the same time, I had to provide enough guidance so that they did not feel abandoned and completely overwhelmed. Finally, I suggested that we narrow our focus to American women for the purposes of ease in researching material. When I had shared *Anonymous Was a Woman* with them, some liked it, but what I sometimes think really convinced them that the lives of rural women could be interesting was their realization that this kind of production would allow them to wear long dresses on the stage!

They shared my desire to focus not on the few famous women whose personalities and accomplishments have been preserved, but rather to explore the lives and feelings of the average women who lived and worked in the nineteenth century. Although my students are all city girls, they were interested in looking at rural women—perhaps because their lives are so different, or so they thought at first. We titled the production *Threads* since we were planning to explore the feelings that the women had about their handiwork and because we were interested in looking at the ways in which lives entwined and connected.

In June the girls left for the summer, full of plans for research and interviews with ancient family members, eccentric relatives, and friends. Several of the girls planned to visit the historical societies and libraries in their summer communities. I spent one sweltering morning in the library in Muncy, Pennsylvania where the library staff and the Historical Society gave me full run of the Pennsylvania Room, a collection of documents and articles about the area in which I spend my summers. I discovered no crumbling love letters or journals. I began to realize that one of the difficulties in documenting the lives of rural women of the nineteenth century was that most of them were too busy to spend time writing down how they felt. And the materials available in print tended to be too impersonal for our purposes. . . .

Later in the summer, I drove to the Laporte Historical Society. One of the members of the society accompanied me through the crowded little building. Crammed full of clothing, farm implements, scrapbooks, and family histories, the collection was fascinating. In seeing real objects that had been used, I had caught a glimpse of the women we were looking for . . . .

In September we returned to New York and our playwriting group reassembled to share information. Our February production dates seemed unreal and far off to them. I, however, was feeling more than a little nervous about how little time we had to write, cast, and rehearse a play. Once again, I encouraged them to explore more primary sources now published about women. The idea of having to do formal research was another hurdle. "Research," they exclaimed, "this is worse than history class!" Many wanted to set about creating characters out of their heads, but I suggested that they browse through some of the books our own library had to offer. Again, I wanted them to understand the value of research that was needed to enrich their work. Our school librarian was wonderful and increased the collection of appropriate materials. Some writers went to the library and copied down bibliographical information and potential quotations. Others were caught up in the process of researching trivia. One heard from her American History teacher that nineteenth century women did not wear under-clothes and she immediately came to report the news to the drama club. English and history teachers commented on the drama girls' fascination with the life of the nineteenth century woman. I was pleased that they were learning because they wanted to find out information in order to bring specific characters to life.

Our writing committee had several conversations about how to begin, how to create characters. The script was slow going. . . .

As a metaphor for the production, I suggested that we create a quilt to hang at the back of the stage. I felt that making a quilt of their own would help the girls to understand the type of creative work the women they were writing about found so important. I also thought that the group effort would be another way to reinforce the ensemble spirit which is important to create with a cast. I had never made a quilt myself and neither had any of the girls, but the club president and I examined several books on quilting and decided to go ahead with it. Each member was to design a 12" by 12" square and we would put them all together. It sounded simple! The girls were later awed when they learned that the sewing skills of a nineteenth century five-year-old far exceeded their own humble abilities.

As our writing sessions continued, we decided to name the protagonist Grace. Naming her helped clarify her character. . . .

*S*tudent production of "Threads," a celebration of the lives of nineteenth-century women, written by students at the Chapin School, New York City. (Ann Klotz, director.)

[*What followed was a detailed description of the elements that the group selected to include in the script. The plot was interspersed with poems, music, narration, and a collage based on a woman's day.*]

Gradually Grace's story took shape as we gathered more and more material. One student came across family letters from the Civil War and another brought into school the cameo her great-grandmother had worn across the Oregon trail . . . .

Early in January, our costume designer came to work on costumes. We were lucky to have a number of simple calico dresses, but because there were twenty-two in the cast, we also had to build and restore many others. Every girl in the club helped with costumes or the quilt. One became our expert ironer; others learned to gather waistbands and pin on trim. The girls ransacked their homes for shawls and aprons. Once we saw the costumes, the whole play began to seem real. We were becoming experts at the very crafts we had been reading about.

During four long Saturday rehearsals we did a combination of acting and tech work. Our set was simple—the frame of a house against the upstage wall and a number of platforms to provide levels and discrete playing areas . . . .

We decided to include several poems and the words to an old folk song about a quilting bee. I had a friend compose music for this and we used it at the end of the first act. At different points in the show, I had several girls enter and speak about the same topics: girlhood, courtship, motherhood, etc. These served as transitions or bridges. Speaking the lines about having a baby, or getting engaged, or going West, the girls noticed that perhaps their 1980s lives were not so very different from those of the young women they were acting after all—at least the feelings were the same across one hundred years. . . .

Until the dress rehearsal I had worried that although the show had taught the girls a great deal, it might be painful to watch. I was not confident that we had had enough rehearsal time, that the understudies could pull off their roles, that the other girls had the confidence to carry on no matter what happened. There were moments in the show I was still dissatisfied with, things I would have changed had the show not been created by the students. The director in me battled with the teacher in me. In short, I was not sure *Threads* would be good theatre. But magically, the opening came and the audience was spellbound . . .

Spring vacation came and went and we returned to school to talk about plans for next year. "How about Shakespeare?" I inquired at a Drama Club meeting. "Shakespeare," one eighth grader muttered indignantly, "you mean we're not going to write our own play?" Another member added, "What if it's not as good as *Threads*?" I laughed and reminded them about their initial misgivings about *Threads*. They looked offended; surely I had been mistaken—they always knew that *Threads* would be wonderful! I smiled back at them. We had learned a lot from one another.[3]

Other Suggestions

The following list of topics includes a wide variety of sources that can be used for simple improvisations but can also be expanded into original plots or even well-developed plays like *Threads*. Many sources are worth time spent on research and may inspire players to work on them over a long period, eventually sharing them with an audience. Some are:

Advertisements	Occupations
Bridges	Time
Rivers	Headlines in newspapers
Cartoons	Letters to the editor
Photographs	"Personals"
Posters	Books (printing and publishing)
Sculpture	Tools
Poetry	Animal welfare
Hands	Space
Coins	Sports (All sports offer material that interests children.)

Some of the best projects come out of field trips. Field trips, because they have been planned for their content, suggest topics that can be noted by the teacher in follow-up discussions. A trip to a seaport or harbor, for instance, might arouse curiosity about the old sailing ships, boats of all kinds, immigration and immigrants, marine life, and so on. Museums of natural history are obvious sources of information and should be explored for ideas on science and social studies. Art museums and special exhibitions can stimulate interest in individual artists, other periods, and foreign countries. Costume and jewelry exhibits as

3. Ann Klotz' report "The Making of *Threads*" by her students at the Chapin School, New York City.

well as crafts and folk art appeal to young people. Trips to factories generate questions, leading to possibilities for study that can lead into drama or documentaries. The latter, incidentally, are splendid sources for T.I.E. (Theatre-in-Education) programs and can be developed by older children, often expressing a strong point of view.

Summary

Many beginning teachers tend to use stories exclusively as material for creative drama. Although good stories and folklore are excellent, there are hundreds of other sources available, and it is in that interest that this chapter was included. Creating plays from researched topics is difficult because the structure must be developed by the teacher and the class, but it is excellent practice in writing and can bring enormous satisfaction to the group that tries it. Yes, it is a risk, but a risk worth taking. If the first attempt is not successful, do not be discouraged; try again. The teacher and the class will learn much in the process.

11 The Possibilities in Poetry

Poetry and dance go well together. *(Courtesy of Lucille Paolillo, Children's Centre for the Creative Arts, Adelphi University; photograph by George Meyer.)*

*C*hildren like poetry. They are sensitive to the rhythm of it and enjoy the repetition of sounds, words, and phrases. The direct approach of the poet is not unlike their own; hence poetry, unless it has been spoiled for them, has a special appeal. The music and language, as well as the ideas, feelings, and images of poetry, reach the younger child particularly, capturing and stimulating his or her imagination. For this reason, poetry can be used in creative dramatics, often with highly successful results.

Many leaders find poetry a more satisfactory springboard than prose for introducing creative playing to a group. This is probably an individual matter, depending as much on the leader as on the participants. If the leader or teacher enjoys poetry, he or she will find that it provides a rich source of material that can be used at all levels of experience and with all ages. For children, poetry and play go together naturally. "The affinity between poetry and play is not external only; it is also apparent in the structure of creative imagination itself. In the turning of a poetic phrase, the development of a motif, the expression of a mood, there is always a play element at work."[1]

For these reasons, the possibilities in poetry as motivation are considered. What kinds of poems are usable? How can poetry and movement be combined? Has choral speaking any place in creative dramatics? For the answers to these questions, one has only to go to children themselves, as they engage in their play. Many of their games are accompanied by chants, which are a form of choral speaking. In action games, rhythm is basic, whereas some games are played to verse with the players often making up their own original stanzas. If we listen, we note the enjoyment of repetition, refrain, and the sounds of words. Only very much later does poetry become a literary form to be taken seriously, and when it does, the element of play is, unfortunately, too often lost.

Choral Speaking

Because poetry lends itself so well to group enjoyment, let us begin with a consideration of choral speaking, its purposes, and its procedures. Choral reading, or speaking, is simply reading or reciting in unison under the direction of a leader. It is not a new technique, for people have engaged in it for centuries. It antedated the theatre in the presentation of ideas and became an important element of the Greek drama. Evidences of choral speaking have been found in the religious ceremonies and festivals of primitive peoples, and today it is still used for ritualistic purposes in church services and on patriotic occasions. In the early twentieth century, however, it was recognized as one of the most effective methods of teaching the language arts and of improving speech habits.

In the past, choral speaking was used as an important means of communication and communion; today it is an art form as well and is employed both ways by

1. Johan Huizinga, *Homo Ludens* (Boston: Beacon Press, 1955), p. 14.

the theatre, the church, and the school. When working with older children or adults, the two major purposes of the activity are:

1. Learning (when the purpose is process and, therefore, participant centered)
2. Performance (when the purpose is program and, therefore, audience centered)

Often the former leads into the latter, but like creative drama, it does not necessarily follow that practice must result in performance. Practice has values of its own, whether or not the product is shared.

Values

One of the values of choral speaking is that it can be used successfully regardless of space or class size. Although a group of twenty or so is more desirable than one of forty or fifty, the larger number need not be a deterrent.

Many teachers consider the greatest value of choral speaking the opportunity it provides for speech improvement. Pitch, volume, rate, and tone quality are important to the effective interpretation of material. The need for clear diction is apparent when a group is reading aloud, whereas the practicing of speech sounds alone is often a tedious and unrelated exercise. During discussion, even young children will make suggestions as to how a poem should be recited. Vocal expression and the clear enunciation of speech sounds are often acquired more easily and with greater motivation when the group works together on meaning.

A third value, and one shared with creative dramatics, is the opportunity it provides for social cooperation. Choral speaking is a group activity and, by its nature, therefore, directs each individual to a common goal. The child with the strident voice learns to soften his or her tone, whereas the shy child can work for more volume without feeling self-conscious. Even the speech-handicapped child may recite without embarrassment, because she is not speaking alone and, therefore, is not conspicuous.

A fourth value of choral speaking is its suitability to any age level. It may be introduced in the kindergarten but is equally effective when used in high school or college classes. Not all material is adapted to choral work, but much of it is, and the major criterion is probably that it be enjoyed and recommended by the readers themselves.

Procedures

There are many ways of beginning choral speaking, but with younger children, it will probably spring from their own enjoyment of a poem and their obvious desire to say it aloud or to the accompaniment of action. With older children who have had no experience in group reading, the teacher will not only select the material with care but will give some thought in advance to its interpretation. Discussion of the meaning and of the various ways of reading the material so as to bring out the meaning give the pupils a part in planning the group reading. A second reading will reveal further meaning, as well as difficulties in phrasing and diction.

As the group becomes more experienced, it will offer suggestions about those lines that may be most effectively taken by the whole group, by part of the group, and by individual voices. Although a structured activity, choral speaking offers a real opportunity for creative thinking, as each group works out its own presentation. The teacher leads, indicating when to start, and watches the phrasing, emphases, and pauses suggested by the readers. The time spent on a poem will vary, but it is more important to keep the enthusiasm alive than it is to work for perfection. With practice, the group will grow increasingly sensitive to the demands of different kinds of material, and their results will improve in proportion to their understanding and enjoyment.

Most authorities on choral speaking suggest dividing the group into light and dark voices. This is not the same as a division into high and low or soprano and alto voices but has to do with quality and resonance as well as pitch. Some leaders, on the other hand, believe that a division in which there are both light and dark in each group makes for more interesting quality. However it is done, some division is necessary for any group of more than ten participants. Some poems can be read by three groups if the class is very large. These groups may include middle voices, though, again, it is the material that will suggest the groupings rather than an arbitrary division.

Ways of Reading

Unison: The whole group reads together. Although the simplest in one sense, this is the most difficult, since using all voices limits variation. Some poems, particularly short ones, are most effective when read or spoken by the entire class.

Antiphonal: This is a division into two groups with each taking certain parts. Many poems are more effective when read in this way. The poem will dictate the way it may be read.

Cumulative: When this technique is used, it is for the purpose of building toward a climax or certain high points in the poem. As the term suggests, it is the accumulation of voices, either individually or by groups.

Solo: Often lines or stanzas call for individual reading. This can be an effective technique, as well as a way of giving an opportunity for individual participation.

Line-Around: This is solo work, in which each line is taken by a different reader. Children enjoy this and are alert to the lines they have been assigned.

As the group progresses and attempts longer and more difficult material, it may suggest using several or all of these techniques in one poem. The results can be remarkably effective, encouraging attentiveness and self-discipline, as well as imaginative planning. Occasionally, sound effects can be added. Music, bells, drums, and vocal sounds, produced by the readers themselves, provide an opportunity for further inventiveness.

Because our primary concern is creative drama, only those poems that suggest movement or pantomime are included here. The following have been used successfully with groups, combining choral speaking and activities suggested by the content or sounds. The first, "Happy New Year," is an old rhyme, suggesting the simplest kind of movement as a beginning.

> Happy New Year! Happy New Year!
> I've come to wish you a Happy New Year.
> I've got a little pocket and it is very thin.
> Please give me a penny to put some money in.
> If you haven't got a penny, a halfpenny will do.
> If you haven't got a halfpenny, well—
> God bless you!

In England, children went caroling from house to house on New Year's Day. Their neighbors gave them money, much as we give candy and apples for trick-or-treat on Halloween. Whether or not they received a contribution, they sang or spoke, and this old rhyme has been handed down. The group can say the verse together, with one child acting the part of the caroler; or half of the group can speak, with the other half playing the carolers. Perhaps the entire group will want to speak and move. There are various possibilities in even as short a rhyme as this.

A very simple verse, but one that offers an unusual opportunity for imaginative movement, is "Jump or Jiggle." Not only children but adult students as well get into the spirit of it and have a good time thinking of movements that characterize the animals mentioned.

JUMP OR JIGGLE
EVELYN BEYER

> Frogs jump.
> Caterpillars hump.
> Worms wiggle.
> Bugs jiggle.
> Rabbits hop.
> Horses clop.
> Snakes slide.
> Sea gulls glide.
> Mice creep.
> Deer leap.
> Puppies bounce.
> Lions stalk—
> But
> I walk.

The next verse suggests the use of sound effects rather than action. Part of the group might say the first and third lines, with the others taking the second and fourth. Or, if two clocks are suggested, a solo voice might take the first and third, with the total group taking the other lines. Even so simple a poem as this provides some opportunity for inventiveness.

> Slowly ticks the big clock:
> Tick-tock; tick-tock!
> But cuckoo clock ticks a double quick:
> Tick-a-tock-a, tick-a-tock-a,
> Tick-a-tock-a, tick!

MERRY-GO-ROUND
DOROTHY BARUCH

> I climbed up on the merry-go-round,
> And it went round and round.
> I climbed up on a big brown horse,
> And it went up and down.
>
> Around and round and up and down.
> Around and round and up and down.
>
> I sat high up on a big brown horse,
> And rode around on the merry-go-round,
> And rode around on the merry-go-round.
> I rode around on the merry-go-round
> Around
> And round
> And
> Round.

This poem is fun for children of all ages because of the action, which requires some coordination. As with the others, half of the group can read it while the other half acts the merry-go-round; or if the group is small, everyone can do the action while repeating the lines. It is probably more satisfactory handled the first way, with variety achieved by having individual voices take the lines beginning with "I." Sometimes children like to imagine the merry-go-round running down until it comes to a stop.

ECHO
AUTHOR UKNOWN

> I sometimes wonder where he lives,
> This Echo that I never see.
> I heard his voice now in the hedge,
> Then down behind the willow tree.

And when I call, "Oh, please come out,"
"Come out," he always quick replies.
"Hello, hello," again I say;
"Hello, hello," he softly cries.

He must be jolly, Echo must,
For when I laugh, "Ho, ho, ho, ho,"
He answers me with "Ho, ho, ho."

I think perhaps he'd like to play;
I know some splendid things to do.
He must be lonely hiding there;
I wouldn't like it. Now, would you?

Echoes are fascinating, and this poem is one that may prompt a group to make up an original story about echoes. It lends itself so well to choral reading that it is suggested the class try it this way first and then discuss whether something else might be done with it. The lines in which the Echo speaks are good solo lines that stimulate speculation as to whom the Echo is, what the Echo is like, where the Echo is hiding, and whether or not the Echo is ever discovered. Some groups have made up delightful stories about the Echo after reading the poem together first.

Both younger and older students find enjoyment in simple folk rhymes. The following are included because they can be interpreted in more than one way: literally, telling the stories; and abstractly, dancing the characters caught in amusing situations.

SIMPLE SIMON

Simple Simon met a pieman,
    Going to the fair;
Says Simple Simon to the Pieman,
    Let me taste your ware.

Says the Pieman to Simple Simon,
    Show me first your penny;
Says Simple Simon to the pieman,
    Indeed I have not any.

Simple Simon went a-fishing,
    For to catch a whale;
All the water he had got
    Was in his mother's pail.

Simple Simon went to look
    If plums grew on a thistle;
He pricked his finger very much,
    Which made poor Simon whistle.

THE QUEEN OF HEARTS

The Queen of Hearts
She made some tarts,
All on a summer's day;
The Knave of Hearts
He stole the tarts,
And took them clean away.
The King of Hearts
Called for the tarts,
And beat the Knave full sore;
The Knave of Hearts
Brought back the tarts,
And vowed he'd steal no more.

Although choral speaking is an effective way to begin pantomime, it is not the only way of using poetry. Often a poem can be introduced by the leader, either before or after improvisation. The poem may serve as a springboard to action in which the whole class participates, but the improvising class does not necessarily repeat or read the verse. One short poem that has proved highly successful with many groups of all ages is "Halloween."

HALLOWE'EN
GERALDINE BRAIN SIKS

Sh! Hst!
Hsst! Shssssh!
It's Hallowe'en.
Eerie creatures now are seen.
Black, bent witches fly
Like ugly shadows through the sky.
White, stiff ghosts do float
Silently, like mystery smoke.

Lighted pumpkins glow
With crooked eyes and grins to show
It's Hallowe'en
Hssst! Shssh!
Sh! Hst!

The period might start off with a discussion of what we think of when we hear the word *Halloween*. Most groups suggest pumpkins, witches, orange and black, elves, broomsticks, cats, night, ghosts, trick-or-treat, and masks. Some pantomime to music can be introduced here, with the whole class becoming witches, cats, or ghosts. After they are thoroughly in the spirit of Halloween, the poem can be read. When the group is small, all may be eerie creatures, witches, and ghosts. When the group is large, it can be divided into several parts, with each one choosing one idea to pantomime. Pumpkins have been suggested in a variety of ways: rolling about on the floor in rounded shapes, squatting with big smiles, and moving in circles to music. Music is helpful, though not necessary. This poem never fails to arouse a response, and on one occasion led to an informal program of Halloween poems and improvisations.

The next poem is one that has been most successful with both children and adults. The universality of its theme appeals to everyone and stimulates an imaginative response at any time of the year. It was the basis for a delightful improvisation by a group of Puerto Rican teachers, who understood and enjoyed it in English, then improvised it with Spanish dialogue.

SING A SONG OF SEASONS
ALICE ELLISON

It's spring.
Such a hippity, happity, hoppity
First spring day.
Let's play! Let's play! Let's play!

It's summer!
Such a swingy, swazy lazy
First hot day.
Let's play! Let's play! Let's play!

It's fall!
Such a brisky, frisky, crispy
First fall day.
Let's play! Let's play! Let's play!

It's winter!
Such a blowy, snowy joy
First winter day.
Let's play! Let's play! Let's play!

Before reading the poem, there can be pantomimes of simple sports and games. Flying kites, skating, tossing a ball, jumping rope, and playing tennis are familiar activities that serve to get the group moving and break down the barriers of self-consciousness. After perhaps fifteen minutes of this kind of activity, the teacher is ready to read the poem. Discussion about games and sports appropriate to each season directs the thinking and often brings some unexpected suggestions. After everyone has had a chance to offer ideas, the teacher can ask how the poem might be played.

If the class is separated into four groups, each group can take a season, showing various games and sports belonging to it. Some groups create situations for each, such as going to the beach in summer, with sunbathing, swimming, picnicking, and the like. More than one group has created a scene with characters for each season, using the poem only as a springboard for an original situation. It is urged that this be done in the round, rather than on a stage or in the front of a room, so as to allow for as much movement as possible and easy passage into the center without breaking the mood.

IMAGININGS
J. PAGET-FREDERICKS

Imagine!
A little red door that leads under a hill
Beneath roots and bright stones and pebbly rill.

Imagine!
A quaint little knocker and shoe scraper, too—
A curious carved key
Is waiting for you.

Imagine!
Tiptoe on doormat, you're turning the key.
The red door would open
And there you'd be.

Imagine!
Shut the door tightly, so no one could see.
And no one would know then
Where you would be.
Imagine, if you can.

A poem such as "Imaginings" lends itself to all kinds of improvisation. Every age will find an answer to the question: What lies behind the little red door? It is a good idea for the teacher to read the poem aloud two or three times before asking what the group sees in it. If the class is not too large, every child may be given a chance to describe what he or she sees. Younger children find buried treasure, a forbidden city, thieves, a ghost town. Some may describe a place they know, with friends or neighbors inhabiting it. This particular poem is a wonderful springboard for the imagination, since it leads listeners to the threshold and then leaves them free to follow their own ideas.

Some groups have been stimulated to plan an original play, involving several characters. If many good suggestions come out of the discussion, the leader may want to break the class into small groups of three or four, who will in turn dramatize their ideas. Occasionally, if a group is very small, or if the teacher wants to plan an individual lesson, each child may pantomime what he or she sees and does behind the red door. The poem can hold a group for two or three sessions, depending on their readiness to use the material and the interest it stimulates.

SOME ONE
WALTER DE LA MARE

Some one came knocking
    At my wee, small door;
Some one came knocking,
    I'm sure—sure—sure;
I listened, I opened,
    I looked to left and right,
But nought there was a-stirring
    In the still dark night;
Only the busy beetle
    Tap-tapping in the wall,
Only from the forest
    The screech owl's call
Only the cricket whistling
    While the dewdrops fall,
So I know not who came knocking
    At all, at all, at all.

"Some One" has the same power as the previous poem to evoke an imaginative response. Though the poem is short, it creates an atmosphere of mystery and wonder. Who can be knocking? How large is the "wee, small door"? Who am "I"? Do I ever find out who my mysterious visitor was? How do I react? Groups of all ages enjoy imagining this situation, and the teacher may expect a variety of responses and interpretations. Some children have insisted that the door can be no more than a few inches high, which leads into the question of whose house it is. Fairies, elves, friendly insects, and mice have all been suggested. Other children have seen it as a cottage door—small compared to the doors of city buildings. Visitors, in this case, vary from mysterious strangers with magic powers to actual persons—frightened and faint with weariness. Indians have been suggested, investigating an early settler's cabin. Because the poet does not say who knocked, the reader is entirely free to create his or her own situation, and some delightful stories have been inspired as a result.

SEA SHELL
AMY LOWELL

Sea Shell, Sea Shell,
    Sing me a song, O please
A song of ships, and sailor men,
    And parrots, and tropical trees.

Of islands lost in the Spanish Main
Which no man ever may find again,
Of fishes and coral under the waves,

And sea-horses stabled in great green caves.

Sea Shell, Sea Shell,
Sing of the things you know so well.

Although "Sea Shell" offers vivid imagery, it leaves the imagination free to roam tropical isles and savor adventure. Every child responds to the singing of a shell, and most will go on to ideas of their own. Perhaps having the group tell their own stories is a good beginning. What did you hear? Where did you find the shell? What is it like? What did it sing when you listened? Tell us its story.

Having a collection of shells adds to the interest as the children feel and examine them. Elaborate plays set on unknown shores have resulted, with the children responding to the thoughts of sailors, pirates, and treasures buried in the sand.

The poems of Robert Louis Stevenson have long appealed to children, and both their content and the suggestions for action make them especially appropriate for creative drama. The two poems that follow can be used with quite young children, who may already be familiar with them.

MY SHADOW
ROBERT LOUIS STEVENSON

I have a little shadow that goes in and out with me.
And what can be the use of him is more than I can see.
He is very, very like me from the heels up to the head;
And I see him jump before me, when I jump into my bed.

The funniest thing about him is the way he likes to grow—
Not at all like proper children, which is always very slow;
For he sometimes shoots up taller like an India-rubber ball;
And he sometimes gets so little that there's none of him at all.

He hasn't got a notion of how children ought to play,
And can only make a fool of me in every sort of way.
He stays so close beside me, he's a coward, you can see;
I'd think shame to stick to nursie as that shadows sticks to me!

One morning, very early, before the sun was up,
I rose and found the shining dew on every buttercup;
But my lazy little shadow, like an arrant sleepy-head,
had stayed at home behind me and was fast asleep in bed.

The idea of a shadow offers all kinds of possibilities. The group might try this one all together—half being children; half, shadows. This could also lead into original stories, with use of shadows as a theme. It could also stimulate the writing of original verse.

The Wind

Robert Louis Stevenson

I saw you toss the kites on high
And blow the birds about the sky;
And all around I heard you pass,
Like ladies' skirts across the grass—
    O wind a-blowing all day long,
    O wind, that sings so loud a song.

I saw the different things you did,
But always you yourself you hid.
I felt you push, I heard you call,
I could not see yourself at all—
    O wind a-blowing all day long,
    O wind, that sings so loud a song.

    O you that are so strong and cold,
    O blower, are you young or old?
Are you a beast of field and tree
    Or just a stranger child than me?
    O wind a-blowing all day long,
    O wind, that sings so loud a song.

Like the preceding verse, "The Wind" offers a wonderful opportunity for strong movement. The group can divide up in many ways, being everything that is mentioned: the wind, the birds, the kites, the skirts, and other things that the children may suggest. Wind is a good topic for discussion, often suggesting original stories as well as the search for other stories such as Aesop's fable *The Sun and the Wind.* A whole unit could be developed on the subject or on the natural elements.

Most children at one time or another have made a mobile. Perhaps there is one in the classroom. The following poem describes a mobile, suggesting how it moves and seems to be alive. How can it be used as a springboard to suggest movement and dramatic action? See what it suggests to the class.

Mobile

David McCord

Our little mobile hangs and swings
And likes a draft and drafty things:

Half-open doors; wide-window breeze,
All people when they cough or sneeze;

Hot dishes giving off their heat;
Big barking dogs, small running feet.

Our mobile's red and made to look
Like fish about to bite a hook:

Six fishes with a hook in front
Of each. They range in size—the runt,

Or baby, up to papa fish,
With hooks to watch and make them wish

That they could reach the nice blue worms
A-dangle there with swirly squirms;

Six fishy mouths all open wide,
Six sets of teeth all sharp inside,

Six fishy holes where eyes should be,
Six fish to swim on airy sea.

I'm eating breakfast now and they are watching me.
And I must say

That every time I take a bite
I see and feel their sorry plight.

Birds, fish, and sailboats are often used as subjects for mobiles. This is because they all move, dip, turn, and swirl as the air circulates around them. There is almost a magic in the way a mobile moves, even when there appears to be no breeze stirring. Without using words, have the class be a mobile:

Moving as separate parts of the mobile
Putting the parts together in a formation
Moving without touching the other parts of the mobile

Now break the class into small groups, each suggesting in movement the images described in the verse. Try adding the images to the moving mobile.

This may lead to the making of a mobile or the creating of a verse. Or it may lead to an entirely different way of suggesting a mobile. See what it makes the class feel, see, do.

Langston Hughes's poetry is rich in images and rhythms. This particular short work suggests strong movement, which older children enjoy using to create the different rivers.

THE NEGRO SPEAKS OF RIVERS
LANGSTON HUGHES

I've known rivers:
I've known rivers ancient as the world and older than
  the flow of human blood in human veins.
My soul has grown deep like the rivers.
I bathed in the Euphrates when dawns were young.

I built my hut near the Congo and it lulled me to
   sleep.
I looked upon the Nile and raised the pyramids above
   it.
I heard the singing of the Mississippi when Abe Lincoln
   went down to New Orleans, and I've seen its muddy
   bosom turn all golden in the sunset.

I've known rivers:
Ancient, dusky rivers.
My soul has grown deep like the rivers.

After some discussion of the places and the different kinds of rivers described in the poem, the children will be ready to use it as a springboard. Strong movement and use of the whole body are called for; perhaps large groups, moving together, can suggest the vast bodies of water better than one or two persons. What else is there to depict besides the waters? Are there any people? Does anything happen? What does the last line mean? How can this be expressed?

THE OLD WIFE AND THE GHOST
JAMES REEVES

There was an old wife and she lived all alone
In a cottage not far from Hitchin:
And one bright night, by the full moon light,
Comes a ghost right into her kitchen.

About that kitchen neat and clean
The ghost goes pottering round.
But the poor old wife is deaf as a boot
And so hears never a sound

The ghost blows up the kitchen fire,
As bold as bold can be;
He helps himself from the larder shelf,
But never a sound hears she.

He blows on his hands to make them warm,
And whistles aloud "Whee-hee!"
But still as a sack the old soul lies
And never a sound hears she.

From corner to corner he runs about,
And into the cupboard he peeps;
He rattles the door and bumps on the floor,
But still the old wife sleeps.

Jangle and bang go the pots and pans,
As he throws them all around;

And the plates and mugs and dishes and jugs,
He flings them all to the ground.

Madly the ghost tears up and down
And screams like a storm at sea;
At last the old wife stirs in her bed—
And it's "Drat those mice," says she.

Then the first cock crows and morning shows
And the troublesome ghost's away.
But oh! what a pickle the poor wife sees
When she gets up next day.

"Them's tidy big mice," the old wife thinks.
And off she goes to Hitchin.
And a tidy big cat she fetches back
To keep the mice from her kitchen.

This amusing verse should stimulate all kinds of ideas for dramatization, characterization, and movement. It can be done entirely in mime or with improvised dialogue. Why not have the entire group work on the ghost's movement and activities? They will enjoy it, and many ideas will be expressed within the security of the group. Music and sound effects are helpful and add atmosphere. This is a good poem for Halloween, but it has a strong appeal for young children at any time of year.

The next selection, *"A Sioux Indian Prayer,"* suggests movement as the spoken word. It can be said in unison by part of the class with the rest of the class expressing it in dance, or spoken by one with the class moving, or spoken by the entire group with one child dancing. It is a lovely piece to which I have found students very responsive. The words and the meaning behind them appeal to both younger and older children. Discussion can be expected because of the cultural differences and the beauty of the form.

A SIOUX INDIAN PRAYER

O' GREAT SPIRIT,
Whose voice I hear in the winds,
And whose breath gives life to all the world,
hear me! I am small and weak, I need your
strength and wisdom.

LET ME WALK IN BEAUTY, and make my eyes
ever behold the red and purple sunset.

MAKE MY HANDS respect the things you have
made and my ears sharp to hear your voice.

MAKE ME WISE so that I may understand the
things you have taught my people.

LET ME LEARN the lessons you have hidden
in every leaf and rock.

I SEEK STRENGTH, not to be greater than my
brother, but to fight my greatest
enemy—myself.

MAKE ME ALWAYS READY to come to you with
clean hands and straight eyes.

SO WHEN LIFE FADES, *as the fading sunset,*
my spirit may come to you
without shame.

The "Blind Men and the Elephant" is a favorite on all levels and begs for
pantomime. Like "A Sioux Indian Prayer," it can be handled in several ways. Not
only is the humor fun, but the idea always causes discussion about how we make
judgments.

THE BLIND MEN AND THE ELEPHANT
JOHN G. SAXE

It was six men of Indostan
  To learning much inclined,
Who went to see the Elephant
  (Though all of them were blind),
That each by observation
  Might satisfy his mind.

The First approached the Elephant,
  And happening to fall
Against his broad and sturdy side,
  At once began to bawl:
"God bless me! but the Elephant
  Is very like a wall!"

The Second, feeling of the tusk,
  Cried, "Ho! what have we here
So very round and smooth and sharp?
  To me 'tis mighty clear
This wonder of an Elephant
  Is very like a spear!"

The Third approached the animal,
  And happening to take
The squirming trunk within his hands,
  Thus boldly up and spake:
"I see," quoth he, "the Elephant
  Is very like a snake!"

The Fourth reached out his eager hand,
    And felt about the knee.
"What most this wondrous beast is like
    Is mighty plain," quoth he;
"'Tis clear enough the Elephant
    Is very like a tree!"

The Fifth, who chanced to touch the ear
    Said, "E'en the blindest man
Can tell what this resembles most;
    Deny the fact who can,
This marvel of an Elephant
Is very like a fan!"

The Sixth no sooner had begun
    About the beast to grope,
Than, seizing on the swinging tail
    That fell within his scope,
"I see," quoth he, "the Elephant
    Is very like a rope."

And so these men of Indostan
    Disputed loud and long,
Each in his own opinion
    Exceeding stiff and strong.
Though each was partly in the right,
    And all were in the wrong!

Younger children enjoy acting out the story as it is being read. However it is handled, the idea provides opportunity for pantomime and or food for thought.

"The Creation" can be read, acted, or danced. Most young people respond to its power and find in its strong, imaginative style a stimulus for expression of one or another of these dramatic forms. It is suggested that it be read aloud first, then performed both in dance and in mime. Because of the numbers of creatures the poet includes, it is an ideal piece for a large group to work on.

THE CREATION
JAMES WELDON JOHNSON

And God stepped out on space,
And he looked around and said:
I'm lonely—
I'll make me a world.

And as far as the eye of God could see
Darkness covered everything,
Blacker than a hundred midnights
Down in a cypress swamp.

Then God smiled,
And the light broke,
And the darkness rolled up on one side,
And the light stood shining on the other,
And God said: That's good!

Then God reached out and took the light in his hands,
And God rolled the light in his hands
Until he made the sun;
And he set that sun a-blazing in the heavens.
And the light that was left from making the sun
God gathered it up in a shining ball
And flung it against the darkness,
Spangling the night with the moon and stars.
Then down between
The darkness and the light
He hurled the world;
And God said: That's good!

Then God himself stepped down—
And the sun was on his right hand,
And the moon was on his left;
The stars were clustered about his head,
And the earth was under his feet.
And God walked, and where he trod
His footsteps hollowed the valleys out
And bulged the mountains up.

Then he stopped and saw
That the earth was hot and barren.
So God stepped over to the edge of the world
And he spat out the seven seas—
He batted his eyes, and the lightnings flashed—
He clapped his hands, and the thunders rolled—
And the waters above the earth came down,
The cooling waters came down.

Then the green grass sprouted,
And the little red flowers blossomed,
The pine tree pointed his finger to the sky,
And the oak spread out his arms,
The lakes cuddled down in the hollows of the ground,
And the rivers ran down to the sea;
And God smiled again,
And the rainbow appeared,
And curled itself around his shoulder.

Then God raised his arm and waved his hand,
Over the sea and over the land,
And he said; Bring forth! Bring forth!

And quicker than God could drop his hand,
Fishes and fowls
And beasts and birds
Swam the rivers and the seas,
Roamed the forests and the woods,
And split the air with their wings.
And God said: That's good!

Then God walked around,
And God looked around
On all that he had made.
He looked at his sun,
And he looked at his moon,
And he looked at his little stars;
He looked on his world
With all its living things,
And God said; I'm lonely still.

Then God sat down—
On the side of a hill where he could think;
By a deep, wide river he sat down;
With his head in his hands,
God thought and thought,
Till he thought; I'll make me a man!

Up from the bed of the river
God scooped the clay;
And by the bank of the river
He kneeled him down;
And there the great God Almighty
Who lit the sun and fixed it in the sky,
Who flung the stars to the most far corner of the night,
Who rounded the earth in the middle of his hand;
This great God,
Like a mammy bending over her baby,
Kneeled down in the dust
Toiling over a lump of clay
Till he shaped it in his own image;

Then into it he blew the breath of life,
And man became a living soul.
Amen. Amen.

I HEAR AMERICA SINGING
WALT WHITMAN

I hear America singing, the varied carols I hear.
Those of mechanics, each one singing his as it
   should be blithe and strong,
The carpenter singing as he measures his plank
   or beam,

The mason singing his as he makes ready for
work, or leaves off work.
The boatman singing what belongs to him in his
boat, the deckhand singing on the steamboat
deck,
The shoemaker singing as he sits on his bench,
the hatter singing as he stands,
The wood-cutter's song, the ploughboy's on his
way in the morning, or at noon intermission or
at sundown,
The delicious singing of the mother, or of the
young wife at work, or of the girl sewing or
washing.
Each singing what belongs to him or her and to
none else.
The day what belongs to the day—at night the
party of young fellows, robust, friendly.
Singing with open mouths their strong
melodious songs.

"I Hear America Singing" is a splendid poem for both choral speaking and dramatization. The various characters and their occupations suggest pantomime to participants of all ages. If playing in a large room, the characters can be scattered about the circle, with any number taking part. Pantomime and speaking may be done simultaneously or separately, as the group prefers. This is a poem that is particularly appealing to older students, who are often stimulated to further reading of the poet's work. The mood is powerful and usually acts as a unifying element.

Puppets and Poetry

An imaginative program combining puppets and poetry was devised by two artist/teachers in New Jersey a few years ago. Its popularity attests the effectiveness of the method, which is described in their brochure as follows:

More and more puppets are used in education to add dimensions to learning. A puppet can add clarity and motion to difficult teaching problems and abstractions, demonstrating to the students a living picture of the offered material.[2]

The artist/teachers make the point that poetry and puppets have certain similarities: the words are the puppets of the poem, just as puppets are the materials of the puppeteer. In each case, total involvement is necessary. The idea is not to be construed as a gimmick but rather as another way of teaching the language arts. Lyric poems are handled with great simplicity to deepen emotion-

2. Leila Weisholz and Lois Koenig. *Poetry and Puppets in Education* (Cedar Grove, NJ).

A member of the audience meets an actor after a performance of "The Magic Word," a poetry program. *(Courtesy of Periwinkle Productions, Inc., Monticello, N.Y.)*

al involvement and not distract by excessive movement. Narrative poetry, on the other hand, is presented differently; puppets mime the story as the poem is read aloud. Puppets demonstrate the basic exaggerations of poetry, the artists say. Results include not only enjoyment and a better understanding of the poetic form but also encouragement of the writing of original verse.

Poetry and Dance

Poetry grew out of dance and song, and so they are natural companions. Bringing a dancer to the class—the dance teacher, perhaps older students who have had more dance experience than the class, or a professional dancer if one is available—adds another dimension when working with poems. For one thing, dance offers an abstract expression rather than the more literal interpretation of mime and improvisation. Dividing the class, with one half moving to the cadence and meaning of the poem and the other half speaking it, calls for imagination and cooperation. This approach is not suggested for older students only; younger children, though lacking well-developed performance skills, are often freer in interpreting poetry through movement.

Working on poetry first in mime and then in dance helps students to experience it more fully. Lyric verse lends itself best to nonverbal interpretation, whereas narrative and dramatic verse stimulate the improvisation of dialogue. Some groups respond to poetry more readily than others but most will enjoy it, if the leader's approach is positive and enthusiastic.

A poet or professional children's theatre company that performs poetry may inspire children. One such company is The Periwinkle Productions of Monticello, New York, which began playing poetry programs more than twenty years ago and retains poetry performance as an important emphasis in an expanding theatrical repertory. In addition to doing poetry reading and performances, the company works in schools with teachers to encourage creative writing, principally poetry. Special classes as well as English classes have responded to the stimulation and have achieved some remarkable results.

Summary

Poetry is an effective springboard for improvisation and improvisation, for poetry. The directness of verse motivates the players to a response that is direct and imaginative. For this reason, poetry is a good starting point for the beginner, though it can be used at any time with even the most advanced players. Because the sounds of poetry have as great an appeal as the content and mood, it is suggested that poetry be spoken as well as acted.

Choral speaking is a group art and can, therefore, be combined with creative dramatics if the teacher so wishes. Some of the reasons for including choral speaking are as follows:

1. It can be done with groups of any size and age.
2. It emphasizes group rather than individual effort.
3. It provides an opportunity to introduce poetry.
4. It offers the shy or handicapped child an opportunity to speak.
5. It promotes good habits of speech through enjoyable exercise, rather than drill.
6. It is a satisfying activity in itself.
7. It can be combined successfully with rhythmic movement and pantomime.

Just as action songs are used with very young children as an approach to creative rhythms, so may poetry be used with older children, to suggest mood, stimulate ideas, and begin the flow of creative energy. Chants and the repetition of words have a natural appeal. Thus poetry and nonsense verse may prove a successful method of introducing creative drama. Skill in movement, rhythms, and pantomime are increased as all children are given opportunities to participate.

12 Speech and Speech-Related Activities

Monologue. *(Courtesy of Diana Kelly, University of Windsor.)*

*I*mproved speech is a shared objective of modern educators and teachers of creative drama. Although this book is not primarily directed toward speech and the language arts but is focused instead upon various aspects of dramatic techniques, the implications for improved speech habits are obvious. As the players, either children or adults, feel the desire to communicate orally with others, they will seek the words they want and try to pronounce and articulate them clearly. This chapter suggests some speech-related activities that may be carried on in addition to creative drama and may act as an incentive for improving oral expression.

Speech depends upon words. The more words one has at one's command, the richer and more precise one's communication. Children love words and enjoy learning new ones, given half a chance and some encouragement. Vocabulary building, moreover, is a never-ending process. Reading good literature is one of the finest ways of meeting new words, and the improvisation of dialogue offers an opportunity for putting them into practice. Different characters speak in different ways. A person's manner of speech distinguishes him or her as much as physical movements and behavior do. In assuming a role, the player learns as much as possible about the character he or she is playing: age, education, occupation, likes and dislikes, strengths, weaknesses, and other personal qualities. Knowledge of a character will help determine the words used as well as the way in which they are said.

The young or inexperienced player will not be able to delineate character at the outset but will slowly develop an awareness of the speech appropriate to a character and in time will be able to handle dialogue that conveys more than rudimentary information. Particularly effective in pointing out individual differences in speech and the possibilities of enriching them is the discussion held after the first and second playing. The leader may ask the player some questions about the character: Would the character talk that way? Use those words? Use slang? Suggest the occupation by the way he or she describes it? Then the leader may proceed to some general questions about characters: How would a father speak? A storekeeper? A general? A television newscaster? Would a child say the same thing in the same words and phrases? Children are quick to discern discrepancies. Moreover, they enjoy finding just the right words for a particular character and delight in using long words. Proof of this can be seen in the way in which very young children memorize repeated phrases and words from favorite stories: any deviation from the text on the part of a reader, in an effort at simplification, will bring an immediate correction from the listening child, who knows and loves the original.

As to clarity and audibility, no activity points up the necessity of being heard and understood any better than taking part in a play. The teacher need not—indeed, should not—stress such failings as indistinct or inaudible speech, but the other players will be aware of it. A far more effective way of telling a player that his or her voice is too soft is to raise questions such as: would an angry man sound like that? What kind of voice do you think a giant would have? How do we know that the boy is calling to someone from a distance?

Too much attention to vocal projection and articulation frequently leads to an artificial manner of delivery, but attention to the reasons for a louder voice or clearer speech will accomplish the desired goals, though admittedly this approach takes longer. Observers are quick to comment when they cannot hear or understand a player. Peer criticism is a far more effective way of improving a player's speech than constant nagging by the teacher. If the player really wants to be understood he or she will make the necessary effort. Again, the player will not accomplish everything in the beginning but, with practice and encouragement as well as criticism, will show improvement in time. Creative drama offers a unique opportunity to enlarge the vocabulary, promote more audible speech, and improve articulation.

In recent years there has been a conscious effort to improve the self-image of the speaker whose verbal skills are poor or for whom English is a second language. To accomplish this, voice and diction have been deemphasized; in other words, *what* is said is considered of greater importance than *how* it is said. The objectives—encouragement of the speaker and the building of pride in a cultural heritage—have been given a priority. Although no one would quarrel with this as the first step in language improvement, it is to be hoped that once a degree of self-confidence has been achieved, the student should be helped to move on to better habits of speech. Clarity, audibility, and a constantly improving vocabulary are still the goals for citizens in a democratic society. Freedom of speech is of little value without the ability to express oneself clearly and effectively. Today that ability affects almost every facet of life and most jobs. Therefore, the speech arts are more important than ever before, and it is condescending to demand anything less than the best of students in this area as well as in others. The teacher's acceptance of a patois or a substandard level of English does the speaker a disservice both now and later. Poor speech, like poor writing, is a handicap that need not exist. What better place than the public school classroom to learn to communicate effectively?

Most people—adults and children—enjoy nonsense verse. Probably the most familiar verse is Lewis Carroll's "Jabberwocky." Reading it with expression is a challenge, to which most students respond readily. Who is to say what it means? This gives the readers carte blanche to do what they want with it. It may also prompt them to want to write nonsense verses of their own. Beyond that is the built-in necessity to articulate clearly. It is a perfect example of an exercise that is regarded as fun.

JABBERWOCKY
from THROUGH THE LOOKING-GLASS

LEWIS CARROLL

'Twas brillig, and the slithy toves
Did gyre and gimble in the wabe:

All mimsy were the borogoves,
    And the mome raths outgrabe.

"Beware the Jabberwock, my son!
    The jaws that bite, the claws that catch!
Beware the Jubjub bird, and shun
    The frumious Bandersnatch!"

He took the vorpal sword in hand:
    Long time the manxome foe he sought—
So rested he by the Tumtum tree,
    And stood awhile tulgey wood,

And as in uffish thought he stood,
    The Jabberwock, with eyes of flame,
Came whiffling through the tulgey wood,
    And burbled as it came!

One, two! One, two! And through and through
    The vorpal blade went snicker-snack!
He left it dead, and with its head
    He went galumphing back.

"And hast thou slain the Jabberwock?
    Come to my arms, my beamish boy!
O frabjous day! Callooh! Callay!"
    He chortled in his joy.

'Twas brillig, and the slithy toves
    Did gyre and gimble in the wabe:
All mimsy were the borogoves,
    And the mome raths outgrabe.

Classroom activities other than those described provide work on oral communication. One of the oldest and best of them is storytelling, a favorite pastime in itself as well as a primary step in the preparation of a dramatization.

Storytelling

Storytelling is an ancient art that continues to be loved in spite of, or perhaps because of, our technical advances in communication. The purpose of storytelling, however, remains unchanged. Its goal is to bring its listeners a heightened awareness that involves a sense of wonder, mystery, and creativity. Television brings a vast array of entertainment into our homes, but it can no more replace the living storyteller than film can take the place of theatre. The reader-audience relationship depends upon the rapport between the one telling the story and the listeners: their involvement in the material and the way it is presented to them, which varies with each telling. The age, background, and interests of the audience, the physical surroundings, and even the time of day affect the development of that rapport. But the most important factor in storytelling is always the storyteller and his or her sensitivity and enthusiasm. Fortunate are the boys and girls who are exposed to a good storyteller; fortunate, also, are the ones who possess the skill to choose just the right story for the occasion and make it live again for their listeners.

Traditionally, stories were told for three purposes: to entertain, to teach, and to transmit the culture. These purposes have not changed essentially, though in an era of mass education the storyteller primarily provides entertainment and aesthetic pleasure. Folk tales, myths, legends, fables, biography, and history offer a wealth of storytelling material. A lively tale, believable characters, and a worthwhile theme are the primary requisites; they are also the requirements for a good play, though not every good story can be adapted to the stage successfully, for a variety of reasons.

Storytellers have the freedom, however, to tell any tales they consider worthwhile and appropriate, for they will not have to cope with the problems of dramatization. A vast supply of good literature is available, but the good storytellers must first be able to find it. They must select material to which they respond and which they want to share with others. They must then decide whether the story will be better read or told. Perhaps they will feel that the language and literary style of the author should not be sacrificed by putting them into the words of another. If this is the case, the story will be better if read. If, on the other hand, they decide that the material will be more effective told, the storytellers' preparation will be somewhat different.

The storytellers have already considered the age of the listeners and have thought about both the length of the story and the time at their disposal. Having satisfied themselves that they have made a wise choice, they will familiarize themselves thoroughly with all details. For the beginning storytellers, making an outline is a good way to organize the material: the beginning, the action, the climax, the denouement. They should practice telling the story aloud, considering carefully the mood as well as the significant details.

Choice of words is important in storytelling. Often, certain words or phrases are repeated a number of times and are so important that the teller will wish to use them. The traditional storytellers did not try to memorize the story, for they thought this would lead to a stilted presentation and the risk of forgetting. Knowing a story so well that it can be told in one's own words was thought to be a far more satisfactory way of sharing it. Descriptive words create vivid pictures; words can suggest seeing, hearing, tasting, smelling, and touching and can help the listener become more deeply interested and involved. Some impersonation makes characters come alive, though the storyteller's aim is to guide interpretation rather than to establish patterns for characterization. Facial expressions and gestures add interest if they are natural and spontaneous. Several rehearsals are needed, however, for the storyteller to polish the sentences and achieve fluency.

Sincerity is a basic requirement in storytelling, for the child in the audience is sensitive to condescension and resents not being taken seriously. Humor, on the other hand, is enjoyed by everyone. A humorous tale, character, joke, or witty remark serves to draw teller and audience together. Indeed, one objective of storytelling is to develop a sense of humor, which is really a sense of proportion.

A pleasing voice and clear speech are to be cultivated, since the storyteller depends primarily on verbal communication, unlike the actor, who uses the entire body to convey the meaning. Storytellers must be able to forget themselves in their preoccupation with the material. Rather than wondering how well they are doing, they will be checking constantly to see if the audience hears, understands, and seems to be appreciating the story.

The techniques of storytelling are changing, however; twenty-five years ago it was emphasized that the storyteller was not an actor and must resist the temptation to become one; today some of the most successful storytellers use movement and mime freely. The recent revival of interest in the oral tradition has resulted in new ways of telling stories. Instead of rejecting the actor's techniques, many younger storytellers are making full use of them, including vocal effects, strong facial expression, and physical activities that border on the acrobatic—for a frankly theatrical effect. Many of them memorize their material, wear costumes, or at least garments that are different from ordinary street clothes. Some add musical accompaniment or work with a musician. Who is to say that this is *not* storytelling because it breaks traditional rules? Librarians and teachers tend to favor the traditional approach when they tell stories: first, because they are not giving a performance; second, because they are telling stories in a quiet place and are concerned with creating a quiet atmosphere; and third, because they are not performers. On the other hand, the professional storyteller who comes in for assembly programs or special occasions *is* a performer, educated in the storytelling techniques, and serves a different purpose. It is not suggested here that either the teacher or the student should discard the old conventions to keep up with the times. The point is simply this: that we can no longer lay down iron-clad rules regarding any art form and refuse to recognize the changes that artists may make in them.

This renaissance in the art of storytelling has resulted in the founding of numerous centers and the popularity of individual artists, who are making significant contributions to the field. Among the better known centers in the East is Weston Woods in Weston, Connecticut, established by Morton Schindel in 1953. Aware of his own children's enjoyment of literature presented in this way, the young filmmaker was inspired to reach many listeners by combining storytelling with the media. He began by adapting picture books to film in a quiet rural area sixty miles from New York. Consulting with authors of children's books, publishers, illustrators, and teachers, he selected material of good literary quality and appropriate to the medium. The slogan "Fidelity to the Original" was a guiding principle from the beginning and has been a major factor in the success of the project. The Weston Woods brochure lists three criteria for selection: desirability, adaptability, and availability. During the more than thirty-five years since its founding, Weston Woods has undergone changes, has enlarged its operation, and has received worldwide recognition, but it has not deviated from its original goals. Although the material is filmed and therefore not live, it is advertised as *storytelling* rather than *filmed stories.*

Vineyard Video Productions in West Tisbury, Massachussets, is another storytelling center, whose work has received high commendation from the National Council of Teachers of English, the National Educational Film Festival, and the American Film Festival. Jay O'Callahan teaches master classes as well as telling stories, old and new, for young people from the primary grades through high school. Videocassettes have enlarged his audiences but have not altered his style of presentation. The sound and rhythm of words and his expressive body language offer young people an additional dimension. O'Callahan called story-telling our oldest art and said we are all storytellers. "As we share experiences and ideas, as we teach and amuse each other, we do so in great measure through storytelling."[1]

Also on the East coast is the New York City Storytelling Center. Founded in 1981, its members include storytellers, teachers, librarians, and any other persons interested in this art form. In spite of television, radio still includes storytelling among its most popular programs. Although I am particularly conscious of the number of storytellers in this region, I am aware of many others in different parts of the country. A recent issue of *The New Yorker* reported on Ray Hicks, a champion storyteller in North Carolina.[2] Now in his late sixties, Hicks has held audiences spellbound since he was a young man. He specializes in the *Jack* tales of the Blue Ridge Mountains, often telling them without charge to tourists who seek him out, to neighbors, and locally at schools and small colleges. Once a year, however, he is persuaded to travel to the town of Jonesboro, Tennessee, for the annual storytelling festival. First in the country, the Jonesboro Festival now has many imitators and many participants, but Hicks is considered the patriarch. Although other storytellers have become professional, doing research and making tapes and videos of their performances, Hicks still works in the simple oral tradition: no agent, no press kits, no fees of any sizable amount.

This brief discussion of some of the aims and techniques of storytelling is directed to the teacher, but telling stories is also a good classroom activity for children. High school and college students not only enjoy the experience but often find use for it in working with camp or play groups. Children in the middle and upper grades take pleasure in sharing their favorite stories; at the same time, they are acquiring new skills in communication. If the group is small, each child should have a chance to tell a story from time to time. If the group is large, then each child may be given a portion of a story to tell, one way of ensuring equal participation for all. Besides providing practice in recall and organization,

1. Brochure for Vineyard Video Productions.
2. Gwen Kinkead, "An Overgrown Jack," *The New Yorker* 64, no. 22 (July 18, 1988): 33–41.

storytelling is a splendid opportunity for work on vocabulary, syntax, and diction. Everyone loves a good story. Being able to tell one clearly and well is a way of providing pleasure for others as well as discovering the satisfaction of an attentive audience.

> It has often been maintained, at times somewhat routinely, that storytelling is the basis of all important prose writing. But storytelling is ultimately—like everything else—a social act. You tell a story in order to relay an experience by means of language, in order to make somebody else listen. From this it follows also that the functions and methods of storytelling must change with society, especially if the change of the latter is so far-reaching that it also affects our ability to use our language.[3]

Joanna Kraus has coined the term "sound and motion stories."[4] This is a conscious use of the young child's natural impulse to participate in a story being read or told. Her collection of tales, suggesting places in the text where sounds and actions can be incorporated, is an excellent example of what the teacher can do to involve the group more actively in the experience. It is also a way of beginning a creative drama session or of encouraging participation where time and space is limited. With a little practice, the storyteller can find places in a text where sounds and motions add a dimension and are fun to do.

Incidentally, because words grow out of sounds, this is a valid approach to the teaching of speech. Children enjoy the sounds of words, and this enjoyment of sound for its own sake should be encouraged. Small children love repetition; through correct repetition better speech habits are built. Difficult sounds can be practiced in this way without the dullness of drill.

Sound and Motion Stories

Sound and motion stories provide a technique that can be used when space is limited or when desks are fastened to the floor. At the same time the imagination is stimulated, providing freedom within the boundaries of space, time, or the ability of the students to handle more demanding material. It is especially popular with children in the lower grades. If a class enjoys the participation, the teacher can find other stories that lend themselves to the technique and mark the participation points accordingly.

The following is a delightful story from Joanna Kraus's collection of tales that children with whom I have worked love. Perhaps because it is modern or a contrast to the folk and fairy tales, they enjoy a situation that they can easily visualize.

---

3. Steve Sem-Sandberg, *Cultural Life in Sweden* (issued by the Swedish Information Service, 825 Third Avenue, New York, N.Y.), no. 37 (December 1988): 7.
4. Joanna H. Kraus, *Seven Sound and Motion Stories* (Rowayton, Conn.: New Plays, 1971).

The Night The Elephants Marched On New York
Joanna Kraus

There they were, stranded in a railway yard in New Jersey, two hundred animals from Gambelli Brothers Circus.

Thirteen miles away in President Gambelli's New York City office, the phone rang. (S)[5]

"What! What! I can barely hear you," President Gambelli yelled into the telephone.

From the other end of the wire came the sound of nineteen hungry elephants. (S) The chief animal trainer was trying to explain, but President Gambelli could only hear half of what he said.

". . . railway strike . . . in the yard at South Kearney, New Jersey . . . can't get the animals through to New York City . . . two o'clock opening tomorrow. . . ."

President Gambelli heard the roars of nine lions and fifteen tigers in the background. (S)

"I'll do what I can," called President Gambelli and hung up the receiver. (A)

He paced his office. On the wall was a large poster of a circus elephant which he knew thousands of school children had seen. He knew thousands of mothers, fathers, aunts, and uncles had bought tickets for the two o'clock performance of the Gambelli Brothers Circus.

Violetta, his assistant, rushed in with the morning papers and put them on his desk. He picked up the first newspaper. (A) "Rail Strike," announced the headlines. He picked up the second newspaper. (A) Large black letters spelled out the disaster. "Nationwide Rail Strike. Country Comes to a Halt."

"If the animals don't arrive on time, there won't be a circus," he said to Violetta. "Do you know there are over two hundred animals in the unit stranded in South Kearney, New Jersey!" Luigi Gambelli put his head in his hands. (A) How was he going to move two hundred animals by two o'clock tomorrow?

"We could put the smaller animals in vans, if we can find some," Violetta suggested, "but eight thousand pound elephants . . . I don't know. There won't be a van big enough anywhere."

"It sounded like the jungle when the chief trainer telephoned me. We've got to do something fast," answered President Gambelli.

"JUNGLE! That's it. That's where they're from—any kid knows that," said Violetta excitedly. "Well, it's only about thirteen miles from South Kearney to midtown Manhattan. In India the elephants walk further than that."

"But they don't have rush hour traffic in the jungle," he reminded Violetta. Then Luigi Gambelli threw back his shoulders and looked sternly at the pile of newspapers on his desk. (A) "Gambelli Brothers Circus has never missed a performance, and it's not going to now! Get the governor on the phone, and then the mayor! I will *not* disappoint all those children."

---

5. In the story (S) calls for a sound; (A), for an action.

The governor found vans to carry the smaller animals. He authorized a yellow permit slip for the larger animals to march to Lincoln Tunnel. (A) The mayor authorized a blue permit slip for the animals to finish their march to Madison Square Garden on the public streets of New York City.

Late that night the gorillas, lions, panthers, and tigers were sent in huge vans across the Hudson River over the George Washington Bridge.

President Gambelli, the chief animal trainer, and his assistants lined up the elephants, trunk to tail, and chained them together. As they worked they fastened each chain carefully. (A) When the elephants moved, you could hear the clinking of the heavy metal chains. (S) At the end of the line was a baby elephant. Tied to her tail were a zebra, a llama, and a Shetland pony.

The chief animal trainer carefully guided the lead elephant by the ear with his bull hook. (A)

A few miles from Lincoln Tunnel, a grocer rushed out to the street. "Luigi Gambelli," he said, "I heard about the animal march on the radio. You and the elephants are invited to have supper in my store." Nineteen elephants flapped their ears happily, as the grocer and his two children fed them thirty-nine cents a pound peanuts and fed carrots to the other animals.

A little later Miss Page, the Lincoln Tunnel toll booth attendant, waved hello to the motorists she recognized who drove through the tunnel every night at that hour. (A)

It was nearly eleven o'clock. Soon she could go home too. At her feet her pet dog, Bouncer, was dozing and dreaming of a bone. (S) For a few minutes there were no cars and she glanced at the new report forms she had to fill out. After "Accidents" she wrote "None." After "Unusual Events" she sighed and wrote "None."

Suddenly Bouncer pricked up his ears and let out a low growl. (S) Miss Page looked up startled. (A) She listened carefully, then looked uncomfortably about. (A) She could not see a car or a person. But way down at the end of the tunnel there was a noise that sounded like a movie she had just seen on television. The movie had been all about the jungle. The sound grew louder . . . and louder, as it got nearer and nearer. (S)

A minute later President Gambelli, the chief animal trainer, and his assistants arrived at the toll booth. Miss Page could only stare at them. President Gambelli took off his hat. (A) "Gambelli Brothers Circus," he explained. "They're part of a mixed animal act," the chief animal trainer added.

Miss Page looked quickly through the pages of *Traffic Rules, Regulations and Toll Rates.* There were twelve categories of vehicles in the little green book. "But there's nothing here about elephants," she told them. Then she turned back to the page on Class 2 Vehicles: "Animals, ridden, led or herded, and motorcycles." "Fifty cents an elephant," she said.

President Gambelli counted out nine crisp new dollar bills. (A) The chief animal trainer counted out five dimes. (A) "What about the zebra, llama, and the Shetland pony," the animal trainer asked.

Miss Page and Bouncer leaned out of the booth. (A) Neither had ever seen a zebra, a llama, or a Shetland pony before. Timidly, Miss Page put out her hand and patted the pony. (A) "Aw, let them have a free ride," she said. "I know there's nothing in the regulations about zebras, llamas, and Shetland ponies."

After they had thanked her, they marched away. Miss Page could hear the elephants trumpeting at the end of the tunnel. (S) She picked up her report. Next to "Unusual Events," she scratched out the word "None." (A) Miss Page wrote rapidly. (A) She could still hear the sounds of nineteen elephants, one zebra, one llama, and one Shetland pony marching away. (S) "They'll never believe it," she said to Bouncer.

The next day at two o'clock exactly, Gambelli Brothers Circus opened. There were loud trumpets as the house lights dimmed. (S) The news photographers snapped pictures of Luigi Gambelli standing with the mayor and the governor. (A) President Gambelli told the press, "Gambelli Brothers Circus has never missed a performance."

The Night the Elephants Marched on New York could tie in with a circus theme. Or it could, on the other hand, be a stimulus to finding stories and local anecdotes in the news to write or tell, as well as discovering good places for sounds and actions. I like to use sound and motion stories for "starters," going on to improvisation and a total involvement after the limited participation required by this technique.

Movement

Sound or verbal participation in a story is a traditional way of involving younger children. When they are interested their response comes spontaneously, particularly if there is repetition of words or phrases. Another, and extremely effective, technique, however, is the encouragement of movement rather than words. The storyteller suggests movement that can be done from a sitting position. Young children love to imitate the action, often creating variations on it. One story, which I saw demonstrated, contained the following characters: jelly fish, big fish, an octopus, little fish, and a lobster. The children had a wonderful time moving arms as each was introduced. Not all stories provide opportunity for movement, but when they do, the storyteller has another choice and will find the listeners responsive.

Monologues

The monologue, a dramatic form that is less in evidence today than it was a generation or so ago, seems to be regaining some of its lost popularity. Although generally done as performance, it has many educational values when prepared thoughtfully and creatively. Most students find it a challenge and a change. One class of undergraduates whom I visited did a particularly effective job of monologue preparation, each selecting and observing a character, improvising his or her actions and imagined actions, writing a monologue from the material, and finally performing it for the class. One of the reasons the monologue lost favor was the artificiality that so often characterized the performance. This particular class, however, guided by a gifted and resourceful professor, helped the students to seek out interesting subjects and then develop them in a natural way.[6] The assignment sharpened the students' powers of observation, offered an

6. Professor Diana Kelly, University of Windsor, Canada.

excellent opportunity for improvisation, and provided them with an exercise in written and oral communication, culminating in performance. The professor's success with her class suggested the value of the assignment for a younger group; for instance, a high school or junior high school class. Prepared as carefully as this assignment was, the monologue can have great value; although not creative drama, it does offer some of the same opportunities and is a change from group work in permitting each student to work on individual projects of choice.

Readers Theatre

Readers theatre, a relatively new concept in the speech arts, is particularly suitable for older children and high school students. The simplicity of production and effectiveness of result make it singularly desirable in schools with inadequate stage facilities and where rehearsal time is at a premium. More than that, it is a way of enjoying good literature through guided study, a mutually agreed-upon interpretation, and clear and expressive oral reading. *Readers theatre* may be defined as the oral presentation of drama, prose, or poetry by two or more readers, with characterization when necessary, narration if desired, coordination of material to constitute a whole, and the development of a special reader-audience relationship as an objective. Although traditionally a reader has handled a single role, recent performances have permitted one person to read several. Readers theatre is neither lecture nor play; rather, it is a staged program that allows the audience to create its own images through the skilled performance of the readers.

The cast (whether large or small) usually remains onstage or on the designated area throughout, reading the various assigned portions. Generally, readers use little movement, suggesting action instead with simple gestures and facial expression. They must understand what the author has to say, the structure of the piece, and the development of characters, and they must be able to interpret a variety of roles in a matter of minutes, if called upon to do so. I have seen many different types of presentation in readers theatre, ranging from some actual movement on stage to formal positions behind lecterns. Stools and steps are sometimes used to sit on, if an effect of informality is desired or if the leader wishes to have the performers seated when they are not reading. Sometimes readers turn their backs to the audience to indicate their absence from a particular scene. The material, as well as the group's experience and preference, will determine how much or how little movement to include. In general, however, movement is minimal.

Readers theatre has grown in popularity in the past fifteen to twenty years, and with this growth has come experimentation. Some groups have abandoned the lectern entirely and are now fully costumed. They use movement and have gone so far along the continuum that their results are scarcely distinguishable from theatre. Indeed, one of the criticisms of readers theatre is its indulgence in novelty for its own sake. I cannot share this concern because it seems to me that exponents of readers theatre are doing what is being done in all of the arts these days: consciously blending and mixing forms in the search for new ones. Sometimes they are successful; sometimes they are not. But I find experimentation that risks failure more interesting than rigid adherence to rules that were established by the originators.

One brilliant example of this mixing of forms was the New York production of *Colored Girls Who Have Considered Suicide/When the Rainbow is Enuf.* Described as a choreo–poem, it combined the oral presentation of poetry with choreographed movement. Simple but effective costumes were worn by the young actresses in the cast, and stage lighting was an important element of the production. First done experimentally, *Colored Girls* moved uptown, where it drew large audiences on Broadway for several months.

Although a good deal of readers theatre has been done by adults for adult audiences (e.g., *John Brown's Body, Under Milkwood, Don Juan in Hell, Spoon River),* the Periwinkle Players of Monticello, New York, have for years been presenting highly effective programs in the genre for elementary school children. This company uses simple costumes to suggest character or period and lighting effects to enrich the performance. With several programs in their repertory, they have proved that poetry—as well as drama and prose—has a strong appeal for children. An awakening interest in words and writing were found to be an additional positive result. Although these players are adult professional actors doing a professional job, their kind of program, on a simplified scale, could be done by children.

One particularly effective program was performed by high school students who selected and arranged a script using a group of the world's great love poems to celebrate St. Valentine's Day. In this instance, a narrator introduced each section of the program, giving some background material. A different but equally successful program for children was arranged by college students on the subject of the American West. Prose and poetry that told about the settlers and the frontier were combined with appropriate background music played on the guitar. When transitions were needed, folk songs were introduced. A chronological progression built interest, with the music adding a unifying colorful element. Children doing readers theatre can select material they like and then decide as a group, just as these groups did, the questions of arrangement and sequence. Choral reading is often incorporated, if group speech is considered more effective than solo reading for some selections.

It should be mentioned that other kinds of literature can be used effectively: history, biography, letters, and various documentary materials. More than one program celebrating the bicentennial of American Independence featured American history and American essays. Black history has been the focus of other programs, whereas topics of current social and political interest can offer powerful and dramatic content. These materials require much more arranging and editing than do drama and short stories. On the other hand, they bring a new dimension to material that is not usually read aloud.

This brings up the point that selections from separate works can be combined. It is not required that one text only be used. Thus there is a wide range of possibilities from which to choose; and the form is one that teachers should consider rather than thinking always in terms of the play, traditionally staged and mounted. Readers theatre features the text, and, because it does so, can serve as an extremely effective tool for learning.

Stories that are partially narrated, with readers assuming the various roles, comprise another way in which readers theatre makes literature come alive for an audience. Plays and scenes from plays can be performed in this way by students of all ages. For older children particularly, readers theatre is a viable activity for the classroom, as well as an appealing vehicle for public sharing. Important to stress here is the fact that readers theatre does not require an audience beyond the class; indeed, the primary values are derived from the selection and interpretation of the material and the practice in reading aloud. Inasmuch as the result is so often worth sharing, this type of presentation is recommended for the opportunity it offers those engaged in it, an opportunity bearing much pleasure and no problems of production detail and lengthy rehearsals.

In 1973 the Institute for Readers Theatre was established in California. Among its services are a Readers Theatre Script Service, an international workshop held each summer in a different locale, and short workshops in the United States and Canada for various organizations such as the Foreign Language Association, the International Reading Association, the Speech Association, and theatre conferences. An impressive list of guest artists, both British and American, and an advisory board composed primarily of educators show the seriousness of the project. According to its brochure, the Institute was founded to encourage academic interest in group performances of literature. Its phenomenal growth proves the interest in this approach to art and education.

The following story, *The Musicians of Bremen,* is included as an example of one way in which readers theatre was used by older students for children. If children do it, they should act the story creatively first and then read it aloud from the script, eliminating stage movement and business. Any story may be treated in this manner. Myths and legends, which often depend upon the supernatural, can be handled with ease, whereas difficulties are encountered when they are dramatized in the usual way. Appropriate music may be added, if desired, to suggest the passage of time, the movement from one scene to another, or changes of mood. Music is not necessary to this story or to readers theatre in general, but it often makes the presentation more effective, just as background music and sound effects lend color and setting to a radio play.

Costumes may be suggested if desired; but they need not, and, indeed, probably should not, be complete or literal. The same thing is true of settings, which, if merely suggested, make demands on the audience that lead to a clearer and more accurate understanding than any attempt to duplicate a place or scene. Platforms, stools, chairs, ladders, and benches do not connote particular places, which has been one reason for their popularity. Although material may be memorized, books or manuscripts are generally used to let the audience know at once that it is going to share literature, not see a play.

THE MUSICIANS OF BREMEN
A Dramatization for Readers Theatre by Nellie McCaslin

NARRATOR	CAT
DONKEY	COCK
DOG	ROBBER

The six readers may stand throughout, reading from their scripts at lecterns or reading stands. Because the story is so simple and informal, they may prefer to sit on steps instead; they will probably be able to get more into the spirit of it if they are seated informally and close to the audience.

NARRATOR: There was once near the town of Bremen a farmer whose Donkey was growing old and was every day less fit for work. The farmer knew that he should soon have to buy a new donkey and so he began to think of how he could get rid of his faithful old beast. Now the Donkey, who was not as stupid as the farmer thought, decided that he would settle the matter himself. So one day, when the farmer was in the house having his dinner, the Donkey took himself off and started down the road toward the city. "For there," he thought, "I may become a musician." He had a powerful voice which, in spite of his advancing years, could be heard for miles around when he put back his head and brayed. Yes, a musician was what he should be.

He had not gone far when he met a Dog lying stretched out by the roadside. The Dog was panting as if he had just run a great distance. The Donkey stopped and greeted him.

DONKEY: Good morning, friend Dog. What may I ask are you doing out here all by yourself? And why are you panting so hard?

DOG: Ah, me. I have run away, but I am an old dog and my strength has all but given out.

DONKEY: Run away? Why should an old fellow like you run away? Pardon me for saying it, but I should think you'd be better off at home where you've someone to care for you than out seeking adventure.

DOG: I agree with you. But the truth of the matter is that my master no longer wants me around. I was a "fine fellow," a "good dog," as long as I was able to work. But now he grows angry when I trail behind and can no longer hunt or herd sheep.

DONKEY: *(sympathetically)* That is too bad.

DOG: That's not the worst of it. He even threatened to knock me on the head and thus be rid of me. Then, with me out of the way, he'll get him a puppy.

DONKEY: Your master is a cruel man, but I can understand how you feel, for the same thing has happened to me. My master is impatient with my slow steps and stiff joints and would replace me with a younger beast.

DOG: It's hard to grow old in this world. I suppose I may as well lie here till I die, for I am of no use to anyone anymore.

DONKEY: Nonsense, my dear friend. Listen, I have an idea. I'm on my way to the city. There I plan to become a musician. Why don't you join me and see what you can do? We may harmonize well together and anyhow, two are always better off than one.

DOG: I have nothing to lose by it. Yes, your words give me courage. I'll go along with you to the city.

NARRATOR: So the two of them set out. Before they had gone very far they came upon a Cat sitting in the middle of the road. They stopped to speak to her.

DONKEY: I beg your pardon, my lady, what is the trouble? You look as unhappy as my friend the Dog did less than an hour ago. Surely life is not all that hard.

CAT: And why shouldn't I look unhappy? You don't know what it is to grow old and no longer be welcome in your very own house.

DONKEY: Indeed? Do tell us what has happened. We, too, have suffered similar misfortunes. Perhaps we can help.

CAT: Very well, I'll tell you, though there's nothing either one of you can do.

DOG: *(sympathetically)* Sometimes it helps just to talk.

CAT: That is true. You see, I used to be loved very much. My mistress thought me the most beautiful cat in the world. She brushed my fur—it was soft and sleek in those days—and gave me cream in a saucer each morning, and meat at night. And she praised me to all the neighbors. She said I kept the place clean of mice.

DOG: Go on.

DONKEY: What happened next?

CAT: You wouldn't believe it! Because I no longer care to run about and catch mice and prefer to curl up by the fire, my mistress has said she would drown me. Is that the way to treat an old friend? I was fortunate enough to escape from her, but how shall I find enough to eat or a warm bed at night, I do not know.

DONKEY: Do not despair, old friend. We share the same sorrow. Instead of sitting here in the road, why not come with us to the city? You are a good musician, I'm sure. Perhaps we can work together. A trio is much more attractive than a duet. Wouldn't you agree, Master Dog?

DOG: Yes, indeed.

CAT: I hadn't thought of being a singer. But it's worth trying and I'm glad to have company, however it turns out.

NARRATOR: So the Cat got up and went with them. The three talked and exchanged stories of their youth and began to feel much better as they got acquainted. Presently they came to a farm yard, where they saw a Cock perched on the gate. He was crowing with all his might.

COCK: Cock-a-doodle-do!

DONKEY: What a fine sound you make, Master Cock. Pray, what great event are you proclaiming?

COCK: Why, that it is a fair day and sunny and my mistress can safely hang out her wash.

DONKEY: She must depend on you very much.

COCK: Indeed she does. She would never know when the sun had come up if it weren't for my crowing.

DOG: You don't looked pleased, somehow. What's the matter?

COCK: I've had a rude shock. Would you believe it, in spite of my years of service to her, I have just heard her say that she plans to cut off my head and roast me for Sunday dinner.

DOG: Oh, that is even worse than what has happened to us, friend Cock. Why don't you leave here at once?

COCK: Where can I go? And how do I know every other farmer's wife might not have the same idea?

CAT: Well, we have a plan. . . .

COCK: What kind of a plan?

CAT: Come along with us and we'll tell you.

COCK: Where are you going?

DONKEY: To the city. We are going to seek our fortune as musicians. With your fine strong voice, I'm sure you will have no trouble finding work.

CAT: And if we practice together, we may work up a concert. Four voices—do come along.

COCK: I'll join you. And I thank you with all my heart.

DOG: Anything is better than staying here, and who knows, things may turn out for the best after all.

NARRATOR: And so the four of them walked on together. The day was fair and their hearts were high, for they were certain that good luck was in store for them. As evening approached, they were still a distance from town, so they decided to stop at the edge of the woods for the night. The Donkey and the Dog made a comfortable bed under a tree and the Cat climbed up on a bough where she felt safer. The Cock, however, who was used to spending the night on a perch, flew up to the very top of the tree and settled himself on a sturdy branch.

COCK: Everyone all right down there?

DONKEY: As right as my old bones can be on this hard ground.

DOG: This is better than being knocked in the head, though I shall be glad when we find proper lodging.

COCK: How about you, Mistress Cat? Are you comfortable?

CAT: Oh, I'm all right. The leaves keep out the draft and anyhow it's not a cold night.

COCK: Well, I'll say goodnight then and I'll wake you up first thing in the morning.

NARRATOR: Before tucking his head under his wing, however, he looked out in all directions, to be sure that nothing was amiss. As he did so, he noticed, not too great a distance anyway, something shining and bright. He called down to the others.

COCK: We can't be as far from the town as we thought. I see lights. There must be a house nearby.

DOG: Are you sure? It looks very dark to me.

CAT: Yes, I see it. It's a house or an inn.

DONKEY: Then perhaps we should push on. I could use a softer bed.

DOG: So could I. And, who knows, the master might throw in a bone and some scraps from his table.

CAT: Yes, indeed. I would willingly exchange this bough for a spot in front of a fire.

COCK: I'm game. Let's find out what it is.

NARRATOR: Having agreed, the four companions got up and followed the Cat, whose eyes served best in the dark. At length they came to a house. It was a very comfortable house, in which there lived a band of robbers. The four stopped outside the door, then the Donkey, who was the tallest, cautiously peered through the window.

COCK: Well, friend Donkey, what do you see? Do they look like kindly folk?

DONKEY: I see an astonishing thing. A table piled with good things to eat and a band of men sitting around it, counting their gold.

CAT: What do you take them to be?

DONKEY: If I'm not mistaken, I'd say they were robbers. This is no farmer's cottage.

COCK: Do you suppose they live here?

DONKEY: Either that or they've taken over the place.

DOG: Perhaps we can scare them away. I used to be good at that years ago. My master always said no robber could get within gunshot when I was around.

CAT: It looks like a fine lodging for us, if we can get in.

DONKEY: Let's think of a way.

DOG: I've got it. I'll get on the Donkey. You, Mistress Cat, jump on my back and the Cock can perch on your shoulders. Then we'll make music.

COCK: A capital idea! Let's do it.

ALL: *(ad lib)* All right—I'm for it—Good idea!

DONKEY: Is everyone in place? Good. Now, altogether . . . *(Each animal makes his own noise at the same time.)*

DONKEY: Now, then, stand back. I'll put my front feet through the window and we'll all go inside. *(Crash of glass.)*

NARRATOR: The robbers, who had been startled by the concert, were terrified when the four musicians tumbled over the sill into the room. They were out the door in a flash and scattered in all directions. The four old friends watched them go.

DONKEY: Well, it looks as if we have the place to ourselves.

DOG: And the dinner.

CAT: Will you see what's on the table! This is a feast.

COCK: It would be too bad to let so much good food go to waste. What say you? Let's eat.

NARRATOR: So the four gobbled up every crumb. Then, their hunger satisfied, each one sought a bed to his liking. The Donkey found a pile of straw outside the back door and bade the others good night. The Dog stretched out on a rug under the table. The Cat curled up on the hearth; and the Cock, who preferred a higher spot even indoors, perched on a beam in the ceiling. Warm and tired from their travels, they were soon fast asleep.

Later on that night, however, the robbers, seeing the house dark, and hearing no noise, crept stealthily back. The leader of the band was the first to venture inside. He struck a match on the fireplace and then out of the darkness blazed two bright eyes. The Cat was on her feet in a flash and flew at him and clawed him with all her might. *(Meow.)* The robber yelled in fright more than pain. As he stumbled back he tripped over the Dog who bit him sharply in the leg. *(Bow-wow.)* Running out the back door, he bumped into the Donkey who woke up with a start and kicked him with both feet. *(Hee-haw.)* All this commotion roused the Cock who crowed at the top of his lungs. *(Cock-a-doodle-do.)* This was too much for the robber who ran off to his companions and told them what had befallen him.

ROBBER: A witch has got into the house. I saw her eyes in the dark. First she scratched me with her long nails; next she stabbed me in the leg. Then, when I tried to escape, I was struck with a club from behind and all the while someone on the roof was yelling, "Throw the rascal out! Throw the rascal out!" I tell you, the place is bewitched.

NARRATOR: Well, after that, the robbers never ventured inside the house again. The four musicians were so pleased with their lodging that they stayed right there. And I shouldn't be surprised if they're living there still.

WITH THE SUNRISE IN HIS POCKET
A Dramatization for Readers Theatre by Nellie McCaslin

FIRST STORYTELLER	MISSISSIPPI, *his alligator*
SECOND STORYTELLER	A STRANGER, *his political opponent*
DAVY CROCKETT	DEATH HUG, *his bear*
RATTLER, *his dog*	PEOPLE *(for applause and animal sounds)*
	SOUND EFFECTS PERSON

With the Sunrise in His Pocket is *an American folk legend with appeal for an older group of children. The storytellers can either read or tell the connecting narration in their own words. Like* The Musicians of Bremen, *it offers an opportunity for participation by the whole class. If children enjoy readers theatre, they may want to create programs of their own based on familiar stories, legends, or materials relating to a particular topic or unit of study. Readers theatre is like improvisation in that it combines reading and speaking, though, admittedly, it is a more formal kind of theatre.*

The dramatization of With the Sunrise in His Pocket *features one of the most delightful personalities to be found in our pre–Civil War South, Davy Crockett. The actual man and his legendary adventures make him a richer character for both storytelling and drama. Hunter, backwoodsman, lover of animals, Indian fighter, and member of Congress, he has an appeal for everyone. His gift for spinning tall tales and his rustic sense of humor have caused some to call him the forerunner of Will Rogers and even Abraham Lincoln. Because his adventures are so fantastic, this play has been put into readers theatre form, in which the imagination can produce the miracles impossible to present on the stage.*

PRODUCTION NOTES: Sound Effects—*animal noises (to be made by the children); whistle; sound of machinery.* Music—*"Pop Goes the Weasel" or "Turkey in the Straw."*

FIRST STORYTELLER: We in America have a great many heroes that we don't know very much about. Of course, we know Abraham Lincoln and George Washington and Thomas Jefferson and we know the things they did are true. On the other hand, we know Paul Bunyan and John Henry and Pecos Bill and we know that most of the stories told about them aren't really true but we like them all the same. Well, about halfway between these two kinds of heroes stands another name—the name of a man who was real enough but the stories they tell about him belong to America's "tall tales." That man was Davy Crockett and he served his country in a great many ways. He was a hunter, a backwoodsman, and an Indian fighter; he was even a member of Congress from 1827 to

1835 and in 1836 he was killed in the defense of the Alamo. Now Mr. Crockett, or Colonel Crockett, as he was known, was born in the hills of Tennessee; but because he went to Washington we think of him as belonging to the whole country instead of just one state. The stories they told about him were so mixed up with the facts that it's pretty hard to tell which is which, but since it doesn't really matter anyhow, we're going to tell them to you just as we heard them.

SECOND STORYTELLER: In a way Davy Crockett was a giant. At least he started out that way. Like all the other giants, he was a most remarkable baby. He himself told how he slept in the shell of a great big snapping turtle instead of a cradle. He had a panther's skin for a cover and a crocodile curled itself right up in a ball to make him a pillow.

FIRST STORYTELLER: I like what he said he ate when he was just a year old.

SECOND STORYTELLER: Yes. He told how he used to get so hungry by eleven o'clock in the morning they'd feed him a sandwich made of a bear's ham and a whole loaf of bread with a few spare ribs thrown in for good measure!

FIRST STORYTELLER: One of the things everybody seemed to remember most about him was his grin. Why, it was famous all over the United States. When he was a boy he used to grin the way other people would shoot a gun—he'd just get what he wanted by grinning at it! They tell how one time he saw a coon up in a tree and since he didn't have his old rifle, Betsy, with him, he just stood there and grinned. Well, after a while, that old coon toppled right off the branch and fell down at his feet. And it was from that coon that he made his famous coonskin cap.

SECOND STORYTELLER: And then there was the other time—later on—he *thought* he saw a coon. He and his hunting dog, Rattler, were out in the forest at night and . . .

CROCKETT: Rattler, old boy, do you see that coon way up there on the top branch of that pine tree?

RATTLER: Arf—arf!

CROCKETT: You don't? Well, you just keep alookin' and pretty soon you'll see him come tumbling down. *(Pause.)* Rattler, what do you mean by layin' down? I know it's night but it ain't time to sleep when we're trying to get that old coon to budge.

RATTLER: Gr-r-r-r.

CROCKETT: What's that you say? You going to sleep anyways? Well, all right but you ain't the hound dog I thought you were—leavin' me grinnin' here in the dark all by myself.

SECOND STORYTELLER: Well, Davy Crockett stood there all night agrinnin' and agrinnin'. And Rattler, he just curled up and went fast asleep. But when morning came Davy made a discovery. . . .

CROCKETT: Why, Rattler, that ain't no coon up there! That's just a big knot in the branch of the tree! You were smarter'n me when you went off to sleep.

RATTLER: Gr-r-r-r.

CROCKETT: But you know something? I grinned at it so hard, I grinned the bark right off the limb! And it's left that knot as smooth as a whistle!

FIRST STORYTELLER: Yes, sir, that was a powerful grin all right. And when Davy Crockett began running for office, he could outgrin every other candidate. Why, he used to get votes just as easy as he got coons.

SECOND STORYTELLER: But he didn't just grin to make people do what he wanted. He meant it. Davy Crockett was friendly, and people and animals, too, all loved him.

FIRST STORYTELLER: You know, he always said he had just as many friends among the animals as he did among the people. And they weren't all tame, either; some of them were wild. Some of them were animals he'd rescued when they were in trouble and they never forgot his kindness. Two of his friends, Death Hug, the bear, and Mississippi, his pet alligator, stayed with him all of his life. He brought them up from tiny little critters and there wasn't anything they wouldn't do for him. He used to ride on their backs just like he'd ride his horse and with a bear and a horse and an alligator, there wasn't much territory he couldn't cover.

SECOND STORYTELLER: Maybe they'd like to hear about the time he rode over Niagara Falls?

FIRST STORYTELLER: I'm sure they would. That was exciting. Davy Crockett and Death Hug and Mississippi were all out ice skating that day. . . .

CROCKETT: Nice skatin' here on this ice, ain't it, Death Hug?

DEATH HUG: *(With great appreciation.)* Gr-r-r-r.

CROCKETT: What about you, Mississippi? I know you don't like the cold climate much but don't you like skatin' around up here above the falls?

MISSISSIPPI: *(With appreciation.)* Cro-cro-cro.

CROCKETT: Wouldn't be safe down south but up here the ice is so thick you can cut any figures you please. Watch out, Mississippi, here I come! *(Pause.)* How's that for a figure eight? Let's see you two do one!

DEATH HUG: *(With great glee as he skates.)* Gr-r-r-r.

MISSISSIPPI: *(With delight, also, as he skates.)* Cro-cro-cro.

CROCKETT: Good! You're both better skaters than most people I know. Now let's all take hands and go around together.

DEATH HUG: *(In sudden excitement and fear.)* Gr-r-r-r.

CROCKETT: What's the matter, Death Hug? You ain't afraid, a big bear like you?

DEATH HUG: *(As if warning of great danger.)* Gr-r-r-r.

CROCKETT: Oh, I see what it's all about! There's a crack in the ice and it's gettin' wider and wider—and why, it's broke off altogether! Now we are in a pickle. We got to do some quick thinking or we'll go right down over the falls!

DEATH HUG: *(In excitement.)* Gr-r-r-r.

CROCKETT: You want me to jump on your back, Death Hug?

DEATH HUG: *(Meaning "yes.")* Gr-r-r.

CROCKETT: All right. I'm aholdin' on so let's go! *(Sound: There is a whistle as they go off together down the falls.)*

CROCKETT: Good for you, Death Hug! Right down over the falls on that old chunk of ice and we didn't even get so much as a ducking!

MISSISSIPPI: Cr-r-r-r.

CROCKETT: What's the matter, Mississippi? You want me to ride down the falls again on *your* back?

MISSISSIPPI: *(Eagerly.)* Cr-r-r-r.

CROCKETT: Well, all right, then. But I got a better idea! You're a good jumper. Instead of going down, we'll just go back up. When I get on your back, you just pick up and JUMP! Now—wait'll I get my arms around you. . . . You all ready, Mississippi?

MISSISSIPPI: Cr-r-r-r.

CROCKETT: All right—here we go! *(Sound: A whistle noise again as they fly right up the falls.)*

CROCKETT: Right up over the topside of the falls in one jump! And we're back where we started from.

FIRST STORYTELLER: Yes, they had lots of fun together and lots of adventures. But one of the best ones came later on when Davy Crockett was running for office. Of course all the animals were there that day as well as all the people who wanted to hear the two candidates speak. Now Davy's opponent was a rich man. He was well-educated, too, and he used a lot of big words when he talked. Davy didn't have any more schooling than he had money but he had good common sense. Well, the people listened in spite of his coonskin cap and his backwoods clothes and they liked what he had to say. But when the stranger began to talk it seemed as if they forgot all about poor Davy Crockett. They flocked around the stranger and the animals began to feel sorry. They didn't like to see their old friend deserted this way for someone so rich and smooth-talking.

STRANGER: *(Orating.)* And so, my friends, a vote for me is a vote for better government. I've been around this great country of ours and . . .

FIRST STORYTELLER: Well, the animals had listened just as long as they were going to. Then Rattler let out a bark.

RATTLER: Arf! Arf!

FIRST STORYTELLER: And Death Hug, he growled.

DEATH HUG: Gr-r-r-r.

FIRST STORYTELLER: And Mississippi, he made all the noise he could.

MISSISSIPPI: Cr-r-r-r.

FIRST STORYTELLER: And then all the other animals—the coons and the woodchucks and the bears—the pigeons and the frogs and the crows—and even the skunks—began to make their own particular noises. But they all sounded like "Crockett."

ANIMALS: *(A great din as they all enter in.)* CR-CR-R-R-R-R-R-CROCKETT.

FIRST STORYTELLER: Now that poor stranger tried harder and harder to speak above the noise but he just couldn't be heard. Every time he'd open his mouth the animals would drown him out.

STRANGER: *(In a louder tone.)* As I said before, I've been all over this great country—

ANIMALS: CR-R-R-CROCKETT! CROCKETT! CROCKETT!

STRANGER: *(Shouting above it and losing his temper.)* All over this great country of ours and I've—

ANIMALS: CROCKETT! CROCKETT! CROCKETT!

FIRST STORYTELLER: Well, it kept up like that. The Stranger trying to make his speech and the animal friends of Davy Crockett keeping him from it. Davy, he just stood on the sidelines and grinned. Well, it worked like a charm. The voters were so tickled that they stopped even trying to listen to the Stranger and they all voted for the man the animals loved—Davy Crockett!

ANIMALS: Crockett! Crockett! Crockett! *(Sound: Great applause.)*

FIRST STORYTELLER: Of course you can imagine how Davy felt about that. He was glad to win the election but he was even more pleased with the loyalty of all his animal friends. And so he decided to give them a party. It was the Fourth of July and Davy started off with a big speech, thanking them for their support.

CROCKETT: . . . and I want to thank you all for the help you gave me in winning this election. There's some folks talks about dumb animals but I know animals are smart. And if it hadn't been for all of you, calling out "Crockett"—"Crockett"—I know I wouldn't be standin' here today as a member of the legislature. It's a great country we have, just like my opponent said, this United States of America. One reason it's great is because a poor man can run for office and get it. You don't have to be rich or well known or even well educated, if you're honest and willing to work. That's democracy and it's something we don't ever want to lose. My opponent has called it "Coonskin Democracy" and I suppose he was referrin' to my cap. But at this meeting, it don't make any difference how I'm dressed. You're all my friends, same as the people of this state, and I'm proud of it. And now let's give three big cheers for our country, the United States of America! Hip-hip-hooray!

ANIMALS: Hip-Hip-hooray!

CROCKETT: HIP-HIP-HOORAY!

ANIMALS: HIP-HIP-HOORAY!

CROCKETT: *HIP-HIP-HOORAY!*

ANIMALS: *HIP-HIP-HOORAY!*

CROCKETT: And now, if you'll all come over here in the meadow, the dancing will begin. I know some of you don't know how to dance, but Death Hug, here, and Mississippi, they'll teach you. We got some right smart fiddlers, too. Are you ready with the music?

VOICES: *(Off mike.)* Ready.

CROCKETT: All right, then. Let's go! *(Music: "Turkey in the Straw" or "Pop Goes the Weasel.")*

FIRST STORYTELLER: *(With the music in the distance, fading by the end of his speech.)* The dancing went on all night and the animals had a wonderful time. Davy Crockett, he was just as happy as anybody is who has a host of loyal friends and a heart that's in the right place.

SECOND STORYTELLER: Well, Davy Crockett went on through life making friends, winning elections, serving his country, and telling his stories. In fact, his stories are what people remembered best about him after he was gone. The things he told about his early life were nothing, though, compared to the adventures he had later on. The one with the sun was probably the best, and this is the story that places him among America's giants.

FIRST STORYTELLER: One winter morning, when Davy Crockett was getting to be an old man, a stranger thing happened. It was so cold in his cabin that morning the old tinder box he'd used all his life wouldn't produce so much as a spark. And the daylight—well, it was so far behind coming that Davy thought all Creation was freezing fast. Like anybody that was as cold as he was, he decided the best thing to do was to start moving and so he went for a walk.

CROCKETT: *(Whistling.)* Can't hardly get my lips to pucker up and whistle. And that ain't ever happened before. *(He tries again but not very successfully.)* Well, here we are anyway, up to the top of Daybreak Hill and just as cold as when we started. Rattler, what you find over there?

RATTLER: Arf! Arf!

CROCKETT: Well, if it ain't a poor old grizzly bear that just plumb froze to death. I'll hoist him up on my back and take him on home. *(Grunts.)* There we are. Now, then, let's keep awalkin'. *(Whistles in surprise.)* Hello there! Rattler, you see what I see? Why, it's the cause of the whole trouble. The old earth has froze in her axis and can't turn around! Now what do you think of that?

RATTLER: Arf! Arf!

CROCKETT: And that ain't all. The sun's got jammed between two cakes of ice under the wheels! The more he tries to get loose, the stiffer he's friz—

RATTLER: Gr-r-r-r.

CROCKETT: Don't you growl at him. He can't help it no more'n you could. But this is serious. Creation—this is the toughest sort of suspension. It mustn't be endured or human creation is done for! Wait, I got an idea! I'll just squeeze the oil out of this old bear I got on my back *(he grunts)*—and pour it over the sun's face *(grunts)*—and give the cog wheel a kick—and there she goes! *(Sound: There is a sound of machinery beginning to move.)*

CROCKETT: The sun's loose and the earth's begun moving. That's all right, Mr. Earth. I'll just put a piece of the sunrise in my pocket and get along home. I can cook one of my bear steaks with it—and there ain't any doubt now about it's being morning.

FIRST STORYTELLER: No, there wasn't and the people all along the way were grateful to Davy Crockett for starting the earth aturning. And Davy, he just went along home, with the sunrise in his pocket.

SECOND STORYTELLER: Well, Davy Crockett didn't live much longer after that, but he left his mark on the people of his time and those that came after him. Sure, he told some tall tales and he was different from the rest. But he never said a mean word and he loved every living creature. His country came first with him always and that's why we list him with our heroes.

Yes, Davy Crockett was a great man. Some say, a giant.

Story Theatre

Story theatre is closely related to readers theatre. According to Paul Sills, whose production by the same name, "Story Theatre," captivated audiences of all ages a number of seasons ago, it evolved from readers theatre. Sills had worked in readers theatre, but in his search for a new form of expression, developed a technique that has become a genre in its own right. He defined this

"Story Theatre" with human actors and puppets. (*Courtesy of Andrew Drummond, Kingsborough Community College.*)

form as an oral story rather than as a piece of literature. In dispensing with the narrator, which Sills often does, the exposition is imbedded in the dialogue of the various characters. They may also speak in the third person, as in the short sketch that follows.

Like readers theatre, story theatre is hard to define because of its flexibility; therefore no hard and fast rules apply. Actors are usually costumed and may speak or perform in pantomine, while a narrator tells the story. There may be musical accompaniment throughout if desired, and the pantomime may approach dance, depending upon the wishes and abilities of the group. When readers theatre is kept motionless and books and lecterns are used, they may be conceived of as distinct and opposite forms. On the other hand, when performers in readers theatre use stage techniques and story theatre is formalized, the two forms may be similar. Inasmuch as both reflect the director's approach rather than any rigid set of rules, one can only enjoy and applaud the results, when they are successful.

The following short play is an illustration of what is usually meant by story theatre.[7]

RIMOUSKI
SHIRLEY PUGH

Music: "Gypsy Rover" melody used throughout.

MARCEL: A peasant named Marcel—

MADELEINE: —lived with his wife Madeleine—*(curtsies)*.

JEANETTE: —and their little daughter Jeanette—*(Madeleine cues Jeanette to curtsey.)*

MARCEL: —in the tiny village of St. Fabien. But he had it in his head to travel.

MADELEINE: Oh!

(A sound of deprecation.)

St. Fabien is good enough for me.

(Mimes cooking and stirring.)

I was born here and I'll die here.

MARCEL: Me, I want to see what is in the world. More than anything else, I want to see Rimouski.

MADELEINE: Rimouski! How can you think of it? So far away!

JEANETTE: Is Papa going to Rimouski?

MADELEINE: Papa is going nowhere, Jeanette. Stop pulling at my skirt.

MARCEL: Today I talked to the blacksmith. There's a good fellow—he has seen Rimouski.

---

7. From *In One Basket* (New Orleans: Anchorage Press, 1972).

MADELEINE: *(adds pepper to the pot.)* That's very fine for the blacksmith. *(She readies herself to sneeze—and the sneeze doesn't come.)*

MARCEL: *(sneezes without warning.)* Ah-choo!

JEANETTE: Bless you, Papa.

MARCEL: Thank you. Listen—Rimouski is a town that could swallow St. Fabien. The blacksmith says that people crowd the streets there. Have you ever seen a crowd in St. Fabien? The blacksmith says—

MADELEINE: Then listen to the blacksmith and be satisfied.

MARCEL: No, listen—he says there are fine shops and large houses in Rimouski. He says—

JEANETTE: When is Papa going to Rimouski?

MADELEINE: Play with your doll, Jeanette. Papa is going nowhere.

MARCEL: No, listen. I am going, me myself, to Rimouski.

MADELEINE: Marcel, you are a peasant. We are poor people. Travel is not for you. So expensive!

MARCEL: I can't rest until I see for myself what is in the world.

MADELEINE: You certainly can't afford to ride such a distance!

MARCEL: Then I will walk.

MADELEINE: What? And wear out your boots? They aren't in good repair anyway.

MARCEL: Then I will walk without my boots.

MADELEINE: Barefooted! Hah! A fine sight he'll be in Rimouski with no boots on his feet.

MARCEL: Then I know what I'll do. I'll carry my boots in my hand. When I see the smoke from the chimneys of Rimouski, I'll put on my boots and go into the town.

JEANETTE: *(weeping.)* Why must you go to Rimouski, Papa?

MARCEL: Don't worry, Jeanette. I will return.

MADELEINE: *(mimes packing a basket.)* What can be done with such a man? Marcel, do you really want to go to Rimouski?

MARCEL: With all my heart.

MADELEINE: Go, then. Here's a basket with sausage and bread and beer—

MARCEL: Sausage and bread and beer—that will be fine. First I'll take off my boots— *(Mime.)*

—and I'll be on my way.

(Mimes taking the basket in one hand and his boots in the other, making ready to leave for Rimouski.)

MADELEINE: Promise me you will stop to rest, Marcel.

MARCEL: Yes, well, I'll do that all right.

MADELEINE: And take time to eat your sausage and bread.

MARCEL: Sausage and bread. I will, I will.

MADELEINE: And whatever you do, Marcel, don't leave your boots at the side of the road or they'll be stolen.

MARCEL: I'm not a nincompoop. I'll keep them right here in my hand.

JEANETTE: How far is it to Rimouski, Papa?

MARCEL: Jeanette, it is a journey of one entire day.

JEANETTE: Oh, Papa! So far!

MADELEINE: And don't lose your way, Marcel. The road will be confusing.

MARCEL: All right! Jeanette, mind your mama. *(Kisses her.)*

MADELEINE: Oh, Marcel, it is such a distance!

MARCEL: *(He kisses her.)* Don't worry, keep well, and when I return I will tell you about the wonders of Rimouski.

MADELEINE: The wonders of Rimouski! Hah! *(Flounces off with Jeanette.)*

MARCEL: *(Music. He walks.)* What a woman to worry, and the little one will be just like her. Do they think I can't keep my wits about me? She should see me now, on the road, a seasoned traveler.

(Music.)

The sun is high in the sky—it's getting hot. A little sausage and bread and a drink of beer will go down well. Here's a spot of shade.

(Music. Mimes eating.)

A swallow of beer—ah, that's good!—a bite of sausage—That's not so good—

(He finishes eating.)

Maybe now a small nap.

(He lies down, immediately sits up.)

But if I sleep, how will I remember which way the road goes?

Ah, that's it! I'll put my boots on the ground—and I'll point the toes of them toward Rimouski.

(Mimes action.)

There. When I wake up, my boots will point the way.

(Lies down and snores gently. Threatening music.)

THIEF: Now a thief happened along the road. There's a pair of boots with no one's feet in them. I could use an extra pair of boots. He's asleep, all right.

(To audience.) Should I, or shouldn't I? I'm going to do it anyway.

(Steals boots.)

These boots, they aren't much. Not worth the stealing. Full of holes and all run down at the heels. They are no better than my own boots.

(Puts boots down with toes pointing the wrong way.)

And he put the boots down with the toes pointing back toward St. Fabien.

(Music. Thief exits.)

MARCEL: *(Wakes, yawns, scratches, stretches.)*

And now it's cooler and I'm on my way. But which way does the road go? See? I'm not such a fool. There are my boots, with the toes pointing to Rimouski.

(Takes boots and basket and follows wrong direction. Music.)

There's smoke! That smoke comes from the chimneys of Rimouski!

Now to put on my boots.

(Mimes action.)

Well, so this is Rimouski! Looks a lot like St. Fabien! The blacksmith said it was so miraculous here. Why, this street could be a street in St. Fabien! These shops look no finer than the shops at home. And the houses—they aren't so large. I expected a town that looked better than this. Rimouski is not so grand!

(Walks.)

I'm really in Rimouski!

(Madeleine appears, sweeping the sidewalk.)

(Jeanette appears, washing a window.)

Ah, well, this street could be my own street. As far as that goes, look. This house could be my own house. See—an ordinary wife like my own wife. A little girl like my own daughter. If I didn't know I was in Rimouski, I'd swear I was in St. Fabien!

MADELEINE: Marcel! Come in the house and have your supper.

MARCEL: She calls me by my name!

Kingsborough Community College production of "Story Theatre" using masks. (*Courtesy of Andrew Drummond.*)

JEANETTE: Did you bring me something, Papa?

MARCEL: It is exactly like St. Fabien! I've never heard of this, but it's true. Imagine—two places so far apart, yet with streets alike, houses alike—even the people are the same! Aha! Now I see! There is someone just like me who lives in this house, here in Rimouski. Maybe at this moment, he is visiting *my* house at St. Fabien.

MADELEINE: Marcel, stop talking to yourself. Go in and eat your supper.

MARCEL: Yes, I know. I know all about it. Tomorrow he'll come back here. Well, I'll stay in Rimouski and wait until he comes.

(Goes into house, sits and eats.)

JEANETTE: *(Puzzled.)* And he's still waiting.

MADELEINE: And he still thinks he's in Rimouski.

(A single minor chord from the musicians.)

(BLACKOUT)

One other term should be mentioned in this discussion of speech-related activities: *chamber theatre.* In defining it, Robert Breen, the originator, called it a method of preparing and presenting undramatized fiction in which changes are made to accommodate time, space, and number of characters.[8] A narrator becomes dramatically involved in the story and speaks for the author.

8. Robert Breen, *Chamber Theatre* (Englewood Cliffs, N.J.: Prentice-Hall, 1978).

Chamber Theatre

Chamber Theatre has been likened to chamber music in its intimacy with the audience. It explores human relationships in a narrative context provided by the narrator's close association with the spectators. First presented at Northwestern in 1947, Chamber Theatre has had a small but devoted following. A primary distinction of the art form is an unwillingness to turn fiction into drama. Chamber Theatre recognizes the value of the novel's contribution to storytelling through the exploration of a character's motivation at the moment of action. By rejecting the possibility of oversimplification, which can happen in the stage play, Chamber Theatre aims toward a deeper and richer understanding of character, at the same time realizing the unique style of the material. Both children's theatre and adult theatre have found it an interesting and viable method of reaching an audience.

Chamber theatre, story theatre, and readers theatre are similar in that the primary virtue is the text. All can be highly successful when used with children, as they offer possibilities for inventive production and nontraditional content.

Summary

The number of activities that can be incorporated into a curriculum to improve speech and teach the language arts are almost limitless. Storytelling, sound and motion stories, group discussion, monologues, improvisation, readers theatre, and story theatre are activities most young people enjoy. We are living in a period of experimentation and change, however, and new forms are being created every day. Hard and fast rules no longer apply. The combining of forms and the use of nondramatic material for oral presentation suggest possibilities to the imaginative teacher and student. Whereas the produced play was once considered the logical outcome of a semester's work or a unit of drama, it is now only one of numerous possibilities. What is more, the loosening of the rules that previously governed form make possible the invention of interesting and often exciting new structures. Not all of these inventions will be successful, but school is a place in which experimentation should be encouraged: The opportunities for learning are enormous, and what better way than through speech?

Speech is our most important means of communication, although the written language often receives the greater emphasis in schools. It is through the oral language, however, that our earliest learnings take place; through it we are able to express our thoughts and feelings, our needs and desires. The actor and public speaker are not necessarily more gifted in its use than the average man or woman; they have simply developed their skill through diligent and daily practice. Good speech is within the reach of everyone, except, perhaps, persons with certain handicapping conditions that speech therapy cannot overcome.

The creative drama class offers a rich opportunity for practice in oral communication. Storytelling, reading aloud, class discussion and planning sessions, participation in plays all demand the ability to use the language and to use it well. Students are motivated to work on voice and diction when they participate in these and other activities. Because drama deals with ideas and literature, vocabularies are enlarged and the ability to express thoughts clearly is strengthened. Interpretation of characters brings color to the voice and melody to the speech as players take a variety of roles.

The student who achieves a good standard of speech does more than present him or herself well; he shows consideration for the listener. Communication, be it oral, written, or sign language, is a two-way affair; the speaker and the receiver have a relationship that is strong or weak, depending on their ability to express and comprehend meanings.

13

Drama as a Teaching Tool

*P*athways to Learning—learning through movement. *(Photograph by Anne Jackson, Morgantown, Penn.)*

The school of the future will, perhaps, not be a school as we understand it—with benches, blackboards, and a teacher's platform—it may be a theatre, a library, a museum, or a conversation.

—TOLSTOY

*T*olstoy's prediction of a century ago has taken place; today, we find both receptivity and active involvement of community resources in the education of children and young people. One of the most effective resources is theatre, a medium that is examined in this and the following chapter.

The use of drama as a tool for teaching is not a new idea: Historically, both drama and theatre have long been recognized as potent means of education and indoctrination. The ways in which they are used today, however, are new, and they differ in a number of respects from the ways in which they have been used in the past.

Most familiar to us in the Western world is the theatre of ancient Greece, which developed from celebration and dance into a golden age of theatre. Athenian education in the fifth century B.C. was based on music, literature, and dance. Physical activities were emphasized, whereas music included the study of rhythms and harmony as well as the instruments of the time. Since dance was basic to religious festivals, it was stressed, and the chorus of young people received a rigorous training subsidized by wealthy citizens. Dramatists were highly respected, and drama was a major educational force. Plato, in *The Republic,* advocated play as a way of learning. Aristotle urged education in the arts, distinguishing between activities that were means and those that were ends.

The medieval church, in its use of mystery plays, taught through the medium of theatre and, in so doing, helped to restore theatre to its proper place as a great art form. By the last half of the sixteenth century, drama was an important part of the curriculum of the English boys' schools. Not only the reading but the staging of classic plays flourished. We could go on through the centuries, nation by nation, and culture by culture, finding examples of the various ways in which drama and theatre have been used to inform, inspire, entertain, and indoctrinate.

The United States has only recently discovered the relationship between theatre and school. Indeed, the twentieth century was well advanced before the arts began to have any real impact on public education in this country. Private schools often offered opportunities in the arts, but usually as extracurricular activities or as minor subjects, rarely placed on a par with the so-called solids. On the secondary school level, they were given even less emphasis. All of the arts tended to be what the teacher made them; thus they reflected the teacher's background, interests, and attitude. In the minds of many, theatre and dance were even questionable as to their inclusion as part of a young person's education. Drama, in fact, followed music, athletics, and the visual arts into the curriculum. Few today would argue against arts education; yet the inclusion, let alone requirement, of drama in the elementary school curriculum is far from widespread. In the high school there is still a greater emphasis on play production as an extracurricular and social activity than there is on drama as a serious subject.

The first major curricular offerings in child drama and theatre in this country appeared in the twenties. These were the result of Winifred Ward's pioneering efforts at Northwestern University, which brought the public schools of Evanston and the Evanston Children's Theatre into sharp focus. For the first time in this country, creative dramatics, as Ward called it, had a place in the public school curriculum, and plays for children were produced and scheduled on a regular, ongoing basis. Ward's own books were among the first to appear on the subject, becoming landmark texts. College courses and textbooks on drama education and children's theatre followed. Since then there has been a steady increase in the number of colleges and universities offering courses and degrees in the theatre arts and in the teaching of drama and theatre. At the same time, there has been fluctuation in both quantity and quality of drama education in our public schools. Budget cuts and the lack of well-prepared teachers have been the most commonly given reasons for eliminating the arts or curtailing established programs.

Despite progress, however, the dispute regarding the importance and function of drama in education continues. Is it to be included in the curriculum as a means or as an end? Are we primarily concerned with its use as a teaching tool, or do we regard it as a discipline in its own right, to be taught for its own sake? Since the twenties, many of the foremost leaders in the field of drama education have warned against the exploitation of drama/theatre to achieve other ends; that is, making it a "handmaiden" to other subject areas. This exploitation, incidentally, has been of concern to teachers of the other arts as well. Are the visual arts, for instance, to be respected as art, or are they to be used for the preparation of school decorations, posters, party invitations, stage sets, and so on? This concern is not to be confused with inclusion of the arts in integrated projects, in which the same activities might be performed, but in which they are related, often brilliantly, to a unit of study.

Integrated Projects

Projects integrating drama, music, dance, creative writing, and the visual arts with social studies and literature have been popular since the early days of the progressive education movement. Even the most traditional schools have found integrated projects an effective way of teaching and learning. Arts educators have generally endorsed them because they placed the arts at the core of the curriculum rather than on the periphery. Accorded an importance equal to the academic subjects, the arts thus became a basic part of the educational system rather than a frill or something of fringe interest. Integrated projects continue to find popularity in schools where staff members are able and willing to work closely together. This is often more easily accomplished in small private schools, where the schedule allows for flexibility and where there is concern for student interest.

The integrated project usually starts in the social studies or English class. With the topic as a base, various aspects of it are explored. Take, for instance, the topic of a foreign country such as Egypt. In the exploration of the topic, Egyptian history, geography, climate, religion, homes, clothing, food, occupations, myths and legends, arts and crafts, would all be included, and from this study a project evolves. At the time of the King Tut Exhibition at the Metropolitan Museum in New York, one fifth-grade class became so fascinated with the subject that the children made shadow puppets and presented them in a program of short plays based on their favorite Egyptian legends. The project lasted for several weeks and involved the art, music, and social studies teachers; the results showed both interest and understanding.

A project might, on the other hand, start with a question on a more specific topic like the *calendar, time, strip mining,* or *peace.* If the children's interest seems sufficiently strong, this could be a beginning for a class project. The teacher would then bring in books, newspapers, and visual aids, thus keeping the study within one class or area, rather than integrating it with other subjects in the curriculum.

Such integrated projects tend to be part of school work, done during school time and seen by an audience of schoolchildren. Occasionally, a project reaches into the community or is of such magnitude that a wider audience is invited to see the work. One program given in New York City early in 1979 celebrated the International Year of the Child. This was an extremely effective project in which performers from Asia, Africa, and Latin America; children from the Third World Institute of Theatre Arts Studies; and children from the United Nations International School worked together on an ecumenical multiethnic pageant. Entitled *A Third World Litany,* it brought dance, chanting, music, and religious rites together, concluding with a pledge to observe the rights of children everywhere. The result was a deeply moving performance given for parents and friends in the community. This program, incidentally, which was conceived by the Childyear Culture Corps, had its beginning in 1978 in San Jose, California; the Pacific Peoples Theatre Arts Festival also brought performers from many lands together to heighten the understanding of our rich cultural diversity in celebration of the International Year of the Child. Other projects, relatively unpublicized, have been reported by teachers at meetings and in professional publications as being highly successful ways of learning in academic areas through the theatre arts.

Whether drama should be taught as a subject in its own right or employed as a medium for the teaching of other subjects is at the heart of a continuing controversy, and each side of the argument has its proponents. Not that the two points of view are necessarily incompatible; they are not. Many teachers holding both points of view achieve successful results. When the teacher subscribes strongly to one point of view, however, that separate point of view is given a priority; it is for this reason that drama/theatre as an art and drama/theatre as a learning medium are examined separately.

Drama as an Art in Its Own Right

When drama is taught as an art form, the goals are both aesthetic and intrinsic: aesthetic, because product is emphasized; intrinsic, because the child is a major concern. Overall objectives in such teaching include range of perception, sincerity, and the deepening of feeling and thought, for arts education is "education of the senses, of the intuition, not necessarily a cognitive or explicit didactic education."[1]

Drama classes include work on movement and rhythms, pantomime, improvisation, character study, and speech. Teachers help students to develop greater awareness as they create dramatic situations and, later, rehearse scenes and plays. The problems of structure, organization, unity, and plot are studied through guided improvisation and group discussion. Characters and their relationships to other characters in a situation or play are analyzed for insights into motivation for their actions. Students are encouraged to express their own ideas and interpretations and to offer suggestions to the group. Indeed, the teacher's first job is to create an atmosphere in which the players feel comfortable and at ease with one another while working together.

The teacher of creative drama on any level usually begins drama instruction with simple group activities and theatre games. As the players develop and grow, they are given longer and more demanding assignments. Folklore and literature that lends itself to dramatization make excellent material for creative playing. Class members plan scenes and try out various roles. The teacher enriches the experience by bringing in appropriate materials: music, pictures, and other visual aids. Properties and bits of colorful costumes help to stimulate the imagination and, if it is available, stage lighting to enhance the mood. A stage, however, is not necessary and is, in fact, undesirable until much later, when students reach the performance level. Even then, performing in an all-purpose room or in a large classroom, arena style, is usually preferable.

There are no right or wrong answers in creative drama; for imagination, the ability to hold an image long enough to see and use it, honesty, and depth of involvement are the major goals. We are not engaged in the training of professional actors; rather, we are helping children discover their own resources,

1. Robert Landy, *A Handbook of Educational Drama and Theatre* (Westport, Conn.: Greenwood Press, 1982), p. 260.

from which their most imaginative ideas and strongest feelings flow. Players gain freedom as self-discipline and the ability to work with others develop. Drama/ theatre, more than any of the other arts, offers opportunities for full human expression: physical, mental, emotional, and verbal. When players are stimulated and freed to make full use of their creative powers, they produce work that is not only satisfying to them but communicates to others. Or, as Suzanne Langer put it, "Art creates perceptible forms expressive of human feeling."[2]

The aesthetic growth of a student has little, if anything, to do with his or her chronological growth, for it is individual and so differs from one person to another. In a sound program of arts education students are encouraged to interpret the world as they see it in their own ways. Far from being an escape from life, art is a deep involvement in life, one that enriches the participant now and afterward. In the lower grades children enjoy the act of creating or pretending. Few little children ask on their own to give plays for an audience. The process of playing itself brings fulfillment. In the middle and upper grades, however, product assumes a greater importance. Performing for an audience carries the experience one step further. It must be emphasized that this is not an essential or automatic outcome of every lesson in creative drama, but older children generally do reach the point where they want a performance. When this happens, the teacher should support the request and help them plan the details, adding the necessary showmanship so that the program or play will be a success. The teacher makes sure, however, that the children's work remains theirs and is not transformed into a show with an adult-imposed structure and style. This turns guidance into exploitation.

In the past few years I have been aware of a slight but visible shift in attitude toward public performance. Many educators since the twenties have shared Winifred Ward's conviction that children under the age of eleven or twelve should not perform for an audience. The reasons were obvious: children's productions were generally wooden and lifeless, teacher dominated, and lacking in imagination. Plays were often of poor quality with too few parts to go around. Adult audiences, not schooled in the values of drama for the child, often responded in inappropriate ways, laughing at mistakes or applauding for the wrong reasons. Because teachers understandably wanted productions to go well, they tended to superimpose their own ideas and to cast the same children repeatedly in leading roles, thus giving a few boys and girls a great deal of experience at the expense of the majority. The rest of the class might be cast as a group of "villagers" or "townsfolk" or, worse yet, might not be in the production at all. Minor roles in themselves should not be scorned. Indeed, they serve a valuable purpose when rotated. It is only when some children seem always destined for crowd scenes that opportunities for learning are lost and, at worst, permanent damage may be done.

2. Suzanne Langer, *The Problems of Art* (New York: Scribner's, 1957), p. 80.

If the program or play is developed through an improvisational method, process can be stressed before product. Even though a script will be used for performance, working for meaning before casting or memorization of dialogue puts the emphasis on the play rather than on pleasing an audience. Thus process leads into product, which is the normal result of studying a performing art. Performance, to be satisfying to both players and spectators, calls for education of the adults in the audience as well as the children in the cast. Parents, teachers, and administrators need to understand what they are looking for and why: to appreciate the work that has gone into the performance; to perceive the growth and share the excitement of the players; to commend the result but not overpraise individuals, laugh at mistakes, or expect skills that are not yet developed. Performing can be a wonderfully rewarding experience if approached in the right spirit and received in the same way.

It is to be hoped that performances by children are confined to school assemblies, where a sympathetic invited audience will view the product with knowledge of the process through which the product was developed. Honesty and understanding are important, not technical skills that children do not have and cannot be expected to acquire until bodies and voices have matured.

Except for such assembly programs performed by children, theatre for children is generally experienced through attendance at plays produced by professional touring companies or university students. In the past, children's plays tended to be dramatizations of well-known folk and fairy tales, presented for their entertainment value rather than for any educational purpose. They were brought into schools as special "treats" with little advance preparation or follow-up, except that which an individual teacher might provide. Children living in big cities or towns with good community theatres might have the added advantage of seeing plays given by serious nonprofessional adult actors.

The seventies, which brought new concepts of drama and theatre education to this country, caused some far-reaching changes in these practices and a reexamination of our methods and goals. These concepts are described later in this chapter; simply stated, however, they represent a shift of emphasis from drama as *end* to drama as *means*. Classroom teachers, more at home with the use of drama as a technique for teaching other subjects than with the production of plays (for which they had little or no background or sufficient time to rehearse), discovered this to be an exciting and useful way of working. Proponents of the new techniques offered the suggestion that administrators might find drama and theatre as an educational medium more acceptable than as aesthetic education and would therefore be willing to lend it support. This argument would be further strengthened, they said, if research could prove that children's learning was enhanced when drama and theatre had been used as teaching tools.

Professional children's theatre companies, influenced by the shift in emphasis, took a look at their offerings, and many of them found that another dimension could be added without changing their work in any substantive way. As a result, many companies prepared study guides and teachers' packets; some offered workshops following their performances to extend the experience, thus making theatre more than an engaging hour of entertainment. Some of the newer companies took a frankly educational approach from the start. They developed their own pieces based on curricular units and social issues of concern to children and young people. They realized that scripts would have to hold the attention of an audience if they were to have impact and challenge thought, for there is an inherent risk involved in presenting either strongly didactic plays or material that is too obviously educational. Theatre that lacks human feeling fails as surely as theatre without substance, for in time both bore an audience, though for different reasons. Some companies have been able to combine content related to the curriculum or to children's interests with artistry, achieving brilliant results. This is not easily accomplished, and the most successful companies performing educational theatre are those composed of actor/teachers with experience in both professions. Teachers who prepare their classes for plays through the use of materials sent in advance by the producing companies and who welcome the suggested follow-up activities have found such theatre a stimulus to learning. In whichever context theatre is used—to heighten appreciation and give aesthetic pleasure or to serve as an aid to learning—good theatre is a rich experience for children.

The other important component of aesthetic education is the experience of seeing good theatre. This is often easier said than done because of the wide variation in both availability and quality of plays for the child audience. Availability depends upon the community and its geographic location; quality, on the standards of the producing groups. There is no single pattern throughout the country. Professional, university, and community theatres all contribute but not all meet the same standard of production. In some areas university theatres offer excellent plays and tour them to nearby villages and towns. In other areas civic or community theatres provide regular and ongoing seasons of plays including one or more for children and youth. In still other communities schools sponsor performances by professional touring companies whose work also varies in quality. Few plays designed for the adult audience are appropriate for elementary schoolchildren, though some adult plays hold interest for the high school students.

Good dramatic literature, well performed and artistically costumed and staged, is welcomed by every drama and classroom teacher as the other aspect of aesthetic education. A fine production nourishes as well as gives pleasure and, moreover, holds up a standard of excellence. Although the involvement of the spectator is rarely as deep as that of the participant, it can bring a child excitement and make a lasting impression. In addition, it helps build an appreciation of an art form that is different from the response one has to film and television. The live performance, in which the audience plays an integral part, touches the child on a deeper level. Not every community provides theatre for its young people, but concerned parents and teachers, by checking local resources, may discover some first-rate work being done by a nonprofessional company in

Playwriting stimulated by creative drama. *(Courtesy of Arts Partners, New York City.)*

the region, and they may even encourage a university theatre to include a children's play among their departmental offerings. Although an occasional mediocre performance does no harm, a diet of poor plays, poorly played with nothing better for comparison, cannot build appreciation. Only the best qualifies as aesthetic education; anything less is unacceptable as a component. Discussion and analysis of the production depend on the teacher and the age of the spectators. A curriculum that includes both drama and theatre is the ideal, though it may take time to build. At present there appears to be a growing interest in arts education that includes both the performing and the visual arts, an excellent approach and one that may prove to be stronger than a collection of separate programs.

Drama as a Learning Medium

Drama employed as a specific teaching technique differs primarily in intent from drama taught as an art form or end in itself. Many of the same procedures may be followed, but in the case of drama as a learning medium the teacher is using these procedures to reach certain extrinsic goals: to gain knowledge, arouse interest, solve problems, and change attitudes. Through the process of studying a conflict and the persons involved in it, material is illuminated and interpreted just as it is in the preparation of a play. Occasionally, an original play with interesting content and good dramatic structure will result; this is more likely to happen when drama is used in teaching the language arts than in other curricular areas.

The language arts include listening, speaking, reading, and writing. When used in teaching the language arts, drama can further the teacher's goals and strengthen the students' abilities in all of these areas. Most teachers find drama to be a strong motivation for reading and vocabulary building. In addition, interpretation of character is deepened through creating dialogue. As to structure, creating a play demands organization of the various elements of which it is comprised.

Drama-in-Education

Many of the innovations in drama and theatre education since the first edition of this book must be attributed to influences from England, where the Drama-in-Education (DIE) program and several well-known drama education leaders have attracted wide attention. Best known of these British leaders, because of their numerous visits to the United States, are Dorothy Heathcote, Gavin Bolton, Brian Way, and Cecily O'Neill. Dorothy Heathcote, who was on the faculty of the University of Newcastle-upon-Tyne for many years, has given workshops and summer sessions in various parts of the country and has been the subject of three films made at Northwestern University.

Heathcote's approach to drama is particularly appealing to classroom teachers, who find in it techniques that they can use in their own teaching. She works, as she said, from the inside out, and her concern is that children use drama to expand their understanding of life experiences, to reflect on a particular circumstance, and to make sense out of their world in a deeper way. Her goal is not the teaching of drama alone but of other subjects as well. In fact, there is no area of the curriculum in which she has not used drama. She begins with process and in time moves to a product that may take an audience into account, though this is not her major concern. Her intent is always the depth and breadth of learning, which excites the class and brings satisfaction to the teacher. She consciously employs the elements of drama to educate, according to Betty Jane Wagner, and aims "to bring out what children already know but don't yet know they know."[3]

In lieu of putting on plays and dramatizing literature, Heathcote prefers to help children find the dramatic moment in an event or unit of study. She believes in helping the teacher use drama to teach more effectively, but not by exploiting it to sugarcoat nondramatic material, and encourages the teacher to work with children as a guide and resource person. When there is a drama specialist in the school, Heathcote advocates having the classroom teacher, or generalist, follow up the lesson with his or her suggestions. When there is no specialist, the classroom teacher must learn how to discover the tension, conflict, or point of greatest interest in a topic, how to collect relevant source materials, and how to guide the class through an original piece of work. This process may last for a few

---

3. Betty Jane Wagner, *Dorothy Heathcote* (Washington, D.C.: National Education Association Press, 1976).

periods or for an entire semester, depending on the scope of the study and the interest of the children.

Dramatizing an event, Heathcote believes, makes it possible to isolate and study it. Like most creative drama teachers, she starts with discussion. She uses the children's ideas and encourages their making decisions. Once the direction is clear, she suggests a choice of procedures: analogy, simulation, and role. Of the three, Heathcote prefers the last because she believes it fixes an emotional response. She will, therefore, assume a role. In other words, she takes part as a character in the drama. She frequently steps out of role, stopping the drama when she believes clarification is needed and taking time for further discussion. She will then resume the improvisation. It is this technique that most differentiates her work from that of the majority of American creative drama teachers, who rarely take an active part or stop a scene that is going well to discuss it. Heathcote's classes, because of their interest in the situation, are able to stop, enter into discussion, and then continue playing.

Teachers following this method collect the best reference materials, literature, and artifacts they can find. The children are encouraged to spend much time studying them in order to build an original drama. Social studies, current events, moral and ethical problems, become grist for the mill because Heathcote is concerned with both cognitive and affective learning. Possible topics for drama might be the study of a particular community, industry, energy, pollution, transportation, immigration, a disaster with social implications, or a great or well-known person like Martin Luther King. The possibilities are endless and may come from any area of the curriculum, but the point is that by employing drama in this way, children are helped to see below the surface of an event or topic and thereby gain a better understanding of it.

Gavin Bolton of the University of Durham has worked with Dorothy Heathcote in the United States on numerous occasions and has also offered workshops of his own. Although they share the same educational philosophy, Bolton's techniques differ in certain respects. His approach is more intellectual and analytical; he spends much time in questioning and discussion. Bolton stated his aims in drama education as follows:

1. To help the student understand himself and the world he lives in
2. To help the student know how and when (and when *not*) to adapt to the world he lives in
3. To help the student gain understanding of and satisfaction from the medium of drama[4]

Bolton admitted to being primarily concerned with the cognitive aspect of the drama experience. Although he did not recommend neglecting the aesthetic element, he said that he teaches through it rather than for it.

4. From notes prepared for London Teachers of Drama by Gavin Bolton, 1973.

The major difference between creative drama as traditionally taught in this country and Drama-in-Education as described here lies in emphasis and techniques. There are as many different approaches to the teaching of drama as there are teachers, but the Heathcote approach is the best known of the newer methods and has had the greatest impact to date on American classroom teachers. Betty Jane Wagner's book *Dorothy Heathcote—Drama as a Learning Medium,* provides the most detailed description available of this dynamic leader's philosophy and methods.

One of the newer voices in Drama-in-Education is that of Cecily O'Neill. Although she has been connected with the Inner London Education Authority for a number of years, she is currently on leave, as visiting professor in the School of Education at Ohio State University in Columbus. As she said in the following pages, she shares the philosophy of Dorothy Heathcote and Gavin Bolton, but realizing that many American teachers and students have difficulty in applying it to their own work, she is trying to clarify the method by working with them over a longer period. The following excerpt from a paper written by Cecily O'Neill for me may help readers understand this popular and practical use of Drama-in-Education.

DRAMA AS A SIGNIFICANT EXPERIENCE

For me, the most important task in drama in education is the creation of a shared dramatic context, a fictional world, in which it is possible to explore and examine ideas, issues, relationships, and content areas. Like theatre, drama is a paradoxical activity. It is both real and not real at the same time. Both drama and theatre require an active engagement with the make-believe, a willingness to be caught up in and accept the rules of the imaginary world which is created on stage or in the classroom. . . . I want my students to experience the pleasure, insight, and satisfaction of balancing these opposites. There will be a growing sense of mastery and delight in cooperatively manipulating the make-believe and sharing perceptions and cognitions with others.

A central concept in my work is role-play. In both theatre and drama the participants adopt roles. They pretend to become what they are not. By taking on roles they transcend their everyday selves, and get a glimpse of their own potential. Roles can be assumed, modified, elaborated, refined and relinquished. But the result is not merely that the participants' role repertoire is expanded. By exploring the different perspectives offered by fictional roles, students may come to recognize, and, if necessary, modify their habitual orientation to the world.

As drama teachers, instead of colluding with our students in their inventions of themselves as failures and incompetents who are unnecessary to society, we can help them re-invent themselves through drama and discover their possible powers, skills, and competencies. Role-play comes easily to children, if their attempts are supported and authenticated by the teacher, especially if the teacher participates in the creation of the make-believe.

What is surprising is how often classroom drama manages to avoid these essential role transformations. Drama lessons that rely on games and exercises to the neglect of the creation of dramatic roles and contexts are lacking what is, for me, the essential activity of drama. Drama is by its nature an experimental, exploratory and ambiguous process. We create a fictional world not to escape from the real world, but to reflect on it, to examine it more closely. Drama, as Peter Brook said of theatre, can be a mirror, a magnifying glass, a microscope or a searchlight. We conduct this experiment within the safety of what Dorothy Heathcote has called the "no penalty" area, where the two parts of people can have equal status. The spectator part, which allows us to stand back and see what it is we are experiencing at the moment, and the participant part, which has to deal with the event. Heathcote taught us the need for living through drama. She used the strategy of teacher-in-role to achieve moments of real encounter, of heightened experience. But she also helped us to understand that experience without reflection will not bring about change. "To be a proper spectator is to be in two places at once," observed Richard Foreman;—"involved in the make-believe and seeing oneself involved in it."[5]

There has to be engagement, but simultaneous contemplation. One is not working for a "hallucinated participation" but for a kind of dual awareness, a critical consciousness which challenges the students to make sense of the experience in terms of their own lives and the world around them. Our task as drama teachers is to set up the kinds of action which will heighten the participants' sense of "seeing," while still demanding meaningful participation in the action. For me, the heart of the drama experience is in the *encounter,* the kind of improvisation which, although it may be structured to include a number of different episodes, produces anticipation, unease, surprise, suspense, recognition, insight. For the experience to be significant this encounter has to be an event, in the present moment, as it is in the theatre. We have to be able to transform the classroom or drama studio into a place where something happens. To achieve this sense of an event, we cannot build our drama wholly on playmaking, or re-enactment, or what Brian Way calls polished improvisation. There may be moments in the dramatic structure which are prepared or rehearsed, but if insights are to be achieved or discoveries made, the heart of the encounter must remain spontaneous. This spontaneity does not imply freedom from the constraints of the medium. It involves a quality of response which balances impulse and restraint, and integrates imagination and reason.

Since I have learned so much from both Heathcote and Bolton, and share the same philosophy, it is difficult to articulate precisely the ways in which my work differs from theirs. A continuing support in structuring my work comes from what I have learned from theatre and dramatic literature—by the kind of themes, conventions and devices which playwrights and theatre workers have used throughout the ages. Much of the theory we have found to support our thinking and practice in drama in education has come from educational philosophy, child development, psychology and sociology.

 . . . In drama we are not seeking solutions or finding answers, as is often the case when role-playing is used as an instrument in the curriculum. We are trying to release students into finding their own questions. The power of the teacher-

---

5. Richard Foreman, *Plays and Manifestos,* The Drama Review Series (New York: New York University Press, 1976), p. 143.

in-role comes not from theatrical skills or a desire to perform but from a capacity for courageous, imaginative, and authentic engagement with students in the co-creation of an imagined world. In my work with teachers I have tried to share this sense of structure. I want them to gain confidence in manipulating elements of the drama experience so that it is satisfying for both leader and participants.

Again, as in every area, similar work is being carried on successfully in America without publicity by classroom teachers, who created their own methods of teaching. One of them is the *Echo Project* designed by two young teachers in Middle College High School of La Guardia Community College, Long Island City, New York. *The Bongo Workbook,* a manual for teachers of science and social studies, was made possible by grants from the National Endowment for the Arts and administered by the Research Foundation of the City University of New York. The teachers, Paul Jablon and Terry Born, realized the special needs of this city's at-risk urban high school population and to that end designed an interdisciplinary, team-teaching program in the late seventies. By the late eighties its success was recognized, and a workbook explaining their methodology was completed. Published in 1987, it is now available for use by other teachers in the field. A popular technique described throughout is creative drama.[6]

Another interesting project was instigated by a teacher of first and second grades in a New York inner city school. Discovering that the children had never experienced sharing a traditional Thanksgiving dinner with a family or community group, the teacher used the holiday as a way of learning about the first Thanksgiving and how some of our customs and practices have evolved. He included songs, arts and crafts, and the enactment of appropriate legends and stories in his plans. The children made Indian headdresses and strings of paper beads to wear for the occasion and paper mats to be used on the tables.

With the cooperation of a parent-teacher committee, a complete Thanksgiving dinner was prepared. The children counted and peeled potatoes, apples and squash, measured brown sugar, made butter and stirred gravy, thus meeting the curriculum goals of science and math, as well as social studies. Local merchants supplied food, including a large turkey, and a florist friend of the teacher contributed flowers for the tables. I was invited to the festivities held at noon of the day before Thanksgiving and I was both charmed and touched by the enjoyment and pride of the children as they presented their simple program and then looked for their places at the tables. It was evident throughout that much learning had taken place, particularly through the use of the arts.[7]

Brian Way, on the other hand, is best known for his textbook *Development through Drama* and for his theory of participatory theatre (briefly described in

6. Terry Born and Paul Jablon, *The Bongo Workbook* (Long Island City, N.Y.: Middle College High School at LaGuardia Community College, 1987).

7. Project described and observed in Marc Janover's classroom, New York City.

The first Thanksgiving. *(Courtesy of Marc Janover.)*

chapter 1). Brian Way shares with Heathcote a concern for the participant, making the same point but in different words: he said that he is not interested in training actors but in developing people. Way does not endorse drama as a teaching tool, however; his primary concern is the human being, not education, aesthetic or otherwise. For the past several years he has been giving lectures and workshops of varying lengths throughout the United States on the subjects of creative dramatics and participatory theatre. In both areas he has brought new ideas and ways of working, though it is in the use of audience participation that his most original work has been done. Here formal theatre and creative drama are combined to create a new form, which is being used by a number of children's theatre companies. His years as director of the Theatre Center in London have given him a wealth of experience, particularly with inner city children. This has won him a ready and receptive following in the United States. Whereas Heathcote, Bolton, and O'Neill's following includes many classroom teachers, Way tends to attract producing groups, both professional and amateur, who work with children in schools. The changes that have taken place in England in the past thirty years and are being seen here today are clearly summarized in the following statement:

> There has been a shift in direction from an interest in the personal development of the individual pupil through the acquiring of theatrical and improvisational skills, to the recognition of drama as a precise teaching instrument, which works best when it is seen as part of the learning process, and when it is embedded firmly within the rest of the school curriculum. Drama is no longer seen only as another branch of art education, but as a unique teaching tool, vital in language

development, and invaluable as a method in the exploration of other subject areas.[8]

Except for a few fears regarding the exploitation of drama for the purpose of teaching other subjects, some questions regarding the relevancy of creative drama today, and occasional misunderstandings about the nature and function of audience participation, I believe that there are more similarities than differences between these two approaches. Drama, when it is used in education, is, as opposed to formal theatre, primarily concerned with process learning and the growth of the individual. Both means and ends are involved, however, because they are inseparable. It is, therefore, a matter of emphasis rather than of opposing goals. In the final analysis, we must each determine our goals and create our own methods. We may find imitating the methods of others a necessary and valuable first step, but we are strengthened by trusting ourselves and risking failure in the beginning in our search for success.

Theatre-in-Education

One of the newest types of performing groups is the Theatre-in-Education touring company. Because of the growing popularity of T.I.E. in America, an entire chapter is devoted to it in this fifth edition, and a teachers' guide is included in the Appendix.

Artists-in-the-Schools

Another approach to drama/theatre education is the Artists-in-the-Schools program, which brings performers into the classroom for a morning, a day, a week, or sometimes a much longer period. Here actors perform, demonstrate, or work directly with the children. This provides an opportunity for the teacher to learn new techniques that help him or her to continue alone after the actors have gone. It also exposes children to the creative artist, whom they would otherwise probably never meet. Throughout the United States, actors, dancers, musicians, painters, puppeteers, and poets have been brought into schools through funded programs. Information on available artists (both groups and individuals) is available through state arts councils and state departments of education. Although not every school has made use of either the program or the concept, many have, and children have had their education enriched as a result.

The Theatre-in-the-Schools program of the National Endowment for the Arts was described in detail by Sr. Kathryn Martin, the theatre coordinator for the education program in 1979. This report is the last comprehensive documentation of the companies involved in the program and selected as exemplary groups. Inasmuch as there is no longer a theatre coordinator, it is difficult to make a precise statement about the number of states that currently have a theatre/drama

8. Cecily O'Neill, Alan Lambert, Rosemary Linnell, and Janet Warr-Wood, *Drama Guidelines* (London: Heinemann Educational Books, 1976), p. 7.

component. According to Sr. Kathryn Martin, however, the probability is that a large majority do have some kind of drama activity within the artist-in-education program. This might be a creative drama specialist, a theatre company in performance or workshop, or a mime and puppetry company. Basic structures vary from state to state because of geographical and educational needs as well as the length of time that such activities have been included.

Playwriting with Young People

Since the last edition of this book there has been a developing interest in playwriting with and by children and young people. It is too soon to tell whether or not this is a trend, but some unusual opportunities have been made available to both elementary and secondary school students and their teachers to learn more about this form of writing. The participation play, by involving the audience in the process as well as in the performance, introduces children to dramatic structure in a way that the formal proscenium production does not do. Whether the idea of bringing a playwright into the classroom is in any way related to participatory theatre is hard to say, but it is obvious to anyone who has ever been in a child audience that children are extremely perceptive regarding character, plot, and motivation. Though children do not necessarily observe a linear pattern in their writing any more than they do in their improvisations, there is a logic in their dramatic writing which, if given encouragement and basic technical help, can lead to some impressive results.

One program that has attracted attention in the New York area is the Young Playwrights' Project, initiated in 1980 by the Dramatists' Guild. To direct it the Guild engaged Gerald Chapman, a young Englishman whose work in playwriting with young people at the Royal Court Theatre in London brought him to their attention. Mr. Chapman launched the project by offering workshops for students and teachers in the New York metropolitan area, and later in other cities. By 1982 the Young Playwrights' Project had become highly successful, with 700 plays submitted that season, ten of which were produced with professional casts. The brochure for the following season announced (1) workshops for young people from fourth through twelfth grades, and (2) a festival in the spring offering professional production of the award-winning scripts at the Circle Repertory Theatre. Critics, educators, and directors have acclaimed the project as "an innovative design for learning" . . . "a bracing theatrical occasion" . . . "an opportunity for children to acquire not only a sensitivity to the art of playwriting and drama but a contribution to their cognitive, social and emotional development." Mr. Chapman elicits the interests and concerns of children, then works with them in their classrooms to help them express these concerns in play form.

A quite different approach is that used by Aurand Harris, a well-known American children's playwright, who has been playwright-in-residence in a number of communities throughout the country. In Cleveland, Ohio, where he spends a month at a time in elementary school classrooms, he works directly with children, stimulating them to writing but without awards or eventual production. His educational objectives are an ongoing interest in the dramatic form and improvement in written communication. The results of his work are reported to be highly successful and, judging from the increasing demands for him to come to other communities, there is little doubt about the popularity of this new direction in drama/theatre education. According to Elizabeth Flory Kelly, "Mr. Harris not only has developed a creative drama–playwriting formula which can simultaneously inspire the beginning student to write; but he is instructing the teacher in the use of a fresh method of motivating children in the basic skill of writing."[9]

Guided experience in writing plays performs a number of services for the student. Its contribution to the language arts, however, can be summed up in the following simple statement concerning plays as literature: "The important feature is that they [plays] are primarily linguistic, narrative constructs; they are all part of the unique relationship between language and form we call literature."[10]

It is heartening to see that children's plays have finally been recognized as literature and accorded a place in some elementary school textbooks and anthologies of children's literature. Stories, poems, and essays have traditionally comprised the contents of these books; today, however, with a growing number of excellent plays by gifted children's playwrights, a new genre of literature has become available, and it is one to which most children respond. It is also interesting to note that the range of subject matter has broadened. Plays with different ethnic and racial backgrounds are being written, and some leaders in the field are also taking an active part in making fine religious dramas available to young people.[11]

A number of colleges and universities now offer courses in playwriting, a few of them in playwriting for the child audience; but the workshops *for* children represent a new direction. Not that some teachers on both elementary and secondary school levels have not included playwriting before now, but the idea of having a professional writer work with the children and the classroom teacher is an innovation.

Child Drama Programs in Colleges and Universities

In 1950 the Children's Theatre Association of America (CTAA) undertook a periodic survey of college and university offerings in child drama. The results of the 1982 survey were reported and tabulated in the 1983 Winter Issue of *The*

9. Letter from Elizabeth Flory Kelly to the author in January, 1983, following Aurand Harris's second playwriting residency in Cleveland.

10. *Plays Considered as Literature as Well as Theatre for Young People from 8 to 18 to Read and Perform,* compiled and discussed by Aidan Chambers (S. Woodchester, Stroud, Eng.: Thimble Press, 1982), p. 6.

11. Correspondence with Pamela Barrager and Norman J. Fedder, Kansas State University.

Children's Theatre Review.[12] The major categories were: (1) graduate programs in child drama; (2) undergraduate programs in child drama; and (3) theatre departments with advanced courses but no declared emphasis on child drama. The 1982 survey, compared to the four previous surveys, indicated a slow but steady increase in offerings and pointed to four particular trends:

1. The number of college and university theatre departments concerned with child drama or offering course work in it is growing;
2. More comprehensive programs tend to develop once a department offers courses and productions for children;
3. The increase in comprehensive programs indicates the growing depth and breadth of the field;
4. A strong thrust toward touring children's productions throughout the country reveals an interest in taking good theatre to young people, especially in areas where no other live theatre exists.

Since 1982, the budget crunch has caused some cutting of curricular offerings, and child drama programs are among these affected. It is to be hoped that they will be restored in an improved economy.

Special Arts Projects

Supplementing curricular offerings are the many special arts projects that have been funded by the United States Office of Education to promote intercultural and interracial communication for students, teachers, and community members. Although all of the programs fluctuate and are subject to budgetary cuts, some of the areas to which they have contributed are as follows:

1. The artist-in-residence program. Before each residency the artist holds a workshop with teachers about his or her craft. Artists include a poet, a dancer, a media specialist, a visual artist, a dramatist, and a musician.
2. Special series programs. In this area there are performances by actors, orchestras, ballet, mimes, and puppet theatres.
3. Speakers and field trips.
4. Arts camps.
5. Publications.
6. School-community relations. The aim is to involve more parents and community organizations in the purpose and implementation of the special arts projects program.
7. Teacher training. Workshops to help teachers in ongoing arts programs.

12. Lin Wright and Rosemarie Willenbrink, "Child Drama, 1982: A Survey of College and University Programs in the United States," *The Children's Theatre Review* 32, no. 1 (January 1983).

8. Project replication. Visits to other school systems and preparation of helpful materials.

Increasingly evident in education are the strong forces that are attempting to change the direction of education from a purely intellectual emphasis to one that recognizes latent potential and therefore includes the arts as a basic component. Also apparent is the growing interest of many teachers in using the arts as a tool for teaching, as well as a discipline in its own right—not to sugarcoat other subject areas but to illuminate and interpret them. This is less a change, however, than it is an expansion of goals. The many and varied approaches to these concepts represent a new vitality.

Circumstances rather than specific methodology, however, should be our guide. Leaders share certain common objectives, but they assign priorities according to their situations, strengths, and needs. In other words, although there have been significant changes in the philosophy and the methods employed by teachers of creative drama, there is perhaps less actual than apparent difference. All subscribe to a primary concern for the child; most place process above product; all hold certain educational goals in common.

Summary

The controversy regarding drama as means or end is not settled and perhaps never will be. Compelling arguments on both sides press for a curriculum in which there is a place for each. Leading educators have declared drama and speech to be central to a language curriculum. They believe that drama can motivate writing and improve oral skills; they believe that it stimulates reading. Some insist that it can be used to teach any subject effectively.

There is agreement among many educators that study of the arts gives form and expression to human feeling and that attending the theatre as a spectator is a rich experience not found in film and television viewing. In the foreword to a publication released by the State University of New York in 1978, a strong stand is taken regarding the place of the arts in education: "The arts are a means of expressing and interpreting human experience. Quality education of individuals is complete only if the arts are an integral part of the daily teaching and learning process. The integration of the arts in the elementary, secondary and continuing education curriculum is a key to the humanistic development of students."[13]

It is such statements of purpose that distinguish the attitude toward arts education today from that held in the past. The hundreds of agencies and foundations—federal, state, and private—that contribute to the arts are a further

---

13. *The Arts as Perception (A Way of Learning),* Project Search, The University of the State of New York (Albany, N.Y.: State Department, Division of Humanities and Arts Education, 1978), p. iii.

expression of support. Although we have far to go before we can point with pride to schools in which the arts and the academic areas have equal emphasis, progress has been made. In this respect the picture today is brighter than at any other time in the history of American education. Whether or not the progress continues if financial support is reduced will be the proof of its strength and the depth of our commitment.

14 Theatre-in-Education

*H*ome Court, a play about crack, produced by the Creative Arts Team, New York University. *(Courtesy of Lynda Zimmerman; photograph by Lou Manna.)*

Theatre-in-Education: a definition of the term was given in the first chapter. What place, therefore, does further discussion of the subject have in a text on creative drama? Simply this: Theatre-in-Education (T.I.E.) has created so much interest in this country in the past fifteen years and is so closely linked with creative drama that it now merits a chapter in itself rather than the few paragraphs it was accorded in earlier editions. Originating in England in the sixties, the T.I.E. concept spread to other English-speaking countries and, soon afterward, to many countries around the world. Because T.I.E. so often uses creative drama in activities preceding and following a performance, it is helpful to teachers not only to be able to work with the teams in this way but also to see how creative drama is a natural method of solving problems and exploring curricular material and social issues.

John O'Toole described T.I.E. as based on an extension of children's play and a combination of theatricality and classroom techniques to provide an experience in its own right, with the glamour of strangers in dramatic role and costume providing both a stimulus and a context that are not normally available to the teacher.[1] Whenever children put themselves in the place of others, they are identifying with them and so are better able to comprehend their concerns and problems in both affective and cognitive ways.

The potential of T.I.E. as an effective means of reaching young people is now generally accepted in the United States, although the approach and techniques used by the various companies are far from uniform. Some groups pattern their work on the British model, whereas others adapt the concept to meet American needs and interests. Many American children's theatre touring companies advertise an educational component, but not all of them interpret this in the same way, nor do they necessarily offer T.I.E. pieces exclusively. Some children's theatre companies give plays that qualify purely as entertainment, and others describe their work as educational. Few, however, attempt the more difficult task of offering controversial subject matter in a theatrically aesthetic form.

The basic difference between traditional children's theatre and T.I.E. is *intent.* The former comes into the school to entertain, whereas the mission of TIE is to effect change or to illuminate subject matter through the medium of the theatre. The desired result is:

1. To change an attitude, thereby leading to a change in behavior
2. To stimulate intellectual curiosity
3. To motivate the pursuit of a particular topic or issue

Although a play may do any or all of these things, it is not the playwright or producer's intent, and there is rarely a follow-up after the performance. Children

1. John O'Toole, *Theatre in Education* (London: Hodder and Stoughton), p. vi.

may, and often do, reenact what they have just seen on the stage, but the motivation comes from their enjoyment of the story or the impression made on them by the actors. Although the T.I.E. has often been criticized as being didactic, at its best it is excellent theatre in both content and form. But let us see how it evolved.

Background of Theatre-in-Education

T.I.E. as a concept originated in England in 1965. The first company was established at the Belgrade Theatre in Coventry, primarily as a way of drawing the young people of the community into the theatre. The first programme was a piece called "Out of the Ashes."[2] It dealt with life in Coventry during the blitz and its aftermath and was developed through improvisation and subsequently put into script form with the assistance of a local playwright. Gordon Vallins, who designed the first programmes at the Belgrade, was concerned not only with building an audience for the future but also with the way in which theatre was being presented to young people. Vallins noted that:

> The local authority bought out two matinee performances a year for particular productions which were felt to be suitable. These tended to include the annual Shakespearean play, an event treated by many schools as a jolly afternoon out. This event was loathed by the actors. Most of the young people came ill-prepared and demonstrated little respect for the play or the actors. Consequently, the actors tended to rush the performance and garble their lines. For most actors it was a negative experience. Although some attempt had been made by the theatre to provide preparatory talks before the theatre visit, it was administratively impossible to visit every school. The situation was embarrassing and obviously needed reassessing. For most of the young audience it was as if the play had been spoken in a foreign tongue, the action remote, played on a platform behind the proscenium arch, with the actors talking to each other and never to their audience.[3]

Vallins was concerned and attacked the situation with a pilot project in which he sought a new way to capture the attention of young audiences and hold their interest. The material, he believed, must be direct, challenging, and relevant to their lives. It need not be current or even familiar, but it must contain an issue or a problem to solve. He was acquainted with Brian Way's work at the Theatre Centre in London and knew the value of audience participation. The Theatre Centre at that time produced specially scripted plays, written and produced to include children's participation. The participation might be vocal,

2. The spelling of the word *programme* is that used by the British and will be used when referring to their material.
3. Gordon Vallins, "The Beginnings of T.I.E.," in *Learning through Theatre,* ed. Tony Jackson (Manchester, Eng.: Manchester University Press, 1960), p. 6.

physical, or verbal and was sometimes necessary to the outcome of the plot, but Way's primary purpose was to entertain rather than to educate the audience. Theatre-in-Education, on the other hand, was created with an awareness of the limitations of the school curriculum and the lack of impact that the theatre was having on young people. If audiences could be moved to participate, Vallins reasoned, the restlessness might be dispelled and replaced by a genuine involvement in the content. "In essence," wrote Tony Jackson, "T.I.E. needs to be seen as a new genre, a form of theatre that has arisen in direct response to the needs of both theatre and schools and which has sought to harness the techniques and imaginative potency of theatre in the service of education."[4]

Kathy Joyce, curriculum development leader for drama in the city of Manchester, described T.I.E. as a

> unique hybrid which combines the skills and techniques of traditional theatre with modern educational philosophy and practice to create a medium for learning with direct emotional and intellectual impact upon the audience. The good T.I.E. company will generally deal with strong, sometimes contentious material related to the real world, refusing to water down or patronize, even for the smallest children.[5]

Although Vallins resigned his position in 1966, the pilot project was continued and deemed a success. During the next few years the leadership of the Belgrade company changed several times, and some members left to set up new companies in Leeds, Bolton, Edinburgh, London, and other sites where there was interest. In the beginning, to ensure quality and an understanding of their audiences and their needs, performers were required to have certification as teachers and to hold membership in Actors' Equity. This did not pertain to teams on college campuses, of which there were a number, but the latter were established with careful faculty supervision and a limited number of performances.

In time T.I.E. companies developed a variety of plays for different age levels. Infant, junior, and secondary school programmes were devised, sometimes even on the same theme but handled in different ways, with increasing complexity on the upper levels. By serving a large population, teams were able to qualify for funding, which came from the British Arts Council and local Authorities, though not necessarily from Local Education Authorities. Many T.I.E. teams were attached to regional theatres and some, as mentioned, to academic institutions. Standards and goals varied, reflecting the individual team's perspective and point of view. Some were highly political; others were not. All, however, researched and prepared their own material and created programmes that they considered relevant to the lives of young people.[6] At the core of the concept was the

---

4. Tony Jackson, ed., *Learning through Theatre* (Manchester, Eng.: Manchester University Press, 1960), p. viii.

5. Ibid., p. 25.

6. Many of the scripts were later published and so made available to other groups.

conviction that the best learning takes place through personal or hands-on experience. Actor/teachers would engage the students' interest in the subject and then give them the details necessary to bring the material to life. From there on it was a cooperative effort with the team guiding the class through an exploration of the problem.

Language development has remained an important objective of T.I.E., for it is an essential means of human communication. Yet although the emphasis was on learning, the enjoyment and appreciation of theatre as an art form was not neglected. A fine balance between learning and aesthetic pleasure must be struck, if the experience were to fulfill its purpose.

The classroom teacher was to be a key person in helping students derive maximum benefit from a visit; therefore, cooperation from the schools was enlisted. Many teachers were enthusiastic about this new and different approach, and it was not long before it had captured the imagination of the English-speaking world and of drama teachers on the continent of Europe. Although there have been changes in T.I.E. since its founding, the basic tenents have remained.

Common Strategies

Children are expected to enter into a situation and are asked to make decisions or solve problems. In this respect it is believed that they will become much more deeply involved than in merely seeing a production that is entertaining or having a lesson taught traditionally in a classroom. Also, with young children, having a teacher participate "in role" (assuming a part) also heightens the experience, although it is not necessarily a part of the programme. Some programmes are humorous, some are serious, but all are thought provoking. When a team goes to a school more than once, an assignment between visits is often given. In this case the teacher using the materials provided by the team can set the stage for the next meeting. In its use of relevant themes, audience participation, improvisation, and discussion with the cast afterward, T.I.E. represents an entirely new method of learning.

Although audience participation is commonly used in T.I.E., the two terms are not synonymous.[7] Indeed, audience participation is frequently used in children's theatre as a device for involving the audience in the entertainment. In the T.I.E. programme, however, participation makes a greater demand on the audience. It means decision making, thoughtful discussion, and cooperative effort that will affect the outcome of the programme. It is both the *intent* and the *extent* of its use that differentiates it from participation used in other types of plays.

7. Audience participation is used just as often in plays in which there is no social problem. Younger children particularly enjoy them.

Creative drama is another technique that is often employed following a performance, but it, too, is only one of many methods suggested by the team to make the most productive use of the visit. In other words, there is no exact formula for a programme or for the varieties of participation and combinations of techniques employed.

One effective method that is sometimes employed is *simulation*. A scene or situation is simulated with an entire group of students taking part. Factory, which took place in the Curtain Theatre in London in the early years, is an example of simulation. The secondary school students, for whom it was planned, were divided into groups with the factory workers on the shop floor and the white-collar employees on an upper floor. Each group was introduced to its responsibilities and then led through the schedule of an entire working day. By experiencing the job, the hierarchy, and the rewards and problems faced by factory personnel, the students had a much better understanding of both the work and labor relations than they had had before. Simulation not only requires much careful planning and supervision, but is time consuming and involves fewer students than a programme that takes place in an auditorium. Nevertheless, it is an effective and unique way of learning. As opposed to traditional learning, simulation aims to help students develop critical judgment and a sense of personal responsibility rather than a passive, unquestioning acceptance of society as it is. By living through a simulated situation, the participant is better

Students in New York University's Program in Educational Theatre preparing for production of "The Crucifixion" from *The Wakefield Cycle* during summer session at Bretton Hall College, Yorkshire.

able to assess it. Imaginative thinking is encouraged and a deeper level of feeling is aroused.

Another effective technique is *anthology.* This is used primarily in the teaching of history. According to John Hodgson of Bretton Hall College, anthology is a collection of authentic material from a period like the Georgian or Elizabethan. It can be music, poetry, prose, plays, or any form of actable, livable, presentable, communicable idea or sound or facility. In other words, explained Hodgson, "It's all about people in history. It's about people living in an age, what they did, what they said to each other, what they thought about each other, what they wrote to each other and about each other."[8]

Tony Jackson, in his introduction to *Learning through Theatre,* described the theatrical event, whatever it may be, as the central stimulus of the T.I.E. programme, but it is only one of several elements. The team provides teachers' workshops in advance to explain the aim and describe the manner in which the programme will be presented. If teachers are to take part "in role," they are taught how to proceed and are given a packet containing research materials and suggestions for further activities. The performance elements come next and, last of all, an opportunity for the team and the classroom teacher to assess the effectiveness of the programme. Assessment of a programme is always difficult because of the subjectivity that is involved in the judgment. The following criteria were suggested early on, as guidelines for engaging a company and reviewing its work.

1. Is the content worth presenting, and how far does it go in arresting, informing, and challenging the audience?
2. Is the material well performed and has the team good audience contact?
3. Is it performed for the right age level and the most appropriate size of audience?
4. To what extent are the teachers involved and does the programme relate to the school curriculum?
5. How committed are the actors to the objectives of their work? Are they open to discussion and criticism? Do they attempt to evaluate their work?
6. What unique contribution will this company make to the children's education?[9]

Although this is by no means a definitive list of questions, it directs the attention of the sponsor or teacher and the team to the most salient points.

By 1973 the T.I.E. concept had proliferated to the extent that a two-week festival was organized and held in London. Two venues were selected to accommodate the thirty-eight companies that responded to the invitation to

8. Robert Landy, *Handbook of Educational Drama and Theatre* (Westport, Conn.: Greenwood Press, 1982), p. 53.

9. Jackson, *Learning through Theatre,* p. 33.

participate. These sites were the Young Vic and The Cockpit, both theatres with active companies of their own and good performance spaces. A wide variety of programmes, ranging from simple pieces for infants to sophisticated programmes for teenagers, was offered to delegates from throughout the United Kingdom and abroad. Companies had not been screened in advance; hence the quality was uneven but the event was nevertheless exciting in its diversity. Since then there has been further growth, despite the tightening of budgets for the arts. One way of solving budgetary problems was to shorten the time spent in a school, thus leaving the follow-up activities to the teacher and freeing the team to go on to another school. This has resulted in further changes, but the concept itself has lost neither its popularity nor integrity.

Bretton Hall College in Yorkshire was one of the colleges in the forefront of the T.I.E. movement from its inception, and it was the campus selected by New York University's Program in Educational Theatre in 1973 for its overseas summer school. John Hodgson of Bretton Hall and Nancy Swortzell of New York University designed a curriculum for graduate students in educational theatre, whereby American students might elect twelve credits in a summer toward a master's or doctoral degree. The majority of students take course work during the fall and spring semesters on the New York campus, with many spending one, two,

Production of "The Crucifixion" from *The Wakefield Cycle* as performed at The National Trust Foundation, Fountain's Abbey, Yorkshire, England, by students in New York University's Program in Educational Theatre (summer session at Bretton Hall College).

or three summers at Bretton Hall. This plan has resulted in a thorough grounding in T.I.E. techniques and the formation of one highly successful project in New York as an outgrowth. This project was the now-well-known company the Creative Arts Team (CAT).

A group of New York University students in the early years of the program were so inspired by the work they had seen and engaged in at Bretton Hall that they decided to establish a similar group in New York. The team was patterned on the British model but adapted to American schools and concerned with American problems. The project met with success. A combination of strong guidance in the beginning, a sound program, a variety of skills and talents in the company, a clear perception of the needs of the New York metropolitan area, and continuity of leadership has led to an increasingly busy schedule and numerous awards. The CAT has grown from a small nucleus of graduate students to a professional company of some seventy actor/teachers, with a playwright in residence and several ongoing community projects. The company is still connected with the university, but it is autonomous, handling its own operation, research, and fund raising.

The CAT defines itself as "a new kind of provocative and challenging theatre which questions, probes, involves, and finally motivates personal response and action . . . a catalyst for thought on social and curricular issues, enriching the

A scene from *The Divider,* a production of the Creative Arts Team, New York University; a piece about prejudice. *(Courtesy of Lynda Zimmerman; photograph by Johan Elbers.)*

lives of both young people and adults by the vitality, immediacy, and pertinence to the concerns of today's society."[10]

Projects change according to sponsors' needs, but there is usually a new one each season. Profiles of three of CAT's current projects are:

Conflict Resolution through Drama: A performance, workshop, and video project designed to develop conflict resolution skills: addressing issues such as child abuse, teen pregnancy, and drug abuse.

Arts Partners: A uniquely designed residency for the New York City Board of Education. Participatory drama workshops addressing specific educational priorities with kindergarten through eighth grade take place throughout the academic year.

Project: Communication: A residency combining a theatre performance on human relations issues and participatory drama workshops designed to enhance students' communication skills.

Recent touring productions have been *I Never Told Anybody,* a program on child abuse; *Home Court,* a program on the tragic consequences of using crack; and *The Divider,* a study of the emotional roots of racial prejudice and the violence it engenders. Although none of the productions is based on a particular case, the playwright and team familiarized themselves thoroughly with the subject matter and its importance.

An interesting project developed by the CAT in 1987 was "Children of Ellis Island." Under a grant from the New York State Council on the Arts, CAT, in collaboration with Community School District 20 in New York, celebrated the centennial of the Statue of Liberty and Ellis Island in the public schools. Beginning with a study of the cultural diversity of the district, the team worked with the children in the intermediate grades of each school. Activities focused on the experiences of the immigrants to their new land. Each school in the district engaged in research, including oral history, discussed the experiences of people leaving their native lands forever, the long journey to New York, and the arrival in America. Scenes, monologues, and music were knit into scripts with the help of the team and were later performed in the schools. Students, teachers, parents, and administrators attended. Not only were performance skills involved but also reading, writing, and social studies were important aspects of the project.

During the summer of 1987 a group of Korean graduate students in the Educational Theatre Program at New York University decided to investigate the problems of the youth in the Korean community of the city. Working closely with the Korean Youth Center in Queens, they initiated a Theatre Festival as a way of reaching this rapidly growing population. The project was operated by a Christian minister and supported by a daily newspaper and a broadcasting company in the community. There was a general assumption that the younger generation had serious problems in adjusting to their new country and its values.

10. CAT brochure, 1988.

By applying theatre techniques and launching a festival, the students thought they could pinpoint these problems and help the young people find ways of coping with and solving them.

Two hundred teenagers responded to the invitation to participate. They were divided into twenty groups scattered throughout metropolitan New York and New Jersey. Each group was guided to discover the major concerns and then to develop and present programs that dealt with them. Beginning in mid-April, under the leadership of the students, the young people planned, wrote, cast, and rehearsed their plays. The result was deemed a great success by both the participants and the adults of the community. One of the most valuable results was what the festival revealed to the parents. Proof of the success of the project for the young people was their request to repeat the Theatre Festival the following year with "Teen-age Problems" the overall theme.

Another student, stimulated by the Bretton Hall experience, developed an unusual project in the Boston area. His use of T.I.E. was aimed at creating a bridge between local historical events and the persons involved in or affected by them. Through research into the lives of actual persons, who had lived in Concord at the time of the Revolutionary War and were known to have taken part in the events that happened on the night of April 19, 1775, a living history piece was developed. It was entitled *Cannon Fields* and played for several weeks during the summer of 1982 at the Visitors' Center in Minutemen Historical Park in Concord, Massachusetts.[11] This is an example of family theatre for both community and tourists in the area, but the procedures followed in creating the piece and the values derived from it are the same as those designed for schools. Many teachers made use of this documentary, but the performance dates and location precluded the kind of follow-up that is part of a regular TIE program.

Today in many parts of the world theatre is reported to be used to teach, entertain, and stimulate discussion about important social issues. For example, in Africa, where tribal societies have used narrative and other forms of theatre to pass on tribal history, religious beliefs, and moral values, today it is being used to educate for the future. From Nigeria to Swaziland, theatre companies similar in structure to T.I.E. are presenting programs on topics such as health care, family planning, conservation, sanitation, and alcoholism. Theatre is found to be a particularly effective way of reaching country people in areas where there is no electricity to run movie projectors or install television sets. The audiences respond to live performance, often joining in the singing and dancing but also engaging in serious discussion afterward.

Some of the plays call for audience participation; some are purposely left open-ended. Most are used for instruction rather than for entertainment. The director of the National Theatre of Zaire described theatre as a particularly useful way of informing illiterate people of local issues and different ways of solving local problems. Often story lines are selected after polling the people for their suggestions. The government of Mozambique has used theatre to show villagers

---

11. Program notes for *Cannon Fields.*

the serious responsibilities that come with independence. Used with adults as well as with young people, drama and theatre are potent techniques for consciousness raising and teaching in developing countries.[12] In reverse order, the South African musical *Sarafina!* came to Broadway in the spring of 1988. American audiences responded to it so enthusiastically that the announced limited engagement was extended indefinitely to accommodate the crowds who stormed the box office. Many high school teachers in the area made use of *Sarafina!* as a field trip for their students. Printed materials explaining the content and process of creating the musical were in the best T.I.E. tradition.

Summary

A "key link with T.I.E. is the word, 'play.' As already implied, both educational drama and simulation games have their roots in the function that children's play seems to have of ritualizing forms of exploration—in both, the process is enjoyable if it is challenging, clear, and progressing toward some kind of satisfying conclusion."[13]

The manner in which Theatre-in-Education is employed varies as greatly as the content and orientation of the company. The age and needs of the groups to be served determine the objectives; the financial aspect offsets the time that can be spent in a school. Nevertheless, three components are always included:

1. Preparatory material, sent in advance of the team's visit to the school or community center in which the program is to appear
2. The presentation by the team
3. Follow-up activities for use in a workshop after the performance or for discussion later with the classroom teacher

As an illustration of these components, the study guide for *The Divider,* a recent program of the Creative Arts Team, is included in the appendix. It addresses the issue of prejudice by exploring different types of prejudice with which we are faced in our daily lives. *The Divider* was written and produced as "a fictional response to the recent surge in racial violence around the country."[14] By viewing human relations in a contemporary multiethnic community in America, the ramifications of discrimination and the tragic consequences that can result are demonstrated. Audience participation in the form of group discussion with the team follows, with further study in the classroom suggested.

---

12. "Drama in Africa Is Used to Educate Audiences," *The New York Times,* April 4, 1983.
13. John O'Toole, *Theatre in Education* (London: Hodder and Stoughton, 1976), p. 39.
14. Study guide for *The Divider.*

15

Creative Drama for the Special Child

Very Special Arts Program. (*Courtesy of Martha Kaiser, The Kennedy Center, Washington, D.C.*)

Let each become all that he was created ca-
pable of being: expand, if possible, to his full
growth; and show himself at length in his own
shape and stature, be these what they may.

—THOMAS CARLYLE

*T*his chapter considers creative drama in one of
the newer areas of education: special education, or the education of the
exceptional child. *Special education* may be defined as any program of teaching
techniques designed to meet the needs of children whose abilities deviate
markedly from those of the majority of boys and girls of their age. Included in
this group are the intellectually gifted as well as the mentally retarded, the
physically handicapped, the emotionally disturbed, the culturally and economically disadvantaged, children for whom English is a second language, and the
underachievers, whose problems may not have been identified.

Until recently very little has been done to help these children, whose basic
needs are the same as those of so-called normal children but whose individual
needs require special educational services. A difference of opinion until recently
has existed about whether, or when, these children should be integrated into
regular classrooms. But there is recognition of the fact that their special needs
must be met and that they should be helped to take their places with their peers
in as many areas as possible and as soon as they are able to do so. One of the
greatest obstacles to this goal has been the widespread notion that these
children are different from the normal children. Modern educators and psychologists have pointed out the value of getting these boys and girls into regular
classrooms while they are receiving remedial help, therapy, or, in the case of the
gifted, additional enrichments. The remediation should be an aid to their
instruction, rather than a separate program of instruction.

Mainstreaming

Mainstreaming is the term used to define the integration of exceptional
children with the so-called normal. The major objective is social: to assist both
groups in working and living together. To this end, the following practices may
be followed.

Speech therapy, remedial reading, language classes for non-Englishspeak-
ing children, psychological counseling, and special classes for the partially
sighted, blind, or deaf may be included in the school day without removing a
child from the group for more than a period or two at a time. Most schools do not
have this extensive a program of special services, but many schools have set up

some programs to meet the more urgent needs of the school or community. In some instances special activities have been added as enrichment for the culturally disadvantaged as well as for the gifted. In all of these programs there is an opportunity to use creative drama as a therapeutic process. As used here, the term *therapeutic* does not imply psychodrama or sociodrama but rather points to an aspect of an art form in which children find pleasure, emotional release, mental stimulation, personal satisfaction through success, and, most of all, a chance to use and stretch their imaginations.

The Gifted Child

One group of children that has received very little attention, perhaps because they are able to move ahead on their own, is the intellectually gifted. Only recently have educators and parents taken constructive steps to enrich the curriculum so that these gifted boys and girls may receive the stimulation they need by participating in extra classes and following individual interests. One of the areas that has been used most successfully for enrichment is the arts. This is not to imply that *all* children should not have wide and continued exposure to the arts, but because this is an area with endless possibilities, it has been selected often for use with the gifted. Arts programs have been designed both as after-school activities and as additional classes during school time. Some programs include field trips to museums, theatres, and concerts, although funds given for this purpose are generally allocated for the use of all children rather than for one specially selected group. Classes in drama, dance, music, and the visual arts offer gifted children a chance to use their abilities in putting on plays—often written by the children themselves—and in designing and making costumes and scenery.

Profiles of gifted children suggest four categories in which such youngsters tend to fall:

The high-achieving studious—Such students work hard in drama as in other subjects, though their work is frequently conventional rather than original. Improvisations are structured and detailed and are likely to be rehearsed and well performed. Their objectives, which they usually succeed in achieving, are a good product, a serious involvement, and better than average performance skills.

The social leaders—They produce superior work in groups. They also work hard but have the additional ability to lead their classmates to desired ends.

The creative intellectuals—These students have originality. They like the freedom to choose situations and they produce work that is original, often humorous.

The rebels—The mavericks in a group who are as likely to be disruptive as to be supportive. With guidance, these students can produce excellent results but they are not always easy for their peers to work with.[1]

Despite these stereotypes, for this is what they are, the gifted student is a challenge, and the results when they are well taught are often brilliant and original. Courses are specifically designed, however, for students of above-average ability; the curriculum of these courses is characterized by intellectual rigor and a challenge to students to make full use of their abilities.

Gifted children have the ability to think of many things at a time; therefore, drama, with its wide range of responsibilities, is an ideal choice. When dealing with gifted children, the leader must always present a challenge. Drama, by its nature, does this.

Programs outside the school day can be somewhat different from those presented during the school day. One particularly interesting program set up specifically for the gifted was described in the *Children's Theatre Review*.[2] In Pennsylvania the Lackawanna County Schools established a program for sixty fifth- and sixth-grade children whose IQs ranged from 130 to 165. A sixteen-week series of Saturday morning classes was held on the Marywood College campus in Scranton, although funds for the program came from the Pennsylvania Department of Public Instruction in Harrisburg. Believing that all children have creative power, the faculty offered a variety of experiences aimed at stimulating this power and giving the participants a chance to express it. Literature was chosen as the focus of the program. During the eight Saturdays of the fall semester, the accent was on the development of the creative process; during the eight weeks of the spring semester, the accent was on the academic, with each child selecting, as an outgrowth of the first semester's activities, work in special areas in which he or she was most interested. The central theme, which coordinated all activities of the second eight-week period, was "What kind of world would I like to live in?"

No homework was required, but the Marywood Children's Library facilities were available, and the children were encouraged to withdraw books each week. A librarian and three teachers, aided by college students, were responsible for the groups of fifteen children each. Films were shown and specialists in the areas of pantomime, creative drama, dance, and puppetry were engaged to come to Scranton to work directly with the children on ideas sparked by the films selected for the day. Specialists came from the Museum of Natural History in New York City, the Woods Hole Oceanographic Research Center, colleges, and art studies centers. Trips to New York City and the Roberson Arts Center in Binghamton, New York, further enriched the program. The Marywood Readers' Theatre interpreted selections from *Alice in Wonderland* and *The Wind in the Willows*,

---

1. Richard Courtney, *Re-Play* (Toronto: The Ontario Institute for Studies in Education, 1982), p. 106.
2. Jeanne R. Spillane, "Stimulating Creativity in the Gifted Child," *Children's Theatre Review* 19, no. 1 (1970): 10–13, 18–19.

Very Special Arts Program, The Kennedy Center, Washington, D.C. (*Photograph by John Whitman.*)

which the children had read and enjoyed. A documentary film showing each of the children's experiences was made during the first year as a record of the project. Plans for the following year included more subject matter in depth, with particular emphasis on creative drama as one of the most successful means of stimulating creativity.

The Lackawanna County project is not unique; it is cited here because it recognized the needs of the gifted child for opportunities beyond the classroom and because it emphasized creative drama in its program.

Another experiment, designed for a doctoral study, was conducted early in the seventies in La Crosse, Wisconsin.[3] Creative drama classes were held for two semesters in three schools for groups of gifted seventh-graders. The results confirmed the hypothesis that creative drama is an effective learning experience in promoting the growth, development, and functioning ability of the imaginative capacities of gifted junior high school pupils. The favorable results of the research indicated that this approach to education is deserving of far more consideration than it has had in the past.

3. Sister Dorothy Prokes, "Exploring the Relationship between Participation in Creative Dramatics and Development of the Imaginative Capacities of Gifted Junior High School Students" (Ph.D. diss., School of Education, New York University, 1971).

A different type of program for gifted youth is located at the Hunter College Center for Lifelong Learning in New York City. There Saturday classes in science, the arts, and social studies are given regularly for young people aged twelve to sixteen who are designated as gifted. Drama workshops are among the offerings, and instruction is by highly qualified and experienced leaders.

A concern for the education of gifted youth in Cleveland, Ohio, led to the formation of a still different type of program designed for both teachers and students. The first such program had been established in the twenties, but it was subsequently dropped for budgetary reasons. In 1979 through special funding Dr. Dorothy Sisk, formerly head of the Office of the Gifted and Talented in Washington, D.C., was secured to help establish a series of workshops and seminars. This is cited as yet another example of the awakened interest in one of our most valuable resources, the gifted child, and the ways in which drama can serve his or her interests and needs. Persons wanting to establish similar programs can get help by writing to this government agency, which has publications and a variety of services to aid educators who are working or preparing to work with gifted and talented youth.

The Mentally Retarded Child

Mental retardation describes a condition rather than a disease. Although it can refer to any degree of retarded mental development, the classifications most commonly used are the following: the educable mentally retarded, the trainable mentally retarded, and the dependent mentally retarded. This discussion of creative drama in the education of the mentally retarded child centers on the first category. It is with this group that play can be most rewarding both as a teaching tool and a pleasure. Inasmuch as play constitutes an important role in the all-around development of the child, it has a special significance for the mentally retarded.

According to a survey taken in the early sixties, the major objectives of teachers using creative drama in the education of the mentally retarded child were to stimulate language and to promote social development.[4] The nature of drama makes it a versatile tool in working with these handicapped youngsters. Rhythms, dramatic play, and pantomime are activities that are widely used by many teachers of the educable and trainable mentally retarded. Adaptations of the techniques used with normal children and developed over a longer period can bring both immediate satisfaction and lasting benefit. According to one teacher who has used creative drama successfully with mentally retarded groups, some of the best material comes from the very social situations that cause the retarded child to be stared at and shunned: entering a restaurant; ordering food

---

4. Geraldine Brain Siks, *Children's Theatre and Creative Dramatics* (Seattle: University of Washington Press, 1961), chap. 17.

and eating it; going on a bus, train, or plane trip; and dressing—simple daily activities that the average child of his age has mastered.

Like all children, the retarded child wants to be a member of a group, to contribute to it, and to have the contribution accepted. Drama offers this opportunity. One characteristic of the retarded child is slowness to use imagination or to deal with abstract ideas. Some teachers believe that retarded children become more imaginative when placed in a class with normal children. Whether they are in a regular classroom or a special class, however, their pace is slow. Recognizing this handicap, the teacher can guide their dramatic play and stimulate their response. Frequently, the leader errs in expecting too much too soon. Retarded children need more help and encouragement than other children; they need to repeat experiences more often; and, finally, they must learn self-confidence and feel the satisfaction of having their contribution, however small, accepted. The game of "pretending" can help them learn to use imagination, to prepare for new experiences, and to lay a firmer foundation for oral communication. Experienced teachers state that dramatic activities help to develop the skills of listening and looking. In this way, attention is engaged.

Rhythms and movement games are excellent beginning exercises. They aid the development of large muscles while they motivate use of imagination. The acting out of simple stories comes much later. At first, retarded children will be more comfortable participating in a group than working individually. They probably have experienced frustration and the sense of being different; their need for praise and encouragement, therefore, will be greater than that of a normal child. When they show interest in moving out of the group to become a specific character—someone other than themselves—they are ready for the next step. Now, instead of general group activities, individual roles may be undertaken. The teacher will need to provide not only stimulation at this stage but must also give clear and simple direction: Who is the character? How does the character walk? What is the character doing? How does he or she do it? What does the character say?

If social ease and a sense of security are our first consideration, oral expression is the second. Guided dramatic play is a way of introducing oral vocabulary and developing concepts that prepare the child for reading. A variety of experiences will help to provide the child with a better understanding of his or her world, and acting out words that describe this world will give them meaning. Action words such as *jump, run, skip, skate, throw a ball*—teach by doing. Nouns such as *farmer, mailman, mother,* or *grocer* can become the basis for dramatic play and pantomime. Mentally retarded children who have been guided carefully and slowly through dramatic play will eventually be ready to dramatize simple stories. By this time they will have achieved some personal freedom and mastered a functional reading vocabulary. The procedure of planning, playing, and evaluating is the same as that followed in the normal classroom, except that with these children, the task and the process must be simpler and will take longer.

One particularly important point to remember is that adjustments in all activities for the retarded child should be made on the basis of the child's interests and needs. Stories selected for dramatization should, in addition to being clear and simple, reflect the interests that give meaning to the child's life. As his or her interests widen, a greater variety of stories may be introduced, with new words to express and describe them.

Not only literature but other subjects as well can be taught through the medium of improvisation. For example, one teacher had the children in her arithmetic class be plus and minus signs and pieces of fruit; through acting out simple problems of subtraction and addition, the children were able to see the correct answers. So-called creative walks, on which children became trees, flowers, stones, birds, and animals, helped them to observe and recall what they had seen after they returned to the classroom. Such use of creative drama is not generally sanctioned; indeed, it was discouraged in an earlier chapter. With these children, however, communication and social development are the primary goals; art is secondary. The potential in drama for motivating and reaching these primary goals validates its use. In time, other objectives can be established, but they are not possible until the child has developed a sense of security, has acquired some freedom of expression, and has mastered a working vocabulary that will enable him or her to take on the role of another.

Participation by the retarded child in the formal play is to be discouraged. A continuing program of creative drama, on the other hand, offers an opportunity for social growth, emotional release, and a way of learning. As one teacher put it after using creative drama techniques successfully for many years: "These children need to be crawled with first—then they can walk." When they have reached the walking stage, they often astonish us with what they have learned.

The Emotionally Disturbed Child

It is in the area of the emotionally disturbed child that the classroom teacher must exercise the greatest caution. We know so little about these children and the causes of their problems that the possibility of doing harm is greater than it is with any other group. Indeed, it is often difficult to distinguish between the emotionally disturbed child and the mentally retarded child because of the frequent similarity of behavior. Frequently, repeated testing must be done to determine the nature of the condition. What might be a rewarding activity for the retarded child might not be good enough for the child who is disturbed. Psychodrama and play therapy are accepted techniques in the treatment of emotionally disturbed children, but they can be damaging in the hands of the lay person, regardless of his or her background and skill as a teacher of creative drama. The seriously disturbed child will probably not be found in the regular classroom but will be enrolled in a special class or special school and provided with special services. These services may or may not include psychiatric help and

A performance of "Sunshine Too" by the National Technical Institute for the Deaf. (*Courtesy of Rochester Institute of Technology; photograph by M. Spencer.*)

play therapy. Often children in special schools are referred to outside clinics or therapists, and drama may be part of the treatment.

Remedial Drama

Remedial drama is an umbrella term used here to cover several specific techniques. As was stated earlier, drama/theatre has historically been an essential part of human development. In preventive and therapeutic work we are primarily concerned with communication and therefore in helping individuals and groups build better relationships. According to Sue Jennings, author of *Remedial Drama:* "[It] does not differ in content or technique from other types of drama, although great care must be taken in selecting and applying drama techniques to remedial work."[5] Her emphasis is on experience, and the goals of drama, used in this way, are *socialization, creativity,* and *insight.*

Eleanor Irwin, well-known drama therapist, drew a distinction between a therapeutic experience and therapy as a treatment. She said that "any experience which helps an individual to feel a greater sense of competence and well-being may be thought of as therapeutic."[6] This is the sense in which the word *therapy* is

---

5. Sue Jennings, *Remedial Drama* (New York: Theatre Arts Books, 1974), p. 4.

6. Eleanor Irwin, "Drama Therapy with the Handicapped," in *Drama/Theatre and the Handicapped,* ed. Ann Shaw and Cj Stevens (Washington, D.C.: American Theatre Association, 1979), p. 23.

used by many persons and the sense in which it would be most accurately applied to the work of most classroom teachers using drama with the children on a regular basis.

Drama therapy, role playing, psychodrama, and *sociodrama* are the terms most frequently heard with reference to remedial drama. They differ both as to technique and thrust. David Johnson of Yale University, a leader in this new field, defined drama therapy as "the intentional use of creative drama toward the psychotherapeutic goals of symptom relief, emotional and physical integration, and personal growth."[7] Drama therapy, like the other arts therapies, applies a creative medium and establishes an understanding or contract between the client and the therapist. Thus it is differentiated from creative drama in an educational setting.

Psychodrama

"Psychodrama is a professional practice based on the philosophy and methodology developed by Jacob L. Moreno, M.D. (1889–1974), which uses action methods of enactment, sociometry, group dynamics, role theory, and social systems analysis to facilitate constructive change in individuals and groups through the development of new perceptions or reorganization of old cognitive patterns and concomitant changes in behavior."[8]

Adam Blatner, M.D., of the School of Medicine at the University of Louisville, stated that he has found that many psychodramatic techniques and ideas can deepen and extend the power of creative drama and vice versa. "Since Moreno's death in 1974, psychodrama has developed in a variety of directions, such as Jonathon Fox's Playback Theatre in Poughkeepsie, New York." He said that some of the frontiers of drama therapy are also sharing in this interdisciplinary process of cross-fertilization and convergence.[9]

Sociodrama

Sociodrama, as the name implies, deals with the group and with group problems or conflicts. A class in creative drama may become a sociodramatic experience when a real life situation is employed, leading to discussion with benefits to all participants. Classroom teachers and recreation leaders sometimes use sociodrama in a limited way to help solve problems that arise and persist in having a damaging effect on the group. Although individuals are involved, it is the group and the group relationships that are the primary concerns.

7. David Johnson, unpublished duplicated material, 1978.

8. D. R. Buchanan, "Psychodrama," in *The Psychosocial Therapies,* Part II of the Psychiatric Therapies, ed. T. B. Karasu (Washington, D.C.: The American Psychiatric Association, 1984)

9. Correspondence with Adam Blatner, M.D. (May 11, 1985). See also J. Fox, "Playback Theater: The Community Sees Itself," in *Drama in Therapy,* vol. 2, ed. Gertrude Schattner and Richard Courtney (New York: Drama Book Specialists, 1981), pp. 295–308.

Another use of sociodrama is described in an article by Robert J. Landy and Deborah Borisoff in the *English Journal,* "Reach for Speech: Communication Skills through Sociodrama."[10]

"Reach for Speech" is a program to help young people in New York City develop speech skills. Departing from conventional methods of skills teaching and debates, it focuses upon sociodrama. It centers on an examination of significant social problems within New York City communities and empowers secondary school students to address these problems in the roles of a wide variety of characters.

The method developed for "Reach for Speech" proceeds in several discrete steps:

1. Students and teacher choose a relevant social issue.
2. The group identifies appropriate roles that relate to the issue.
3. Group members select roles.
4. Research through readings and interviews of role models in the community for roles.
5. Students enact roles in class; they act "as if" they were particular characters, presenting their character's point of view through speech and movement. The role-playing is deepened through a process that includes role-reversal and a critique of the role-playing.
6. Students shape their role-playing, preparing for a final presentation.
7. In a final presentation the students, in role, present the dimensions of the social issue to a particular audience.

There is a difference of opinion as to the desirability of drama of any kind, however, for the seriously disturbed child. Some teachers believe that role playing is beneficial; others, that the child's problems present difficulties that may make this form of expression less desirable than participation in the other arts. Seriously disturbed children need to make sense out of their own environment before they can enter another; moreover, until they know whom *they* are, they will have difficulty being someone else. Their greatest needs frequently include the ability to interact and to develop language. Until they can express themselves, they will find it difficult, if not impossible, to enter into the simplest form of dramatic play, according to Dr. Haim Ginott: "The playroom behavior of immature and neurotic children is characterized by an excess of inhibition or aggression."[11] Inasmuch as play therapy requires special training techniques, we shall confine ourselves to the consideration of appropriate activities for the child with emotional problems who is to be found in the regular classroom.

10. Reprinted from *English Journal* 76, no. 5 (September 1987): pp. 68–71. Copyright © 1987 by the National Council of Teachers of English.
11. Haim G. Ginott, *Group Psychotherapy with Children* (New York: McGraw-Hill, 1961), p. 40.

The child who functions well enough to be in a class with normal children may derive great benefit from dramatic play and dramatization. Under these circumstances, engaging in creative drama may be both an emotional release and a socializing experience. Bear in mind, however, that because the child's language and speech are frequently poor, he or she is likely to meet with frustration and difficulty in the oral expression of ideas and the improvisation of dialogue. An inhibited child cannot be expected to function at as high a level as the child's classmates and needs much more support and encouragement. The aggressive child, on the other hand, needs to be restrained in his or her tendency to take over or to distract others. The attention span of children with emotional problems is apt to be shorter than that of other children who have demonstrated poor attention in other classes.

According to some experienced teachers, dramatic play, when first introduced to the child with emotional problems, should include reality-based situations rather than fantasy. Highly imaginative situations may cause young children who are not in touch with reality to meld with the idea or to identify too closely with the characters played. All children tend to become deeply involved in the dramatic play. The normal child can suspend disbelief for the duration of the period and then return to reality. The disturbed child may not be able to shake off the role so easily, however, and may continue to be the character long after the play period has ended. As said earlier, however, we are dealing here with the child who is able to be in a normal group and therefore may be helped by more reality-oriented peers.

There is a general agreement that dance, rhythms, and ritual movement are excellent for disturbed children. Physical activity gives them a sense of the body; the large movements, such as skipping, galloping, stretching, and moving the arms, are wonderful exercises for those who are poorly coordinated. "Reaching for the sky or pushing away the clouds," "feeling big," "growing tall"—all are movements that contain an element of drama. The Dance Therapy Center in New York City works for release through the improvisational method, whereby the student is made conscious of new insights through bodily action. The philosophy of this unusual center is based on the "restoration of spontaneous movement to break the tenacity of the neurotic hold of body memory and on the experience of new psychophysical action as health is regained."[12] This is a relatively new field, and it is interesting that it recognizes movement as a specific therapeutic technique in dealing with emotional problems.

Many teachers have reported that the nonverbal child can develop the ability to express feelings and knowledge through the use of movement and pantomime. In this the child finds a means of communication and from it may find motivation for speech. The teacher may also discover capabilities and awareness that remain hidden in the usual classroom situation.

12. Dance Therapy Center brochure, New York, 1972–73.

A good exercise for any group of children but particularly good for the disturbed is the following:

1. One child begins a pantomime. This might be a man shoveling snow. Another child, who knows what the first child is doing, steps up and joins in. The second child may also shovel snow or do something that relates to it. The pantomime is kept up until the whole group has entered into the activity, one at a time. This is an excellent means of focusing attention and assisting each to "join" the group in a natural and logical way. If the class is large, two smaller groups can be formed, each taking a turn at the same exercise.

2. Another suggestion is a variation on the old game of "statues." One person comes into the center of the room and strikes a pose. The child freezes as another person joins in. Each one stays in a pose until the entire group has come together, forming a large sculpture. This exercise is not drama therapy but is pantomime with possible therapeutic benefits, inasmuch as it encourages both observation of others and movement that relates to them.

3. The mirror game is often suggested for children with problems. It focuses the attention and encourages concentration. Although it is only an exercise, repeating it from time to time makes for greater precision, and most people of all ages enjoy it.

4. Role playing and role reversal are particularly helpful and appropriate for children and teenagers with emotional problems.

5. Storytelling, followed by story acting, offers work on speech, language, concentration, and a sense of sharing. Stories should be short and, if acted, good for dramatization. For a group of immigrant children, stories with ethnic backgrounds are particularly appropriate. Children benefit from sharing their backgrounds with one another and enjoy learning stories, dances, and music of other lands. Sue Jennings in her book *Remedial Drama* suggested improvising "shopping" in ethnic neighborhoods.[13] Players lead others into stores and describe what they see and what they are used for. For some groups, if the interest is keen, cross-cultural celebrations or folk festivals might be a culmination of the study. She made a point of stories being short, clear, and clearly told, with satisfying endings. For disturbed children "calming down" endings are important.

6. Choral speaking is an activity that can be carried far beyond the activity stage. A value here is that the group works together rather than singling out individuals for reading or performance.

13. Sue Jennings, *Remedial Drama* (New York: Theatre Arts Books, 1974).

Large spaces like gymnasiums should be avoided. Smaller rooms have boundaries, important for children with problems. The exception to this is the player in the wheelchair, who needs more space.

Although it is suggested that all groups benefit from starting a session with movement, it is essential for children with problems. Through ritual, they find security; through warm-ups, use of the body; through moving as a group, a lessening of self-consciousness. It is further suggested that dance involving physical touch is often helpful, and patterned dance with its structure is a better starting place for some children than freer dance forms. Under any circumstances, rhythms that involve the whole body, clapping the hands, and making sounds to a beat are all good ways of getting and holding attention. Sue Jennings warned against imposing "end of session" discussions on children with problems. "Let them happen," she advised. The first job is to establish trust and security. Verbalization may be slow, and any analytical discussion should be a future goal.

Both finger puppets and hand puppets have been found to work successfully with children too inhibited to assume roles themselves. Such children usually have a poor self-image; thus it takes longer to build interest and ego strength to the point where they are able to move out of the group to assume roles and sustain them through improvised situations. Again, we are speaking of children with knowledge of themselves and their reality. When they can enter into dramatic situations with relative ease, these emotionally disturbed children will begin to derive some of the same benefits found by other children. In terms of objectives, interaction with the group, ability to concentrate, ability to express themselves orally, and ability to take the part of another come first on the list. After these objectives have been met, the children should be able to work with joy, accomplishing as much and sometimes more than the others in the group. Their sensitivity, if properly guided, can be an asset to their understanding of a character and creation of a characterization. Drama, because of its total involvement—physical, mental, emotional, and social—offers a wealth of activities, all of which have therapeutic value, if properly handled.

A professional organization, The National Association for Drama Therapy, was formed in 1978 to set standards and goals. Both specialist and generalist should benefit from this formalization of principals and practices. Annual conventions and regional conferences offer programs featuring speakers, demonstrations, and discussion groups, as well as an opportunity to view new films and publications. Like all national organizations, meetings rotate, taking place in different parts of the country every year so as to enable members to attend as frequently as possible.

The Physically Handicapped Child

In many ways the physically handicapped children present fewer difficulties to the classroom teacher than the emotionally disturbed or the mentally retarded children. Their handicaps are visible and their limitations obvious. Their problems are easier to identify, and depending upon the seriousness of the disability, decisions have already been made as to whether or not they can function in a regular classroom. As with all exceptional children, the physically handicapped children are thought to be better off in a normal situation rather than segregated; if their disability is so severe that they require special services, however, they may have to be enrolled, at least for a time, in a special school or in a hospital.

For our purposes we shall consider the physically handicapped to include the deaf, the partially sighted or blind child, as well as the child unable to function normally because of some other physical disability. Frequently, children with physical problems have emotional problems as well; for both of these reasons they will need all the support and encouragement that the teacher can give as the children struggle to reach their goals. Because of the conspicuousness of their handicap, however, they are generally treated with more compassion and understanding than a classmate with emotional problems whose behavior is inappropriate or immature. People whose psychological problems cause them to behave in a socially unacceptable manner are often criticized or ridiculed, prompting the comment, "Why must they act that way?" The person on crutches, on the other hand, never prompts this response, for we know that person is walking as well as possible. In spite of, or perhaps because of, physical limitations, the child who cannot hear, see, or speak clearly or who lacks physical coordination or cannot walk needs an opportunity to escape the walls of this prison on the wings of his or her imagination. Creative drama offers this opportunity, though admittedly the goals must be modified for physically handicapped children.

The Little Theatre of the Deaf, which achieved national prominence at the end of the sixties, is a shining example of what can be done by actors for children who cannot hear. Because oral communication is emphasized in early education, the deaf child is at a disadvantage when attending theatrical performances, just as he or she is in ordinary classroom situations. Pantomime is the obvious means of reaching the hard-of-hearing, and it is in this form that The Little Theatre of the Deaf has succeeded so brilliantly. A cue can be taken from this experiment: Pantomime is an area of drama in which the child with hearing loss can participate as well as enjoy as a spectator. Incidentally, we have recently become accustomed to seeing interpreters using sign language on television to bring important programs to nonhearing viewers.

Again, movement is an ideal way to begin activities. Large physical movements come first and then rhythms and dance. Small muscle movements follow. Sensitive to the deaf child's keen visual perception, the leader can move from dance to pantomime. There will be motivation for speech in drama, but the easiest communication will be through pantomime, in which the deaf child can achieve success. Stories may be told in this medium, giving pleasure both to player and observer. My observation of creative drama classes in a school for the deaf revealed remarkable possibilities for learning and emotional release.

Graduate students from the New York University Deafness Center frequently share some of their techniques and experiences with my classes. On a recent occasion, a cast of hearing and nonhearing students, using mime, sign language, and a speech choir, presented a program of unusual artistry. One of the greatest values of the production was the opportunity it offered the actors and the audience to share ideas and insights.

Blind or partially sighted children face different problems. They are at home with speech, so storytelling is an excellent beginning activity. Choral speaking, like music, is also an art in which they can excel and at the same time find pleasure. Original poetry composed by the group offers them a chance to express feelings and personal responses. Free movement is more difficult for them than for the sighted children, but it is not impossible. Carefully guided improvisation may be attempted, although the formal play, where movement is predetermined and not changed in rehearsal, is by its nature easier. One director who has had great success with a blind drama group stressed the fact that she never moves scenery or props once the placement has been established. A knowledge of where things are enables the players to move freely and easily about the stage. For the blind or partially sighted player, formal drama offers greater security than improvisation.

Children with physical problems that prevent them from running, walking, or even using their arms or legs easily have also found drama to be within the range of their capabilities. Group participation while the children are seated is an excellent way of involving everyone in pantomime, choral speech, and puppetry. In preparing a dramatization, the roles of narrator and storyteller are highly regarded and can be handled by a child who may not be able to engage in more active participation. The imaginative teacher can find a place for the handicapped children, where they are able to add their bit to the group endeavor, thus enhancing their self-image and giving them a sense of achievement. The philosophy of all therapeutic recreation includes this sense of pride in a job well done and the joy of creative accomplishment.

Physically handicapped persons are able to do and enjoy a much wider range of dramatic activities than was formerly thought possible. Most obvious but little used in the past is puppetry. The puppeteer in a wheelchair is able to run, jump, dance, fly—in short, to perform every physical activity through the puppet. In most cases, the child is at no disadvantage. There are now a number of theatre groups for the handicapped across the nation. Robert Landy's *Handbook of Educational Drama and Theatre* lists Theatre Unlimited in San Francisco; Process Theatre with the Handicapped of the Alan Short Center in Stockton, California; The San Diego Theatre for the Disabled; and The National Theatre Workshop of the Handicapped in New York.[14] One group that must be given special mention is The Rainbow Company in Las Vegas. There classes in creative

14. Robert J. Landy, *Handbook of Educational Drama and Theatre* (Westport, Conn.: Greenwood Press, 1982).

drama, mime, technical theatre, makeup, costuming, and playwriting are held for children from preschool age through high school. The Rainbow Company has received national acclaim for the quality of its work with handicapped performers; in 1982 it was selected as a model site for the fourth consecutive year by the National Committee: Arts for the Handicapped.[15]

The National Theatre Workshop of the Handicapped in New York is an integrated group of physically disabled and ablebodied persons founded by Rick Curry in 1977. Its stated objectives are the same as those of any other drama school. Through training in mime, improvisation, and acting, students develop an appreciation of the theatre arts, learn theatre techniques, and improve their own performance skills. Most important, they gain confidence and a better understanding of themselves. Curry believes that the time has come for physically disabled actors to find employment in the theatre; meanwhile, the theatre is becoming more accessible to them as spectators.

Two other companies, which do not fall precisely in the above categories, merit mention because of the extensive work they are doing for persons with handicapping conditions. They are Facets Performance Ensemble and Imagination Theatre, Inc., both Chicago based. Neither company was originally founded for the purpose of performing for the handicapped, but they have recognized a need and are presently directing a major effort toward these audiences. Facets' statement of purpose differs from the objectives of most T.I.E. companies in its "attempt to increase the ability of elementary school children to learn by confronting the problems of concentration, discipline, and an understanding of communication, through the ability to express thoughts and feelings." Another description states that Facets' "Handicapped Children's Workshop Program gives children a reason to concentrate. . . . children learn to hear, see, and act in a unified activity which is simply otherwise unavailable to them."[16] Imagination Theatre, Inc., in adding Specialized Playmaker Programs to its programming, expanded its offerings to include two new types of audiences: physically and mentally handicapped children and young people, and senior adults. Audiences participate, and although the Playmaker Programs are presented as entertainment, they incorporate creative drama techniques that can be used later in follow-up activities. Unlike the other companies described, Imagination Theatre is completely participant centered; however, participants do not give public performances. They are involved in process and what process can do for them. In 1982 Imagination Theatre received the Governor's Award for the Arts in Illinois for its work in providing programs and/or workshops for schoolchildren; the mentally, physically, and emotionally handicapped; senior citizens; therapists; teachers; and parents.

15. A brochure of The Rainbow Company, 1982, reported that "this designation has been made to only ten sites in the country and indicates 'exemplary programming in the arts by, with, and for the handicapped.' "

16. Facets Performance Ensemble brochure.

The Kids' Project, a puppet troupe created in 1977 in response to the problems of mainstreaming, has become an effective and growing medium for reaching handicapped schoolchildren.[17] The puppets represent a variety of disabling conditions: blindness, deafness, cerebral palsy, mental retardation, and learning disabilities. Two nondisabled puppets are also included in the skits, in which they learn to accept the others. One segment of the performance is devoted to each of the handicapped puppets, followed by a question and answer period. The originator of The Kids' Project, Barbara Aiello, was a special education teacher in Washington, who realized that putting handicapped children into regular classrooms in compliance with The Education for All Handicapped Children Act of 1975 demanded attitudinal changes, if true integration were to take place. After years of separation, both handicapped and nonhandicapped needed to understand each other.

Aiello used the puppets in her own program, "Kids on the Block," but she also made it possible for others to purchase them. Buyers pay a one-time fee, which includes puppets, props, and scripts, but they are restricted to nonprofit use. By 1983 five hundred groups, including fifty in foreign countries, were reported using the puppets. New York State alone had sixteen troupes funded at both state and local levels. Although the New York troupes use the same curriculum, they vary their styles to fit the area in which they are performing. For example, urban children experience problems on the street that are unknown among rural children.

Extensions of the project may be found in some high schools and at the time of this writing are being planned for adults in the workplace. The values of puppets are described in an earlier chapter, but the impact of this program demonstrates their effectiveness in reaching youngsters who have trouble relating to others and to nondisabled persons who have trouble establishing a rapport with the handicapped. One of the most remarkable aspects that I have discovered about the years 1968–84 is the ingenuity teachers and children's theatre directors have shown in finding new ways of reaching young people and of including heretofore excluded populations. The Kids' Project is an example.

In all of these companies and groups the main focus is on giving the disabled person the advantage of the drama/theatre experience rather than preparation for the professional stage. Nevertheless, successful plays featuring the disabled like *Children of a Lesser God,* plays presented by the National Theatre of the Deaf, and a few television productions in which a disabled actor is used are proof of the unexplored possibilities for employment. Creative drama, however, is not theatre training, and whatever an interested student may wish to pursue professionally later is not our concern in this text. What is our concern is the added dimension that participation in the performing arts gives the disabled; as educators and community leaders, we have an opportunity through the arts to open doors and expand the horizons of this too-long-neglected population.

17. "Puppets Depict Life of Disabled," *The New York Times,* July 10, 1983.

Very Special Arts Program, The Kennedy Center, Washington, D.C. (*Courtesy of Martha Kaiser.*)

There have been some major developments in this country since the publication of the first edition of this book in 1968. One of them was the founding of the National Committee: Arts for the Handicapped, now called Very Special Arts. In June 1974 the John F. Kennedy Foundation provided funding for a national conference on arts for the mentally retarded. As a result of the interest engendered by the Alliance for Arts Education, the Department of Health, Education, and Welfare, and the Bureau of Education for the Handicapped, a new national committee was formed. The purpose of this committee was to plan and coordinate an arts program for all handicapped children. The committee's belief in the creative arts experience as a powerful means of bringing joy and beauty into the lives of children burdened by physical, emotional, or mental handicaps has resulted in a strong, ongoing program. In 1983 Very Special Arts inaugurated a Young Playwrights Project, to which writers between the ages of twelve and eighteen were invited to submit scripts dealing with some aspect of disability in contemporary society. A selected script would be produced at the John F. Kennedy Center for the Performing Arts in Washington in May. By challenging disabled and nondisabled students to express ideas and feelings in playroom, many areas of the theatre arts might be explored.

The other and much more comprehensive development that is affecting arts programs, as well as others, inasmuch as educational institutions are involved, is the Rehabilitation Act of 1973 regarding Handicapped Persons. Section 504 of this act states: "No otherwise qualified handicapped individual in the United States . . . shall, solely by reason of his handicap, be excluded from the participation in, be denied the benefits of, or be subjected to discrimination under any program or activity receiving Federal financial assistance."

In 1977 a final Section 504 regulation was issued for all recipients of funds from HEW, including elementary and secondary schools, colleges, social service agencies, and hospitals. Already the results of this legislation have been felt in numerous ways, and they are bound to increase in the future. The arts will be affected as part of the educational system; and, as with any changed condition, so will public attitudes. The concept of "mainstreaming," mentioned earlier, will be strengthened and, it is also to be hoped, the quality as well as the quantity of arts experiences for all children and youth. Indirectly, drama/theatre education will be expanded.

Related but not germane to this text is the current interest in and recent legislation regarding the aged. It is mentioned here only because some creative drama teachers and group leaders have successfully applied the same techniques that they have used in the classroom with senior citizens and nursing home patients. This opens up a new area and one in which very little has been done as yet. Funds are becoming available for programs for the senior adult, however, and it would appear that teachers of the arts, particularly those experienced in working with children and the arts therapies, will have much to offer. Texts and articles dealing with the arts and this population are beginning to appear;

Creative drama as a tool for teaching speech. (*Courtesy of Victoria Brown; photograph by Kelly Butterworth.*)

meanwhile, the basic principles and practices of creative drama are finding a new use.

There are a number of special courses and workshops where one can be trained in drama therapy. Robert Landy, in his *Handbook of Educational Drama and Theatre,* published in 1982, listed California State University in Los Angeles, Avila College in Kansas City, Antioch University in San Francisco, and Loyola University in New Orleans. He described New York University as having one of the most comprehensive programs available within its Program in Educational Theatre. In 1988 it had the only program in the United States to offer both the master's degree in drama therapy and a doctorate in educational theatre with a concentration in drama therapy. Students are required to take work in the related fields of drama/theatre and psychology and to do supervised field work in one of New York's hospitals, special schools, or community institutions that serve disabled persons. Certification under the title of Registered Drama Therapist is now offered by the National Association for Drama Therapy.

On the undergraduate level a unique example is the curriculum of Gallaudet College located in Washington, D.C. This is a well-known institution specializing in the education of deaf and hearing-impaired students. The college theatre arts department at this school recently reviewed its goals and objectives, which resulted in a new program designed to prepare students to work with children in educational, recreational, and social settings, where the arts can be integrated to facilitate learning. The Gallaudet major in "developmental drama," as it is called there, represents a collaboration between the theatre arts department and the

Signing a creative drama activity. (Courtesy of Victoria Brown; *photograph by Kelly Butterworth.*)

Reaching for a goal. (*Courtesy of Jody Johnson, The Rainbow Company, Las Vegas.*)

departments of psychology, education, and sociology. Theories of dramatic play, creative drama techniques, the use of a visual/gestural approach to working with hearing-impaired children, classes in the theatre arts, and leadership training comprise the major features of the program.

In addition to taking course work in the Gallaudet program, students present plays with and for deaf children. According to the staff, more than four thousand deaf and hearing children from the District of Columbia and surrounding states attend these productions every year. One faculty member reported: "It's an excellent opportunity for hearing children to learn about deafness and for deaf children to be exposed to theatre, many for the first time."[18]

18. Letter from Vickie Brown, Gallaudet College, March 15, 1983.

Extensive outreach services for teachers of deaf children are offered by the Gallaudet staff. The college also works closely with the Wolf Trap Foundation in training teachers of Head Start children and their families to use a visual/gestural approach as a more effective way of teaching English as a second language. Improvisation, role playing, movement, puppetry, storytelling, and mime are taught through visual/gestural communication.

An outreach program, Sunshine Too, was founded in 1980 at the National Technical Institute for the Deaf at the Rochester Institute of Technology. Deaf and hearing actors comprise a company of six, which tours shows for children and youth. More than six hundred and fifty performances a year are given, as well as appearances on television, residencies in schools and colleges, and participation in national and regional conferences. Sunshine Too stated that it is the only college in the world that offers a full program of theatre, dance, and music for deaf students.

Mention must also be made of Sesame in England, a school founded by Marion Lindkvist. Graduates of Sesame are prepared through training in movement and drama to work with mentally, emotionally, and physically disabled persons. Many Americans have visited this well-known institution. The growing interest in this new field is creating a need for special preparation, which will be met as more colleges and universities establish training programs.

The Culturally and Economically Disadvantaged Child

Since the advent of the Head Start program, we have been hearing much about the culturally disadvantaged child, or the child in the disadvantaged urban area. This is not a new problem in our society but one that, for a variety of reasons, is now attracting wide attention, with government and private foundation funds having been allocated for the establishment of educational and recreational programs. The arts, including dramatic play and creative drama, are emphasized in many of these programs. The values cited in chapter 1 have tremendous implications for these children, who have been born into an environment lacking books, playing space, supervision, the arts—and, in many cases, language itself. According to one group of leaders at a conference on the subject of Creative Drama in Special Education, the problems of these children are manifold. For example, poverty may preclude treatment of a physical handicap; the handicap causes feelings of inadequacy; and this results in emotional disturbance. Hence we have a combination of problems requiring understanding and skill beyond the qualifications of the average well-prepared teacher.

The need for special training is recognized, and many universities and organizations are offering courses in this area. Because this is a subject of specialized interest and content, it is beyond the scope of this book. But for those teachers and recreation leaders who are interested in working in disadvantaged areas, let it be said that creative drama and theatre are approved and exciting techniques.

Nevertheless, the classroom teacher can do much for ghetto children. Actually, the first work in children's drama in this country was initiated in the settlement houses of our large cities at the turn of the century. It is significant that the first children's theatre in America was established at the Educational Alliance in New York City in 1903 for the children of immigrant families of the lower East Side. This enterprise attracted wide attention, and in the following twenty-five years many settlement houses and playgrounds introduced storytelling and drama to the children of the poor. Most of the classes were conducted by social workers and Junior League members, some of whom had had theatre training but all of whom realized the potential of drama in teaching the language, brightening the lives of the boys and girls, and bringing strangers together socially in a new land.

Since that time the schools have taken up the challenge, although the social settlements have by no means abdicated their responsibilities. During the sixties and seventies the phenomenon of street theatre began to appear in our cities: free performances of drama, music, and dance in ghetto neighborhoods, where strength is drawn even as it is given. Some of these productions have been subsidized by state arts councils, some by municipalities, others by churches and universities. Some have been part of a two-pronged program, involving both participation and spectator enjoyment. Many school districts have reported pilot projects in the arts for culturally disadvantaged youngsters, and drama is a frequent inclusion.

The schools have been concerned in recent years with bilingual education and the teaching of English as a second language. Particularly in large urban areas has the need been felt for teachers with a knowledge of Spanish and the ability to teach English in the early grades to children who enter school speaking a foreign language. One technique used and discussed today involves movement and pantomime.

For over a century, body movement has been recognized as bearing a relationship to the acquisition of a second language. Indeed, several methods making use of mime, rhythm, and sign language have been devised for teaching foreign languages. Movement is, therefore, not a new technique; rather, it is now recognized as an integral part of the learning process. Movement plus oral activities offer a great variety of opportunities for learning on any level.

The child who is learning a second language is faced with a problem not unlike the others we have discussed. It is therefore suggested that the procedures be much the same. Dance is recommended as a beginning because it forces more concentration than does pure verbal exercise. Folk dances involve a physical response to oral commands. Pantomime makes the spectator guess what the performer is doing and thereby ties the word to the act. Choral speech, on the other hand, has great value because it offers practice in talking, pronunciation, and interpretation. It is, in addition, an enjoyable exercise that does not single out the less able speaker.

A number of experiments have been conducted to determine the value of movement in the learning of language and to create new teaching procedures. One research project conducted at New York University merits special mention, since it revealed that daily participation in oral language activities derived from children's literature expanded skill significantly. The study was conducted with five hundred black children in twenty classrooms—kindergarten through third grade—over a period of one year. Selected books were read aloud; this was followed by sessions in creative drama, puppetry, role playing, and storytelling. The objective was to teach standard English without negating the dialect spoken by the children. One important finding was that the earlier the program was begun, the more susceptible children were to language expansion. The research team recognized the importance of self-image to the nonstandard speaker, a point of view that differs from that commonly held a generation ago. The acquisition of language is not an isolated aspect of intellectual development but rather is a part of the process of socialization.

Creative drama with bilingual children does not differ from creative drama with other groups except in the matter of vocabulary. The most common error in dealing with these children is underestimating their ability and overestimating their verbal skill. By giving them very short but interesting activities they can be successful and thus at the same time improve their self-image.

One gifted young drama teacher, whose work with a bilingual sixth grade I observed recently, used television commercials as assignments. Each child wrote and performed a commercial for a well-known product. They were clear, brief, and, in some cases, humorous; in every instance they were within the capabilities of the youngsters, who enjoyed creating and improvising them. An activity of this kind could be done on almost any level and can be assured of being understood. Incidentally, a few bilingual plays have been written and published. The play *¡Zas!* by Virginia Boyle incorporates English and Spanish in the dialogue. This is an example of one approach to language learning through theatre.[19]

A particularly interesting experiment was originated by Jearnine Wagner of Trinity University for nonachieving children in San Antonio. Called Learning about Learning, it is based on a philosophy of the consideration of the whole child—at school, at home, at church, in the neighborhood: his or her world. Federally funded, a staff of twenty-five worked for two and a half years on a special curriculum directed primarily at the fourth, fifth, and sixth grades. Special books relating to the child's world were written and used to stimulate children's interest in themselves, their problems, and the people around them. The first objective was to develop a more positive attitude in the children toward themselves. This accomplished, they were free to learn, and an exciting program of community-oriented activities was set up. Creative activities, including drama, formed an important part of this curriculum, which was aimed at helping children discover who they were and to value this discovery.

19. Virginia A. Boyle, *¡Zas!* (Chicago: Coach House Press, 1980).

The need for special training in working with the disadvantaged is widely recognized, and many universities and organizations are offering programs toward this end. Because of the emphasis on the urban child, there has been less recognition of the disadvantaged rural child. In both instances, experienced teachers urge beginning with children's own experiences and interests rather than forcing preconceived ideas on them. Encouragement of their efforts helps build confidence and motivate interest in exploring new ideas and new interests.

Funding programs giving support to professional and community theatre groups benefit the economically deprived by making performances and workshops available. Drama experiences that would otherwise not be available to the inner-city child are now possible, if school administrators take advantage of Artists-in-the-Schools programs, Theatre-in-Education teams, and professional and highly competent nonprofessional performers in the community. Free and half-price tickets to plays in cities where live theatre exists provide enrichment for older students.

It is to be hoped that all agencies and organizations that have taken such positive action in establishing programs will be able to continue and to expand. Only through ample subsidy can all children be provided with regular arts experiences of quality. *Perspectives: A Handbook in Drama and Theatre,* edited by Ann M. Shaw, Wendy Perks, and Cj Stevens, includes a most useful chapter on

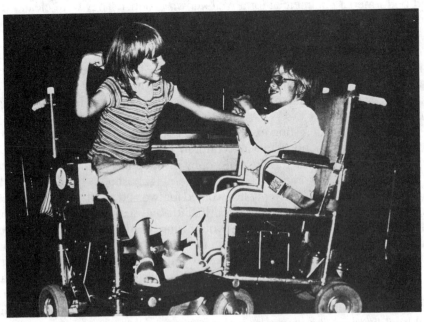

*M*embers of the Rainbow Company enjoy creative drama class. (*Courtesy of Jody Johnston.*)

grants and proposal writing.[20] Inasmuch as programs for the handicapped generally fall outside established budgets, this information is of special value. The book also carries a section listing resources, a little known but nationwide network among those working to expand opportunities for persons with disabilities. Handicapped children should be enabled to enjoy participation in the daily activities of life so that they may share the opportunities for self-realization that other persons experience. A later chapter on circus arts describes new and innovative methods of reaching academically disadvantaged children in this country.

Summary

This chapter has dealt with the subject of the special, or exceptional, child in the most cursory way, and it is hoped that leaders of any handicapped group or class in which there is a child with a handicapping condition will avail themselves of the growing literature in the field. Each condition cited merits a book in itself. The purpose of discussing them here is to:

1. Raise the consciousness of the leader to make him or her become more aware of the needs of the disabled or special person in the group
2. Offer encouragement to try creative drama and puppetry with disabled persons
3. Give an introduction to some of the materials in the field

A practical starting place for the beginner is with assessment—of oneself, of existing programs, and of the facilities that are available.

The exceptional child, regardless of the condition that sets him or her apart, suffers isolation and unhappiness. Life is said to be dependent on one's social network, which in the case of the exceptional child is all too often lacking.[21] *Social isolation* is defined as nonparticipation in activities that require interpersonal contact. Drama is an ideal way of meeting and working with others and of establishing interpersonal relationships through a shared interest.

The exceptional child merits individual attention, and each teacher knows the capabilities as well as the disabilities of the various children in the group. We are not discussing here the special services school; we are, rather, concerned with the exceptional child in the regular classroom and the ways in which creative drama techniques can be used to meet that child's needs and potential. Although the child cannot do everything that the normal child does, the

20. Ann M. Shaw, Wendy Perks, and Cj Stevens, *Perspectives* (Washington, D.C.: American Theatre Association, 1981).
21. Joseph Zubin, *Aging, Isolation, and Resocialization* (New York: Van Nostrand Reinhold, 1980), p. viii.

exceptional child can do some things well and, from this experience, can move forward, thus gaining pleasure and a sense of accomplishment. One successful teacher stressed *listening* as the first and most important element of the teaching process. What are the children trying to tell about themselves, their desires, their frustrations? What is unspoken and why? Important cues are there to be picked up by a sensitive ear.

Every teacher recalls with clarity those handicapped children and college students who have been able to meet the challenge of learning and succeed beyond all expectation. The child with muscular dystrophy who participated in the enactment of an Indian legend by sitting around an improvised campfire with the rest of the braves. The boy with the broken leg who beat a drum because he could not walk, yet was able to lead the group. The child labeled "slow," who memorized a lengthy part in a play although she was failing in her academic work; after that, she improved in all areas—was it, perhaps, because of increased self-confidence? The high school stutterer who was able to perform without hesitation in her class play. The college student with an arm partially paralyzed by polio, who not only participated actively in workshop drama but who later went on the professional stage as a singer. Not all will attain this degree of success, but all can achieve in some measure if we hold the belief articulated by the late Emily Gillies in an article describing the Institute of Physical Medicine and Rehabilitation in New York: "Here is a child's world where we can concentrate on the abilities, not the disabilities, which brought him here. Hopefully, if given enough sense of accomplishment, he can come through to a discovery and recognition of himself as a person."[22]

The classroom teacher does not presume to be a therapist, but by knowing the exceptional child in the class—his or her problems and needs—the teacher may apply the techniques of drama to effect growth, strengthen abilities, and build a more positive self-concept. Moreover, the teacher can work with the therapists to their mutual benefit. These are our goals.

22. Emily Pribble Gillies, "The Katherine Lilly Nursery School," *IMPR* 2, no. 3 (1962): 11.

16

Playgoing
for Appreciation
and Learning

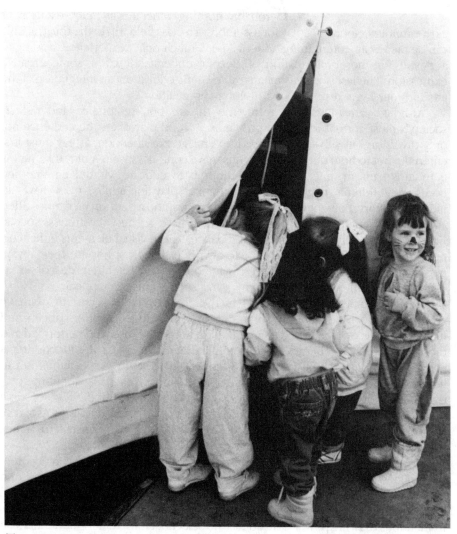

Taking a peek backstage. *(Vancouver Children's Festival, courtesy of Valerie Hennell; photograph by May Henderson.)*

*P*robably nothing generates as much excitement as the announcement of a play for assembly or a class field trip to the theatre. This can be merely an entertaining hour or so or a much richer experience, leading to a desire for more information, a deeper understanding, or some creative expression. The last is what is meant by aesthetic education: an integration of the arts into our lives, resulting in a lifelong appreciation.

Although an ancient art form, the theatre both entertains and reflects society's most current ideas and problems. A good play offers the audience not only diversion but substance; indeed, to engage our attention, a play must first entertain, but to hold our interest, it must have content as well. A play that merely entertains palls in time; a play that attempts to educate without entertaining bores. A children's play, even more than a play for adults, must have an interesting story, content worth spending time on, and a performance by a skilled and talented company. Beyond that, it may have scenery, costumes, special lighting effects, and perhaps music and dance. These visual elements enhance a performance, but they are not found in every production, nor are they always necessary. They explain, however, why the theatre is often described as encompassing all of the arts and why it has such a universal appeal.

In early societies, all members of the community took part in dramatic celebrations. As time went on, some persons emerged as superior dancers and musicians. This eventually led to a separation between those who performed and those who watched—between actors and audience. Today, except for children's participatory plays, when we attend a performance, we go as spectators. But to get the most out of the experience, we need to know something about the play that we are going to see—not every detail or the outcome but the theme, some idea of the plot, and the style and quality of the production. As adult theatregoers, we read what the critics have to say in advance, or we talk to friends who have already seen a performance.

Children's plays are not, as a rule, professionally reviewed. This may account, in part, for the popularity of the traditional folk and fairy tales with both children and adults who select their entertainment. The appeal of the familiar is strong, and the announcement of a well-loved story brought to life on the stage has tremendous drawing power. The adult who selects a child's entertainment is also inclined to respond to the known over the unknown title. A growing number of playwrights are bringing new stories and modern themes to the theatre, however, including some of the troubling problems that young people face today. To help children better understand and enjoy these plays, it is more important than it has been in the past for the teacher to take on the role of reviewer. The orientation that he or she can provide will stimulate interest and prepare a class for a valuable and exciting experience.

There are a number of criteria for evaluating plays for the child audience, and adults responsible for sponsoring them should be aware of them.

1. Is the story suitable for the children who are going to see it?
2. Is the story worth telling? Does it have content and meaning?
3. Is it entertaining?
4. Does the play develop along clear, dramatic lines—that is, does it have a beginning, a properly built climax, and a satisfying conclusion?
5. Is the story told without interruption or without the introduction of extraneous action or characters?
6. Is it clearly established to which character the story belongs?
7. Is there an opportunity for identification? Usually, a play is stronger if the audience can identify with the character to whom the story belongs.
8. Do characters react to one another naturally?
9. Are character and story developed through interaction?
10. If it is an adaptation, are the essential elements of the source material retained so that the audience will not be offended by the change?[1]

Values of Attending the Theatre

Much has been said about the values of theatre for children, and basic to this subject is the script. The children's playwright has a special and difficult task, since he or she cannot anticipate the age level of the audience. The chances are that those who will be attending the play will range in age from five to twelve, perhaps a span even greater. Efforts have been made in some communities to try to control the age of the audience, either by a statement in the publicity or by two series of plays. Age-level programming is controversial and exists as a problem with which the playwright is faced.

Children's interests change. Although fairy and animal tales are popular with younger children, the eleven- or twelve-year-old prefers adventure, history, biography, and stories of real life. The attention span of the older child is longer; hence the older child can be absorbed for as long as two hours, in contrast to the younger child, who probably cannot give full attention for more than an hour.

To younger children, a character is all good or all bad. As they grow older, children begin to comprehend motives and can see a combination of faults and

---

1. Adapted from "CTAA Guidelines for Writing Children's Plays." By permission of the Children's Theatre Association of America.

The Potato People in "Double Play." *(Courtesy of Theatre Beyond Words, Niagara-on-the-Lake, Ontario.)*

virtues, or weakness and strength, in a single person. Children identify with characters of high motives and brave deeds. Through this experience they grow, gaining appreciation for the ideals and standards by which people live. Values, therefore, are important to both young and old. Material that confirms values such as honesty, integrity, and social concern holds the interest of all and may be presented without condescension.

In our preoccupation with ideals and values, we sometimes forget the appeal that comedy holds. Children of all ages love humor, though what is funny to the younger child—riddles, jokes, repetition, slapstick, the chase—does not appeal to an older brother or sister. Comical characters, ridiculous situations, and amusing lines are the materials of comedy and may even teach more effectively than the serious play. Some of our social critics have used comedy to point up the defects and flaws of society.

Some criticism has been directed at those playwrights and producers who give children only the musical play. This seems to be a trend of the times, with the adult theatre having an equally large portion. However, whatever the medium, if the ingredients of taste and credibility are combined with a worthwhile idea, a hero with whom the audience can identify, action, poetic justice, substance, and literary quality, the playwright will have accomplished his or her purpose. Children today are exposed to so much television that they come to expect technical expertise and take spectacular effects for granted. In spite of this, however, they can be absorbed in honest work, well done and simply staged.

In children's theatre the values may be categorized simply as *aesthetic, educational,* and *social,* to which the following elements contribute:

1. *A good story.* A good story holds the interest of the audience from beginning to end. Something happens as the result of a conflict or problem that must be solved. Beyond that, a good story has literary value, vocabulary that enriches, ideas that challenge, and dialogue that strikes our ears as true.

2. *Credible characters.* Credible characters are those in whom the audience can believe, whether or not they are real. In other words, the characters may be witches, giants, ghosts, or elves, but the audience must accept them as real. Children are quick to detect the false or inconsistent, but they will accept the most fantastic characters when they are well developed and consistently played.

3. *Well-developed performance skills.* Well-developed performance skills include speech that is clear and audible; music, well played or sung; dances, choreographed and performed by disciplined dancers; and other skills such as juggling, fencing, and acrobatics that may be called for. These things must not detract from the story but should be so well integrated that unity, as well as a high standard of performance, is maintained throughout. Sometimes a director will add songs and dances to enliven a show, but unless they are an integral part of it, they will take away from the production, actually weakening it.

4. *Beautiful visual effects.* Although not every play requires elaborate mounting and costumes or special lighting effects, many do, and children respond with delight to them. The word *beautiful* includes color, a sense of proportion, and good composition; therefore, even a slum setting or a simple screen can achieve an aesthetic quality. Likewise, a costumer can use color and design so as to bring beauty to the poorest garments without sacrificing the authenticity of the wardrobe. I shall always remember the inner-city children who attended plays at a college where I once taught. Their response to a beautiful scenic effect was as thrilling to the cast and backstage crew as the set was to the audience. The gasp of appreciation that was heard when the curtains opened was clear proof of the joy that color brought into their lives, contrasting with the drab neighborhoods from which they came.

Many producers today dress their actors in a uniform costume, such as jump suits or leotards. There are reasons for this choice, and in many cases, the

"The Further Adventures of the Potato People." *(Courtesy of Theatre Beyond Words, Niagara-on-the-Lake, Ontario.)*

uniform is appropriate and effective. The Paper Bag Players, cited in Chapter 18, aim to stimulate the imagination of the audience and so are always dressed alike, except for color. With their succession of short skits, the actors simply add bits of clothing to save time and suggest different characters. As a general practice, however, the elimination of costumes deprives the audience of one of the theatre's most colorful components, spectacle, and one of its aesthetic values.

5. *Challenging ideas.* Challenging ideas stimulate thinking about attitudes, solutions to problems posed in the play, or social values. Consciousness often can be raised more effectively through theatre than in any other way. Even the folk and fairy tales that have been handed down to us convey valuable lessons,

which is one of the reasons for their survival, according to Bruno Bettelheim.[2] Modern plays and Theatre-in-Education programs present issues more directly, but unless the plays are too didactic, children are affected by them and are concerned with the message. Children want to see justice done, an almost universal response reflecting their strong sense of fair play.

6. *Experience as a member of an audience.* Going to a play, unlike reading a book or even watching television, is a social experience. It involves being part of a large group, sharing a common experience. It also provides material for discussion later, either at home or at school.

7. *Involvement with the players.* This relates to being part of the audience. The living theatre differs from television and film in that the response of the audience affects the performance. Theatre is communication; hence, the rapport between actor and audience is an essential element. Actors are quick to state that no two performances of the same play are ever alike because of the differences in audience response.

8. *The opportunity to learn about other persons and different cultures.* In the theatre, we are able to view other cultures and learn about persons different from ourselves. Characters living in foreign lands or at different times come alive on the stage, often making an indelible impression. This, incidentally, is another reason for truthful and accurate portrayals. Far too many stereotypes have been imposed on children, both in the theatre and on television, for us to ignore misrepresentations. Aware of this, responsible producers are making a conscious effort to show characters as they really are, by treating them with respect as individuals and as members of a social group. This principle, incidentally, should always hold, even in comedy. To be genuinely funny, characters should not be consistently presented in a derogatory light, for it is the exception that amuses us and the unusual situation that makes us laugh.

A stereotype, in which all members of a particular group are presented as identical, reinforces an impression that not only is untrue but is difficult to erase. The villain should not always be presented as foreign and dark; the hero, as tall, handsome, clever, and strong; the heroine, as blonde and beautiful. On stage, as in life, human beings come in a wide assortment of colors, ages, and backgrounds, each one possessing individual strengths and weaknesses. An honest portrayal helps children to distinguish between them and, in doing so, to develop the values and insights that are believed to be the characteristics of an educated adult.

9. *A strong emotional response.* Aristotle wrote of the catharsis of theatre. Anyone who has ever been in a children's audience can readily understand what he meant, for their emotional responses are strong and spontaneous. Children are caught up in the excitement of the drama. They cheer the hero or heroine and may even "boo" the villain, and they often participate vocally by calling out advice to the actors. Unless it gets out of hand (and an experienced cast will see that it does not), this is a natural outlet for emotion. The children have a vicarious

2. Bruno Bettelheim, *The Uses of Enchantment* (New York: Knopf, 1976).

experience, one that they probably would never have in real life. They participate in a great adventure; they identify with the protagonist; and in the end, they win through just and honorable actions. In some modern plays, the spectator is left with an ethical or a moral question to think about after the final curtain has closed. The emotional response has come first, however, and now comes the time to consider alternative solutions and their consequences.

10. *The foundation for an appreciation of the theatre.* Good theatre experienced when one is young often leads to lifelong pleasure. Few persons pursue the theatre as a profession, but all of us may enjoy it as members of the audience. The opportunity to see even a few fine plays, well produced, under optimum conditions, is the best possible preparation.

The values of theatre can scarcely be overestimated. Granted that not all children's entertainment is of the quality we would like to see offered, but much of it is, and it is improving constantly, thanks to better-educated producers and the numerous funding sources now available. By orienting children to the best at an early age and helping them to extend the experience, we are able to increase these values immeasurably. Let us see how we can best go about it.

Although teachers ordinarily do not have an opportunity to preview productions that children will see in school assemblies, their opinion is often sought afterward. This is particularly true when attention has been poor or the audience has appeared to lack interest. The following Evaluation Form was prepared by a committee of the Children's Theatre Association of America as an instrument to use in selecting plays for a showcase of children's entertainment.

Adapted From

EVALUATION FORM FOR CHILDREN'S THEATRE PREVIEWERS

Production Title _____
Date Previewed _____ Estimated Number in Audience _____
Name of Auditorium _____ Seating Capacity _____
Producer _____
       (Name)   (Address)   (Tel. No.)

Note to Previewers: The prime criteria we use in children's theatre is a respect of the production for the audience—of the audience for the production. Does the production present an idea worthy of a child's consideration? Does it do so in a manner which honors his intelligence and integrity? Does it evoke his honest responses to quality in the theatre?

Report on this form by applying this rating code:

Excellent	Good	Adequate	Fair	Poor	TOTAL:	
5	4	3	2	1		

Using the question as a guide, rate each category by the NUMBERS SHOWN ABOVE. Feel free to comment in answer to any specific question and enlarge on it.

1. DOES THE PRESENTATION RESPECT THE AUDIENCE IN THE PLAYSCRIPT?
   - ☐ *Content:*
     Is it worth doing?
     Did you feel the children were involved enough to care about the people in the story and what happened to them?
   - ☐ *Dramatic Development:*
     Is the story line clear and forward moving?
     Is the piece well paced, or does it drag? (Or, is it too hectic?)
   - ☐ *Dialogue:*
     Does the vocabulary, which is essential to the comprehension of the plot, come within the range of the audience?
     Beyond that, does it offer enrichment?
     Is the dialogue suitable to the style and mood of the piece?
   COMMENT:

2. DOES THE PRESENTATION RESPECT THE AUDIENCE IN THE PRODUCTION?
   - ☐ *Direction:*
     Is stage business pertinent to the situation and style? (Or, inserted for its own sake?)
     Does the director have a point of view through which he unifies the elements of the play?
     Is the physical movement in keeping with character and style?
     Does the director achieve an ensemble performance?
   - ☐ *Mounting:*(Costumes—Scenery—Lighting—Music)
     Are settings and costumes expressive of the style, the characters, the locale, and the period?
     If there is available equipment, is the lighting also consistent?
     Are settings and costumes fresh looking and attractively executed?
   - ☐ *Acting:*
     Do you believe the actor in his character? In relation to the style of the piece? (Or, does he ever step out of character?)
     Is there a sense of joy in the performance? (Or, is it flat?)
     Is dialogue well spoken (Voice? Diction? Interpretation?)
     Are songs and dances well performed?
   COMMENT:

Question: *DID YOU ENJOY IT?* _____

The Paper Bag Players preparing for a play. *(Courtesy of Judith Martin; photograph by Ken Howard.)*

Preparing Children for the Occasion

By the time children are in the fourth or fifth grade, the chances are that they have attended several plays and are looking forward to seeing others. It is equally possible, however, that some children have attended only informal performances in an all-purpose room or gymnasium and so have never been to a community or university theatre or seen a play produced formally in an auditorium. In that case, the subject of theatre etiquette and conventions should be part of the orientation. This should not be presented as a disciplinary measure; rather, it should be explained as courteous and expected behavior.

Orientation

By the time children have reached the middle grade, they are ready for substantial background material that will spark interest and enrich the performance. Many producers send packets of teaching material to the school in advance; these materials are well worth using, since they provide additional information for the class before seeing the play. Producers often list books they have found useful in doing their own research on the subject. These books are usually available and may even be in the school library. Sometimes, when a company tours a region on a regular basis, it will develop a program for a particular grade-level curriculum. In this case, it is easy to relate the play to the unit of study. The class already may be familiar with the major character, in which case the children will be eager to see him or her brought to life on the stage.

In contrast, the protagonist may be a well-known figure in real life. I am reminded of a production I saw recently based on the career of Jackie Robinson. He was a hero to the audience as a result of television sports news, so the story of his boyhood and struggle as he rose to fame had a strong attraction. The background the children brought with them made the play twice as meaningful as it would have been had it involved the struggle of an unknown protagonist.

Assuming that the class does not know what the play is about and that the title is also unfamiliar, the teacher will want first to introduce the theme and then, if it is important to their understanding, to give the class an idea of the plot. In the Bicentennial year, many children's theatre companies wrote their own plays based on historical events or, if they toured a particular area extensively, on a topic of regional interest. Since the children might not have been familiar with the material, some study of it in advance was necessary. Schools were appreciative of the cooperation that these companies offered, for it enriched and extended the learning.

Preliminary study has the same effect as knowing a story and then seeing it dramatized. It is the time to bring in relevant background material—historical, biographical, cultural—so that the class may gain a better idea of where and how the characters lived or live. If the play takes place at a former time or in another place, not only will the clothing be different from ours, but so will the furnishings of the homes, the occupations, the props, and the lives of the people. Social attitudes may differ also; therefore, the class will get more from the play if it understands why the characters behave as they do. Speech patterns may be strange, so that some knowledge of the dialect used makes for appreciation rather than amusement. The extent of the orientation that teachers give varies, depending on the play and the amount of time they have at their disposal. I believe that some information about the prospective assembly program or excursion is always desirable in order for the audience to derive maximum pleasure and benefit.

Play structure was treated in chapter 8. By the middle and upper grades, children should have some knowledge of dramatic form. They know the difference between comedy and tragedy and are familiar with a few of the more common theatrical terms. Opportunities for attending plays as well as creating and writing them help young people gain a deeper understanding of an art form that involves the work of many artists, yet does not live until it is shared with an audience.

Audience Participation

Some theatre companies, both commercial and educational, perform what is called participatory drama. This means that instead of acting on a stage, they perform in the round in an all-purpose room or a gymnasium, with the audience seated on three or four sides, where it can become actively involved in the performance. The actors request help from the children from time to time, in response to their questions or to a request to come into the playing space as fellow actors. Occasionally, a company will invite suggestions about what course of action to take, and the responses may alter the outcome of the story. An experienced cast is able to handle audience participation skillfully, thus giving children a dual experience: that of spectator and that of participant.

Before a participatory play is given, actors usually go into the classrooms of the children who are going to attend. They discuss the play and may rehearse the scenes in which the class will be taking part. This can be a richly rewarding experience, when it is carefully planned and rehearsed. Participatory theatre is most effective with younger children; beyond the fifth or sixth grades, there is an inherent risk involved in asking the audience to take part, unless the techniques are sophisticated and the children are used to participation. The majority of companies that offer plays for middle and upper grades perform on a proscenium stage in a traditional manner. Although this does not require the same kind of preparation as does the participatory play, it does warrant some pointers on theatre conventions and etiquette. Everyone will enjoy the performance more when these simple ground rules are observed.

Theatre Etiquette

One aspect of theatregoing that must be treated is etiquette. Accustomed to television, with its frequent breaks for commercials, younger children must be told that the theatre makes certain demands on the audience so that all may see and hear well. Although older children do not have to be oriented in the same way, they may have to be reminded that a good audience:

1. *Does not talk aloud or annoy others.* Once seated, the members of the audience should refrain from whispering, standing up, or leaving without permission.
2. *Does not bring food into the auditorium.* Candy, gum, potato chips, and other easily accessible foods interfere with attention in addition to causing clutter on the floor. The practice of eating while watching television has cultivated a habit that should be discouraged in the theatre.

Eating should take place before or after the performance but never during the play.

3. *Does not run around the auditorium during the intermission.* An intermission need not be a trying period for teachers and ushers, if its purpose is explained. It is a time to move and stretch, to go out for a drink, or to use the rest rooms while scenery is being changed. Some producers are afraid of intermissions, but I have never seen one misused when the play held the interest of the audience.

4. *Does not destroy printed programs.* Some companies provide printed programs. This is a theatre convention that children should understand. Programs are not to be made into airplanes or balls and thrown around the auditorium. They are to be read. In addition to information about the play, they often include activities for children to try at home or in class afterward.

5. *Waits for applause and curtain calls.* Applause and curtain calls are theatre conventions. Applause is our way of thanking the actors for the good time they have given us, and curtain calls let us see the actors as people instead of as characters in the play.

6. *Leaves the auditorium in an orderly manner.* Putting on coats, getting up before the curtain is closed, slamming seats, and running noisily up the aisles are bad manners. If children realize this, the majority of them will wait till the lights in the auditorium are turned on, and it is time for the audience to go.

"*The* Sleeping Beauty" staged in the Japanese Kabuki style. *(Photograph by Fred Ricard.)*

7. *Meets the cast afterward, if invited.* Some casts make a practice of meeting the children in the lobby on their way out, and many youngsters enjoy it. I have mixed feelings about this practice, for it removes the mystique that the cast has taken pains to establish. But some older boys and girls have questions about the play or technical effects that they want to ask, and this is an ideal way to have them answered.

The Performance

The day of the play has finally come. Ideally, the class has been well prepared and are in the auditorium in their seats five to ten minutes before the curtain opens. If the play is presented in the school auditorium, the teacher can

"Patches of Oz" performed at Brigham Young University. *(Courtesy of Harold Oaks.)*

easily gauge the time it will take to go from the classroom to the reserved section of seats. If it takes place in a community theatre or the auditorium of another school or university, more planning is involved to be sure that the group arrives on time, neither late nor too early. When school buses are employed, this may present problems, but it is important to arrange the arrival in plenty of time to hang up wraps, or at least to remove them, and to be comfortably seated before the performance begins. I have often seen classes come into a darkened auditorium fifteen to twenty minutes late, which is unfortunate because they can never catch up on what happened before they arrived, not to mention the disturbance they cause for others who are absorbed in the story.

By the time children have reached the third or fourth grade and have attended a number of programs and plays, they are accustomed to listening carefully to the dialogue and to refraining from whispering or annoying their neighbors. Indeed, when children can see and hear well, this rarely happens. Only when plays are given in huge auditoriums with poor acoustics and poor sightlines is the audience restless and uninvolved. Some companies stipulate the size of audience they will play for, refusing to perform for more than two hundred or three hundred spectators. This is ideal, but it is not always possible to arrange; nevertheless, it is a safe bet that children who can see and hear everything that happens on the stage not only will be a better audience but also will get far more out of the play than if they had missed lines or had trouble seeing the actors.

Should the audience be restless under ideal conditions, there is something wrong. It may be that the script is geared to a younger age level than is present or is over the heads of the audience. Most children are willing to reach up to the latter, but they are bored by anything they consider "babyish." It also may be a poor production. This is another matter altogether, which should have been discovered before the contract was signed. There are so many excellent university theatre departments sending out student groups and so many good professional touring companies available that there is little excuse for engaging a mediocre company. It can happen, however, and when it does, it is a problem for the faculty and administration. Good companies are expensive, but one good show is worth far more than half a dozen poor ones. When university troupes are available, they are an ideal resource. Not only are they less expensive, but their standards tend to be consistently high, their choice of material usually is excellent, and the student actors are sensitive to the interests and needs of children.

Although carrying on conversations during the performance has been termed inconsiderate, it does not mean that an audience should observe total silence. Indeed, it is a pity when children are made to think they cannot utter a sound. There is nothing wrong with laughter, cheers, even calling out spontaneously to the actors when the comments are appropriate; an experienced cast can handle such responses, and most actors enjoy having this rapport with the audience.

*"P*lay to Win" won a 1984 Audelco Award for "best writing of a new show by black authors for the noncommercial theatre." *(Courtesy of Theatreworks/USA.)*

Extending the Experience

Although a good performance of a fine play will certainly stand by itself, it can be enriched by a follow-up period afterward. As adults, we like to discuss a play or film we have seen, and children respond in much the same way. They will discuss the play on their own, but with proper guidance, the discussion can be made richer and more lasting. There are many ways of starting. Least likely to lead to discussion is the question "Did you like it?" But questions relating to the underlying theme or the characters and their solutions to problems will usually generate a lively discussion. Depending on when and where the action took place, the way of life, or the social attitudes of the characters, questions will be raised, offering an ideal opportunity for further exploration. Although children find many programs diverting, they are capable of remarkable insights, when guided toward a more discriminating point of view.

As in all teaching, we are most successful when we begin where the children's interests lie, following their lead before making suggestions. The following are some of the successful ways in which teachers have followed up a performance.

A traditional but still worthwhile activity is writing letters to the cast. This should not be imposed on children as a tedious assignment, but when it represents an honest expression of appreciation, it is an outlet for feelings, a courteous act, and a valid exercise in writing. Actors, incidentally, love the letters children write and often keep them in their scrapbooks.

Painting or drawing pictures of the play is another favorite activity. The Paper Bag Players of New York, aware of the effect that their performances have on young children, put up yards of brown wrapping paper on the walls of the lobby, where space permits, so that audiences can draw pictures during the intermission and after the production.

Some teachers' packets include folk songs and dances that children can learn. Many folk tales, particularly those of the Indians and Eskimos, suggest tools and artifacts that children can make. Masks, jewelry, woven fabrics, pictures of the clothes the Indians and Eskimos wear, and photographs of the land are always fascinating, especially to children in urban areas. I have seen many excellent exhibits of art work stimulated by a performance of Joanna Kraus's *Ice Wolf,* a serious drama that invariably arouses discussion. Stories of the American Indians never fail to stimulate interest in learning their dances and making totem poles and masks.

Many children are eager to enact scenes from the play. Although this is a sure sign of interest, it is also a way to encourage further improvisation. New scenes, action that might have taken place, different endings—these things can begin with questions such as "How else?" or "What if?" Creative drama and the scripted play are different, but the one often leads to the other. Seeing a play may stimulate creative drama, whereas creative drama may result in an original play.

Some teachers find that other forms of writing come more easily as well. The release of emotion into verse is not uncommon. The theatre reaches us on many levels, and because it embodies all of the arts, it makes for various verbal, visual, and physical responses. Older children are often led to further study of a culture and will share their findings in oral or written reports. Whatever form the expression takes, the ramifications of theatre go far beyond the enjoyment of the performance, when time and opportunity are offered.

A word of caution. Although there is no doubt that preparation and follow-up enhance the experience, the teacher must never give the impression that he or she is testing for right or wrong answers. Children who think that they are

"Deep Wood Boy" by Xan S. Johnson, based on an Oscar Wilde fairy tale. (Courtesy Xan Johnson, University of Utah.)

expected to reply in a certain way are robbed of spontaneous, honest responses. The response to a work of art is an individual matter. Adults do not always agree about what they have seen, and we should not expect agreement among children. Appreciation of any art form is difficult to assess, if, indeed, it is even possible. Sometimes it takes days, weeks, or years to integrate what one has thought and felt. This does not mean that everything a child sees should embody a lesson or aim to teach. There is a time for serious study, but there is also a time for fun. Children love humor, and a good comedy has many values, not the least of them laughter. In her book *Understanding Your Child's Entertainment,* Muriel Broadman discusses concerns we all share, but implicit and explicit throughout is a plea for quality, whatever the material may be.[3] Integrity, performance skills, respect for the young audience, and "heart"—in her opinion, these things are of equal importance. Although her text is addressed to parents, the points she makes are valid for anyone responsible for selecting children's programs or guiding young people in the development of aesthetic awareness, critical judgment, and appreciation of the living theatre. Since many college students have not seen productions for children, at least as adults, they need some guidelines about content, form, audience behavior, and ways of getting the most out of the experience.

Summary

Theatregoing can be one of the richest experiences of a child's life. With its aesthetic, educational, and social potential, a good play, well produced, can lead to appreciation of a great art form and add to knowledge and deeper understanding of humankind. Orientation to the event prepares children by familiarizing them with the theme, the style of the production, and any other aspects that will enhance their enjoyment. In the case of a traditional story, less preparation is needed. But for the majority of children, who have grown up watching television, some orientation to live performers is necessary. For many, the school assembly program may be the first exposure to theatre they have.

Theatre etiquette, simple as it sounds, is also necessary, if we are going to teach consideration for the right of others to enjoy the play and to show respect for the actors. The theatre makes demands not only on our hearts and minds but also on our social awareness, for the living theatre, unlike television, is shared enjoyment.

Follow-up activities in the classroom offer a further opportunity for enrichment. Most children enjoy reliving a performance; hence giving them the time and place in which to do it is a welcome extension. Theatre can be a one-time hour of entertainment, but it can be much more than that, as teachers and producers have discovered.

3. Muriel Broadman, *Understanding Your Child's Entertainment* (New York: Harper & Row, 1977).

17 Sharing Work with an Audience

Kimchi Kid by Joanna Halpert Kraus, Packer Collegiate Institute. *(Photograph by Dorothy Napp Schindel, director.)*

*T*he formal play, in contrast to creative drama, is primarily audience centered and has, from the beginning, public performance as its goal. A script is either written or selected in advance and memorized by the players. It does not matter whether the lines were written by a playwright or the teacher or composed by the children themselves. The use of a script distinguishes the formal play from creative drama and supplies the structure—plot, theme, characters, dialogue—that will be followed.

It would be unwise to attempt to cover both informal and formal dramatic techniques in one book, whatever its length. It is hoped that teachers of young children will confine their efforts to creative drama exclusively. But for teachers of older children and junior high school students, who may wish to share their work with others, a few elementary suggestions are offered as to the smoothest way of moving the play to the stage.

A momentary digression: as I stated in the Preface, my attitude toward children's performing has undergone change since the first edition of this book more than twenty years ago. There are a number of reasons for this. First, theatre is a performing art, and to refuse the performance, when actors are eager and ready to share their work, is to frustrate a natural desire. Second, after fifty years of drama education in America, there is the fact that plays by very young players, often taught gestures by imitation and lines by rote, are disappearing, if they have not almost vanished from the scene. Third, and less a philosophic conviction than a fact of life, is the effect that television has had on young people. Spectators from birth, children see skilled performers and technical scenic effects daily and so take for granted the idea of performance as the natural goal of rehearsal. Whereas before the advent of television children were taken to an occasional movie or play, statistics show that many children spend more hours before the screen each week than they spend in the classroom. For better or worse, television has conditioned them to want to communicate their work or to move from drama to theatre at a much earlier age than their forebears. Although this may appear to be a pragmatic and therefore questionable reason for change, it is a fact of modern life, which added to my basic belief is part of a rationale for supporting performance. It does not, however, justify exploitation of child actors, but it does, I hope, urge understanding on the part of the responsible adult, whether it be teacher, administrator, recreation leader or parent.

The transition from classroom to stage should come easily and naturally to the group that has spent many hours in improvisation. For boys and girls who have played together informally for some time, the result is more likely to be one of "sharing" than "showing," and to this end the teacher should be able to help the players achieve their goal—successful communication with an audience. Public performances, regardless of their popularity, should be infrequent, however, and then planned only for other classes or parents. This chapter has been included to help the teacher move, if necessary, from informal classroom drama to the sharing of an experience with others or to the experiencing of performance as the natural outcome of creative playing.

Unless the teacher has had some theatre training, directing the formal play can be a difficult experience. That is the reason for emphasizing simplicity: a long script, requiring elaborate scenery and costumes, poses problems for the most seasoned director. The average teacher does not have the background, time, or facilities to cope with such problems, but he or she can support and help enthusiastic young players prepare and demonstrate their work. In guiding beginners of any age, the most important single element is the approach of the leader. Enthusiasm and guidance help young players to cross the bridge between self-expression and successful communication.

Creativity is less dependent upon training and past experience than it is upon a special way of feeling, thinking, and responding. It is, therefore, possible for the teacher to be a highly creative person without having specialized in the theatre arts. Nevertheless, the formal play does make technical demands that the teacher must realize; an audience is involved, and, therefore, a product. The teacher must be prepared to take an additional step by supplying showmanship and maintaining discipline.

Kimchi Kid by Joanna Halpert Kraus, Packer Collegiate Institute. *(Photograph by Dorothy Napp Schindel, director.)*

Choosing the Script

It is to be hoped that the play presented by children in the lower and middle grades will be one they have written themselves. When the script comes as the result of enthusiasm over a good story or the culmination of their study of a subject, it is much more likely to have meaning for the class. If, for example, a class has been studying another culture (the Native Americans, China, the Middle Ages), and they dramatize material relating to it, the play emerges from this background as a natural result. The class may decide they want to dramatize one of the stories or legends they have read. After playing it creatively a number of times, they will be ready to write, or have the teacher write, the dialogue as they suggest it. The results will be childlike and crude, but the story itself has stood the test of time and, therefore, serves as a good scenario.

Sometimes a group wants to try an original plot. This is infinitely more difficult. Again, if it comes as the result of great interest in a subject the class has been studying, they will know something of the background (time, place, occupations of the people, beliefs, superstitions, education, food, housing, folk or tribal customs). Their very enthusiasm is the primary requisite. Beyond that, they will need the guidance of the teacher in planning a story and developing characters who motivate the action. Inexperienced playwrights of any age cannot be expected to turn out well-made plays. What they *can* do is demonstrate their understanding of the subject matter about which they are writing and show believable characters involved in the story. The play that comes as the result of integrating drama with social studies, music, literature, dance, or art will have its greatest value to the players. Another class will enjoy seeing their work and perhaps will be stimulated to try a play of its own. These are sufficient reasons for deciding to share the project, but unless the children are older and the teacher has had considerable experience in drama, it should probably not go beyond the school-assembly audience.

Occasionally, however, a class of older children will want to do a play that is not related to class work. When this request comes, the problem is somewhat different. There is the question of finding a good script that will offer as many opportunities as possible, without featuring three or four talented players. There is a scarcity of such material, though there are some good short plays available that have been written with the class or drama club group specifically in mind. The values cited in an earlier chapter should be considered when making the decision. Is it worthwhile material? Are the characters believable? Does the dialogue offer enrichment? Is the play interesting to the players? Has it substance? Beyond that, we must ask if it has enough parts and opportunities for participation to involve the whole group.

The text, by whomever it is written, should be a literate entity. Language should help to create character, provoke action, further plot, offer color and credibility. The construction of the play is of equal importance, for content and form should work together. A good play will offer opportunity for young people to interpret not only its literary content but its production requirements—scenery, costumes, lighting effects. Finally, a good play generates interest beyond itself—beyond its subject matter, ideas, or characters. It should move and stimulate thought in both performers and audience. This is a big order and not all plays meet these demands equally, but material that is worth working on must contain some of them. Students work best when challenged and tire or become bored when too quickly satisfied.

Within the past few years a number of good collections of plays for children have appeared on the market. Consult the catalogues of publishers who specialize in this area of dramatic literature. Visit bookstores that carry their material. If you have no resources of this kind in your community, write for scripts; most publishers are helpful in supplying information and books for examination.

There are also many short plays by major dramatists that are suitable and challenging for junior and senior high school students. These plays are seldom considered, but they make excellent material on which to work. Moreover, one of these plays will hold the attention of an audience of peers if the cast enjoys the play and can project its meaning and dramatic value. The choice of play is important because it is the foundation of the production. A play of good quality is worth all the time, effort, and study that will be required in the weeks that follow.

Often a play written expressly for classroom use will have several major characters and groups of townsfolk or a chorus. This structure gives everyone a chance, makes double casting possible, and may even offer an opportunity to add music or dance. Production problems are another consideration. What are the staging facilities? Or will the play be performed in the classroom? If so, will it be in the round or in proscenium style? Are scenery and costumes essential, or can the script be simply performed with the tables and chairs that are available?

Sometimes the teacher will find a play based on a favorite story. Other times, the children will want to work on a particular kind of play—for example, a mystery. Whatever the choice, it should be a short script, requiring as little time as possible for rehearsals; long periods spent in rehearsing difficult scenes rarely make for a lively experience. If the group does a play for an audience, the choice of a script is the first important consideration.

Occasionally, a junior high school group will want to do a Shakespearean play. This is a challenge to the teacher as well as to the class, but it can be done intelligently and effectively, if approached in the right way. First, the play will be far too long as it stands. If the teacher familiarizes the class with the story, has them improvise scenes from the play, and then cuts the play to a manageable length, the project will be realistic. Rather than cutting within the play, it is better to select key scenes on which to work. In this way there is no dilution of the literature; what is done has been carefully selected to be performed as written.

Shakespeare requires more time to prepare than a modern play because of the language and the necessary orientation. On the other hand, children who can experience Shakespeare as *theatre* rather than a textbook assignment are amazingly quick to grasp meanings and see its humor. *A Midsummer Night's Dream, Twelfth Night, As You Like It, Julius Caesar,* and *The Merchant of Venice* are among the plays I have seen or have done with seventh and eighth graders, and they have all been successful.

Not only Shakespeare but Molière, Goldoni, and Rostand as well have appeal for older children. Again, scenes only should be performed rather than the full-length play; however, the actors must have knowledge of the entire work. An advantage of working on classics is the fact that scenery is rarely important. Two or three chairs, a bench, a table, perhaps some sturdy boxes, a screen—these are all pieces of furniture and props that schools and community centers have on hand. The classics are certainly not for beginners or for the very young. Still, for children who have had previous work in creative drama, they provide a real challenge and can establish a lifelong love for some of the world's greatest dramatic literature.

Few modern Broadway plays are appropriate for children. Older plays like *Our Town, Abe Lincoln in Illinois,* and some of the comedies of the modern stage are. The big musicals and the ultrasophisticated script should be avoided. Children under high school age rarely suggest doing them; but in addition to their problematical content, the need for skilled dancers and singers to perform them is another reason for excluding them from consideration.

The Director

The teacher moves from being guide to being director during the rehearsal periods. Some directors are permissive and allow much opportunity for individual interpretation. Others plan action carefully in advance and supervise every detail. The director of inexperienced casts often finds the greatest success in an approach that is somewhere between the two extremes: giving enough direction to make the cast feel secure but providing enough leeway for individual interpretation and inventiveness. Regardless of method, however, the use of a script and the anticipation of an audience automatically place the emphasis on product rather than process.

Production also implies scenery and costumes; hence time and effort must be given to their design and construction. These things need not be elaborate; indeed, they seldom are in school or club situations, but the mounting is an important aspect of the formal play. When children can assume some responsibility for scenery, costumes, and properties, additional learning experiences are provided, as well as the opportunity for integrating arts and crafts with drama. Cooperation between the players and the backstage crew is essential to success and is certainly one of the greatest satisfactions a group can experience.

For younger children, however, these values are all too frequently outweighed by anxiety or boredom or both; the results tend to be wooden, lacking freshness and charm. For the child in the middle grades, however, there is occasionally reason for producing a play, provided the script is not too demanding or the direction too rigid. For the older child, on the other hand, the produced play is frequently of great value in teaching dramatic techniques and sharing an art with an audience. For the seventh- or eighth-grader, there are values to be found in the sustained work of production. Older children delight in the sharing of an activity and enjoy the discipline required to bring the performance to a high level.

The Alliance Children's Theatre production of "A Wrinkle in Time," an adaption of Madeleine L'Engles' novel by Sandra Deer. *(Courtesy of Edith Love; photograph by Charles Rafshoon.)*

It is suggested that before any work on the play is begun, the director have the group play the story creatively. Improvisation helps the players become familiar with the plot, get acquainted with the characters, and remain free in their movement. When the cast is thoroughly acquainted with the story, it is a relatively easy matter to rehearse more formally.

Floor Plans

The director should make a floor plan or diagram of the playing space in advance. On this he or she will sketch in the essential pieces of scenery or furniture and indicate the entrances. This is not a picture of the set but rather a careful diagram of the floor area, which indicates where each piece of scenery will be placed, its relative size, and the space left on the stage for easy movement. The director will be careful to put entrances where the actors can use them most comfortably and effectively. Although the scenery will probably not be available much before final rehearsals, the director will try to find pieces of comparable size so that the cast becomes used to the plan and will have as little trouble as possible adjusting to the setting when it appears. For example, three or four folding chairs will suggest a sofa, coat trees, trees, and so on.

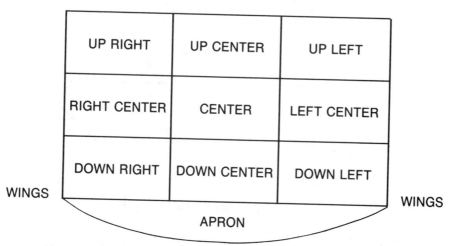

The areas of the stage. *Left* and *right* always refer to the *actor's* left and right.

The director will also want to list all pieces of scenery so that they can be checked off as he or she collects or makes them. The beginner will find that the simpler the setting, the fewer the problems and, incidentally, the more effective the stage will probably be. Children can be involved in all of the details of the production; they will enjoy it and learn from the experience.

Arena Stage

The term *arena stage* is used to describe a center playing space. Some smaller theatres are built with the playing space in the center and the audience seated on all four sides; others, often called "thrust stages," have seats on only

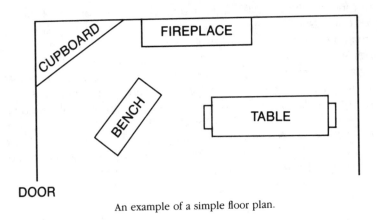

An example of a simple floor plan.

ARENA STYLE

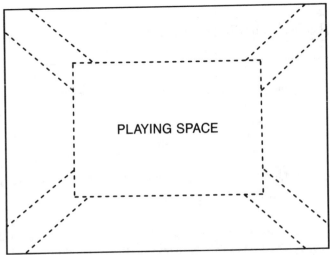

The audience is seated on three or four sides of the indicated playing space.

three sides. In either case a different style of acting is demanded from that required by the proscenium stage, but it is one that is often easier for the less experienced player than for the professional adult actor, accustomed to the techniques of the proscenium stage. In schools with an all-purpose room, plays are frequently given in the round. Although such areas lack proper lighting and good acoustics, they have the advantage of being familiar territory to the students and they require little in the way of scenery. What scenery there is should be simple and low so as not to block the view and so lightweight that it can be carried on and off the stage in front of the audience. Entrances may be indicated by putting masking tape on the floor. The audience must be told when it is seated that the taped-off areas will be used by the actors and must therefore be kept open. If the play calls for audience participation, it is much easier to handle in the round than on an elevated proscenium platform.

Whatever the space, it should be small, with as good acoustics as possible. This will not only put the actors at ease but will help to prevent the constant reminders to "speak up" or "louder, please!" These admonitions all too often lead to a stilted, unnatural performance, with children talking to the audience rather than to the other characters in the play. Large high school auditoriums are probably the worst possible places for children to perform. A small room, on the other hand, deemphasizes the lack of performance skills and puts the attention where it should be, on the play.

The Stage Manager

The job of stage manager is important and one that responsible girls and boys can do and enjoy. A stage manager should be appointed at the same time the cast is selected and given a script. A stage manager attends all scheduled rehearsals and keeps a record of all cuts, action, and business. It is a good idea for the stage manager to sit at one side of the stage where he or she can not only see and hear but also call the actors for their entrances.

Under most circumstances, the stage manager will be able to pull the curtains and handle or give cues for the lights. The stage manager works closely with the director and assumes as much authority as the director feels he or she can when the play is presented. The stage manager has a chance to grow in the job, for this person is important to every aspect of the production, and he or she learns, by doing, the meaning of the word *responsibility.*

Casting the Play

This preliminary work done, the director is now ready to give attention to casting the play. In creative drama the cast changes with every playing. In the formal production, however, there is one cast that rehearses each scene a number of times in preparation for the performance. The matter of casting is therefore, important. The director tries to get the best possible cast together and usually does it by means of tryouts. The director is obligated to do a certain amount of typecasting. For example, a giant must be played by a very large child; a dwarf or elf, by a child who is small; other characters who may have certain specified physical characteristics, by children with similar characteristics. To cast for any other reason than theatrical effectiveness is a questionable practice.

The audience must believe in the reality of the characters, and if they are too obviously different from the description or implications in the script, an audience cannot find them acceptable. Likewise, older players will feel uncomfortable if they realize that they are not believable, and so the good that the experience may do them is negated by their own feelings of inadequacy. This is one of the strong arguments against public performance by children. An actor cannot grow if he or she is constantly cast in the same type of role; yet the actor cannot experiment with a part for which he or she is conspicuously miscast, in front of an audience.

Casting should be done carefully, for a mistake made in the beginning may be disastrous later. Some directors like to have two casts. This is a good idea, provided there is sufficient time for a double set of rehearsals. It is a precaution against illness and accidents and gives the entire group a feeling of security. It also provides twice as many opportunities for participation and should work out well if there is time enough to rehearse both groups equally. Both casts, then, must be given a chance to perform.

Stage Movement

Stage movement is the movement of actors about the stage. The director who plots it in advance will find that valuable time is saved in rehearsal. Writing notations in the script, or even making diagrams, will help the director see at a glance where the various characters are. Although most published scripts have action included, it seldom works, because no two stages are alike. For example, an important entrance, which the script indicates should be from the right, may have to be reversed if the wing space in the school auditorium cannot accommodate it.

If the movement is memorized along with the lines and not changed, it is an advantage. Once the general movement is set, the cast is free to develop appropriate business and work on characterization. Early memorization of lines also helps the group move ahead, giving attention to the rhythm of the play, the building of climaxes, projection of voice, and general polishing. Perfection is never the aim when working with children, but their satisfaction will certainly be greater if they can feel well prepared, comfortable, and able to enter into the performance with a sense of security. Encouragement, plus necessary constructive criticism, help to make the rehearsal period one of pleasure and learning.

Business

Business is the small movements the actors make to suggest character, occupation, emotional state, and necessary mime or use of required props. Knitting, setting a table, reading, sweeping, putting on gloves, cleaning glasses, coats, playing with jewelry, arranging flowers, and smoking cigarettes are common bits of business that help to establish character and move the play forward.

Music

Many children's plays require music. It may be taped or live. Instrumental music is often suggested or demanded by the playwright (guitar, flute, recorder, drum). Live music is best if musicians are available; otherwise taped music works well.

Lighting

Lighting is the area in which children are usually least involved. Lighting equipment is dangerous, expensive, and too sophisticated for a young and inexperienced crew. An all-purpose room is rarely equipped with stage lights so that the problem does not exist there. Occasionally, a school auditorium will have a few simple spotlights that can be added to the general lighting; in this case children in the intermediate grades and up can learn how to operate them, and they enjoy the magic of transforming a scene with colored lights and dimmers.

Scenery

Scenery means the large pieces that suggest the locale of the play. There is always controversy as to the difference between scenery and properties, or "props." Scenery is background, whereas properties are those items used by the actors.

The trend today (and a fortunate trend for inexperienced and young groups) is toward curtains rather than box sets and toward suggested rather than realistic settings. For example, a bench, a table, chairs, stools, perhaps a fireplace or a hutch—if available—will suggest a peasant's cottage, without the necessity of building flats, putting in doors, or painting an elaborate representational background. Some of the most effective modern settings, both on Broadway and in community theatres, have been abstract or so simple as to focus all attention on the play and the players.

Platforms and steps are helpful in creating different levels, thus adding variety in appearance and making for interesting movement. A bright tablecloth, a few large flowers, two or three benches or stools, can often provide all that is needed. Children have wonderfully imaginative ideas for suggesting scenery; what they do need is practical help in constructing it and in supporting the pieces. If the director works closely with the art department of the school, most backstage problems can easily be solved. Best of all, the stage crew or scenery committee will have an ideal opportunity to learn techniques of painting and handling materials.

Scenery is usually not needed until the final rehearsals. It is suggested that if it can be ready a week in advance of the first dress rehearsal, the players will have a chance to get used to it and not have to add that adjustment to costumes and other last-minute details. A few *dos* and *don'ts* may be helpful:

1. Scenery should enhance, not distract.
2. Scenery should be firm, not flimsy.
3. Scenery should unify the production.
4. Scenery should be in keeping with the mood of the play.
5. Scenery should suggest the time and place of the story and the circumstances of the characters.
6. Scenery and costumes should be planned together.
7. Scenery should help the players, not get in their way.

Properties

Very little needs to be said about properties. They are all the objects (usually small) used by the players. If the school has a property closet, many commonly used items can be kept and brought out when needed. A creative drama teacher should have these items anyhow, for they are often used in class. Baskets, canes, wooden bowls, china (better yet, plastic dishes), swords, and the like are basic equipment. Some things must be borrowed, some made. It is a challenge to the ingenuity of the property committee when, for example, things such as a "golden goose," a "snowman," a "roast chicken," or a "birthday cake" are called for. Papier-mâché and styrofoam are excellent materials for the unusual item, but, again, the young or inexperienced committee needs help in construction.

One other word regarding props: the property committee learns through its assignment what responsibility is all about, for objects are often needed at particular moments in the play, and the absence of them can ruin an otherwise excellent scene. Properties should be checked before and after every rehearsal and performance and, if damaged or missing, replaced. It is a good idea to begin gathering the properties as soon as the play goes into rehearsal to give the actors ample time to get used to handling them.

Costumes

Costumes, like scenery, can be a source of worry and frustration to the teacher whose group is too young or inexperienced to assume responsibility for them. Sometimes parents take a hand with the costumes, and sometimes the art department offers assistance. The former may be a satisfactory arrangement, but all too often it builds what should have been a simple performance into a major production. Too much emphasis is put on the mounting, and the public performance with adult contributions takes precedence over the learning. The second arrangement—assistance from the art department—is decidedly preferable, since it keeps the play within the framework of the school and may give the class an opportunity to help design or even make some part of the costumes. If neither type of cooperation is available the teacher should try to solve the matter of clothing by merely suggesting it or adapting easily obtainable garments to the play.

For example, aprons, hats, vests, capes, boots, and shawls are easily acquired and go a long way toward suggesting various kinds of characters. Children accept simple suggestions readily and do not demand complete or authentic outfits. Blue jeans, tights, and colored T-shirts are in the wardrobes of most children and young people today, regardless of economic circumstances. If these things can be chosen with a color scheme in mind, they can be used as costumes for many folk tales or for plays with historical backgrounds.

Paper should be avoided. It tears easily and so is hazardous. It is suggested that all good costumes, whether made for a particular occasion or given to the school, be saved and kept clean and in good repair. The collection of basic garments should be a continuing project; in time it will provide many, sometimes all, of the costumes needed for future productions.

It is generally better not to put old and authentic garments and inexpensive, newly made costumes on the stage at the same time. The effect is usually that of making the old look faded and dirty and the new cheap and too bright. Occasionally, the two can be combined, but in general, it is better to use one or the other for a unified overall impression.

Here a few suggestions are offered as to the function of costumes:

1. Costumes should suggest the personality, age, occupation, and financial circumstances of the characters.
2. Costumes should belong to the period and setting of the play.
3. Costumes should be appropriate to the season of the year, as suggested by the story.
4. Costumes should help to unify the production.
5. Costumes should be planned with the scenery in mind; they should carry out the color scheme and look well against the background.
6. Costumes should not distract for reasons of brightness, richness, or design, unless there is a reason for it.

A play for assembly. *(Photograph by Milton Polsky, director.)*

7. Costumes should fit the wearers and be clean and well pressed.
8. Costumes should be secure, neither carelessly made nor too fragile to be safe.
9. Costumes should make the wearers feel appropriately dressed and comfortable, not self-conscious.

Rehearsals

In the beginning, the director, regardless of the group, will have many decisions to make and many details to organize. Once the director has cast the play, has decided upon the floor plan, and has made arrangements for settings and costumes, he or she can get down to the serious business of rehearsing. As stated earlier, time spent on improvisation will be time well spent; the cast will become thoroughly acquainted with the characters and the plot. Better yet is the play that evolves from a comprehensive unit of study. When children have been deeply immersed in a situation, a period, or a place for a long time, the play they build will have much greater meaning for them and for the audience.

The director is now ready to set up a rehearsal schedule. It is hoped that, for the teacher or director of children, this will be an informal procedure. Even though a performance date has been set and the work planned, the director must try to avoid the anxiety and boredom that mar rehearsals of so many nonprofessional productions. For this reason, rehearsals should be frequent but short. Scenes, rather than the entire play, should be rehearsed first; complete run-throughs come later.

Early memorization of lines is advocated, since it frees the players to move and develop pertinent business. People memorize at different rates of speed, but the sooner it is done, the more productive the rehearsal periods will become. Most important is probably interpretation. Discussions along the way help the actors to learn who the characters are and why they behave as they do. First, there should be an oral reading of the whole play. Then questions such as these should be answered.

1. How would you describe the character you are playing?
2. What does he/she have to say about him/herself?
3. What do others have to say about him/her?
4. What are his/her relationships to other persons in the play?
5. What are his/her aims? Motivations?
6. What are his/her individual qualities? Details that help in understanding him/her (personality, temperament, age, occupation, background, likes, dislikes, education, beliefs)?
7. What are the main events of the play? How does each character fit into them?

It is suggested that improvising scenes from the play precede memorization and blocking. Any misunderstanding or lack of understanding will be cleared up if plays create their own dialogue, characters, and motivations.

One word of caution: the dramatist's intention must be respected in interpreting the play. Altering the meaning is dangerous and disrespectful. If the group does not like the play as written, better give it up and select something else. Changing mood or meaning will throw the play out of focus. Leave the "spoofs" for older and more experienced players, if they wish to tamper; it is a questionable practice at best and not for young players.

Blocking the scenes comes next. If the director plans the movement in advance, he or she will be able to approach a rehearsal knowing when characters enter and leave, by what door, and where they sit or stand. It is a good idea to note all movements on a master script. Often, when a few days have passed between rehearsals, there is disagreement about what was done before. A careful record will answer the questions so that the rehearsal can proceed.

Business, which is individual action in keeping with the character, can be developed next. For example, knitting, sweeping, eating, and so on add to the reality of the characters and give young players something definite to do. The more times business is repeated, the more natural it becomes. As was mentioned earlier, if properties are available at the beginning of the rehearsal period, the players grow used to them and can handle them with ease and naturalness.

Composition, or "stage picture," is another thing for the director to bear in mind. Even an experienced actor cannot see the grouping on the stage when he or she is part of it; hence the director, who is watching closely from the front, must be aware of the composition. Are the players hiding each other? Can important business be seen? Are entrances blocked? If there are several players together, do they make a pleasing picture? Does one composition flow into another? All of this pertains much more to the play designed for an outside audience; yet, even under the most informal circumstances, it is important that the players be clearly seen and heard.

If dances or songs are included, they should be rehearsed and integrated as early as possible. It is always a temptation to let them go, but the director will find that this makes for a weak spot or a slow transition. Such business should appear to spring from the play and belong to it; it should not be imposed for the purpose of adding more people or relieving monotony.

As with scenery, any cooperation between the drama and music teachers is an advantage. The more a staff can work together on a project, the better the learning and the better the production. If a player is absent, the stage manager or another person should step into the part. When the director reads the lines from out front, the cast is at a disadvantage; for while the lines are delivered the space is empty, and the scene very often breaks down. Incidentally, this is another good reason for double casting. It ensures each group of a substitute at a moment's notice.

As the rehearsal period proceeds, the play should grow in feeling, understanding, technical competence, and unity. Smoothness will come as lines are learned, the business perfected, and the actors develop rapport with each other. Rough spots should be ironed out in the beginning, rather than left to the end for polishing. Finally, if the director can maintain a spirit of fun, the rehearsal period will be a source of pleasure as the cast shares the satisfaction of building something together.

As in creative drama, the director occasionally finds a show-off or clown in the cast. The director does not want to inhibit inventiveness, but he or she cannot afford byplay, which disrupts the rehearsal and takes the attention away from the script. Clowning must be stopped at once, for it can jeopardize the entire performance. Most children and young people, if approached constructively, will see that practical and private joking are out of order, and for the good of the production, their energy must be used to build, not break up, a scene. For children of junior and senior high school age, this experience may be the highlight of the year and leave a lasting impression.

Teamwork is both a necessity to a good performance and a source of deep satisfaction to the players. There is probably no experience comparable to the camaraderie that develops during rehearsals. A special feeling binds a group together when it shares the hard work, the creative effort, the interdependence, and the fun of rehearsing and presenting a play.

The Dress Rehearsal

The dress rehearsal can be either a day of confusion or a satisfying and joyous culmination of weeks of group effort. When details have been well planned and the scenery and costumes are ready, there is no reason why it should not be the high point of the rehearsal period. The old adage "a poor dress rehearsal makes a good show" is fallacious. It is true to a degree only when the dress rehearsal is so bad that the cast makes one last mighty effort to prevent the play from being a disaster. This always involves work that should have been done weeks before; with this work completed, the cast is ready to add the final details with a sense of security.

Two, or even three, dress rehearsals are desirable and should be planned from the beginning. At the first one, the scenery should be finished and in place. At the second and third, costumes should be worn, so that by the time the play goes on, the cast and backstage crew have mastered all of the problems. After each dress rehearsal and performance, costumes should be hung up carefully and properties checked. This not only helps to keep things in good order but also instills a sense of responsibility in the players. Even in the most informal of plays, the actors should remain backstage and not mingle with the audience. Food and other refreshments have no place in a dressing room. They are a risk to the costumes and divert the players.

Children absorbed in performance of *The Magic Word. (Courtesy of Periwinkle Productions, Inc.; photograph by Joe Lippincott, Detroit.)*

If makeup is used (and with children it is nearly always unnecessary), it should be tried out first for effectiveness. Teenagers like working with makeup; therefore, for them, another learning experience is provided. Again, makeup extends or enhances a character; it does not create one. Sometimes a player will say, "I'll be all right when I'm made up and get into my costume." The actor will be better, perhaps, but if he or she has not succeeded in creating a character by that time, costumes and makeup cannot do it.

If there is a curtain call, it should be rehearsed so that the players are ready to come out and take a bow to the audience. One curtain call is sufficient for the audience to show its appreciation. Although there is some difference of opinion about this, the curtain call is a convention of the formal theatre, and an audience should be given a chance to observe it.

The Performance

Once again, a performance by beginners or children should be simple and informal. The director has the greatest responsibility here, for his or her attitude of calm encouragement will be contagious. If the director regards the play as a good piece of work that the cast and crew take pleasure in sharing, they will view it much the same way. They will look forward to the performance with anticipation rather than with anxiety. Both excessive criticism and excessive praise are as harmful at this stage as at any other. The most satisfying response a group can be accorded is the appreciation of the audience. The players will know that they have succeeded in achieving their goal: successful communication.

One performance of a play is recommended for younger children, for they plan and anticipate it as a special event. Repeating the experience rarely recaptures the fun; the play lacks the original spontaneity and the players become bored with what was once a lively involvement. Junior and senior high school students, however, can gain a great deal from the experience of giving a play two or three times. As the product assumes more importance, there is the challenge of trying to improve it and discovering in the process the responses of different audiences.

In a children's production the director supplies the necessary showmanship. This does not mean dictating the way lines should be read or imposing a style that is unnatural to young players. It means being sensitive to their ideas and helping them express those ideas most effectively. It means checking costumes and props, watching that the players look and are comfortable in their clothes and that the clothes they wear add to the individual and overall effect. Attention to cleanliness, color, design, and fit need not take up much time, but it is worth every minute spent and will avoid the amateur look of the old-fashioned school play. Simplicity, selectivity, appropriateness, will always outweigh elaborate mounting and will be easier for everyone involved.

The Auditorium

One aspect of producing a play that is frequently overlooked is that of the auditorium seating area. Ushers may be members of the class who have worked on play committees and so are free when the dress rehearsals are over. Ushering is an excellent way for them to perform a necessary function. If there are programs, they may hand them out, although in an informal situation a narrator is a preferred way of imparting necessary information to the audience.

Attendance should be by invitation only, rather than by ticket. When tickets are sold, there is an added emphasis on perfection and a felt obligation to make elaborate settings and costumes. Young players feel the strain, and the "sharing with" too often turns into "showing-off." Publicity, also, should be restricted to posters made by the group and oral announcements. The greater the participation of the class in every aspect of the production and the fewer contributions from outside, the more positive values the experience will have.

Summary

The presentation of a play for an audience should be done only when older children are involved and then infrequently. Informality and simplicity should be stressed if the basic values of communication and sharing are to be realized. There is real difference of opinion about whether children should ever appear before an audience, for fear of destroying their spontaneity and naturalness. This is a valid argument, but my contention is that performance does no harm if it is done without pressure, thus avoiding drudgery. The teacher must become director, supplying showmanship and making certain decisions. As teacher, however, he or she tries to involve every member of the group so that the procedure is as democratic as possible. Most important, children should not be exploited to show the value of the content or of the instruction.

In the school, club, or camp play, the educational and social values come first. The product will hold interest for the viewers if they are properly oriented and their appreciation is the natural consequence of a successful attempt at communication. If these emphases are preserved, the leader and group will find producing a play a rewarding experience. There is probably nothing that binds a group together more closely than the production of a play and no joy more lasting than the memory of a play in which all the contributions of all participants have dovetailed so well that each has had a share in its success. This can and should happen when exploitation does not enter the picture. If teacher and class work together on a play from the beginning, discussion of costumes, set, and style will expand the learnings. Although the director is the final authority when important decisions are made, showing the cast pictures and photographs; relating costume to period, place, and role; and helping them visualize the scene will provide further opportunities for learning.

Children design the backdrop for an original play. *(Courtesy of CAT, New York University.)*

Finally, theatre is a performing art. Let us not forget it. The suspicions that have surrounded the theatre in our country from the beginning are still here, if masked. When we cut the arts from the budget in times of depression and deemphasize *acting* in favor of the word *learning,* we are giving tacit acceptance to an old prejudice. Some funding agencies request a product as proof of the effectiveness of the programs to which they have given financial support. A product need not be interpreted as a full-fledged production, however; in fact, a good demonstration can meet the requirement just as well, often better. You may find a production desirable, but if not, consider a demonstration of creative drama or an open class by showing what it is, what it does, and how it works. If there is one thing that recent experimentation in the arts has shown us, it is that there are few, if any, rules that must be obeyed. Children experiment freely,

mixing media, ignoring conventional forms, being "horse and rider" simultaneously, and erasing the line that exists between actor and audience. Therefore, an
opportunity to observe children working creatively together may satisfy the
funding agency and be a far more effective presentation than the traditional
school play.

18
Creative Drama
in Alternative Spaces

After the performance, children play on stage with the Paper Bag Players' props. *(Courtesy of Judith Martin; photograph by Ken Howard.)*

Not all creative drama is taking place in class-rooms and community centers. Some very imaginative work is being done in or under the auspices of other social and cultural institutions and in the streets and playgrounds of the city as well. It is with these alternative locations that this chapter is concerned. The years since the original publication of this textbook have witnessed a dramatic spread of activities and the acceptance of an expanding arena for learning. The open classroom, the magnet schools, the university without walls programs and their various permutations have increased our awareness of the possibilities for learning beyond the boundaries of our public and private educational institutions.

There are many reasons for this phenomenon, and any one answer would be simplistic. Recent budget cuts for the arts is one; this has caused many communities to look elsewhere for places in which to hold classes in drama, puppetry, dance, music, painting, and pottery, as well as the meetings of special crafts and hobby groups popular in individual neighborhoods. Another reason is the superior facilities of some community centers and civic theatres and the closely related asset of a central or accessible location that these centers usually offer. Some Y's and community centers have simply continued a long-standing tradition of classes in the visual and performing arts; as school programs are curtailed or cut altogether, these organizations find themselves again providing an important community service. Still another source of creative energy is to be found in some of the alternative and magnet schools, which came into being during the late sixties and seventies. Although not all of these programs have survived, enough of them remain to account for an important contribution to education in the arts.

The goals and values of drama in alternative spaces do not differ from those of the classroom; therefore the suggestions of literature and other activities in the earlier chapters are still appropriate. There are some differences in the situations, however, and this chapter is concerned with the special environment and features that these outside locations possess and some of the ways in which to use them. The environment does not alter goals, but it may modify procedures. It may also offer unique resources that the leader can use. Among the more common sites of activities are libraries, churches, and museums. There are also some spacious cultural centers with programs expressly designed for children. Among them are the Minneapolis Children's Theatre, which has become a school; the Nashville Theatre and Academy; the Empire State Institute for the Performing Arts in Albany; Lincoln Center in New York; and the Kennedy Center in Washington, whose programs are discussed in chapter 16. Each center has developed a format of its own, depending on the interests and needs of the community and the particular resources it has to offer.

Free of board of education guidelines, these alternative sites are able to be flexible regarding organization, schedule, workshops for teachers and students, and programs in general. This is not to state that they have no restrictions; they have. Their programs differ from those of the schools in that the classes are not

Drama in the playground. *(Courtesy of Tom Behm, University of North Carolina.)*

part of a required curriculum, students are not graded (though they may be evaluated), and the classes fall within the category of leisure-time interests.

Drama in Libraries

Not all libraries offer classes in creative drama, but many include storytelling, puppetry, and children's films among their special services. Story dramatization grows naturally from storytelling and librarians who have worked with it report its popularity. Older children are eager to enact favorite stories, whereas little children are drawn to tales they have just heard told and they want to try on the various roles. Surrounded by walls of books, children meeting in libraries have literary resources at their fingertips—an advantage over groups meeting in schoolrooms. Whether the creative drama class is conducted by the children's librarian or by an expert who comes in each week, the environment is conducive to the pursuit of creative drama, particularly story acting.

According to Nancy Pereira, author of *Creative Drama in the Library,* there are benefits to the library as well as to its young patrons. First, drama brings children into the library and encourages their returning. Children discover its resources and in the process get acquainted with the staff. They find persons there who will answer their questions, show them film strips and materials, and help them locate periodicals and books. When television viewing is claiming many hours a week in a child's life, a strong connection with the local public library has mutual benefits.

One question that always comes up has to do with noise and space. If there is an activity room, and many libraries have one, this is no problem. Some libraries have more than one room available for storytelling, lectures, and classes. Large urban libraries often have auditoriums with stages, where films are shown and plays can be given. Because of the noise level when a group of children get

Drama group in a library. *(Courtesy of Magie Dominic, Woodstock, N.Y.; photograph by Susan Kain.)*

together, the most soundproof quarters available should be chosen for classes in creative drama. If, on the other hand, the library is small or consists of a single room, the hours for creative drama have to be set when the fewest persons tend to use it. This will affect the program, but a way can usually be found if drama is really wanted. Storytelling and puppets, which require very little space, make a good beginning. It may be that a simple rearrangement of furniture is all that is necessary to create a larger space for human actors. The cooperation of the staff, however, is essential under any circumstances.

One interesting drama program evolved through the efforts of a librarian in Woodstock, New York. Her interest in history prompted an unusual focus on material relating to a particular person, event, or culture. Calling itself "The Children's History Theatre," the children meet on a regular basis during the school year, doing their research on the chosen topic and rehearsing the play they develop and present as a culmination of their work. Because the project exists outside the classroom, the librarian is free to select a topic that particularly interests the children and, on occasion, to enlist the help of local professional artists, dancers, and musicians. Posters in the library and school inform the public as to when plays are being performed.[1]

Drama in Museums

Museums play a central role in preserving the cultural, artistic, and historical heritage of each generation. Through their education departments they have become more than repositories of treasures; lectures, films, special exhibits, and programs are offered to attract a larger public. Some art museums, in expanding their community services, are providing not only more educational programs than they offered in the past but are providing space for outside groups to use and in which to perform. Some museums now offer classes in the performing as well as the visual arts. One example is the Brooklyn Museum in New York, where a number of years ago an innovative drama program was inaugurated. Paintings and sculpture provide stimulation and inspiration, whereas galleries are used for playing space. Actually, the drama program is one of several offerings of the museum education department. Shrinking funds for community services in the past few years challenged the museum to find new ways to involve and educate children and family audiences. One way that has proved successful is drama/theatre. The visual images and emotional impact of the museum's collections motivate interest and learning. At the Brooklyn Museum, the use of theatre techniques is said to parallel Piaget's contention that children are motivated to gain a greater understanding of their world and to restructure their knowledge when they encounter experiences that are dissonant with their previous assumptions.

1. Magie Dominic was formerly director of The Children's History Theatre, Woodstock, N.Y.

In the museum children find objects removed from their original context. Helped to understand that these objects once belonged to a particular society and were expressive of that society, children recreate a cultural context for dramatization. In this context they explore the environment and the relationship between the objects of art and the people who created them. Aesthetic standards that differ from their own, as well as cognitive learnings, result when children visit the museum in this way. They also view plays as well as create them in a special gallery that seats no more than one hundred persons.

The Brooklyn Museum has several other educational and theatre-related programs. *Museum/School Collaboration* creates an educational experience that meets the needs of both institutions. *Holiday Programs* provide family audiences with programs to stimulate interest in particular collections. *Summer Day Camp Programs* provide activities for ad hoc groups, often representing a wide age range and little past experience of the museum. *Informal Theatre Events for Special Exhibitions* create quick theatrical "happenings" to point up or highlight an exhibit. These vignettes are written and performed by staff members and student actors. Staff involvement in theatre encourages participation on the part of both children and adults. Furthermore, the museum has found that audiences who participate are motivated to return.

Additional programs are also made available to children and planned as field trips for different grade levels. Previsit kits for teachers prepare children coming from schools in school time. "What's Up?" on the other hand, is a free year-round program for elementary school children. Storytelling, drawing, and painting aid participants in learning about a different collection every time they attend. A film entitled "Statues Hardly Ever Smile" was made up of the drama work at the Brooklyn Museum, showing how one museum opened its doors to the children of the community at little cost and with great success.

An example of one of the museum/school collaborations was the Chinese mythology theatre "collage" entitled *Can You Hear the River Calling the Moon?* This piece was created and performed by elementary school children for the general public over the Christmas holidays. A class of schoolchildren visited the Brooklyn Museum for ten weekly sessions, during which time Chinese art and culture were the subject of study. The children acted Chinese myths improvisationally and made their own costumes and props in the museum workshops. The script that evolved was based on the myths and put into written form by the museum instructor. As described in a museum newsletter, the protagonist of the "collage" was a river that flowed from a landscape painting and introduced the various components of the production: a shadow puppet play, showing the creation of the land; large puppets in a morality legend; and a group of children performing a dragon myth.

The play told of the relationship of the people to the land and explained the convention of Chinese landscape painting. A Chinese musician accompanied the performance with music played on traditional instruments. Following each performance the audience was invited to tour the galleries, where they viewed the original paintings of the characters, dragons, waterfalls, and landscapes that they had just seen portrayed. After the weekend performances at the museum the play was given in the school auditorium for the rest of the children. This is an illustration of one way in which school, museum, and community can work together on a project involving all of the arts, with educational and aesthetic values receiving equal emphasis.

The Children's Museum in Boston is another example of a museum with an extensive program of activities including classes in drama and weekly children's theatre performances. Both a Sunday series and a Friday night series of entertainments are open to the public and are held in a small area called the "Sit Around Space." Because the space is small, puppet shows, storytelling, magic shows, and singers are featured, though plays are also offered on occasion.

Classes in creative drama include those held at regular meeting times and in special workshops. Two examples of the latter were conducted in the summer of 1981. Under the direction of Carol Korty, children created plays from folktales, which were then performed in the "Sit Around Space." Advanced drama classes were taught at the museum by the Boston Shakespeare Company. Wheelock College has also held acting workshops and given performances for children at the museum. Brochures from the museum describe teacher workshops as well, and they include drama among a variety of arts and crafts.

Although many museums are serving their communities in similar ways, the Boston Children's Museum is cited for the quantity and quality of its offerings as part of an ongoing program.

Museums are also serving as hosts for theatre performances and workshops. Cleveland's new Museum of Natural History was the principal venue chosen for a children's theatre festival held in that city in the spring of 1982. The imaginative architectural design of the building afforded a variety of playing spaces for performances of plays, dance, and music. Large museums have traditionally offered educational programs for both adults and children, but these informal grassroots programs in which children are active participants define the museum in new terms. The museum, once a hushed and awesome sanctuary, is proving to be a lively and suitable location for classes in drama, movement, and mime.

Bruno Bettelheim, commenting on the value of the museum to the child, said that irrespective of what a museum's content might be, it serves "to stimulate his imagination, to arouse his curiosity so that he wishes to penetrate ever more deeply the meaning of what he is expected to admire in the museum, to give him a chance to admire in his own good time things that are beyond his ken, and, most important of all, to give him a feeling of awe for the wonders of the world. Because a world that is not full of wonders is one hardly worth the effort of growing up in."[2] Bettelheim was not writing of drama when he made that statement, but the role of children's drama in the museum serves two of his

---

2. Bruno Bettelheim, "Children and Museums," *Children Today* 9, no. 1 (January–February 1980): 23.

purposes: to offer an aesthetic experience in a welcoming cultural institution and to bring the child into the museum, which he might otherwise not have entered.

Drama in Parks

Parks and playgrounds since the early part of this century have included drama among their activities for children. In many cases this has meant an informal program of storytelling, improvisation, puppetry, and traveling theatre companies who performed free of charge in parks. In recent years, however, more structured programs have been designed with well-qualified leaders and better facilities for both classes and performances. An example of the latter is Wolf Trap Farm Park for the Performing Arts in Virginia, where programs for adults and children take place all summer with children's productions in both indoor and outdoor settings. Drama lends itself to this type of structure, which combines recreational opportunities and picnic and sport areas with performances of drama, mime, dance, and music. Although the emphasis is on performance at Wolf Trap, participation is included. Today, Wolf Trap's program includes classes in creative drama, with a text book designed especially for its own use. This beautiful facility with its fine staff and superb location is an example of what can be done when a community sets out to do the best possible job, making maximum use of its resources. Not all parks or community centers are blessed with so much, but every place, like every individual, has a unique character. The trick is to find and build on its distinction and advantages. Again, this is not an isolated example, but it is probably one of the better known parks providing excellence in entertainment. On a recent visit to Wolf Trap I watched a group of students with their professor from Georgetown University giving a performance of a participatory play. The situation was ideal for this kind of production, and the director was skilled in handling it. Performing daily had helped the actors to achieve a high level of artistry, which could not normally be expected in an informal activity in a park.

Drama in Churches

The church has historically had a close relationship with the theatre. The medieval theatre was born in the church, and despite the repudiation that theatre has suffered periodically at its hands, an unquestionable connection and acceptance of certain common values and goals exist between them. It is therefore no surprise to discover the growing number of drama and theatre groups that are housed in church buildings of various faiths. Some of these groups are companies that produce plays on religious themes. Others are groups to whom space is given for classes in acting, creative drama, and dance. Many churches support extensive programs in the performing arts, including profes-

A church offers a space for drama. "God loved variety; each tree according to its own kind." *(Courtesy of Elizabeth Rike, Knoxville, Tenn.)*

sional resident companies; like museums and libraries, they also offer space to outside groups for whom commercial studios are unavailable or financially beyond their ability to pay. Indeed, one has only to look at a history of the community theatre movement in this country to see how many successful ventures were begun in the church. Large meeting rooms; a stage, if or when one is needed; after school and Saturday morning hours for classes; low rent (or no rent)—these are the services that many churches provide. In large cities, where rents are prohibitive, the church house is often a haven for the performing arts.

In addition, there is now an awakened interest in drama written on religious themes, modern plays posing moral and ethical questions relevant to life today. Both educators and church people are involved in writing, directing, and promoting this new kind of religious drama. Also available is a body of information on choral reading, monologues, clowning, and textbooks on creative drama and improvisation. Successful Broadway plays like *Joseph and the Amazing Technicolor Dreamcoat, Godspell,* and recent productions with religious themes may have been the precursors of this new wave of interest; they may also account for the strengthened relationship between theatre and church.

*A*n American company in street theatre for a Spanish-speaking audience. *(Courtesy of FACETS Performance Ensemble. Chicago: photograph by Nicole E. Dreiske, director.)*

Paralleling this development is the church's receptivity to theatre companies as cited above.

The American Alliance for Theatre and Education has a Religious Drama Committee, which publishes a newsletter and bibliographies of religious plays for children and books on creative drama in religious education.[3] It also sponsors programs at the annual convention of the organization each August, thus helping other groups initiate programs in their local churches and parishes. Although the goal of many of these groups is public performance, often followed by audience discussion, classes in creative drama and mime for children are also popular. They may be taught by staff members, scout leaders, or by experts from outside; children who attend are not necessarily affiliated with the church.

3. Pam W. Barrager, comp., *Creative Dramatics as a Subject or Method in Religious Education (Washington, D.C.: American Theatre Association, 1975); Religious Plays for Children, Youth, and Family Audiences* (Washington, D.C.: American Teachers' Association, 1975).

Other Locations

Classes in creative drama are to be found in a variety of other places as well, both indoors and out. Among them are department stores, shopping centers, parks, playgrounds, hospitals, housing complexes, grange halls, and beaches. In some cases they are established, ongoing programs; in other cases, they are little more than informal play groups to which children may come while parents are shopping. One cannot expect a high level of accomplishment when attendance is irregular or when weather conditions affect the meeting of the class. Nevertheless, these informal drama groups are not to be written off as lacking direction or continuity, for a number of highly successful ventures were begun in playgrounds and parks under skillful leadership. The key to success is the leader: a dedicated, well-prepared man or woman, who is able to work with prevailing conditions while seeking funding and more permanent quarters.

Procedures vary according to place, time, length, and frequency of meetings and the experience of the leader. The suggestion given in earlier chapters for improvisation and mime and the materials for dramatization may be used under most circumstances, although not all are suitable everywhere. More than one informal program has attracted regional and even national attention for its originality and success. These examples are what James Reany calls "root ideas that uncurl in a community until you find yourself taking a workshop to a school gym or helping 129 teachers in Niagara Falls improvise a play."[4]

One example of a project that has found a generous sharing of space in several institutions is the Creative Theatre Unlimited of Princeton, New Jersey. The McCarter Theatre, the one hundred fifty-year-old Trinity Church, and selected historic sites in the area have all contributed to its continuing growth. In 1983–84 public creative drama workshops were funded by the Mercer County Cultural and Heritage Commission. Sites for these workshops were selected on the basis of their relationship to labor and industry. Summer and winter programs make for a year-round community service and illustrate clearly how local facilities can enable a fledgling group to gain a foothold in these precarious times. The availability of a lawn is an attractive feature of the summer program, which culminates in a work-in-progress on the stage of the McCarter.

On the practical side, most leaders recommend charging a fee for the informal drama group, albeit a small one. This payment constitutes a commitment ensuring, or at least encouraging, regular attendance. The after-school program is elected by the participants, a feature that has both its positive and negative aspects. The child who *chooses* to attend and becomes an interested member will in all probability stay in the group; the child who is uncommitted is the one who tends to drop out. The leader of a leisure time activity should make a special effort to reach every child in the class in order to build a strong, ongoing

---

4. James Reany, *Apple Butter and Other Plays for Children* (Vancouver: Talonbooks, 1973), introduction.

Drama in a shopping mall. *(Courtesy of Eunice Joffe, Imagination Theatre, Inc., Chicago.)*

group. A modest fee will not affect registration; boredom or casual attitude toward the class will.

Environmental Theatre

An alternative space of a different sort is what in avant garde adult theatre is called "environmental." This is the deliberate staging of a play in a venue in which the action could logically take place or the creation of an environment as near like it as possible. Sometimes, where there is enough space to accommodate several settings simultaneously, scenery is arranged around the area with the audience moving from one location to another. The backstage crew does not shift sets but, rather, moves chairs during intermissions so that when the audience returns, it is facing in a different direction and, therefore, another setting. One example of this could be a play that is based on a court trial that is given in a local court house where trials once took place or a historical play given in a park, which was the site of the event. This can be an extremely effective device, especially if the location provides the appropriate scenery and atmosphere.

One group in Vermont, the Montiverdi Players, offered a summer production of *The Tempest* in an outdoor woodland setting. A film, describing the production, shows the company planning the action, rehearsing the dances and the music, and building the ship for the opening and later scenes. It also shows the audience streaming in across the meadow and seating itself on the grass. Actors appear through the trees, hiding behind bushes and disappearing into the forest beyond. The play could have been staged in a theatre in the village but the Montiverdi Players chose the outdoor setting for its environmental value.[5]

A play that I once directed for a college group was laid in a dormitory. We gave the play first on a stage; then, as an experiment, gave it again in a dormitory drawing room. We were fortunate in having a small raised platform at one end of the room, with a step down into the main section. This was an ideal location for the small invited audience. The room could accommodate no more than fifty persons, and lighting was simply what was already there with the addition of two spotlights. The result was realistic and appealing. The obvious drawbacks were the space limitation for regular performances and the fact that we were taking over a popular room in a college building. There was no objection to a one-night stand, but it could not have been done on a regular basis.

Another idea, reported by a young teacher in a junior high school, was the creation of a setting for a Halloween show that the children in her class wrote. They wanted to put on a spooky play, but instead of staging it conventionally, they chose an old building on the edge of the school yard that was used as a potting shed and place for storing lawn mowers, wheel barrows, and so on. The class was granted permission to convert it for one night into a haunted house, designing it so that the audience would walk through a dark corridor to find seats on the floor close to the actors. Audience participation was required from the moment one walked in the door and throughout the performance. Although the evening could hardly be described as anything other than entertaining and social, it demanded imagination and hard work to execute it; however, as the children discovered, it was far from being an easy way out, but it was satisfying and fun for everyone.

Many Theatre-in-Education (T.I.E.) programs are handled in this way because of the opportunities that are offered for simulation and credibility.

Summary

The leader of a group meeting in a nontraditional setting is wise to take stock of its assets: to consider what the facility has, not what it lacks. For instance:

The *library* has rich resources in literature, visual aids, and research materials. Make use of them. In addition to finding favorite stories, you have a

---

5. John Carroll, director of the Montiverdi Plays, artist in Residence in the GALLATIN Division, New York University.

Summer class on the church lawn. *(Courtesy of Joan Robinson and Jacqueline Johnson. Creative Theatre Unlimited, Princeton, N.J.)*

unique opportunity at the library to introduce children to new literature and authors they do not know.

The *museum* has collections and special exhibitions, and its education department can provide a wealth of resources. Discover the possibilities of the museums and how you can work with the staff to add another dimension to the creative drama experience.

The *church* has meeting rooms, often a stage, and access to a piano. Its staff is accustomed to having groups of young people around, and you will probably find more time there in which to work or rehearse.

Other spaces vary so widely that one has to discover their unique advantages. Most will have some positive features. If not, look for another place in which to hold the class. A room, a leader, a group, imagination, and a regular meeting time: these are the prerequisites. A drama program, unlike all of the other arts, and contrary to public opinion, is the least expensive to launch. One warning: remember that alternative spaces were not designed for classes in creative drama and will therefore lack some of the features teachers expect. Respect them, use them, but do not abuse the hospitality of the institution. Your successful use of its resources is a measure of your *own* creativity—and perhaps a new program will grow tomorrow from the roots you put down today.

One further suggestion involves the planning of a single workshop in creative drama. So far we have been thinking in terms of a course or series of classes; however, an occasional workshop held in a particular place, or planned for a special occasion, has a unique value that must be mentioned. It cannot have the depth of the well-planned sequence of lessons, but it may hold an excitement that the participants will remember for the rest of their lives. The fact that it happens only once sets it apart—much like the experience of going to the theatre.

Workshops of this sort are generally held in places not normally available to students, at least for this purpose. For example, the site might be the location of a historical event; the original house of a well-known person, who once lived in the community; or a landmark building such as a courthouse, church, or farm museum. An imaginative teacher, seeing the possibilities of extending a field trip to include the dramatization of material at the site, might arrange ahead for a full morning or afternoon visit. Museums are generally glad to cooperate with a plan made in advance. Familiarity with the place and, in the case of older children, research into its past can make a single such workshop an inspiring occasion.

Dramatizing history or taking the roles of real or imagined persons who lived at that time or in that place makes an indelible impression on young participants. Follow-up activities in the classroom afterward (if the workshop is a school event) may include further improvisation, creative writing, or arts and crafts. Teachers find these experiences an opportunity for greater enrichment and another dimension in learning. During the bicentennial year both historic sites and significant dates led to imaginative workshops throughout the country. I have heard children and college students recall with pleasure their experiences in both seeing and creating plays arranged by their teachers with local children's theatre companies. Their memories of the learnings that took place during that period are still amazingly vivid.

Creative Theatre Unlimited, described earlier in this chapter, held three workshops, all funded in part by a local cultural commission, held "on location." They included trips in which drama was created on the following sites:

1. The Port Mercer Canal House, where participants would dramatize life along the working Delaware–Raritan Canal at the turn of the century
2. The Kuser Farm Mansion, where participants might imagine the response to the first movie with sound in the year 1928
3. The New Jersey State Museum in Trenton, where participants would reenact the Potters' Strike of 1923

Every community has a multitude of possibilities that an enterprising teacher or theatre company can exploit, often at little or no extra cost. Workshops may be one-time events or represent a high point in the semester; either way, they are examples of the unique value that a special space has to offer.

19

Clowning and Circus Arts

The clown and the child. *(Courtesy of Andrew Burnstine, Clown and Barbara Walz, photographer.)*

There is a mutual love affair between the clown and the child—a love affair that the adult permits.

—TONY MONTANARO, MIME

*U*ntil a few years ago the circus arts were enjoyed by the American public primarily as popular entertainment and spectacle. Audiences were drawn by the skill of the performers, the dazzling feats of the aerialists, the wild animal acts, the comic characters, and the traditional sounds and smells of the big tent. The circus possesses a special mystique, different from all of the other performing arts. Beyond that, it is the only form that can be labeled family entertainment. With the sixties and seventies, however, came changes. The three- and four-ring spectacular was giving way to the more intimate one-ring show. The word *acts* in the advertisements was replaced by the more felicitous term *arts,* which suggested a change in status. By the late eighties the changes could be perceived in many quarters but chiefly in the involvement of the circus performer in education, in the arts therapies, and even in the church. Values that extended beyond entertainment were getting recognition.

Because of these changes, clowning and circus arts may now claim a legitimate place in a textbook on creative drama. In a narrow sense, one might question the rationale for this inclusion, but in a broader sense, there is justification, since circus arts and creative drama share many of the same values and goals. Among them are use of the body, stimulation of the imagination, the development of spatial awareness, expression through pantomime, self-confidence as the performer's skills are honed, and teamwork involving trust and cooperation.

Children's theatre requires competence in all of these areas; the folk and fairy tales, as well as many dramatized events in history, include fencing, juggling, clowning, acrobatics, magic acts, and dancing. Children, playing these same stories creatively, also face the need to develop these skills, if not on a high professional level, at least to whatever degree they are able.

Although few classroom and physical education teachers have studied the circus arts, interest in this form of entertainment has grown, until today there are many trained performers and performer/teachers in the United States. Although they tend to be located in our larger cities, it is in the cities that we find the greatest number of children for whom these skills are proving their value. They are children with learning problems, children for whom English is a second language, school dropouts, "hotel kids," adolescents with a poor self-image, and boys and girls "at risk" in suburban as well as inner-city neighborhoods. Many of them have responded so positively to the challenge of the circus arts that special schools and classes have been established to serve their needs. Not only is there a record of success among these young people in their ability to acquire new skills, but a belief in themselves is credited for improvement in academic areas.

This has brought with it the respect of their peers, for the ability to ride a unicycle, walk on stilts, juggle, and perform difficult acrobatic acts, both alone and in groups, elicits a type of admiration that these young people have never before experienced. Just as drama enriches the lives of the handicapped, so can clowning and circus arts bring satisfaction to others.

These changes, incidentally, have brought a new vitality to the circus. The concept of the single ring, where individual performers, lost in the three-ring spectacular, can once more be recognized for their unique abilities, is spreading. Some clowns have taken to the streets. Others have joined groups like The Flying Karamazov Brothers, The Big Apple Circus in New York, the Pickle Family Circus, the Vaudeville Nouvelle in San Francisco, and the Cirque du Soleil of Montreal. A recent article in *Backstage* called them "The New Vaudevillians,"

Learning to juggle. (Courtesy of Jean Paul Jenack, Westbury, N.Y.)

clowns who are bringing back the traditions of the past in productions that combine virtuosity with modern technical equipment and lighting. Michael Pedretti, director of Movement International (MI) in Philadelphia, identified their common traits as follows:

1. *Continuity*—Sketches linked together in a plot with character, as opposed to an unrelated series of short pieces;
2. *Audience Interaction*—Members of the audience joining performers, and performers going down into the audience, rather than maintaining a separation;
3. *A Sense of Joy*—A treatment of the madness of life as buffoonery;
4. *Politics*—Using performance to make points, something the theatre has always done but the circus rarely;
5. *Virtuosity*—The development of at least three skills to perfection, no amateurishness permitted.[1]

A new aesthetic, dependent on the artistry of the performance, rather than on pyrotechnics, is replacing many of the traditional animal acts. In some cases, animals no longer appear at all. The sideshow, once a popular attraction, has been questioned and abandoned in a new awareness of human feelings and a respect for the dignity of the individual.

Clowning is also being employed very successfully as one of the arts therapies, and special centers, staffed by certified teachers and therapists, are being established. Circus performers, once living in a subculture outside society, now work side by side with other professionals, at least to the extent that their travel schedules permit. Today, career clowns may be found teaching in universities and elementary schools, assisting ministers in churches, and going out into the communities where they interact with children, serving in capacities that could not have been imagined a generation ago. But are these changes wholly without precedent? Perhaps the best way to examine the circus arts is in their historical context.

Historical Overview of the Circus Arts

From earliest times the clown has played an important part in human celebration, religion, and entertainment. Clowns have participated in sacred rites and have been permitted special privileges, including the right to criticize society, use coarse language, and perform vulgar tricks. At the same time, some cultures have believed them to have sacred healing powers. Since antiquity clowns have been found in the temples, on the streets, and in the palaces of

---

1. "Clowns on Center Stage: The New Vaudevillians," *Backstage*, June 3, 1988, section 2, p. 22A.

kings; on the stage as performers and in play scripts, where their role advances the plot and provides comic relief. "The clown's first appearance on the historical stage can be safely dated around the year 2270 B.C., at the beginning of the reign of Pepi II, a pharaoh of the Egyptian Sixth Dynasty."[2]

Clowns appeared in Greece in the first century and went on to enliven the Western world, sometimes as solo performers and sometimes as members of a troupe. Their popularity reached new heights in Rome, where their skill as a mime, an acrobat, a singer, or a dancer pleased the crowds and inspired the writers of comedy. Clowns and the circus were often thought of as having a symbiotic relationship, although the clown also performed occasionally alone. After the fall of Rome clowns reappeared as wandering players, displaced persons traveling from one market place to another, offering their wares—tumbling, juggling, telling stories, and singing songs—for whatever coins were tossed to them. Sometimes they made out well, sometimes not, but their independence and resilience kept them going through good times and bad. In 1555 a play entitled *Jack Juggler* entertained audiences in England with a character who was to appear in many plays thereafter, even to the present. This was in the role of practical joker, whose wit not only affected the outcome of the plot but taught a lesson to all those who encountered him.

The fools and jesters of the Middle Ages and Renaissance were the special property of kings and noblemen. These clowns lived well, performed at their masters' pleasure, and were often regarded as wise men, savants whose advice was sought in matters of state and romance. Often grotesque, brightly costumed, and highly prized, they occupied a unique status on into the seventeenth century. Probably the best known clowns were members of the commedia dell'arte, the Italian acting troupes, who toured Western Europe for nearly two centuries. From the middle of the sixteenth to the middle of the eighteenth century, they delighted audiences with their improvised performances. One thing distinguished them from other comedians; they created the roles of particular characters, whom they always played: Harlequin, Pantalone, Capitano, the Inamorata. The actors developed and polished their characters, who, in the case of the comic characters, performed stock tricks known as "lazzi."

Elizabethan England loved the theatre in all of its forms; hence the wandering players and minstrels enjoyed another period of relative prosperity. Clowns and acrobats performed on the streets of London and in the courts, while playwrights wrote parts for jesters in their plays. Shakespeare's fools were integral to the plots, requiring often, in addition, special skills such as the ability to sing and play musical instruments.

In France, Italy, and England during the Restoration, the clown continued to be an important character but more often as social critic than entertainer. Since 1792 America has had its clowns, though the majority learned their craft in Europe. Grimaldi, Durang, Dan Rice, Harrigan, and Hart are names that strike a

---

2. Lowell Swortzell, *Here Come the Clowns* (New York: Viking Press, 1978), p. 8.

familiar note to Americans today. In fact, "Joey," the nickname given to a clown, comes from Joseph Grimaldi.

The clown's counterpart in the Orient was a beloved entertainer, singer, storyteller, and purveyor of the culture. He could be found in both the classical drama and in the folk theatre of India, China, and Japan. Indeed, he was referred to throughout the Chow Dynasty, from 1000 to 300 B.C. He may be seen today in the Peking Opera. His appearance in Japan came later, in the Kyogen plays of the twelfth century and in the Kabuki. Clown characters were used to provide relief from the violence, and the stylized form of the Japanese dramas. Clowns and puppets, often performing together, are still to be seen in theatres throughout Asia, although changes there are also taking place as in the Western world.

In America we recognize three popular types of clowns: the white-faced traditional clown derived from Pierrot of France and the commedia dell'arte of Italy (sometimes described as the "classy clown"); the Auguste or character clown, originating in Germany, but known throughout Europe as a simple, well-meaning fellow with a red nose, big feet, and bald head; and the Grotesque, or tramp, whose physical characteristics are exaggerated through costume and padding. As to makeup, it is generally known that a clown's face is his or her personal property, designed by him or her, and may not be copied or used by another during the clown's lifetime. Marcel Marceau's "Bip," Charlie Chaplin's little tramp, the Marx Brothers, and the familiar comedians of stage, screen, and television, have continued to entertain the public, thus carrying on an ancient tradition in a high tech world.

Although we are aware of this changing world of entertainment, the aspect of greatest interest to the teacher and student is the appearance of the clown in the classroom. Viewed in the past as storyteller, conduit of the culture, social critic, nonjudgmental friend of the child, and sometimes wise man, the clown's role as educator/therapist should not astonish us. The clown's skills have been found to teach children where conventional methods have failed. Although these skills are popular with most children who have the opportunity of learning them, it is in the populations that have not succeeded in mastering the basic requirements of education that clowning and the circus arts are proving most successful.

The Circus Arts in Education

Some startling facts emerge in a study of circus arts in modern education. Although it is generally known that some schools and colleges offer them on an after-school or extracurricular basis, the extent to which they are being offered is not. Today, according to Jean Paul Jenack, there are more than one hundred fifty colleges and universities with well-developed programs in circus skills, with many of the courses offered for credit.

Since there are several approaches to education in the circus arts, one way of examining them is to view a few of the successful and better-known companies individually. Some approach the work from a cultural or performing-arts point of view; some from a physical education base; still others as entertainment. Recently, with recognition of the psychological values in clowning, education and therapy are stressed. Some companies emphasize production, preparing and sending out teachers' study guides in advance of a performance and giving a follow-up session afterward in the classroom.

Other groups have schools or studios, which enroll children as well as adults in a carefully structured curriculum. Still other circus professionals work closely in or with the schools, using the circus arts as tools for reaching boys and girls who show little motivation in academic areas. One thing the new circus professionals have in common is a strong academic background, often including a graduate degree. It would be a mistake to think that circus performers of the past were roustabouts, or runaways, lured by a romantic notion of life under the big tent. They were not formally educated, for a variety of reasons, but this did not mean that they were ignorant or illiterate. To the contrary, they were highly educated in discrete areas, generally taught by their families, with daily practice for perfection. The tradition was for families to hand down their expertise, if the child showed promise. Education began at an early age, much like the training of the ballet dancer. Whether the young performer followed in his or her parents' footsteps as aerialist, equestrian, clown, or animal trainer, early acquaintance with the field was necessary to ensure success in a demanding and often dangerous profession.

Formal schooling was out of the question because of the heavy touring schedule, which made regular attendance impossible. As to mathematics and science, basic elements were mastered through the rigging of tents and wires, where errors of judgment could be fatal. Animal trainers in those days did not mistreat their animals anymore than their counterparts of today do, according to former circus performers. On the contrary, a close relationship of trust is essential not only for the successful execution of their acts but for their lives. The trainer of fifty to seventy-five years ago had no knowledge of veterinary science, but sensitivity, common sense, and experience were then, as now, vital to partners in the act, whether they be dogs, horses, elephants, or big cats. Performers of an earlier period belonged to a subculture with practical know-how and intuitive judgment. Released from the confinement of this subculture, today's performers not only are able to acquire a broad background, including the liberal arts, but as a result are allowed to teach in the schools or establish schools of their own. The first circus arts programs to appear in American schools were actually in the mid-twenties, but there was no further record of activity until the thirties. This took the form of magic shows, popular as entertainment both in and outside the classroom. Again, this did not lead to any well-developed programs in the circus arts. After World War II, circus skills were introduced into physical education departments as new body-building techniques. By the eighties a combination of many of these techniques reappeared and was followed by a pattern of real growth. In England circus arts were equestrian

*N*ational Circus Project instructor John Foss coaching unicycle act for Children's Village circus. *(Courtesy of Jean Paul Jenack; photograph by Mary Fennell.)*

based, whereas in the Eastern European countries troupes worked for excellence in professional performance. The trend in America, on the other hand, has been to join in partnership with educators and community leaders. In recent years psychologists and the clergy have found therapeutic values in this area.

In addition, the changing times demand more than a liberal education provides; many circus specialists seek graduate study in business, sports medicine, kinesiology, science, law, and veterinary medicine. Whereas the artists of yesterday were well educated within their own culture, many of today's artists are acquiring an education comparable or, in some instances, superior to that of the average American citizen. This means that the teacher/performer or performer/teacher, as the case may be, is equipped to work in the elementary schools and high schools with other professionals, understanding their goals and problems; to negotiate contracts; to be a partner in therapeutic programs; and to be a respected member of a fine arts faculty in a university or conservatory.

The Big Apple Circus

One company that fits the description of the new circus is The Big Apple Circus in New York. It was founded in 1977 by Paul Binder, a graduate of

Dartmouth College with a master's degree in business administration from Columbia University. His knowledge of the circus came from Le Nouveau Circus de Paris, which inspired him to bring the European one-ring circus back to America and to found a school, which he did, called the New York School for Circus Arts. It is a nonprofit organization, with support from foundation grants, government agencies, corporations, private organizations, and the box office. Binder's productions were an instant success. Very few animals were used in lieu of developing human performance skills; the small size of the ring made for excellent visibility, hence audiences' appreciation of this new approach and style. The participants include some professionals and many street people. One of his most interesting acts early on was called "The Back Street Flyers," a group of teenagers, whose first experience with the circus was being in it. "Street kids," said Binder in describing them, "have an unmatchable energy, which translates into something that can change their circumstances, and make them the most highly motivated, most responsive and responsible students you could find. For years street wisdom has had it that the only ways out of the ghetto were crime and professional sports. Now the circus has become an unlikely addition to the list of opportunities."[3]

In his classes for students preparing to perform professionally and those for whom the circus arts are an interest, Binder included the following subjects, all taught by experts:

> tumbling, partnered acrobatics, ensemble improvisation, ballet, individual skills (unicycle, juggling, object balancing, wire work, and physical conditioning)

Binder's teachers' guides, to be used after children have attended a performance, include suggestions such as the following:

> *Making a clown mask*
> *Writing about the character*   for whom the mask was created
> *Writing a story about the circus,*   using a "lead in" or "one liner" like "the
>   ringmaster blew his whistle and I knew it was my turn to enter the ring"; or
>   "a dark figure was lurking outside the big top; quietly he moved toward the
>   giant elephant with a handful of peanuts"; or "the circus performers were
>   about to begin their show when—"
> *Vocabulary* (words like *resplendent, breathtaking, pachyderm, extrava-*
>   *ganza, pantomime, equestrian,* etc.)
> *Crossword puzzles,*   in which all words relate to the circus
> *A study of exotic animals*

Lecture-demonstration programs round out the multiofferings of The Big Apple Circus. Not only has this group won many awards and citations but it is dignified

---

3. Mimeographed materials.

by an annual month-long residency in Lincoln Center's Walter Damrosch Park, next to the Metropolitan Opera building.

Le Cirque du Soleil

A circus that has taken Canada and the United States by storm is Montreal's Le Cirque du Soleil. Founded in 1980, it is praised not only for its brilliance but also for its National Circus School, enrolling children aged eleven to seventeen and adults, both those interested in the circus as a career and those enjoying it as an avocation. Le Cirque du Soleil eliminated animals altogether in favor of acrobatics, choreographed movement, mime, and sketches that demonstrate artistry of the highest order. The stated goals of the company are:

Discipline
Physical coordination
Grace and balance
Teamwork
Communication
Creativity and imagination

The point is made in the program that acrobatics is not just performing feats of skill, although these things are important, but the expression of feelings. This attitude represents the philosophy of the new aesthetic.

Reg Bolton's Suitcase Circus

Leaving North America for the moment, let us take a look at the work of Reg Bolton, a British clown and certified teacher. Bolton has worked in England, Scotland, Wales, and the United States; at present he is in Australia. His work in America has consisted of short-term residencies and individual performances and workshops on the East Coast; however, his book *Circus in a Suitcase,* published here in 1982 by New Plays, Inc., has the distinction of being the only text directed to the teacher and community leader who want to teach clowning and circus arts to young people. Bolton does not encourage children to attempt dangerous acts, but he believes that many skills can be mastered by children with benefits and pleasure as a result.

Bolton and his wife, Annie Stainer, a dancer, ran the Long Green Theatre Company in Edinburgh for several years during the seventies. While there, he established Scotland's first Circus School. One of his most successful projects, however, was the Pilton Circus Club (1979), a community enterprise involving teenagers who were not "joiners." He attributed its success to the strong structure of self-discipline that developed within the group as members worked together in a constructive way. By the end of the first year the group was giving two or three shows a month for children, old people, and at local galas. The "mums" made the costumes and the dads built the stilts. By summer the youthful performers were ready for a tour of western Scotland. "Whereas back home the name Pilton was synonymous with trouble; far from home the name came to be associated with the aspiration, enterprise, and success of this group."[4] The Pilton Circus Club gave the boys and girls the opportunity of gaining new experiences, and doing something exciting and worthwhile with their time was the expressed attitude of the community.

Bolton founded a similar community project in Flint, Wales, in 1980. This was a new concept in Flint, but within the next four years it had spread into twelve towns in England and Scotland. Bolton listed the advantages of amateur circus troupes:

Adults, teenagers and children can all work together.
There's something for everybody to do, from grannies to toddlers.
It provides scope for the clever, the quiet, the bold and the noisy.
You can work indoors and out.
You can really put your neighborhood on the map.
It's fun.[5]

Bolton's preparation for this work began with his education as an elementary school teacher in England when "project learning" was a popular technique. Getting a class interested in a topic and exploring it with them analytically, historically, creatively, environmentally, and so on was the approach that Bolton said is ideally suited to the circus. Furthermore, he believes that the circus arts and acrobatics are far more suitable for schools than are Olympic gymnastics. Group skills he thinks are preferable to individual work for the young, since teamwork, grace, solidity, and buffoonery are realistic goals rather than striving for medals and trying to win top place.

Among the skills that Bolton said young people can develop are:

Acrobatics—the forward roll
   the backward roll
   headstands
   cartwheels
   handsprings
   somersaults
   the crab
   pyramids
   two-person balances
Animal acts (fake)—costumes and mime to create a horse
   the snake charmer; a trick, in which a cobra is pulled out of a basket
Magic

4. Reg Bolton, *Circus in a Suitcase* (Bethel, Conn.; New Plays, 1982), p. 8.
5. Ibid., p. 11.

Juggling—one to four balls (beginning with bean bags)
  Indian clubs
  rings
Stilts—footed tie-on stilts (the usual kind of any height)
  Chinese stilts (no feet, making it necessary for the wearer to keep on the move)
Animal acts (real)—using your own pet, if he has been taught tricks
  the parade (some animals, especially dogs, enjoy being in costume and marching in a parade with their masters and mistresses)
Giants—a smaller person on the shoulders of a taller
A clown—any of the ones described
Clown troupes—several clowns who have worked up acts together
Unicycles
Strong men—faked, but impressive
Wrestlers
Hoop work—diving through hoops, rolling hoops, etc.
Roller skates and skate boards
Balancing acts
Tight rope (no higher than two feet from the ground)
The parade with ringmaster, music, costumes, and all participants

Once a student has learned a skill, such as walking on stilts, for example, he or she is ready to do something with it, and this may be drama. Focus, concentration, imagination, and timing all come together, channeling energy and turning what may have been disruptive behavior into a performance of skill and charm. The shy, the brash, and the nonachiever are enabled to reach levels of success not reached before, through the power of clowning and the circus arts. Bolton and his wife both perform, but it is through teaching and community projects that their influence has been strongest.

The National Circus Project

The National Circus Project of Westbury, New York, is a division of Circus Education Specialists, Inc., "a non-profit, tax exempt organization dedicated to the preservation of circus skills and arts in America. . . . Its aim is to foster an interest in the circus arts by providing relevant educational programs for schools, libraries, and other educational organizations throughout the United States."[6] One way of achieving this is through an Artist-in-Residence program. Professional circus artist/teachers work in schools with physical education and/or performing arts faculty, offering workshops for students and teachers. In elementary schools, workshops include the entire student body rather than selected groups.

Activities are carefully planned for motor skill and cognitive skill levels according to age, grade, and abilities. However, an important point is made by

6. Brochure of the National Circus Project.

the staff that the same skills can be taught on all levels, but the same degree of achievement is not expected of the young child that can be expected of the eighth grader. Introductory, intermediate, and long-term programs are available. Introductory programs include scarf and ball juggling, plate spinning, and devil stick manipulation. Intermediate workshops include ring, club, and nontraditional object juggling; lariat manipulation; stilt walking; rola bola; tumbling; acrobatics; and unicycling. Long-term programs include all of the above but may also teach tight wire and slack rope walking, vaulting, and trapeze. In addition, there are expressive movement, character, mime, and clowning skills. Although the teaching is highly disciplined, it is the process rather than the product that is emphasized.

Jean Paul Jenack, founder and executive director of the National Circus Project, was a professional performer from childhood until a serious accident in 1973 caused him to seek physiotherapy. (He is quick to point out that the injury was not circus related.) Discouraged with the lack of progress he was making with conventional treatment, he tried applying some of the circus techniques he knew and found them effective. For the next decade, Jenack studied trends in physical education and school curriculum, suspecting that circus skills had an unrealized potential. The result was the founding of the National Circus Project in 1984. Four years later, he had a staff of eight full-time instructors, including himself and his partner, Meryl Schaffer; six part-time teachers; another six with special abilities; and some to be called on, if and when needed.

Jenack's first teaching position was at Nassau Community College on Long Island. Unlike most teachers, who move from lower to higher levels, Jenack went from college to high school and elementary levels. His usual school visit begins with a performance in the gymnasium or auditorium the first thing in the morning, with the rest of the day spent in working with individual classes. Unlike games and sports, circus skills are noncompetitive and individualized. For most children they are a new experience, so that everyone, regardless of age, is starting from square one. According to John Foss, the National Circus Project's senior field instructor, students with motor problems or learning disabilities often excel, even though they may have to work a little harder than the others. Jenack said that the underachievers in academic areas are usually the ones who do the best work because they have no record of failure. Circus skills have also proved to be effective diagnostic tools, and remedial activities for certain motor-learning problems. They offer children an opportunity to express themselves in a new way, using the body rather than speech. Meryl Schaffer summed it up in the following statement:

> By integrating circus skills with physical education, children can have the best of both worlds, participating in a cultural arts experience that helps them grow and improve, artistically and physically.[7]

7. Brochure.

The Starlight Foundation

Different from all of the preceding is an organization called The Starlight Foundation, dedicated to performance for, and work with, terminally ill children in New York. It may or may not include clowning. The purpose of the foundation is to grant wishes for children for whom there is little time left and for whom there is no hope for recovery. As far as it is possible and realistic, the wishes are granted. For instance, the wish for a pony by a child unable to ride would not be granted, whereas a trip to Disneyland or the Ringling Brothers' headquarters in

"Granpa Giggles" delights audiences of all ages. (*Courtesy of Andy Burnstine; photograph by Gideon Lewin.*)

Florida could be. Andrew Burnstine is a popular entertainer because of his skill as a clown and his love for children.

Andrew Burnstine

Burnstine, in his clown's persona of "Grandpa Giggles," works regularly with the foundation. In some ways, Burnstine is the quintessential "new clown." He has a bachelor's degree in the liberal arts with a concentration in theatre and business administration, a master's degree in theatre, two years at the Stella Adler Studio, and a diploma from Clown College in Sarasota. Following his graduation from Clown College he traveled with Ringling Brothers for a year. Burnstine also worked with the Pixie Judy Troupe, a touring children's theatre company, in the Northeast; was artistic director of Poinciana Children's Theatre in Palm Beach, Florida; and has performed with small circuses such as Bertolini Brothers European Circus, Circus Kingdom, and Pan American Circus.

Celebration Mime Theatre

Although Tony Montanaro's Celebration Mime Theatre is technically not part of the circus world, mime is so closely related to it, and Montanaro so involved in the art of clowning, that his work deserves mention. Indeed, Tony Montanaro considers himself a clown, as the excerpts that follow state. It was during the sixties that the art of mime became popular in this country. At that time Montanaro was a popular and respected performer in children's theatre. Later he played to adult audiences, who admired his skill and appreciated his particular brand of humor. In the seventies he moved his studio from New York to Maine, where he felt he could work more peacefully away from the tensions and distractions of the city.

Although he gave up performing on a regular basis, he accepted residencies of varying lengths on college campuses, where he was a master teacher of the art of mime. The move to Maine enabled him to expand his school and shift his emphasis to teaching and preparing young artists for a professional career in the theatre. Increasingly, his work and the work of his students has shown the influence of the circus. His touring troupe, Celebration Mime Theatre, represents the conservatory approach—education of the young adult in mime, acrobatics, juggling, sounds that suggest insects, animals and mechanical equipment, and commedia dell'arte techniques. Performances are given in Portland's Theatre of Fantasy, an intimate space, seating eighty persons, another resemblance to the "new circus."

Summary

Tony Montanaro summarized the special relationship that exists between the child and the clown in an article, "Ramblings on the Clown." In it he made some cogent points that most of us have not considered but would not dispute.

The link between the clown and the child is a very intimate one, and is nearly as powerful as the relationship of parent to child or brother to sister; it is very special and very private.

I think that the clown is the first adult that the child dreams of being, after dreaming of being just like Mommy and Daddy. . . .

Why does the child love the clown so much?

A child feels a personal victory if he can cause an adult to laugh joyously at something he says or does. . . . The clown is the escape valve for human nature; the pressure point that gives. In fact, the adult likes the clown, too, because he rather likes the clown representing his mistakes; underneath it all, the adult would like to admit his weaknesses. The clown represents the middle ground between two worlds.

The child's vocabulary is limited, but his visual sense is keen. Seeing, at this young stage, is more exciting than hearing. The clown falls on his face, opens a tiny umbrella in a giant rainfall, loses his shoe, walks into a wall while watching a pretty person pass by, is chased by a duck. The clown is like a bright bird of paradise, preening and strutting, making the best of things, and not caring who is looking.

Why do clowns love children?

For one thing, the child is more responsive to his antics than older folks. I like being a clown because, like a child, I want to be appreciated. Clowns need children to survive.[8]

Whether we call them the "new vaudevillians" or the "new circus," there is a conspicuous break with the past. The spectacular is being replaced by the intimate performance, whose company is committed to the community and to education. Not all companies are following this trend, but some are in sufficient numbers to declare that there is, indeed, a change.

One noteworthy aspect of the circus of the eighties is the network that has evolved. The field is still small enough for the artists to know each other and the philosophy on which their programs are based. Therefore, questions asked of one company lead easily from one to another, until the desired information is found. Many new books and articles on the circus arts are being written and published not just by scholars but by the performers themselves. What was previously enjoyed by the general public as popular entertainment is now viewed for its other contributions to education and human service. In demystifying the circus, without destroying the romance, performer/teachers have given it a new dimension in which all stand to gain.

First welcomed by the physical education departments of our schools and colleges for its body-building techniques and later by the theatre departments for its aesthetic appeal, the circus arts are now finding acceptance in the education and psychology departments as well. No longer considered trivial or "fringe" entertainment, the circus arts have earned a legitimate niche in the academic community. Still something of a hybrid, they take a holistic approach to

8. "Ramblings on the Clown," reprint from *Mime Times,* November 1976, pp. 1–2.

education that is embraced by many modern theorists. In short, the circus arts are seen as both process and product, with some groups emphasizing the former; others, the latter, depending on philosophic commitment and local interests, needs, and priorities.

20 New Directions

Intergenerational Drama. *(Courtesy of Milton Polsky, director.)*

The life of the arts, far from being an interruption,
a distraction, in the life of the nation, is very close
to the center of a nation's purpose—and is a test
of the quality of a nation's civilization.

—JOHN F. KENNEDY

Many changes have taken place in drama and theatre education within the past few years. Whether or not they indicate a trend is uncertain, but the fact that they are happening in all sections of the country suggests that there are definitely new directions in the education and practices of creative drama teachers. Although some of these changes can be attributed to the economy, there are other influences at work. The most conspicuous are the introduction of programs for and with the handicapped, which grew out of a concerned legislation in the midseventies; the use of drama as a teaching tool; the growing number of state-mandated programs for education in the theatre arts; better articulated school and community resources; more artists in the schools; and new research in the field. Recognition of minorities continues, though at a slower pace since funding for programs serving them has been reduced. Many arts programs have suffered similar cutbacks, but as a result, we are witnessing some highly imaginative ways of reaching children, including the circus arts and new community programs.

Newer Programs

The newer programs are sponsored by museums, libraries, community and recreation centers, civic theatres, and churches. As recreation and leisure time activities, drama classes and clubs have always enjoyed popularity. These recreational activities are important for a variety of reasons, not the least of them being that they are elected "for fun." Many leaders doing outstanding work in such programs today hold degrees in recreation and theatre; some volunteers are teachers, dancers, and writers who conduct workshops in the arts because they, also, enjoy them. We find colleges and universities around the country touring plays on a much larger scale than ever before, in order to provide wholesome entertainment for children in concert with the education of students in theatre departments.

The Children's Theatre Association of America, a division of the American Theatre Association, had been instrumental since 1944 in bringing leaders together, holding conferences and disseminating information through its publications. When the American Theatre Association ceased operation in 1986, the

Children's Theatre Association and the Secondary School Theatre Association formed a new organization, the American Alliance for Theatre and Education (AATE). National conventions continue to be held every August, providing programs that demonstrate work being done in the various regions of the country, as well as talks, symposia, and panel discussions on topics of interest to teachers and leaders, kindergarten through grade twelve. Workshops in creative drama and puppetry, under the direction of outstanding leaders, are often planned before the opening of the conference, in response to the members' demand for further specialized training. Although the principal interest at present is the introduction of drama education into the school curriculum, there is a growing enthusiasm for its inclusion in camps, hospitals, and special education classes. Reports on research in the field indicate the effectiveness of this aspect of drama as a social and educational technique.

During the past two decades a number of experimental and pilot projects have been initiated in the arts. Some of them have been funded by state arts councils, some by private foundations, and some by interested organizations such as PTAs. All have a common goal: to bring the arts to the children of communities in which little has been done or where more exposure to the arts is desired and to bring the arts to the handicapped. Such projects have not been confined to any particular regions; they have been nationwide. Nor have they followed identical patterns.

An example of a particularly extensive project was the Arts in General Education program, financed by the John D. Rockefeller III Fund, for the eight thousand-pupil school system of University City, a suburb of Saint Louis. In this program, painting, music, photography, dance, poetry, drama, and other visual and performing arts were integrated into the curriculum from kindergarten through the twelfth grade. The major objective of the program was to give children experience in the arts and to increase their knowledge of the arts. In-school participation, field trips, and exhibitions were among the experiences offered. One problem discovered by the evaluators initially was a general feeling of inadequacy on the part of the educators. Because few teachers have had enough training and experience to feel comfortable with the arts, they did not introduce a variety of arts activities into their classrooms on any regular basis. Moreover, arts education, particularly in the upper grades, is often considered a separate area and is segregated from other studies, if not neglected.

Through the financial support of the Rockefeller fund, the community support of the University City School Board and the staff and resources of the Central Midwestern Regional Educational Laboratory (CEMREL), an extensive educational program was carried on over a three-year period. Both specialists and classroom teachers participated in an effort to realize present and long-term goals, with the result that many of the ideals and objectives of the three-year program have become a part of the University City Arts Program.

The CEMREL's long-range curriculum program, including drama/theatre for children, was founded in the hope that its materials and philosophy would have a lasting effect on education throughout the United States. The CEMREL is reported to be the first educational laboratory established under the provisions of the Elementary and Secondary Education Act of 1965 (ESEA), which included all of the arts in its program. An example of a citywide experiment is Arts Partners in New York. Carol Sterling, director, adds new companies and artists to this highly successful program each year. Newsletters and reports are published on a regular basis and sent to concerned agencies and citizens.

This chapter does not purport to enumerate or describe programs in detail but simply states that they exist both at the state level and in institutions of higher learning. The spread of activity is impressive, but there is no single pattern or area of emphasis. *Coming to Our Senses, The Significance of the Arts in American Education,* generally referred to as The Rockefeller Report of 1977 (discussed later in this chapter), indicated strong public support for the arts, but the present state of the economy does not augur well for their growth in the immediate future. Nevertheless, imaginative steps have been taken, and it is to be hoped that new types of arts programs will be designated in the near future.

Although the arts in America are not yet included as a significant part of public education, such efforts as these represent positive steps in the direction of constructive change in the curriculum. Drama, a relative newcomer, is finding recognition as an art that contributes to the emotional, intellectual, and social development of the child, with values to be derived from active participation on all levels.

Artist-in-residence. *(Courtesy of Milton Polsky; photograph by Ken Korsh.)*

The Arts-Centered Schools

The Mead School in Byram, Connecticut, attracted national attention in 1977 when it was featured in an article in the *Saturday Review* entitled "Why Children Should Draw."[1] The unique character of this school lay in its belief in the arts as basic to education. The Mead catalog stated that learning is multisensory. "Children need to touch, taste, see, talk," and to that end it is suggested that they should follow a curriculum that gives the arts and traditional subjects equal status. In fact, the arts in a sense are predominant. "Art gets the largest space here," according to Mead's director, who explained that a child uses his or her mind in concert with the hands and eyes. Through experiential learning (the arts), the child reaches the symbolic (traditional). This small private school, after fifteen years, was able to point to scores at or above Standard Achievement Test (SAT) averages in every subject.

The *Saturday Review* article also cited some other schools that had embarked on innovative arts programs. Project IMPACT, begun in 1970 and located in five areas, lasted only a few years but developed into other institutions like the Magnet Arts School in Eugene, Oregon, and The Eastgate School in Columbus, Ohio. In these schools, and in The Magic Mountain School in Berkeley, California, the emphasis was placed on the role of the arts in the development of human capacities, rather than on arts education as traditionally taught. The magnet schools, with their alternative curricula, often provide more time for the arts than the more traditional public schools.

Creative Drama in the Camp

Except in the arts camp, drama/theatre is rarely one of the more important activities of the camp program. Camps exist primarily to give city children an experience in group living in an outdoor setting. An opportunity to engage in a variety of sports is provided, with nature study, music, arts and crafts, and drama, as well as other activities from which to choose. Because of this broad emphasis, children should not be expected to spend long hours indoors, in rehearsals, but rather to enjoy drama and share the results of their work in occasional informal programs. Creative drama is an ideal activity for campers of all ages and backgrounds. Pantomime, improvisation, and simple out-of-door pageantry can contribute both to the participants and to those occasions when the group comes together for programs. Full productions with scenery and costumes have no place in camp; the drama counselor might better prepare by studying creative drama techniques so as to be able to work informally with campers of all ages, rather than formally for an audience. Class and rehearsal periods should be short and flexible. This, however, does not mean that time should be wasted or results

1. Roger M. Williams, *Saturday Review* 4, no. 23 (September 1977): 10–16.

sloppy. No activity brings satisfaction unless it is looked upon with respect; hence, informal drama, seriously undertaken, has as much to offer the camp as it has the community center or school.

Workshops and Training

Workshops in creative drama are held in the United States each year under a variety of sponsorships. Some are part of the summer school offerings of universities and colleges. Others are sponsored by organizations such as the American Alliance for Theatre and Education, the Association for Childhood Education International, and the National Recreation Association. Still others are among the in-service courses for public school teachers held after school or on Saturdays. The consortium of arts organizations in a city is also an effective way of bringing classroom teachers together to work with a master teacher. Cleveland, Ohio, is a prime example of this approach. Although surveys have been made from time to time in an effort to determine the amount and kind of training being offered by educational institutions throughout the country, it would be difficult to list or assess the numbers and types of workshops conducted by the alternative institutions and organizations mentioned. It is significant, however, that they seem to be on the increase and that hundreds of teachers and leaders take part in them each year for the purpose of broadening their own backgrounds and adding another dimension to their programs.

Most successful seem to be the workshops that include demonstrations with children and participation in acting on the adult level. Reading, lectures, and discussion are to be taken for granted, but practical laboratory experience is essential for any study of the arts. It has been my experience that the class members most reluctant to participate in drama in the beginning have always mentioned it first when evaluating the course. Only a concentrated workshop, or a semester's class, permits enough hours to include all of these activities. The acquisition of fine technical skills should not be expected, for techniques are a developmental process, attained over a much longer period of time spent in practice and study.

The Naropa Institute Teacher Re-Training Program in Boulder, Colorado, is one of a number of programs designed to bring the teacher into a closer and more comfortable relationship with the arts. Despite such excellent resources as Young Audiences and Artists-in-the-Schools, the classroom teacher often feels personally alienated and inadequate when it comes to continuing the programs they have initiated. Administrators, farther removed from these programs, have even greater difficulty relating to them; hence a good start all too often dies out before it has accomplished its purpose. At the Naropa Institute, the objectives are (1) to change the attitudes of nonarts teachers and administrators and (2) to introduce the arts to this population through direct personal experience. In its first summer session in 1977, eighty-five students from throughout the United

States were immersed in the performing arts; during the following summer, the visual arts were added.

The aim is not to provide either "recipes" or workshops in sensitivity training. Rather, it is to try to develop awareness and appreciation of the arts that will enable nonarts teachers to continue on their own after the summer is over. This includes the development of greater self-confidence; a basic understanding of the elements of the arts; an appreciation of the interrelatedness of the arts; a belief in the creative spirit in all human beings, not just the artist; and a desire to relate all of this to education.

A number of American universities have brought visiting lecturers in the arts from abroad and have established overseas study programs for credit. Among the universities that have done extensive work in the area of drama/theatre education are Northwestern University, which has brought Dorothy Heathcote and Gavin Bolton for several summer sessions on the Evanston campus; and New York University, which has conducted a program since 1973 at Bretton Hall College of Education in England. In Cleveland, in-service drama/theatre courses for area teachers have been held for the past few winters under a joint sponsorship of Cleveland State University, the Cleveland Playhouse, and the Board of Education. Many other colleges and universities in the West, the South, and in New England have sponsored teacher workshops and exchange programs for students in the field of drama education. Brian Way has spent much of the past several years traveling throughout the United States and Canada, lecturing and giving workshops on creative drama and on participation theatre. In addition to leaders already named, there have been other educators who have come for conferences and short-term engagements. Among them are Cecily O'Neill of the Inner London Education Authority, who is at present at the Ohio State University in Columbus; Tony Jackson, London; Margaret Faulkes-Jendyk, cofounder with Brian Way of the Theatre Centre in London and now on the faculty of the University of Alberta, Canada; John Hodgson of Bretton Hall; and Marian Lindkvist of Sesame in London. There have been additional programs in other foreign countries, but the ones mentioned here are among the very successful and are cited because of their content, common language, and duration.

With improved travel, American teachers have been able to meet with colleagues overseas and, on occasion, to lecture, give workshops, and to attend conferences and festivals—in short, to extend the perimeters of their own experience as no generation of educators has until now been able to do. This appears to be a trend in drama/theatre education, which can only enrich our offerings.

A valuable guide to resources in the field of educational drama is the *Theatre Resources Directory/Handbook*, prepared in 1980 by the Education Division of the National Endowment for the Arts. It was designed to help Artists-in-Schools coordinators for state arts agencies in locating and selecting theatre companies and resource persons that are capable of providing successful in-school theatre residencies. The fourfold purpose of the *Directory/Handbook* is to:

1. Provide descriptive information about those companies who have developed or are willing to develop programs for residencies in schools
2. Provide lists of individual theatre artists willing to participate in artist-in-residence programs in schools or communities
3. Provide companies with sample educational materials of a preperformance and postperformance nature
4. Provide in-school coordinators with examples of schedules for planning residencies and suggestions for curriculum materials related to theatre artists and performance groups

More than mention must be made of the 334-page Rockefeller Report released in the spring of 1977. Entitled *Coming to Our Senses: The Significance of the Arts in American Education,* it was by far the most comprehensive survey of the subject ever made in this country. A panel of experts for two years studied arts education in elementary schools, secondary schools, and colleges, with funding provided by the Office of Education, the National Endowment for the Arts, and several private foundations. Professional organizations assisted in the research, which revealed a widespread belief in the arts in education, despite inadequate programs in many areas. Among the ninety-eight recommendations that were made, the panel called for the creation of a National Center for Arts in Education and a federal agency to coordinate information about artists, funding, programs, and research; it also recommended that the existing federal council on the Arts and the Humanities carry out a ten-year strategy for art in education, in cooperation with the states.

The panel suggested that school districts allow students to earn credit for work done in community arts programs and that curricula should be expanded to include dance, film, drama, poetry, and design. In the area of teacher education and in-service training, the panel urged that all prospective teachers have experience in a variety of arts and learn how to relate them to each other and to other disciplines. The reception of the report was generally favorable, and some results have already taken place. One was the formation, in 1978, of a new organization called Arts, Education, and Americans, which aimed to:

1. Organize several regional conferences, in which there would be an opportunity to discuss the Rockefeller Report, develop specific plans for local or regional implementation, and to make recommendations toward the national plan
2. Maintain a speakers' bureau that would include panel members and others connected with the report
3. Establish a central communications center in the New York office
4. Promote distribution of the report
5. Participate in developing a national plan for the arts in education

As a private organization, Arts, Education, and Americans was designed to seek all possible means to foster the development of a national program for strengthening the role of the arts from kindergarten through college. One chapter suggested cooperation between schools and nonacademic institutions as a way of increasing funds that were available for the arts. In addition, the organization suggested that children's experiences could be enriched by making use of community resources such as museums, theatres, studios, film libraries, and local artists.

Ten years later a new book appeared, entitled "Can We Rescue the Arts for America's Children?" The author, Charles Fowler, took a pessimistic view of the implementation of the recommended suggestions. He discovered that many of these suggestions were not being followed and that others had been abandoned for lack of staff, facilities, or money. Teachers in the public schools often carried heavy loads, including the education of children for whom English is a second language. Although America's teachers have always had this problem with which to deal, today's teachers have many more students requiring remedial help. But teachers with no background in drama and theatre arts cannot see the possibilities of using it as a way of teaching the language arts and at the same time fulfilling the recommendations of the panel and the request of the public.

If it is true that it takes at least fifty years for a new idea to find acceptance, it is high time for drama to be included in the curriculum with the other arts. On the other hand, I am heartened by the fact that the numerous programs I have cited are being carried on with vigor, excitement, and a sense of purpose. The new directions have solid underpinnings that are neither trendy nor impractical. Winifred Ward gave us a new direction in the twenties; now, more than sixty-five years later, we are witnessing a phenomenon of growth as a result of her clarification of terms, goals, and values. They have not changed. Rather, they have pointed the way to a bright and creative future.

The American Association of Community Theatre (ACT) is a particularly active force in establishing contacts for its members in different parts of the United States and the world. The ACT embraces all areas: children's theatre, high school theatre, and adult theatre. It publishes a calendar listing theatre festivals in the United States and abroad; it assists Americans wanting to attend festivals overseas; and it assumes a responsibility for entertaining out-of-town and foreign visitors and showing them work of interest going on here.

The ASSITEJ is an international organization for children's theatre. The United States center was established in 1965. ASSITEJ holds a congress in a different country every three years, but American members meet annually during the American Alliance for Theatre and Education national convention. Among the values of belonging to the ASSITEJ are the opportunity it affords to meet with children's theatre artists in other parts of the world in a spirit of cooperation and sharing and to see children's theatre productions presented by companies of the member nations. Although formal theatre is not the primary concern of the teacher of creative drama, the ASSITEJ is mentioned here because it is an important organization to which many American teachers now belong, thus further enriching our field.

One of the most heartening developments in drama education was the position taken by the ATA in 1983; it was reported as follows in *Theatre News:* "The commission on Theatre Education of the American Theatre Association early in 1979 issued the following statement on general education."

That drama/theatre must be an integral part of general education and that at the same time such involvement should affirm the integrity of drama/theatre as an art form.

"Any consideration of drama/theatre in general education must:"

1. Recognize the arts as fundamental to the learning process;
2. Recognize drama/theatre as a major component of the arts;

Experiments with scale: oversize puppets and live actors. (Courtesy of Bread and Puppet Theatre, Glover, Vt.; photograph by Alex Williams.)

3. Acknowledge the values of studying drama/theatre as an art form in its own right as a significant part of general education;
4. Acknowledge the value of drama/theatre processes when skillfully applied as a pedagogical tool to facilitate learning in many areas of the curriculum.[2]

The Arts and the States

Paralleling this statement was the report of the Arts Task Force prepared by the National Conference of State Legislatures in 1981 and recommended for state action. Among the several proposals included in the report were the following:

Basic Education: Amend the state education act to redefine basic education to include arts education at the elementary and secondary levels.

In-Service Teacher Training: Make state funds available to interested school districts to provide in-service arts education training for elementary school teachers. Training programs should emphasize both arts experiences and appreciation, and integration of the arts into the educational curriculum as a means of teaching math, reading, science, and other basic subjects.

Gifted and Talented: Include children gifted and talented in the arts within categorical state funding of gifted and talented programs.

Schools for the Arts: Consider funding schools for the arts to provide intensive training opportunities for artistically gifted and talented school-age children. The schools may be organized as (1) summer schools for the arts, (2) schools where a substantial portion of the day is devoted to arts instruction, or (3) after-school arts instruction programs.[3]

Community Arts Agencies

In 1974 there were approximately 200 community arts agencies in the United States. By 1984 there were two thousand, and they are increasing. Most of these agencies were established through local initiative because citizens wanted arts programs in their own communities. The purpose, regardless of structure, is "mainstreaming the arts into all areas of the community—working with seniors, in the schools, with redevelopment, among many other areas. . . . Community arts agencies can be catalysts for new approaches to problems in urban and rural

2. *Theatre News* 15, no. 1 (January/February 1983): 1.
3. *Arts and the States* (A Report of the Arts Task Force, National Conference of State Legislatures), comp. Larry Briskin (Denver: National Conference of State Legislatures, 1981), p. 7.

areas."[4] Rural communities, which heretofore were isolated from the arts, are now bringing in professional artists and nationally known arts companies. Government-supported public television programs, arts periodicals, artists' residency programs, and improved transportation have made the arts accessible to rural citizens. Most encouraging has been the support of local artists and the increased opportunities for participation in the arts that the community programs provide. Although there is great variation in type and quality of programs, this seems to be a grass-roots movement supporting the stated belief in the arts as essential to an enlightened and humane society.

Artists-in-Education Program

The artists-in-education program is an illustration of a partnership between the National Endowment for the Arts and the state arts agencies. According to a recent report, more than 21,000 artists participated in arts-in-education projects in 42,000 schools and communities across the country between 1969 and 1980; 10.3 million schoolchildren and 328,000 teachers were involved in the projects. In a larger context, however, a National Assessment of Educational Progress Study, conducted in 1978–79, showed a disappointing picture. Of the 95,000 students, aged nine to seventeen, who were surveyed, the following results indicated that:

1. Students' knowledge of music had declined since the early seventies.
2. Teenagers were less inclined to pursue arts activities outside school hours.
3. Many students received formal instruction in the arts only in the seventh and eighth grades. Subsequent courses emphasized only the development and refinement of skills.
4. Courses in art history and appreciation were a rarity.[5]

As a result of the survey, arts education was declared an important area of concern for the Endowment and the state arts agencies; both realized the need to design a more effective plan for dealing with the situation. The eighties, the report continued, would not be like the seventies, for the factors affecting the arts must be identified and a response made. Enhanced arts education must assume a top priority; the public had expressed a desire for the arts; hence there was an obligation on the part of the established agencies to the taxpayers and to the artists.

4. Ibid., p. 88.
5. Frank Hodsoll, "Dealing with Reality," excerpts from an address delivered to the National Assembly of State Arts Agencies, October 29, 1982, published in National Endowment for the Arts journal *The Cultural Post* 8, no. 6 (January/February 1983): 3.

Overlife-size puppets in the Bread and Puppet Museum in Glover, Vt. *(Photograph by Alex Williams.)*

Arts Centers

One of the most exciting developments of the past twenty-five years has been the growth of large cultural centers with programs in the performing arts for young people. Some of them are large arts complexes that have incorporated services for children and youth; others were designed specifically for children and have since extended their services to include workshops and training programs for teachers. Best known among the former is the Kennedy Center for the Performing Arts in Washington, D.C. There an extensive series is offered to children free of charge under the aegis of its Education Department.

During the construction period of the Kennedy Center the U.S. Office of Education created twenty-two educational research and development laboratories across the country. Two of these laboratories, the South West Regional Laboratory (SWRL) in Los Angeles and the Central Mid-West Regional Educational Laboratory (CEMREL) in St. Louis, involved themselves in teacher training and curriculum development. As CEMREL's interest in arts education and the Kennedy Center's mandate coincided, a collaboration was established between them. In 1976 the National Aesthetic Education Learning Center (NAELC) was opened at the Kennedy Center. From it a model for collaborative programming by educational institutions and arts centers evolved. Twenty-five years ago the large centralized performing arts center was all but unknown in the United States; today, according to the NAELC, many exist.

In New York City, Lincoln Center has developed a somewhat different program. The Lincoln Center Institute is responsible for bringing children to performances and for taking artists into the schools. In addition, numerous teacher and student workshops in all of the performing arts supplement and enrich the program.

The organizations, each different in inception and program, are the Children's Theatre Company and School (CTC) in Minneapolis, Minnesota; the Empire State Institute for the Performing Arts (ESIPA) in Albany, New York; the Nashville Academy Theatre in Nashville, Tennessee; The Dallas Theatre Center in Dallas, Texas; The Mark Taper Forum in Los Angeles; and the Alliance Theatre Company in Atlanta, Georgia. Although already well-known for its artistry and innovative approach, the Children's Theatre Company and School burst on the scene nationally with the August 1982 issue of the *Smithsonian*. Beautiful color photographs of productions and a description of its program told the story of a successful community institution. Founded in 1961 in humble surroundings, it is now housed in a splendid theatre complex designed especially for children. The building was officially opened in 1974.

The Empire State Institute for the Performing Arts, also established in 1974, was the first state-mandated theatre for young people in the United States. It is housed in the "Egg," an imaginative structure in which a series of plays and concerts is offered each season. In addition, and of equal importance, is an extensive touring schedule and teacher education program, including the training of interns. As part of our cultural exchange program, the ESIPA has twice sent a production to Moscow and has been host to the Moscow Musical Theatre for Children.

The Nashville Academy Theatre, on the other hand, has served that city for more than fifty-five years. Its growth and success led to the establishment of a fully accredited theatre school in 1970, in which members of the company teach classes on all age levels. Performances in the theatre, a local touring program, and numerous appearances abroad distinguish its work and make it a model for other communities.

An unusual center also deserving of mention is the O'Neill Memorial Theatre Center in Waterford, Connecticut. Best known for its Theatre of the Deaf and its Playwrights' Conferences, the O'Neill Center is involved in numerous other programs. The following is a summary of its major areas of activity:

Ensuring That New Voices Are Heard
  National Playwrights' Conference
  Second Step Program
  The O'Neill Playwrights
  Playwrights Catalogue

Developing New Forms and Uses
  National Theatre of the Deaf
  Creative Arts in Education

Training a New Generation
National Theatre Institute
Professional School for Deaf Theatre Personnel

Raising the Standards of Appreciation and Judgment
National Critics Institute
Children's Theatre Conferences

Reaching Out to Young Audiences
Showboat
Little Theatre of the Deaf
Summer Theatre Camp

Preserving a Heritage
Eugene O'Neill Theatre Museum
American Theatre Treasury Recollection Series

Learning about Learning is an educational foundation for research, development, and training at Trinity University in San Antonio, Texas. Established in 1971 as a program for children, it has grown and gained prominence as a resource center for teachers, parents, and community organizations. Books, films, and a variety of attractive curricular materials are available from the foundation, and special-interest and after-school workshops are regularly offered for children and adults. Learning about Learning, in meeting area needs, has grown in a special way, different from the other centers cited, and has gained national prominence and prestige.

On the West Coast, the Civic Conservatory of Theatre Arts San Diego Junior Theatre offers instruction for young people from eight to eighteen, in addition to giving five productions a year. Under the sponsorship of the city's Recreation and Parks Department, this thirty-five-year-old institution is among the nation's oldest and largest centers of its kind. It began as a summer project, but its popularity led to a year-round program, a large paid staff, and a home of its own. An estimated fifteen hundred children and teenagers attend classes which, added to audiences, are reported to total around thirty-five-thousand persons served each year.

Although only in its fourth year, the Performing Arts Council Music Center of Los Angeles County has achieved national recognition with its extensive and progressive programs. Best known are:

The Holiday Festival, an annual event in which sixteen thousand children participate in music, dance, mime, and drama and take part in a performance at the Music Center.

The Very Special Arts Festival, a day-long festival in which handicapped and special-education children participate in performing arts workshops, meet film and television actors, display their work, and view performances by special education students.

Music Center on Tour   features a roster of twenty artists and performing groups who, during the 1982–83 season, planned six hundred fifty performances in a tour of seventy cities.

Workshops for Teachers   are held on Saturday mornings at the Music Center. They are offered in a variety of disciplines including drama/theatre techniques and mime.

The Summer Institute for Educators   is a three-week period of study offered to teachers and administrators. Learning about different arts includes spending time at various cultural institutions throughout Los Angeles County as well as the Music Center.

The Bravo Award   is the newest addition to the program. It applauds educators for their outstanding achievement in arts education.

Attractive brochures describe the various activities held in the Mark Taper Forum, the Music Center, the Ahmanson Theatre, public schools, and local community centers.

Fees are minimal for the programs sponsored by the Performing Arts Council, and some activities and events are free. This unusual structure involves children and adults, school and community, nonprofessional and professional artists, and is an example of the trend toward cooperative, collaborative enterprises. Although a large city like Los Angeles is better equipped to launch a comprehensive program of this sort than a small town, it represents a type of organization that seems to be gaining ground and financial support in a number of places. Given continued interest and available artists and locations for activities, we may see more such programs in the future. Certainly, if school budgets suffer further cuts, community programs may be the means whereby youth and the arts are brought together until the time when the arts are again included in the public school curriculum.

Other arts center programs could be described, but the ones mentioned here are cited because of the magnitude of their operations, their special services to the community, or the imaginative design of their structure. What is interesting is the fact that theatre and education are at last coming together. Today workshops and classes emphasize creative drama and improvisation rather than the production of plays. Encouraging as all of this is, however, there is cause for concern. Funds for the arts at the time of this writing have been cut on all sides, with "back to basics" as the slogan of the day. Of equal concern is the sense of discouragement that prevails. With budget cuts, curtailment of funding programs, and staff reduction, schools and community centers are finding it increasingly difficult to maintain quality programs. It is to be hoped that they may weather these difficult times so as not to lose the remarkable progress that has been made.

Arts centers and educational institutions have special skills and competencies and by working together they can achieve their desired goal of better

Children watching a "Jack Tale" enacted in an all-purpose room. *(Courtesy of Rex Stephenson, Ferrum College, Va.)*

education in the arts. The arts center has access to the finest performers, contacts in the community, and often special funds at its disposal, whereas the schools and universities have other kinds of resources that complement it. Teacher workshops and seminars were instituted by the arts centers in response to the need of educators to learn more about the arts in order to use the materials that were prepared for them. It is to be hoped that these imaginative programs will not be lost during a temporary period of recession.

One way in which some communities are finding support for the arts is through forming a consortium. The consortium is a group of local organizations that band together to pool their resources and approach funding agencies cooperatively. This unified effort is often far more successful than the efforts of a single organization struggling alone toward the same goal.

Young Audiences

An organization that does not fit any of the above categories but has been a help and source of inspiration to many communities is Young Audiences. Founded in 1952 as a national nonprofit organization, it has as its stated purpose to enhance the education and, in doing so, the quality of life for young people by introducing them to the performing arts. To achieve this purpose, Young Audiences sponsors professional musicians, dancers, and actors, who present programs in public and private schools. Students learn about the creative process directly from the performers. In 1983, thirty years after its founding, Young Audiences had thirty-eight local chapters throughout the United States with twenty-eight hundred professional artists participating. More than six thousand workshops and twelve thousand performances annually were reported with the totals rising. Although music has been emphasized, drama/theatre is included in the offerings, and it is hoped that these offerings will grow as the organization continues to expand. Young Audiences offers:

Programs for Students: Young Audiences offers performances and demonstrations in primary and secondary schools. Workshop and residency programs are also offered to teach students about the arts in a series of presentations, conducted over a longer period of time.

Programs for the Education Community: Young Audiences advocates arts education in education systems at the local, regional, state, and national levels. It encourages the integration of the arts into the training of teachers, as well as students.

Programs for Artists: Young Audiences designs its programs and trains its artists to meet the educational and cultural needs of the individual communities it serves. It provides—and sustains—career opportunities for performing artists.

Programs for Growth: Young Audiences works to expand its representation throughout the United States. It is committed to strengthening affiliations among the thirty-eight chapters in its national network. Young Audiences researches techniques for developing arts education programs and distributes the published results to professionals in the field of arts education.[6]

A word must be said here regarding the scope and quality of productions for young audiences. Although traditional plays continue to lead in popularity across the country, many children's theatres are broadening their offerings to include a wide variety of programs. As an illustration, and many other arts centers could be cited, the ESIPA in Albany, New York, lists the following attractions for the 1988–89 season at The Egg: *Once Upon a Mattress, The Manteo Family Sicilian Marionettes, From the Mississippi Delta, Hizzoner! Yellow Fever, Sherlock Holmes, The Pied Piper, Gl'Innamorati, Peter Pan, A Man for All Seasons.* Consideration is given to appropriate material for all age levels, and unlike the case in many children's theatres, Friday night performances there are offered for older audiences.

One of the benefits of a high-quality performance is the stimulating effect it has on students' own creative work. When the teacher makes use of the excite-

6. Young Audiences, Inc., brochure, 1982.

ment engendered by the artist, the results are often imaginative and strong: On occasion when performers come into the classroom, another point is made: that art can be created and enjoyed anywhere; it is not confined to the concert hall. Young children have no problem with this. It is only the adult who thinks in terms of auditoriums, lights, curtains, and so on. This brings up a point rarely made: that drama is the least expensive of all arts to implement. It requires no elaborate equipment and no special materials. A room, a leader, and a group of children are all that are needed. A piano and tape recorder are useful but not necessary. Nor is stage lighting needed, although it adds atmosphere if it is available. Costumes and props can be supplied by teacher and students, but they act as stimuli rather than as dressing for players or stage. Education of the leader *is* important, however; but the many classes and workshops that are available today in most communities make it relatively easy for the interested teacher to find the help he or she needs. Pointing out the fact that creative drama is not the production of plays and therefore does not require a theatre rules out the first objection of an administration that believes "drama is too expensive."

Federal Funding for the Arts

With the inauguration of a new president comes the inevitable question regarding appropriation for the arts. Although no big changes appear to be in store for the 1989 federal arts budget, the last budget proposed by former President Reagan called for increases in funds for the National Endowment for the Arts and for the National Endowment for the Humanities. This gave an increase of $1 million to the former and $153 million to the latter. Frank Hodsoll, chairman of the National Endowment for the Arts, expressed pleasure at the time that these increases had taken place during a period of fiscal cuts. He was particularly pleased that $1 million was earmarked for arts education. Spending levels for grants in programs in dance, theatre, and music remained the same. Government officials anticipate that the culture budget will stay the same under President Bush.[7]

Research

In reviewing the achievements and new directions of drama and theatre in America, I am reminded of a statement made by Professor Judith Kase-Polisini of the University of South Florida at the ATA convention in 1981. She described the leaders of the three periods through which creative drama has passed and is presently engaged as being the *pioneers,* the *practitioners,* and the *researchers.*

---

7. Irvin Molotsky, "No Big Changes in '89 Federal Arts Budget," *The New York Times,* January 29, 1989, section 2, p. 49.

We are today indeed engaged in a variety of research projects having to do with testing the effectiveness of our work, its impact on learning in other subject areas, and the changes in social attitudes as the result of experience in drama. Some of the research is being done by doctoral students; some, under the auspices of government agencies or universities with government grants. Money is needed for projects of any size extending over a period of time, however, and the reality is that such monies are today in increasingly short supply. One of the largest and possibly the last of the large grants in the foreseeable future was given to the Arts Council of Tampa-Hillsborough County and the University of South Florida department of arts education. Under this grant Kase-Polisini, project director, completed two years of work evaluating a school-systemwide Artists-in-the-Schools program. Included for testing were theatre, dance, music, architecture, sculpture, photography, filmmaking, creative writing, and poetry. The theatre component was one of the largest tested and received more than one-fourth of the $150,000 budget. The report included one thousand on-site observations and interviews. A special research portion of the project focused on creative drama (Artists-in-the-Schools program) and revealed new information to support previous findings that creative drama is a valuable inclusion in the elementary school curriculum.[8]

Since the fourth edition of *Creative Drama in the Classroom* was published, much more research has been done. In 1982 a series of symposia on child drama was organized and took place during the following three years (1982–86). Under the direction of Kase-Polisini, five locations were selected with speakers from other disciplines invited to present papers during a two-day conference, with respondents from Children's Theatre Association of America (CTAA). The disciplines included psychology, anthropology, and education. The symposia were held at Harvard in 1983, at the Ontario Institute for Studies in Education in Toronto also in 1983, at the University of Texas at Austin in 1984, at Arizona State University in 1985, and at Rutgers in New Brunswick, New Jersey in 1986. Attendance was limited to two hundred CTAA members; however, the proceedings were recorded, and the first collection of papers was published by the University Press of America in 1985. The second collection came out in 1986. This scholarly project was unique in the history of child drama and children's theatre in America.

Interest in research is further manifested by the presentation of an award for outstanding scholarly research by the American Alliance for Theatre and Education at its national convention in August.

Other new directions include both disciplines previously regarded as not relevant to creative drama, and an emphasis on those that were but distantly related. For example, since the publication of the last edition of this book, I have met, observed, talked with, and invited as guest speakers to my classes both

8. "Florida Survey Studies School Arts Activities," *Theatre News* 14, no. 9 (December 1982): 11.

The Alliance Theatre Company's production of *Don Quixote.* *(Courtesy of Edith Love.)*

clowns and other professionals who use clowning in their work. These skills have proved effective in helping children with academic and behavioral problems, adult patients, and parishioners. In some cases it is the acquisition of these special skills that enhances a child's or adolescent's self-image, which, in turn, enables him or her to do better work and improve social relationships. Some ministers and social workers use clowning to reach persons who respond to the nonthreatening personality of the clown and the distance that separates the clown from society. Thus the circus arts have a closer relationship to drama and education than was previously realized.

Another new direction, which became obvious to me during my research for *A Historical Guide to Children's Theatre in America,* was the prevalence of the educational component in professional and educational touring companies. No doubt many of the professional companies seized on this for survival, for funding agencies often give monies to companies that serve schools in this way. Residencies of varying lengths and the preparation of useful study guides have transcended the former superficial appearance after the show, and actors find they enjoy working seriously with young people. In the same category is the Artists-in-the-Schools program. Some artists spend more time with the classroom teachers and some with the students, but both add a special dimension to the curriculum.

Drama therapy, discussed in chapter 15, is a growing area of interest. Still in its infancy as far as degree programs are concerned, its popularity is apparent in the enrollment of drama therapy classes and the letters of inquiry in universities that offer course work in it.

Theatre organizations have long worked for state mandates that would add drama/theatre to the other arts in the elementary curricula. If these programs are carried out according to a specific timetable, we shall be seeing a growing number within the next few years. Even mild recessions can retard the growth or cancel programs, however, so complacency is not in order. But the trend is heartening, and universities are ready to prepare classroom teachers as well as specialists to handle it.

Another direction that drama has been taking is intergenerational. Although the combining of the elderly with children in creative drama classes is not widely practiced, leaders who have tried it believe in its value for both age groups.

Storytelling, an ancient art form, which had become a simple but nonetheless favorite way of sharing literature, is having a rebirth. We are discovering more and more professional storytellers who make a living with colorful presentations of literature in schools, churches, and community centers. Often in costume and accompanied by music either live or taped, their work has taken on the character of theatre, and audiences are apparently enthusiastic about it. Storytelling centers, new courses in storytelling in universities, radio programs, and confer-

Festivals of the arts in foreign countries attract visitors from all over the world. *(Courtesy of Sibenik Festival of the Child, Yugoslavia.)*

ences devoted to the subject all point to a renewed interest in the live performance.

Ethnic theatre groups and groups using ethnic material are springing up throughout the United States. Along with mature themes and subject matter previously considered taboo for the child audience, this is having an effect on youth theatre of the eighties. Although the folk and fairy tales still outnumber the new scripts in subscription seasons, there is an unmistakable trend toward the acceptance and use of current themes and a recognition of racial and ethnic groups in our society.

Wheelock Family Theatre

An unusual theatre group was founded in the early eighties at Wheelock College in Boston. Although located on a college campus, the Wheelock Family Theatre is a professional theatre serving the community. It is distinguished by its policy of casting minorities in roles traditionally performed by white actors. Black, Oriental, and white actors, handicapped and elderly, are given opportunities to audition and participate in all productions. A nonprofit organization, in agreement with Actors Equity, its goal is that of Wheelock College, a private teacher education institution: to improve the quality of life for children and their families. The age range of the actors is reported to be from two to seventy-eight, and parts are open to amateurs as well as professionals.

Among the productions offered to the public have been *The Sound of Music, Our Town, Carousel, The Diary of Anne Frank,* and *The Miracle Worker.* Many of the plays are classics and all are given two performances in American Sign Language. The new direction that this experiment represents is the deliberate casting of actors previously excluded from the theatre for reasons of color, accent, handicapping condition, and age. The results of the enterprise have been highly successful with a majority of the performances sold out. A second look at the Wheelock Family Theatre reveals that some of the earlier experiments were incorporated in its philosophy and design, demonstrating how creativity can be stimulated and encouraged.[9]

Las Posadas

Las Posadas is another interesting project developed in and for the Boston Public Schools. A bilingual, multicultural children's theatre festival and in-school folk-arts-in-education project, it was begun in 1982 to increase children's awareness of the rich cultural traditions of Hispanic, Afro-American, Oriental,

9. Anne Driscoll, "Recasting the Mold in Theatre," *The New York Times,* January 29, 1989, section 2, p. 49.

and other ethnic communities in the Boston metropolitan area. The *Las Posadas* celebration is the transportation of an American tradition that is still observed annually in Mexico and the southwestern part of the United States. Like the celebration that inspired it, the Boston celebration became an ongoing historical event that uses the resources of local artists, musicians, storytellers, and anthropologists. According to the 1988 project report, nineteen artists from diverse backgrounds—Ugandan, Nigerian, Mexican, Argentinian, African, Guatemalan, Portugese, Bolivian, Chinese, Afro-American, and Italian—had participated in the program.

Elena Dodd, director and founder, conceived of the project in 1982 and coordinated a performance in Dorchester with the help of Sara Garcia, a Mexican–American actress and teacher. Within the next six years the festival was engaging hundreds of Boston-area schoolchildren, storytellers, visual artists, playwrights, actors, musicians, and dancers in a pageant of magnitude. Project goals are summarized as follows:

1. To introduce outstanding folk artists, selected to represent specific ethnic/cultural communities as positive work and role models for Boston public school children
2. To promote and promulgate the African concept of collective work and cooperation to students and teachers
3. To strengthen students' grasp of geography and develop in them a basic understanding of the history and culture of the specific groups of peoples who make up the largest portion of Boston's ethnic minorities

In addition, an in-service component for each school includes teacher workshops in history, geography, and cultural expressions of the individual artists working in the schools. Curriculum resource materials and teachers' guides are available upon request. These resources list books on folk tales, handicrafts, slides, tapes, films, maps, and bibliographies on a variety of appropriate subjects. The project director for *Las Posadas* is Lois Berggren, an artist/teacher with a dedication to its goals and a willingness to share information on the development of this most successful community event with interested educators in other parts of the country.[10]

Aesthetic Education

What may be another new direction is a revival of interest in drama as aesthetic education. Theatre is, above all, an art form, which has been cherished in its own right through the ages. Its use as a means of learning is currently enjoying wide popularity, as is its value as a therapeutic agent. These are not in

10. Project description from Lois Berggren.

themselves new ideas, for they were understood and practiced by early societies. The Greeks taught the performing arts. Medieval priests used theatre to explain the Christian religion to the masses. During the Renaissance schoolmasters took the classical plays of Greece and Rome as models for teaching literature and writing. Indeed, drama as literature has been an important element in the education of Western people up to and including the present. What is new are the *specific uses* that are being made of theatre for teaching that distinguish the present from the past.

As for the use of drama in therapy, primitive societies cast out demons through dance and mime. Aristotle wrote of the cathartic effect of plays on audiences. Children play out their experiences and problems. What is new is the *scientific* approach to therapy in which drama, dance, and circus skills are used in the treatment of problems. Nor should we omit the value of theatre as recreation. Too often considered trivial, recreation is a potent force in the revitalization of the human spirit. Far from having lost ground in this period of the high tech, nonprofit theatre is stronger than ever, according to Mort Clark, president of the Association of Community Theatre of America. Martha Coigney, director of the U.S. center of the International Theatre Institute (ITI) and president of ITI worldwide, corroborates this observation with the further statement that the line between professional and nonprofessional theatre has blurred. Whether or not it is stronger, she does not know, but that it is alive and well throughout the world is obvious from her point of view.

Therefore, although we applaud the new uses of theatre as important, it appears obvious that they cannot supplant the value of theatre as an art; considering the growing number of states requiring the performing arts in the curriculum, aesthetic education in America is on the rise.

The Teacher or Leader

With so much concern for the future of creative drama, is it not appropriate to raise some questions regarding the teacher? What special qualifications should he or she have? What kind of education best prepares a person to teach creative drama at this time? Is a pure theatrical background a disadvantage? Is a workshop experience sufficient preparation? Dare the teacher embark on a program without some specialized training? Is certification necessary?

Without discrediting academic preparation, what seems most important to me are those personal attributes that make a good teacher. If a person already possesses the qualities of sympathetic leadership, imagination, and respect for the ideas of others, he or she has the basic requirements. Sensitivity to the individuals in a class is necessary to an activity that is participant centered, with the growth of each child an objective. In other words, although one is teaching an art and should therefore have some knowledge and appreciation of it as a form, a genuine concern for the players is of equal importance.

Successful creative drama teachers guide rather than direct. They are able to work with others, offering and accepting ideas. To them, sharing is more important than showing; thus their satisfaction will come through the process as well as from the product. When they do show the work of their group, they will be clear as to what is demonstration and what is performance. Unless they are working with groups over the age of ten or eleven, they will avoid the latter, in favor of informal class demonstrations.

Teachers of creative drama find their own way. No methods courses can prepare them perfectly, for no two groups are alike. What works well with one class does not work with another. Materials and methods that arouse a response in one group may be totally inadequate in a second, whose cultural background, age, and experiences are different. Knowledge of the neighborhood in which one is working is just as important as a knowledge of literature and drama. Teachers must find out for themselves what stimulates and what fails to elicit a response. Familiarity with techniques is an invaluable asset, but the imaginative leader will, in the end, create his or her own methods.

A sense of humor helps teachers over those periods when nothing goes right. Their ability to laugh with the group, as well as at themselves, enables them to carry on, in spite of failures and frustrations. Because they are interested in all kinds of things, they will have an expanding background of information on which to draw. They learn constantly from their pupils. They must also learn not to expect good results each time the class meets. Many efforts will be pedestrian and disappointing, but, as Hughes Mearns pointed out: "Those who work with children creatively are compelled to discard or ignore a hundred attempts while they are getting a mere half-dozen good ones."[11] It is these "good ones" that inspire others and encourage the leader to keep on trying.

Teachers maintain high standards, knowing that what they accept in the beginning is what the group is capable of at the time, but that they can expect more from them later. By establishing an atmosphere in which all feel important, teachers will challenge their class to give only their best; a teacher will wait for this, without demanding or pushing. For this reason, it is more difficult to teach creative drama than formal theatre. The absence of a basic structure, or script, demands flexibility, judgment, a willingness to accept the efforts of the shy and inarticulate, patience, and the confidence that something of value is eventually forthcoming. This is not easy for the teacher whose only previous experience has been with the formal play or whose theatre background has conditioned him or her to expect technically perfect results within a stipulated period.

The teacher must, at the same time, set limits. The establishment of boundaries does not limit freedom but, rather, gives a sense of security to the young or inexperienced player. As in any class, discipline must be maintained at all times to ensure, for each member, the freedom to experiment. In his book *Child Drama*, Peter Slade observed that "the manner of handling is what matters,

---

11. Hughes Mearns, *Creative Power* (New York: Dover Publications, 1958), p. 33.

and, because of this, some of the best work with children is done by experienced teachers who really understand what they are doing and yet, strangely enough, have very little knowledge of drama."[12]

All of this is not meant to imply that specialized training is unnecessary; what is meant is that successful teachers of creative drama seems to possess certain attitudes and qualities of personality that distinguish and qualify them. A background that includes both education and theatre is ideal, but interested leaders, whatever their preparation, may acquire, through course work and reading, additional information and techniques. Some knowledge of music and dance is invaluable and should be part of the teacher's preparation. Classroom teachers, professional actors, and social workers have all achieved notable results in creative drama with children. Because of their belief that creative drama has a contribution to make, they have adapted their own individual skills to its use, with intelligence and imagination.

Finally, a successful creative drama leader keeps abreast of the times. The world is changing rapidly. With constant exposure to television, children and adults have access to the same information. Children are no longer excluded from discussion of subjects once considered inappropriate or taboo. In his book *The Disappearance of Childhood,* Neil Postman documented the ways in which modern technology has destroyed the boundaries separating the world of the child from the world of the adult. This has important implications for the teacher, both generalist and specialist. For us to assume, however, that children today "know more" than children of previous generations is a facile and easy assumption. They no longer inhabit a protected environment, but this does not mean they have a mature understanding of complex social, psychological, and political issues. What it does suggest is that the teacher must be prepared for a variety of new subjects and problems to come up, and he or she must be ready and able to handle them. Children today are bombarded with sex, violence, and news of crime in high places; many of them experience divorce, drugs, alcoholism, and death in their own homes or neighborhoods. Often they suggest situations dealing with these topics for improvisation. This is where the teacher must be able to accept what is offered and help the group deal with it or question wisely suggestions such as one made by a nine-year-old in a middle-class city school: "Let's do an improvisation about a girl getting raped!" Through drama, some understanding may be reached and relevant information given. It means a greater openness on our part than has been expected of us in the past, and this presents both difficulties and rewards. The teacher's role is critical in a successful teacher/artist collaboration. It works well when:

The teacher is excited about the program.
The teacher makes time to talk with the artist.

12. Peter Slade, *Child Drama* (London: University of London Press, 1954), p. 271.

Creating statues. *(Courtesy of Kelsey E. Collie, Howard University.)*

The teacher is flexible.

The teacher is actively involved with the artist and students in the classroom.

The teacher, ideally, is eager to integrate the program into his or her classroom curriculum.[13]

13. Shari Davis and Benny Ferdman, "The Teacher/Artist Collaboration—How It Works," *Arts Partners Newsletter* 5, no. 1 (Winter 1987): 1, 4, 6.

Summary

Most of the new directions in drama/theatre education are heartening. The greatest challenges we face in the next few years may be finding the monies to finance these programs and overcoming the discouragement that prevails regarding employment. The programs that the pioneers envisioned, the practitioners have created, and the researchers are finding viable and of value are in jeopardy; it is up to us to discover new ways to support and preserve them.

I believe that a third challenge has grown out of our own zeal to make drama/theatre meaningful: to preserve the *fun* of theatre (a word chosen consciously and with care). In our effort to enrich education through drama, and to sponsor theatre with greater substance than it has had in the past, we sometimes lose sight of the *fun* that it brings to our lives. We who have worked to improve the quality of dramatic literature and performance skills risk losing the spirit with which the best theatre is endowed. Fun in this sense is not to be confused with the trivial and banal or with poorly presented camp; rather, fun may be the joy that comes from creating drama or from watching superb performers in vehicles that may or may not be concerned with a serious subject matter. Not that we should settle for mediocrity; on the contrary, we must continue to strive for excellence but to remember that the spirit is of the utmost importance and fun is a part of it. A good season of children's theatre will contain a variety of plays, including both serious and amusing subject matter, produced equally well. A good class in creative drama will use varied material appropriate to the age, experience, and interests of the children.

Creative drama may be viewed as an art form, a way of learning, a means of self-expression, a leisure-time activity, or a therapeutic tool. In each instance, learnings include self-knowledge, knowledge of others, information acquired through the process of drama, and aesthetic appreciation.

Self-Knowledge

Through drama, players think, plan, and organize. They feel deeply but learn to channel and control their emotions. Their communication skills are involved as they speak and express their ideas. Through rhythms and physical movement, they make use of their bodies. Working with others teaches the meaning of cooperation. They come to understand their own strengths and weaknesses. Benedetti called acting self-extension rather than self-expression, which describes in a word what we are talking about.

Knowledge of Others

By trying on characters, players learn about other people. Acting a variety of parts helps them to think and feel like persons different from themselves. Being part of a group not only teaches them something of teamwork but sensitizes them to the feelings of those with whom they are working. Finally, through the material the teacher brings in and that brought in by classmates, they are exposed to other people's customs, to ideas and values that may be foreign to their own.

Intellectual Development

Play has long been recognized by nursery educators as experimentation that offers unlimited possibilities for learning. Jean Piaget has written extensively on the function of play in the intellectual development of young children. He saw conceptual thinking as originating in spontaneous play through manipulation of objects and social collaboration with other children. Recent research indicates that an appropriate balance between spontaneous and more structured play is desirable.[14] No activity provides a greater variety of opportunities for learning than creative drama, regardless of the level.

Aesthetic Appreciation

The most difficult aspect to assess is aesthetic appreciation. Although the child who has been taken to museums, concerts, and theatres will have the advantage of knowledge about the nature of these art forms, what meanings they hold for the child may not be immediately evident. Research reveals learnings but cannot measure the extent of appreciation. Nevertheless, one can observe involvement through the attention and behavior of children in an audience. Those who are exposed to the best tend to be more deeply engaged, often paint pictures of the experience afterward, speak of it, or use it in creative drama classes as a springboard to further exploration. Erwin Edman described the aesthetic experience as "reinstating the emotions, clarifying experience, interpreting life and giving pleasure."[15] In an ordered society these opportunities can and should be accessible to all children, regardless of intellectual, social, physical, cultural, or economic differences.

Peter Slade capitalized the word *Joy* in writing of child drama. This is an emotion we may be overlooking rather than emphasizing in our concern for substance and the social experience a group activity provides. Joy, however, implies another dimension, for it reaches a deeper level of consciousness than enjoyment or fun in providing an ultimate human fulfillment. Let us not forget joy.

Recent research indicates that there may be an important connection between the arts and learning. Jean Houston, director of the Foundation for Mind Research in Pomona, New York, has produced some new and challenging questions in the past few years. She goes beyond the integration of subject matter into methods of enhancing concentration and freedom from distraction. She advocates a holistic approach to education; in other words, if a start is made from

14. Millie Almay, "Spontaneous Play: An Avenue for Intellectual Development," *Bulletin of the Institute of Child Study* (University of Toronto) 28, no. 2 (1966).

15. Erwin Edman, *Arts and the Man* (New York: New American Library, 1950), p. 25.

a deep aesthetic base, everything related to the subject at hand can be learned more quickly, easily, and thoroughly. A richer sensory perception, kinesthetic thinking, and the use of rhythms and movement to facilitate learning form an important part of her theory.

Her workshops in discovering latent human capacities are being offered to teachers on elementary and secondary school levels, to religious leaders, and to social workers. Houston's goal is a fuller development of the human being, and she is convinced of the important role the arts play in this.

Conclusion

A basic requirement of any activity is that it be a satisfying experience for both leader and group. The more successful the project, the greater the degree of satisfaction. As leaders grow in experience, they will recognize the possibilities in a variety of materials and methods, and their groups will likewise grow in security and the ability to tackle problems more imaginatively. This is true of the creative drama leader and a group on any age level, whether in a school or recreational setting.

Through the spread of our mass media, we have become known as a "spectator society." Our lives have become increasingly programmed and our experiences packaged. Participation in any of the arts is, therefore, more needed today than at any other period in our history. Drama, of all of the arts, demands of the practitioner a total involvement. By offering an opportunity for participation in drama, we are helping to reserve something of the play impulse in all of its joy, freedom, and order.

Educational and social goals are closely related in drama; therefore a climate in which the player feels good about himself or herself and others is conducive to learning. When the questions of peace and survival concern us deeply, drama can serve a twofold purpose in the lives of children: it offers an opportunity to learn more about others, including the values and customs of different racial and ethnic groups, and a place where fears of nuclear war and destruction (often unvoiced) may be relieved and examined. This is not to suggest that drama is a panacea for the world's ills, but it has the power to bring people together through cooperative endeavors and mutual understanding. Although the word *child* is used throughout this text, the basic principles apply to all ages, and the concept of a warm and supportive environment as a positive influence is applicable everywhere. It is this kind of environment that we should try to create, an environment in which all persons can grow. I am more convinced than ever of the truth of Robert Benedetti's statement, in a text written for the adult actor, that "acting is neither seeming nor being; it is becoming."[16]

16. Robert Benedetti, *Seeming, Being, and Becoming* (New York: Drama Book Specialists, 1976), p. 87.

Appendix A

Glossary of Some Common Dramatic Terms

Many of the following terms will not be part of an elementary school child's vocabulary, but in the event that they come up in class discussion after seeing a play, the teacher will have brief definitions to share at his or her discretion.

Act. To perform or play a role; a division of a drama.

Actor. A person who performs in a play, who assumes the role of a character.

Adaptation. A play based on a story or novel rather than being an original plot.

Amateur. A person who engages in an art or a sport for love of it, rather than for a livelihood.

Backstage. The area behind the stage, not visible to the audience.

Border lights. Overhead lighting at the front of the stage.

Box office. The office where tickets are sold, located either in or in front of the lobby.

Choreographer. A person who designs and directs a dance.

Choreography. The design for a dance; the written representation of the steps of dancing.

Climax. The highest point of interest, usually near the end of the play.

Comedy. A play that ends satisfactorily for the hero or heroine; it is entertaining and usually lively, as opposed to a tragedy.

Community theatre. Theatre organized and run by persons living in the community; actors generally perform for the enjoyment of the experience rather than as a profession.

Cue. The signal for an actor to speak or perform an action, usually a line spoken by another actor.

Curtain call. The return of the entire cast to the stage after the end of a performance, when they acknowledge applause.

Dénouement. The final unraveling of the plot of a play; the solution or outcome.

Dialogue. The lines of the play spoken by the actors.

Director. The person in charge; the one who gives directions to the actors and assumes ultimate responsibility for the production.

Double cast. To prepare two casts for a play, both of which will play the same number of performances.

Downstage. The front of the stage; the area nearest the audience.

Dramatist. Another name for a playwright.

Dramatization. The creation of a play from a story or poem.

Dress rehearsal. The final rehearsal or rehearsals of a play, when costumes are worn and all stage effects are completed.

Epilogue. A short scene or speech at the end of the play; it is not often found in modern plays.

Footlights. The row of lights across the front of the stage, on a level with the actors' feet.

Hero. The central male character in a play; a man distinguished for valor.

Heroine. The central female character in a play.

The house. The auditorium or seating area of a theatre.

Houselights. The auditorium lights, turned off or dimmed when the performance starts.

Intermission. A recess or temporary stopping of action, usually about halfway through a play.

Lines. The dialogue or words spoken by the actors.

Lobby. The foyer or hall at the front of a theatre.

Mounting. The scenery and costumes used to dress the production.

Musical. A theatrical production characterized by music, songs, dances, and often spectacular settings and costumes.

Performance. A representation before spectators; an entertainment.

Playwright. A person who writes plays.

Plot. The story.

Production. The total theatrical product, including the play, the acting, the direction, scenery, costumes, lighting, and special effects.

Professional theatre. Theatre in which actors and all other employees earn their living.

Prologue. An introduction to a play, usually spoken by one of the actors; it occasionally is employed in plays for children to orient the audience to the piece or engage its attention.

Prompter. The person who watches the script backstage during the performance of a play; he or she gives the lines to the actors, if they should forget.

Scenery. The large pieces (flats, backdrops, furniture, and so on) that are placed on the stage to represent the location.

Script. The manuscript or form in which the play is written; it contains the dialogue, stage directions, and time and place of each act and scene.

Soliloquy. Lines in a play spoken by one character alone on the stage, in which his or her thoughts are revealed.

Spatial perception. A sense of space as related to body movement; something happening or existing in space.

Sponsor. A person or an organization engaging a theatrical company.

Spotlight. A strong beam of light used to illuminate a particular person or area of the stage, as opposed to floodlights.

Stage manager. The person in charge backstage; he or she helps the director during rehearsals and then takes charge backstage when the play is given.

Straight play. A drama without music or dance.

Subplot. A plot subordinate to the principal plot.

Theme. A topic or subject developed in a play; the subject on which the plot is based.

Thrust stage. A stage or platform that extends into the auditorium, with the audience seated on three sides.

Touring company. A company of actors who take their show on the road, as opposed to a resident company.

Tragedy. A play that ends with the defeat or death of the main character; it is based on a serious theme or conflict, as opposed to a comedy.

Understudy. The actor who learns the part of another actor playing a major role; he or she is ready to go onstage in the unexpected absence of the original actor.

Upstage. The rear of the stage; the area farthest from the audience.

Villain. A character who commits a crime; the opponent of the hero or heroine.

Wings. The side areas of the stage, out of view of the audience; the area where the actors wait for their entrances.

APPENDIX B

Pupil Evaluation

To evaluate children's work in any area it is necessary to know the *characteristics, abilities, needs,* and *interests* of the particular age level. Not that these are present to the same degree in all children, but they serve as guidelines for expectations. Human beings grow at different rates of speed, so there can be no arbitrary rules governing growth and development. Experienced teachers know what children of different ages are like, but for the inexperienced teacher, or the teacher working with drama for the first time, the following explanations may be helpful.

Characteristics of the First-Grade Child

Physical. Energetic, alert, active; responds with the entire body; enjoys frequent change of activity and position; needs quiet time after active periods; follows rules of the game.

Mental. Capable of reproductive images and concrete operations as well as movement for its own sake; has ability to think independently; short attention span; is curious and investigative; enjoys symbolic play.

Social. Begins decentering in cognitive and social areas; likes to be with other children of the same age; has strong feelings and is expressive; must learn to take turns.

Interests. Family, home, local activities, and occupations; toys, animals, machinery; holidays and field trips.

Activities. Fifteen to twenty minutes recommended; rhythms, imitative movements, and simple pantomimes; likes to enact short verses and nursery rhymes; favorite stories often played many times; should work in large groups rather than individually; enjoys having the teacher participate with class.

Characteristics of the Second-Grade Child

Physical. Enjoys using the entire body; active, eager to participate; improved coordination and better control of small muscle movements than the six-year-old.

Mental. Is moving from concrete thinking to more conceptual mode of thought; vocabulary is expanding; developing critical ability; enjoys short discussion periods; creates anticipatory images as well as reproductive images.

Social. Greater enjoyment of other children; more socialized and more independent.

Interests. The community; holidays, guessing games, and riddles; animals; stories, both familiar and new.

Activities. Thirty-minute periods of drama recommended; enjoys dramatizing stories and poems; likes fairy tales and fantasy; "Show and Tell" is a favorite activity; easily stimulated and can work in groups of two, three, or four as well as in large groups; enjoys pantomime.

Characteristics of the Third-Grade Child

Physical. Developing well-coordinated movements; likes to run, jump, skip, gallop, and dance; noticeably finer development of small movements.

Mental. Capable of critical and evaluative observation; able to organize ideas more quickly and clearly; plans scenes and sequences with ease; enjoys humor.

Social. Strong sense of justice and fair play; often cites the moral of a story or fable; follows directions and works well with peers.

Interests. Interests broadening to include other peoples and other lands; interested in fantasy, royalty, folk and fairy tales, but moving toward stories of the here and now.

Activities. Thirty to forty-five minutes recommended; enjoys challenging work on literature, projects, and exercises; will bring in relevant materials such as pictures, games, stories, songs, and other items of interest; likes to work on integrated projects involving social studies, literature, and the arts.

Characteristics of the Fourth-Grade Child

Physical. Constantly gaining better control of the body as he or she grows older, taller, and stronger; works and plays hard; is active, spontaneous, eager to try new things and to learn.

Mental. Becoming more self-motivated; enjoys discussion and group planning periods; likes to solve problems.

Social. Independent but likes working with others; can share ideas and work cooperatively on scenes and class projects.

Interests. Adventure, sports, strong heroes and heroines; enjoys new stories and more demanding exercises.

Activities. Forty to sixty minutes recommended for drama period. Classes may include exercises, stories, poems, suggestions for creating scenes; interest in play structure; can handle more complicated plots and create original plays; able to work for longer periods and study subjects in greater depth.

Characteristics of the Fifth-Grade Child

Physical. Continued improvement of physical skills, including tumbling, acrobatics, circus acts, and clowning.

Mental. Growing ability to solve problems and create well-rounded characters; motivation for characters' behavior becomes important; likes words and can create dialogue appropriate to characters and situations or periods in which the story is laid; accepts constructive suggestions from the teacher or leader.

Social. Able to analyze feelings; continues to work well in a team; fair play important; still needs help in commenting on the work of others so as not to hurt feelings.

Interests. Similar to the fourth grader but with a constantly widening spread of interests; fantasy and fairy tales become less interesting as interest in the lives of real persons and tales of heroic acts grows.

Activities. Forty minutes to an hour or more can be spent on a variety of activities; can handle longer and more complicated stories; still childlike in spontaneity but more perceptive and thoughtful; able to sustain interest in one activity for a longer period.

Characteristics of the Sixth-Grade Child

Physical. The preadolescent is undergoing change; physical growth is reflected in the finer muscle coordination; often self-conscious because of body change but capable of refined movements, well-developed pantomime, and circus skills.

Mental. Interested in detail and motivation of characters; talkative and investigative; enjoys discussion, shows more mature reasoning ability; has keener critical judgment; is often surprisingly perceptive.

Social. Interested in the opposite sex; sensitive and aware; has had more experiences on which to draw; vocabulary much larger; can be expected to offer well-thought-out ideas and well-expressed criticism.

Interests. Many and varied interests; romantic interests as well as love of adventure, mystery, and adolescent problems.

Activities. Can work for an hour to an hour and a half. Likes writing and may enjoy playwriting as well as performing; can integrate learnings and engage in long-range project involving social studies, literature, and the arts; may want to put on a play for an audience.

Characteristics of the Seventh-Grade Child

Physical. Growing rapidly at this age; some preadolescents are more mature than others; energetic, strong, capable of fine physical coordination, including the mastery of some circus skills.

Mental. Curious; enjoys the challenge of more difficult material; continued eagerness to discuss ideas with classmates; developing good reasoning power and critical judgment.

Social. Uneven development as some children now show considerable social growth, whereas others are self-conscious and sensitive to criticism; experience in dramatic activities an effective way of facilitating social growth and poise.

Interests. Interests broaden, including those noted in the sixth grader.

Activities. Now has ability to sustain an interest over a longer period; definite desire to perform for an audience outside the class.

Characteristics of the Eighth-Grade Child

Physical. As teenagers, children show greater physical maturity, with girls often appearing two or three years older than their chronological age; awkwardness in some cases because of this rapid growth; dance and physical activities should be included in drama sessions.

Mental. Capable of solving more complex problems; eager for the challenge of new ideas to pursue and discuss with peers.

Social. Uneven social development and skills; many now comfortable, however, working with peer groups, including opposite sex; expanding vocabulary contributes to improved communication.

Interests. Wide range of interests, especially among children who read; most young people of this age concerned with adolescent problems and ways of solving them; Theatre-in-Education companies coming into the school of particular interest and a source of stimulation.

Activities. Ability to work for two hours on projects of interest, often exhibiting unusual ability in writing and knowledge of theatre production; most children of this age are ready and eager to perform plays for outside audiences.

Characteristics of Ninth- and Tenth-Grade Children

Physical, mental and social growth continues but now at a slower pace. In some school systems these students are in high school, where they are pursuing a more advanced curriculum. Interests may shift sharply toward performance and the production of full-length plays, although pantomime and improvisation are still popular. Young people of this age are capable of difficult and often remarkably artistic work, showing a preference for *improvisation,* rather than creative drama.

Using an Evaluation Chart

Although grading children in the arts is to be avoided, a simple checklist may be helpful in evaluating growth and development. The evaluation chart on page 457 was designed to show the major areas of concern and should serve as (1) a guide to the emphases in teaching creative drama and (2) an aid to the identification of children's individual needs and progress. It is suggested that children be evaluated three or four times a semester to note change and improvement.

We do not look for performance skills in elementary school children, nor expect the level of achievement possible among high school students. Involvement, sincerity, imagination, freedom of movement, and cooperation with the group are the basic goals in teaching creative drama. Beyond that, vocal expression, vocabulary, and the ability to plan and to organize material are important, but they come with experience. The criteria applied to adult actors are inappropriate for children and should not be used. These criteria are audience centered and therefore do not belong to creative drama, in which the participant is central. Even when children's work is shared with others, the goals remain the same, with the audience prepared for the occasion rather than the players drilled for a performance.

It is suggested that instead of giving children letter grades, teachers use the following three numbers to indicate quality of response in the specific category:

1. Shows good response
2. Is adequate
3. Needs special attention and, perhaps, help

The Areas of Concentration

1. *Listening.* Listening is an important skill for hearing instructions, discussing topics in class, responding to questions, and helping to create a climate in which all children are able to express themselves freely.
2. *Concentration.* The ability to hold an idea long enough to respond thoughtfully or creatively is essential in any discipline. It is particularly important in drama, for a breakdown in concentration on the part of one participant invariably affects the concentration of all. Group work requires the concentrated attention of every member.
3. *Response.* Responses can be varied; the important thing to note is whether or not the child is able to respond physically, verbally, or emotionally to the challenge.
4. *Imagination.* Imagination is the element that distinguishes a response as original, creative, or interesting.
5. *Movement.* Young children tend to be free in the use of their bodies as a primary means of expression. As they grow older, children become more inhibited in their physical responses. Tight, constricted movement suggests self-consciousness or fear. Unlocking the muscles, therefore, helps the performer to express ideas and feelings more openly.
6. *Verbal Ability.* The older the student, the greater verbal ability is to be expected. Increased vocabulary and added experience in speaking should improve oral communication. Creative drama offers a unique opportunity to develop this skill.

7. *Cooperation.* Cooperation includes the ability to offer and accept the ideas of others easily and graciously. It is an important part of successful living in a democracy.

8. *Organization.* Planning, seeing relationships, making choices, and arranging the components of a project require thought, maturity, and patience. As children work together, they develop the ability to organize materials in such a way as to communicate with others.

9. *Attitude.* Attitude is the feeling or disposition toward the work and the other members of the class. A positive attitude not only enhances the quality of the individual student's work but also contributes to the combined efforts of the group. A negative attitude, on the contrary, detracts and may even be a destructive force. A *good* attitude, therefore, is the most important element for achieving growth and success.

10. *Understanding.* Understanding means more than comprehension of meaning. It includes the ability to use the material: what it is and how to handle it.

Although there are other important goals in teaching creative drama, those listed above are the most important in assessing the progress of children in the elementary and intermediate grades or, indeed, of beginners on any level. The evaluation sheet was designed for easy duplication. Teachers may also want to keep brief anecdotal records as well as a checklist. The space at the right, marked "Comments," provides for such entries. Specific instances of change, "breakthroughs," or problems of individual children can be written here.

"Class Progress" is the overall picture of the group at work. In the adult theatre, this often is referred to as ensemble. Ensemble means the quality of work done as a group rather than by individual actors. It is not developed in a day or a week; after a month or so, a tentative evaluation can be made. This is because individuals develop at different rates, and some have problems that must be resolved before it is possible for them to become absorbed in a group project. An accurate statement of group progress, therefore, cannot often be made until near the end of a semester.

Other Yardsticks

The best method of evaluating student progress is personal observation made on a daily basis. These observations lead to the information needed for a checklist later. Because the teacher's attention is on the lesson and the group, however, and because he or she must move on to other lessons, daily rating is impractical and actually undesirable. If there are student teachers in the room, ask them to be responsible for watching response and variations in behavior from day to day. Should there be more than one student teacher assigned to the class, each can be given a group of children to observe over a period of time. This has two advantages: (1) it is a help to the classroom teacher, freeing him or her for teaching the group; and (2) it sharpens the student teacher's ability to discern growth and development. Again, it must be stressed that teaching comes first and that at no time should evaluation become important to the children or take on the appearance of assigning letter grades. When children try to *please* adults, they lose the most important value of the experience.

Another yardstick, possible in some schools but not in most, is videotaping of the class. This is an ideal way to compare work done at different periods in the semester and to take a second look at a performance that one does not clearly remember. The obvious disadvantage of taping is that when children know they are being filmed, they tend to become self-conscious, thus negating two of our

Date: _____

Students' names	Listening	Concentration	Response	Imagination	Movement	Verbal ability	Cooperation	Organization	Attitude	Comments
Doe, John	1	2	2	1	3	1	3	1	2	

Teacher's evaluation of class progress:

Evaluation key:
1. Shows good response
2. Is adequate
3. Needs special attention and, perhaps, help

principal goals: sincerity and involvement. Therefore, where videotaping is possible, it is suggested that it not be done until halfway through the semester, by which time the class is comfortable and working easily together. This should make it seem a natural way of recording group work and not like filming a show.

Books on Child Development

BRUNER, JEROME. *The Process of Education.* Cambridge: Harvard University Press, 1960.

DAY, B. D. *Early Childhood Education: Creative Learning Activities.* New York: Macmillan, 1983.

DITTMAN, L. L., and M. E. RAMSEY, eds. *Today Is for Children.* Washington, D.C.: Association for Childhood Education International, 1982.

FLAVELL, J. H. *The Developmental Psychology of Jean Piaget.* Princeton, N.J.: Van Nostrand, 1963.

GESELL, ARNOLD, and FRANCES ILG. *The Child from Five to Ten.* New York: Harper & Row, 1946.

HENDRICK, J. *Total Learning for the Whole Child.* St. Louis: Mosby, 1980.

MAXIM, G. *The Very Young Child: Guiding Children from Infancy through the Early Years,* 2d ed. Belmont, Calif.: Wadsworth, 1985.

MAYNARD, OLGA. *Children and Dance and Music.* New York: Scribner's, 1968.

PIAGET, JEAN, and BARBEL INHELDER. *The Child's Conception of Movement and Speed.* New York: Basic Books, 1969.

———. *The Psychology of the Child.* New York: Basic Books, 1969.

SPODEK, B., ed. *Handbook of Research in Early Childhood Education.* New York: Free Press, 1982.

APPENDIX C

A Sample Drama Session

Famous People. Prepared by Cecily O'Neill
An account of a drama session with a class of high school students.

I began by asking the group to imagine that they were very famous people—all celebrities in some branch of human endeavor. They were at the peak of their profession, and their names were known throughout the world. I told them that even if they could not decide immediately what exactly they were famous for, they could still join in the activity.

ACTIVITIES	TEACHING POINTS
I asked the group to sit in a circle, with me. I explained that I was a talk-show host and had invited them all to appear on my program. As famous people, they would be accustomed to appearing on television, but it would be unusual for so many celebrities to appear on the same show.	It was important at this stage to give the group the confidence to join in the activity. I wanted them to hold off, if necessary, from deciding on their profession until they began to understand the rules of the game and saw the possibilities it offered them.
In role, I welcomed the celebrities to the program and said how grateful I was to them for agreeing to appear on the show. I told them I would begin by asking them all the same question. "What is the best thing for you about being famous?"	My role, as the talk-show host, is designed to support and authenticate the roles the students adopt. I must accept them as the celebrities I have asked them to role-play.
One by one I went round the circle, asking the same question to each member of the class.	The activity is limited and therefore gives the students a sense of security. They are asked to answer only one question.
The answers they gave were fairly simple and included items such as money, power, respect, recognition, the knowledge that one is the best in one's field, fans, freedom to choose one's	

459

work. In role, I accepted each answer and, when appropriate, elaborated on it.

Next, I asked the group another question.

"What, for you, is the worst thing about being famous?"

This time, answers were much longer and less superficial. They focused on loss of privacy, the effect on their family and private lives, the fear of failure, pressure from the media, the need for security, the sense of exploitation, envy from others, the inability to know who one's true friends are.

Finally, I thanked them for taking part in the program.

It is important that I make it clear to the group that many of them may choose the same answers. If some students find it difficult to think of something to say, I can help them by mentioning a few alternatives.

Again, my acceptance of their answers signals my belief in their roles and helps them articulate their understandings of the pressures and problems of being famous.

Out of role, we discussed what had taken place. Some of them from their answers to the questions had made it obvious what they were famous for. Others had not shared this information.

I asked the students to work in groups of three or four. Could they imagine that each of the famous people had a family photograph album and that one of the photos taken when they were children shows a hint of what they were to become.

Each group presented its photos to the rest of the class. The spectators were encouraged to speculate about what was happening in each photo and to articulate the qualities that each famous person possessed, even at such an early age.

I gave them examples of what I meant —the young writer receiving a prize, the lawyer on the debate team, the famous doctor as a child playing at hospitals, the boxer in a playground brawl.

It is important that this activity doesn't turn into a guessing game. There will be a lot to see in each group's work and a great deal of information about the famous person and his or her background.

In the next part of the work, I asked the students to imagine that, as famous people with a great deal of money and power, they constantly received many requests or demands for their time, money, or support. How would they respond to this kind of pressure?

The students worked in pairs. One of them remained in role as the famous person. The partner became someone

Now the students themselves are supporting each other in role, as well as putting pressure on each other. Some who was asking the celebrity for help —perhaps for a very worthy cause to do with young people or those in need.

students will prove very skillful at getting the celebrity to agree.

Sitting in a circle with the half of the class who had been the people asking for help, I talked to them while the celebrities listened. They reported on the success or otherwise their attempts at persuasion. Some were generous and unselfish, others were too busy or too callous to give any support.

It is interesting for the famous people to hear how they are perceived by others. Dividing the class in half is a very useful way of getting feedback in role. The private activity in role becomes public. A useful way of getting feedback.

In later sessions we explored their responses to pressure from the media, tensions between work and family life, and the need for friends. A very compelling moment was a spontaneous scene created by one group in which a famous sports hero visited his family whom he had been neglecting. We watched his wife and children try to make clear to him that they needed him more than his fans or his team. Another group explored what happened when the famous person went back to his home town and met his boyhood friends and teenage sweetheart.

The students wrote headlines and newspaper stories about the celebrities, shared journal entries, wrote letters to their families and their fans, and created a dance drama, in two large groups, of the nightmares suffered as a result of the pressures of fame.

Richard Mennen pointed out that "conscious invention is a beginning place for games and improvisation, but the event can only happen if invention is transcended."[1] In the piece of work I have described, the students took on a variety roles that were modified and elaborated in the process, worked together in both spontaneous and prepared drama modes, transcended their own limitations, and developed insights that had relevance for their own lives.

1. Richard Mennen, "Grotofsky's Para-Theatrical Project," *The Drama Review* 19, no. 4 (1975):58–69.

Appendix D

Classroom Resource Guide for *The Divider*

The Creative Arts Team's 1987–88 touring production *The Divider* takes a look at prejudice and social discrimination in a contemporary American community. The play is a fictional response to the recent surge of racially motivated violence around the country and particularly in New York City.

Lin Pang, a recent immigrant to the United States, is seriously injured by a car as she dashes across a busy highway. What is this girl's relationship to the community? What caused her to run out on a dangerous highway?

Alva Simpson, a television reporter, returns to the community where she grew up, more than twenty years ago, to investigate the incident. The once exclusively white community is now a predominantly black neighborhood. During Alva's investigation she meets Frank Turner, the pharmacist who employed Lin. As a former classmate of Turner's and one of the first blacks to move into the community, Alva is reminded of the prejudices she faced many years ago, particularly from Turner. From Monroe, another of his employees, she learns of the intricate set of relationships that existed among him, Lin, her boy friend Darell, and Priscilla, her Hispanic friend from school.

All of these teenagers tell her of their memories of Lin's arrival in the community. Revealed in a series of flashbacks, the story is filled with contradictions and half-truths. A web of false assumptions, lies, and fears emerge. It is revealed that Lin was physically attacked just before her dash onto the highway. Lying unconscious in the hospital, she cannot shed light on the story herself. Eventually, though, Alva Simpson discovers Lin's diary, which finally leads the reporter to the truth of what happened.

In the end, all members of the community, though not directly involved in the attack on Lin, are forced to examine their responsibility for the incident. At the end of the play, the audience is given an opportunity to challenge and confront the characters directly about their prejudicial statements and attitudes.

The play exposes the audience to the many misconceptions that exist about people from other cultures and highlights the deep-seated emotional roots of prejudice in a provocative, theatrical context.

To the Teacher

The *purpose* of this study guide is to explore the play through follow-up activities which will make the themes, issues and theatrical elements of *The Divider* more personally relevant to your students.

Our *goal* is to address the issue of *prejudice* by identifying moments in the play when a character shows prejudicial behavior, and by exploring the different types of prejudice.

We hope this is a resource well worth your time and effort, and that it will stimulate and challenge your students.

Prejudice

> *a judgement or opinion formed before the facts are known.*
>
> —WEBSTER'S NEW WORLD DICTIONARY

Recognizing Prejudice

In *The Divider,* three examples of prejudice are clearly expressed.

1. A *stereotype* about a group or race is used to discriminate against an individual.
2. A person or group is made the *scapegoat* for problems they have not caused.
3. A *derogatory remark* is made about a member of a different race.

Scapegoating

When people transfer anger or frustration onto an object or a person that is not the source of the frustration, they are making that person or thing a substitute for the real person or thing that is causing the problem. This substitute is called a *scapegoat.*

As you discuss this concept with the students, ask them for examples of scapegoating in the play.

Who Is the Scapegoat?

Preparation and Discussion Near the end of the play, Priscilla becomes very upset with Lin and she says:

> *"Liar! Your family just bought . . . the whole building. Now you listen to this. You're on thin ice with me. Pang, you got that? So keep your distance."*

Activity

1. Read the above line to the students and ask them:

   —What are Priscilla's feelings about Lin in this scene? What are Lin's feelings? How do you know?

   —Why does Priscilla seem to be turning against Lin? Is she justified in feeling this way?

   —Was it Lin's fault that Priscilla and her family had their rent doubled?

   —Who is the scapegoat in this scene? Why?

   —To whom should Priscilla have talked about this?

2. Are there any other characters in the play who were treated as a scapegoat? Who were they and who were the characters involved?

   —Choose one of the scenes and have the students improvise or write a scene where scapegoating is avoided and the conflict is constructively solved.

Goal The students will be able to recognize examples of scapegoating in the play *The Divider*.

Follow-Up What are other situations, outside of the play, in which people are treated as scapegoats?

EXAMPLE: A parent has a bad day at work and takes out his/her frustrations on other members of the family.

Have the students improvise two versions of a chosen scene.

Version One: We see an example of scapegoating.

Version Two: Scapegoating is avoided and the characters find a constructive solution.

Derogatory Remarks

Is making an insulting remark about another person's race, creed, sex, or ethnic origin.

Activity I Read the following line of dialogue to the students:

MONROE: *Well, well, well, if it isn't chop suey herself.*

Ask the students:

—Which character from *The Divider* spoke this line of dialogue?

—What words would best describe the character of Monroe?

(Point out to the students that what Monroe said to Lin was an example of a derogatory remark.)

—What other derogatory remarks do you remember from *The Divider* that Monroe said to Lin?

—In what way could Lin have responded to Monroe's derogatory remarks?

Have the students write a scene in which Lin confronts Monroe about his insults toward her. The setting of the scene is Mr. Turner's store. Begin with the following lines of dialogue:

LIN: (She enters the store and takes off her coat.) *Monroe, I have to speak to you for a minute.*

MONROE: *Yeah? What do you want?* (He puts his hands on his hips and looks at her.)

Goal Students will be able to write a short scene in which a character recognizes and responds to a derogatory remark.

Follow-Up Ask the students what other characters in *The Divider* spoke derogatory remarks toward Lin? Have the students write a short scene in which Lin confronts those characters.

Stereotyping

Is considering an entire race, nationality, or religion to be alike and without individuality.

Activity II Read the following line of dialogue to the students:

MR. TURNER: *I thought I could trust you. Blacks, Chinese, Puerto Ricans, you're all the same.*

Ask the students:

—Which character from *The Divider* spoke this line of dialogue?
—What word could best describe the character of Mr. Turner?

(Point out to the students that Mr. Turner's attitude and words are an example of stereotyping.)

—If you were able to speak to the character of Mr. Turner, what would you say to him, or ask him about his actions toward Lin?
—What would you say to him about his actions toward the other characters in *The Divider?*

Have the students write one statement and one question that you would like to ask or say to Mr. Turner.

Put yourself, or one of your students who is willing and able, into the role of Mr. Turner and have the students confront Mr. Turner with their statements and questions.

Goal The students will be able to recognize the prejudicial behavior of characters in *The Divider* and clearly respond to this behavior.

Follow-Up Follow this same process with the other characters in *The Divider* who express themselves with stereotypes.

Personally Speaking . . . What Do You Think?

Activity III Copy the three previous pages and hand these out to the students; or post them on a board; or read the quotes to them. Ask the students to consider the theme of prejudice and to write their own personal opinion on a 3 × 5 index card.

Perhaps these cards could be displayed on a bulletin board in the classroom with the title "Personally Speaking."

Goal The students will be able to clearly express their personal opinion about prejudice through writing.

Follow-Up Once a week, or whenever is appropriate, choose a new theme such as Drugs, Family, Jobs, etc., and have the students write their personal opinion as they consider that particular theme.

Selected Bibliography

Creative Drama

BARNFIELD, GABRIEL. *Creative Drama in Schools*. New York: Macmillan, 1971.
A British publication with an emphasis on the secondary school. It gives ideas that the author has used and found successful. He begins with movement and rhythm and dance and describes the use of music as a technique for encouraging imagination.

BARRAGER, PAMELA. *Spiritual Understanding through Creative Drama*. Valley Forge, Pa.: Judson Press, 1981.
An up-to-date text on the use and values of creative drama in religious education. Written by an experienced teacher and well-known authority in the field.

BOLTON, REG. *Circus in a Suitcase*. Rowayton, Conn.: New Plays, 1982.
This is a clear and delightful presentation of teaching circus skills to young people. The author is an English clown and a certified teacher with years of experience in clowning with and for amateurs. Highly recommended and the only book of its kind in the field for children and young people.

BURGER, ISABEL B. *Creative Drama in Religious Education*. Wilton, Conn.: Morehouse-Barlow, 1976.
One of the few books on the use of creative dramatics in religious education. Burger's years of successful teaching make this a practical and authoritative text for leaders in this field.

BYERS, RUTH. *Creating Theatre*. San Antonio: Trinity University, 1968.
This is a handsome book with a focus on a creative approach to playwriting with children and teenagers. Pantomime and improvisation lead to exercises in writing. Many beautiful photographs and nine scripts illustrate the work done in classes under the guidance of the author, who is director of the Teen-Children's Theatre and assistant professor of drama at Baylor University in the Dallas Theatre Center.

CHAMBERS, DEWEY W. *Storytelling and Creative Drama*. Dubuque, Iowa: William C. Brown, 1970.

This is an invaluable little book for the teacher, librarian, or group leader who wants to learn something of the ancient art of storytelling. Clear and succinct, it guides selection of material and offers simple techniques for effective presentation.

CHARTERS, JILL, AND ANNA GATELY. *Drama Anytime.* Portsmouth, N.H.: Heinemann Educational Books, 1986.

This is a short paperback, excellent for young children. Dramatic play is developed into guided drama; activities are designed for use in the language arts and also across the curriculum.

CHEIFITZ, DAN. *Theatre in My Head.* Boston: Little, Brown, 1971.

This book describes an experimental workshop in creative drama conducted by the author in an inner-city New York church. Cheifitz communicates the need to look *into* not merely *at,* the child, as he reports his successes and failures.

CROSSCUP, RICHARD. *Children and Dramatics.* New York: Scribner's, 1966.

Crosscup's book is an autobiographical account of his twenty-seven years' experience in one school. Of greatest value is the view he gives of a gifted teacher, able to stimulate the creativity of his pupils. Social values are stressed.

EHRLICH, HARRIETT, AND PATRICIA GRASTRY. *Creative Dramatics Handbook.* Philadelphia: School District of Philadelphia Instructional Services, 1971.

This handbook offers a wealth of ideas for the teacher wishing to include creative drama in the curriculum. Since the material grew directly from the authors' experiences, it is fresh and practical.

FITZGERALD, BURDETTE. *World Tales for Creative Dramatics and Storytelling.* New York: Prentice-Hall, 1962.

In this book the author introduces a wide variety of stories not usually found in collections of this sort. She has drawn from the folklore of countries rarely represented in anthologies of children's literature, thus making an interesting contribution to the field.

FOX, MEM. *Teaching Drama to Young Children.* Portsmouth, N.H.: Heinemann, 1987.

Fox has written a simple, highly readable and sensible book for the teacher of the very young. It is one of the few in the field addressed to the needs and interests of this level.

GOODWILLIE, BARBARA. *Breaking Through: Drama Strategies for Ten's to Fifteen's.* Rowayton, Conn.: New Plays, 1986.

Breaking Through is highly recommended for teachers of upper grades and junior high school students. Simply written with humor and sympathy.

HAAGA, AGNES, AND PATRICIA RANDLES. *Supplementary Material for Use in Creative Dramatics with Younger Children.* Seattle: University of Washington, 1952.

This outline of lessons, planned and evaluated by the authors, is of great practical value to teachers of younger children. It is unique in describing the activities of each session in detail, the music and literature used, and the children's reactions.

HAGGERTY, JOAN. *Please Can I Play God?* Indianapolis: Bobbs-Merrill, 1967.
Haggerty's book tells of her first teaching experience in a ghetto school in London. Throughout her account, which is both amusing and touching, runs her concern for these disadvantaged children as she guides them in creative dramatic activities. It is not a textbook but a sympathetic account of a beginning teacher's classroom experiences.

HEINIG, RUTH. *Creative Drama for the Classroom Teacher.* Englewood Cliffs, N.J.: Prentice-Hall, 1981.
This is a second edition of a text originally written by two experienced teachers but this time by one, who is well known in the field. Pantomime, improvisation, songs, and games are among the activities suggested. They are arranged to guide the classroom teacher through simple to more advanced techniques, and each chapter has suggestions and assignments for the college student.

————. *Creative Drama for Kindergarten through Grade 3.* Englewood Cliffs, N.J. Prentice-Hall, 1987.

————. *Creative Drama Resource Book for Grades 4 through 6.* Englewood Cliffs, N.J.: Prentice-Hall, 1987.
These two texts are addressed to the classroom teacher, who has no background in drama but is interested in using it. Practical and clearly written by an experienced and respected leader in the field.

HODGSON, JOHN, AND ERNEST RICHARDS. *Improvisation.* London: Methuen, 1967.
This book on improvisation is not directed exclusively to work with children. The aim is to use two elements from everyday life: spontaneous response to unexpected situations and the employment of this response in controlled conditions. Exercises are given.

KASE, ROBERT. *Stories for Creative Acting.* New York: Samuel French, 1961.
Kase has collected stories recommended to him by experts in the field. All stories have been used with success, thus making this a valuable addition to any teacher's library.

KASE-POLISINI, JUDITH. *The Creative Drama Book: Three Approaches.* New Orleans: Anchorage Press, 1988.
The author gives three approaches to the subject in a book that is different from all the other texts in the field. Written by an experienced and well-known leader, it should be of interest to specialists and generalists. Recommended reading for persons working in schools, recreation programs, and therapeutic settings.

KEYSELL, PAT. *Motives for Mime.* London: Evans, 1975.
This little paperback is divided into three parts: the first deals with beginning activities for children from five to seven; the second, with development for the seven- to nine-year-olds; and the third, application for those aged nine to twelve. Starting with real objects, the author progresses to mime. She works for awareness of size, weight, shape, and the use of space. Although the material is organized according to age levels, it also follows a logical progression from simple to complicated

and is, therefore, a useful text on any level.

KRAUS, JOANNA HALPERT. *Sound and Motion Stories*. Rowayton, Conn.: New Plays, 1971.
Although not a textbook, the way in which sounds and actions can be used to capture attention to stimulate the imagination of younger children qualifies it for inclusion in this bibliography. The reader can learn from the author's suggestions how to use other material in this way.

McCASLIN, NELLIE. *Children and Drama*. 2d ed. Lanham, Md.: University Press of America, 1986.
This is a collection of essays on creative drama written by twenty experts in the field. A variety of viewpoints is represented and different methodologies suggested. It is of greater interest to the experienced teacher than to the beginner.

———. *Creative Drama in the Intermediate Grades*. White Plains, N.Y.: Longman, 1987.

———. *Creative Drama in the Primary Grades*. White Plains, N.Y.: Longman, 1987.
The two books on creative drama were written specifically for the classroom teacher. Theory and lesson plans are combined with scope and sequence of objectives in mind.

NOBLEMAN, ROBERTA. *Fifty Projects for Creative Dramatics*. Bethel, Conn.: New Plays, 1986.
An excellent source for activities that can be used by classroom teachers and recreation leaders. Written by an experienced teacher, all activities have been tried out and used successfully by the author.

———. *Using Creative Drama Outside the Classroom*. Bethel, Conn.: New Plays, 1974.
In this book the author tells how creative drama may be taught successfully in nontraditional spaces and places. As valuable, however, for the teacher as for the leader in community and camp situations.

POLSKY, MILTON. *Let's Improvise!* Lanham, Md.: University Press of America, 1989.
A popular book filled with short and lively suggestions for improvisations. The text can be used in class and in afterschool interest groups.

PEREIRA, NANCY. *Creative Dramatics in the Library*. Rowayton, Conn.: New Plays, 1974.
Although the content is not substantially different from other books on the subject, the consideration of the neighborhood library as a location for dramatic activities is. The author offers suggestions for starting points, games, use of time and space, and handling of groups, visual aids, and culminating activities.

ROSENBERG, HELANE. *Creative Drama and Imagination: Transforming Ideas into Action*. New York: Holt, Rinehart and Winston, 1987.
The subtitle describes the thrust of this book by a well-known author. Beginning with a brief history of the field, it goes into imagery, the Rutgers Method, drama structures, and "starters." The book was several years in the making and should be of interest to teachers and drama leaders.

SALISBURY, BARBARA; *Theatre Arts in the Elementary School (K-3) and (4-6)*. New Orleans: Anchorage Press, 1987.
This text is designed for the use of the classroom teacher who is

required to teach creative drama along with the other arts but has had little or no preparation for it. Consequently, the guidelines are clear, the exercises and activities practical and on the level for which it was intended. A most useful and simple text by an expert in the field.

SCHER, ANNA, AND CHARLES VERRALL. *100+ Ideas for Drama*. London: Heinemann Educational Books, 1975.
Here is a small paperback filled with good ideas for games, warm-ups, mime and movement, and activities using props and costumes. Improvised plays are described with suggested techniques to create them.

———. *Another 100+ Ideas for Drama*. London: Heinemann Educational Books, 1987.
An excellent text for developed work in improvisation and guidance in the production of an end-of-term play for older students.

SCHWARTZ, DOROTHY, AND DOROTHY ALDRICH, eds. *Give Them Roots and Wings*. 2d ed. New Orleans: Anchorage Press, 1987.
This is a guide to drama in the elementary school, prepared by leaders in the field and edited by Dorothy Schwartz and Dorothy Aldrich as cochairmen of a project for the Children's Theatre Association. Published in workbook form, it offers the classroom teacher goals and dramatic activities with checklists for rating children's development. Usable and attractively illustrated.

SIKS, GERALDINE BRAIN. *Children's Literature for Dramatization*. New York: Harper & Row, 1964.
This is a collection of stories and poems, old and new, for the classroom teacher and group leader. The introductions to the stories make the book particularly valuable to less experienced teachers, but it is useful to anyone working in the field.

———. *Drama with Children*. 2d ed. New York: Harper & Row, 1983.
This latest book by a well-known creative drama leader and author of other texts in the field is of particular interest to the more experienced teacher or graduate student. It is divided into three parts: the philosophy of drama, the teaching of drama, and individual experiences and uses of drama. In this new edition the author expands on what she calls the "process-concept structure approach" and includes a selected bibliography and a few short plays.

SLADE, PETER. *Child Drama*. London: University of London Press, 1954.
Written by an expert in children's dramatics in England, this lengthy book presents a philosophy and way of working. It is detailed and informative and should be of interest to all leaders and teachers of creative dramatics. The author takes an unequivocal stand against children in public performances.

———. *An Introduction to Child Drama*. London and Toronto: Hodder and Stoughton, 1976.
All the fundamental principles of Slade's methods are here. Children, if unhampered by adult imposition, can find self-expression and reach toward full human development. It is simply written, short, and to the

point. Highly recommended for the beginner.

SPOLIN, VIOLA. *Improvisation for the Theatre*. Evanston, Ill.: Northwestern University Press, 1963.

This is a comprehensive handbook of teaching and directing techniques, not specifically designed for use with children but nevertheless appropriate and useful to the more experienced teacher. It contains a variety of exercises and theatre games.

―――. *Theatre Games for the Classroom*. Evanston, Ill.: Northwestern University Press, 1987.

An adaptation of her popular and well-known text for adult actors, *Improvisation for the Theatre*. This book, however, is written to meet the needs of the classroom teacher who is required to teach drama and knows little about it or how to present it to children.

STRAUSS, JOYCE. *Imagine That! Exploring Make-Believe*. New York: Human Sciences Press, 1985.

Less well-known than most of the creative drama books on the lists of texts in the field, it contains some good material that leaders should find useful. The title gives an idea of the spirit that prevails.

VAN TASSEL, KATRINA, and MILLIE GREIMANN. *Creative Dramatization*. New York: Threshold Division, Macmillan, 1973.

Here is a book with special value for the teacher of very young children. Based on sound educational principles, it is a guidebook for the stimulation of creativity through music, mime, movement, and language arts. It is clearly written and presented in an attractive format. Illustrated. Highly recommended.

WAGNER, JEARNINE, AND KITTY BAKER. *A Place for Ideas: Our Theatre*. Rev. ed. New Orleans: Anchorage Press, 1978.

This is a unique book in that it describes with appreciation and beauty the theatre in which the authors work. It is not a children's theatre in the usual sense but rather a "place for ideas," where the arts can be explored and experienced. Illustrations show children experimenting with color, movement, and music, as well as creative drama. This is less a textbook than an inspiration to others who work with children in the arts.

WARD, WINIFRED. *Playmaking with Children*. New York: Appleton-Century-Crofts, 1957.

This book by a distinguished leader is a landmark text. It is arranged both as to age levels and use, including dramatics in school, recreation, religious education, and therapy. Highly readable, it is valuable both for the beginning and the experienced teacher.

―――. *Stories to Dramatize*. Anchorage, Ky.: Anchorage Press, 1952.

In this collection, the author includes a rich variety of stories and some poems for use in school and recreation groups. It is arranged for children on various age levels (from six to fourteen) and contains material that the author tested and found rewarding in her many years of teaching.

WAY, BRIAN. *Development through Drama*. New York: Humanities, 1972.

The development of the whole child is the thesis of this book, directed particularly to teachers of older children. Many practical exercises in improvisational drama are included. Highly recommended.

WILDER, ROSILYN. *A Space Where Anything Can Happen.* Rowayton, Conn.: New Plays, 1977.

The author brings a wealth of experience to this text, directed to the teacher of older children. Challenges, projects, descriptions of her own classes and students, discipline, and clear guidelines for leading modern youngsters in creative work are the most valuable aspects.

Play

BARRAGER, PAMELA. *Spiritual Understanding through Creative Drama.* Valley Forge, Pa.: Judson Press, 1981.

The author's specialization in religious drama gives her the background necessary for the approach used in this book. Recommended particularly for teachers in parochial schools and religious education programs.

BETTELHEIM, BRUNO. *The Uses of Enchantment.* New York: Knopf, 1976.

This landmark book validated the fairy tale, thus giving teachers of younger children the confidence they sought to use these popular, age-old stories in drama classes. Children love them and teachers can see their value pyschologically as well as dramatically.

BLATNER, ADAM, AND ALLEE BLATNER. *The Art of Play: An Adult's Guide to Reclaiming Imagination and Spontaneity.* New York: Human Sciences Press, 1988.

This is an excellent book for parents, teachers and community program leaders in the arts. Written by specialists, it is readable and interesting; recommended to both the experienced and inexperienced teacher.

GROOS, KARL. *The Play of Animals.* New York: D. Appleton and Co., 1898.

Written nearly a hundred years ago, Groos is still considered an important scholar and scientist. This book provides a detailed and comprehensive classification of the play of animals from an instinctive point of view. Recommended for teachers particularly interested in the phenomenon of play.

HARTLEY, RUTH, LAWRENCE FRANK, AND ROBERT GOLDENSON. *The Complete Book of Children's Play.* New York: Cromwell, 1975.

This book is of particular interest to teachers of younger children. Readable and clear, it has held its place in the forefront of texts on child behavior.

———. *Understanding Children's Play.* New York: Columbia University Press, 1964.

A continuation of the study of play listed above. Also highly recommended.

HUIZINGA, JOHAN. *Homo Ludens.* Boston: Beacon Press, 1950.

A classic text to be found on all lists of persons interested in psychology, philosophy, and drama. A "must" for creative drama leaders, who will see the relationship of play to all aspects of life and necessary for full human development.

KOSTE, VIRGINIA GLASGOW. *Dramatic Play in Childhood: Rehearsal for Life.* University Press of America, Lanham, Md.: 1987.

A delightful collection of observations made by the author in the study of the dramatic play of young children. She eschews scholarly writing deliberately in keeping with the spirit of her study. Highly recommended for teachers of the young but enjoyable reading for everyone.

LOWENFELD, MARGARET. *Play in Childhood.* New York: Wiley, 1967.

Another book by an American educator, written for the teacher and highly readable. Not new but still good and recommended.

MEARNS, HUGHES. *Creative Power.* New York: Dover Publications, 1958.

An inspiring book, written during the height of the progressive education movement. Out of print for a number of years, it was reprinted nearly thirty years ago and is to be found on the reading lists of all teachers of the arts. Simple and sound.

MONTAGU, ASHLEY. *Growing Young.* New York: McGraw-Hill, 1981.

A highly popular book by a respected and well-known author. In examining play, he finds it a key to staying young and living a richer life. Recommended for persons of all ages and occupations.

PIAGET, JEAN. *Play, Dreams and Imitation in Childhood.* New York: W. W. Norton, 1962.

Probably our most respected and best known educator, Piaget describes the value of play and of imitation in the development of the human being. His five developmental stages give the teacher of creative drama more than a grid; they help to understand the materials to use and the responses to expect on each of the levels.

PIERS, MARIA W., ed. *Play and Development: A Symposium with Contributions by Piaget and Others.* New York: W. W. Norton, 1972.

The book does exactly what the title promises. Instead of one author, it is written by specialists in the field. Important for teachers particularly interested in the subject.

RASMUSSEN, MARGARET, ed. *Play.* Washington, D.C.: Association for Childhood Education International, 1963.

Another book by a well-known educator, who in this instance acts as editor. Articles by specialists on the subject.

REILLY, MARY. *Play as Exploratory Learning: Studies of Curiosity Behavior.* Beverly Hills, Calif.: Sage, 1974.

This book stresses a special area of the subject of play. Recommended as sound but more limited than many of the above texts.

SCHECHNER, RICHARD, AND MADY SCHUMAN. *Ritual, Play, and Performance.* New York: Seabury Press, 1976.

Richard Schechner's interest in ritual has led him into an analysis of play and its relationship to theatre. One of the best known proponents of the subject, his work is recommended to teachers of older and adult students.

TORRANCE, PAUL. *Encouraging Creativity in Children.* Dubuque, Iowa: William C. Brown, 1970.

Torrance is a well-known name among educators. He writes with clarity and enthusiasm as he describes his research into the subject. Still recommended reading.

Theatre for Children

BREEN, ROBERT. *Chamber Theatre.* Englewood Cliffs, N.J.: Prentice-Hall, 1978.

The originator of chamber theatre describes the technique clearly and simply. Although it is not practiced widely, chamber theatre is still a good way of handling literary material that is not written in dramatic form.

BROADMAN, MURIEL. *Understanding Your Child's Entertainment.* New York: Harper & Row, 1977.

Although this book has been out of print for several years, it is still the only one in the field that strikes every area of children's theatre with a clear point of view and a professional approach. Interesting and understandable.

CHORPENNING, CHARLOTTE. *Twenty-One Years with Children's Theatre.* Anchorage, Ky.: Anchorage Press, 1955.

This book has been out of print for a long time but it is included in this list because a few copies are around and the author was the first to prescribe rules for writing plays for young audiences. Times have changed and the rules are no longer strictly observed but there is much valid material here.

COREY, ORLIN. *Theatre for Children — Kids' Stuff or Theatre?* Anchorage, Ky.: Anchorage Press, 1974.

A short collection of essays written by the publisher of the Anchorage Press, Inc. The author knows the field well and writes with honesty and conviction.

CUNNINGHAM, REBECCA. *The Magic Garment: Principles of Costume Design.* White Plains, N.Y.: Longman, 1989.

This book on costume goes into some detail about history and principles of costume. Recommended for the experienced costumer.

DAVIS, JED, AND MARY JANE EVANS. *Theatre for Children and Youth.* New Orleans: Anchorage Press, 1982.

Written by two lifelong practitioners of theatre for children, this college text was revised and republished in 1987. A handsome book, covering all major areas of the subject. Invaluable for students and directors.

FISHER, CAROLINE, AND HAZEL ROBERTSON. *Children and the Theatre.* Palo Alto, Calif.: Stanford University Press, 1950.

Long out of print, this book tells the story of the Palo Alto community theatre in California. The authors were pioneers and their book gives serious students of the subject some valuable insights.

FORKERT, MAURICE. *Children's Theatre That Captures Its Audience.* Chicago: Coach House, 1962.
The story of the Goodman Theatre of the Art Institute of Chicago Children's Program. Valuable but difficult to find in many libraries.

GOLDBERG, MOSES. *Children's Theatre: A Philosophy and a Method.* Englewood Cliffs, N.J.: Prentice-Hall, 1974.
This is one of the best books on the subject. Written by a professional children's theatre producer with years of experience behind him, it is an invaluable college text that is now out of print but still available.

HALL, JEANNE. "An Analysis of the Content of Selected Children's Plays with Special Reference to the Developmental Values Inherent in Them." Ph.D. dissertation, University of Michigan, 1966.

HEALY, DATY, *Dress the Show.* Bethel, Conn.: New Plays, 1976.
An excellent resource for the classroom teacher working on a limited budget with limited time. Practical, simple text, illustrated by the author.

JOHNSON, ALBERT, AND BERTHA JOHNSON. *Drama for Junior High.* New York: A. S. Barnes, 1971.
This is a text for older children to be used by both inexperienced and experienced teachers. It includes exercises for diction, acting, and scene study. Unlike most texts in the field, it contains a bit of stage history and profiles of well-known actors.

JOHNSON, RICHARD. *Producing Plays for Children.* New York: Rosen, 1971.
Recommended for high school teachers. The author is a teacher with many years of experience and well-known as a leader in the field.

KLEIN, JEANNE, ed. *Theatre for Young Audiences: Principles and Strategies for the Future.* Lawrence, Kans.: University of Kansas at Lawrence, 1988.
Proceedings of a conference held in honor of Jed H. Davis.

KORTY, CAROL. *Writing Your Own Play.* New York: Scribner's, 1986.
An excellent guide for young people in writing original plays.

LEVY, JONATHON. *A Theatre of the Imagination.* Rowayton, Conn.: New Plays, 1986.
A splendid collection of essays on children's theater.

MCCASLIN, NELLIE. *Historical Guide to Children's Theatre in America.* Westport, Conn.: Greenwood Press, 1987.
This is a reference book designed for library use. It contains information on children's theatre and profiles all known children's theatres past and present that have been in existence for at least five years and have given at least fifty performances a year.

———. *Shows on a Shoestring.* Bethel, Conn.: New Plays, 1989.
This is a book that falls somewhere between creative drama and children's theatre. It offers suggestions to older children about preparing shows of various kinds for fun, street fairs, community events, and so on. Not only short plays but mime, fashion shows, pet shows, puppet shows, and clowning are among the inclusions.

MCSWEENY, MAXINE. *Creative Children's Theatre.* New York: A. S. Barnes, 1974.

The text follows the procedure from play to creative drama to story dramatization and formal theatre. It would be useful to drama leaders in recreation programs, on playgrounds, and in camp, as well as to classroom teachers.

MILGRIM, SALLY-ANNE. *Plays to Play with in Class.* San Jose, Calif.: Resource Publications, 1986.
Here is a collection of short one-act plays with language arts activities. The plays can be played as they are or used as exercises in which students may change dialogue, characters, and endings. An interesting and different book to use with older children.

ROSENBERG, HELANE S., AND CHRISTINE PRENDERGAST. *Theatre for Young People: A Sense of Occasion.* New York: Holt, Rinehart and Winston, 1983.
Here is a good, comprehensive text for college students. It covers all areas of theatre and is profusely illustrated. The authors represent educational theatre and professional theatre for children, respectively.

SIKS, GERALDINE BRAIN, AND HAZEL DUNNINGTON, eds. *Children's Theatre and Creative Dramatics: Principles and Practices.* Seattle: University of Washington Press, 1961.
A collection of monographs written by specialists in the field. It needs up-dating but is still an important record of the movement in this country.

WHITTON, PAT HALE. *Participation Theatre for Young Audiences.* Bethel, Conn.: New Plays, 1972.
A collection of articles by directors who have used participation.

WAY, BRIAN. *Audience Participation.* Boston: Baker's Plays, 1981.
The only thorough book on the subject. It lists goals and values and describes in detail the method devised by the author.

Drama in Education

ALLEN, JOHN. *Drama in Schools: Its Theory and Practice.* London: Heinemann Educational Books, 1979.
The author of this book is both well known and well qualified to write on drama education. After giving a brief history of the subject in England, he proceeds to discuss current practices and to take a strong stand on a number of controversial issues. This should be required reading for every specialist and recommended for the generalist.

BAKER, DONALD. *Understanding the Under Fives.* London: Evans, 1975.
The author combines background and expertise in early childhood education as well as theatre and drama education. It is a unique, practical, and highly readable text.

BISSINGER, KRISTEN, AND NANCY RENFRO. *Leap into Learning: Curriculum Taught through Creative Dramatics and Dance* (Photographs by Anne Jackson). Austin, Tex.: Nancy Renfro Studios, 1989.
A recent text written by a teacher of dance and a puppeteer. Highly recommended for teachers in the elementary grades.

BOLTON, GAVIN. *Drama as Education.* London: Longman, 1984.
A theoretical and practical book by one of England's most respected leaders.

———. *Toward a Theory of Drama in Education.* London: Longman, 1979.
Written by one of England's outstanding drama educators, this is a theoretical treatment of the subject. It is of greatest interest to the specialist or experienced classroom teacher.

CHARTERS, JILL, AND ANNE GATELY. *Drama Anytime.* London: Heinemann, 1986.
Drama Anytime explores the place of drama in the primary curriculum and provides guidelines for planning a variety of activities in movement, role play, improvisation, and performance. A practical short handbook for the classroom teacher.

COURTNEY, RICHARD. *Play, Drama and Thought.* New York: Drama Book Specialists, 1974.
There are many useful sections in this British publication directed toward the philosophy and practice of drama in the school.

———. *Re-Play: Studies of Human Drama in Education.* Toronto: Ontario Institute for Studies in Education, 1982.
The author deals with the process of education as spontaneous drama. He begins by examining developmental drama and proceeds to the drama of learning. A rationale for including the arts in education is provided. Detailed and theoretical rather than practical.

CULLUM, ALBERT. *Aesop in the Afternoon.* New York: Citation, 1972.
This is a most usable collection of Aesop's fables, which can be played creatively by children of all ages.

———. *Push Back the Desks.* New York: Citation, 1967.
The author has written an account of some creative projects and techniques he has used in the public school classroom to enhance learning. History, reading, vocabulary, and math are included units of study.

———. *Shake Hands with Shakespeare.* New York: Citation, 1968.
Eight of Shakespeare's plays are adapted for children. The results are filled with action and are relatively simple to produce. They do require time to prepare but could also be improvised, if desired. The value of using Shakespeare is the richness of the language and is a further recommendation for this text.

DAVIES, GEOFF. *Practical Primary Drama.* London: Heinemann, 1985.
A short useful text for the generalist. It contains suggestions on how to prepare and conduct drama sessions, particularly in schools where space and time are limited. Ideas for lessons are included.

DAVIS, DAVID, AND CHRIS LAWRENCE, eds. *Gavin Bolton: Selected Writings.* London: Longman, 1986.

DODD, NIGEL, AND WINIFRED HICKSON, eds. *Drama and Theatre in Education.* London: Heinemann, 1971.
This is a collection of essays by well-known British experts including Gavin Bolton, Dorothy Heathcote, Veronica Sherbourn, and others. Of interest to the more experienced leader.

DOYLE, DONALD P. "An Investigation of Elementary Teacher Education Related to the Preparation of Teachers in the Use of Creative Drama in Teaching Language Arts," Ph.D. dissertation, University of Minnesota, 1974.
The findings of this study advocate the use of creative drama as an aid in teaching of language arts in the elementary grades; research showed preparation inadequate and in general not required.

FOX, MEM. *Teaching Drama to Young Children.* Portsmouth, N.H.: Heinemann Educational Books, 1987.
One of the best books available directed to the classroom teacher working with young children. The author, an Australian educator, writes with a sense of humor and great simplicity. Highly recommended.

GREEN, HARRIET H., AND SUE MARTIN. *Sprouts.* Carthage, Ill.: Good Apple, 1981.
This is an amply illustrated collection of ideas for use with younger children. Highly recommended.

HALL, MARY ANN, AND PAT HALE. *Capture Them with Magic.* Rowayton, Conn.: New Plays, 1982.
A wonderful and useful collection of ideas to help kindergarten and primary school teachers enliven classes in language arts and science, encourage reading, and improve self-esteem. Described by the authors as "real life" lessons, they deal with the magic of everyday experiences and activities.

HASEMAN, BRAD, AND JOHN O'TOOLE. *Dramawise.* Richmond, Victoria: Heinemann Educational Books Australia, 1987.
An extremely helpful and clear how-to book on understanding the construction of and the writing of a play with young people.

KASE-POLISINI, JUDITH, ed. *Creative Drama in a Developmental Context.* Lanham, Md.: University Press of America, 1985.
———. *Creative Drama and Learning.* Lanham, Md.: University Press of America, 1986.
Both books came out of symposia on creative drama over a five-year period. Recommended only for graduate students or scholars. Excellent but strictly theoretical.

KELLY, ELIZABETH. *Dramatics in the Classroom: Making Lessons Come Alive.* Bloomington, Ind.: Phi Delta Kappa Educational Foundation, 1976.
This small pamphlet gives, in a nutshell, a philosophy of education as well as practical help in showing how drama can be used to teach curricular material effectively. Of greatest value to the beginning or general classroom teacher.

LANDY, ROBERT J. *A Handbook of Educational Drama and Theatre.* Westport, Conn.: Greenwood Press, 1982.
A book based on New York University's Sunrise Semester, in which the various uses of drama and theatre currently found in schools and communities are described. The author describes interviews with experts in all of the fields covered.

McGREGOR, LYNN, MAGGIE TATE, AND KEN ROBINSON. *Learning through Drama.* London: Heinemann, 1977.
Here is another book for the specialist, particularly for one who knows

something about drama education in England. It represents a comprehensive survey done by three well-qualified researchers. An important contribution to the field.

MEARNS, HUGHES. *Creative Power.* 2d rev. ed. New York: Dover Publications, 1958.
This classic text by the gifted educator offers a philosophy of education in the creative arts and techniques with which to implement it. Long out of print, it was republished in paperback at the instigation of the Children's Theatre Association of America, a strong supporter of his views.

MOFFETT, JAMES, AND BETTY JANE WAGNER. *Student Centered Language Arts and Reading, K–13.* Boston: Houghton Mifflin, 1976.
Written by two well-known educators, this book is an argument for the use of drama in language learning and comprehension.

NEELANDS, JONOTHAN. *Making Sense of Drama: A Guide to Classroom Practice.* London: Heinemann, 1984.
A short text that suggests how the teacher can plan and evaluate drama lessons. Different approaches are discussed as well as the relationship between classroom drama and performance.

O'NEILL, CECILY, AND ALAN LAMBERT. *Drama Structures: A Practical Handbook for Teachers.* London: Heinemann Educational Books, 1982.
The subtitle describes its intent, which is how to teach drama in the classroom. Structures show how to take themes and use them in small group work and how to build drama across the curriculum. An excellent text for college students planning to teach.

PIAGET, JEAN. *Play, Dreams, and Imitation in Childhood.* New York: W. W. Norton, 1962.
A study of child development in terms of systematic and representative imitation, the structure and symbolism of games and dreams, and the movement from sensory-motor schemas to conceptual schemas. A landmark book.

SAXTON, JULIANA, AND NORA MORGAN. *Teaching Drama.* Portsmouth, N.H.: Heinemann, 1987.
The authors are experienced teachers who write from the standpoint of education in which drama is used as an effective tool. Highly recommended as a Drama-in-Education resource.

SHUMAN, R. BAIRD, ed. *Educational Drama for Today's Schools.* Metuchen, N.J.: Scarecrow, 1978.
This collection of articles came about as a result of workshops given in this country by Dorothy Heathcote, who has written the lead chapter. Drama-in-Education is defined as "anything which involves persons in active role-taking situations in which attitudes, not characters, are the chief concern . . . at this moment, not memory based." Each chapter, written by a different person, deals with values clarification, language development, moral education, and so on.

STABLER, TOM. *Drama in Primary Schools* (Schools Council Drama 5–11 Project). London: Macmillan Education, 1978.
This is a one-year study of forty schools in England, including infant,

primary, junior, and middle schools. Objectives are clear, with material for teachers and administrators in areas of language, writing, and literature.

STEWIG, JOHN WARREN. *Informal Drama in the Elementary Language Arts Program.* New York: Teachers College Press, 1983.
This text focuses on the value of drama in the development of language skills. The author deals with the various ways in which the classroom teacher can use movement and improvisation and can evaluate sessions in terms of the language arts. Greatest value is for the generalist or classroom teacher.

————. *Teaching Language Arts in Early Childhood.* New York: Holt, Rinehart and Winston, 1980.
Although a text on language arts by a specialist in the field, drama is stressed as to its value in English teaching. The author shares his enthusiasm with readers.

TIEDT, IRIS M. *Drama in Your Classroom.* Champaign, Ill.: National Council of Teachers of English, 1974.
Written by and for the teacher of English, the text advocates drama as an aid to more effective classroom teaching.

TYNAS, BILLI. *Child Drama in Action: A Practical Guide for Teachers.* Toronto: Gage, 1971.
This is an instructor's manual, which opens with a brief but clear introduction and then moves directly into a series of lesson plans. Each of these plans follows a theme and gives the activity to be emphasized. This very beautiful book will be of most use to teachers with a background in creative drama rather than to beginners.

WAGNER, BETTY JANE. *Dorothy Heathcote: Drama as a Learning Medium.* Washington, D.C.: National Education Association, 1976.
The author has done a masterful job of describing the methods of this distinguished English drama teacher. Wagner explains how Heathcote finds material, helps children build an imagined situation, and leads them to see and feel the elements of human experience. Most important, she shows how the learning takes place. It is apparent from this book why Heathcote has so great a following among elementary school teachers.

WATSON, CHARLES M., ed. and proj. supv. *Theatre Resources Directory/Handbook.* Washington, D.C.: National Endowment for the Arts, Artists in the Schools, 1980.

Puppetry and Masks

ALKEMA, CHESTER J. *Mask Making.* New York: Sterling, 1981.
A variety of masks made from a variety of materials. Beautiful illustrations in both black and white and color, ranging from simple paper bags to elaborately decorated masks.

BOYLAN, ELEANOR. *Puppet Plays for Special Days.* Rowayton, Conn.: New Plays, 1976.
This delightful collection of short plays should prove helpful to class-

room teachers and community leaders engaged in puppetry. Focus is on the play rather than on methods of construction.

BROOKS, COURTANEY. *Plays and Puppets Etcetera.* Claremont, Calif.: Belnice Books, 1981. This book is designed as a starting point for readers who have little or no knowledge of puppets. Written in a conversational style, the text encourages the inexperienced person; yet it does not talk down to the reader.

CHAMPLIN, CONNIE. *Puppetry and Creative Drama in Storytelling.* Austin, Tex.: Nancy Renfro Studios, 1980. The Renfro Studios are known for work in puppetry but they also include other uses of puppets, such as an aid to storytelling and therapy for children with special problems. Highly recommended, especially for teachers of younger children.

CHAMPLIN, JOHN, AND CONNIE BROOKS. *Puppets and the Mentally Retarded Student.* Austin, Tex.: Nancy Renfro Studios, 1980. Developing literary comprehension with the mentally retarded child. The text shows how to adapt books for telling stories and offers special techniques for using puppets in programs K–6.

COLE, NANCY. *Puppet Theatre in Performance.* New York: William Morrow, 1978. What distinguishes this book is its emphasis on performance. Whereas many texts on puppetry offer detailed instructions for making puppets, Cole gives ideas and clear directions for handling them. An unusually good book for advanced as well as older puppeteers.

CUMMINGS, RICHARD. *101 Hand Puppets: A Guide for Puppeteers of All Ages.* New York: McKay, 1962. This is an extremely comprehensive book offering step-by-step instruction for making every conceivable kind of hand puppet from the simplest to the most elaborate. It includes scripts and has more than sixty diagrams and illustrations. For older and more experienced classes.

DEAN, AUDREY VINCENT. *Puppets That Are Different.* New York: Taplinger, 1973. This book was specially designed to teach beginners how to bring the hand puppet to life and how to develop the skills needed to mount a successful show. Every detail is included in a clear, attractive step-by-step primer.

ENGLER, LARRY, AND CAROL FIJAN. *Making Puppets Come Alive.* New York: Taplinger, 1973. This is a charming and practical text for the beginner of any age. To be used by the teacher, it offers help in making and handling puppets, including exercises to develop the skills needed to produce a show. Beautifully illustrated.

FERGUSON, HELEN. *Bring on the Puppets.* New York: Morehouse–Barlow, 1975. Here is another good book on puppetry, less well-known than most of the others on this list. The publisher handles books in specialized areas, such as the handicapped and the elderly.

FREERICKS, MARY, AND JOYCE SEGAL. *Creative Puppets in the Classroom.* Rowayton, Conn.: New Plays, 1979. As the title states, this book gives instruction for using puppets in the curriculum. Inexpensive materials and simple techniques add to its value for the teacher.

HUNT, TAMARA, AND NANCY RENFRO. *Puppetry in Early Childhood Education.* Austin, Tex.: Nancy Renfro Studios, 1982.
One of the most comprehensive books on the subject. Teachers, librarians, and recreation leaders will find this enormously helpful. Highly recommended.

JAGENDORF, MORITZ. *Puppets for Beginners.* Boston: Plays, 1952.
A simple, comprehensive book with attractive illustrations. Recommended for school and community use.

HANFORD, ROBERT TEN EYCK. *The Complete Book of Puppets and Puppeteering.* New York and London: Drake, 1976.
A 157-page paperback concentrating on an overview of puppetry—past, present, and to come; the tools of the trade; the production; and techniques and tips from the pros. An excellent book written in clear, definitive style with simple, yet complete instructions on all aspects of puppets and puppet productions.

KRINSKY, NORMAN, AND BILL BERRY. *Paper Construction for Children.* New York: Reinhold, 1966.
Masks and puppets are among many projects described in this book. Delightful text with drawings and photographs to illustrate the brief but adequate explanations.

LUSKIN, JOYCE. *Easy to Make Puppets.* Boston: Plays, 1975.
Instructions, patterns, and photographs show how to create twenty-four puppets: hand, glove and marionette. Simple, attractive format.

MCCASLIN, NELLIE. *Puppet Fun: Performance, Production and Plays.* New York: McKay, 1977.
This text, directed to the child from ages seven to ten, can be used equally well by the inexperienced teacher or recreation leader who wants to include puppetry but who has never worked with it. Diagrams and illustrations show the rudiments of making and manipulating hand puppets. Currently out of print.

NOBLEMAN, ROBERTA. *Mime and Masks.* Rowayton, Conn.: New Plays, 1979.
A gifted teacher brings two areas together in this book: mime, which is an actor's tool, and the mask, used for dramatic projection. In this text the performing and visual arts meet.

PEYTON, JEFFREY, AND BARBARA KOENIG. *Puppetry: A Tool for Teaching.* New Haven, Conn.: P.O. Box 270, 1973.
Simplicity and economy characterize this one-hundred-page guide to puppetry for the curriculum. Originally prepared for the New Haven Public Schools, it is adaptable to other systems and a variety of subject areas.

RENFRO, NANCY. *Puppetry and the Art of Story Creation.* Austin, Tex.: Nancy Renfro Studios, 1979.
A guide to story creating with simple puppet ideas. There is a special section on puppetry for the disabled.

ROLFE, BARI. *Behind the Mask.* Oakland, Calif.: Personabooks, 1977.
One of the few books on the mask. For teachers and students looking for
material on masks, this book is recommended.

ROSS, LAURA. *Scrap Puppets.* New York: Holt, Rinehart and Winston, 1978.
A clearly illustrated book that describes four basic kinds of puppets. A
list of materials supplements the directions for making them.

SCHMIDT, HANS J., and KARL J. SCHMIDT. *Learning with Puppets.* Chicago: Coach House
Press, 1980.
A guide to making and using puppets in the elementary school. Stress on
acquisition of academic and social skills, as well as artistic expression.

SIMS, JUDY. *Puppets for Dreaming and Scheming.* Walnut Creek, Calif.: Early Stages, 1978.
A source book for those using puppetry in the elementary classroom.
Especially well suited to the needs of teachers of younger children;
many ideas and simple, clear directions.

WHITTAKER, VIOLET. *Give Puppets a Hand.* Grand Rapids, Mich.: Baker Book House, 1982.
Here is another book on puppetry, recommended for school use. Good
material, well organized, and practical for the teacher or group leader.

Movement and Dance

BARLIN, ANN, AND PAUL BARLIN. *The Art of Learning through Movement.* New York: Ritchie
Ward, 1971.
The authors have had wide experience in public school teaching. They
present their material clearly with enthusiasm and practicality.

BLATT, GLORIA T., AND JEAN CUNNINGHAM. *It's Your Move.* New York: Teachers College
Press, 1981.
The authors' aim is the integration of expressive movement and the
language arts. Lessons in movement help the teacher in reaching
language and literature.

CARR, RACHEL. *See and Be: Yoga and Creative Movement for Children.* Englewood Cliffs,
N.J.: Prentice-Hall, 1980.
This beautifully illustrated book shows parents and teachers ways of
helping preschool-age children to develop self-awareness and confidence through yoga and creative movement.

CONNER, NORMA, AND HARRIET KLEBANOFF. *And a Time to Dance.* Boston: Beacon Press,
1967.
This is a sensitively illustrated book that explains, encourages, and
shows the reader how to involve children in creative dance. Simply
written, it also shows what can be done with the mentally retarded.

DORIAN, MARGERY. *Ethnic Stories for Children to Dance.* San Mateo, Calif.: BBB, 1978.
Here is a second book by the author of *Telling Stories through Movement.* It includes stories from around the world with suggestions for
rhythmic accompaniment on drums and other instruments. Years of
experience as a dancer and as teacher of dance give the author
knowledge and insight. The choice of material is a valuable addition to

the resources available to teachers in lower grades.

DORIAN, MARGERY, AND FRANCES GULLAND. *Telling Stories through Movement.* Belmont, Calif.: Fearon, 1974.
This is an invaluable little book for creative drama teachers working with young children. The authors bring a rich background in dance, education, and drama to the task, and the result is practical and clear. Creative movement and rhythms are used to tell stories from many lands.

GRAY, VERA, AND RACHEL PERCIVAL. *Music, Movement, and Mime for Children.* Oxford: Oxford University Press, 1962.
The emphases in this book are on music and movement, and the authors give a good basic introduction to those planning to teach in these areas. It is clear and concise with many exercises and procedures suggested.

KING, NANCY. *The Actor and His Space.* New York: Drama Book Specialists, 1971.
This book explains the importance of movement in an actor's training. Many exercises are given. It is probably less useful to the elementary and secondary school teacher than the author's other text, *Giving Form to Feeling,* but is good material nevertheless.

———. *Giving Form to Feeling.* New York: Drama Book Specialists, 1975.
This is a sound and useful handbook with many exercises and ideas. The author states that it is a book of beginnings. This is true, but it is not necessarily written for the beginner; the actor, dancer, and teacher on any level will find help in expressing ideas and feelings through movement, rhythm, sounds, and words.

———. *A Movement Approach to Acting.* Englewood Cliffs, N.J.: Prentice-Hall, 1981.
A text that goes from breathing and body awareness exercises to circus skills, stage combat, and nonverbal elements of drama. Written by an experienced teacher, this book is highly recommended.

LA SALLE, DOROTHY. *Rhythms and Dance for Elementary Schools.* Rev. ed. New York: Ronald, 1951.
This collection of rhythms and dances should be extremely useful to the teacher of dramatic play and creative drama or to the children's theatre director. It contains movement fundamentals, singing games, and folk dances, ranging from simple to advanced.

LABAN, RUDOLF. *Modern Educational Dance.* Boston: Plays, 1980.
Published first in England in 1973, this book is now available in the United States. It is an excellent guide for teachers and parents in the techniques of modern dance. It provides information on movement and dance, also suggesting themes suitable for different age groups.

LOWNDES, BETTY. *Movement and Creative Drama for Children.* Boston: Plays, 1971.
First published in England, this practical and stimulating book should find enthusiastic readers in the United States as well. The author, an experienced teacher, explains the value and use of improvised movement and follows with chapters on body awareness, locomotion, mime, sensory awareness, and creative movement.

MAYNARD, OLGA. *Children and Dance and Music.* New York: Scribner's, 1968.
This book includes material not usually found in texts on creative drama. A good supplement to any text.

MURRAY, RUTH LOVELL. *Dance in Elementary Education.* 3d ed. New York: Harper & Row, 1963.
An extremely helpful dance guide for teachers of beginners and advanced students. The author includes a variety of approaches. The fact that it went into a third edition indicates its popularity.

ROWAN, BETTY. *Learning through Movement Activities for the Preschool and Elementary Grades.* New York: Teachers College Press, 1982.
The author suggests ways to use the child's natural movement for the teaching of language, science, numbers, and social studies. Lists of literature and recordings add to its value as a reference book.

SLADE, PETER. *Natural Dance.* London: Hodder and Stoughton, 1977.
This is particularly recommended for the teacher of creative drama. In it Slade discusses "natural dance," or dance that is improvised, as opposed to formal dance techniques. It deals with all ages, levels of experience, and levels of ability; the therapeutic aspects of dance are also included.

Choral Speaking

ABNEY, LOUISE. *Choral Speaking Arrangements for the Lower Grades.* Boston: Expression, 1937.

GULLAN, MARJORIE. *The Speech Choir.* New York: Harper & Row, 1937.

HUCKLEBERRY, ALAN W., and EDWARD S. STROTHER. *Speech Education for the Elementary Teacher.* Boston: Allyn & Bacon, 1966, chap. 6.

RASMUSSEN, CARRIE. *Choral Speaking for Speech Improvement.* Boston: Expression, 1942.

RASMUSSEN, CARRIE. *Let's Say Poetry Together and Have Fun.* Minneapolis: Burgess, 1962.
The above books all appeared during the time when there was great interest in choral speech. They are all excellent and to be recommended for any age level but particularly for use in the elementary classroom. Although the technique is not used widely today, some teachers like it and need help in arranging groups and practicing reading or speaking together. Not all are to be found in all libraries but any one of the books is of practical value.

Storytelling and Reading

BAKER, AUGUSTA, AND ELLIN, GREENE. *Storytelling: Art and Technique.* New York, London: R. R. Bowker. 1977.
An excellent book by two well-known teachers. With the renewed interest in this form of oral communication, the availability of this text is welcome.

BLAKE, JAMES NEAL. *Speech Education Activities for Children.* Springfield, Ill.: Charles C. Thomas, 1970.

Although not a recent book, the content is good and the activities practical and useful for the elementary school.

COGER, LESLIE, AND MELVIN WHITE. *Readers Theatre Handbook.* Chicago: Scott, Foresman, 1967.

Here is an excellent text on this new technique written by experts in the field. Directed toward the adult reader, it is nevertheless equally useful to the high school teacher or to any teacher interested in trying this concept of theatre.

COLWELL, EILEEN. *A Storyteller's Choice.* New York: Henry Z. Walck, 1965.

Although this book has been on the market for some twenty-five years, the content is still practical and the suggestions valid. Recommended.

MACLAY, JOANNA HAWKINS. *Readers Theatre: Toward a Grammar of Practice.* New York: Random House, 1971.

This is an excellent text on the subject. It covers a definition of readers theatre, gives a selection of material, and also describes performance techniques. It is most useful to teachers of upper grades.

MCGUIRE, JACK. *Creative Storytelling: Choosing, Inventing, and Sharing Tales for Children.* New York: McGraw-Hill, 1984.

A relatively new book that teachers will find of great value. The author covers all the important areas in a clear and helpful manner.

SAWYER, RUTH. *The Way of the Storyteller.* New York: Viking, 1962.

Probably the best known of the books in the field, *The Way of the Storyteller* still takes its place at the top of the list. Available in most libraries even after nearly thirty years.

SLOYER, SHIRLEE EPSTEIN. *Readers Theatre: Story Dramatization in the Classroom.* Champaign, Ill.: National Council of Teachers of English, 1981.

An excellent book for teachers of junior and senior high school students. It offers good ideas and a clear description of a technique that appeals to students and gives good training in voice and diction as well as appreciation of literary material.

Drama for the Special Child

Creative Dramatics. Washington, D.C.: American Alliance for Health, Physical Education, and Recreation, 1977.

Creative drama with handicapped and nonhandicapped children and adults is described. Games, activities, story drama, and role playing are included for the purpose of expressing one's own feelings and helping one to work cooperatively with others.

The Eagle Soars: The Artist, the Teacher, and the Handicapped. Chappaqua, N.Y.: New York State Poets in the Schools, 1977.

Activities used in an interdisciplinary arts program with both moderately and severely handicapped students are described. Objectives, procedures, and lesson plans are included.

BETTLEHEIM, BRUNO. *The Uses of Enchantment: The Meaning and Importance of Fairy Tales.* New York: Knopf, 1976.
A landmark book, generally well-known and highly respected. The author gives psychological reasons for the longevity of fairy tales and of their value for young children.

BLATNER, ADAM. *Acting-In (Practical Applications of Psychodramatic Methods).* New York: Springer, 1973.
This book is well-known in psychological circles but is readable and practical for the classroom teacher as well. Recommended for all age levels.

GAY, ELIZABETH. "Gert Schattner's Drama Sessions for Short-Term In-Patients" (Video tape and Report of the Methods of a Founder of Drama Therapy in the United States). Ph.D. dissertation, New York University, 1986.

GILLIES, EMILY P. *Creative Dramatics for All Children.* Washington, D.C.: Association for Childhood Education International, 1973.
Gillies, whose years of experience qualify her to speak authoritatively, discusses drama for the emotionally disturbed and physically handicapped child, as well as its use in the education of children for whom English is a second language.

JENNINGS, SUE. *Creative Drama in Groupwork.* London: Winslow Press, 1986.
A second book by a well-known drama therapist. Simply written and easily understood by the nonspecialist.

———.*Remedial Drama.* New York: Theatre Arts, 1974.
The message in this book is that the experience of drama can enrich everyone's life, whether one is mentally or physically handicapped or socially disadvantaged. For nonspecialists. It is clear and easy to read and will help the teacher to work with the therapist.

———, ed. *Dramatherapy: Theory and Practice for Teachers and Clinicians.* London & Sydney: Croom Helm, 1987.
The value of this book lies in its theoretical content. Not a textbook for classroom teachers, it is to be recommended for college students preparing to teach.

LANDY, ROBERT J. *Drama Therapy: Concepts and Practices.* Springfield, Ill.: Charles C. Thomas, 1986.
One of the few books on drama therapy for students preparing to work in this new field. Readable and sound, by a leader with a background in drama, education, and therapy.

———. *Handbook of Educational Drama and Theatre.* Westport, Conn.: Greenwood Press, 1982.
This book came out of a Sunrise Semester course given at New York University and aired by CBS. It covers all areas of drama in the classroom, and theatre as an art form. The material is arranged in the same interview format as the program, including many specialized with Professor Landy as the anchorman. Interesting to teachers on all levels.

McINTYRE, BARBARA. *Informal Dramatics: A Language Arts Activity for the Special Child.* Pittsburgh: Stanwix, 1963.

This book is a useful guide for teachers of special education and is one of the first directed toward this new area.

Materials on Creative Arts (Arts, Crafts, Dance, Drama, and Music) for Persons with Handicapping Conditions. Washington, D.C.: American Alliance for Health, Physical Education, and Recreation, 1975.

This guide provides information on resources for use in the arts for persons with various handicapping conditions. It suggests activities, guidelines, and implications for programming in art, crafts, dance, drama, and music; materials, references, and suppliers of equipment add to the usefulness.

PIAGET, JEAN. *Play, Dreams, and Imitation in Childhood.* New York: W. W. Norton, 1962. This is one of the books that is recommended for students of drama therapy and teachers of education as well as theatre. The author is one of the world's most respected educators.

PORTNER, ed., updated by Robert Landy, Roberta Zito, and Renee Emunah. *Drama Therapy in Print: A Bibliography.* New York: National Association for Drama Therapy Publications, 1986.

PROKES, SR. DOROTHY. "Exploring the Relationship between Participation in Creative Dramatics and Development of the Imaginative Capacities of Gifted Junior High School Students." Ph.D. dissertation, New York University, 1971. This is one of the few studies made in the field of the arts for the gifted child and is unique in its focus on creative dramatics. The study is available in microfilm and at the New York University Library.

SCHATTNER, GERTRUDE, AND RICHARD, COURTNEY, eds. *Drama in Therapy.* Vol. 1. New York: Drama Book Specialists, 1981. The editors have collected and assembled two volumes of essays written by a large group of experts in a variety of specialized areas. The first books of their kind, *Drama in Therapy* should be of enormous interest and value to teacher and student, as well as to specialist and generalist in drama education.

Related Fields

Aesthetics

ANDRES, MICHAEL F. *Aesthetic Form and Education.* Syracuse: Syracuse University Press, 1958.

BALFE, JUDITH H., AND JONI CHERBO HEINE, eds. *Arts Education beyond the Classroom.* New York: American Council on the Arts, 1987. One of the books available from the American Council on the Arts. Recommended for teachers interested in finding community resources outside the school that will supplement or enhance the classroom experience.

Coming to Our Senses: The Significance of the Arts for American Education. Panel Report, David Rockefeller, Jr., chairman. New York: McGraw-Hill, 1977.

This long-awaited survey of the state of arts education in America is of greatest interest to the specialist and the administrator. It represents years of collecting, compiling, and writing down information gathered from many sources, both persons and organizations.

EDMAN, IRWIN. *Arts and the Man.* New York: New American Library, Mentor Book, 1950. Written by a well-known philosopher over thirty years ago, this is still an important text on aesthetic education. Recommended college students.

ENGEL, MARTIN, AND JEROME HAUSMAN, eds. *Curriculum and Instruction in Arts and Aesthetic Education.* St. Louis: Central Midwestern Regional Educational Laboratory, 1981.

FOWLER, CHARLES. *Can We Rescue the Arts for America's Children? (Coming to Our Senses Ten Years Later).* New York: American Council for the Arts. 1987. A response to the 1977 book, *Coming to Our Senses.* The author takes a look at our goals and how far we have gone toward reaching them. His findings are disappointing and the outlook less bright than it appeared at the time the original research was done.

GARDNER, HOWARD, *Art, Mind, and Brain.* New York: Basic Books, 1982. Written by a Harvard Medical School professor, the author draws together the two areas, cognitive and affective, in a study of human development and learning. This is a brilliant study but of greater interest to the specialist than to the generalist.

KATZ, JONATHAN, ed. *Arts and Education Handbook.* New York: American Council on the Arts, 1987. This is another fine contribution from the American Council on the Arts. Of particular interest to administrators and arts administrators.

KNIETER, GERARD L., AND JANE STALLINGS, eds. *The Teaching Process and Arts and Aesthetics.* St. Louis: Central Midwestern Regional Educational Laboratory, 1979. This is one of the publications of CEMREL, the Central Midwestern Regional Educational Laboratory. Emphasis is on aesthetic education, theory, and practice. CEMREL was a very popular educational service in the seventies.

LANGER, SUZANNE. *Problems of Art.* New York: Scribner's, 1957. Although the book was written more than thirty years ago, the material is still good and of interest. Langer is a well-known philosopher, highly regarded among artists and students of aesthetics.

LINDERMAN, EARL W., AND DONALD W. HEBERHOLZ. *Developing Artistic and Perceptual Awareness.* Dubuque, Iowa: William C. Brown, 1964. One of the best books on the market for both the specialist and the generalist. Written simply by two master teachers, it gives guidance and confidence to teachers of all the arts, not just teachers of the visual arts.

LOWENFIELD, VIKTOR. *Creative and Mental Growth.* New York: Macmillan, 1952.

MADEJA, STANLEY S., ed. *Art and Aesthetics: An Agenda for the Future.* St. Louis: Central Midwestern Regional Educational Laboratory, 1977. This book has been on the market for over thirty-five years but it is still popular with teachers of the visual arts and of great value to teachers of all the arts. Recommended on all levels but particularly for teachers in the elementary schools.

MCLAUGHLIN, JOHN, ed. *A Guide to National and State Arts Education Services.* New York: American Council on the Arts, 1987.

————. *Toward a New Era in Arts Education: The Interlochen Symposium.* New York: American Council on the Arts, 1988.
The two books by McLaughlin are available from the American Council on the Arts and present both a picture of arts education today and how it can be up-graded and enhanced in the future. The author, a former teacher, is knowledgeable and sensitive to the problems of the American educator.

PLOWITZ, KATHRYN A. "Artists-in-Schools: Background Information." Mimeographed report. Washington D.C.: National Endowment for the Arts, April 7, 1980.
This report is often referred to by scholars and administrators. Recommended to arts administrators primarily; an important document.

PORTER, ROBERT. "State Appropriations: Will They Be Enough?" *ACA Update: News for Arts Leaders* (New York: American Council for the Arts) 3, no. 2 (February 12, 1982): 10–12.
An article that deals with the serious question of funding for the arts. Recommended to arts administrators.

SCHIFF, BENNETT. *Artists-in-Schools.* Washington, D.C.: National Endowment for the Arts, 1973.
A popular way of supplementing arts education today, written under the sponsorship of our most prestigious government agency, the National Endowment for the Arts. Recommended for any teacher, administrator or artist interested in working with the board of education as sponsor or artist.

SIKS, GERALDINE BRAIN. "Drama in Education—A Changing Scene." In *Children and Drama.* 2d ed. Edited by Nellie McCaslin. New York: Longman, 1981.
A short but very valuable article on the state of drama in the American classroom today. The author, a well-known and highly respected educator, has followed the scene for many years and brings her research to the reader in a short, clear presentation.

Media and Music

ARONOFF, FRANCES WEBBER. *Music and Young Children.* New York: Turning Wheel Press, 1969.
A widely used text for music teaching, this book has much to offer both specialist and generalist in drama. Ways in which music can enrich the lives of children are suggested and explained. An excellent resource.

CONCANNON, TOM. *Using Media for Creative Teaching.* Bethel, Conn.: New Plays, 1980.
A text for today's classroom, in which a media specialist explains how skills may be developed through the use of camera, video tape, tape recorders, and even the human body. Methods and specific suggestions for using media in the curriculum areas from K to 8 are given.

LIST, LYNNE K. *Music, Art, and Drama Experiences for the Elementary Curriculum.* New York: Teachers College Press, 1982.

This book differs from most in that it focuses on all the arts, showing how they can stimulate learning and enhance teaching. Games and projects are described, as well as suggestions for using them with children who have special problems and needs.

RAVOSA, CARMINO. *Songs Children Act up For.* Rowayton, Conn.: New Plays, 1974.
Twenty-two action songs collected by an experienced teacher and composer for use with children. This is a good and seldom used way of stimulating creative drama.

SHAW, ANN M., AND CJ STEVENS. *Drama, Theatre, and the Handicapped.* Washington, D.C.: American Theatre Association, 1979.
This collection of articles is the work of a committee of the American Theatre Association, funded under a Special Project Program Grant of the National Committee: Arts for the Handicapped, and chaired by the editors. Contributors are experienced in their respective areas and address themselves to the potential of the arts for handicapped persons, the removal of barriers, programs that have already been established, and a review of the existing literature. This is recommended reading for all teachers and recreation leaders.

SHAW, ANN M., WENDY PERKS, AND CJ STEVENS, eds. *Perspectives: A Handbook in Drama and Theatre by, with, and for Handicapped Individuals.* Washington, D.C.: American Theatre Association, 1981.
An invaluable handbook for persons working with the handicapped. Developed by a committee of the American Theatre Association with support from the National Committee: Arts for the Handicapped, it includes articles and plans from eighteen contributors in all areas: the blind, deaf, retarded, emotionally disturbed, elderly, and so on. Although each contributor has a point of view, the collection is practical rather than theoretical. Exercises and resources include proposal and grant writing.

SIMOS, JACK. *Social Growth through Play Production.* New York: Association Press, 1957.
The author is a social worker who describes the step-by-step process of producing plays with emotionally disturbed children in a treatment center. Although he deals with teenagers in this book, his observations and techniques are useful on any age level.

SINGER, DOROTHY G., AND JEROME L. SINGER. *Make Believe.* Glencoe, Ill.: Scott, Foresman 1985.
An excellent text by a highly respected writer and clinician with particular interest in human imagination. Psychological aspect emphasized.

WETHERED, AUDREY G. *Drama and Movement in Therapy.* London: Macdonald and Evans, 1973.
The therapeutic use of movement, mime, and drama are covered in this short text. It is simple and clear and should be useful to both nonspecialist and specialist.

Circus Arts

BALLENTINE, BILL. *Clown Alley.* Boston: Little, Brown, 1982.
This is a collection of anecdotes and memories of circus life. With profiles of well-known performers, it has been termed by reviewers "a salty and affectionate memoir."

BOLTON, REG. *Circus in a Suitcase.* Bethel, Conn.: New Plays, 1982.
An excellent resource for the nonprofessional teacher, or physical education leader who wants to work with circus skills in the community.

———. *New Circus.* London: The Calouste Gulbenkian Foundation, 1977.
This is both a different kind of book and an important book in that it is a survey of the community or regional circus programs of several countries. Written by a man who is interested in the process-oriented circus, it shows clearly the move away from the elitism of the traditional show toward a community-based concept, often amateur by choice, with an emphasis on innovation.

BURGESS, HOVEY. *Circus Techniques.* New York: Drama Book Specialists, 1976.
A comprehensive book for teachers by a master teacher of circus arts at New York University. Includes a series of structured lessons.

CROWTHER, CAROL. *Clowns and Clowning.* London: Macdonald Educational, 1978.
A book for children, including a history of clowning, with many suggestions for activities.

DUCHARTRE, PIERRE LOUIS. *The Italian Comedy.* New York: Dover Publications, 1966.
Valuable material on the commedia dell' arte.

HAMMARSTROM, DAVID LEWIS. *Behind the Big Top.* New York: A. S. Barnes, 1980.
The American circus seen from backstage, this book contains interesting information about performers.

JENKINS, RON. *Acrobats of the Soul.* New York: Theatre Communication Group, 1988.
Former clown, now teaching at Emerson College in Boston, traces the geneology of the New Vaudeville movement, describing how the various groups began and have crossed paths repeatedly.

NICOLL, ALLARDYCE. *Masks, Mimes, and Miracles: Studies in the Popular Theatre.* New York: Cooper Square Publishers, 1963, pp. 135–214.
Nicoll's work is a comprehensive survey and scholarly history of the drama of the Middle Ages. By using extant illustrations, pictures, and texts, Nicoll attempts to provide a kind of "perspective arrangement" of the centuries between the third and the sixteenth, departing somewhat from a formal and direct analysis, first, to summarizing the chief records regarding shows, spectacles, and entertainments until the tenth century (when the religious drama is supposed to take its rise); then, to discussing whatever relics remain of secular drama during the period; and finally, to casting a glance at the origin and development of the religious plays themselves.

———. *The World of Harlequin.* London: Cambridge University Press, 1963.

Distinguished theatre historian describes the classic clown in detail.

NIKLAUS, THELMA. *Harlequin.* New York: George Braziller, 1956.

The author recounts the four hundred years of this colorful clown and progenitor of today's comedians in what she subtitles "The Rise and Fall of a Bergamask Rogue."

SPEIGHT, GEORGE. *A History of the Circus.* New York: A. S. Barnes, 1980.

A reference work filled with details, anecdotes, and photographs.

STOLZENBERG, MARK. *Clowns for Circus and Stage.* New York: Sterling, 1981.

An excellent how-to book for persons interested in learning circus techniques.

———. *How to be Really Funny.* New York: Sterling, 1988.

Another text giving valuable information on circus skills by a clown who is also a teacher and writer. Clearly written, the emphasis is on comedy, a necessary quality in a clown but not always treated in textbooks featuring techniques.

TOWSEN, JOHN. *Clowns.* New York: Hawthorn, 1976.

A highly recommended book written by a clown and scholar, who describes the buffoons and fools who have made audiences laugh.

TROMPETT, ANN. *The Greatest Show on Earth: A Biography of P. T. Barnum.* Minneapolis: Dillon Press, 1987.

This is a short book for young readers. According to performers acquainted with the material, it is historically accurate and accessible to older children and teenagers. Biographical anecdotes and adventures of the famous P. T. Barnum make for fascinating sidelights on a unique period in America and American show business.

WILLEFORD, WILLIAM. *The Fool and His Scepter: A Study in Clowns and Jesters and Their Audience.* Evanston, Ill.: Northwestern University Press, 1969, pp. 3–257.

Willeford examines certain unique questions of "why" that may still be profitably asked about "The Fool" and the secret of his enduring popularity. Why are we so attracted to the clowns and jesters "who from widely diverse times and places reveal such striking similarities"? What is the significance of the "interaction between the court jester of the Middle Ages and his king"?

Further Information

Because thousands of teachers from all parts of the country have asked for information about the circus, to help them plan teaching units, Ringling Brothers has prepared the following information, which can be duplicated and distributed (second edition).

RINGLING BROS.-BARNUM & BAILEY COMBINED SHOWS, INC.
Department of Educational Services
1015 18th Street, N.W.
Washington, DC 20036
Dr. Mildred S. Fenner, Director

Circus Fans Association of America Was founded in 1926, to create a broader understanding of the educational and recreative value of the circus and a better appreciation of the art of the Big Top. Its growing membership is kept informed of circus activities through its bimonthly magazine, "The White Tops." For more information:

> J. Allen Duffield
> Secretary–Treasurer
> P.O. Box 69
> Camp Hill, PA 17011

Circus Historical Society Is made up of persons interested in the circus past and present. Information and photos of circuses of years ago are brought to its members by *The Bandwagon,* the Society's bimonthly magazine. For more information:

> Johann W. Dahlinger
> Secretary–Treasurer
> 743 Beverly Park Place
> Jackson, MI 49203

Circus World Museum (Baraboo, Wisconsin) Circus history comes to life at Circus World Museum, located at original Ringling Brothers circus winterquarters.
World's largest, grandest and most exciting circus attraction!
Magnificent collection of restored circus wagons.

Big Top performances-Circus Acts
Circus Train loading and unloading
Antique Carousel and Ferris Wheel rides
Circus memorabilia
Circus World Museum Library

For more information:

> Circus World Museum
> Baraboo, WI 53913

Circus Model Builders Was founded in 1936 to bring together builders and owners of models of circus equipment, either single units or complete shows, who generate broader public interest in the circus through displays of their models.
Publishes *The Little Circus Wagon* six times a year.
For more information:

> Sally Conover Weitlauf
> Secretary–Treasurer
> 347 Lonsdale Avenue
> Dayton, OH 45419

Anthologies of Children's Literature

ARBUTHNOT, MAY HILL, ed. *The Arbuthnot Anthology of Children's Literature.* Rev. ed. Glenview, Ill.: Scott, Foresman, 1961.

This anthology contains the 3 classic Arbuthnot texts for children's literature: *Time for Fairy Tales, Time for Poetry,* and *Time for True Tales and Almost True.* Not all the stories and poems lend themselves to dramatization, but many of the poems can be used for choral speaking.

ARBUTHNOT, MAY HILL, eds. *Children's Books Too Good to Miss.* 7th ed. Cleveland: The Press of Case Western Reserve University, 1980.

Here is a treasury of materials for the elementary school classroom. Poetry, stories, biography, and study guides and explanations of literary and other items make this a useful and an authoritative source.

BUTLER, FRANCELIA, ed. *Sharing Literature with Children.* New York: Longman. 1977.

This well-known anthology is divided in a unique way: "Toys and Games," "Fools," "Masks and Shadows," "Sex Roles," and "Circles." The editor has included material for all age levels and provided a rich resource for the teacher to tell, read aloud, and use in creative playing.

CIARDI, JOHN. *I Met a Man.* Boston: Houghton Mifflin, 1961.

These amusing verses for children, written by a well-known American poet, are useful for both creative drama and choral speaking.

———. *The Man Who Sang the Sillies.* Philadelphia: Lippincott, 1961.

Here is another collection of amusing verse for both younger and older children.

COLE, WILLIAM, ed. *Poem Stew.* New York: Harper & Row, 1981.

Fun for children, this collection has more than fifty poems for reading and dramatic enactment.

CUMMINGS, E. E. *Poems for Children.* New York: Liveright, 1983.

These twenty poems offer an introduction to the poet's work and provide an avenue to other modern experimental forms.

DE LA MARE, WALTER, ed. *Come Hither: A Collection of Rhymes and Poems for the Young of All Ages.* New York: Knopf, 1957.

This collection of more than five hundred traditional poems with notes is interesting to children of all ages.

FARGEON, ELEANOR. *Eleanor Fargeon's Poems for Children.* Philadelphia: Lippincott, 1951.

Some of these favorite poems by a well-known poet are good for dramatization, and many are suitable for choral speaking.

FISHER, AILEEN. *Out in the Dark and Daylight.* New York: Harper & Row, 1980.

Selections from Fisher's books are compiled in a collection that is varied and representative of her work.

FITZGERALD, BURDETTE, ed. *World Tales for Creative Dramatics and Storytelling.* Englewood Cliffs, N.J.: Prentice-Hall, 1962.

This is a splendid collection of folk tales from around the world, many of which are little known.

GEORGIOU, CONSTANTINE. *Children and Their Literature.* Englewood Cliffs, N.J.: Prentice-Hall, 1969.

An excellent resource for teachers of all grades, this book treats the history and criticism of children's literature; divisions, genres, and analyses of old and new books. It includes extensive lists of stories for primary, intermediate, and upper grades.

GRUENBERG, SIDONI M., ed. *More Favorite Stories.* Garden City, N.Y.: Doubleday, 1948.
This old but still good collection for primary and intermediate grades usually is available in public libraries.

JENNINGS, COLEMAN A., AND AURAND HARRIS, eds. *Plays Children Love.* Garden City, N.Y.: Doubleday, 1981.
This is an excellent collection of plays edited by two of our best-qualified practitioners: a child-drama specialist and a leading children's playwright. In the first part are plays for children to enjoy as spectators; in the second part are plays for older children to perform. The latter are shorter, making them suitable for children to memorize and produce.

JOHNSON, EDNA, CARRIE E. SCOTT, AND EVELYN R. SICKLES, eds. *Anthology of Children's Literature.* Boston: Houghton Mifflin, 1948.
This classic text, still available, is filled with selections arranged according to subject matter and age level. Sections include fables, folk tales, myths, nature stories, travel, biography, literary fairy tales, and poetry.

KASE, ROBERT, ed. *Stories for Creative Acting.* New York: French, 1961.
Although compiled in 1961, this selection is well worth having in the library, for it includes stories used and recommended by leading creative-drama teachers. Many of them would be included today, if another such book were being assembled. The editor was a leading figure in the field and still devotes much time to drama/theatre but with senior adults.

LEAR, EDWARD. *A Book of Nonsense.* New York: Viking, 1980.
This collection of the poet's amusing limericks is always fun and good for all ages.

McCORD, DAVID. *One at a Time.* Boston: Little, Brown, 1977.
A collection of the poet's most popular work, this book is most useful to teachers of intermediate grades.

MAYER, MERCER. *A Poison Tree and Other Poems.* New York: Scribner's, 1977.
For intermediate grades, these verses express children's feelings: anger, sadness, wishes, as well as less serious themes.

MERRIAM, EVE. *Rainbow Writing.* New York: Atheneum, 1976.
Light, descriptive verses covering a wide range of subjects, they are most useful on the intermediate level.

MOORE, LILLIAN. *See My Lovely Poison Ivy.* New York: Atheneum, 1975.
These short verses with appeal for children in grades three to six are light and amusing.

MORTON, MIRIAM, ed. *A Harvest of Russian Children's Literature.* Berkeley: University of California Press, 1967.
In this comprehensive collection of prose and poetry, the editor has included material for ages five to seven, eight to eleven, twelve to fifteen,

and young adults. She has translated some material from the Russian, told some of the folk tales in her own words, and written introductions to each section. A wealth of material is presented for the classroom teacher as well as for the specialist.

OPIE, IONA, AND PETER OPIE, eds. *The Oxford Book of Children's Verse*. New York: Oxford University Press, 1973.
In this classic text, teachers will find a wealth of material, some of which is suitable for choral speaking and creative drama.

PRELUTSKY, JACK. *The New Kid on the Block*. New York: Greenwillow Books, 1984.
These modern, childlike verses with a sense of humor can be enjoyed by children in lower and middle grades. The book is good for both creative-drama classes and choral speaking.

———, ed. *The Random House Book of Poetry for Children*. New York: Random House, 1984.
A collection of more than five hundred poems with more than four hundred illustrations, this is a valuable addition to the library of books for creative playing. Amusing verse, witty rhymes, and serious poetry are all included in a source book for teachers and creative-drama leaders of children of all ages.

SAWYER, RUTH, ed. *The Way of the Storyteller*. Rev. ed. New York: Penguin Books, 1977.
This well-known book contains ways of telling and choosing stories, stories to tell, and a reading list.

SHEDLOCK, MARIE, ed. *The Art of the Story Teller*. 3d ed. rev. New York: Dover Publications, 1977.
This is well known and still one of the best books on the art of storytelling. In addition to having chapters dealing with how to tell stories, it includes eighteen selections and a list of others.

SIKS, GERALDINE BRAIN, ed. *Children's Literature for Dramatization: An Anthology*. New York: Harper & Row, 1964.
An anthology of poems and stories suitable for dramatization, it was assembled by a leader in the field. The stories are arranged for younger and older children. The poetry is categorized as "inviting action," "suggesting characterization," and "motivating conflict."

STEVENSON, ROBERT LOUIS. *A Child's Garden of Verses*. New York: Random House, 1978.
These familiar verses are still interesting to children and good to use for both creative drama and choral speaking.

VIORST, JUDITH. *If I Were in Charge of the World and Other Worries*. New York: Atheneum, 1981.
The poet gives a variety of children's most secret thoughts, worries, and wishes in this collection. It is perceptive and humorous.

WARD, WINIFRED, ed. *Stories to Dramatize*. New Orleans: Anchorage Press, 1952.
In this volume, the author includes a rich collection of stories and poems from her own years of experience as a creative-drama teacher. It is arranged for players of various ages and contains material both classical and contemporary.

Annotated Bibliographies of Children's Literature

KIMMEL, MARGARET MARY, AND ELIZABETH SEGEL. *For Reading Out Loud!* New York: Dell (Delacorte Press), 1983.

This book shows adults how to enrich children's lives and stimulate their interest by reading aloud to them. The authors explain why it is important to start early and how to do it successfully. The most valuable part of the book is a bibliography in which almost one hundred fifty books are described in detail. A long list of titles aids the teacher (or parent) in finding material for all age levels and interests.

TRELEASE, JIM. *The Read-Aloud Handbook.* New York: Penguin Books, 1982.

The author tells how reading aloud awakens the listener's imagination, improves language arts, and opens doors to a new world of entertainment. An important inclusion is an annotated list of more than three hundred fairy tales, short stories, poems, and novels that the author describes in detail, with suggested age and grade levels.

Suggested Music for Creative Drama

Mood Music

The following mood music is suggested for creative drama. It is listed in categories, implying different moods and conditions. Many leaders find music a great asset in freeing children and inducing creative movement. All of the selections are well known and available. This is by no means an exhaustive list, and many teachers will have ideas of their own.

It is suggested that children first listen to the music, and then either move to it or talk about the feelings it suggests. It often is a good idea to play it a second or even a third time before attempting to do anything with it.

Music Suggesting Activity

Beethoven, Ludwig van	Sonata op. 10, no. 2 [fourth movement]
Bizet, Georges	March and Impromptu from *Jeux d'enfants*
Chopin, Frédéric	Mazurka in B-flat
Gershwin, George	*An American in Paris*
Grainger, Percy	"Country Gardens"
Mendelssohn, Felix	Tarantella from *Songs Without Words* op. 102, no. 3
Paganini, Niccolò	"Perpetual Motion"
Prokofiev, Sergei	Symphony no. 1 in D [fourth movement]
Rimsky-Korsakov, Nicolai	"Flight of the Bumble Bee"

| Strauss, Johann, Jr. | "Thunder and Lightning, Galop" |
| Wagner, Richard | "Spinning Song" from *The Flying Dutchman* |

Music Suggesting Animals, Birds and Insects

Dvořák, Antonin	"Legend no. 7"
Grieg, Edvard	"Little Bird"
———	"Papillon [Butterfly]"
Respighi, Ottorino	*The Birds*
Rimsky-Korsakov, Nicolai	"Flight of the Bumble Bee"
Saint-Saëns, Camille	*Carnival of the Animals*
Schumann, Robert	*Papillons*
Stravinsky, Igor	Suite from *The Firebird*

Ballads and Folk Songs

Many well-known ballads and folk songs are appropriate for creative drama.

Environmental Music

Britten, Benjamin	"4 Sea Interludes" from *Peter Grimes*
Debussy, Claude	*La Mer [The Sea]*
Delius, Frederick	"Summer Night on the River"
Mendelssohn, Felix	*Fingal's Cave* Overture
Respighi, Ottorino	*The Fountains of Rome*
Smetana, Bedřich	"The Moldau" from *My Fatherland*
Strauss, Johann, Jr.	"Blue Danube" Waltz

Happy Music

Dvořák, Antonin	Slavonic Dances
Mozart, Wolfgang Amadeus	Serenade in G *(Eine Kleine Nachtmusik)*
	Symphony no. 40 in G Minor [first movement]
Nicolai, Otto	Overture to *Merry Wives of Windsor*
Offenbach, Jacques	*Gaité Parisienne*
Rossini, Gioacchino	*La Boutique Fantastique*
Scarlatti, Domenico	Harpsichord sonatas
Schumann, Robert	*Carnaval*
Telemann, Georg Philipp	*Don Quixote*

Lullabies

| Brahms, Johannes | "Lullaby" |
| Godard, Benjamin Louis Paul | "Berceuse" from *Jocelyn* |

Grieg, Edvard	"Cradle Song" from *Peer Gynt*
Khatchaturian, Aram	"Lullaby" from *Gayne*

Military Music

Elgar, Edward	*Pomp and Circumstance* marches
Sousa, John Philip	Any marches
Suppé, Franz von	*Light Cavalry* Overture
Tchaikovsky, Peter Ilyich	*1812* Overture

Music Suggesting Mystery

Dukas, Paul	*The Sorcerer's Apprentice*
Grieg, Edvard	"Abduction of the Bride" from *Peer Gynt*
———	"March of the Dwarfs" from *Huldigungmarsch*
———	"The Hall of the Mountain King" from *Peer Gynt*
Mussorgsky, Modest	*Night on Bald Mountain*
———	*Songs and Dances of Death*
Saint-Saëns, Camille	"Danse Macabre"
Schubert, Franz	"The Erlking"
Sibelius, Jean	*The Swan of Tuonela*
Strauss, Richard	*Death and Transfiguration*

Romantic Music

Beethoven, Ludwig van	Sonata no. 23 for Piano *(Appassionata)*
Brahms, Johannes	"Valse"
Liszt, Franz	"Liebestraum [Love Dream]"
Mendelssohn, Felix	*Songs without Words* op. 38, no. 2
———	*Songs without Words* op. 102, no. 1
Paderewski, Ignace	"Love Song"
Rubinstein, Anton	"Melody"
Tchaikovsky, Peter Ilyich	Overture to *Romeo and Juliet*
———	Symphony no. 5 [selections]
Wagner, Richard	Prelude to *Tristan and Isolde*

Music Suggesting the Seasons

Beethoven, Ludwig van	Sonata op. 24, no. 5 for Violin and Piano *(Spring)*
———	Sonata op. 27, no. 2 *(Moonlight)*
———	Symphony no. 6 *(Pastoral)*

Debussy, Claude   "Clair de Lune"
Delius, Frederick   "Summer Night on the River"
Grieg, Edvard   "Morning Mood"
————   "To the Spring" from *Lyric Pieces*
Grofé, Ferde   *Grand Canyon* Suite
Mendelssohn, Felix   Melody in F ("Spring Song")
Prokofiev, Sergei   "In Autumn"
————   *Summer Day* Suite
Ravel, Maurice   *Daphnis and Chloe*
Rossini, Gioacchino   "The Storm" from the Overture to
                                     William Tell
Sibelius, Jean   "Night Ride and Sunrise"
Vivaldi, Antonio   "Spring" from *The Four Seasons*

Serene Music

Bach, Johann Sebastian   Cantata no. 147 ("Sheep May Safely
                                     Graze")
Barber, Samuel   "Adagio for Strings" from Quartet for
                                     Strings, op. 11
Bizet, Georges   *L'Arlésienne* [third movement]
Debussy, Claude   *Afternoon of a Faun*
————   *Songs without Words* op. 102, no. 6
Mendelssohn, Felix   *A Midsummer Night's Dream*
Schubert, Franz   Quintet in A Major for Piano and
                                     Strings *(Trout)*
Schumann, Robert   *Traumerei*

Music Suggesting Strong Movement

Beethoven, Ludwig van   Sonata op. 27, no. 2 *(Moonlight* [third
                                     movement])
Falla, Manuel de   "Ritual Fire Dance" from *El Amor
                                     Brujo*
Holst, Gustav   "Mars" from *The Planets*
Khatchaturian, Aram   "Saber Dance" from *Gayne*
Prokofiev, Sergei   *Scythian* Suite [selections]
Shostakovich, Dimitri   Symphony no. 5 [fourth movement]
Tchaikovsky, Peter Ilyich   "Marche Slav"
————   Symphony no. 4

Music Suggesting Toys and Puppets

Bratton, John   "Teddy Bears' Picnic"
Coates, Eric   *Cinderella*
————   *The Three Bears*

Debussy, Claude	*Children's Corner*
Delibes, Léo	*Coppelia*
Elgar, Edward	*Nursery* Suite
————	*The Wand of Youth* Suites nos. 1 and 2
Herbert, Victor	"March of the Toys" from *Babes in Toyland*
Humperdinck, Engelbert	*Hansel and Gretel*
Jessel, Leon	"Parade of the Tin Soldiers"
————	"Tubby the Tuba"
Kleinsinger, George	"Peewee the Piccolo"
Mozart, Leopold	"Toy Symphony" from Cassation for Orchestra and Toys in G
Pierne, Gabriel	"March of the Little Lead Soldiers"
Prokofiev, Sergei	*Cinderella*
————	*The Love for Three Oranges*
————	*Peter and the Wolf*
Ravel, Maurice	*Mother Goose*
Rossini, Gioacchino	*La Cenerentola*
Tchaikovsky, Peter Ilyich	*The Nutcracker*
————	*The Sleeping Beauty*
————	*Swan Lake*

Whimsical Music

Grieg, Edvard	*Humoresque*
Mozart, Leopold	"Toy Symphony" from Cassation for Orchestra and Toys in G
Ponchielli, Amilcare	"Dance of the Hours" from *La Gioconda*
Strauss, Richard	*Till Eulenspiegel*
Tchaikovsky, Peter Ilyich	*Humoresque*

Films

Animal Films for Humane Education. New York: Argus Archives, Dept. AF-4, 228 East 49th Street, New York, NY 10017.

There are 136 entries in this new and expanded version of the earlier Argus Archives collection. Reviews, discussion techniques, and suggestions about how to integrate humane education with other subjects in the curriculum. Many of the films are excellent for creative drama, stimulating original work and raising consciousness of this area in urban children.

BERGGRENN, LOIS, AND VERY SPECIAL ARTS, MASSACHUSETTS. *The Great Escape.* 50
Sippiwissett Road, Falmouth, MA 02540.
This is a National Education Association award-winning teacher-training
videotape, showing multiple handicapped children at the Kennedy
Memorial Hospital School. The creator of the film is an artist–teacher,
dedicated to making the folk traditions accessible to low-income,
minority, and disabled children. Los Posadas, a bilingual Mexican–
American Children's Theatre Festival, which she founded, celebrated its
fifth year in 1987, at which time this film was introduced.

Creative Dramatics: The First Steps. 29 min. color, sound. Northwestern Film Library, 614
Davis Street, Evanston, IL 60201
This is a vintage film that demonstrates the teaching of creative dramatics
to a group of fourth-grade children. Guided by an experienced teacher,
the group moves from the faltering first steps to the creation of a drama.

Creativity: A Way of Learning. 11 min. color, sound. NEA Distribution Center, The
Academic Bldg. Saw Mill Rd., West Haven, CT 06516.
This film explores creativity, how it is related to life in and out of school,
and how it can be encouraged.

Dorothy Heathcote Talks to Teachers—Part I. 30 min. color. Northwestern University Film
Library, 1735 Benson Avenue, Evanston, IL 60201.

Dorothy Heathcote Talks to Teachers—Part II. 32 min. color. Northwestern University
Film Library, 1735 Benson Avenue, Evanston, IL 60201.

Drama with the Kindergarten (Videotape Presentation). 1987 Arizona State University,
Tempe, AZ.
Jennifer Akridge introduces this color tape of creative drama classes
taught by Lin Wright, Donald Doyle, and Johnny Saldana. Three approaches to creative drama are shown documenting the first year's work
in a seven-year longitudinal study of drama with and theatre for children.

Everyman in the Streets. 30 min. color. Channel 13 NET—New York (no charge), 304 W.
58th Street, New York, NY 10019.

FEIL, EDWARD, producer. *Aurand Harris Demonstrating Playwriting with Children,* 1983.
24 min., color (3/4″ U-MATIC; 1/2″ VHS; 1/2″ BETA). Distributed by Edward Feil
Production, 4614 Prospect Avenue, Cleveland, OH 44103.
Children's playwright demonstrates teaching playwriting to a class of
fifth and sixth graders. The lesson is interspersed with Harris's discussion of what he is doing and how playwriting strengthens writing.

Ideas and Me. 17 min. color. Dallas Theatre Center, 3636 Turtle Creek Boulevard, Dallas,
TX 75200.
In this film children participate in the various aspects of creative drama.

One of a Kind. 58 min. color, sound. Phoenix Films, Inc., 470 Park Avenue South, New
York, NY 10016.
Intended for audiences of all ages, this powerful film deals with the
relationship between a child and a troubled mother. Through participation in a traveling puppet show, the child is able to express her anguish
and needs. The film can be used effectively for classes in special
education, psychology, creative drama, and language arts.

Playing: Pretending Spontaneous Drama with Children. 20 min. b/w. Community Services Department, Pittsburgh Child Guidance Center, 201 De Soto Street, Pittsburgh, PA 15213.

This film, by Eleanor C. Irwin, describes a number of different forms of spontaneous drama with primary- and elementary-age children. Activities showing creative movement, puppetry, role play, and improvisation are demonstrated. The nature of creativity, the developmental roots of drama, the importance of impulse control as well as impulse expression, the individuality of children and their fantasies, and the value of dramatic play for children in both cognitive and affective learning are discussed.

Statues Hardly Ever Smile. 25 min. color. Brooklyn Museum, Eastern Parkway and Washington Avenue, Brooklyn, NY 11238.

This film shows work done at the museum. Although several years old, it is unique in content, form, and approach to creative drama.

Take 3. 70 min. 16-mm, color, sound. National Audio-Visual Aids Library, Paxton Place, Gipsy Road, London SE27 9SR.

This English film describes the work of three drama teachers and is intended to provoke thought and raise questions about the nature of drama, assessment, and evaluation. Although not available for rental in the United States at the time of publication of this book, it is recommended because it shows three teachers at work in three entirely different situations, each using individual techniques.

Three Looms Waiting. 52 min. color. BBC Production. Distributed by Time-Life Films, Inc., 43 W. 16th Street, New York, NY 10016.

This film shows Dorothy Heathcote, one of the leading British teachers of creative drama, working with a group of children. An excellent demonstration of her method.

Why Man Creates. 25 min. color. Pyramid Films, P.O. Box 1048, Santa Monica, CA 90406.

This is a popular film to be shown more than once. It inquires into the human need to create in an unusual way.

Index

Action, 76–77, 161, 171, 220, 234, 240–241, 256, 294, 345, 365. *See also* Movement
Actors, 9, 10, 123–124, 344, 349, 357
Acts, 158, 401
Aesthetics, 347–350, 361, 440–441, 446–447
Africa, 313–314, 440
Aged, 334–335, 438
Aiello, Barbara, 332
Alan Short Center [Stockton, California], 330
Allen, John, 20, 163
Alliance for Arts Education, 333
Alliance Theatre Company [Atlanta, Georgia], 430
Alternative schools, 385
Alternative space. *See name of specific type of space*
American Alliance for Theatre and Education, 393, 418–419, 422, 436
American Association of Community Theatres [ACT], 425
American Teachers' Association [ATA], 425–426
American Theatre Association, 418–419
Analogy, 292
Anthology, 309
Antiphonal reading, 232
Applause, 355
"Apples in the Wilderness" [story], 162, 163–170
Arena stages, 370–371
Artist-in-Education program, 428
Artist-in-Residence program, 300, 411, 424
Artists-in-the-Schools program, 297–298, 340, 418, 422, 436, 437
Art Partners [CAT project], 312
Arts, Education, and Americans [organization], 424–425
Arts
  See also name of specific type of art
  definition of, 41–44
  funding for the, 385, 432, 433, 435–439
  importance of the, 37
  and play, 41–44
  and state government, 427
Arts-centered schools, 421
Arts centers, 429–433
Arts education, 286, 296–297. *See also* Drama as a teaching tool; Theatre education
Arts in General Education program, 419
Arts Partners in New York, 420
Assembly programs, 288, 350, 353, 361, 365
Association for Childhood Education International, 422
Atkin, Flora, 154
Attending the theatre
  and characters, 345–346, 347, 349
  and comedy/humor, 346–347, 349, 360–361
  and communication, 349

and costumes, 347–348
and emotions, 349–350
and etiquette, 354–356, 361
follow-up after, 358–361, 398
and improvisation, 398
and participatory theatre, 354
and the performance, 347, 356–357
and plot/story, 347, 353
preparation for, 352–356, 359–360, 389
and social development, 349
and television, 347, 349, 361
and themes, 345, 353, 361
values of, 345–351, 361
and visual effects, 347
Audience
  See also Attending the theatre; Participatory theatre; Performances
  actors' relationships with the, 9, 344, 349, 357
  age of the, 345
  and chamber theatre, 280
  and children's theatre, 6–7
  and the circus/circus arts, 403
  and creative drama, 5
  and directors, 367
  and drama as a teaching tool, 287, 289, 294, 298, 301, 305–306, 307, 313, 314
  and formal productions, 363
  and storytelling, 173, 255–256, 263, 265
  and theatre-in-education [TIE], 10–11
Auditorium, 381
Baker, Donald, 39
Bandana puppets, 125
"The Bat's Choice" [legend], 62
Behavior problems, 31–35, 378, 411
Belgrade Theatre [Coventry, England], 305, 306
Benedetti, Robert, 445, 447
Berggren, Lois, 440
Bettelheim, Bruno, 16, 42, 178, 348–349, 390–391
Big Apple Circus, 407–409
Bilingual education. *See* Language arts
Binder, Paul, 407–408
Blatner, Adam, 41, 47, 324
"The Blind Men and the Elephant" [poem for choral speaking], 245–246
Blocking, 377
"Blue Bonnets" [story], 198–200
Body language, 50–51, 53, 71, 256
Bolton, Gavin, 291, 292, 294, 295, 296, 423
Bolton, Reg, 409–411
The Bongo Workbook [drama as a teaching tool], 295
Borisoff, Deborah, 325
Born, Terry, 295
Boston Shakespeare Company, 390
Boundaries, 442–443
Brainstorming, 26–27